ABA Compendium of Professional Responsibility Rules and Standards

1999 Edition

Cover and interior design by Laurie Crane.

Printed in the United States of America.

ISBN: 1-57073-701-0

Discounts are available for books ordered in bulk. Special consideration is given to state bars, CLE programs and other bar-related organizations. Inquire at Center for Professional Responsibility, American Bar Association, 541 N. Fairbanks Court, Chicago, Illinois 60611.

03 02 01 00 99 5 4 3 2 1

ABA Compendium of Professional Responsibility Rules and Standards

Contents

Model Rules and Codes

Related Materials

Preface

This second edition of the American Bar Association Center for Professional Responsibility *Compendium of Professional Responsibility Rules and Standards* gathers together for immediate reference the essential legal ethics materials needed by lawyers and judges in their daily practice, law students in their exploration of the standards of their new profession, and legal scholars in their analysis of the changing currents that influence professional regulation.

The first section of the *Compendium* presents models for ethical and professional conduct and standards for enforcing that conduct that have been developed by the American Bar Association. These models have been used as the foundation for most state regulations and as interpretive guidance for the courts in their resolution of professional responsibility issues. Despite the local variations in the way they have been adopted (occasionally significant), they serve to familiarize the reader with the philosophy of lawyer regulation and can be used to initiate review of substantive issues unfamiliar to the lawyer, student or scholar.

In addition, the *Compendium* contains a selection of Federal Rules of Civil and Appellate Procedure that are commonly needed in the general practice of law, and that impact upon a number of ethical rules of conduct, such as the rules regarding competence and meritorious claims and contentions.

The New York Domestic Relations Procedures have been included in the *Compendium* because they represent a significant attempt to further regulate the conduct of lawyers in a particular area of practice that has come under much scrutiny in regard to various aspects of the client-lawyer relationship.

Six recent and much discussed Formal Ethics Opinions issued by the ABA Standing Committee on Ethics and Professional Responsibility are reprinted in the *Compendium* to further interpret the Model Rules of Professional Conduct in important areas of lawyer conduct that have raised considerable debate. With the debate that has accompanied these opinions and other issuances of the Committee in mind, the Composition, Jurisdiction and Procedures of the Committee also have been included to better inform the user of the way in which the ethical rules and their interpretations are formulated.

For the benefit of the many law students who will be using the *Compendium* as a supplement to their professional responsibility textbook, the *Compendium* also includes sample questions, answers and analysis that can be used to help study for a law school exam or for the Multistate Professional Responsibility Exam.

Finally, the *Compendium* presents the status of the adoption of the Model Rules of Professional Conduct at the time of publication.

The American Bar Association Center for Professional Responsibility greatly appreciates the contributions of Nathan H. Crystal, Professor of Law at South

Carolina School of Law, for preparing the review questions and analysis and Erica Moeser, President, National Conference of Bar Examiners, for granting permission to reprint questions from previous Multi-State Professional Responsibility Exams.

The Center also thanks the West Group for its generous gift of the West Professional Responsibility Law Library, the resource for much of the research performed at the Center.

ABA MODEL RULES OF PROFESSIONAL CONDUCT

The ABA Model Rules of Professional Conduct, including Preamble, Scope, Terminology and Comment, were adopted by the ABA House of Delegates on August 2, 1983, and amended in 1987, 1989, 1990, 1991, 1992, 1993, 1994, 1995, 1997 and 1998.

ABA COMMISSION ON EVALUATION OF PROFESSIONAL STANDARDS (1977-1983)

ROBERT W. MESERVE*, *Chair*
Boston, Massachusetts

ALAN BARTH*
Washington, D.C.

ARNO H. DENECKE*
Salem, Oregon

THOMAS EHRLICH
Washington, D.C.

JANE FRANK-HARMAN
Washington, D.C.

MARVIN E. FRANKEL
New York, New York

LOIS C. HARRISON
Lakeland, Florida

ROBERT O. HETLAGE
St. Louis, Missouri

ROBERT B. McKAY*
New York, New York

L. CLAIR NELSON*
Washington, D.C.

RICHARD H. SINKFIELD
Atlanta, Georgia

WILLIAM B. SPANN, JR.*
Atlanta, Georgia

SAMUEL D. THURMAN
Salt Lake City, Utah

ROBERT J. KUTAK*
Omaha, Nebraska
Former Chair

LIAISONS

MICHAEL FRANCK*
Lansing, Michigan
Standing Committee on Professional Discipline

JOHN C. DEACON
Jonesboro, Arkansas
Board of Governors

H. WILLIAM ALLEN
Little Rock, Arkansas
Standing Committee on Ethics and Professional Responsibility

THOMAS Z. HAYWARD, JR.
Chicago, Illinois

CONSULTANTS

BETTY B. FLETCHER
Seattle, Washington

L. RAY PATTERSON
Atlanta, Georgia

JOHN F. SUTTON, JR.
Austin, Texas

REPORTER

GEOFFREY C. HAZARD, JR.
New Haven, Connecticut

ASSISTANT REPORTERS

THOMAS J. McCORMICK
Washington, D.C.

DANIEL S. REYNOLDS
DeKalb, Illinois

*Deceased

ABA STANDING COMMITTEE ON ETHICS AND PROFESSIONAL RESPONSIBILITY (1998-1999)

M. PETER MOSER, *Chair*
Baltimore, Maryland

LORETTA C. ARGRETT
Washington, D.C.

JACKSON M. BRUCE, JR.
Milwaukee, Wisconsin

WILLIAM B. DUNN
Detroit, Michigan

ALBERT C. HARVEY
Memphis, Tennessee

NANCY MCREADY HIGGINS
Seattle, Washington

DANIEL W. HILDEBRAND
Madison, Wisconsin

DONALD B. HILLIKER
Chicago, Illinois

WILLIAM H. JEFFRESS, JR.
Washington, D.C.

BRUCE A. MANN
San Francisco, California

CLARENCE W. WALKER
Charleston, North Carolina
Liaison, Board of Governors

CENTER FOR PROFESSIONAL RESPONSIBILITY

Director
JEANNE P. GRAY

Ethics Counsel
GEORGE A. KUHLMAN

Associate Ethics Counsel
EILEEN B. LIBBY

Contents

Transactions with Persons Other Than Clients

Law Firms and Associations

Public Service

Information About Legal Services

Maintaining the Integrity of the Profession

PREFACE

For more than eighty years, the American Bar Association has provided leadership in legal ethics and professional responsibility through the adoption of professional standards which serve as models of the regulatory law governing the legal profession.

On August 27, 1908, the Association adopted the original Canons of Professional Ethics. These were based principally on the Code of Ethics adopted by the Alabama Bar Association in 1887, which in turn had been borrowed largely from the lectures of Judge George Sharswood, published in 1854 as *Professional Ethics*, and from the fifty resolutions included in David Hoffman's *A Course of Legal Study* (2d ed. 1836). Piecemeal amendments to the Canons occasionally followed.

In 1913, the Standing Committee on Professional Ethics of the American Bar Association was established to keep the Association informed about state and local bar activities concerning professional ethics. In 1919 the name of the Committee was changed to the Committee on Professional Ethics and Grievances; its role was expanded in 1922 to include issuing opinions "concerning professional conduct, and particularly concerning the application of the tenets of ethics thereto." In 1958 the Committee on Professional Ethics and Grievances was separated into two committees: a Committee on Professional Grievances, with authority to investigate charges of professional misconduct, and a Committee on Professional Ethics with responsibility to express its opinion concerning proper professional and judicial conduct. The Committee on Professional Grievances was discontinued in 1971. The name of the Committee on Professional Ethics was changed to the Committee on Ethics and Professional Responsibility in 1971 and remains so.

In 1964, at the request of President Lewis F. Powell Jr., the House of Delegates of the American Bar Association created a Special Committee on Evaluation of Ethical Standards (the "Wright Committee") to assess whether changes should be made in the then-current Canons of Professional Ethics. In response, the Committee produced the Model Code of Professional Responsibility. The Model Code was adopted by the House of Delegates on August 12, 1969, and subsequently by the vast majority of state and federal jurisdictions.

In 1977, the American Bar Association created the Commission on Evaluation of Professional Standards to undertake a comprehensive rethinking of the ethical premises and problems of the legal profession. Upon evaluating the Model Code and determining that amendment of the Code would not achieve a comprehensive statement of the law governing the legal profession, the Commission commenced a six-year study and drafting process which produced the Model Rules of Professional Conduct. The Chair's Introduction to the Model Rules, which is reprinted following the Editor's Note to this volume, details the history of this process. The Model Rules were adopted by the House of Delegates of the American Bar Association on August 2, 1983. At the time this edition went to press, more than two-thirds of the jurisdictions had adopted new professional standards based on these Model Rules.

Twenty-nine amendments have been made to the Rules and Comment since their initial promulgation in 1983. A synopsis of these amendments, most of which, with the notable exception of those dealing with lawyer advertising, have been minor, is included as an appendix to this volume.

The American Bar Association continues to pursue its goal of assuring the highest standards of professional competence and ethical conduct. The Standing Committee on Ethics and Professional Responsibility, charged with interpreting the professional standards of the Association and recommending appropriate amendments and clarifications, issues opinions interpreting the Model Rules of Professional Conduct and the Model Code of Judicial Conduct. So long as a significant number of jurisdictions continue to base their professional standards on the predecessor Model Code of Professional Responsibility, the opinions will also continue to refer to the Model Code. The opinions of the Committee are published by the American Bar Association in the 1967 volume *Opinions on Professional Ethics*, the 1975 two-volume set *Informal Ethics Opinions*, the 1984 volume *Formal and Informal Ethics Opinions*, the 1999 volume *Formal and Informal Ethics Opinions: 1983 to 1998*, and the current loose-leaf subscription service, *Recent Ethics Opinions*.

Requests that the Committee issue opinions on particular questions of professional and judicial conduct should be directed to the American Bar Association, Center for Professional Responsibility, 541 North Fairbanks Court, Chicago, Illinois 60611.

CHAIRPERSON'S INTRODUCTION

The Commission on Evaluation of Professional Standards was appointed in the summer of 1977 by former ABA President William B. Spann, Jr. Chaired by Robert J. Kutak until his death in early 1983, the Commission was charged with evaluating whether existing standards of professional conduct provided comprehensive and consistent guidance for resolving the increasingly complex ethical problems in the practice of law. For the most part, the Commission looked to the former ABA Model Code of Professional Responsibility, which served as a model for the majority of state ethics codes. The Commission also referred to opinions of the ABA Standing Committee on Ethics and Professional Responsibility, as well as to decisions of the United States Supreme Court and of state supreme courts. After thoughtful study, the Commission concluded that piecemeal amendment of the Model Code would not sufficiently clarify the profession's ethical responsibilities in light of changed conditions. The Commission therefore commenced a drafting process that produced numerous drafts, elicited voluminous comment, and launched an unprecedented debate on the ethics of the legal profession.

On January 30, 1980, the Commission presented its initial suggestions to the bar in the form of a Discussion Draft of the proposed Model Rules of Professional Conduct. The Discussion Draft was subject to the widest possible dissemination and interested parties were urged to offer comments and suggestions. Public hearings were held around the country to provide forums for expression of views on the draft.

In the year following the last of these public hearings, the Commission conducted a painstaking analysis of the submitted comments and attempted to integrate into the draft those which seemed consistent with its underlying philosophy. The product of this analysis and integration was presented on May 31, 1981 as the proposed Final Draft of the Model Rules of Professional Conduct. This proposed Final Draft was submitted in two formats. The first format, consisting of blackletter Rules and accompanying Comments in the so-called restatement format, was submitted with the Commission's recommendation that it be adopted. The alternative format was patterned after the Model Code and consisted of Canons, Ethical Considerations, and Disciplinary Rules. In February 1982, the House of Delegates by substantial majority approved the restatement format of the Model Rules.

The proposed Final Draft was submitted to the House of Delegates for debate and approval at the 1982 Annual Meeting of the Association in San Francisco. Many organizations and interested parties offered their comments in the form of proposed amendments to the Final Draft. In the time allotted on its agenda, however, the House debated only proposed amendments to Rule 1.5. Consideration of the remainder of the document was deferred until the 1983 Midyear Meeting in New Orleans. The proposed Final Draft, as amended by the House in San Francisco, was reprinted in the November 1982 issue of the *ABA Journal*.

At the 1983 Midyear Meeting the House resumed consideration of the Final Draft. After two days of often vigorous debate, the House completed its review of the proposed amendments to the blackletter Rules. Many amendments, particularly in the area of confidentiality, were adopted. Debate on a Preamble, Scope, Terminology and Comments, rewritten to reflect the New Orleans amendments, was deferred until the 1983 Annual Meeting in Atlanta, Georgia.

On March 11, 1983, the text of the blackletter rules as approved by the House in February, together with the proposed Preamble, Scope, Terminology and Comments, was circulated to members of the House, Section and Committee chairmen, and all other interested parties. The text of the Rules reflected the joint efforts of the Commission and the House Drafting Committee to incorporate the changes approved by the House and to ensure stylistic continuity and uniformity. Recipients of the draft were again urged to submit comments in the form of proposed amendments. The House Committees on Drafting and Rules and Calendar met on May 23, 1983 to consider all of the proposed amendments that had been submitted in response to this draft. In addition, discussions were held among concerned parties in an effort to reach accommodation of the various positions. On July 11, 1983, the final version of the Model Rules was again circulated.

The House of Delegates commenced debate on the proposed Preamble, Scope, Terminology and Comments on August 2, 1983. After four hours of debate, the House completed its consideration of all the proposed amendments and, upon motion of the Commission, the House voted to adopt the Model Rules of Professional Conduct, together with the ancillary material as amended. The task of the Commission had ended and it was discharged with thanks.

Throughout the drafting process, active participants included not only the members of the Commission but also the Sections and Committees of the American Bar Association and national, state and local bar organizations. The work of the Commission was subject to virtually continuous scrutiny by academicians, practicing lawyers, members of the press, and the judiciary. Consequently, every provision of the Model Rules reflects the thoughtful consideration and hard work of many dedicated professionals. Because of their input, the Model Rules are truly national in derivation. The Association can take immense pride in its continued demonstration of leadership in the area of professional responsibility.

The Model Rules of Professional Conduct are intended to serve as a national framework for implementation of standards of professional conduct. Although the Commission endeavored to harmonize and accommodate the views of all the participants, no set of national standards that speaks to such a diverse constituency as the legal profession can resolve each issue to the complete satisfaction of every affected party. Undoubtedly there will be those who take issue with one or another of the Rules' provisions. Indeed, such dissent from individual provisions is expected. And the Model Rules, like all model legislation, will be subject to modification at the level of local implementation. Viewed as a whole, however, the Model Rules represent a responsible approach to the ethical practice of law and are consistent with professional obligations imposed by other law, such as constitutional, corporate, tort, fiduciary and agency law.

I should not end this report without speaking of the Commission's debt to many people who have aided us in our deliberations, and have devoted time, energy and goodwill to the advancement of our work over the last six years. It would probably be impossible to name each of the particular persons whose help was significant to us, and it surely would be unfortunate if the name of anyone were omitted from the list. We are, and shall remain, deeply grateful to the literally hundreds of people who aided us with welcome and productive suggestions. We think the bar should be grateful to each of them, and to our deceased members, Alan Barth of the District of Columbia, who we hardly had time to know; Bill Spann, who became a member after the conclusion of his presidential term; and our original chairman, Bob Kutak.

The long work of the Commission and its resulting new codification of the ethical rules of practice demonstrate, it is submitted, the commitment of the American lawyer to his or her profession and to its achievement of the highest standards.

Robert W. Meserve*
September 1983

*Robert W. Meserve was chairperson of the American Bar Association Commission on Evaluation of Professional Standards.

PREAMBLE, SCOPE AND TERMINOLOGY

PREAMBLE: A LAWYER'S RESPONSIBILITIES

[1] A lawyer is a representative of clients, an officer of the legal system and a public citizen having special responsibility for the quality of justice.

[2] As a representative of clients, a lawyer performs various functions. As advisor, a lawyer provides a client with an informed understanding of the client's legal rights and obligations and explains their practical implications. As advocate, a lawyer zealously asserts the client's position under the rules of the adversary system. As negotiator, a lawyer seeks a result advantageous to the client but consistent with requirements of honest dealing with others. As intermediary between clients, a lawyer seeks to reconcile their divergent interests as an advisor and, to a limited extent, as a spokesperson for each client. A lawyer acts as evaluator by examining a client's legal affairs and reporting about them to the client or to others.

[3] In all professional functions a lawyer should be competent, prompt and diligent. A lawyer should maintain communication with a client concerning the representation. A lawyer should keep in confidence information relating to representation of a client except so far as disclosure is required or permitted by the Rules of Professional Conduct or other law.

[4] A lawyer's conduct should conform to the requirements of the law, both in professional service to clients and in the lawyer's business and personal affairs. A lawyer should use the law's procedures only for legitimate purposes and not to harass or intimidate others. A lawyer should demonstrate respect for the legal system and for those who serve it, including judges, other lawyers and public officials. While it is a lawyer's duty, when necessary, to challenge the rectitude of official action, it is also a lawyer's duty to uphold legal process.

[5] As a public citizen, a lawyer should seek improvement of the law, the administration of justice and the quality of service rendered by the legal profession. As a member of a learned profession, a lawyer should cultivate knowledge of the law beyond its use for clients, employ that knowledge in reform of the law and work to strengthen legal education. A lawyer should be mindful of deficiencies in the administration of justice and of the fact that the poor, and sometimes persons who are not poor, cannot afford adequate legal assistance, and should therefore devote professional time and civic influence in their behalf. A lawyer should aid the legal profession in pursuing these objectives and should help the bar regulate itself in the public interest.

[6] Many of a lawyer's professional responsibilities are prescribed in the Rules of Professional Conduct, as well as substantive and procedural law. However, a lawyer is also guided by personal conscience and the approbation of professional peers. A lawyer should strive to attain the highest level of skill, to improve the law and the legal profession and to exemplify the legal profession's ideals of public service.

[7] A lawyer's responsibilities as a representative of clients, an officer of the

legal system and a public citizen are usually harmonious. Thus, when an opposing party is well represented, a lawyer can be a zealous advocate on behalf of a client and at the same time assume that justice is being done. So also, a lawyer can be sure that preserving client confidences ordinarily serves the public interest because people are more likely to seek legal advice, and thereby heed their legal obligations, when they know their communications will be private.

[8] In the nature of law practice, however, conflicting responsibilities are encountered. Virtually all difficult ethical problems arise from conflict between a lawyer's responsibilities to clients, to the legal system and to the lawyer's own interest in remaining an upright person while earning a satisfactory living. The Rules of Professional Conduct prescribe terms for resolving such conflicts. Within the framework of these Rules, many difficult issues of professional discretion can arise. Such issues must be resolved through the exercise of sensitive professional and moral judgment guided by the basic principles underlying the Rules.

[9] The legal profession is largely self-governing. Although other professions also have been granted powers of self-government, the legal profession is unique in this respect because of the close relationship between the profession and the processes of government and law enforcement. This connection is manifested in the fact that ultimate authority over the legal profession is vested largely in the courts.

[10] To the extent that lawyers meet the obligations of their professional calling, the occasion for government regulation is obviated. Self-regulation also helps maintain the legal profession's independence from government domination. An independent legal profession is an important force in preserving government under law, for abuse of legal authority is more readily challenged by a profession whose members are not dependent on government for the right to practice.

[11] The legal profession's relative autonomy carries with it special responsibilities of self-government. The profession has a responsibility to assure that its regulations are conceived in the public interest and not in furtherance of parochial or self-interested concerns of the bar. Every lawyer is responsible for observance of the Rules of Professional Conduct. A lawyer should also aid in securing their observance by other lawyers. Neglect of these responsibilities compromises the independence of the profession and the public interest which it serves.

[12] Lawyers play a vital role in the preservation of society. The fulfillment of this role requires an understanding by lawyers of their relationship to our legal system. The Rules of Professional Conduct, when properly applied, serve to define that relationship.

SCOPE

[13] The Rules of Professional Conduct are rules of reason. They should be interpreted with reference to the purposes of legal representation and of the law itself. Some of the Rules are imperatives, cast in the terms "shall" or "shall not." These define proper conduct for purposes of professional discipline. Others, generally cast in the term "may," are permissive and define areas under the Rules in which the lawyer has professional discretion. No disciplinary action should be taken when the lawyer chooses not to act or acts within the bounds of such discre-

tion. Other Rules define the nature of relationships between the lawyer and others. The Rules are thus partly obligatory and disciplinary and partly constitutive and descriptive in that they define a lawyer's professional role. Many of the Comments use the term "should." Comments do not add obligations to the Rules but provide guidance for practicing in compliance with the Rules.

[14] The Rules presuppose a larger legal context shaping the lawyer's role. That context includes court rules and statutes relating to matters of licensure, laws defining specific obligations of lawyers and substantive and procedural law in general. Compliance with the Rules, as with all law in an open society, depends primarily upon understanding and voluntary compliance, secondarily upon reinforcement by peer and public opinion and finally, when necessary, upon enforcement through disciplinary proceedings. The Rules do not, however, exhaust the moral and ethical considerations that should inform a lawyer, for no worthwhile human activity can be completely defined by legal rules. The Rules simply provide a framework for the ethical practice of law.

[15] Furthermore, for purposes of determining the lawyer's authority and responsibility, principles of substantive law external to these Rules determine whether a client-lawyer relationship exists. Most of the duties flowing from the client-lawyer relationship attach only after the client has requested the lawyer to render legal services and the lawyer has agreed to do so. But there are some duties, such as that of confidentiality under Rule 1.6, that may attach when the lawyer agrees to consider whether a client-lawyer relationship shall be established. Whether a client-lawyer relationship exists for any specific purpose can depend on the circumstances and may be a question of fact.

[16] Under various legal provisions, including constitutional, statutory and common law, the responsibilities of government lawyers may include authority concerning legal matters that ordinarily reposes in the client in private client-lawyer relationships. For example, a lawyer for a government agency may have authority on behalf of the government to decide upon settlement or whether to appeal from an adverse judgment. Such authority in various respects is generally vested in the attorney general and the state's attorney in state government, and their federal counterparts, and the same may be true of other government law officers. Also, lawyers under the supervision of these officers may be authorized to represent several government agencies in intragovernmental legal controversies in circumstances where a private lawyer could not represent multiple private clients. They also may have authority to represent the "public interest" in circumstances where a private lawyer would not be authorized to do so. These Rules do not abrogate any such authority.

[17] Failure to comply with an obligation or prohibition imposed by a Rule is a basis for invoking the disciplinary process. The Rules presuppose that disciplinary assessment of a lawyer's conduct will be made on the basis of the facts and circumstances as they existed at the time of the conduct in question and in recognition of the fact that a lawyer often has to act upon uncertain or incomplete evidence of the situation. Moreover, the Rules presuppose that whether or not discipline should be

imposed for a violation, and the severity of a sanction, depend on all the circumstances, such as the willfulness and seriousness of the violation, extenuating factors and whether there have been previous violations.

[18] Violation of a Rule should not give rise to a cause of action nor should it create any presumption that a legal duty has been breached. The Rules are designed to provide guidance to lawyers and to provide a structure for regulating conduct through disciplinary agencies. They are not designed to be a basis for civil liability. Furthermore, the purpose of the Rules can be subverted when they are invoked by opposing parties as procedural weapons. The fact that a Rule is a just basis for a lawyer's self-assessment, or for sanctioning a lawyer under the administration of a disciplinary authority, does not imply that an antagonist in a collateral proceeding or transaction has standing to seek enforcement of the Rule. Accordingly, nothing in the Rules should be deemed to augment any substantive legal duty of lawyers or the extra-disciplinary consequences of violating such a duty.

[19] Moreover, these Rules are not intended to govern or affect judicial application of either the attorney-client or work product privilege. Those privileges were developed to promote compliance with law and fairness in litigation. In reliance on the attorney-client privilege, clients are entitled to expect that communications within the scope of the privilege will be protected against compelled disclosure. The attorney-client privilege is that of the client and not of the lawyer. The fact that in exceptional situations the lawyer under the rules has a limited discretion to disclose a client confidence does not vitiate the proposition that, as a general matter, the client has a reasonable expectation that information relating to the client will not be voluntarily disclosed and that disclosure of such information may be judicially compelled only in accordance with recognized exceptions to the attorney-client and work product privileges.

[20] The lawyer's exercise of discretion not to disclose information under Rule 1.6 should not be subject to reexamination. Permitting such reexamination would be incompatible with the general policy of promoting compliance with law through assurances that communications will be protected against disclosure.

[21] The Comment accompanying each Rule explains and illustrates the meaning and purpose of the Rule. The Preamble and this note on Scope provide general orientation. The Comments are intended as guides to interpretation, but the text of each Rule is authoritative. Research notes were prepared to compare counterparts in the ABA Model Code of Professional Responsibility (adopted 1969, as amended) and to provide selected references to other authorities. The notes have not been adopted, do not constitute part of the Model Rules, and are not intended to affect the application or interpretation of the Rules and Comments.*

*These research notes have been superseded by the Legal Background sections of the *Annotated Model Rules of Professional Conduct* (2d ed. 1992). – *Ed.*

TERMINOLOGY

"Belief" or "believes" denotes that the person involved actually supposed the fact in question to be true. A person's belief may be inferred from circumstances.

"Consult" or "consultation" denotes communication of information reasonably sufficient to permit the client to appreciate the significance of the matter in question.

"Firm" or "law firm" denotes a lawyer or lawyers in a private firm, lawyers employed in the legal department of a corporation or other organization and lawyers employed in a legal services organization. See Comment, Rule 1.10.

"Fraud" or "fraudulent" denotes conduct having a purpose to deceive and not merely negligent misrepresentation or failure to apprise another of relevant information.

"Knowingly," "known," or "knows" denotes actual knowledge of the fact in question. A person's knowledge may be inferred from circumstances.

"Partner" denotes a member of a partnership and a shareholder in a law firm organized as a professional corporation.

"Reasonable" or "reasonably" when used in relation to conduct by a lawyer denotes the conduct of a reasonably prudent and competent lawyer.

"Reasonable belief" or "reasonably believes" when used in reference to a lawyer denotes that the lawyer believes the matter in question and that the circumstances are such that the belief is reasonable.

"Reasonably should know" when used in reference to a lawyer denotes that a lawyer of reasonable prudence and competence would ascertain the matter in question.

"Substantial" when used in reference to degree or extent denotes a material matter of clear and weighty importance.

CLIENT-LAWYER RELATIONSHIP

RULE 1.1 COMPETENCE

A lawyer shall provide competent representation to a client. Competent representation requires the legal knowledge, skill, thoroughness and preparation reasonably necessary for the representation.

Comment

Legal Knowledge and Skill

[1] In determining whether a lawyer employs the requisite knowledge and skill in a particular matter, relevant factors include the relative complexity and specialized nature of the matter, the lawyer's general experience, the lawyer's training and experience in the field in question, the preparation and study the lawyer is able to give the matter and whether it is feasible to refer the matter to, or associate or consult with, a lawyer of established competence in the field in question. In many instances, the required proficiency is that of a general practitioner. Expertise in a particular field of law may be required in some circumstances.

[2] A lawyer need not necessarily have special training or prior experience to handle legal problems of a type with which the lawyer is unfamiliar. A newly admitted lawyer can be as competent as a practitioner with long experience. Some important legal skills, such as the analysis of precedent, the evaluation of evidence and legal drafting, are required in all legal problems. Perhaps the most fundamental legal skill consists of determining what kind of legal problems a situation may involve, a skill that necessarily transcends any particular specialized knowledge. A lawyer can provide adequate representation in a wholly novel field through necessary study. Competent representation can also be provided through the association of a lawyer of established competence in the field in question.

[3] In an emergency a lawyer may give advice or assistance in a matter in which the lawyer does not have the skill ordinarily required where referral to or consultation or association with another lawyer would be impractical. Even in an emergency, however, assistance should be limited to that reasonably necessary in the circumstances, for ill-considered action under emergency conditions can jeopardize the client's interest.

[4] A lawyer may accept representation where the requisite level of competence can be achieved by reasonable preparation. This applies as well to a lawyer who is appointed as counsel for an unrepresented person. See also Rule 6.2.

Thoroughness and Preparation

[5] Competent handling of a particular matter includes inquiry into and analysis of the factual and legal elements of the problem, and use of methods and procedures meeting the standards of competent practitioners. It also includes adequate preparation. The required attention and preparation are determined in part

by what is at stake; major litigation and complex transactions ordinarily require more elaborate treatment than matters of lesser consequence.

Maintaining Competence

[6] To maintain the requisite knowledge and skill, a lawyer should engage in continuing study and education. If a system of peer review has been established, the lawyer should consider making use of it in appropriate circumstances.

Model Code Comparison

DR 6-101(A)(1) provided that a lawyer shall not handle a matter "which he knows or should know that he is not competent to handle, without associating himself with a lawyer who is competent to handle it." DR 6-101(A)(2) required "preparation adequate in the circumstances." Rule 1.1 more fully particularizes the elements of competence. Whereas DR 6-101(A)(3) prohibited the "[N]eglect of a legal matter," Rule 1.1 does not contain such a prohibition. Instead, Rule 1.1 affirmatively requires the lawyer to be competent.

RULE 1.2 SCOPE OF REPRESENTATION

(a) A lawyer shall abide by a client's decisions concerning the objectives of representation, subject to paragraphs (c), (d) and (e), and shall consult with the client as to the means by which they are to be pursued. A lawyer shall abide by a client's decision whether to accept an offer of settlement of a matter. In a criminal case, the lawyer shall abide by the client's decision, after consultation with the lawyer, as to a plea to be entered, whether to waive jury trial and whether the client will testify.

(b) A lawyer's representation of a client, including representation by appointment, does not constitute an endorsement of the client's political, economic, social or moral views or activities.

(c) A lawyer may limit the objectives of the representation if the client consents after consultation.

(d) A lawyer shall not counsel a client to engage, or assist a client, in conduct that the lawyer knows is criminal or fraudulent, but a lawyer may discuss the legal consequences of any proposed course of conduct with a client and may counsel or assist a client to make a good faith effort to determine the validity, scope, meaning or application of the law.

(e) When a lawyer knows that a client expects assistance not permitted by the rules of professional conduct or other law, the lawyer shall consult with the client regarding the relevant limitations on the lawyer's conduct.

Comment

Scope of Representation

[1] Both lawyer and client have authority and responsibility in the objectives and means of representation. The client has ultimate authority to determine the

purposes to be served by legal representation, within the limits imposed by law and the lawyer's professional obligations. Within those limits, a client also has a right to consult with the lawyer about the means to be used in pursuing those objectives. At the same time, a lawyer is not required to pursue objectives or employ means simply because a client may wish that the lawyer do so. A clear distinction between objectives and means sometimes cannot be drawn, and in many cases the client-lawyer relationship partakes of a joint undertaking. In questions of means, the lawyer should assume responsibility for technical and legal tactical issues, but should defer to the client regarding such questions as the expense to be incurred and concern for third persons who might be adversely affected. Law defining the lawyer's scope of authority in litigation varies among jurisdictions.

[2] In a case in which the client appears to be suffering mental disability, the lawyer's duty to abide by the client's decisions is to be guided by reference to Rule 1.14.

Independence from Client's Views or Activities

[3] Legal representation should not be denied to people who are unable to afford legal services, or whose cause is controversial or the subject of popular disapproval. By the same token, representing a client does not constitute approval of the client's views or activities.

Services Limited in Objectives or Means

[4] The objectives or scope of services provided by a lawyer may be limited by agreement with the client or by the terms under which the lawyer's services are made available to the client. For example, a retainer may be for a specifically defined purpose. Representation provided through a legal aid agency may be subject to limitations on the types of cases the agency handles. When a lawyer has been retained by an insurer to represent an insured, the representation may be limited to matters related to the insurance coverage. The terms upon which representation is undertaken may exclude specific objectives or means. Such limitations may exclude objectives or means that the lawyer regards as repugnant or imprudent.

[5] An agreement concerning the scope of representation must accord with the Rules of Professional Conduct and other law. Thus, the client may not be asked to agree to representation so limited in scope as to violate Rule 1.1, or to surrender the right to terminate the lawyer's services or the right to settle litigation that the lawyer might wish to continue.

Criminal, Fraudulent and Prohibited Transactions

[6] A lawyer is required to give an honest opinion about the actual consequences that appear likely to result from a client's conduct. The fact that a client uses advice in a course of action that is criminal or fraudulent does not, of itself, make a lawyer a party to the course of action. However, a lawyer may not knowingly assist a client in criminal or fraudulent conduct. There is a critical distinction between presenting an analysis of legal aspects of questionable conduct and rec-

ommending the means by which a crime or fraud might be committed with impunity.

[7] When the client's course of action has already begun and is continuing, the lawyer's responsibility is especially delicate. The lawyer is not permitted to reveal the client's wrongdoing, except where permitted by Rule 1.6. However, the lawyer is required to avoid furthering the purpose, for example, by suggesting how it might be concealed. A lawyer may not continue assisting a client in conduct that the lawyer originally supposes is legally proper but then discovers is criminal or fraudulent. Withdrawal from the representation, therefore, may be required.

[8] Where the client is a fiduciary, the lawyer may be charged with special obligations in dealings with a beneficiary.

[9] Paragraph (d) applies whether or not the defrauded party is a party to the transaction. Hence, a lawyer should not participate in a sham transaction; for example, a transaction to effectuate criminal or fraudulent escape of tax liability. Paragraph (d) does not preclude undertaking a criminal defense incident to a general retainer for legal services to a lawful enterprise. The last clause of paragraph (d) recognizes that determining the validity or interpretation of a statute or regulation may require a course of action involving disobedience of the statute or regulation or of the interpretation placed upon it by governmental authorities.

Model Code Comparison

Paragraph (a) has no counterpart in the Disciplinary Rules of the Model Code. EC 7-7 stated: "In certain areas of legal representation not affecting the merits of the cause or substantially prejudicing the rights of a client, a lawyer is entitled to make decisions on his own. But otherwise the authority to make decisions is exclusively that of the client . . . ." EC 7-8 stated that "[I]n the final analysis, however, the . . . decision whether to forego legally available objectives or methods because of nonlegal factors is ultimately for the client . . . . In the event that the client in a nonadjudicatory matter insists upon a course of conduct that is contrary to the judgment and advice of the lawyer but not prohibited by Disciplinary Rules, the lawyer may withdraw from the employment." DR 7-101(A)(1) provided that a lawyer "shall not intentionally . . . fail to seek the lawful objectives of his client through reasonably available means permitted by law . . . . A lawyer does not violate this Disciplinary Rule, however, by . . . avoiding offensive tactics . . . ."

Paragraph (b) has no counterpart in the Model Code.

With regard to Paragraph (c), DR 7-101(B)(1) provided that a lawyer may, "where permissible, exercise his professional judgment to waive or fail to assert a right or position of his client."

With regard to Paragraph (d), DR 7-102(A)(7) provided that a lawyer shall not "counsel or assist his client in conduct that the lawyer knows to be illegal or fraudulent." DR 7-102(A)(6) provided that a lawyer shall not "participate in the creation or preservation of evidence when he knows or it is obvious that the evidence is false." DR 7-106 provided that a lawyer shall not "advise his client to disregard a standing rule of a tribunal or a ruling of a tribunal . . . but he may take appropriate steps in good faith to test the validity of such rule or ruling." EC 7-5 stated that a lawyer "should never encourage or aid his client to commit criminal acts or counsel his client on how to violate the law and avoid punishment therefor."

With regard to Paragraph (e), DR 2-110(C)(1)(c) provided that a lawyer may withdraw from representation if a client "insists" that the lawyer engage in "conduct that is illegal or that is prohibited under the Disciplinary Rules." DR 9-101(C) provided that "a lawyer shall not state or imply that he is able to influence improperly . . . any tribunal, legislative body or public official."

RULE 1.3 DILIGENCE

A lawyer shall act with reasonable diligence and promptness in representing a client.

Comment

[1] A lawyer should pursue a matter on behalf of a client despite opposition, obstruction or personal inconvenience to the lawyer, and may take whatever lawful and ethical measures are required to vindicate a client's cause or endeavor. A lawyer should act with commitment and dedication to the interests of the client and with zeal in advocacy upon the client's behalf. However, a lawyer is not bound to press for every advantage that might be realized for a client. A lawyer has professional discretion in determining the means by which a matter should be pursued. See Rule 1.2. A lawyer's work load should be controlled so that each matter can be handled adequately.

[2] Perhaps no professional shortcoming is more widely resented than procrastination. A client's interests often can be adversely affected by the passage of time or the change of conditions; in extreme instances, as when a lawyer overlooks a statute of limitations, the client's legal position may be destroyed. Even when the client's interests are not affected in substance, however, unreasonable delay can cause a client needless anxiety and undermine confidence in the lawyer's trustworthiness.

[3] Unless the relationship is terminated as provided in Rule 1.16, a lawyer should carry through to conclusion all matters undertaken for a client. If a lawyer's employment is limited to a specific matter, the relationship terminates when the matter has been resolved. If a lawyer has served a client over a substantial period in a variety of matters, the client sometimes may assume that the lawyer will continue to serve on a continuing basis unless the lawyer gives notice of withdrawal. Doubt about whether a client-lawyer relationship still exists should be clarified by the lawyer, preferably in writing, so that the client will not mistakenly suppose the lawyer is looking after the client's affairs when the lawyer has ceased to do so. For example, if a lawyer has handled a judicial or administrative proceeding that produced a result adverse to the client but has not been specifically instructed concerning pursuit of an appeal, the lawyer should advise the client of the possibility of appeal before relinquishing responsibility for the matter.

Model Code Comparison

DR 6-101(A)(3) required that a lawyer not "[n]eglect a legal matter entrusted to him." EC 6-4 stated that a lawyer should "give appropriate attention to his legal work." Canon 7 stated that "a lawyer should represent a client zealously within the bounds of the law." DR 7-101(A)(1) provided that a lawyer "shall not intentionally . . . fail to seek the lawful objectives of his client through reasonably available means permitted by law and the Disciplinary Rules . . . ." DR 7-101(A)(3) provided that a lawyer "shall not intentionally . . . [p]rejudice or damage his client during the course of the relationship . . . ."

RULE 1.4 COMMUNICATION

(a) A lawyer shall keep a client reasonably informed about the status of a matter and promptly comply with reasonable requests for information.

(b) A lawyer shall explain a matter to the extent reasonably necessary to permit the client to make informed decisions regarding the representation.

Comment

[1] The client should have sufficient information to participate intelligently in decisions concerning the objectives of the representation and the means by which they are to be pursued, to the extent the client is willing and able to do so. For example, a lawyer negotiating on behalf of a client should provide the client with facts relevant to the matter, inform the client of communications from another party and take other reasonable steps that permit the client to make a decision regarding a serious offer from another party. A lawyer who receives from opposing counsel an offer of settlement in a civil controversy or a proffered plea bargain in a criminal case should promptly inform the client of its substance unless prior discussions with the client have left it clear that the proposal will be unacceptable. See Rule 1.2(a). Even when a client delegates authority to the lawyer, the client should be kept advised of the status of the matter.

[2] Adequacy of communication depends in part on the kind of advice or assistance involved. For example, in negotiations where there is time to explain a proposal, the lawyer should review all important provisions with the client before proceeding to an agreement. In litigation a lawyer should explain the general strategy and prospects of success and ordinarily should consult the client on tactics that might injure or coerce others. On the other hand, a lawyer ordinarily cannot be expected to describe trial or negotiation strategy in detail. The guiding principle is that the lawyer should fulfill reasonable client expectations for information consistent with the duty to act in the client's best interests, and the client's overall requirements as to the character of representation.

[3] Ordinarily, the information to be provided is that appropriate for a client who is a comprehending and responsible adult. However, fully informing the client according to this standard may be impracticable, for example, where the client is a

child or suffers from mental disability. See Rule 1.14. When the client is an organization or group, it is often impossible or inappropriate to inform every one of its members about its legal affairs; ordinarily, the lawyer should address communications to the appropriate officials of the organization. See Rule 1.13. Where many routine matters are involved, a system of limited or occasional reporting may be arranged with the client. Practical exigency may also require a lawyer to act for a client without prior consultation.

Withholding Information

[4] In some circumstances, a lawyer may be justified in delaying transmission of information when the client would be likely to react imprudently to an immediate communication. Thus, a lawyer might withhold a psychiatric diagnosis of a client when the examining psychiatrist indicates that disclosure would harm the client. A lawyer may not withhold information to serve the lawyer's own interest or convenience. Rules or court orders governing litigation may provide that information supplied to a lawyer may not be disclosed to the client. Rule 3.4(c) directs compliance with such rules or orders.

Model Code Comparison

Rule 1.4 has no direct counterpart in the Disciplinary Rules of the Model Code. DR 6-101(A)(3) provided that a lawyer shall not "[n]eglect a legal matter entrusted to him." DR 9-102(B)(1) provided that a lawyer shall "[p]romptly notify a client of the receipt of his funds, securities, or other properties." EC 7-8 stated that a lawyer "should exert his best efforts to insure that decisions of his client are made only after the client has been informed of relevant considerations." EC 9-2 stated that "a lawyer should fully and promptly inform his client of material developments in the matters being handled for the client."

RULE 1.5 FEES

(a) A lawyer's fee shall be reasonable. The factors to be considered in determining the reasonableness of a fee include the following:

(1) the time and labor required, the novelty and difficulty of the questions involved, and the skill requisite to perform the legal service properly;

(2) the likelihood, if apparent to the client, that the acceptance of the particular employment will preclude other employment by the lawyer;

(3) the fee customarily charged in the locality for similar legal services;

(4) the amount involved and the results obtained;

(5) the time limitations imposed by the client or by the circumstances;

(6) the nature and length of the professional relationship with the client;

(7) the experience, reputation, and ability of the lawyer or lawyers performing the services; and

(8) whether the fee is fixed or contingent.

(b) When the lawyer has not regularly represented the client, the basis or rate

of the fee shall be communicated to the client, preferably in writing, before or within a reasonable time after commencing the representation.

(c) A fee may be contingent on the outcome of the matter for which the service is rendered, except in a matter in which a contingent fee is prohibited by paragraph (d) or other law. A contingent fee agreement shall be in writing and shall state the method by which the fee is to be determined, including the percentage or percentages that shall accrue to the lawyer in the event of settlement, trial or appeal, litigation and other expenses to be deducted from the recovery, and whether such expenses are to be deducted before or after the contingent fee is calculated. Upon conclusion of a contingent fee matter, the lawyer shall provide the client with a written statement stating the outcome of the matter and, if there is a recovery, showing the remittance to the client and the method of its determination.

(d) A lawyer shall not enter into an arrangement for, charge, or collect:

(1) any fee in a domestic relations matter, the payment or amount of which is contingent upon the securing of a divorce or upon the amount of alimony or support, or property settlement in lieu thereof; or

(2) a contingent fee for representing a defendant in a criminal case.

(e) A division of a fee between lawyers who are not in the same firm may be made only if:

(1) the division is in proportion to the services performed by each lawyer or, by written agreement with the client, each lawyer assumes joint responsibility for the representation;

(2) the client is advised of and does not object to the participation of all the lawyers involved; and

(3) the total fee is reasonable.

Comment

Basis or Rate of Fee

[1] When the lawyer has regularly represented a client, they ordinarily will have evolved an understanding concerning the basis or rate of the fee. In a new client-lawyer relationship, however, an understanding as to the fee should be promptly established. It is not necessary to recite all the factors that underlie the basis of the fee, but only those that are directly involved in its computation. It is sufficient, for example, to state that the basic rate is an hourly charge or a fixed amount or an estimated amount, or to identify the factors that may be taken into account in finally fixing the fee. When developments occur during the representation that render an earlier estimate substantially inaccurate, a revised estimate should be provided to the client. A written statement concerning the fee reduces the possibility of misunderstanding. Furnishing the client with a simple memorandum or a copy of the lawyer's customary fee schedule is sufficient if the basis or rate of the fee is set forth.

Terms of Payment

[2] A lawyer may require advance payment of a fee, but is obliged to return any

unearned portion. See Rule 1.16(d). A lawyer may accept property in payment for services, such as an ownership interest in an enterprise, providing this does not involve acquisition of a proprietary interest in the cause of action or subject matter of the litigation contrary to Rule 1.8(j). However, a fee paid in property instead of money may be subject to special scrutiny because it involves questions concerning both the value of the services and the lawyer's special knowledge of the value of the property.

[3] An agreement may not be made whose terms might induce the lawyer improperly to curtail services for the client or perform them in a way contrary to the client's interest. For example, a lawyer should not enter into an agreement whereby services are to be provided only up to a stated amount when it is foreseeable that more extensive services probably will be required, unless the situation is adequately explained to the client. Otherwise, the client might have to bargain for further assistance in the midst of a proceeding or transaction. However, it is proper to define the extent of services in light of the client's ability to pay. A lawyer should not exploit a fee arrangement based primarily on hourly charges by using wasteful procedures. When there is doubt whether a contingent fee is consistent with the client's best interest, the lawyer should offer the client alternative bases for the fee and explain their implications. Applicable law may impose limitations on contingent fees, such as a ceiling on the percentage.

Division of Fee

[4] A division of fee is a single billing to a client covering the fee of two or more lawyers who are not in the same firm. A division of fee facilitates association of more than one lawyer in a matter in which neither alone could serve the client as well, and most often is used when the fee is contingent and the division is between a referring lawyer and a trial specialist. Paragraph (e) permits the lawyers to divide a fee on either the basis of the proportion of services they render or by agreement between the participating lawyers if all assume responsibility for the representation as a whole and the client is advised and does not object. It does not require disclosure to the client of the share that each lawyer is to receive. Joint responsibility for the representation entails the obligations stated in Rule 5.1 for purposes of the matter involved.

Disputes over Fees

[5] If a procedure has been established for resolution of fee disputes, such as an arbitration or mediation procedure established by the bar, the lawyer should conscientiously consider submitting to it. Law may prescribe a procedure for determining a lawyer's fee, for example, in representation of an executor or administrator, a class or a person entitled to a reasonable fee as part of the measure of damages. The lawyer entitled to such a fee and a lawyer representing another party concerned with the fee should comply with the prescribed procedure.

Model Code Comparison

DR 2-106(A) provided that a lawyer "shall not enter into an agreement for, charge, or collect an illegal or clearly excessive fee." DR 2-106(B) provided that a fee is "clearly excessive when, after a review of the facts, a lawyer of ordinary prudence would be left with a definite and firm conviction that the fee is in excess of a reasonable fee." The factors of a reasonable fee in Rule 1.5(a) are substantially identical to those listed in DR 2-106(B). EC 2-17 states that a lawyer "should not charge more than a reasonable fee . . . ."

There was no counterpart to paragraph (b) in the Disciplinary Rules of the Model Code. EC 2-19 stated that it is "usually beneficial to reduce to writing the understanding of the parties regarding the fee, particularly when it is contingent."

There was also no counterpart to paragraph (c) in the Disciplinary Rules of the Model Code. EC 2-20 provided that "[c]ontingent fee arrangements in civil cases have long been commonly accepted in the United States," but that "a lawyer generally should decline to accept employment on a contingent fee basis by one who is able to pay a reasonable fixed fee . . . ."

With regard to paragraph (d), DR 2-106(C) prohibited "a contingent fee in a criminal case." EC 2-20 provided that "contingent fee arrangements in domestic relation cases are rarely justified."

With regard to paragraph (e), DR 2-107(A) permitted division of fees only if: "(1) The client consents to employment of the other lawyer after a full disclosure that a division of fees will be made. (2) The division is in proportion to the services performed and responsibility assumed by each. (3) The total fee does not exceed clearly reasonable compensation . . . ." Paragraph (e) permits division without regard to the services rendered by each lawyer if they assume joint responsibility for the representation.

RULE 1.6 CONFIDENTIALITY OF INFORMATION

(a) A lawyer shall not reveal information relating to representation of a client unless the client consents after consultation, except for disclosures that are impliedly authorized in order to carry out the representation, and except as stated in paragraph (b).

(b) A lawyer may reveal such information to the extent the lawyer reasonably believes necessary:

(1) to prevent the client from committing a criminal act that the lawyer believes is likely to result in imminent death or substantial bodily harm; or

(2) to establish a claim or defense on behalf of the lawyer in a controversy between the lawyer and the client, to establish a defense to a criminal charge or civil claim against the lawyer based upon conduct in which the client was involved, or to respond to allegations in any proceeding concerning the lawyer's representation of the client.

Comment

[1] The lawyer is part of a judicial system charged with upholding the law. One of the lawyer's functions is to advise clients so that they avoid any violation of the law in the proper exercise of their rights.

[2] The observance of the ethical obligation of a lawyer to hold inviolate confidential information of the client not only facilitates the full development of facts essential to proper representation of the client but also encourages people to seek early legal assistance.

[3] Almost without exception, clients come to lawyers in order to determine what their rights are and what is, in the maze of laws and regulations, deemed to be legal and correct. The common law recognizes that the client's confidences must be protected from disclosure. Based upon experience, lawyers know that almost all clients follow the advice given, and the law is upheld.

[4] A fundamental principle in the client-lawyer relationship is that the lawyer maintain confidentiality of information relating to the representation. The client is thereby encouraged to communicate fully and frankly with the lawyer even as to embarrassing or legally damaging subject matter.

[5] The principle of confidentiality is given effect in two related bodies of law, the attorney-client privilege (which includes the work product doctrine) in the law of evidence and the rule of confidentiality established in professional ethics. The attorney-client privilege applies in judicial and other proceedings in which a lawyer may be called as a witness or otherwise required to produce evidence concerning a client. The rule of client-lawyer confidentiality applies in situations other than those where evidence is sought from the lawyer through compulsion of law. The confidentiality rule applies not merely to matters communicated in confidence by the client but also to all information relating to the representation, whatever its source. A lawyer may not disclose such information except as authorized or required by the Rules of Professional Conduct or other law. See also Scope.

[6] The requirement of maintaining confidentiality of information relating to representation applies to government lawyers who may disagree with the policy goals that their representation is designed to advance.

Authorized Disclosure

[7] A lawyer is impliedly authorized to make disclosures about a client when appropriate in carrying out the representation, except to the extent that the client's instructions or special circumstances limit that authority. In litigation, for example, a lawyer may disclose information by admitting a fact that cannot properly be disputed, or in negotiation by making a disclosure that facilitates a satisfactory conclusion.

[8] Lawyers in a firm may, in the course of the firm's practice, disclose to each other information relating to a client of the firm, unless the client has instructed that particular information be confined to specified lawyers.

Disclosure Adverse to Client

[9] The confidentiality rule is subject to limited exceptions. In becoming privy to information about a client, a lawyer may foresee that the client intends serious harm to another person. However, to the extent a lawyer is required or permitted to disclose a client's purposes, the client will be inhibited from revealing facts which would enable the lawyer to counsel against a wrongful course of action. The

public is better protected if full and open communication by the client is encouraged than if it is inhibited.

[10] Several situations must be distinguished.

[11] First, the lawyer may not counsel or assist a client in conduct that is criminal or fraudulent. See Rule 1.2(d). Similarly, a lawyer has a duty under Rule 3.3(a)(4) not to use false evidence. This duty is essentially a special instance of the duty prescribed in Rule 1.2(d) to avoid assisting a client in criminal or fraudulent conduct.

[12] Second, the lawyer may have been innocently involved in past conduct by the client that was criminal or fraudulent. In such a situation the lawyer has not violated Rule 1.2(d), because to "counsel or assist" criminal or fraudulent conduct requires knowing that the conduct is of that character.

[13] Third, the lawyer may learn that a client intends prospective conduct that is criminal and likely to result in imminent death or substantial bodily harm. As stated in paragraph (b)(1), the lawyer has professional discretion to reveal information in order to prevent such consequences. The lawyer may make a disclosure in order to prevent homicide or serious bodily injury which the lawyer reasonably believes is intended by a client. It is very difficult for a lawyer to "know" when such a heinous purpose will actually be carried out, for the client may have a change of mind.

[14] The lawyer's exercise of discretion requires consideration of such factors as the nature of the lawyer's relationship with the client and with those who might be injured by the client, the lawyer's own involvement in the transaction and factors that may extenuate the conduct in question. Where practical, the lawyer should seek to persuade the client to take suitable action. In any case, a disclosure adverse to the client's interest should be no greater than the lawyer reasonably believes necessary to the purpose. A lawyer's decision not to take preventive action permitted by paragraph (b)(1) does not violate this Rule.

Withdrawal

[15] If the lawyer's services will be used by the client in materially furthering a course of criminal or fraudulent conduct, the lawyer must withdraw, as stated in Rule 1.16(a)(1).

[16] After withdrawal the lawyer is required to refrain from making disclosure of the client's confidences, except as otherwise provided in Rule 1.6. Neither this rule nor Rule 1.8(b) nor Rule 1.16(d) prevents the lawyer from giving notice of the fact of withdrawal, and the lawyer may also withdraw or disaffirm any opinion, document, affirmation, or the like.

[17] Where the client is an organization, the lawyer may be in doubt whether contemplated conduct will actually be carried out by the organization. Where necessary to guide conduct in connection with this Rule, the lawyer may make inquiry within the organization as indicated in Rule 1.13(b).

Dispute Concerning a Lawyer's Conduct

[18] Where a legal claim or disciplinary charge alleges complicity of the lawyer in a client's conduct or other misconduct of the lawyer involving representation of

the client, the lawyer may respond to the extent the lawyer reasonably believes necessary to establish a defense. The same is true with respect to a claim involving the conduct or representation of a former client. The lawyer's right to respond arises when an assertion of such complicity has been made. Paragraph (b)(2) does not require the lawyer to await the commencement of an action or proceeding that charges such complicity, so that the defense may be established by responding directly to a third party who has made such an assertion. The right to defend, of course, applies where a proceeding has been commenced. Where practicable and not prejudicial to the lawyer's ability to establish the defense, the lawyer should advise the client of the third party's assertion and request that the client respond appropriately. In any event, disclosure should be no greater than the lawyer reasonably believes is necessary to vindicate innocence, the disclosure should be made in a manner which limits access to the information to the tribunal or other persons having a need to know it, and appropriate protective orders or other arrangements should be sought by the lawyer to the fullest extent practicable.

[19] If the lawyer is charged with wrongdoing in which the client's conduct is implicated, the rule of confidentiality should not prevent the lawyer from defending against the charge. Such a charge can arise in a civil, criminal or professional disciplinary proceeding, and can be based on a wrong allegedly committed by the lawyer against the client, or on a wrong alleged by a third person; for example, a person claiming to have been defrauded by the lawyer and client acting together. A lawyer entitled to a fee is permitted by paragraph (b)(2) to prove the services rendered in an action to collect it. This aspect of the rule expresses the principle that the beneficiary of a fiduciary relationship may not exploit it to the detriment of the fiduciary. As stated above, the lawyer must make every effort practicable to avoid unnecessary disclosure of information relating to a representation, to limit disclosure to those having the need to know it, and to obtain protective orders or make other arrangements minimizing the risk of disclosure.

Disclosures Otherwise Required or Authorized

[20] The attorney-client privilege is differently defined in various jurisdictions. If a lawyer is called as a witness to give testimony concerning a client, absent waiver by the client, paragraph (a) requires the lawyer to invoke the privilege when it is applicable. The lawyer must comply with the final orders of a court or other tribunal of competent jurisdiction requiring the lawyer to give information about the client.

[21] The Rules of Professional Conduct in various circumstances permit or require a lawyer to disclose information relating to the representation. See Rules 2.2, 2.3, 3.3 and 4.1. In addition to these provisions, a lawyer may be obligated or permitted by other provisions of law to give information about a client. Whether another provision of law supersedes Rule 1.6 is a matter of interpretation beyond the scope of these Rules, but a presumption should exist against such a supersession.

Former Client

[22] The duty of confidentiality continues after the client-lawyer relationship has terminated.

Model Code Comparison

Rule 1.6 eliminates the two-pronged duty under the Model Code in favor of a single standard protecting all information about a client "relating to representation." Under DR 4-101, the requirement applied to information protected by the attorney-client privilege and to information "gained in" the professional relationship that "the client has requested be held inviolate or the disclosure of which would be embarrassing or would be likely to be detrimental to the client." EC 4-4 added that the duty differed from the evidentiary privilege in that it existed "without regard to the nature or source of information or the fact that others share the knowledge." Rule 1.6 imposes confidentiality on information relating to the representation even if it is acquired before or after the relationship existed. It does not require the client to indicate information that is to be confidential, or permit the lawyer to speculate whether particular information might be embarrassing or detrimental.

Paragraph (a) permits a lawyer to disclose information where impliedly authorized to do so in order to carry out the representation. Under DR 4-101(B) and (C), a lawyer was not permitted to reveal "confidences" unless the client first consented after disclosure.

Paragraph (b) redefines the exceptions to the requirement of confidentiality. Regarding paragraph (b)(1), DR 4-101(C)(3) provided that a lawyer "may reveal [t]he intention of his client to commit a crime and the information necessary to prevent the crime." This option existed regardless of the seriousness of the proposed crime.

With regard to paragraph (b)(2), DR 4-101(C)(4) provided that a lawyer may reveal "[c]onfidences or secrets necessary to establish or collect his fee or to defend himself or his employers or associates against an accusation of wrongful conduct." Paragraph (b)(2) enlarges the exception to include disclosure of information relating to claims by the lawyer other than for the lawyer's fee; for example, recovery of property from the client.

RULE 1.7[1] CONFLICT OF INTEREST: GENERAL RULE

(a) A lawyer shall not represent a client if the representation of that client will be directly adverse to another client, unless:

(1) the lawyer reasonably believes the representation will not adversely affect the relationship with the other client; and

(2) each client consents after consultation.

---

1. Amended February 17, 1987, American Bar Association House of Delegates, New Orleans, Louisiana, per Report No. 121.

(b) A lawyer shall not represent a client if the representation of that client may be materially limited by the lawyer's responsibilities to another client or to a third person, or by the lawyer's own interests, unless:

(1) the lawyer reasonably believes the representation will not be adversely affected; and

(2) the client consents after consultation. When representation of multiple clients in a single matter is undertaken, the consultation shall include explanation of the implications of the common representation and the advantages and risks involved.

Comment

Loyalty to a Client

[1] Loyalty is an essential element in the lawyer's relationship to a client. An impermissible conflict of interest may exist before representation is undertaken, in which event the representation should be declined. The lawyer should adopt reasonable procedures, appropriate for the size and type of firm and practice, to determine in both litigation and non-litigation matters the parties and issues involved and to determine whether there are actual or potential conflicts of interest.

[2] If such a conflict arises after representation has been undertaken, the lawyer should withdraw from the representation. See Rule 1.16. Where more than one client is involved and the lawyer withdraws because a conflict arises after representation, whether the lawyer may continue to represent any of the clients is determined by Rule 1.9. See also Rule 2.2(c). As to whether a client-lawyer relationship exists or, having once been established, is continuing, see Comment to Rule 1.3 and Scope.

[3] As a general proposition, loyalty to a client prohibits undertaking representation directly adverse to that client without that client's consent. Paragraph (a) expresses that general rule. Thus, a lawyer ordinarily may not act as advocate against a person the lawyer represents in some other matter, even if it is wholly unrelated. On the other hand, simultaneous representation in unrelated matters of clients whose interests are only generally adverse, such as competing economic enterprises, does not require consent of the respective clients. Paragraph (a) applies only when the representation of one client would be directly adverse to the other.

[4] Loyalty to a client is also impaired when a lawyer cannot consider, recommend or carry out an appropriate course of action for the client because of the lawyer's other responsibilities or interests. The conflict in effect forecloses alternatives that would otherwise be available to the client. Paragraph (b) addresses such situations. A possible conflict does not itself preclude the representation. The critical questions are the likelihood that a conflict will eventuate and, if it does, whether it will materially interfere with the lawyer's independent professional judgment in considering alternatives or foreclose courses of action that reasonably should be pursued on behalf of the client. Consideration should be given to whether the client wishes to accommodate the other interest involved.

Consultation and Consent

[5] A client may consent to representation notwithstanding a conflict. However, as indicated in paragraph (a)(1) with respect to representation directly adverse to a client, and paragraph (b)(1) with respect to material limitations on representation of a client, when a disinterested lawyer would conclude that the client should not agree to the representation under the circumstances, the lawyer involved cannot properly ask for such agreement or provide representation on the basis of the client's consent. When more than one client is involved, the question of conflict must be resolved as to each client. Moreover, there may be circumstances where it is impossible to make the disclosure necessary to obtain consent. For example, when the lawyer represents different clients in related matters and one of the clients refuses to consent to the disclosure necessary to permit the other client to make an informed decision, the lawyer cannot properly ask the latter to consent.

Lawyer's Interests

[6] The lawyer's own interests should not be permitted to have an adverse effect on representation of a client. For example, a lawyer's need for income should not lead the lawyer to undertake matters that cannot be handled competently and at a reasonable fee. See Rules 1.1 and 1.5. If the probity of a lawyer's own conduct in a transaction is in serious question, it may be difficult or impossible for the lawyer to give a client detached advice. A lawyer may not allow related business interests to affect representation, for example, by referring clients to an enterprise in which the lawyer has an undisclosed interest.

Conflicts in Litigation

[7] Paragraph (a) prohibits representation of opposing parties in litigation. Simultaneous representation of parties whose interests in litigation may conflict, such as coplaintiffs or codefendants, is governed by paragraph (b). An impermissible conflict may exist by reason of substantial discrepancy in the parties' testimony, incompatibility in positions in relation to an opposing party or the fact that there are substantially different possibilities of settlement of the claims or liabilities in question. Such conflicts can arise in criminal cases as well as civil. The potential for conflict of interest in representing multiple defendants in a criminal case is so grave that ordinarily a lawyer should decline to represent more than one codefendant. On the other hand, common representation of persons having similar interests is proper if the risk of adverse effect is minimal and the requirements of paragraph (b) are met. Compare Rule 2.2 involving intermediation between clients.

[8] Ordinarily, a lawyer may not act as advocate against a client the lawyer represents in some other matter, even if the other matter is wholly unrelated. However, there are circumstances in which a lawyer may act as advocate against a client. For example, a lawyer representing an enterprise with diverse operations may accept employment as an advocate against the enterprise in an unrelated matter if doing so will not adversely affect the lawyer's relationship with the enterprise or conduct of the suit and if both clients consent upon consultation. By the same

token, government lawyers in some circumstances may represent government employees in proceedings in which a government agency is the opposing party. The propriety of concurrent representation can depend on the nature of the litigation. For example, a suit charging fraud entails conflict to a degree not involved in a suit for a declaratory judgment concerning statutory interpretation.

[9] A lawyer may represent parties having antagonistic positions on a legal question that has arisen in different cases, unless representation of either client would be adversely affected. Thus, it is ordinarily not improper to assert such positions in cases pending in different trial courts, but it may be improper to do so in cases pending at the same time in an appellate court.

Interest of Person Paying for a Lawyer's Service

[10] A lawyer may be paid from a source other than the client, if the client is informed of that fact and consents and the arrangement does not compromise the lawyer's duty of loyalty to the client. See Rule 1.8(f). For example, when an insurer and its insured have conflicting interests in a matter arising from a liability insurance agreement, and the insurer is required to provide special counsel for the insured, the arrangement should assure the special counsel's professional independence. So also, when a corporation and its directors or employees are involved in a controversy in which they have conflicting interests, the corporation may provide funds for separate legal representation of the directors or employees, if the clients consent after consultation and the arrangement ensures the lawyer's professional independence.

Other Conflict Situations

[11] Conflicts of interest in contexts other than litigation sometimes may be difficult to assess. Relevant factors in determining whether there is potential for adverse effect include the duration and intimacy of the lawyer's relationship with the client or clients involved, the functions being performed by the lawyer, the likelihood that actual conflict will arise and the likely prejudice to the client from the conflict if it does arise. The question is often one of proximity and degree.

[12] For example, a lawyer may not represent multiple parties to a negotiation whose interests are fundamentally antagonistic to each other, but common representation is permissible where the clients are generally aligned in interest even though there is some difference of interest among them.

[13] Conflict questions may also arise in estate planning and estate administration. A lawyer may be called upon to prepare wills for several family members, such as husband and wife, and, depending upon the circumstances, a conflict of interest may arise. In estate administration the identity of the client may be unclear under the law of a particular jurisdiction. Under one view, the client is the fiduciary; under another view, the client is the estate or trust, including its beneficiaries. The lawyer should make clear the relationship to the parties involved.

[14] A lawyer for a corporation or other organization who is also a member of its board of directors should determine whether the responsibilities of the two roles may conflict. The lawyer may be called on to advise the corporation in matters

involving actions of the directors. Consideration should be given to the frequency with which such situations may arise, the potential intensity of the conflict, the effect of the lawyer's resignation from the board and the possibility of the corporation's obtaining legal advice from another lawyer in such situations. If there is material risk that the dual role will compromise the lawyer's independence of professional judgment, the lawyer should not serve as a director.

Conflict Charged by an Opposing Party

[15] Resolving questions of conflict of interest is primarily the responsibility of the lawyer undertaking the representation. In litigation, a court may raise the question when there is reason to infer that the lawyer has neglected the responsibility. In a criminal case, inquiry by the court is generally required when a lawyer represents multiple defendants. Where the conflict is such as clearly to call in question the fair or efficient administration of justice, opposing counsel may properly raise the question. Such an objection should be viewed with caution, however, for it can be misused as a technique of harassment. See Scope.

Model Code Comparison

DR 5-101(A) provided that "[e]xcept with the consent of his client after full disclosure, a lawyer shall not accept employment if the exercise of his professional judgment on behalf of the client will be or reasonably may be affected by his own financial, business, property, or personal interests." DR 5-105(A) provided that a lawyer "shall decline proffered employment if the exercise of his independent professional judgment in behalf of a client will be or is likely to be adversely affected by the acceptance of the proffered employment, or if it would be likely to involve him in representing differing interests, except to the extent permitted under DR 5-105(C)." DR 5-105(C) provided that "a lawyer may represent multiple clients if it is obvious that he can adequately represent the interest of each and if each consents to the representation after full disclosure of the possible effect of such representation on the exercise of his independent professional judgment on behalf of each." DR 5-107(B) provided that a lawyer "shall not permit a person who recommends, employs, or pays him to render legal services for another to direct or regulate his professional judgment in rendering such services."

Rule 1.7 clarifies DR 5-105(A) by requiring that, when the lawyer's other interests are involved, not only must the client consent after consultation but also that, independent of such consent, the representation reasonably appears not to be adversely affected by the lawyer's other interests. This requirement appears to be the intended meaning of the provision in DR 5-105(C) that "it is obvious that he can adequately represent" the client, and was implicit in EC 5-2, which stated that a lawyer "should not accept proffered employment if his personal interests or desires will, or there is a reasonable probability that they will, affect adversely the advice to be given or services to be rendered the prospective client."

RULE 1.8[2] CONFLICT OF INTEREST: PROHIBITED TRANSACTIONS

(a) A lawyer shall not enter into a business transaction with a client or knowingly acquire an ownership, possessory, security or other pecuniary interestadverse to a client unless:

(1) the transaction and terms on which the lawyer acquires the interest are fair and reasonable to the client and are fully disclosed and transmitted in writing to the client in a manner which can be reasonably understood by the client;

(2) the client is given a reasonable opportunity to seek the advice of independent counsel in the transaction; and

(3) the client consents in writing thereto.

(b) A lawyer shall not use information relating to representation of a client to the disadvantage of the client unless the client consents after consultation, except as permitted or required by Rule 1.6 or Rule 3.3.

(c) A lawyer shall not prepare an instrument giving the lawyer or a person related to the lawyer as parent, child, sibling, or spouse any substantial gift from a client, including a testamentary gift, except where the client is related to the donee.

(d) Prior to the conclusion of representation of a client, a lawyer shall not make or negotiate an agreement giving the lawyer literary or media rights to a portrayal or account based in substantial part on information relating to the representation.

(e) A lawyer shall not provide financial assistance to a client in connection with pending or contemplated litigation, except that:

(1) a lawyer may advance court costs and expenses of litigation, the repayment of which may be contingent on the outcome of the matter; and

(2) a lawyer representing an indigent client may pay court costs and expenses of litigation on behalf of the client.

(f) A lawyer shall not accept compensation for representing a client from one other than the client unless:

(1) the client consents after consultation;

(2) there is no interference with the lawyer's independence of professional judgment or with the client-lawyer relationship; and

(3) information relating to representation of a client is protected as required by Rule 1.6.

(g) A lawyer who represents two or more clients shall not participate in making an aggregate settlement of the claims of or against the clients, or in a criminal case an aggregated agreement as to guilty or nolo contendere pleas, unless each client consents after consultation, including disclosure of the existence and nature of all the claims or pleas involved and of the participation of each person in the settlement.

2. Amended February 7, 1987, American Bar Association House of Delegates, New Orleans, Louisiana, per Report No. 121.

(h) A lawyer shall not make an agreement prospectively limiting the lawyer's liability to a client for malpractice unless permitted by law and the client is independently represented in making the agreement, or settle a claim for such liability with an unrepresented client or former client without first advising that person in writing that independent representation is appropriate in connection therewith.

(i) A lawyer related to another lawyer as parent, child, sibling or spouse shall not represent a client in a representation directly adverse to a person whom the lawyer knows is represented by the other lawyer except upon consent by the client after consultation regarding the relationship.

(j) A lawyer shall not acquire a proprietary interest in the cause of action or subject matter of litigation the lawyer is conducting for a client, except that the lawyer may:

(1) acquire a lien granted by law to secure the lawyer's fee or expenses; and

(2) contract with a client for a reasonable contingent fee in a civil case.

Comment

Transactions Between Client and Lawyer

[1] As a general principle, all transactions between client and lawyer should be fair and reasonable to the client. In such transactions a review by independent counsel on behalf of the client is often advisable. Furthermore, a lawyer may not exploit information relating to the representation to the client's disadvantage. For example, a lawyer who has learned that the client is investing in specific real estate may not, without the client's consent, seek to acquire nearby property where doing so would adversely affect the client's plan for investment. Paragraph (a) does not, however, apply to standard commercial transactions between the lawyer and the client for products or services that the client generally markets to others, for example, banking or brokerage services, medical services, products manufactured or distributed by the client, and utilities' services. In such transactions, the lawyer has no advantage in dealing with the client, and the restrictions in paragraph (a) are unnecessary and impracticable.

[2] A lawyer may accept a gift from a client, if the transaction meets general standards of fairness. For example, a simple gift such as a present given at a holiday or as a token of appreciation is permitted. If effectuation of a substantial gift requires preparing a legal instrument such as a will or conveyance, however, the client should have the detached advice that another lawyer can provide. Paragraph (c) recognizes an exception where the client is a relative of the donee or the gift is not substantial.

Literary Rights

[3] An agreement by which a lawyer acquires literary or media rights concerning the conduct of the representation creates a conflict between the interests of the client and the personal interests of the lawyer. Measures suitable in the repre-

sentation of the client may detract from the publication value of an account of the representation. Paragraph (d) does not prohibit a lawyer representing a client in a transaction concerning literary property from agreeing that the lawyer's fee shall consist of a share in ownership in the property, if the arrangement conforms to Rule 1.5 and paragraph (j).

Person Paying for a Lawyer's Services

[4] Paragraph (f) requires disclosure of the fact that the lawyer's services are being paid for by a third party. Such an arrangement must also conform to the requirements of Rule 1.6 concerning confidentiality and Rule 1.7 concerning conflict of interest. Where the client is a class, consent may be obtained on behalf of the class by court-supervised procedure.

Limiting Liability

[5] Paragraph (h) is not intended to apply to customary qualifications and limitations in legal opinions and memoranda.

Family Relationships Between Lawyers

[6] Paragraph (i) applies to related lawyers who are in different firms. Related lawyers in the same firm are governed by Rules 1.7, 1.9, and 1.10. The disqualification stated in paragraph (i) is personal and is not imputed to members of firms with whom the lawyers are associated.

Acquisition of Interest in Litigation

[7] Paragraph (j) states the traditional general rule that lawyers are prohibited from acquiring a proprietary interest in litigation. This general rule, which has its basis in common law champerty and maintenance, is subject to specific exceptions developed in decisional law and continued in these Rules, such as the exception for reasonable contingent fees set forth in Rule 1.5 and the exception for certain advances of the costs of litigation set forth in paragraph (e).

Model Code Comparison

With regard to paragraph (a), DR 5-104(A) provided that a lawyer "shall not enter into a business transaction with a client if they have differing interests therein and if the client expects the lawyer to exercise his professional judgment therein for the protection of the client, unless the client has consented after full disclosure." EC 5-3 stated that a lawyer "should not seek to persuade his client to permit him to invest in an undertaking of his client nor make improper use of his professional relationship to influence his client to invest in an enterprise in which the lawyer is interested."

With regard to paragraph (b), DR 4-101(B)(3) provided that a lawyer should not use "a confidence or secret of his client for the advantage of himself, or of a third person, unless the client consents after full disclosure."

There was no counterpart to paragraph (c) in the Disciplinary Rules of the Model Code. EC 5-5 stated that a lawyer "should not suggest to his client that a gift be made to himself or for his benefit. If a lawyer accepts a gift from his client, he is peculiarly susceptible to the charge that he unduly influenced or overreached the client. If a client voluntarily offers to make a gift to his lawyer, the lawyer may accept the gift, but before doing so, he should urge that the client secure disinterested advice from an independent, competent person who is cognizant of all the circumstances. Other than in exceptional circumstances, a lawyer should insist that an instrument in which his client desires to name him beneficially be prepared by another lawyer selected by the client."

Paragraph (d) is substantially similar to DR 5-104(B), but refers to "literary or media" rights, a more generally inclusive term than "publication" rights.

Paragraph (e)(1) is similar to DR 5-103(B), but eliminates the requirement that "the client remains ultimately liable for such expenses."

Paragraph (e)(2) has no counterpart in the Model Code.

Paragraph (f) is substantially identical to DR 5-107(A)(1).

Paragraph (g) is substantially identical to DR 5-106.

The first clause of paragraph (h) is similar to DR 6-102(A). There was no counterpart in the Model Code to the second clause of paragraph (h).

Paragraph (i) has no counterpart in the Model Code.

Paragraph (j) is substantially identical to DR 5-103(A).

RULE 1.9[3] CONFLICT OF INTEREST: FORMER CLIENT

(a) A lawyer who has formerly represented a client in a matter shall not thereafter represent another person in the same or a substantially related matter in which that person's interests are materially adverse to the interests of the former client unless the former client consents after consultation.

(b) A lawyer shall not knowingly represent a person in the same or a substantially related matter in which a firm with which the lawyer formerly was associated had previously represented a client

(1) whose interests are materially adverse to that person; and

(2) about whom the lawyer had acquired information protected by Rules 1.6 and 1.9(c) that is material to the matter;

unless the former client consents after consultation.

(c) A lawyer who has formerly represented a client in a matter or whose present or former firm has formerly represented a client in a matter shall not thereafter:

(1) use information relating to the representation to the disadvantage of the former client except as Rule 1.6 or Rule 3.3 would permit or require with respect to a client, or when the information has become generally known; or

3. Amended February 17, 1987, American Bar Association House of Delegates, New Orleans, Louisiana, per Report No. 121; February 7, 1989, American Bar Association House of Delegates, Denver, Colorado, per Report No. 120A.

(2) reveal information relating to the representation except as Rule 1.6 or Rule 3.3 would permit or require with respect to a client.

Comment

[1] After termination of a client-lawyer relationship, a lawyer may not represent another client except in conformity with this Rule. The principles in Rule 1.7 determine whether the interests of the present and former client are adverse. Thus, a lawyer could not properly seek to rescind on behalf of a new client a contract drafted on behalf of the former client. So also a lawyer who has prosecuted an accused person could not properly represent the accused in a subsequent civil action against the government concerning the same transaction.

[2] The scope of a "matter" for purposes of this Rule may depend on the facts of a particular situation or transaction. The lawyer's involvement in a matter can also be a question of degree. When a lawyer has been directly involved in a specific transaction, subsequent representation of other clients with materially adverse interests clearly is prohibited. On the other hand, a lawyer who recurrently handled a type of problem for a former client is not precluded from later representing another client in a wholly distinct problem of that type even though the subsequent representation involves a position adverse to the prior client. Similar considerations can apply to the reassignment of military lawyers between defense and prosecution functions within the same military jurisdiction. The underlying question is whether the lawyer was so involved in the matter that the subsequent representation can be justly regarded as a changing of sides in the matter in question.

Lawyers Moving Between Firms

[3] When lawyers have been associated within a firm but then end their association, the question of whether a lawyer should undertake representation is more complicated. There are several competing considerations. First, the client previously represented by the former firm must be reasonably assured that the principle of loyalty to the client is not compromised. Second, the rule should not be so broadly cast as to preclude other persons from having reasonable choice of legal counsel. Third, the rule should not unreasonably hamper lawyers from forming new associations and taking on new clients after having left a previous association. In this connection, it should be recognized that today many lawyers practice in firms, that many lawyers to some degree limit their practice to one field or another, and that many move from one association to another several times in their careers. If the concept of imputation were applied with unqualified rigor, the result would be radical curtailment of the opportunity of lawyers to move from one practice setting to another and of the opportunity of clients to change counsel.

[4] Reconciliation of these competing principles in the past has been attempted under two rubrics. One approach has been to seek per se rules of disqualification. For example, it has been held that a partner in a law firm is conclusively presumed to have access to all confidences concerning all clients of the firm. Under this analy-

sis, if a lawyer has been a partner in one law firm and then becomes a partner in another law firm, there may be a presumption that all confidences known by the partner in the first firm are known to all partners in the second firm. This presumption might properly be applied in some circumstances, especially where the client has been extensively represented, but may be unrealistic where the client was represented only for limited purposes. Furthermore, such a rigid rule exaggerates the difference between a partner and an associate in modern law firms.

[5] The other rubric formerly used for dealing with disqualification is the appearance of impropriety proscribed in Canon 9 of the ABA Model Code of Professional Responsibility. This rubric has a two-fold problem. First, the appearance of impropriety can be taken to include any new client-lawyer relationship that might make a former client feel anxious. If that meaning were adopted, disqualification would become little more than a question of subjective judgment by the former client. Second, since "impropriety" is undefined, the term "appearance of impropriety" is question-begging. It therefore has to be recognized that the problem of disqualification cannot be properly resolved either by simple analogy to a lawyer practicing alone or by the very general concept of appearance of impropriety.

Confidentiality

[6] Preserving confidentiality is a question of access to information. Access to information, in turn, is essentially a question of fact in particular circumstances, aided by inferences, deductions or working presumptions that reasonably may be made about the way in which lawyers work together. A lawyer may have general access to files of all clients of a law firm and may regularly participate in discussions of their affairs; it should be inferred that such a lawyer in fact is privy to all information about all the firm's clients. In contrast, another lawyer may have access to the files of only a limited number of clients and participate in discussions of the affairs of no other clients; in the absence of information to the contrary, it should be inferred that such a lawyer in fact is privy to information about the clients actually served but not those of other clients.

[7] Application of paragraph (b) depends on a situation's particular facts. In such an inquiry, the burden of proof should rest upon the firm whose disqualification is sought.

[8] Paragraph (b) operates to disqualify the lawyer only when the lawyer involved has actual knowledge of information protected by Rules 1.6 and 1.9(b). Thus, if a lawyer while with one firm acquired no knowledge or information relating to a particular client of the firm, and that lawyer later joined another firm, neither the lawyer individually nor the second firm is disqualified from representing another client in the same or a related matter even though the interests of the two clients conflict. See Rule 1.10(b) for the restrictions on a firm once a lawyer has terminated association with the firm.

[9] Independent of the question of disqualification of a firm, a lawyer changing professional association has a continuing duty to preserve confidentiality of information about a client formerly represented. See Rules 1.6 and 1.9.

Adverse Positions

[10] The second aspect of loyalty to a client is the lawyer's obligation to decline subsequent representations involving positions adverse to a former client arising in substantially related matters. This obligation requires abstention from adverse representation by the individual lawyer involved, but does not properly entail abstention of other lawyers through imputed disqualification. Hence, this aspect of the problem is governed by Rule 1.9(a). Thus, if a lawyer left one firm for another, the new affiliation would not preclude the firms involved from continuing to represent clients with adverse interests in the same or related matters, so long as the conditions of paragraphs (b) and (c) concerning confidentiality have been met.

[11] Information acquired by the lawyer in the course of representing a client may not subsequently be used or revealed by the lawyer to the disadvantage of the client. However, the fact that a lawyer has once served a client does not preclude the lawyer from using generally known information about that client when later representing another client.

[12] Disqualification from subsequent representation is for the protection of former clients and can be waived by them. A waiver is effective only if there is disclosure of the circumstances, including the lawyer's intended role in behalf of the new client.

[13] With regard to an opposing party's raising a question of conflict of interest, see Comment to Rule 1.7. With regard to disqualification of a firm with which a lawyer is or was formerly associated, see Rule 1.10.

Model Code Comparison

There was no counterpart to this Rule in the Disciplinary Rules of the Model Code. Representation adverse to a former client was sometimes dealt with under the rubric of Canon 9 of the Model Code, which provided: "A lawyer should avoid even the appearance of impropriety." Also applicable were EC 4-6 which stated that the "obligation of a lawyer to preserve the confidences and secrets of his client continues after the termination of his employment" and Canon 5 which stated that "[a] lawyer should exercise independent professional judgment on behalf of a client."

The provision for waiver by the former client in paragraphs (a) and (b) is similar to DR 5-105(C).

The exception in the last clause of paragraph (c)(1) permits a lawyer to use information relating to a former client that is in the "public domain," a use that was also not prohibited by the Model Code, which protected only "confidences and secrets." Since the scope of paragraphs (a) and (b) is much broader than "confidences and secrets," it is necessary to define when a lawyer may make use of information about a client after the client-lawyer relationship has terminated.

RULE 1.10[4] IMPUTED DISQUALIFICATION: GENERAL RULE

(a) While lawyers are associated in a firm, none of them shall knowingly represent a client when any one of them practicing alone would be prohibited from doing so by Rules 1.7, 1.8(c), 1.9 or 2.2.

(b) When a lawyer has terminated an association with a firm, the firm is not prohibited from thereafter representing a person with interests materially adverse to those of a client represented by the formerly associated lawyer and not currently represented by the firm, unless:

(1) the matter is the same or substantially related to that in which the formerly associated lawyer represented the client; and

(2) any lawyer remaining in the firm has information protected by Rules 1.6 and 1.9(c) that is material to the matter.

(c) A disqualification prescribed by this rule may be waived by the affected client under the conditions stated in Rule 1.7.

Comment

Definition of "Firm"

[1] For purposes of the Rules of Professional Conduct, the term "firm" includes lawyers in a private firm, and lawyers in the legal department of a corporation or other organization, or in a legal services organization. Whether two or more lawyers constitute a firm within this definition can depend on the specific facts. For example, two practitioners who share office space and occasionally consult or assist each other ordinarily would not be regarded as constituting a firm. However, if they present themselves to the public in a way suggesting that they are a firm or conduct themselves as a firm, they should be regarded as a firm for the purposes of the Rules. The terms of any formal agreement between associated lawyers are relevant in determining whether they are a firm, as is the fact that they have mutual access to information concerning the clients they serve. Furthermore, it is relevant in doubtful cases to consider the underlying purpose of the Rule that is involved. A group of lawyers could be regarded as a firm for purposes of the rule that the same lawyer should not represent opposing parties in litigation, while it might not be so regarded for purposes of the rule that information acquired by one lawyer is attributed to the other.

[2] With respect to the law department of an organization, there is ordinarily no question that the members of the department constitute a firm within the meaning of the Rules of Professional Conduct. However, there can be uncertainty as to the identity of the client. For example, it may not be clear whether the law department of a corporation represents a subsidiary or an affiliated corporation, as well as the corporation by which the members of the department are directly

4. Amended February 17, 1987, American Bar Association House of Delegates, New Orleans, Louisiana, per Report No. 121.

employed. A similar question can arise concerning an unincorporated association and its local affiliates.

[3] Similar questions can also arise with respect to lawyers in legal aid. Lawyers employed in the same unit of a legal service organization constitute a firm, but not necessarily those employed in separate units. As in the case of independent practitioners, whether the lawyers should be treated as associated with each other can depend on the particular rule that is involved, and on the specific facts of the situation.

[4] Where a lawyer has joined a private firm after having represented the government, the situation is governed by Rule 1.11 (a) and (b); where a lawyer represents the government after having served private clients, the situation is governed by Rule 1.11(c)(1). The individual lawyer involved is bound by the Rules generally, including Rules 1.6, 1.7 and 1.9.

[5] Different provisions are thus made for movement of a lawyer from one private firm to another and for movement of a lawyer between a private firm and the government. The government is entitled to protection of its client confidences and, therefore, to the protections provided in Rules 1.6, 1.9 and 1.11. However, if the more extensive disqualification in Rule 1.10 were applied to former government lawyers, the potential effect on the government would be unduly burdensome. The government deals with all private citizens and organizations and, thus, has a much wider circle of adverse legal interests than does any private law firm. In these circumstances, the government's recruitment of lawyers would be seriously impaired if Rule 1.10 were applied to the government. On balance, therefore, the government is better served in the long run by the protections stated in Rule 1.11.

Principles of Imputed Disqualification

[6] The rule of imputed disqualification stated in paragraph (a) gives effect to the principle of loyalty to the client as it applies to lawyers who practice in a law firm. Such situations can be considered from the premise that a firm of lawyers is essentially one lawyer for purposes of the rules governing loyalty to the client, or from the premise that each lawyer is vicariously bound by the obligation of loyalty owed by each lawyer with whom the lawyer is associated. Paragraph (a) operates only among the lawyers currently associated in a firm. When a lawyer moves from one firm to another, the situation is governed by Rules 1.9(b) and 1.10(b).

[7] Rule 1.10(b) operates to permit a law firm, under certain circumstances, to represent a person with interests directly adverse to those of a client represented by a lawyer who formerly was associated with the firm. The Rule applies regardless of when the formerly associated lawyer represented the client. However, the law firm may not represent a person with interests adverse to those of a present client of the firm, which would violate Rule 1.7. Moreover, the firm may not represent the person where the matter is the same or substantially related to that in which the formerly associated lawyer represented the client and any other lawyer currently in the firm has material information protected by Rules 1.6 and 1.9(c).

Model Code Comparison

DR 5-105(D) provided that "[i]f a lawyer is required to decline or to withdraw from employment under a Disciplinary Rule, no partner, or associate, or any other lawyer affiliated with him or his firm, may accept or continue such employment."

RULE 1.11[5] SUCCESSIVE GOVERNMENT AND PRIVATE EMPLOYMENT

(a) Except as law may otherwise expressly permit, a lawyer shall not represent a private client in connection with a matter in which the lawyer participated personally and substantially as a public officer or employee, unless the appropriate government agency consents after consultation. No lawyer in a firm with which that lawyer is associated may knowingly undertake or continue representation in such a matter unless:

(1) the disqualified lawyer is screened from any participation in the matter and is apportioned no part of the fee therefrom; and

(2) written notice is promptly given to the appropriate government agency to enable it to ascertain compliance with the provisions of this rule.

(b) Except as law may otherwise expressly permit, a lawyer having information that the lawyer knows is confidential government information about a person acquired when the lawyer was a public officer or employee, may not represent a private client whose interests are adverse to that person in a matter in which the information could be used to the material disadvantage of that person. A firm with which that lawyer is associated may undertake or continue representation in the matter only if the disqualified lawyer is screened from any participation in the matter and is apportioned no part of the fee therefrom.

(c) Except as law may otherwise expressly permit, a lawyer serving as a public officer or employee shall not:

(1) participate in a matter in which the lawyer participated personally and substantially while in private practice or nongovernmental employment, unless under applicable law no one is, or by lawful delegation may be, authorized to act in the lawyer's stead in the matter; or

(2) negotiate for private employment with any person who is involved as a party or as lawyer for a party in a matter in which the lawyer is participating personally and substantially, except that a lawyer serving as a law clerk to a judge, other adjudicative officer or arbitrator may negotiate for private employment as permitted by Rule 1.12(b) and subject to the conditions stated in Rule 1.12(b).

(d) As used in this Rule, the term "matter" includes:

5. Amended February 17, 1987, American Bar Association House of Delegates, New Orleans, Louisiana, per Report No. 121.

(1) any judicial or other proceeding, application, request for a ruling or other determination, contract, claim, controversy, investigation, charge, accusation, arrest or other particular matter involving a specific party or parties, and

(2) any other matter covered by the conflict of interest rules of the appropriate government agency.

(e) As used in this Rule, the term "confidential government information" means information which has been obtained under governmental authority and which, at the time this rule is applied, the government is prohibited by law from disclosing to the public or has a legal privilege not to disclose, and which is not otherwise available to the public.

Comment

[1] This Rule prevents a lawyer from exploiting public office for the advantage of a private client. It is a counterpart of Rule 1.10(b), which applies to lawyers moving from one firm to another.

[2] A lawyer representing a government agency, whether employed or specially retained by the government, is subject to the Rules of Professional Conduct, including the prohibition against representing adverse interests stated in Rule 1.7 and the protections afforded former clients in Rule 1.9. In addition, such a lawyer is subject to Rule 1.11 and to statutes and government regulations regarding conflict of interest. Such statutes and regulations may circumscribe the extent to which the government agency may give consent under this Rule.

[3] Where the successive clients are a public agency and a private client, the risk exists that power or discretion vested in public authority might be used for the special benefit of a private client. A lawyer should not be in a position where benefit to a private client might affect performance of the lawyer's professional functions on behalf of public authority. Also, unfair advantage could accrue to the private client by reason of access to confidential government information about the client's adversary obtainable only through the lawyer's government service. However, the rules governing lawyers presently or formerly employed by a government agency should not be so restrictive as to inhibit transfer of employment to and from the government. The government has a legitimate need to attract qualified lawyers as well as to maintain high ethical standards. The provisions for screening and waiver are necessary to prevent the disqualification rule from imposing too severe a deterrent against entering public service.

[4] When the client is an agency of one government, that agency should be treated as a private client for purposes of this Rule if the lawyer thereafter represents an agency of another government, as when a lawyer represents a city and subsequently is employed by a federal agency.

[5] Paragraphs (a)(1) and (b) do not prohibit a lawyer from receiving a salary or partnership share established by prior independent agreement. They prohibit directly relating the lawyer's compensation to the fee in the matter in which the lawyer is disqualified.

[6] Paragraph (a)(2) does not require that a lawyer give notice to the government agency at a time when premature disclosure would injure the client; a require-

ment for premature disclosure might preclude engagement of the lawyer. Such notice is, however, required to be given as soon as practicable in order that the government agency will have a reasonable opportunity to ascertain that the lawyer is complying with Rule 1.11 and to take appropriate action if it believes the lawyer is not complying.

[7] Paragraph (b) operates only when the lawyer in question has knowledge of the information, which means actual knowledge; it does not operate with respect to information that merely could be imputed to the lawyer.

[8] Paragraphs (a) and (c) do not prohibit a lawyer from jointly representing a private party and a government agency when doing so is permitted by Rule 1.7 and is not otherwise prohibited by law.

[9] Paragraph (c) does not disqualify other lawyers in the agency with which the lawyer in question has become associated.

Model Code Comparison

Paragraph (a) is similar to DR 9-101(B), except that the latter used the terms "in which he had substantial responsibility while he was a public employee."

Paragraphs (b), (c), (d) and (e) have no counterparts in the Model Code.

RULE 1.12[6] FORMER JUDGE OR ARBITRATOR

(a) Except as stated in paragraph (d), a lawyer shall not represent anyone in connection with a matter in which the lawyer participated personally and substantially as a judge or other adjudicative officer, arbitrator or law clerk to such a person, unless all parties to the proceeding consent after consultation.

(b) A lawyer shall not negotiate for employment with any person who is involved as a party or as lawyer for a party in a matter in which the lawyer is participating personally and substantially as a judge or other adjudicative officer or arbitrator. A lawyer serving as a law clerk to a judge, other adjudicative officer or arbitrator may negotiate for employment with a party or lawyer involved in a matter in which the clerk is participating personally and substantially, but only after the lawyer has notified the judge, other adjudicative officer or arbitrator.

(c) If a lawyer is disqualified by paragraph (a), no lawyer in a firm with which that lawyer is associated may knowingly undertake or continue representation in the matter unless:

(1) the disqualified lawyer is screened from any participation in the matter and is apportioned no part of the fee therefrom; and

(2) written notice is promptly given to the appropriate tribunal to enable it to ascertain compliance with the provisions of this rule.

(d) An arbitrator selected as a partisan of a party in a multimember arbitration panel is not prohibited from subsequently representing that party.

6. Amended February 17, 1987, American Bar Association House of Delegates, New Orleans, Louisiana, per Report No. 121.

Comment

[1] This Rule generally parallels Rule 1.11. The term "personally and substantially" signifies that a judge who was a member of a multimember court, and thereafter left judicial office to practice law, is not prohibited from representing a client in a matter pending in the court, but in which the former judge did not participate. So also the fact that a former judge exercised administrative responsibility in a court does not prevent the former judge from acting as a lawyer in a matter where the judge had previously exercised remote or incidental administrative responsibility that did not affect the merits. Compare the Comment to Rule 1.11. The term "adjudicative officer" includes such officials as judges pro tempore, referees, special masters, hearing officers and other parajudicial officers, and also lawyers who serve as part-time judges. Compliance Canons A(2), B(2) and C of the Model Code of Judicial Conduct provide that a part-time judge, judge pro tempore or retired judge recalled to active service, may not "act as a lawyer in any proceeding in which he served as a judge or in any other proceeding related thereto." Although phrased differently from this Rule, those rules correspond in meaning.

Model Code Comparison

Paragraph (a) is substantially similar to DR 9-101(A), which provided that a lawyer "shall not accept private employment in a matter upon the merits of which he has acted in a judicial capacity." Paragraph (a) differs, however, in that it is broader in scope and states more specifically the persons to whom it applies. There was no counterpart in the Model Code to paragraphs (b), (c) or (d).

With regard to arbitrators, EC 5-20 stated that "a lawyer [who] has undertaken to act as an impartial arbitrator or mediator, . . . should not thereafter represent in the dispute any of the parties involved." DR 9-101(A) did not permit a waiver of the disqualification applied to former judges by consent of the parties. However, DR 5-105(C) was similar in effect and could be construed to permit waiver.

RULE 1.13 ORGANIZATION AS CLIENT

(a) A lawyer employed or retained by an organization represents the organization acting through its duly authorized constituents.

(b) If a lawyer for an organization knows that an officer, employee or other person associated with the organization is engaged in action, intends to act or refuses to act in a matter related to the representation that is a violation of a legal obligation to the organization, or a violation of law which reasonably might be imputed to the organization, and is likely to result in substantial injury to the organization, the lawyer shall proceed as is reasonably necessary in the best interest of the organization. In determining how to proceed, the lawyer shall give due consideration to the seriousness of the violation and its consequences, the scope and nature of the lawyer's representation, the responsibility in the organization and the apparent motivation of the person involved, the policies of the organization concerning such matters and any other relevant considerations. Any measures taken shall be

designed to minimize disruption of the organization and the risk of revealing information relating to the representation to persons outside the organization. Such measures may include among others:

(1) asking reconsideration of the matter;

(2) advising that a separate legal opinion on the matter be sought for presentation to appropriate authority in the organization; and

(3) referring the matter to higher authority in the organization, including, if warranted by the seriousness of the matter, referral to the highest authority that can act in behalf of the organization as determined by applicable law.

(c) If, despite the lawyer's efforts in accordance with paragraph (b), the highest authority that can act on behalf of the organization insists upon action, or a refusal to act, that is clearly a violation of law and is likely to result in substantial injury to the organization, the lawyer may resign in accordance with Rule 1.16.

(d) In dealing with an organization's directors, officers, employees, members, shareholders or other constituents, a lawyer shall explain the identity of the client when it is apparent that the organization's interests are adverse to those of the constituents with whom the lawyer is dealing.

(e) A lawyer representing an organization may also represent any of its directors, officers, employees, members, shareholders or other constituents, subject to the provisions of Rule 1.7. If the organization's consent to the dual representation is required by Rule 1.7, the consent shall be given by an appropriate official of the organization other than the individual who is to be represented, or by the shareholders.

Comment

The Entity as the Client

[1] An organizational client is a legal entity, but it cannot act except through its officers, directors, employees, shareholders and other constituents. Officers, directors, employees and shareholders are the constituents of the corporate organizational client. The duties defined in this Comment apply equally to unincorporated associations. "Other constituents" as used in this Comment means the positions equivalent to officers, directors, employees and shareholders held by persons acting for organizational clients that are not corporations.

[2] When one of the constituents of an organizational client communicates with the organization's lawyer in that person's organizational capacity, the communication is protected by Rule 1.6. Thus, by way of example, if an organizational client requests its lawyer to investigate allegations of wrongdoing, interviews made in the course of that investigation between the lawyer and the client's employees or other constituents are covered by Rule 1.6. This does not mean, however, that constituents of an organizational client are the clients of the lawyer. The lawyer may not disclose to such constituents information relating to the representation except for disclosures explicitly or impliedly authorized by the organizational client in order to carry out the representation or as otherwise permitted by Rule 1.6.

[3] When constituents of the organization make decisions for it, the decisions ordinarily must be accepted by the lawyer even if their utility or prudence is doubt-

ful. Decisions concerning policy and operations, including ones entailing serious risk, are not as such in the lawyer's province. However, different considerations arise when the lawyer knows that the organization may be substantially injured by action of a constituent that is in violation of law. In such a circumstance, it may be reasonably necessary for the lawyer to ask the constituent to reconsider the matter. If that fails, or if the matter is of sufficient seriousness and importance to the organization, it may be reasonably necessary for the lawyer to take steps to have the matter reviewed by a higher authority in the organization. Clear justification should exist for seeking review over the head of the constituent normally responsible for it. The stated policy of the organization may define circumstances and prescribe channels for such review, and a lawyer should encourage the formulation of such a policy. Even in the absence of organization policy, however, the lawyer may have an obligation to refer a matter to higher authority, depending on the seriousness of the matter and whether the constituent in question has apparent motives to act at variance with the organization's interest. Review by the chief executive officer or by the board of directors may be required when the matter is of importance commensurate with their authority. At some point it may be useful or essential to obtain an independent legal opinion.

[4] In an extreme case, it may be reasonably necessary for the lawyer to refer the matter to the organization's highest authority. Ordinarily, that is the board of directors or similar governing body. However, applicable law may prescribe that under certain conditions highest authority reposes elsewhere, for example, in the independent directors of a corporation.

Relation to Other Rules

[5] The authority and responsibility provided in paragraph (b) are concurrent with the authority and responsibility provided in other Rules. In particular, this Rule does not limit or expand the lawyer's responsibility under Rule 1.6, 1.8, 1.16, 3.3 or 4.1. If the lawyer's services are being used by an organization to further a crime or fraud by the organization, Rule 1.2(d) can be applicable.

Government Agency

[6] The duty defined in this Rule applies to governmental organizations. However, when the client is a governmental organization, a different balance may be appropriate between maintaining confidentiality and assuring that the wrongful official act is prevented or rectified, for public business is involved. In addition, duties of lawyers employed by the government or lawyers in military service may be defined by statutes and regulation. Therefore, defining precisely the identity of the client and prescribing the resulting obligations of such lawyers may be more difficult in the government context. Although in some circumstances the client may be a specific agency, it is generally the government as a whole. For example, if the action or failure to act involves the head of a bureau, either the department of which the bureau is a part or the government as a whole may be the client for purpose of this Rule. Moreover, in a matter involving the conduct of government officials, a government lawyer may have authority to question such conduct more

extensively than that of a lawyer for a private organization in similar circumstances. This Rule does not limit that authority. See note on Scope.

Clarifying the Lawyer's Role

[7] There are times when the organization's interest may be or become adverse to those of one or more of its constituents. In such circumstances the lawyer should advise any constituent, whose interest the lawyer finds adverse to that of the organization of the conflict or potential conflict of interest, that the lawyer cannot represent such constituent, and that such person may wish to obtain independent representation. Care must be taken to assure that the individual understands that, when there is such adversity of interest, the lawyer for the organization cannot provide legal representation for that constituent individual, and that discussions between the lawyer for the organization and the individual may not be privileged.

[8] Whether such a warning should be given by the lawyer for the organization to any constituent individual may turn on the facts of each case.

Dual Representation

[9] Paragraph (e) recognizes that a lawyer for an organization may also represent a principal officer or major shareholder.

Derivative Actions

[10] Under generally prevailing law, the shareholders or members of a corporation may bring suit to compel the directors to perform their legal obligations in the supervision of the organization. Members of unincorporated associations have essentially the same right. Such an action may be brought nominally by the organization, but usually is, in fact, a legal controversy over management of the organization.

[11] The question can arise whether counsel for the organization may defend such an action. The proposition that the organization is the lawyer's client does not alone resolve the issue. Most derivative actions are a normal incident of an organization's affairs, to be defended by the organization's lawyer like any other suit. However, if the claim involves serious charges of wrongdoing by those in control of the organization, a conflict may arise between the lawyer's duty to the organization and the lawyer's relationship with the board. In those circumstances, Rule 1.7 governs who should represent the directors and the organization.

Model Code Comparison

There was no counterpart to this Rule in the Disciplinary Rules of the Model Code. EC 5-18 stated that a "lawyer employed or retained by a corporation or similar entity owes his allegiance to the entity and not to a stockholder, director, officer, employee, representative, or other person connected with the entity. In advising the entity, a lawyer should keep paramount its interests and his professional judgment should not be influenced by the personal desires of any person or organization. Occasionally, a lawyer for an entity is requested by a stockholder, director, officer, employee, representative, or other person connected with the entity to represent him in an individual capacity; in such case the lawyer may serve the individual only if the lawyer is convinced that differing interests are not present." EC 5-24 stated that although a lawyer "may be employed by a business corporation with non-lawyers serving as directors or officers, and they necessarily have the right to make decisions of business policy, a lawyer must decline to accept direction of his professional judgment from any layman." DR 5-107(B) provided that a lawyer "shall not permit a person who . . . employs . . . him to render legal services for another to direct or regulate his professional judgment in rendering such legal services."

RULE 1.14[7] CLIENT UNDER A DISABILITY

(a) When a client's ability to make adequately considered decisions in connection with the representation is impaired, whether because of minority, mental disability or for some other reason, the lawyer shall, as far as reasonably possible, maintain a normal client-lawyer relationship with the client.

(b) A lawyer may seek the appointment of a guardian or take other protective action with respect to a client only when the lawyer reasonably believes that the client cannot adequately act in the client's own interest.

Comment

[1] The normal client-lawyer relationship is based on the assumption that the client, when properly advised and assisted, is capable of making decisions about important matters. When the client is a minor or suffers from a mental disorder or disability, however, maintaining the ordinary client-lawyer relationship may not be possible in all respects. In particular, an incapacitated person may have no power to make legally binding decisions. Nevertheless, a client lacking legal competence often has the ability to understand, deliberate upon, and reach conclusions about matters affecting the client's own well-being. Furthermore, to an increasing extent the law recognizes intermediate degrees of competence. For example, children as young as five or six years of age, and certainly those of ten or twelve, are regarded as having opinions that are entitled to weight in legal proceedings concerning their custody. So also, it is recognized that some persons of advanced age can be quite capable of handling routine financial matters while needing special legal protection concerning major transactions.

[2] The fact that a client suffers a disability does not diminish the lawyer's obligation to treat the client with attention and respect. If the person has no guardian or legal representative, the lawyer often must act as de facto guardian. Even if the person does have a legal representative, the lawyer should as far as possible accord the represented person the status of client, particularly in maintaining communication.

[3] If a legal representative has already been appointed for the client, the lawyer should ordinarily look to the representative for decisions on behalf of the client. If a legal representative has not been appointed, the lawyer should see to

7. Amended February 3, 1997, American Bar Association House of Delegates, San Antonio, Texas, per Report No. 113.

such an appointment where it would serve the client's best interests. Thus, if a disabled client has substantial property that should be sold for the client's benefit, effective completion of the transaction ordinarily requires appointment of a legal representative. In many circumstances, however, appointment of a legal representative may be expensive or traumatic for the client. Evaluation of these considerations is a matter of professional judgment on the lawyer's part.

[4] If the lawyer represents the guardian as distinct from the ward, and is aware that the guardian is acting adversely to the ward's interest, the lawyer may have an obligation to prevent or rectify the guardian's misconduct. See Rule 1.2(d).

Disclosure of the Client's Condition

[5] Rules of procedure in litigation generally provide that minors or persons suffering mental disability shall be represented by a guardian or next friend if they do not have a general guardian. However, disclosure of the client's disability can adversely affect the client's interests. For example, raising the question of disability could, in some circumstances, lead to proceedings for involuntary commitment. The lawyer's position in such cases is an unavoidably difficult one. The lawyer may seek guidance from an appropriate diagnostician.

Emergency Legal Assistance

[6] In an emergency where the health, safety or a financial interest of a person under a disability is threatened with imminent and irreparable harm, a lawyer may take legal action on behalf of such a person even though the person is unable to establish a client-lawyer relationship or to make or express considered judgments about the matter, when the disabled person or another acting in good faith on that person's behalf has consulted the lawyer. Even in such an emergency, however, the lawyer should not act unless the lawyer reasonably believes that the person has no other lawyer, agent or other representative available. The lawyer should take legal action on behalf of the disabled person only to the extent reasonably necessary to maintain the status quo or otherwise avoid imminent and irreparable harm. A lawyer who undertakes to represent a person in such an exigent situation has the same duties under these Rules as the lawyer would with respect to a client.

[7] A lawyer who acts on behalf of a disabled person in an emergency should keep the confidences of the disabled person as if dealing with a client, disclosing them only to the extent necessary to accomplish the intended protective action. The lawyer should disclose to any tribunal involved and to any other counsel involved the nature of his or her relationship with the disabled person. The lawyer should take steps to regularize the relationship or implement other protective solutions as soon as possible. Normally, a lawyer would not seek compensation for such emergency actions taken on behalf of a disabled person.

Model Code Comparison

There was no counterpart to this Rule in the Disciplinary Rules of the Model Code. EC 7-11 stated that the "responsibilities of a lawyer may vary according to the intelligence, experience, mental condition or age of a client . . . . Examples include the representation of an illiterate or an incompetent." EC 7-12 stated that "[a]ny mental or physical condition of a client that renders him incapable of making a considered judgment on his own behalf casts additional responsibilities upon his lawyer. Where an incompetent is acting through a guardian or other legal representative, a lawyer must look to such representative for those decisions which are normally the prerogative of the client to make. If a client under disability has no legal representative, his lawyer may be compelled in court proceedings to make decisions on behalf of the client. If the client is capable of understanding the matter in question or of contributing to the advancement of his interests, regardless of whether he is legally disqualified from performing certain acts, the lawyer should obtain from him all possible aid. If the disability of a client and the lack of a legal representative compel the lawyer to make decisions for his client, the lawyer should consider all circumstances then prevailing and act with care to safeguard and advance the interests of his client. But obviously a lawyer cannot perform any act or make any decision which the law requires his client to perform or make, either acting for himself if competent, or by a duly constituted representative if legally incompetent."

RULE 1.15 SAFEKEEPING PROPERTY

(a) A lawyer shall hold property of clients or third persons that is in a lawyer's possession in connection with a representation separate from the lawyer's own property. Funds shall be kept in a separate account maintained in the state where the lawyer's office is situated, or elsewhere with the consent of the client or third person. Other property shall be identified as such and appropriately safeguarded. Complete records of such account funds and other property shall be kept by the lawyer and shall be preserved for a period of [five years] after termination of the representation.

(b) Upon receiving funds or other property in which a client or third person has an interest, a lawyer shall promptly notify the client or third person. Except as stated in this rule or otherwise permitted by law or by agreement with the client, a lawyer shall promptly deliver to the client or third person any funds or other property that the client or third person is entitled to receive and, upon request by the client or third person, shall promptly render a full accounting regarding such property.

(c) When in the course of representation a lawyer is in possession of property in which both the lawyer and another person claim interests, the property shall be kept separate by the lawyer until there is an accounting and severance of their interests. If a dispute arises concerning their respective interests, the portion in dispute shall be kept separate by the lawyer until the dispute is resolved.

Comment

[1] A lawyer should hold property of others with the care required of a professional fiduciary. Securities should be kept in a safe deposit box, except when some other form of safekeeping is warranted by special circumstances. All proper-

ty which is the property of clients or third persons should be kept separate from the lawyer's business and personal property and, if monies, in one or more trust accounts. Separate trust accounts may be warranted when administering estate monies or acting in similar fiduciary capacities.

[2] Lawyers often receive funds from third parties from which the lawyer's fee will be paid. If there is risk that the client may divert the funds without paying the fee, the lawyer is not required to remit the portion from which the fee is to be paid. However, a lawyer may not hold funds to coerce a client into accepting the lawyer's contention. The disputed portion of the funds should be kept in trust and the lawyer should suggest means for prompt resolution of the dispute, such as arbitration. The undisputed portion of the funds shall be promptly distributed.

[3] Third parties, such as a client's creditors, may have just claims against funds or other property in a lawyer's custody. A lawyer may have a duty under applicable law to protect such third-party claims against wrongful interference by the client, and accordingly may refuse to surrender the property to the client. However, a lawyer should not unilaterally assume to arbitrate a dispute between the client and the third party.

[4] The obligations of a lawyer under this Rule are independent of those arising from activity other than rendering legal services. For example, a lawyer who serves as an escrow agent is governed by the applicable law relating to fiduciaries even though the lawyer does not render legal services in the transaction.

[5] A "clients' security fund" provides a means through the collective efforts of the bar to reimburse persons who have lost money or property as a result of dishonest conduct of a lawyer. Where such a fund has been established, a lawyer should participate.

Model Code Comparison

With regard to paragraph (a), DR 9-102(A) provided that "funds of clients" are to be kept in an identifiable bank account in the state in which the lawyer's office is situated. DR 9-102(B)(2) provided that a lawyer shall "identify and label securities and properties of a client . . . and place them in . . . safekeeping . . . ." DR 9-102(B)(3) required that a lawyer "[m]aintain complete records of all funds, securities, and other properties of a client . . . ." Paragraph (a) extends these requirements to property of a third person that is in the lawyer's possession in connection with the representation.

Paragraph (b) is substantially similar to DR 9-102(B)(1), (3) and (4).

Paragraph (c) is similar to DR 9-102(A)(2), except that the requirement regarding disputes applies to property concerning which an interest is claimed by a third person as well as by a client.

RULE 1.16 DECLINING OR TERMINATING REPRESENTATION

(a) Except as stated in paragraph (c), a lawyer shall not represent a client or, where representation has commenced, shall withdraw from the representation of a client if:

(1) the representation will result in violation of the rules of professional conduct or other law;

(2) the lawyer's physical or mental condition materially impairs the lawyer's ability to represent the client; or

(3) the lawyer is discharged.

(b) except as stated in paragraph (c), a lawyer may withdraw from representing a client if withdrawal can be accomplished without material adverse effect on the interests of the client, or if:

(1) the client persists in a course of action involving the lawyer's services that the lawyer reasonably believes is criminal or fraudulent;

(2) the client has used the lawyer's services to perpetrate a crime or fraud;

(3) a client insists upon pursuing an objective that the lawyer considers repugnant or imprudent;

(4) the client fails substantially to fulfill an obligation to the lawyer regarding the lawyer's services and has been given reasonable warning that the lawyer will withdraw unless the obligation is fulfilled;

(5) the representation will result in an unreasonable financial burden on the lawyer or has been rendered unreasonably difficult by the client; or

(6) other good cause for withdrawal exists.

(c) When ordered to do so by a tribunal, a lawyer shall continue representation notwithstanding good cause for terminating the representation.

(d) Upon termination of representation, a lawyer shall take steps to the extent reasonably practicable to protect a client's interests, such as giving reasonable notice to the client, allowing time for employment of other counsel, surrendering papers and property to which the client is entitled and refunding any advance payment of fee that has not been earned. The lawyer may retain papers relating to the client to the extent permitted by other law.

Comment

[1] A lawyer should not accept representation in a matter unless it can be performed competently, promptly, without improper conflict of interest and to completion.

Mandatory Withdrawal

[2] A lawyer ordinarily must decline or withdraw from representation if the client demands that the lawyer engage in conduct that is illegal or violates the Rules of Professional Conduct or other law. The lawyer is not obliged to decline or withdraw simply because the client suggests such a course of conduct; a client may make such a suggestion in the hope that a lawyer will not be constrained by a professional obligation.

[3] When a lawyer has been appointed to represent a client, withdrawal ordinarily requires approval of the appointing authority. See also Rule 6.2. Difficulty may be encountered if withdrawal is based on the client's demand that the lawyer engage in unprofessional conduct. The court may wish an explanation for the withdrawal,

while the lawyer may be bound to keep confidential the facts that would constitute such an explanation. The lawyer's statement that professional considerations require termination of the representation ordinarily should be accepted as sufficient.

Discharge

[4] A client has a right to discharge a lawyer at any time, with or without cause, subject to liability for payment for the lawyer's services. Where future dispute about the withdrawal may be anticipated, it may be advisable to prepare a written statement reciting the circumstances.

[5] Whether a client can discharge appointed counsel may depend on applicable law. A client seeking to do so should be given a full explanation of the consequences. These consequences may include a decision by the appointing authority that appointment of successor counsel is unjustified, thus requiring self-representation by the client.

[6] If the client is mentally incompetent, the client may lack the legal capacity to discharge the lawyer, and in any event the discharge may be seriously adverse to the client's interests. The lawyer should make special effort to help the client consider the consequences and, in an extreme case, may initiate proceedings for a conservatorship or similar protection of the client. See Rule 1.14.

Optional Withdrawal

[7] A lawyer may withdraw from representation in some circumstances. The lawyer has the option to withdraw if it can be accomplished without material adverse effect on the client's interests. Withdrawal is also justified if the client persists in a course of action that the lawyer reasonably believes is criminal or fraudulent, for a lawyer is not required to be associated with such conduct even if the lawyer does not further it. Withdrawal is also permitted if the lawyer's services were misused in the past even if that would materially prejudice the client. The lawyer also may withdraw where the client insists on a repugnant or imprudent objective.

[8] A lawyer may withdraw if the client refuses to abide by the terms of an agreement relating to the representation, such as an agreement concerning fees or court costs or an agreement limiting the objectives of the representation.

Assisting the Client upon Withdrawal

[9] Even if the lawyer has been unfairly discharged by the client, a lawyer must take all reasonable steps to mitigate the consequences to the client. The lawyer may retain papers as security for a fee only to the extent permitted by law. Whether or not a lawyer for an organization may under certain unusual circumstances have a legal obligation to the organization after withdrawing or being discharged by the organization's highest authority is beyond the scope of these Rules.

Model Code Comparison

With regard to paragraph (a), DR 2-109(A) provided that a lawyer "shall not accept employment . . . if he knows or it is obvious that [the prospective client] wishes to . . . [b]ring a legal action . . . or otherwise have steps taken for him, merely for the purpose of harassing or maliciously injuring any person . . . ." Nor may a lawyer accept employment if the lawyer is aware that the prospective client wishes to "[p]resent a claim or defense . . . that is not warranted under existing law, unless it can be supported by good faith argument for an extension, modification, or reversal of existing law." DR 2-110(B) provided that a lawyer "shall withdraw from employment . . . if:

"(1) He knows or it is obvious that his client is bringing the legal action . . . or is otherwise having steps taken for him, merely for the purpose of harassing or maliciously injuring any person.

"(2) He knows or it is obvious that his continued employment will result in violation of a Disciplinary Rule.

"(3) His mental or physical condition renders it unreasonably difficult for him to carry out the employment effectively.

"(4) He is discharged by his client."

With regard to paragraph (b), DR 2-110(C) permitted withdrawal regardless of the effect on the client if:

"(1) His client: (a) Insists upon presenting a claim or defense that is not warranted under existing law and cannot be supported by good faith argument for an extension, modification, or reversal of existing law; (b) Personally seeks to pursue an illegal course of conduct; (c) Insists that the lawyer pursue a course of conduct that is illegal or that is prohibited under the Disciplinary Rules; (d) By other conduct renders it unreasonably difficult for the lawyer to carry out his employment effectively; (e) Insists, in a matter not pending before a tribunal, that the lawyer engage in conduct that is contrary to the judgment and advice of the lawyer but not prohibited under the Disciplinary Rules; (f) Deliberately disregards an agreement or obligation to the lawyer as to expenses and fees.

"(2) His continued employment is likely to result in a violation of a Disciplinary Rule.

"(3) His inability to work with co-counsel indicates that the best interest of the client likely will be served by withdrawal.

"(4) His mental or physical condition renders it difficult for him to carry out the employment effectively.

"(5) His client knowingly and freely assents to termination of his employment.

"(6) He believes in good faith, in a proceeding pending before a tribunal, that the tribunal will find the existence of other good cause for withdrawal."

With regard to paragraph (c), DR 2-110(A)(1) provided: "If permission for withdrawal from employment is required by the rules of a tribunal, the lawyer shall not withdraw . . . without its permission."

The provisions of paragraph (d) are substantially identical to DR 2-110(A)(2) and (3).

RULE 1.17[8] SALE OF LAW PRACTICE

A lawyer or a law firm may sell or purchase a law practice, including good will, if the following conditions are satisfied:

(a) The seller ceases to engage in the private practice of law [in the geographic area] [in the jurisdiction] (a jurisdiction may elect either version) in which the practice has been conducted;

(b) The practice is sold as an entirety to another lawyer or law firm;

(c) Actual written notice is given to each of the seller's clients regarding:

(1) the proposed sale;

(2) the terms of any proposed change in the fee arrangement authorized by paragraph (d);

(3) the client's right to retain other counsel or to take possession of the file; and

(4) the fact that the client's consent to the sale will be presumed if the client does not take any action or does not otherwise object within ninety (90) days of receipt of the notice.

If a client cannot be given notice, the representation of that client may be transferred to the purchaser only upon entry of an order so authorizing by a court having jurisdiction. The seller may disclose to the court in camera information relating to the representation only to the extent necessary to obtain an order authorizing the transfer of a file.

(d) The fees charged clients shall not be increased by reason of the sale. The purchaser may, however, refuse to undertake the representation unless the client consents to pay the purchaser fees at a rate not exceeding the fees charged by the purchaser for rendering substantially similar services prior to the initiation of the purchase negotiations.

Comment

[1] The practice of law is a profession, not merely a business. Clients are not commodities that can be purchased and sold at will. Pursuant to this Rule, when a lawyer or an entire firm ceases to practice and another lawyer or firm takes over the representation, the selling lawyer or firm may obtain compensation for the reasonable value of the practice as may withdrawing partners of law firms. See Rules 5.4 and 5.6.

Termination of Practice by the Seller

[2] The requirement that all of the private practice be sold is satisfied if the seller in good faith makes the entire practice available for sale to the purchaser. The fact that a number of the seller's clients decide not to be represented by the purchaser but take their matters elsewhere, therefore, does not result in a violation. Neither does a return to private practice as a result of an unanticipated change in circumstances result in a violation. For example, a lawyer who has sold the practice

8. Added February 7, 1990, American Bar Association House of Delegates, Los Angeles, California, per Report No. 8A.

to accept an appointment to judicial office does not violate the requirement that the sale be attendant to cessation of practice if the lawyer later resumes private practice upon being defeated in a contested or a retention election for the office.

[3] The requirement that the seller cease to engage in the private practice of law does not prohibit employment as a lawyer on the staff of a public agency or a legal services entity which provides legal services to the poor, or as in-house counsel to a business.

[4] The Rule permits a sale attendant upon retirement from the private practice of law within the jurisdiction. Its provisions, therefore, accommodate the lawyer who sells the practice upon the occasion of moving to another state. Some states are so large that a move from one locale therein to another is tantamount to leaving the jurisdiction in which the lawyer has engaged in the practice of law. To also accommodate lawyers so situated, states may permit the sale of the practice when the lawyer leaves the geographic area rather than the jurisdiction. The alternative desired should be indicated by selecting one of the two provided for in Rule 1.17(a).

Single Purchaser

[5] The Rule requires a single purchaser. The prohibition against piecemeal sale of a practice protects those clients whose matters are less lucrative and who might find it difficult to secure other counsel if a sale could be limited to substantial fee-generating matters. The purchaser is required to undertake all client matters in the practice, subject to client consent. If, however, the purchaser is unable to undertake all client matters because of a conflict of interest in a specific matter respecting which the purchaser is not permitted by Rule 1.7 or another rule to represent the client, the requirement that there be a single purchaser is nevertheless satisfied.

Client Confidences, Consent and Notice

[6] Negotiations between seller and prospective purchaser prior to disclosure of information relating to a specific representation of an identifiable client no more violate the confidentiality provisions of Model Rule 1.6 than do preliminary discussions concerning the possible association of another lawyer or mergers between firms, with respect to which client consent is not required. Providing the purchaser access to client-specific information relating to the representation and to the file, however, requires client consent. The Rule provides that before such information can be disclosed by the seller to the purchaser the client must be given actual written notice of the contemplated sale, including the identity of the purchaser and any proposed change in the terms of future representation, and must be told that the decision to consent or make other arrangements must be made within 90 days. If nothing is heard from the client within that time, consent to the sale is presumed.

[7] A lawyer or law firm ceasing to practice cannot be required to remain in practice because some clients cannot be given actual notice of the proposed pur-

chase. Since these clients cannot themselves consent to the purchase or direct any other disposition of their files, the Rule requires an order from a court having jurisdiction authorizing their transfer or other disposition. The Court can be expected to determine whether reasonable efforts to locate the client have been exhausted, and whether the absent client's legitimate interests will be served by authorizing the transfer of the file so that the purchaser may continue the representation. Preservation of client confidences requires that the petition for a court order be considered in camera. (A procedure by which such an order can be obtained needs to be established in jurisdictions in which it presently does not exist.)

[8] All the elements of client autonomy, including the client's absolute right to discharge a lawyer and transfer the representation to another, survive the sale of the practice.

Fee Arrangements Between Client and Purchaser

[9] The sale may not be financed by increases in fees charged the clients of the practice. Existing agreements between the seller and the client as to fees and the scope of the work must be honored by the purchaser, unless the client consents after consultation. The purchaser may, however, advise the client that the purchaser will not undertake the representation unless the client consents to pay the higher fees the purchaser usually charges. To prevent client financing of the sale, the higher fees the purchaser may charge must not exceed the fees charged by the purchaser for substantially similar service rendered prior to the initiation of the purchase negotiations.

[10] The purchaser may not intentionally fragment the practice which is the subject of the sale by charging significantly different fees in substantially similar matters. Doing so would make it possible for the purchaser to avoid the obligation to take over the entire practice by charging arbitrarily higher fees for less lucrative matters, thereby increasing the likelihood that those clients would not consent to the new representation.

Other Applicable Ethical Standards

[11] Lawyers participating in the sale of a law practice are subject to the ethical standards applicable to involving another lawyer in the representation of a client. These include, for example, the seller's obligation to exercise competence in identifying a purchaser qualified to assume the practice and the purchaser's obligation to undertake the representation competently (see Rule 1.1); the obligation to avoid disqualifying conflicts, and to secure client consent after consultation for those conflicts which can be agreed to (see Rule 1.7); and the obligation to protect information relating to the representation (see Rules 1.6 and 1.9).

[12] If approval of the substitution of the purchasing lawyer for the selling lawyer is required by the rules of any tribunal in which a matter is pending, such approval must be obtained before the matter can be included in the sale (see Rule 1.16).

Applicability of the Rule

[13] This Rule applies to the sale of a law practice by representatives of a deceased, disabled or disappeared lawyer. Thus, the seller may be represented by a non-lawyer representative not subject to these Rules. Since, however, no lawyer may participate in a sale of a law practice which does not conform to the requirements of this Rule, the representatives of the seller as well as the purchasing lawyer can be expected to see to it that they are met.

[14] Admission to or retirement from a law partnership or professional association, retirement plans and similar arrangements, and a sale of tangible assets of a law practice, do not constitute a sale or purchase governed by this Rule.

[15] This Rule does not apply to the transfers of legal representation between lawyers when such transfers are unrelated to the sale of a practice.

Model Code Comparison

There was no counterpart to this Rule in the Model Code.

COUNSELOR

RULE 2.1 ADVISOR

In representing a client, a lawyer shall exercise independent professional judgment and render candid advice. In rendering advice, a lawyer may refer not only to law but to other considerations such as moral, economic, social and political factors, that may be relevant to the client's situation.

Comment

Scope of Advice

[1] A client is entitled to straightforward advice expressing the lawyer's honest assessment. Legal advice often involves unpleasant facts and alternatives that a client may be disinclined to confront. In presenting advice, a lawyer endeavors to sustain the client's morale and may put advice in as acceptable a form as honesty permits. However, a lawyer should not be deterred from giving candid advice by the prospect that the advice will be unpalatable to the client.

[2] Advice couched in narrowly legal terms may be of little value to a client, especially where practical considerations, such as cost or effects on other people, are predominant. Purely technical legal advice, therefore, can sometimes be inadequate. It is proper for a lawyer to refer to relevant moral and ethical considerations in giving advice. Although a lawyer is not a moral advisor as such, moral and ethical considerations impinge upon most legal questions and may decisively influence how the law will be applied.

[3] A client may expressly or impliedly ask the lawyer for purely technical advice. When such a request is made by a client experienced in legal matters, the

lawyer may accept it at face value. When such a request is made by a client inexperienced in legal matters, however, the lawyer's responsibility as advisor may include indicating that more may be involved than strictly legal considerations.

[4] Matters that go beyond strictly legal questions may also be in the domain of another profession. Family matters can involve problems within the professional competence of psychiatry, clinical psychology or social work; business matters can involve problems within the competence of the accounting profession or of financial specialists. Where consultation with a professional in another field is itself something a competent lawyer would recommend, the lawyer should make such a recommendation. At the same time, a lawyer's advice at its best often consists of recommending a course of action in the face of conflicting recommendations of experts.

Offering Advice

[5] In general, a lawyer is not expected to give advice until asked by the client. However, when a lawyer knows that a client proposes a course of action that is likely to result in substantial adverse legal consequences to the client, duty to the client under Rule 1.4 may require that the lawyer act if the client's course of action is related to the representation. A lawyer ordinarily has no duty to initiate investigation of a client's affairs or to give advice that the client has indicated is unwanted, but a lawyer may initiate advice to a client when doing so appears to be in the client's interest.

Model Code Comparison

There was no direct counterpart to this Rule in the Disciplinary Rules of the Model Code. DR 5-107(B) provided that a lawyer "shall not permit a person who recommends, employs, or pays him to render legal services for another to direct or regulate his professional judgment in rendering such legal services." EC 7-8 stated that "[a]dvice of a lawyer to his client need not be confined to purely legal considerations .... In assisting his client to reach a proper decision, it is often desirable for a lawyer to point out those factors which may lead to a decision that is morally just as well as legally permissible .... In the final analysis, however, ... the decision whether to forego legally available objectives or methods because of nonlegal factors is ultimately for the client ...."

RULE 2.2 INTERMEDIARY

(a) A lawyer may act as intermediary between clients if:

(1) the lawyer consults with each client concerning the implications of the common representation, including the advantages and risks involved, and the effect on the attorney-client privileges, and obtains each client's consent to the common representation;

(2) the lawyer reasonably believes that the matter can be resolved on terms compatible with the clients' best interests, that each client will be able to make adequately informed decisions in the matter and that there is little risk of mate-

rial prejudice to the interests of any of the clients if the contemplated resolution is unsuccessful; and

(3) the lawyer reasonably believes that the common representation can be undertaken impartially and without improper effect on other responsibilities the lawyer has to any of the clients.

(b) While acting as intermediary, the lawyer shall consult with each client concerning the decisions to be made and the considerations relevant in making them, so that each client can make adequately informed decisions.

(c) A lawyer shall withdraw as intermediary if any of the clients so requests, or if any of the conditions stated in paragraph (a) is no longer satisfied. Upon withdrawal, the lawyer shall not continue to represent any of the clients in the matter that was the subject of the intermediation.

Comment

[1] A lawyer acts as intermediary under this Rule when the lawyer represents two or more parties with potentially conflicting interests. A key factor in defining the relationship is whether the parties share responsibility for the lawyer's fee, but the common representation may be inferred from other circumstances. Because confusion can arise as to the lawyer's role where each party is not separately represented, it is important that the lawyer make clear the relationship.

[2] The Rule does not apply to a lawyer acting as arbitrator or mediator between or among parties who are not clients of the lawyer, even where the lawyer has been appointed with the concurrence of the parties. In performing such a role the lawyer may be subject to applicable codes of ethics, such as the Code of Ethics for Arbitration in Commercial Disputes prepared by a joint Committee of the American Bar Association and the American Arbitration Association.

[3] A lawyer acts as intermediary in seeking to establish or adjust a relationship between clients on an amicable and mutually advantageous basis; for example, in helping to organize a business in which two or more clients are entrepreneurs, working out the financial reorganization of an enterprise in which two or more clients have an interest, arranging a property distribution in settlement of an estate or mediating a dispute between clients. The lawyer seeks to resolve potentially conflicting interests by developing the parties' mutual interests. The alternative can be that each party may have to obtain separate representation, with the possibility in some situations of incurring additional cost, complication or even litigation. Given these and other relevant factors, all the clients may prefer that the lawyer act as intermediary.

[4] In considering whether to act as intermediary between clients, a lawyer should be mindful that if the intermediation fails the result can be additional cost, embarrassment and recrimination. In some situations the risk of failure is so great that intermediation is plainly impossible. For example, a lawyer cannot undertake common representation of clients between whom contentious litigation is imminent or who contemplate contentious negotiations. More generally, if the relationship between the parties has already assumed definite antagonism, the possibility that the clients' interests can be adjusted by intermediation ordinarily is not very good.

[5] The appropriateness of intermediation can depend on its form. Forms of intermediation range from informal arbitration, where each client's case is presented by the respective client and the lawyer decides the outcome, to mediation, to common representation where the clients' interests are substantially though not entirely compatible. One form may be appropriate in circumstances where another would not. Other relevant factors are whether the lawyer subsequently will represent both parties on a continuing basis and whether the situation involves creating a relationship between the parties or terminating one.

Confidentiality and Privilege

[6] A particularly important factor in determining the appropriateness of intermediation is the effect on client-lawyer confidentiality and the attorney-client privilege. In a common representation, the lawyer is still required both to keep each client adequately informed and to maintain confidentiality of information relating to the representation. See Rules 1.4 and 1.6. Complying with both requirements while acting as intermediary requires a delicate balance. If the balance cannot be maintained, the common representation is improper. With regard to the attorney-client privilege, the prevailing rule is that as between commonly represented clients the privilege does not attach. Hence, it must be assumed that if litigation eventuates between the clients, the privilege will not protect any such communications, and the clients should be so advised.

[7] Since the lawyer is required to be impartial between commonly represented clients, intermediation is improper when that impartiality cannot be maintained. For example, a lawyer who has represented one of the clients for a long period and in a variety of matters might have difficulty being impartial between that client and one to whom the lawyer has only recently been introduced.

Consultation

[8] In acting as intermediary between clients, the lawyer is required to consult with the clients on the implications of doing so, and proceed only upon consent based on such a consultation. The consultation should make clear that the lawyer's role is not that of partisanship normally expected in other circumstances.

[9] Paragraph (b) is an application of the principle expressed in Rule 1.4. Where the lawyer is intermediary, the clients ordinarily must assume greater responsibility for decisions than when each client is independently represented.

Withdrawal

[10] Common representation does not diminish the rights of each client in the client-lawyer relationship. Each has the right to loyal and diligent representation, the right to discharge the lawyer as stated in Rule 1.16, and the protection of Rule 1.9 concerning obligations to a former client.

Model Code Comparison

There was no direct counterpart to this Rule in the Disciplinary Rules of the Model Code. EC 5-20 stated that a "lawyer is often asked to serve as an impartial arbitrator or mediator in matters which involve present or former clients. He may serve in either capacity if he first discloses such present or former relationships." DR 5-105(B) provided that a lawyer "shall not continue multiple employment if the exercise of his independent judgment in behalf of a client will be or is likely to be adversely affected by his representation of another client, or if it would be likely to involve him in representation of differing interests, except to the extent permitted under DR 5-105(C)." DR 5-105(C) provided that "a lawyer may represent multiple clients if it is obvious that he can adequately represent the interests of each and if each consents to the representation after full disclosure of the possible effect of such representation on the exercise of his independent professional judgment on behalf of each."

RULE 2.3 EVALUATION FOR USE BY THIRD PERSONS

(a) A lawyer may undertake an evaluation of a matter affecting a client for the use of someone other than the client if:

(1) the lawyer reasonably believes that making the evaluation is compatible with other aspects of the lawyer's relationship with the client; and

(2) the client consents after consultation.

(b) Except as disclosure is required in connection with a report of an evaluation, information relating to the evaluation is otherwise protected by Rule 1.6.

Comment

Definition

[1] An evaluation may be performed at the client's direction but for the primary purpose of establishing information for the benefit of third parties; for example, an opinion concerning the title of property rendered at the behest of a vendor for the information of a prospective purchaser, or at the behest of a borrower for the information of a prospective lender. In some situations, the evaluation may be required by a government agency; for example, an opinion concerning the legality of the securities registered for sale under the securities laws. In other instances, the evaluation may be required by a third person, such as a purchaser of a business.

[2] Lawyers for the government may be called upon to give a formal opinion on the legality of contemplated government agency action. In making such an evaluation, the government lawyer acts at the behest of the government as the client but for the purpose of establishing the limits of the agency's authorized activity. Such an opinion is to be distinguished from confidential legal advice given agency officials. The critical question is whether the opinion is to be made public.

[3] A legal evaluation should be distinguished from an investigation of a person with whom the lawyer does not have a client-lawyer relationship. For example, a lawyer retained by a purchaser to analyze a vendor's title to property does not have a client-lawyer relationship with the vendor. So also, an investigation into a

person's affairs by a government lawyer, or by special counsel employed by the government, is not an evaluation as that term is used in this Rule. The question is whether the lawyer is retained by the person whose affairs are being examined. When the lawyer is retained by that person, the general rules concerning loyalty to client and preservation of confidences apply, which is not the case if the lawyer is retained by someone else. For this reason, it is essential to identify the person by whom the lawyer is retained. This should be made clear not only to the person under examination, but also to others to whom the results are to be made available.

Duty to Third Person

[4] When the evaluation is intended for the information or use of a third person, a legal duty to that person may or may not arise. That legal question is beyond the scope of this Rule. However, since such an evaluation involves a departure from the normal client-lawyer relationship, careful analysis of the situation is required. The lawyer must be satisfied as a matter of professional judgment that making the evaluation is compatible with other functions undertaken in behalf of the client. For example, if the lawyer is acting as advocate in defending the client against charges of fraud, it would normally be incompatible with that responsibility for the lawyer to perform an evaluation for others concerning the same or a related transaction. Assuming no such impediment is apparent, however, the lawyer should advise the client of the implications of the evaluation, particularly the lawyer's responsibilities to third persons and the duty to disseminate the findings.

Access to and Disclosure of Information

[5] The quality of an evaluation depends on the freedom and extent of the investigation upon which it is based. Ordinarily a lawyer should have whatever latitude of investigation seems necessary as a matter of professional judgment. Under some circumstances, however, the terms of the evaluation may be limited. For example, certain issues or sources may be categorically excluded, or the scope of search may be limited by time constraints or the noncooperation of persons having relevant information. Any such limitations which are material to the evaluation should be described in the report. If after a lawyer has commenced an evaluation, the client refuses to comply with the terms upon which it was understood the evaluation was to have been made, the lawyer's obligations are determined by law, having reference to the terms of the client's agreement and the surrounding circumstances.

Financial Auditors' Requests for Information

[6] When a question concerning the legal situation of a client arises at the instance of the client's financial auditor and the question is referred to the lawyer, the lawyer's response may be made in accordance with procedures recognized in the legal profession. Such a procedure is set forth in the American Bar Association Statement of Policy Regarding Lawyers' Responses to Auditors' Requests for Information, adopted in 1975.

Model Code Comparison

There was no counterpart to this Rule in the Model Code.

ADVOCATE

RULE 3.1 MERITORIOUS CLAIMS AND CONTENTIONS

A lawyer shall not bring or defend a proceeding, or assert or controvert an issue therein, unless there is a basis for doing so that is not frivolous, which includes a good faith argument for an extension, modification or reversal of existing law. A lawyer for the defendant in a criminal proceeding, or the respondent in a proceeding that could result in incarceration, may nevertheless so defend the proceeding as to require that every element of the case be established.

Comment

[1] The advocate has a duty to use legal procedure for the fullest benefit of the client's cause, but also a duty not to abuse legal procedure. The law, both procedural and substantive, establishes the limits within which an advocate may proceed. However, the law is not always clear and never is static. Accordingly, in determining the proper scope of advocacy, account must be taken of the law's ambiguities and potential for change.

[2] The filing of an action or defense or similar action taken for a client is not frivolous merely because the facts have not first been fully substantiated or because the lawyer expects to develop vital evidence only by discovery. Such action is not frivolous even though the lawyer believes that the client's position ultimately will not prevail. The action is frivolous, however, if the client desires to have the action taken primarily for the purpose of harassing or maliciously injuring a person, or, if the lawyer is unable either to make a good faith argument on the merits of the action taken or to support the action taken by a good faith argument for an extension, modification or reversal of existing law.

Model Code Comparison

DR 7-102(A)(1) provided that a lawyer may not "[f]ile a suit, assert a position, conduct a defense, delay a trial, or take other action on behalf of his client when he knows or when it is obvious that such action would serve merely to harass or maliciously injure another." Rule 3.1 is to the same general effect as DR 7-102(A)(1), with three qualifications. First, the test of improper conduct is changed from "merely to harass or maliciously injure another" to the requirement that there be a basis for the litigation measure involved that is "not frivolous." This includes the concept stated in DR 7-102(A)(2) that a lawyer may advance a claim or defense unwarranted by existing law if "it can be supported by good faith argument for an extension, modification, or reversal of existing law." Second, the test in Rule 3.1 is an objective test, whereas DR 7-102(A)(1) applied only if the lawyer "knows or when it is obvious" that the litigation is frivolous. Third, Rule 3.1 has an exception that in a criminal case, or a case in which incarceration of the client may result (for example, certain juvenile proceedings), the lawyer may put the prosecution to its proof even if there is no nonfrivolous basis for defense.

RULE 3.2 EXPEDITING LITIGATION

A lawyer shall make reasonable efforts to expedite litigation consistent with the interests of the client.

Comment

[1] Dilatory practices bring the administration of justice into disrepute. Delay should not be indulged merely for the convenience of the advocates, or for the purpose of frustrating an opposing party's attempt to obtain rightful redress or repose. It is not a justification that similar conduct is often tolerated by the bench and bar. The question is whether a competent lawyer acting in good faith would regard the course of action as having some substantial purpose other than delay. Realizing financial or other benefit from otherwise improper delay in litigation is not a legitimate interest of the client.

Model Code Comparison

DR 7-101(A)(1) stated that a lawyer does not violate the duty to represent a client zealously "by being punctual in fulfilling all professional commitments." DR 7-102(A)(1) provided that a lawyer "shall not . . . file a suit, assert a position, conduct a defense [or] delay a trial . . . when he knows or when it is obvious that such action would serve merely to harass or maliciously injure another."

RULE 3.3 CANDOR TOWARD THE TRIBUNAL

(a) A lawyer shall not knowingly:

(1) make a false statement of material fact or law to a tribunal;

(2) fail to disclose a material fact to a tribunal when disclosure is necessary to avoid assisting a criminal or fraudulent act by the client;

(3) fail to disclose to the tribunal legal authority in the controlling jurisdiction known to the lawyer to be directly adverse to the position of the client and not disclosed by opposing counsel; or

(4) offer evidence that the lawyer knows to be false. If a lawyer has offered material evidence and comes to know of its falsity, the lawyer shall take reasonable remedial measures.

(b) The duties stated in paragraph (a) continue to the conclusion of the proceeding, and apply even if compliance requires disclosure of information otherwise protected by Rule 1.6.

(c) A lawyer may refuse to offer evidence that the lawyer reasonably believes is false.

(d) In an ex parte proceeding, a lawyer shall inform the tribunal of all material facts known to the lawyer which will enable the tribunal to make an informed decision, whether or not the facts are adverse.

Comment

[1] The advocate's task is to present the client's case with persuasive force. Performance of that duty while maintaining confidences of the client is qualified by the advocate's duty of candor to the tribunal. However, an advocate does not vouch for the evidence submitted in a cause; the tribunal is responsible for assessing its probative value.

Representations by a Lawyer

[2] An advocate is responsible for pleadings and other documents prepared for litigation, but is usually not required to have personal knowledge of matters asserted therein, for litigation documents ordinarily present assertions by the client, or by someone on the client's behalf, and not assertions by the lawyer. Compare Rule 3.1. However, an assertion purporting to be on the lawyer's own knowledge, as in an affidavit by the lawyer or in a statement in open court, may properly be made only when the lawyer knows the assertion is true or believes it to be true on the basis of a reasonably diligent inquiry. There are circumstances where failure to make a disclosure is the equivalent of an affirmative misrepresentation. The obligation prescribed in Rule 1.2(d) not to counsel a client to commit or assist the client in committing a fraud applies in litigation. Regarding compliance with Rule 1.2(d), see the Comment to that Rule. See also the Comment to Rule 8.4(b).

Misleading Legal Argument

[3] Legal argument based on a knowingly false representation of law constitutes dishonesty toward the tribunal. A lawyer is not required to make a disinterested exposition of the law, but must recognize the existence of pertinent legal authorities. Furthermore, as stated in paragraph (a)(3), an advocate has a duty to disclose directly adverse authority in the controlling jurisdiction which has not been disclosed by the opposing party. The underlying concept is that legal argument is a discussion seeking to determine the legal premises properly applicable to the case.

False Evidence

[4] When evidence that a lawyer knows to be false is provided by a person who is not the client, the lawyer must refuse to offer it regardless of the client's wishes.

[5] When false evidence is offered by the client, however, a conflict may arise between the lawyer's duty to keep the client's revelations confidential and the duty of candor to the court. Upon ascertaining that material evidence is false, the lawyer should seek to persuade the client that the evidence should not be offered or, if it

has been offered, that its false character should immediately be disclosed. If the persuasion is ineffective, the lawyer must take reasonable remedial measures.

[6] Except in the defense of a criminal accused, the rule generally recognized is that, if necessary to rectify the situation, an advocate must disclose the existence of the client's deception to the court or to the other party. Such a disclosure can result in grave consequences to the client, including not only a sense of betrayal but also loss of the case and perhaps a prosecution for perjury. But the alternative is that the lawyer cooperate in deceiving the court, thereby subverting the truth-finding process which the adversary system is designed to implement. See Rule 1.2(d). Furthermore, unless it is clearly understood that the lawyer will act upon the duty to disclose the existence of false evidence, the client can simply reject the lawyer's advice to reveal the false evidence and insist that the lawyer keep silent. Thus the client could in effect coerce the lawyer into being a party to fraud on the court.

Perjury by a Criminal Defendant

[7] Whether an advocate for a criminally accused has the same duty of disclosure has been intensely debated. While it is agreed that the lawyer should seek to persuade the client to refrain from perjurious testimony, there has been dispute concerning the lawyer's duty when that persuasion fails. If the confrontation with the client occurs before trial, the lawyer ordinarily can withdraw. Withdrawal before trial may not be possible, however, either because trial is imminent, or because the confrontation with the client does not take place until the trial itself, or because no other counsel is available.

[8] The most difficult situation, therefore, arises in a criminal case where the accused insists on testifying when the lawyer knows that the testimony is perjurious. The lawyer's effort to rectify the situation can increase the likelihood of the client's being convicted as well as opening the possibility of a prosecution for perjury. On the other hand, if the lawyer does not exercise control over the proof, the lawyer participates, although in a merely passive way, in deception of the court.

[9] Three resolutions of this dilemma have been proposed. One is to permit the accused to testify by a narrative without guidance through the lawyer's questioning. This compromises both contending principles; it exempts the lawyer from the duty to disclose false evidence but subjects the client to an implicit disclosure of information imparted to counsel. Another suggested resolution, of relatively recent origin, is that the advocate be entirely excused from the duty to reveal perjury if the perjury is that of the client. This is a coherent solution but makes the advocate a knowing instrument of perjury.

[10] The other resolution of the dilemma is that the lawyer must reveal the client's perjury if necessary to rectify the situation. A criminal accused has a right to the assistance of an advocate, a right to testify and a right of confidential communication with counsel. However, an accused should not have a right to assistance of counsel in committing perjury. Furthermore, an advocate has an obligation, not only in professional ethics but under the law as well, to avoid implication in the commission of perjury or other falsification of evidence. See Rule 1.2(d).

Remedial Measures

[11] If perjured testimony or false evidence has been offered, the advocate's proper course ordinarily is to remonstrate with the client confidentially. If that fails, the advocate should seek to withdraw if that will remedy the situation. If withdrawal will not remedy the situation or is impossible, the advocate should make disclosure to the court. It is for the court then to determine what should be done—making a statement about the matter to the trier of fact, ordering a mistrial or perhaps nothing. If the false testimony was that of the client, the client may controvert the lawyer's version of their communication when the lawyer discloses the situation to the court. If there is an issue whether the client has committed perjury, the lawyer cannot represent the client in resolution of the issue, and a mistrial may be unavoidable. An unscrupulous client might in this way attempt to produce a series of mistrials and thus escape prosecution. However, a second such encounter could be construed as a deliberate abuse of the right to counsel and as such a waiver of the right to further representation.

Constitutional Requirements

[12] The general rule—that an advocate must disclose the existence of perjury with respect to a material fact, even that of a client—applies to defense counsel in criminal cases, as well as in other instances. However, the definition of the lawyer's ethical duty in such a situation may be qualified by constitutional provisions for due process and the right to counsel in criminal cases. In some jurisdictions these provisions have been construed to require that counsel present an accused as a witness if the accused wishes to testify, even if counsel knows the testimony will be false. The obligation of the advocate under these Rules is subordinate to such a constitutional requirement.

Duration of Obligation

[13] A practical time limit on the obligation to rectify the presentation of false evidence has to be established. The conclusion of the proceeding is a reasonably definite point for the termination of the obligation.

Refusing to Offer Proof Believed to Be False

[14] Generally speaking, a lawyer has authority to refuse to offer testimony or other proof that the lawyer believes is untrustworthy. Offering such proof may reflect adversely on the lawyer's ability to discriminate in the quality of evidence and thus impair the lawyer's effectiveness as an advocate. In criminal cases, however, a lawyer may, in some jurisdictions, be denied this authority by constitutional requirements governing the right to counsel.

Ex Parte Proceedings

[15] Ordinarily, an advocate has the limited responsibility of presenting one side of the matters that a tribunal should consider in reaching a decision; the conflicting position is expected to be presented by the opposing party. However, in any ex parte proceeding, such as an application for a temporary restraining order, there

is no balance of presentation by cpposing advocates. The object of an ex parte proceeding is nevertheless to yield a substantially just result. The judge has an affirmative responsibility to accord the absent party just consideration. The lawyer for the represented party has the correlative duty to make disclosures of material facts known to the lawyer and that the lawyer reasonably believes are necessary to an informed decision.

Model Code Comparison

Paragraph (a)(1) is substantially identical to DR 7-102(A)(5), which provided that a lawyer shall not "knowingly make a false statement of law or fact."

Paragraph (a)(2) is implicit in DR 7-102(A)(3), which provided that "a lawyer shall not . . . knowingly fail to disclose that which he is required by law to reveal."

Paragraph (a)(3) is substantially identical to DR 7-106(B)(1).

With regard to paragraph (a)(4), the first sentence of this subparagraph is similar to DR 7-102(A)(4), which provided that a lawyer shall not "knowingly use" perjured testimony or false evidence. The second sentence of paragraph (a)(4) resolves an ambiguity in the Model Code concerning the action required of a lawyer who discovers that the lawyer has offered perjured testimony or false evidence. DR 7-102(A)(4), quoted above, did not expressly deal with this situation, but the prohibition against "use" of false evidence can be construed to preclude carrying through with a case based on such evidence when that fact has become known during the trial. DR 7-102(B)(1), also noted in connection with Rule 1.6, provided that a lawyer "who receives information clearly establishing that ... [h]is client has . . . perpetrated a fraud upon . . . a tribunal shall [if the client does not rectify the situation] . . . reveal the fraud to the . . . tribunal . . . ." Since use of perjured testimony or false evidence is usually regarded as "fraud" upon the court, DR 7-102(B)(1) apparently required disclosure by the lawyer in such circumstances. However, some states have amended DR 7-102(B)(1) in conformity with an ABA-recommended amendment to provide that the duty of disclosure does not apply when the "information is protected as a privileged communication." This qualification may be empty, for the rule of attorney-client privilege has been construed to exclude communications that further a crime, including the crime of perjury. On this interpretation of DR 7-102(B)(1), the lawyer had a duty to disclose the perjury.

Paragraph (c) confers discretion on the lawyer to refuse to offer evidence that the lawyer "reasonably believes" is false. This gives the lawyer more latitude than DR 7-102(A)(4), which prohibited the lawyer from offering evidence the lawyer "knows" is false.

There was no counterpart in the Model Code to paragraph (d).

RULE 3.4 FAIRNESS TO OPPOSING PARTY AND COUNSEL

A lawyer shall not:

(a) unlawfully obstruct another party's access to evidence or unlawfully alter, destroy or conceal a document or other material having potential evidentiary

value. A lawyer shall not counsel or assist another person to do any such act;

(b) falsify evidence, counsel or assist a witness to testify falsely, or offer an inducement to a witness that is prohibited by law;

(c) knowingly disobey an obligation under the rules of a tribunal except for an open refusal based on an assertion that no valid obligation exists;

(d) in pretrial procedure, make a frivolous discovery request or fail to make reasonably diligent effort to comply with a legally proper discovery request by an opposing party;

(e) in trial, allude to any matter that the lawyer does not reasonably believe is relevant or that will not be supported by admissible evidence, assert personal knowledge of facts in issue except when testifying as a witness, or state a personal opinion as to the justness of a cause, the credibility of a witness, the culpability of a civil litigant or the guilt or innocence of an accused; or

(f) request a person other than a client to refrain from voluntarily giving relevant information to another party unless:

(1) the person is a relative or an employee or other agent of a client; and

(2) the lawyer reasonably believes that the person's interests will not be adversely affected by refraining from giving such information.

Comment

[1] The procedure of the adversary system contemplates that the evidence in a case is to be marshalled competitively by the contending parties. Fair competition in the adversary system is secured by prohibitions against destruction or concealment of evidence, improperly influencing witnesses, obstructive tactics in discovery procedure, and the like.

[2] Documents and other items of evidence are often essential to establish a claim or defense. Subject to evidentiary privileges, the right of an opposing party, including the government, to obtain evidence through discovery or subpoena is an important procedural right. The exercise of that right can be frustrated if relevant material is altered, concealed or destroyed. Applicable law in many jurisdictions makes it an offense to destroy material for purpose of impairing its availability in a pending proceeding or one whose commencement can be foreseen. Falsifying evidence is also generally a criminal offense. Paragraph (a) applies to evidentiary material generally, including computerized information.

[3] With regard to paragraph (b), it is not improper to pay a witness's expenses or to compensate an expert witness on terms permitted by law. The common law rule in most jurisdictions is that it is improper to pay an occurrence witness any fee for testifying and that it is improper to pay an expert witness a contingent fee.

[4] Paragraph (f) permits a lawyer to advise employees of a client to refrain from giving information to another party, for the employees may identify their interests with those of the client. See also Rule 4.2.

Model Code Comparison

With regard to paragraph (a), DR 7-109(A) provided that a lawyer "shall not suppress any evidence that he or his client has a legal obligation to reveal." DR

7-109(B) provided that a lawyer "shall not advise or cause a person to secrete himself . . . for the purpose of making him unavailable as a witness . . . ." DR 7-106(C)(7) provided that a lawyer shall not "[i]ntentionally or habitually violate any established rule of procedure or of evidence."

With regard to paragraph (b), DR 7-102(A)(6) provided that a lawyer shall not participate "in the creation or preservation of evidence when he knows or it is obvious that the evidence is false." DR 7-109(C) provided that a lawyer "shall not pay, offer to pay, or acquiesce in the payment of compensation to a witness contingent upon the content of his testimony or the outcome of the case. But a lawyer may advance, guarantee or acquiesce in the payment of: (1) Expenses reasonably incurred by a witness in attending or testifying; (2) Reasonable compensation to a witness for his loss of time in attending or testifying; (or) (3) A reasonable fee for the professional services of an expert witness." EC 7-28 stated that witnesses "should always testify truthfully and should be free from any financial inducements that might tempt them to do otherwise."

Paragraph (c) is substantially similar to DR 7-106(A), which provided that "A lawyer shall not disregard . . . a standing rule of a tribunal or a ruling of a tribunal made in the course of a proceeding, but he may take appropriate steps in good faith to test the validity of such rule or ruling."

Paragraph (d) has no counterpart in the Model Code.

Paragraph (e) substantially incorporates DR 7-106(C)(1), (2), (3) and (4). DR 7-106(C)(2) proscribed asking a question "intended to degrade a witness or other person," a matter dealt with in Rule 4.4. DR 7-106(C)(5), providing that a lawyer shall not "fail to comply with known local customs of courtesy or practice," was too vague to be a rule of conduct enforceable as law.

With regard to paragraph (f), DR 7-104(A)(2) provided that a lawyer shall not "give advice to a person who is not represented . . . other than the advice to secure counsel, if the interests of such person are or have a reasonable possibility of being in conflict with the interests of his client."

RULE 3.5 IMPARTIALITY AND DECORUM OF THE TRIBUNAL

A lawyer shall not:

(a) seek to influence a judge, juror, prospective juror or other official by means prohibited by law;

(b) communicate ex parte with such a person except as permitted by law; or

(c) engage in conduct intended to disrupt a tribunal.

Comment

[1] Many forms of improper influence upon a tribunal are proscribed by criminal law. Others are specified in the ABA Model Code of Judicial Conduct, with which an advocate should be familiar. A lawyer is required to avoid contributing to a violation of such provisions.

[2] The advocate's function is to present evidence and argument so that the cause may be decided according to law. Refraining from abusive or obstreperous conduct is a corollary of the advocate's right to speak on behalf of litigants. A lawyer may stand firm against abuse by a judge but should avoid reciprocation; the judge's default is no justification for similar dereliction by an advocate. An advocate can present the cause, protect the record for subsequent review and preserve professional integrity by patient firmness no less effectively than by belligerence or theatrics.

Model Code Comparison

With regard to paragraphs (a) and (b), DR 7-108(A) provided that "[b]efore the trial of a case a lawyer . . . shall not communicate with . . . anyone he knows to be a member of the venire . . . ." DR 7-108(B) provided that during the trial of a case a lawyer "shall not communicate with . . . any member of the jury." DR 7-110(B) provided that a lawyer shall not "communicate . . . as to the merits of the cause with a judge or an official before whom the proceeding is pending, except . . . upon adequate notice to opposing counsel," or as "otherwise authorized by law."

With regard to paragraph (c), DR 7-106(C)(6) provided that a lawyer shall not engage in "undignified or discourteous conduct which is degrading to a tribunal."

RULE 3.6[9] TRIAL PUBLICITY

(a) A lawyer who is participating or has participated in the investigation or litigation of a matter shall not make an extrajudicial statement that a reasonable person would expect to be disseminated by means of public communication if the lawyer knows or reasonably should know that it will have a substantial likelihood of materially prejudicing an adjudicative proceeding in the matter.

(b) Notwithstanding paragraph (a), a lawyer may state:

(1) the claim, offense or defense involved and, except when prohibited by law, the identity of the persons involved;

(2) information contained in a public record;

(3) that an investigation of a matter is in progress;

(4) the scheduling or result of any step in litigation;

(5) a request for assistance in obtaining evidence and information necessary thereto;

(6) a warning of danger concerning the behavior of a person involved, when there is reason to believe that there exists the likelihood of substantial harm to an individual or to the public interest; and

(7) in a criminal case, in addition to subparagraphs (1) through (6):

(i) the identity, residence, occupation and family status of the accused;

(ii) if the accused has not been apprehended, information necessary to aid in apprehension of that person;

9. Amended August 10, 1994, American Bar Association House of Delegates, New Orleans, Louisiana, per Report No. 100.

(iii) the fact, time and place of arrest; and

(iv) the identity of investigating and arresting officers or agencies and the length of the investigation.

(c) Notwithstanding paragraph (a), a lawyer may make a statement that a reasonable lawyer would believe is required to protect a client from the substantial undue prejudicial effect of recent publicity not initiated by the lawyer or the lawyer's client. A statement made pursuant to this paragraph shall be limited to such information as is necessary to mitigate the recent adverse publicity.

(d) No lawyer associated in a firm or government agency with a lawyer subject to paragraph (a) shall make a statement prohibited by paragraph (a).

Comment

[1] It is difficult to strike a balance between protecting the right to a fair trial and safeguarding the right of free expression. Preserving the right to a fair trial necessarily entails some curtailment of the information that may be disseminated about a party prior to trial, particularly where trial by jury is involved. If there were no such limits, the result would be the practical nullification of the protective effect of the rules of forensic decorum and the exclusionary rules of evidence. On the other hand, there are vital social interests served by the free dissemination of information about events having legal consequences and about legal proceedings themselves. The public has a right to know about threats to its safety and measures aimed at assuring its security. It also has a legitimate interest in the conduct of judicial proceedings, particularly in matters of general public concern. Furthermore, the subject matter of legal proceedings is often of direct significance in debate and deliberation over questions of public policy.

[2] Special rules of confidentiality may validly govern proceedings in juvenile, domestic relations and mental disability proceedings, and perhaps other types of litigation. Rule 3.4(c) requires compliance with such rules.

[3] The Rule sets forth a basic general prohibition against a lawyer's making statements that the lawyer knows or should know will have a substantial likelihood of materially prejudicing an adjudicative proceeding. Recognizing that the public value of informed commentary is great and the likelihood of prejudice to a proceeding by the commentary of a lawyer who is not involved in the proceeding is small, the rule applies only to lawyers who are, or who have been involved in the investigation or litigation of a case, and their associates.

[4] Paragraph (b) identifies specific matters about which a lawyer's statements would not ordinarily be considered to present a substantial likelihood of material prejudice, and should not in any event be considered prohibited by the general prohibition of paragraph (a). Paragraph (b) is not intended to be an exhaustive listing of the subjects upon which a lawyer may make a statement, but statements on other matters may be subject to paragraph (a).

[5] There are, on the other hand, certain subjects which are more likely than not to have a material prejudicial effect on a proceeding, particularly when they refer to a civil matter triable to a jury, a criminal matter, or any other proceeding

that could result in incarceration. These subjects relate to:

(1) the character, credibility, reputation or criminal record of a party, suspect in a criminal investigation or witness, or the identity of a witness, or the expected testimony of a party or witness;

(2) in a criminal case or proceeding that could result in incarceration, the possibility of a plea of guilty to the offense or the existence or contents of any confession, admission, or statement given by a defendant or suspect or that person's refusal or failure to make a statement;

(3) the performance or results of any examination or test or the refusal or failure of a person to submit to an examination or test, or the identity or nature of physical evidence expected to be presented;

(4) any opinion as to the guilt or innocence of a defendant or suspect in a criminal case or proceeding that could result in incarceration;

(5) information that the lawyer knows or reasonably should know is likely to be inadmissible as evidence in a trial and that would, if disclosed, create a substantial risk of prejudicing an impartial trial; or

(6) the fact that a defendant has been charged with a crime, unless there is included therein a statement explaining that the charge is merely an accusation and that the defendant is presumed innocent until and unless proven guilty.

[6] Another relevant factor in determining prejudice is the nature of the proceeding involved. Criminal jury trials will be most sensitive to extrajudicial speech. Civil trials may be less sensitive. Non-jury hearings and arbitration proceedings may be even less affected. The Rule will still place limitations on prejudicial comments in these cases, but the likelihood of prejudice may be different depending on the type of proceeding.

[7] Finally, extrajudicial statements that might otherwise raise a question under this Rule may be permissible when they are made in response to statements made publicly by another party, another party's lawyer, or third persons, where a reasonable lawyer would believe a public response is required in order to avoid prejudice to the lawyer's client. When prejudicial statements have been publicly made by others, responsive statements may have the salutary effect of lessening any resulting adverse impact on the adjudicative proceeding. Such responsive statements should be limited to contain only such information as is necessary to mitigate undue prejudice created by the statements made by others.

Model Code Comparison

Rule 3.6 is similar to DR 7-107, except as follows: First, Rule 3.6 adopts the general criterion of "substantial likelihood of materially prejudicing an adjudicative proceeding" to describe impermissible conduct. Second, Rule 3.6 makes clear that only attorneys who are, or have been involved in a proceeding, or their associates, are subject to the Rule. Third, Rule 3.6 omits the particulars in DR 7-107(b), transforming them instead into an illustrative compilation as part of the Rule's commentary that is intended to give fair notice of the kinds of statements that are generally thought to be more likely than other kinds of statements to pose unacceptable dangers to the fair administration of justice. Whether any statement will have a substantial likelihood of materially prejudicially an adjudicatory proceeding will depend upon the facts of each case. The particulars of DR 7-107(c) are retained in Rule 3.6(b), except DR 7-107(C)(7), which provided that a lawyer may reveal "[a]t the time of seizure, a description of the physical evidence seized, other than a confession, admission or statement." Such revelations may be substantially prejudicial and are frequently the subject of pretrial suppression motions whose success would be undermined by disclosure of the suppressed evidence to the press. Finally, Rule 3.6 authorizes a lawyer to protect a client by making a limited reply to adverse publicity substantially prejudicial to the client.

RULE 3.7 LAWYER AS WITNESS

(a) A lawyer shall not act as advocate at a trial in which the lawyer is likely to be a necessary witness except where:

(1) the testimony relates to an uncontested issue;

(2) the testimony relates to the nature and value of legal services rendered in the case; or

(3) disqualification of the lawyer would work substantial hardship on the client.

(b) A lawyer may act as advocate in a trial in which another lawyer in the lawyer's firm is likely to be called as a witness unless precluded from doing so by Rule 1.7 or Rule 1.9.

Comment

[1] Combining the roles of advocate and witness can prejudice the opposing party and can involve a conflict of interest between the lawyer and client.

[2] The opposing party has proper objection where the combination of roles may prejudice that party's rights in the litigation. A witness is required to testify on the basis of personal knowledge, while an advocate is expected to explain and comment on evidence given by others. It may not be clear whether a statement by an advocate-witness should be taken as proof or as an analysis of the proof.

[3] Paragraph (a)(1) recognizes that if the testimony will be uncontested, the ambiguities in the dual role are purely theoretical. Paragraph (a)(2) recognizes that where the testimony concerns the extent and value of legal services rendered in the action in which the testimony is offered, permitting the lawyers to testify avoids the need for a second trial with new counsel to resolve that issue. Moreover, in such a situation the judge has firsthand knowledge of the matter in issue; hence, there is less dependence on the adversary process to test the credibility of the testimony.

[4] Apart from these two exceptions, paragraph (a)(3) recognizes that a balancing is required between the interests of the client and those of the opposing party. Whether the opposing party is likely to suffer prejudice depends on the nature of the case, the importance and probable tenor of the lawyer's testimony, and

the probability that the lawyer's testimony will conflict with that of other witnesses. Even if there is risk of such prejudice, in determining whether the lawyer should be disqualified, due regard must be given to the effect of disqualification on the lawyer's client. It is relevant that one or both parties could reasonably foresee that the lawyer would probably be a witness. The principle of imputed disqualification stated in Rule 1.10 has no application to this aspect of the problem.

[5] Whether the combination of roles involves an improper conflict of interest with respect to the client is determined by Rule 1.7 or 1.9. For example, if there is likely to be substantial conflict between the testimony of the client and that of the lawyer or a member of the lawyer's firm, the representation is improper. The problem can arise whether the lawyer is called as a witness on behalf of the client or is called by the opposing party. Determining whether or not such a conflict exists is primarily the responsibility of the lawyer involved. See Comment to Rule 1.7. If a lawyer who is a member of a firm may not act as both advocate and witness by reason of conflict of interest, Rule 1.10 disqualifies the firm also.

Model Code Comparison

DR 5-102(A) prohibited a lawyer, or the lawyer's firm, from serving as advocate if the lawyer "learns or it is obvious that he or a lawyer in his firm ought to be called as a witness on behalf of his client." DR 5-102(B) provided that a lawyer, and the lawyer's firm, may continue representation if the "lawyer learns or it is obvious that he or a lawyer in his firm may be called as a witness other than on behalf of his client . . . until it is apparent that his testimony is or may be prejudicial to his client." DR 5-101(B) permitted a lawyer to testify while representing a client: "(1) If the testimony will relate solely to an uncontested matter; (2) If the testimony will relate solely to a matter of formality and there is no reason to believe that substantial evidence will be offered in opposition to the testimony; (3) If the testimony will relate solely to the nature and value of legal services rendered in the case by the lawyer or his firm to the client; (4) As to any matter if refusal would work a substantial hardship on the client because of the distinctive value of the lawyer or his firm as counsel in the particular case."

The exception stated in paragraph (a)(1) consolidates provisions of DR 5-101(B)(1) and (2). Testimony relating to a formality, referred to in DR 5-101(B)(2), in effect defines the phrase "uncontested issue," and is redundant.

RULE 3.8[10] SPECIAL RESPONSIBILITIES OF A PROSECUTOR

The prosecutor in a criminal case shall:

(a) refrain from prosecuting a charge that the prosecutor knows is not supported by probable cause;

10. Amended February 12, 1990, American Bar Association House of Delegates, Los Angeles, California, per Report No. 118.

(b) make reasonable efforts to assure that the accused has been advised of the right to, and the procedure for obtaining, counsel and has been given reasonable opportunity to obtain counsel;

(c) not seek to obtain from an unrepresented accused a waiver of important pretrial rights, such as the right to a preliminary hearing;

(d) make timely disclosure to the defense of all evidence or information known to the prosecutor that tends to negate the guilt of the accused or mitigates the offense, and, in connection with sentencing, disclose to the defense and to the tribunal all unprivileged mitigating information known to the prosecutor, except when the prosecutor is relieved of this responsibility by a protective order of the tribunal;

(e) exercise reasonable care to prevent investigators, law enforcement personnel, employees or other persons assisting or associated with the prosecutor in a criminal case from making an extrajudicial statement that the prosecutor would be prohibited from making under Rule 3.6;

(f)[11] not subpoena a lawyer in a grand jury or other criminal proceeding to present evidence about a past or present client unless the prosecutor reasonably believes:

(1) the information sought is not protected from disclosure by any applicable privilege;

(2) the evidence sought is essential to the successful completion of an ongoing investigation or prosecution; and

(3) there is no other feasible alternative to obtain the information.

(g)[12] except for statements that are necessary to inform the public of the nature and extent of the prosecutor's action and that serve a legitimate law enforcement purpose, refrain from making extrajudicial comments that have a substantial likelihood of heightening public condemnation of the accused.

Comment

[1] A prosecutor has the responsibility of a minister of justice and not simply that of an advocate. This responsibility carries with it specific obligations to see that the defendant is accorded procedural justice and that guilt is decided upon the basis of sufficient evidence. Precisely how far the prosecutor is required to go in this direction is a matter of debate and varies in different jurisdictions. Many jurisdictions have adopted the ABA Standards of Criminal Justice Relating to the Prosecution Function, which in turn are the product of prolonged and careful deliberation by lawyers experienced in both criminal prosecution and defense. See also Rule 3.3(d), governing *ex parte* proceedings, among which grand jury proceedings are included. Applicable law may require other measures by the prosecutor and knowing disregard of those obligations or a systematic abuse of prosecutorial discretion could constitute a violation of Rule 8.4.

---

11. Amended August 8, 1995, American Bar Association House of Delegates, Chicago, Illinois, per Report No. 101.

12. Added August 10, 1994, American Bar Association House of Delegates, New Orleans, Louisiana, per Report No. 100.

[2] Paragraph (c) does not apply to an accused appearing *pro se* with the approval of the tribunal. Nor does it forbid the lawful questioning of a suspect who has knowingly waived the rights to counsel and silence.

[3] The exception in paragraph (d) recognizes that a prosecutor may seek an appropriate protective order from the tribunal if disclosure of information to the defense could result in substantial harm to an individual or to the public interest.

[4] Paragraph (f) is intended to limit the issuance of lawyer subpoenas in grand jury and other criminal proceedings to those situations in which there is a genuine need to intrude into the client-lawyer relationship.

[5] Paragraph (g) supplements Rule 3.6, which prohibits extrajudicial statements that have a substantial likelihood of prejudicing an adjudicatory proceeding. In the context of a criminal prosecution, a prosecutor's extrajudicial statement can create the additional problem of increasing public condemnation of the accused. Although the announcement of an indictment, for example, will necessarily have severe consequences for the accused, a prosecutor can, and should, avoid comments which have no legitimate law enforcement purpose and have a substantial likelihood of increasing public opprobrium of the accused. Nothing in this Comment is intended to restrict the statements which a prosecutor may make which comply with Rule 3.6(b) or 3.6(c).

Model Code Comparison

DR 7-103(A) provided that a "public prosecutor . . . shall not institute . . . criminal charges when he knows or it is obvious that the charges are not supported by probable cause." DR 7-103(B) provided that "[a] public prosecutor . . . shall make timely disclosure . . . of the existence of evidence, known to the prosecutor . . . that tends to negate the guilt of the accused, mitigate the degree of the offense, or reduce the punishment."

RULE 3.9 ADVOCATE IN NONADJUDICATIVE PROCEEDINGS

A lawyer representing a client before a legislative or administrative tribunal in a nonadjudicative proceeding shall disclose that the appearance is in a representative capacity and shall conform to the provisions of Rules 3.3(a) through (c), 3.4(a) through (c), and 3.5.

Comment

[1] In representation before bodies such as legislatures, municipal councils, and executive and administrative agencies acting in a rule-making or policy-making capacity, lawyers present facts, formulate issues and advance argument in the matters under consideration. The decision-making body, like a court, should be able to rely on the integrity of the submissions made to it. A lawyer appearing before such a body should deal with the tribunal honestly and in conformity with applicable rules of procedure.

[2] Lawyers have no exclusive right to appear before nonadjudicative bodies, as they do before a court. The requirements of this Rule therefore may subject lawyers to regulations inapplicable to advocates who are not lawyers. However, legislatures and administrative agencies have a right to expect lawyers to deal with them as they deal with courts.

[3] This Rule does not apply to representation of a client in a negotiation or other bilateral transaction with a governmental agency; representation in such a transaction is governed by Rules 4.1 through 4.4.

Model Code Comparison

EC 7-15 stated that a lawyer "appearing before an administrative agency, regardless of the nature of the proceeding it is conducting, has the continuing duty to advance the cause of his client within the bounds of the law." EC 7-16 stated that "[w]hen a lawyer appears in connection with proposed legislation, he . . . should comply with applicable laws and legislative rules." EC 8-5 stated that [f]raudulent, deceptive, or otherwise illegal conduct by a participant in a proceeding before a . . . legislative body . . . should never be participated in . . . by lawyers."

DR 7-106(B)(1) provided that "[i]n presenting a matter to a tribunal, a lawyer shall disclose . . . [u]unless privileged or irrelevant, the identity of the clients he represents and of the persons who employed him."

TRANSACTIONS WITH PERSONS OTHER THAN CLIENTS

RULE 4.1 TRUTHFULNESS IN STATEMENTS TO OTHERS

In the course of representing a client a lawyer shall not knowingly:

(a) make a false statement of material fact or law to a third person; or

(b) fail to disclose a material fact to a third person when disclosure is necessary to avoid assisting a criminal or fraudulent act by a client, unless disclosure is prohibited by Rule 1.6.

Comment

Misrepresentation

[1] A lawyer is required to be truthful when dealing with others on a client's behalf, but generally has no affirmative duty to inform an opposing party of relevant facts. A misrepresentation can occur if the lawyer incorporates or affirms a statement of another person that the lawyer knows is false. Misrepresentations can also occur by failure to act.

Statements of Fact

[2] This Rule refers to statements of fact. Whether a particular statement should be regarded as one of fact can depend on the circumstances. Under generally accepted conventions in negotiation, certain types of statements ordinarily are not taken as statements of material fact. Estimates of price or value placed on the subject of a transaction and a party's intentions as to an acceptable settlement of a claim are in this category, and so is the existence of an undisclosed principal except where nondisclosure of the principal would constitute fraud.

Fraud by Client

[3] Paragraph (b) recognizes that substantive law may require a lawyer to disclose certain information to avoid being deemed to have assisted the client's crime or fraud. The requirement of disclosure created by this paragraph is, however, subject to the obligations created by Rule 1.6.

Model Code Comparison

Paragraph (a) is substantially similar to DR 7-102(A)(5), which stated that "[i]n his representation of a client, a lawyer shall not . . . [k]nowingly make a false statement of law or fact."

With regard to paragraph (b), DR 7-102(A)(3) provided that a lawyer shall not "[c]onceal or knowingly fail to disclose that which he is required by law to reveal."

RULE 4.2[13] COMMUNICATION WITH PERSON REPRESENTED BY COUNSEL

In representing a client, a lawyer shall not communicate about the subject of the representation with a person the lawyer knows to be represented by another lawyer in the matter, unless the lawyer has the consent of the other lawyer or is authorized by law to do so.

Comment

[1] This Rule does not prohibit communication with a represented person, or an employee or agent of such a person, concerning matters outside the representation. For example, the existence of a controversy between a government agency and a private party, or between two organizations, does not prohibit a lawyer for either from communicating with nonlawyer representatives of the other regarding a separate matter. Also, parties to a matter may communicate directly with each other and a lawyer having independent justification or legal authorization for communicating with a represented person is permitted to do so. Communications authorized by law include, for example, the right of a party to a controversy with a government agency to speak with government officials about the matter.

13. Amended August 8, 1995, American Bar Association House of Delegates, Chicago, Illinois, per Report No. 100.

[2] Communications authorized by law also include constitutionally permissible investigative activities of lawyers representing governmental entities, directly or through investigative agents, prior to the commencement of criminal or civil enforcement proceedings, when there is applicable judicial precedent that either has found the activity permissible under this Rule or has found this Rule inapplicable. However, the Rule imposes ethical restrictions that go beyond those imposed by constitutional provisions.

[3] This Rule also applies to communications with any person, whether or not a party to a formal adjudicative proceeding, contract or negotiation, who is represented by counsel concerning the matter to which the communication relates.

[4] In the case of an organization, this Rule prohibits communications by a lawyer for another person or entity concerning the matter in representation with persons having a managerial responsibility on behalf of the organization, and with any other person whose act or omission in connection with that matter may be imputed to the organization for purposes of civil or criminal liability or whose statement may constitute an admission on the part of the organization. If an agent or employee of the organization is represented in the matter by his or her own counsel, the consent by that counsel to a communication will be sufficient for purposes of this Rule. Compare Rule 3.4(f).

[5] The prohibition on communications with a represented person only applies, however, in circumstances where the lawyer knows that the person is in fact represented in the matter to be discussed. This means that the lawyer has actual knowledge of the fact of the representation; but such actual knowledge may be inferred from the circumstances. See Terminology. Such an inference may arise in circumstances where there is substantial reason to believe that the person with whom communication is sought is represented in the matter to be discussed. Thus, a lawyer cannot evade the requirement of obtaining the consent of counsel by closing eyes to the obvious.

[6] In the event the person with whom the lawyer communicates is not known to be represented by counsel in the matter, the lawyer's communications are subject to Rule 4.3.

Model Code Comparison

This Rule is substantially identical to DR 7-104(A)(1) except for the substitution of the term "person" for "party."

RULE 4.3 DEALING WITH UNREPRESENTED PERSON

In dealing on behalf of a client with a person who is not represented by counsel, a lawyer shall not state or imply that the lawyer is disinterested. When the lawyer knows or reasonably should know that the unrepresented person misunderstands the lawyer's role in the matter, the lawyer shall make reasonable efforts to correct the misunderstanding.

Comment

[1] An unrepresented person, particularly one not experienced in dealing with legal matters, might assume that a lawyer is disinterested in loyalties or is a disinterested authority on the law even when the lawyer represents a client. During the course of a lawyer's representation of a client, the lawyer should not give advice to an unrepresented person other than the advice to obtain counsel.

Model Code Comparison

There was no direct counterpart to this Rule in the Model Code. DR 7-104(A)(2) provided that a lawyer shall not "[g]ive advice to a person who is not represented by a lawyer, other than the advice to secure counsel . . . ."

RULE 4.4 RESPECT FOR RIGHTS OF THIRD PERSONS

In representing a client, a lawyer shall not use means that have no substantial purpose other than to embarrass, delay, or burden a third person, or use methods of obtaining evidence that violate the legal rights of such a person.

Comment

[1] Responsibility to a client requires a lawyer to subordinate the interests of others to those of the client, but that responsibility does not imply that a lawyer may disregard the rights of third persons. It is impractical to catalogue all such rights, but they include legal restrictions on methods of obtaining evidence from third persons.

Model Code Comparison

DR 7-106(C)(2) provided that a lawyer shall not "[a]sk any question that he has no reasonable basis to believe is relevant to the case and that is intended to degrade a witness or other person." DR 7-102(A)(1) provided that a lawyer shall not "take . . . action on behalf of his client when he knows or when it is obvious that such action would serve merely to harass or maliciously injure another." DR 7-108(D) provided that "[a]fter discharge of the jury . . . the lawyer shall not ask questions or make comments to a member of that jury that are calculated merely to harass or embarrass the juror . . . ." DR 7-108(E) provided that a lawyer "shall not conduct . . . a vexatious or harassing investigation of either a venireman or a juror."

LAW FIRMS AND ASSOCIATIONS

RULE 5.1 RESPONSIBILITIES OF A PARTNER OR SUPERVISORY LAWYER

(a) A partner in a law firm shall make reasonable efforts to ensure that the firm has in effect measures giving reasonable assurance that all lawyers in the firm conform to the Rules of Professional Conduct.

(b) A lawyer having direct supervisory authority over another lawyer shall make reasonable efforts to ensure that the other lawyer conforms to the Rules of Professional Conduct.

(c) A lawyer shall be responsible for another lawyer's violation of the Rules of Professional Conduct if:

(1) the lawyer orders or, with knowledge of the specific conduct, ratifies the conduct involved; or

(2) the lawyer is a partner in the law firm in which the other lawyer practices, or has direct supervisory authority over the other lawyer, and knows of the conduct at a time when its consequences can be avoided or mitigated but fails to take reasonable remedial action.

Comment

[1] Paragraphs (a) and (b) refer to lawyers who have supervisory authority over the professional work of a firm or legal department of a government agency. This includes members of a partnership and the shareholders in a law firm organized as a professional corporation; lawyers having supervisory authority in the law department of an enterprise or government agency; and lawyers who have intermediate managerial responsibilities in a firm.

[2] The measures required to fulfill the responsibility prescribed in paragraphs (a) and (b) can depend on the firm's structure and the nature of its practice. In a small firm, informal supervision and occasional admonition ordinarily might be sufficient. In a large firm, or in practice situations in which intensely difficult ethical problems frequently arise, more elaborate procedures may be necessary. Some firms, for example, have a procedure whereby junior lawyers can make confidential referral of ethical problems directly to a designated senior partner or special committee. See Rule 5.2. Firms, whether large or small, may also rely on continuing legal education in professional ethics. In any event, the ethical atmosphere of a firm can influence the conduct of all its members and a lawyer having authority over the work of another may not assume that the subordinate lawyer will inevitably conform to the Rules.

[3] Paragraph (c)(1) expresses a general principle of responsibility for acts of another. See also Rule 8.4(a).

[4] Paragraph (c)(2) defines the duty of a lawyer having direct supervisory authority over performance of specific legal work by another lawyer. Whether a lawyer has such supervisory authority in particular circumstances is a question of fact. Partners of a private firm have at least indirect responsibility for all work being done by the firm, while a partner in charge of a particular matter ordinarily has direct authority over other firm lawyers engaged in the matter. Appropriate remedial action by a partner would depend on the immediacy of the partner's involvement and the seriousness of the misconduct. The supervisor is required to intervene to prevent avoidable consequences of misconduct if the supervisor knows that the misconduct occurred. Thus, if a supervising lawyer knows that a subordinate

misrepresented a matter to an opposing party in negotiation, the supervisor as well as the subordinate has a duty to correct the resulting misapprehension.

[5] Professional misconduct by a lawyer under supervision could reveal a violation of paragraph (b) on the part of the supervisory lawyer even though it does not entail a violation of paragraph (c) because there was no direction, ratification or knowledge of the violation.

[6] Apart from this Rule and Rule 8.4(a), a lawyer does not have disciplinary liability for the conduct of a partner, associate or subordinate. Whether a lawyer may be liable civilly or criminally for another lawyer's conduct is a question of law beyond the scope of these Rules.

Model Code Comparison

There was no direct counterpart to this Rule in the Model Code. DR 1-103(A) provided that a lawyer "possessing unprivileged knowledge of a violation of DR 1-102 shall report such knowledge to . . . authority empowered to investigate or act upon such violation."

RULE 5.2 RESPONSIBILITIES OF A SUBORDINATE LAWYER

(a) A lawyer is bound by the Rules of Professional Conduct notwithstanding that the lawyer acted at the direction of another person.

(b) A subordinate lawyer does not violate the Rules of Professional Conduct if that lawyer acts in accordance with a supervisory lawyer's reasonable resolution of an arguable question of professional duty.

Comment

[1] Although a lawyer is not relieved of responsibility for a violation by the fact that the lawyer acted at the direction of a supervisor, that fact may be relevant in determining whether a lawyer had the knowledge required to render conduct a violation of the Rules. For example, if a subordinate filed a frivolous pleading at the direction of a supervisor, the subordinate would not be guilty of a professional violation unless the subordinate knew of the document's frivolous character.

[2] When lawyers in a supervisor-subordinate relationship encounter a matter involving professional judgment as to ethical duty, the supervisor may assume responsibility for making the judgment. Otherwise a consistent course of action or position could not be taken. If the question can reasonably be answered only one way, the duty of both lawyers is clear and they are equally responsible for fulfilling it. However, if the question is reasonably arguable, someone has to decide upon the course of action. That authority ordinarily reposes in the supervisor, and a subordinate may be guided accordingly. For example, if a question arises whether the interests of two clients conflict under Rule 1.7, the supervisor's reasonable resolu-

tion of the question should protect the subordinate professionally if the resolution is subsequently challenged.

Model Code Comparison

There was no counterpart to this Rule in the Model Code.

RULE 5.3 RESPONSIBILITIES REGARDING NONLAWYER ASSISTANTS

With respect to a nonlawyer employed or retained by or associated with a lawyer:

(a) a partner in a law firm shall make reasonable efforts to ensure that the firm has in effect measures giving reasonable assurance that the person's conduct is compatible with the professional obligations of the lawyer;

(b) a lawyer having direct supervisory authority over the nonlawyer shall make reasonable efforts to ensure that the person's conduct is compatible with the professional obligations of the lawyer; and

(c) a lawyer shall be responsible for conduct of such a person that would be a violation of the Rules of Professional Conduct if engaged in by a lawyer if:

(1) the lawyer orders or, with the knowledge of the specific conduct, ratifies the conduct involved; or

(2) the lawyer is a partner in the law firm in which the person is employed, or has direct supervisory authority over the person, and knows of the conduct at a time when its consequences can be avoided or mitigated but fails to take reasonable remedial action.

Comment

[1] Lawyers generally employ assistants in their practice, including secretaries, investigators, law student interns, and paraprofessionals. Such assistants, whether employees or independent contractors, act for the lawyer in rendition of the lawyer's professional services. A lawyer should give such assistants appropriate instruction and supervision concerning the ethical aspects of their employment, particularly regarding the obligation not to disclose information relating to representation of the client, and should be responsible for their work product. The measures employed in supervising nonlawyers should take account of the fact that they do not have legal training and are not subject to professional discipline.

Model Code Comparison

There was no direct counterpart to this Rule in the Model Code. DR 4-101(D) provided that a lawyer "shall exercise reasonable care to prevent his employees, associates, and others whose services are utilized by him from disclosing or using confidences or secrets of a client . . . ." DR 7-107(J) provided that "[a] lawyer shall exercise reasonable care to prevent his employees and associates from making an extrajudicial statement that he would be prohibited from making under DR 7-107."

RULE 5.4[14] PROFESSIONAL INDEPENDENCE OF A LAWYER

(a) A lawyer or law firm shall not share legal fees with a nonlawyer, except that:

(1) an agreement by a lawyer with the lawyer's firm, partner, or associate may provide for the payment of money, over a reasonable period of time after the lawyer's death, to the lawyer's estate or to one or more specified persons;

(2) a lawyer who purchases the practice of a deceased, disabled, or disappeared lawyer may, pursuant to the provisions of Rule 1.17, pay to the estate or other representative of that lawyer the agreed-upon purchase price; and

(3) a lawyer or law firm may include nonlawyer employees in a compensation or retirement plan, even though the plan is based in whole or in part on a profit-sharing arrangement.

(b) A lawyer shall not form a partnership with a nonlawyer if any of the activities of the partnership consist of the practice of law.

(c) A lawyer shall not permit a person who recommends, employs, or pays the lawyer to render legal services for another to direct or regulate the lawyer's professional judgment in rendering such legal services.

(d) A lawyer shall not practice with or in the form of a professional corporation or association authorized to practice law for a profit, if:

(1) a nonlawyer owns any interest therein, except that a fiduciary representative of the estate of a lawyer may hold the stock or interest of the lawyer for a reasonable time during administration;

(2) a nonlawyer is a corporate director or officer thereof; or

(3) a nonlawyer has the right to direct or control the professional judgment of a lawyer.

Comment

[1] The provisions of this Rule express traditional limitations on sharing fees. These limitations are to protect the lawyer's professional independence of judgment. Where someone other than the client pays the lawyer's fee or salary, or recommends employment of the lawyer, that arrangement does not modify the lawyer's obligation to the client. As stated in paragraph (c), such arrangements should not interfere with the lawyer's professional judgment.

Model Code Comparison

Paragraph (a) is substantially identical to DR 3-102(A).
Paragraph (b) is substantially identical to DR 3-103(A).
Paragraph (c) is substantially identical to DR 5-107(B).
Paragraph (d) is substantially identical to DR 5-107(C).

14. Amended February 12, 1990, American Bar Association House of Delegates, Los Angeles, California, per Report No. 8A.

RULE 5.5 UNAUTHORIZED PRACTICE OF LAW

A lawyer shall not:

(a) practice law in a jurisdiction where doing so violates the regulation of the legal profession in that jurisdiction; or

(b) assist a person who is not a member of the bar in the performance of activity that constitutes the unauthorized practice of law.

Comment

[1] The definition of the practice of law is established by law and varies from one jurisdiction to another. Whatever the definition, limiting the practice of law to members of the bar protects the public against rendition of legal services by unqualified persons. Paragraph (b) does not prohibit a lawyer from employing the services of paraprofessionals and delegating functions to them, so long as the lawyer supervises the delegated work and retains responsibility for their work. See Rule 5.3. Likewise, it does not prohibit lawyers from providing professional advice and instruction to nonlawyers whose employment requires knowledge of law; for example, claims adjusters, employees of financial or commercial institutions, social workers, accountants and persons employed in government agencies. In addition, a lawyer may counsel nonlawyers who wish to proceed pro se.

Model Code Comparison

With regard to paragraph (a), DR 3-101(B) of the Model Code provided that "[a] lawyer shall not practice law in a jurisdiction where to do so would be in violation of regulations of the profession in that jurisdiction."

With regard to paragraph (b), DR 3-101(A) of the Model Code provided that "[a] lawyer shall not aid a non-lawyer in the unauthorized practice of law."

RULE 5.6[15] RESTRICTIONS ON RIGHT TO PRACTICE

A lawyer shall not participate in offering or making:

(a) a partnership or employment agreement that restricts the right of a lawyer to practice after termination of the relationship, except an agreement concerning benefits upon retirement; or

(b) an agreement in which a restriction on the lawyer's right to practice is part of the settlement of a controversy between private parties.

Comment

[1] An agreement restricting the right of partners or associates to practice after leaving a firm not only limits their professional autonomy but also limits the freedom of clients to choose a lawyer. Paragraph (a) prohibits such agreements except for restrictions incident to provisions concerning retirement benefits for service with the firm.

15. Amended February 12, 1990, American Bar Association House of Delegates, Los Angeles, California, per Report No. 8A.

[2] Paragraph (b) prohibits a lawyer from agreeing not to represent other persons in connection with settling a claim on behalf of a client.

[3] This Rule does not apply to prohibit restrictions that may be included in the terms of the sale of a law practice pursuant to Rule 1.17.

Model Code Comparison

This Rule is substantially similar to DR 2-108.

RULE 5.7[16] RESPONSIBILITIES REGARDING LAW-RELATED SERVICES

(a) A lawyer shall be subject to the Rules of Professional Conduct with respect to the provision of law-related services, as defined in paragraph (b), if the law-related services are provided:

(1) by the lawyer in circumstances that are not distinct from the lawyer's provision of legal services to clients; or

(2) by a separate entity controlled by the lawyer individually or with others if the lawyer fails to take reasonable measures to assure that a person obtaining the law-related services knows that the services of the separate entity are not legal services and that the protections of the client-lawyer relationship do not exist.

(b) The term "law-related services" denotes services that might reasonably be performed in conjunction with and in substance are related to the provision of legal services, and that are not prohibited as unauthorized practice of law when provided by a nonlawyer.

Comment

[1] When a lawyer performs law-related services or controls an organization that does so, there exists the potential for ethical problems. Principal among these is the possibility that the person for whom the law-related services are performed fails to understand that the services may not carry with them the protections normally afforded as part of the client-lawyer relationship. The recipient of the law-related services may expect, for example, that the protection of client confidences, prohibitions against representation of persons with conflicting interests, and obligations of a lawyer to maintain professional independence apply to the provision of law-related services when that may not be the case.

[2] Rule 5.7 applies to the provision of law-related services by a lawyer even when the lawyer does not provide any legal services to the person for whom the

16. Added February 2, 1994, American Bar Association House of Delegates, Kansas City, Missouri, per Report No. 113; a previous Rule 5.7, denominated "Provision of Ancillary Services," was added August 12, 1991, American Bar Association House of Delegates, Atlanta, Georgia, per Report No. 121 and was rescinded August 12, 1993, American Bar Association House of Delegates, San Francisco, California, per Report No. 10D.

law-related services are performed. The Rule identifies the circumstances in which all of the Rules of Professional Conduct apply to the provision of law-related services. Even when those circumstances do not exist, however, the conduct of a lawyer involved in the provision of law-related services is subject to those Rules that apply generally to lawyer conduct, regardless of whether the conduct involves the provision of legal services. See, e.g., Rule 8.4.

[3] When law-related services are provided by a lawyer under circumstances that are not distinct from the lawyer's provision of legal services to clients, the lawyer in providing the law-related services must adhere to the requirements of the Rules of Professional Conduct as provided in Rule 5.7(a)(1).

[4] Law-related services also may be provided through an entity that is distinct from that through which the lawyer provides legal services. If the lawyer individually or with others has control of such an entity's operations, the Rule requires the lawyer to take reasonable measures to assure that each person using the services of the entity knows that the services provided by the entity are not legal services and that the Rules of Professional Conduct that relate to the client-lawyer relationship do not apply. A lawyer's control of an entity extends to the ability to direct its operation. Whether a lawyer has such control will depend upon the circumstances of the particular case.

[5] When a client-lawyer relationship exists with a person who is referred by a lawyer to a separate law-related service entity controlled by the lawyer, individually or with others, the lawyer must comply with Rule 1.8(a).

[6] In taking the reasonable measures referred to in paragraph (a)(2) to assure that a person using law-related services understands the practical effect or significance of the inapplicability of the Rules of Professional Conduct, the lawyer should communicate to the person receiving the law-related services, in a manner sufficient to assure that the person understands the significance of the fact, that the relationship of the person to the business entity will not be a client-lawyer relationship. The communication should be made before entering into an agreement for provision of or providing law-related services, and preferably should be in writing.

[7] The burden is upon the lawyer to show that the lawyer has taken reasonable measures under the circumstances to communicate the desired understanding. For instance, a sophisticated user of law-related services, such as a publicly held corporation, may require a lesser explanation than someone unaccustomed to making distinctions between legal services and law-related services, such as an individual seeking tax advice from a lawyer-accountant or investigative services in connection with a lawsuit.

[8] Regardless of the sophistication of potential recipients of law-related services, a lawyer should take special care to keep separate the provision of law-related and legal services in order to minimize the risk that the recipient will assume that the law-related services are legal services. The risk of such confusion is especially

acute when the lawyer renders both types of services with respect to the same matter. Under some circumstances the legal and law-related services may be so closely entwined that they cannot be distinguished from each other, and the requirement of disclosure and consultation imposed by paragraph (a)(2) of the Rule cannot be met. In such a case a lawyer will be responsible for assuring that both the lawyer's conduct and, to the extent required by Rule 5.3, that of nonlawyer employees in the distinct entity which the lawyer controls complies in all respects with the Rules of Professional Conduct.

[9] A broad range of economic and other interests of clients may be served by lawyers' engaging in the delivery of law-related services. Examples of law-related services include providing title insurance, financial planning, accounting, trust services, real estate counseling, legislative lobbying, economic analysis, social work, psychological counseling, tax preparation, and patent, medical or environmental consulting.

[10] When a lawyer is obliged to accord the recipients of such services the protections of those Rules that apply to the client-lawyer relationship, the lawyer must take special care to heed the proscriptions of the Rules addressing conflict of interest (Rules 1.7 through 1.11, especially Rules 1.7(b) and 1.8(a), (b) and (f)), and to scrupulously adhere to the requirements of Rule 1.6 relating to disclosure of confidential information. The promotion of the law-related services must also in all respects comply with Rules 7.1 through 7.3, dealing with advertising and solicitation. In that regard, lawyers should take special care to identify the obligations that may be imposed as a result of a jurisdiction's decisional law.

[11] When the full protections of all of the Rules of Professional Conduct do not apply to the provision of law-related services, principles of law external to the Rules, for example, the law of principal and agent, govern the legal duties owed to those receiving the services. Those other legal principles may establish a different degree of protection for the recipient with respect to confidentiality of information, conflicts of interest and permissible business relationships with clients. See also Rule 8.4 (Misconduct).

Model Code Comparison

There was no counterpart to this Rule in the Model Code.

PUBLIC SERVICE

RULE 6.1[17] VOLUNTARY *PRO BONO PUBLICO* SERVICE

A lawyer should aspire to render at least (50) hours of pro bono publico legal services per year. In fulfilling this responsibility, the lawyer should:

17. Amended February 12, 1990, American Bar Association House of Delegates, Los Angeles, California, per Report No. 8A; February 8, 1993, American Bar Association House of Delegates, Boston, Massachusetts, per Report No. 8A.

(a) provide a substantial majority of the (50) hours of legal services without fee or expectation of fee to:

(1) persons of limited means or

(2) charitable, religious, civic, community, governmental and educational organizations in matters which are designed primarily to address the needs of persons of limited means; and

(b) provide any additional services through:

(1) delivery of legal services at no fee or substantially reduced fee to individuals, groups or organizations seeking to secure or protect civil rights, civil liberties or public rights, or charitable, religious, civic, community, governmental and educational organizations in matters in furtherance of their organizational purposes, where the payment of standard legal fees would significantly deplete the organization's economic resources or would be otherwise inappropriate;

(2) delivery of legal services at a substantially reduced fee to persons of limited means; or

(3) participation in activities for improving the law, the legal system or the legal profession.

In addition, a lawyer should voluntarily contribute financial support to organizations that provide legal services to persons of limited means.

Comment

[1] Every lawyer, regardless of professional prominence or professional work load, has a responsibility to provide legal services to those unable to pay, and personal involvement in the problems of the disadvantaged can be one of the most rewarding experiences in the life of a lawyer. The American Bar Association urges all lawyers to provide a minimum of 50 hours of pro bono services annually. States, however, may decide to choose a higher or lower number of hours of annual service (which may be expressed as a percentage of a lawyer's professional time) depending upon local needs and local conditions. It is recognized that in some years a lawyer may render greater or fewer hours than the annual standard specified, but during the course of his or her legal career, each lawyer should render on average per year, the number of hours set forth in this Rule. Services can be performed in civil matters or in criminal or quasi-criminal matters for which there is no government obligation to provide funds for legal representation, such as post-conviction death penalty appeal cases.

[2] Paragraphs (a)(1) and (2) recognize the critical need for legal services that exists among persons of limited means by providing that a substantial majority of the legal services rendered annually to the disadvantaged be furnished without fee or expectation of fee. Legal services under these paragraphs consist of a full range of activities, including individual and class representation, the provision of legal advice, legislative lobbying, administrative rule making and the provision of free training or mentoring to those who represent persons of limited means. The variety of these activities should facilitate participation by government attorneys, even when restrictions exist on their engaging in the outside practice of law.

[3] Persons eligible for legal services under paragraphs (a)(1) and (2) are those who qualify for participation in programs funded by the Legal Services Corporation and those whose incomes and financial resources are slightly above the guidelines utilized by such programs but nevertheless, cannot afford counsel. Legal services can be rendered to individuals or to organizations such as homeless shelters, battered women's centers and food pantries that serve those of limited means. The term "governmental organizations" includes, but is not limited to, public protection programs and sections of governmental or public sector agencies.

[4] Because service must be provided without fee or expectation of fee, the intent of the lawyer to render free legal services is essential for the work performed to fall within the meaning of paragraphs (a)(1) and (2). Accordingly, services rendered cannot be considered pro bono if an anticipated fee is uncollected, but the award of statutory attorneys' fees in a case originally accepted as pro bono would not disqualify such services from inclusion under this section. Lawyers who do receive fees in such cases are encouraged to contribute an appropriate portion of such fees to organizations or projects that benefit persons of limited means.

[5] While it is possible for a lawyer to fulfill the annual responsibility to perform pro bono services exclusively through activities described in paragraphs (a)(1) and (2), to the extent that any hours of service remained unfulfilled, the remaining commitment can be met in a variety of ways as set forth in paragraph (b). Constitutional, statutory or regulatory restrictions may prohibit or impede government and public sector lawyers and judges from performing the pro bono services outlined in paragraphs (a)(1) and (2). Accordingly, where those restrictions apply, government and public sector lawyers and judges may fulfill their pro bono responsibility by performing services outlined in paragraph (b).

[6] Paragraph (b)(1) includes the provision of certain types of legal services to those whose incomes and financial resources place them above limited means. It also permits the pro bono lawyer to accept a substantially reduced fee for services. Examples of the types of issues that may be addressed under this paragraph include First Amendment claims, Title VII claims and environmental protection claims. Additionally, a wide range of organizations may be represented, including social service, medical research, cultural and religious groups.

[7] Paragraph (b)(2) covers instances in which attorneys agree to and receive a modest fee for furnishing legal services to persons of limited means. Participation in judicare programs and acceptance of court appointments in which the fee is substantially below a lawyer's usual rate are encouraged under this section.

[8] Paragraph (b)(3) recognizes the value of lawyers engaging in activities that improve the law, the legal system or the legal profession. Serving on bar association committees, serving on boards of pro bono or legal services programs, taking part in Law Day activities, acting as a continuing legal education instructor, a mediator or an arbitrator and engaging in legislative lobbying to improve the law, the legal system or the profession are a few examples of the many activities that fall within this paragraph.

[9] Because the provision of pro bono services is a professional responsibility, it is the individual ethical commitment of each lawyer. Nevertheless, there may be times when it is not feasible for a lawyer to engage in pro bono services. At such times a lawyer may discharge the pro bono responsibility by providing financial support to organizations providing free legal services to persons of limited means. Such financial support should be reasonably equivalent to the value of the hours of service that would have otherwise been provided. In addition, at times it may be more feasible to satisfy the pro bono responsibility collectively, as by a firm's aggregate pro bono activities.

[10] Because the efforts of individual lawyers are not enough to meet the need for free legal services that exists among persons of limited means, the government and the profession have instituted additional programs to provide those services. Every lawyer should financially support such programs, in addition to either providing direct pro bono services or making financial contributions when pro bono service is not feasible.

[11] The responsibility set forth in this Rule is not intended to be enforced through disciplinary process.

Model Code Comparison

There was no counterpart of this Rule in the Disciplinary Rules of the Model Code. EC 2-25 stated that the "basic responsibility for providing legal services for those unable to pay ultimately rests upon the individual lawyer . . . . Every lawyer, regardless of professional prominence or professional work load, should find time to participate in serving the disadvantaged." EC 8-9 stated that "[t]he advancement of our legal system is of vital importance in maintaining the rule of law . . . [and] lawyers should encourage, and should aid in making, needed changes and improvements." EC 8-3 stated that "[t]hose persons unable to pay for legal services should be provided needed services."

RULE 6.2 ACCEPTING APPOINTMENTS

A lawyer shall not seek to avoid appointment by a tribunal to represent a person except for good cause, such as:

(a) representing the client is likely to result in violation of the Rules of Professional Conduct or other law;

(b) representing the client is likely to result in an unreasonable financial burden on the lawyer; or

(c) the client or the cause is so repugnant to the lawyer as to be likely to impair the client-lawyer relationship or the lawyer's ability to represent the client.

Comment

[1] A lawyer ordinarily is not obliged to accept a client whose character or cause the lawyer regards as repugnant. The lawyer's freedom to select clients is, however, qualified. All lawyers have a responsibility to assist in providing pro bono

publico service. See Rule 6.1. An individual lawyer fulfills this responsibility by accepting a fair share of unpopular matters or indigent or unpopular clients. A lawyer may also be subject to appointment by a court to serve unpopular clients or persons unable to afford legal services.

Appointed Counsel

[2] For good cause a lawyer may seek to decline an appointment to represent a person who cannot afford to retain counsel or whose cause is unpopular. Good cause exists if the lawyer could not handle the matter competently, see Rule 1.1, or if undertaking the representation would result in an improper conflict of interest, for example, when the client or the cause is so repugnant to the lawyer as to be likely to impair the client-lawyer relationship or the lawyer's ability to represent the client. A lawyer may also seek to decline an appointment if acceptance would be unreasonably burdensome, for example, when it would impose a financial sacrifice so great as to be unjust.

[3] An appointed lawyer has the same obligations to the client as retained counsel, including the obligations of loyalty and confidentiality, and is subject to the same limitations on the client-lawyer relationship, such as the obligation to refrain from assisting the client in violation of the Rules.

Model Code Comparison

There was no counterpart to this Rule in the Disciplinary Rules of the Model Code. EC 2-29 stated that when a lawyer is "appointed by a court or requested by a bar association to undertake representation of a person unable to obtain counsel, whether for financial or other reasons, he should not seek to be excused from undertaking the representation except for compelling reasons. Compelling reasons do not include such factors as the repugnance of the subject matter of the proceeding, the identity or position of a person involved in the case, the belief of the lawyer that the defendant in a criminal proceeding is guilty, or the belief of the lawyer regarding the merits of the civil case." EC 2-30 stated that "a lawyer should decline employment if the intensity of his personal feelings, as distinguished from a community attitude, may impair his effective representation of a prospective client."

RULE 6.3[18] MEMBERSHIP IN LEGAL SERVICES ORGANIZATION

A lawyer may serve as a director, officer or member of a legal services organization, apart from the law firm in which the lawyer practices, notwithstanding that the organization serves persons having interests adverse to a client of the lawyer. The lawyer shall not knowingly participate in a decision or action of the organization:

(a) if participating in the decision or action would be incompatible with the lawyer's obligations to a client under Rule 1.7; or

18. Amended February 17, 1987, American Bar Association House of Delegates, New Orleans, Louisiana, per Report No. 121.

(b) where the decision or action could have a material adverse effect on the representation of a client of the organization whose interests are adverse to a client of the lawyer.

Comment

[1] Lawyers should be encouraged to support and participate in legal service organizations. A lawyer who is an officer or a member of such an organization does not thereby have a client-lawyer relationship with persons served by the organization. However, there is potential conflict between the interests of such persons and the interests of the lawyer's clients. If the possibility of such conflict disqualified a lawyer from serving on the board of a legal services organization, the profession's involvement in such organizations would be severely curtailed.

[2] It may be necessary in appropriate cases to reassure a client of the organization that the representation will not be affected by conflicting loyalties of a member of the board. Established, written policies in this respect can enhance the credibility of such assurances.

Model Code Comparison

There was no counterpart to this Rule in the Model Code.

RULE 6.4 LAW REFORM ACTIVITIES AFFECTING CLIENT INTERESTS

A lawyer may serve as a director, officer or member of an organization involved in reform of the law or its administration notwithstanding that the reform may affect the interests of a client of the lawyer. When the lawyer knows that the interests of a client may be materially benefitted by a decision in which the lawyer participates, the lawyer shall disclose that fact but need not identify the client.

Comment

[1] Lawyers involved in organizations seeking law reform generally do not have a client-lawyer relationship with the organization. Otherwise, it might follow that a lawyer could not be involved in a bar association law reform program that might indirectly affect a client. See also Rule 1.2(b). For example, a lawyer specializing in antitrust litigation might be regarded as disqualified from participating in drafting revisions of rules governing that subject. In determining the nature and scope of participation in such activities, a lawyer should be mindful of obligations to clients under other Rules, particularly Rule 1.7. A lawyer is professionally obligated to protect the integrity of the program by making an appropriate disclosure within the organization when the lawyer knows a private client might be materially benefitted.

Model Code Comparison

There was no counterpart to this Rule in the Model Code.

INFORMATION ABOUT LEGAL SERVICES

RULE 7.1 COMMUNICATIONS CONCERNING A LAWYER'S SERVICES

A lawyer shall not make a false or misleading communication about the lawyer or the lawyer's services. A communication is false or misleading if it:

(a) contains a material misrepresentation of fact or law, or omits a fact necessary to make the statement considered as a whole not materially misleading;

(b) is likely to create an unjustified expectation about results the lawyer can achieve, or states or implies that the lawyer can achieve results by means that violate the Rules of Professional Conduct or other law; or

(c) compares the lawyer's services with other lawyers' services, unless the comparison can be factually substantiated.

Comment

[1] This Rule governs all communications about a lawyer's services, including advertising permitted by Rule 7.2. Whatever means are used to make known a lawyer's services, statements about them should be truthful. The prohibition in paragraph (b) of statements that may create "unjustified expectations" would ordinarily preclude advertisements about results obtained on behalf of a client, such as the amount of a damage award or the lawyer's record in obtaining favorable verdicts, and advertisements containing client endorsements. Such information may create the unjustified expectation that similar results can be obtained for others without reference to the specific factual and legal circumstances.

Model Code Comparison

DR 2-101 provided that "[a] lawyer shall not . . . use . . . any form of public communication containing a false, fraudulent, misleading, deceptive, self-laudatory or unfair statement or claim." DR 2-101(B) provided that a lawyer "may publish or broadcast . . . the following information . . . in the geographic area or areas in which the lawyer resides or maintains offices or in which a significant part of the lawyer's clientele resides, provided that the information . . . complies with DR 2-101(A), and is presented in a dignified manner . . . ." DR 2-101(B) then specified twenty-five categories of information that may be disseminated. DR 2-101(C) provided that "[a]ny person desiring to expand the information authorized for disclosure in DR 2-101(B), or to provide for its dissemination through other forums may apply to [the agency having jurisdiction under state law] . . . . The relief granted in response to any such application shall be promulgated as an amendment to DR 2-101(B), universally applicable to all lawyers."

RULE 7.2[19] ADVERTISING

(a) Subject to the requirements of Rules 7.1 and 7.3, a lawyer may advertise services through public media, such as a telephone directory, legal directory, newspaper or other periodical, outdoor advertising, radio or television, or through written or recorded communication.

(b) A copy or recording of an advertisement or communication shall be kept for two years after its last dissemination along with a record of when and where it was used.

(c) A lawyer shall not give anything of value to a person for recommending the lawyer's services except that a lawyer may

(1) pay the reasonable costs of advertisements or communications permitted by this Rule;

(2) pay the usual charges of a not-for-profit lawyer referral service or legal service organization; and

(3) pay for a law practice in accordance with Rule 1.17.

(d) Any communication made pursuant to this rule shall include the name of at least one lawyer responsible for its content.

Comment

[1] To assist the public in obtaining legal services, lawyers should be allowed to make known their services not only through reputation but also through organized information campaigns in the form of advertising. Advertising involves an active quest for clients, contrary to the tradition that a lawyer should not seek clientele. However, the public's need to know about legal services can be fulfilled in part through advertising. This need is particularly acute in the case of persons of moderate means who have not made extensive use of legal services. The interest in expanding public information about legal services ought to prevail over considerations of tradition. Nevertheless, advertising by lawyers entails the risk of practices that are misleading or overreaching.

[2] This Rule permits public dissemination of information concerning a lawyer's name or firm name, address and telephone number; the kinds of services the lawyer will undertake; the basis on which the lawyer's fees are determined, including prices for specific services and payment and credit arrangements; a lawyer's foreign language ability; names of references and, with their consent, names of clients regularly represented; and other information that might invite the attention of those seeking legal assistance.

[3] Questions of effectiveness and taste in advertising are matters of speculation and subjective judgment. Some jurisdictions have had extensive prohibitions against television advertising, against advertising going beyond specified facts about a lawyer, or against "undignified" advertising. Television is now one of the most powerful media for getting information to the public, particularly persons of

19. Amended February 7, 1989, American Bar Association House of Delegates, New Orleans, Louisiana, per Report No. 120B; February 12, 1990, American Bar Association House of Delegates, Los Angeles, California, per Report No. 8A.

low and moderate income; prohibiting television advertising, therefore, would impede the flow of information about legal services to many sectors of the public. Limiting the information that may be advertised has a similar effect and assumes that the bar can accurately forecast the kind of information that the public would regard as relevant.

[4] Neither this Rule nor Rule 7.3 prohibits communications authorized by law, such as notice to members of a class in class action litigation.

Record of Advertising

[5] Paragraph (b) requires that a record of the content and use of advertising be kept in order to facilitate enforcement of this Rule. It does not require that advertising be subject to review prior to dissemination. Such a requirement would be burdensome and expensive relative to its possible benefits, and may be of doubtful constitutionality.

Paying Others to Recommend a Lawyer

[6] A lawyer is allowed to pay for advertising permitted by this Rule and for the purchase of a law practice in accordance with the provisions of Rule 1.17, but otherwise is not permitted to pay another person for channeling professional work. This restriction does not prevent an organization or person other than the lawyer from advertising or recommending the lawyer's services. Thus, a legal aid agency or prepaid legal services plan may pay to advertise legal services provided under its auspices. Likewise, a lawyer may participate in not-for-profit lawyer referral programs and pay the usual fees charged by such programs. Paragraph (c) does not prohibit paying regular compensation to an assistant, such as a secretary, to prepare communications permitted by this Rule.

Model Code Comparison

With regard to paragraph (a), DR 2-101(B) provided that a lawyer "may publish or broadcast, subject to DR 2-103, . . . in print media . . . or television or radio . . . ."

With regard to paragraph (b), DR 2-101(D) provided that if the advertisement is "communicated to the public over television or radio, . . . a recording of the actual transmission shall be retained by the lawyer."

With regard to paragraph (c), DR 2-103(B) provided that a lawyer "shall not compensate or give anything of value to a person or organization to recommend or secure his employment . . . except that he may pay the usual and reasonable fees or dues charged by any of the organizations listed in DR 2-103(D)." (DR 2-103(D) referred to legal aid and other legal services organizations.) DR 2-101(I) provided that a lawyer "shall not compensate or give anything of value to representatives of the press, radio, television, or other communication medium in anticipation of or in return for professional publicity in a news item."

There was no counterpart to paragraph (d) in the Model Code.

RULE 7.3[20] DIRECT CONTACT WITH PROSPECTIVE CLIENTS

(a) A lawyer shall not by in-person or live telephone contact solicit professional employment from a prospective client with whom the lawyer has no family or prior professional relationship when a significant motive for the lawyer's doing so is the lawyer's pecuniary gain.

(b) A lawyer shall not solicit professional employment from a prospective client by written or recorded communication or by in-person or telephone contact even when not otherwise prohibited by paragraph (a), if:

(1) the prospective client has made known to the lawyer a desire not to be solicited by the lawyer; or

(2) the solicitation involves coercion, duress or harassment.

(c) Every written or recorded communication from a lawyer soliciting professional employment from a prospective client known to be in need of legal services in a particular matter, and with whom the lawyer has no family or prior professional relationship, shall include the words "Advertising Material" on the outside envelope and at the beginning and ending of any recorded communication.

(d)[21] Notwithstanding the prohibitions in paragraph (a), a lawyer may participate with a prepaid or group legal service plan operated by an organization not owned or directed by the lawyer which uses in-person or telephone contact to solicit memberships or subscriptions for the plan from persons who are not known to need legal services in a particular matter covered by the plan.

Comment

[1] There is a potential for abuse inherent in direct in-person or live telephone contact by a lawyer with a prospective client known to need legal services. These forms of contact between a lawyer and a prospective client subject the layperson to the private importuning of the trained advocate in a direct interpersonal encounter. The prospective client, who may already feel overwhelmed by the circumstances giving rise to the need for legal services, may find it difficult fully to evaluate all available alternatives with reasoned judgment and appropriate self-interest in the face of the lawyer's presence and insistence upon being retained immediately. The situation is fraught with the possibility of undue influence, intimidation, and over-reaching.

[2] This potential for abuse inherent in direct in-person or live telephone solicitation of prospective clients justifies its prohibition, particularly since lawyer advertising and written and recorded communication permitted under Rule 7.2 offer alternative means of conveying necessary information to those who may be in need of legal services. Advertising and written and recorded communications

20. Amended February 7, 1989, American Bar Association House of Delegates, New Orleans, Louisiana, per Report No. 120B.

21. Added February 7, 1989, American Bar Association House of Delegates, New Orleans, Louisiana, per Report No. 115.

which may be mailed or autodialed make it possible for a prospective client to be informed about the need for legal services, and about the qualifications of available lawyers and law firms, without subjecting the prospective client to direct in-person or telephone persuasion that may overwhelm the client's judgment.

[3] The use of general advertising and written and recorded communications to transmit information from lawyer to prospective client, rather than direct in-person or live telephone contact, will help to assure that the information flows cleanly as well as freely. The contents of advertisements and communications permitted under Rule 7.2 are permanently recorded so that they cannot be disputed and may be shared with others who know the lawyer. This potential for informal review is itself likely to help guard against statements and claims that might constitute false and misleading communications, in violation of Rule 7.1. The contents of direct in-person or live telephone conversations between a lawyer to a prospective client can be disputed and are not subject to third-party scrutiny. Consequently, they are much more likely to approach (and occasionally cross) the dividing line between accurate representations and those that are false and misleading.

[4] There is far less likelihood that a lawyer would engage in abusive practices against an individual with whom the lawyer has a prior personal or professional relationship or where the lawyer is motivated by considerations other than the lawyer's pecuniary gain. Consequently, the general prohibition in Rule 7.3(a) and the requirements of Rule 7.3(c) are not applicable in those situations.

[5] But even permitted forms of solicitation can be abused. Thus, any solicitation which contains information which is false or misleading within the meaning of Rule 7.1, which involves coercion, duress or harassment within the meaning of Rule 7.3(b)(2), or which involves contact with a prospective client who has made known to the lawyer a desire not to be solicited by the lawyer within the meaning of Rule 7.3(b)(1) is prohibited. Moreover, if after sending a letter or other communication to a client as permitted by Rule 7.2 the lawyer receives no response, any further effort to communicate with the prospective client may violate the provisions of Rule 7.3(b).

[6] This Rule is not intended to prohibit a lawyer from contacting representatives of organizations or groups that may be interested in establishing a group or prepaid legal plan for their members, insureds, beneficiaries or other third parties for the purpose of informing such entities of the availability of and details concerning the plan or arrangement which the lawyer or lawyer's firm is willing to offer. This form of communication is not directed to a prospective client. Rather, it is usually addressed to an individual acting in a fiduciary capacity seeking a supplier of legal services for others who may, if they choose, become prospective clients of the lawyer. Under these circumstances, the activity which the lawyer undertakes in communicating with such representatives and the type of information transmitted to the individual are functionally similar to and serve the same purpose as advertising permitted under Rule 7.2.

[7] The requirement in Rule 7.3(c) that certain communications be marked "Advertising Material" does not apply to communications sent in response to

requests of potential clients or their spokespersons or sponsors. General announcements by lawyers, including changes in personnel or office location, do not constitute communications soliciting professional employment from a client known to be in need of legal services within the meaning of this Rule.

[8] Paragraph (d) of this Rule would permit a lawyer to participate with an organization which uses personal contact to solicit members for its group or prepaid legal service plan, provided that the personal contact is not undertaken by any lawyer who would be a provider of legal services through the plan. The organization referred to in paragraph (d) must not be owned by or directed (whether as manager or otherwise) by any lawyer or law firm that participates in the plan. For example, paragraph (d) would not permit a lawyer to create an organization controlled directly or indirectly by the lawyer and use the organization for the in-person or telephone solicitation of legal employment of the lawyer through memberships in the plan or otherwise. The communication permitted by these organizations also must not be directed to a person known to need legal services in a particular matter, but is to be designed to inform potential plan members generally of another means of affordable legal services. Lawyers who participate in a legal service plan must reasonably assure that the plan sponsors are in compliance with Rules 7.1, 7.2 and 7.3(b). See 8.4(a).

Model Code Comparison

DR 2-104(A) provided with certain exceptions that "[a] lawyer who has given in-person unsolicited advice to a layperson that he should obtain counsel or take legal action shall not accept employment resulting from that advice . . . ." The exceptions include DR 2-104(A)(1), which provided that a lawyer "may accept employment by a close friend, relative, former client (if the advice is germane to the former employment), or one whom the lawyer reasonably believes to be a client." DR 2-104(A)(2) through DR 2-104(A)(5) provided other exceptions relating, respectively, to employment resulting from public educational programs, recommendation by a legal assistance organization, public speaking or writing and representing members of a class in class action litigation.

RULE 7.4[22] COMMUNICATION OF FIELDS OF PRACTICE

A lawyer may communicate the fact that the lawyer does or does not practice in particular fields of law. A lawyer shall not state or imply that the lawyer has been recognized or certified as a specialist in a particular field of law except as follows:

(a) a lawyer admitted to engage in patent practice before the United States Patent and Trademark Office may use the designation "Patent Attorney" or a substantially similar designation;

22. Amended February 7, 1989, American Bar Association House of Delegates, Denver, Colorado, per Report No. 121; August 12, 1992, American Bar Association House of Delegates, San Francisco, California, per Revised Report No. 128; August 10, 1994, American Bar Association House of Delegates, New Orleans, Louisiana, per Report No. 121.

(b) a lawyer engaged in Admiralty practice may use the designation "Admiralty," "Proctor in Admiralty" or a substantially similar designation; and

(c) [for jurisdictions where there is a regulatory authority granting certification or approving organizations that grant certification] a lawyer may communicate the fact that the lawyer has been certified as a specialist in a field of law by a named organization or authority but only if:

(1) such certification is granted by the appropriate regulatory authority or by an organization which has been approved by the appropriate regulatory authority to grant such certification; or

(2) such certification is granted by an organization that has not yet been approved by, or has been denied the approval available from, the appropriate regulatory authority, and the absence or denial of approval is clearly stated in the communication, and in any advertising subject to Rule 7.2, such statement appears in the same sentence that communicates the certification.

(c) [for jurisdictions where there is no procedure either for certification of specialties or for approval of organizations granting certification] a lawyer may communicate the fact that the lawyer has been certified as a specialist in a field of law by a named organization, provided that the communication clearly states that there is no procedure in this jurisdiction for approving certifying organizations. If, however, the named organization has been accredited by the American Bar Association to certify lawyers as specialists in a particular field of law, the communication need not contain such a statement.

Comment

[1] This Rule permits a lawyer to indicate areas of practice in communications about the lawyer's services. If a lawyer practices only in certain fields, or will not accept matters except in a specified field or fields, the lawyer is permitted to so indicate. A lawyer is generally permitted to state that the lawyer is a "specialist," practices a "specialty," or "specializes in" particular fields, but such communications are subject to the "false and misleading" standard applied in Rule 7.1 to communications concerning a lawyer's services.

[2] However, a lawyer may not communicate that the lawyer has been recognized or certified as a specialist in a particular field of law, except as provided by this Rule. Recognition of specialization in patent matters is a matter of long-established policy of the Patent and Trademark Office, as reflected in paragraph (a). Paragraph (b) recognizes that designation of admiralty practice has a long historical tradition associated with maritime commerce and the federal courts.

[3] Paragraph (c) provides for certification as a specialist in a field of law when a state authorizes an appropriate regulatory authority to grant such certification or when the state grants other organizations the right to grant certification. Certification procedures imply that an objective entity has recognized a lawyer's higher degree of specialized ability than is suggested by general licensure to practice law. Those objective entities may be expected to apply standards of competence, experience and knowledge to insure that a lawyer's recognition as a special-

ist is meaningful and reliable. In order to insure that consumers can obtain access to useful information about an organization granting certification, the name of the certifying organization or agency must be included in any communication regarding the certification.

[4] Lawyers may also be certified as specialists by organizations that either have not yet been approved to grant such certification or have been disapproved. In such instances, the consumer may be misled as to the significance of the lawyer's status as a certified specialist. The Rule therefore requires that a lawyer who chooses to communicate recognition by such an organization also clearly state the absence or denial of the organization's authority to grant such certification. Since lawyer advertising through public media and written or recorded communications invites the greatest danger of misleading consumers, the absence or denial of the organization's authority to grant certification must be clearly stated in such advertising in the same sentence that communicates the certification.

[5] In jurisdictions where no appropriate regulatory authority has a procedure for approving organizations granting certification, the Rule requires that a lawyer clearly state such lack of procedure. If, however, the named organization has been accredited by the American Bar Association to certify lawyers as specialists in a particular field of law, the communication need not contain such a statement.

Model Code Comparison

DR 2-105(A) provided that a lawyer "shall not hold himself out publicly as a specialist, as practicing in certain areas of law or as limiting his practice . . . except as follows:

> "(1) A lawyer admitted to practice before the United States Patent and Trademark Office may use the designation 'Patents,' 'Patent Attorney,' 'Patent Lawyer,' or 'Registered Patent Attorney' or any combination of those terms, on his letterhead and office sign.
>
> "(2) A lawyer who publicly discloses fields of law in which the lawyer . . . practices or states that his practice is limited to one or more fields of law shall do so by using designations and definitions authorized and approved by [the agency having jurisdiction of the subject under state law].
>
> "(3) A lawyer who is certified as a specialist in a particular field of law or law practice by [the authority having jurisdiction under state law over the subject of specialization by lawyers] may hold himself out as such, but only in accordance with the rules prescribed by that authority."

EC 2-14 stated that "In the absence of state controls to insure the existence of special competence, a lawyer should not be permitted to hold himself out as a specialist, . . . other than in the fields of admiralty, trademark, and patent law where a holding out as a specialist historically has been permitted."

RULE 7.5 FIRM NAMES AND LETTERHEADS

(a) A lawyer shall not use a firm name, letterhead or other professional designation that violates Rule 7.1. A trade name may be used by a lawyer in private

practice if it does not imply a connection with a government agency or with a public or charitable legal services organization and is not otherwise in violation of Rule 7.1.

(b) A law firm with offices in more than one jurisdiction may use the same name in each jurisdiction, but identification of the lawyers in an office of the firm shall indicate the jurisdictional limitations on those not licensed to practice in the jurisdiction where the office is located.

(c) The name of a lawyer holding a public office shall not be used in the name of a law firm, or in communications on its behalf, during any substantial period in which the lawyer is not actively and regularly practicing with the firm.

(d) Lawyers may state or imply that they practice in a partnership or other organization only when that is the fact.

Comment

[1] A firm may be designated by the names of all or some of its members, by the names of deceased members where there has been a continuing succession in the firm's identity or by a trade name such as the "ABC Legal Clinic." Although the United States Supreme Court has held that legislation may prohibit the use of trade names in professional practice, use of such names in law practice is acceptable so long as it is not misleading. If a private firm uses a trade name that includes a geographical name such as "Springfield Legal Clinic," an express disclaimer that it is a public legal aid agency may be required to avoid a misleading implication. It may be observed that any firm name including the name of a deceased partner is, strictly speaking, a trade name. The use of such names to designate law firms has proven a useful means of identification. However, it is misleading to use the name of a lawyer not associated with the firm or a predecessor of the firm.

[2] With regard to paragraph (d), lawyers sharing office facilities, but who are not in fact partners, may not denominate themselves as, for example, "Smith and Jones," for that title suggests partnership in the practice of law.

Model Code Comparison

With regard to paragraph (a), DR 2-102(A) provided that "[a] lawyer . . . shall not use . . . professional announcement cards . . . letterheads, or similar professional notices or devices, except . . . if they are in dignified form . . . ." DR 2-102(B) provided that "[a] lawyer in private practice shall not practice under a trade name, a name that is misleading as to the identity of the lawyer or lawyers practicing under such name, or a firm name containing names other than those of one or more of the lawyers in the firm, except that . . . a firm may use as . . . its name the name or names of one or more deceased or retired members of the firm or of a predecessor firm in a continuing line of succession."

With regard to paragraph (b), DR 2-102(D) provided that a partnership "shall not be formed or continued between or among lawyers licensed in different jurisdictions unless all enumerations of the members and associates of the firm on its letterhead and in other permissible listings make clear the jurisdictional limitations on those members and associates of the firm not licensed to practice in all listed jurisdictions; however, the same firm name may be used in each jurisdiction."

With regard to paragraph (c), DR 2-102(B) provided that "[a] lawyer who assumes a judicial, legislative, or public executive or administrative post or office shall not permit his name to remain in the name of a law firm . . . during any significant period in which he is not actively and regularly practicing law as a member of the firm . . . ."

Paragraph (d) is substantially identical to DR 2-102(C).

MAINTAINING THE INTEGRITY OF THE PROFESSION

RULE 8.1 BAR ADMISSION AND DISCIPLINARY MATTERS

An applicant for admission to the bar, or a lawyer in connection with a bar admission application or in connection with a disciplinary matter, shall not:

(a) knowingly make a false statement of material fact; or

(b) fail to disclose a fact necessary to correct a misapprehension known by the person to have arisen in the matter, or knowingly fail to respond to a lawful demand for information from an admissions or disciplinary authority, except that this rule does not require disclosure of information otherwise protected by Rule 1.6.

Comment

[1] The duty imposed by this Rule extends to persons seeking admission to the bar as well as to lawyers. Hence, if a person makes a material false statement in connection with an application for admission, it may be the basis for subsequent disciplinary action if the person is admitted, and in any event may be relevant in a subsequent admission application. The duty imposed by this Rule applies to a lawyer's own admission or discipline as well as that of others. Thus, it is a separate professional offense for a lawyer to knowingly make a misrepresentation or omission in connection with a disciplinary investigation of the lawyer's own conduct. This Rule also requires affirmative clarification of any misunderstanding on the part of the admissions or disciplinary authority of which the person involved becomes aware.

[2] This Rule is subject to the provisions of the fifth amendment of the United States Constitution and corresponding provisions of state constitutions. A person relying on such a provision in response to a question, however, should do so openly and not use the right of nondisclosure as a justification for failure to comply with this Rule.

[3] A lawyer representing an applicant for admission to the bar, or representing a lawyer who is the subject of a disciplinary inquiry or proceeding, is governed by the rules applicable to the client-lawyer relationship.

Model Code Comparison

DR 1-101(A) provided that a lawyer is "subject to discipline if he has made a materially false statement in, or if he has deliberately failed to disclose a material fact requested in connection with, his application for admission to the bar." DR 1-101(B) provided that a lawyer "shall not further the application for admission to the bar of another person known by him to be unqualified in respect to character, education, or other relevant attribute." With respect to paragraph (b), DR 1-102(A)(5) provided that a lawyer shall not engage in "conduct that is prejudicial to the administration of justice."

RULE 8.2 JUDICIAL AND LEGAL OFFICIALS

(a) A lawyer shall not make a statement that the lawyer knows to be false or with reckless disregard as to its truth or falsity concerning the qualifications or integrity of a judge, adjudicatory officer or public legal officer, or of a candidate for election or appointment to judicial or legal office.

(b) A lawyer who is a candidate for judicial office shall comply with the applicable provisions of the Code of Judicial Conduct.

Comment

[1] Assessments by lawyers are relied on in evaluating the professional or personal fitness of persons being considered for election or appointment to judicial office and to public legal offices, such as attorney general, prosecuting attorney and public defender. Expressing honest and candid opinions on such matters contributes to improving the administration of justice. Conversely, false statements by a lawyer can unfairly undermine public confidence in the administration of justice.

[2] When a lawyer seeks judicial office, the lawyer should be bound by applicable limitations on political activity.

[3] To maintain the fair and independent administration of justice, lawyers are encouraged to continue traditional efforts to defend judges and courts unjustly criticized.

Model Code Comparison

With regard to paragraph (a), DR 8-102(A) provided that a lawyer "shall not knowingly make false statements of fact concerning the qualifications of a candidate for election or appointment to a judicial office." DR 8-102(B) provided that a lawyer "shall not knowingly make false accusations against a judge or other adjudicatory officer."

Paragraph (b) is substantially identical to DR 8-103.

RULE 8.3[23] REPORTING PROFESSIONAL MISCONDUCT

(a) A lawyer having knowledge that another lawyer has committed a violation of the Rules of Professional Conduct that raises a substantial question as to that lawyer's honesty, trustworthiness or fitness as a lawyer in other respects, shall inform the appropriate professional authority.

(b) A lawyer having knowledge that a judge has committed a violation of applicable rules of judicial conduct that raises a substantial question as to the judge's fitness for office shall inform the appropriate authority.

23. Amended August 15, 1991, American Bar Association House of Delegates, Atlanta, Georgia, per Report No. 108C.

(c) This Rule does not require disclosure of information otherwise protected by Rule 1.6 or information gained by a lawyer or judge while serving as a member of an approved lawyers assistance program to the extent that such information would be confidential if it were communicated subject to the attorney-client privilege.

Comment

[1] Self-regulation of the legal profession requires that members of the profession initiate disciplinary investigation when they know of a violation of the Rules of Professional Conduct. Lawyers have a similar obligation with respect to judicial misconduct. An apparently isolated violation may indicate a pattern of misconduct that only a disciplinary investigation can uncover. Reporting a violation is especially important where the victim is unlikely to discover the offense.

[2] A report about misconduct is not required where it would involve violation of Rule 1.6. However, a lawyer should encourage a client to consent to disclosure where prosecution would not substantially prejudice the client's interests.

[3] If a lawyer were obliged to report every violation of the Rules, the failure to report any violation would itself be a professional offense. Such a requirement existed in many jurisdictions but proved to be unenforceable. This Rule limits the reporting obligation to those offenses that a self-regulating profession must vigorously endeavor to prevent. A measure of judgment is, therefore, required in complying with the provisions of this Rule. The term "substantial" refers to the seriousness of the possible offense and not the quantum of evidence of which the lawyer is aware. A report should be made to the bar disciplinary agency unless some other agency, such as a peer review agency, is more appropriate in the circumstances. Similar considerations apply to the reporting of judicial misconduct.

[4] The duty to report professional misconduct does not apply to a lawyer retained to represent a lawyer whose professional conduct is in question. Such a situation is governed by the Rules applicable to the client-lawyer relationship.

[5] Information about a lawyer's or judge's misconduct or fitness may be received by a lawyer in the course of that lawyer's participation in an approved lawyers or judges assistance program. In that circumstance, providing for the confidentiality of such information encourages lawyers and judges to seek treatment through such program. Conversely, without such confidentiality, lawyers and judges may hesitate to seek assistance from these programs, which may then result in additional harm to their professional careers and additional injury to the welfare of clients and the public. The Rule therefore exempts the lawyer from the reporting requirements of paragraphs (a) and (b) with respect to information that would be privileged if the relationship between the impaired lawyer or judge and the recipient of the information were that of a client and a lawyer. On the other hand, a lawyer who receives such information would nevertheless be required to comply with the Rule 8.3 reporting provisions to report misconduct if the impaired lawyer or judge indicates an intent to engage in illegal activity, for example, the conversion of client funds to his or her use.

Model Code Comparison

DR 1-103(A) provided that "[a] lawyer possessing unprivileged knowledge of a violation of [a Disciplinary Rule] shall report such knowledge to . . . authority empowered to investigate or act upon such violation."

RULE 8.4 MISCONDUCT

It is professional misconduct for a lawyer to:

(a) violate or attempt to violate the Rules of Professional Conduct, knowingly assist or induce another to do so, or do so through the acts of another;

(b) commit a criminal act that reflects adversely on the lawyer's honesty, trustworthiness or fitness as a lawyer in other respects;

(c) engage in conduct involving dishonesty, fraud, deceit or misrepresentation;

(d) engage in conduct that is prejudicial to the administration of justice;

(e) state or imply an ability to influence improperly a government agency or official; or

(f) knowingly assist a judge or judicial officer in conduct that is a violation of applicable rules of judicial conduct or other law.

Comment

[1] Many kinds of illegal conduct reflect adversely on fitness to practice law, such as offenses involving fraud and the offense of willful failure to file an income tax return. However, some kinds of offense carry no such implication. Traditionally, the distinction was drawn in terms of offenses involving "moral turpitude." That concept can be construed to include offenses concerning some matters of personal morality, such as adultery and comparable offenses, that have no specific connection to fitness for the practice of law. Although a lawyer is personally answerable to the entire criminal law, a lawyer should be professionally answerable only for offenses that indicate lack of those characteristics relevant to law practice. Offenses involving violence, dishonesty, breach of trust, or serious interference with the administration of justice are in that category. A pattern of repeated offenses, even ones of minor significance when considered separately, can indicate indifference to legal obligation.

[2] A lawyer may refuse to comply with an obligation imposed by law upon a good faith belief that no valid obligation exists. The provisions of Rule 1.2(d) concerning a good faith challenge to the validity, scope, meaning or application of the law apply to challenges of legal regulation of the practice of law.

[3] Lawyers holding public office assume legal responsibilities going beyond those of other citizens. A lawyer's abuse of public office can suggest an inability to fulfill the professional role of lawyers. The same is true of abuse of positions of private trust such as trustee, executor, administrator, guardian, agent and officer, director or manager of a corporation or other organization.

Model Code Comparison

With regard to paragraphs (a) through (d), DR 1-102(A) provided that a lawyer shall not:

"(1) Violate a Disciplinary Rule.

"(2) Circumvent a Disciplinary Rule through actions of another.

"(3) Engage in illegal conduct involving moral turpitude.

"(4) Engage in conduct involving dishonesty, fraud, deceit, or misrepresentation.

"(5) Engage in conduct that is prejudicial to the administration of justice.

"(6) Engage in any other conduct that adversely reflects on his fitness to practice law."

Paragraph (e) is substantially similar to DR 9-101(C).

There was no direct counterpart to paragraph (f) in the Disciplinary Rules of the Model Code. EC 7-34 stated in part that "[a] lawyer . . . is never justified in making a gift or a loan to a [judicial officer] except as permitted by . . . the Code of Judicial Conduct." EC 9-1 stated that a lawyer "should promote public confidence in our [legal] system and in the legal profession."

RULE 8.5[24] DISCIPLINARY AUTHORITY; CHOICE OF LAW.

(a) Disciplinary Authority. A lawyer admitted to practice in this jurisdiction is subject to the disciplinary authority of this jurisdiction, regardless of where the lawyer's conduct occurs. A lawyer may be subject to the disciplinary authority of both this jurisdiction and another jurisdiction where the lawyer is admitted for the same conduct.

(b) Choice of Law. In any exercise of the disciplinary authority of this jurisdiction, the rules of professional conduct to be applied shall be as follows:

(1) for conduct in connection with a proceeding in a court before which a lawyer has been admitted to practice (either generally or for purposes of that proceeding), the rules to be applied shall be the rules of the jurisdiction in which the court sits, unless the rules of the court provide otherwise; and

(2) for any other conduct,

(i) if the lawyer is licensed to practice only in this jurisdiction, the rules to be applied shall be the rules of this jurisdiction, and

(ii) if the lawyer is licensed to practice in this and another jurisdiction, the rules to be applied shall be the rules of the admitting jurisdiction in which the lawyer principally practices; provided, however, that if particular conduct clearly has its predominant effect in another jurisdiction in which the lawyer is licensed to practice, the rules of that jurisdiction shall be applied to that conduct.

Comment

Disciplinary Authority

[1] Paragraph (a) restates longstanding law.

24. Amended August 11, 1993, American Bar Association House of Delegates, New York, New York, per Report No. 114.

Choice of Law

[2] A lawyer may be potentially subject to more than one set of rules of professional conduct which impose different obligations. The lawyer may be licensed to practice in more than one jurisdiction with differing rules, or may be admitted to practice before a particular court with rules that differ from those of the jurisdiction or jurisdictions in which the lawyer is licensed to practice. In the past, decisions have not developed clear or consistent guidance as to which rules apply in such circumstances.

[3] Paragraph (b) seeks to resolve such potential conflicts. Its premise is that minimizing conflicts between rules, as well as uncertainty about which rules are applicable, is in the best interest of both clients and the profession (as well as the bodies having authority to regulate the profession). Accordingly, it takes the approach of (i) providing that any particular conduct of a lawyer shall be subject to only one set of rules of professional conduct, and (ii) making the determination of which set of rules applies to particular conduct as straightforward as possible, consistent with recognition of appropriate regulatory interests of relevant jurisdictions.

[4] Paragraph (b) provides that as to a lawyer's conduct relating to a proceeding in a court before which the lawyer is admitted to practice (either generally or pro hac vice), the lawyer shall be subject only to the rules of professional conduct of that court. As to all other conduct, paragraph (b) provides that a lawyer licensed to practice only in this jurisdiction shall be subject to the rules of professional conduct of this jurisdiction, and that a lawyer licensed in multiple jurisdictions shall be subject only to the rules of the jurisdiction where he or she (as an individual, not his or her firm) principally practices, but with one exception: if particular conduct clearly has its predominant effect in another admitting jurisdiction, then only the rules of that jurisdiction shall apply. The intention is for the latter exception to be a narrow one. It would be appropriately applied, for example, to a situation in which a lawyer admitted in, and principally practicing in, State A, but also admitted in State B, handled an acquisition by a company whose headquarters and operations were in State B of another, similar such company. The exception would not appropriately be applied, on the other hand, if the lawyer handled an acquisition by a company whose headquarters and operations were in State A of a company whose headquarters and main operations were in State A, but which also had some operations in State B.

[5] If two admitting jurisdictions were to proceed against a lawyer for the same conduct, they should, applying this rule, identify the same governing ethics rules. They should take all appropriate steps to see that they do apply the same rule to the same conduct, and in all events should avoid proceeding against a lawyer on the basis of two inconsistent rules.

[6] The choice of law provision is not intended to apply to transnational practice. Choice of law in this context should be the subject of agreements between jurisdictions or of appropriate international law.

Model Code Comparison

There was no counterpart to this Rule in the Model Code.

APPENDIX A: AMENDMENTS TO THE MODEL RULES OF PROFESSIONAL CONDUCT 1983 – 1999

The Model Rules of Professional Conduct, together with the Comment sections, have been amended by the ABA House of Delegates twenty-nine times since their initial adoption in 1983. The amendments were made in 1987, 1989, 1990, 1991, 1992, 1993, 1994, 1995, 1997 and 1998.

The reader should be cautioned that not all of these amendments have been considered and/or adopted by the thirty-nine jurisdictions that have adopted the Model Rules to date. Furthermore, the rules of any adopting jurisdiction must be checked for amendments unique to that jurisdiction.

Rule 1.7 Comment

Amended 1987 per Midyear Meeting Report 121.

Added last sentence of first paragraph, favoring adoption of reasonable conflicts-checking procedures.

Rule 1.8(b)

Amended 1987 per Midyear Meeting Report 121.

Added exception for disclosure required or permitted by Rule 1.6 or 3.3.

Rule 1.9(b)

Amended 1987 per Midyear Meeting Report 121.

Added exception for using information when permitted or required to by Rule 3.3.

Rule 1.9(c) and Comment

Amended 1989 per Midyear Meeting Report 120A.

Added new paragraph (b), regarding clients of a lawyer's former firm [taken from Rule 1.10(b) as originally adopted]; broadened the renumbered paragraph (c) to include former representation of a client by lawyer's present or former firm, rather than by lawyer individually; added subparagraph (c)(2), covering revelation (as opposed to use) of information; amended Comment accordingly [substance of Comment was moved from Rule 1.10 Comment].

Rule 1.10 and Comment

Amended 1989 per Midyear Meeting Report 120A.

Moved original paragraph (b) to Rule 1.9; renumbered original paragraphs (c) and (d) as (b) and (c); added "and not currently represented by the firm" before subparagraphs (b)(1) and (2); moved Comment dealing with imputation to Rule 1.9 in accordance with Rule amendment.

Rule 1.11(c)(2)

Amended 1987 per Midyear Meeting Report 121.

Added exception permitting judicial clerks to negotiate for private employment in accordance with Rule 1.12(b).

Rule 1.12(a)
Amended 1987 per Midyear Meeting Report 121.

Changed requirement of consent after disclosure to one of consent after consultation.

Rule 1.14 Comment
Amended 1997 per Midyear Meeting Report 113.

Amended Comment to describe certain narrowly defined circumstances in which a lawyer may take emergency legal action on behalf of an individual who, by reason of disability, is unable to form a bona fide client/lawyer relationship with the lawyer.

Rule 1.17 and Comment
Added 1990 per Midyear Meeting Report 8A.

Added rule permitting sale of law practice; added relevant Comment.

Rule 3.6 and Comment
Amended 1994 per Annual Meeting Report 100.

Amended paragraph (a) to apply only to a lawyer who is participating in or has participated in the investigation or litigation of a matter; moved the list of statements ordinarily likely to have a prejudicial effect from paragraph (b) to the Comment section of the Rule; moved the paragraph (c) listing of ordinarily acceptable statements to new paragraph (b), deleting the terms "without elaboration" and "general nature"; in a new paragraph (c) provided for a lawyer's limited right of response to protect a client from substantial undue prejudicial effect of recent publicity not initiated by the lawyer or the client; and added a new paragraph, (d), making the Rule applicable to other lawyers in the lawyer's firm or government agency.

Rule 3.8(f) and Comment
Added 1990 per Midyear Meeting Report 118.

Added rule limiting prosecutors' subpoenas of lawyers; added relevant Comment.

Rule 3.8(f)(2) and Comment
Deleted 1995 per Annual Meeting Report 101.

Deleted provision requiring an adversarial hearing and judicial approval prior to subpoenaing lawyers; deleted relevant Comment.

Rule 3.8(g)
Added 1994 per Annual Meeting Report 100.

Added a provision prohibiting prosecutors from making statements likely to heighten public condemnation of an accused, except under limited circumstances.

Rule 4.2
Amended 1995 per Annual Meeting Report 100.

Amended to make clear that Rule 4.2 applies to contacts with represented persons whether or not they are, in a formal sense, actual or prospective "parties" to a proceeding or a transaction. The Comment was also amended to (1) acknowledge the case law limiting the application of "anti-contact" prohibitions in the context of pre-indictment, non-custodial contacts, and (2) make clear that a lawyer may not evade the Rule by avoiding actual knowledge that a person is represented by counsel. The amendment addresses the need to protect represented persons from possible overreaching by a trained advocate who represents differing or potentially differing interests.

Rule 5.4(a)(2)

Amended 1990 per Midyear Meeting Report 8A.

Language changed to reflect contemporaneously enacted Rule 1.17.

Rule 5.6 Comment

Amended 1990 per Midyear Meeting Report 8A.

Sentence added to conform to contemporaneously enacted Rule 1.17.

Rule 5.7 and Comment

Added 1994 per Midyear Meeting Report 113.

Rule and Comment added regarding law-related services.

[A previous Rule 5.7 and Comment, denominated "Provision of Ancillary Services," was added 1991 per Annual Meeting Report 121 and was rescinded 1993 per Annual Meeting Report 10D.]

Rule 6.1 and Comment

Amended 1993 per Midyear Meeting Report 8A.

Added aspirational goal of at least (5) hours of free legal services with substantial majority of hours devoted to persons of limited means or organizations in matters designed primarily to assist those of limited means. Word "voluntary" added to title of Rule.

Rule 6.3(a), (b)

Amended 1987 per Midyear Meeting Report 121.

Added "or action" after "the decision," in order to parallel "decision or action" in the introductory portion of the Rule.

Rule 7.2(a)

Amended 1989 per Midyear Meeting Report 120B.

Technical amendment substituting "except as prohibited by Rule 7.3(b)" for "... not involving solicitation as defined in Rule 7.3," in order to reflect contemporaneous amendment of Rule 7.3.

Rule 7.2(c)(3)

Amended 1990 per Midyear Meeting Report 8A.

Added to reflect contemporaneous enactment of Rule 1.17, permitting sale of law practice.

Rule 7.3 and Comment

Amended 1989 per Midyear Meeting Report 120B.

Changed “may not” to “shall not” (for consistency with other rules); amended paragraph (a) and Comment to permit direct mail solicitation of prospective client [reflecting *Shapero v. Kentucky Bar Ass'n*, 486 U.S. 466 (1988)]; added paragraph (b) prohibiting any kind of solicitation when prospective client has made known contrary desire; added paragraph (c) labeling requirement.

Rule 7.3(d) and Comment
Added 1989 per Midyear Meeting Report 115.

Added to allow participation in prepaid legal service organizations that solicit.

Rule 7.4 and Comment
Amended 1994 per Annual Meeting Report 121.

Amended to provide that where a lawyer's certification as a specialist is granted by an organization accredited by the American Bar Association to issue such certification, the lawyer need not refer to the jurisdiction's lack of its own accrediting process.

Rule 7.4 and Comment
Amended 1992 per Annual Meeting Revised Report 128.

Language added to bring Model Rule 7.4 in compliance with the U.S. Supreme Court decision in *Peel v. Attorney Registration and Disciplinary Commission*, 496 U.S. 91 (1990), holding that states may not constitutionally impose a blanket prohibition on a lawyer's truthful communication that he or she is certified as a specialist by a bona fide organization.

Rule 7.4 Comment
Amended 1989 per Midyear Meeting Report 121.

Amended (1) to delete restriction on lawyer stating that practice is “limited to” or “concentrated in” particular area of law, and (2) to make exception where state provides certification or specialization procedures.

Rule 8.3(c) and Comment
Amended 1991 per Midyear Meeting Report 108C.

Language added to exempt from reporting requirement information gained while serving on lawyer assistance program, to extent information would be confidential if communicated by a client.

Rule 8.4 Comment
Amended 1998 per Annual Meeting Report 117.

Language added specifically to include a lawyer's biased or prejudicial conduct (in the representation of a client) as an example of behavior that may violate Rule 8.4.

Rule 8.5 and Comment
Amended 1993 per Annual Meeting Report 114.

Added choice of law provisions to resolve conflicts when lawyer is licensed or admitted to practice in jurisdictions with differing rules. Title of Rule changed from “Jurisdiction” to “Disciplinary Authority; Choice of Law.”

APPENDIX B: CORRELATION TABLES

TABLES A AND B: RELATED SECTIONS IN THE ABA MODEL CODE OF PROFESSIONAL RESPONSIBILITY

TABLE A*

ABA MODEL RULES	ABA MODEL CODE
Competence	
Rule 1.1	EC 1-1, EC 1-2, EC 6-1, EC 6-2, EC 6-3, EC 6-4, EC 6-5, DR 6-101(A)
Scope of Representation	
Rule 1.2(a)	EC 5-12, EC 7-7, EC 7-8, DR 7-101(A)(1)
Rule 1.2(b)	EC 7-17
Rule 1.2(c)	EC 7-8, EC 7-9, DR 7-101(B)(1)
Rule 1.2(d)	EC 7-1, EC 7-2, EC 7-5, EC 7-22, DR 7-102(A)(6), (7) & (8), DR 7-106
Rule 1.2(e)	DR 2-110(C)(1)(c), DR 9-101(C)
Diligence	
Rule 1.3	EC 2-31, EC 6-4, EC 7-1, EC 7-38, DR 6-101(A)(3), DR 7-101(A)(1) & (3)
Communication	
Rule 1.4(a)	EC 7-8, EC 9-2, DR 6-101(A)(3), DR 9-102(B)(1)
Rule 1.4(b)	EC 7-8
Fees	
Rule 1.5(a)	EC 2-16, EC 2-17, EC 2-18, DR 2-106(A) & (B)
Rule 1.5(b)	EC 2-19
Rule 1.5(c)	EC 2-20, EC 5-7
Rule 1.5(d)	EC 2-20, DR 2-106(C)
Rule 1.5(e)	EC 2-22, DR 2-107(A)

*Table A provides cross-references to related provisions, but only in the sense that the provisions consider substantially similar subject matter or reflect similar concerns. A cross-reference does not indicate that a provision of the ABA Model Code of Professional Responsibility has been incorporated by the provision of a Model Rule. The Canons of the Code are not cross-referenced.

TABLE A
(Continued)

ABA MODEL RULES	ABA MODEL CODE
Confidentiality of Information	
Rule 1.6(a)	EC 4-1, EC 4-2, EC 4-3, EC 4-4, DR 4-101(A), (B) & (C)
Rule 1.6(b)(1)	EC 4-2, DR 4-101(C)(3), DR 7-102(B)
Rule 1.6(b)(2)	DR 4-101(C)(4)
Conflict of Interest	
Rule 1.7(a)	EC 5-1, EC 5-14, EC 5-15, EC 5-17, EC 5-21, EC 5-22, DR 5-101(A), DR 5-105(A) & (B), DR 5-107(B)
Rule 1.7(b) & (b)(1)	EC 2-21, EC 5-1, EC 5-2, EC 5-3, EC 5-9, EC 5-11, EC 5-13, EC 5-14, EC 5-15, EC 5-16, EC 5-17, EC 5-19, EC 5-21, EC 5-22, EC 5-23, DR 5-101(A) & (B), DR 5-102, DR 5-104(A), DR 5-105(A), (B) & (C), DR 5-107(A)
Rule 1.7(b)(2)	EC 5-16, EC 5-17, DR 7-106(B)(2)
Prohibited Transactions	
Rule 1.8(a)	EC 5-3, EC 5-5, DR 5-104(A)
Rule 1.8(b)	EC 4-5, DR 4-101(B)
Rule 1.8(c)	EC 5-1, EC 5-2, EC 5-5, EC 5-6
Rule 1.8(d)	EC 5-1, EC 5-3, EC 5-4, DR 5-104(B)
Rule 1.8(e)	EC 5-1, EC 5-3, EC 5-7, EC 5-8, DR 5-103(B)
Rule 1.8(f)	EC 2-21, EC 5-1, DR 5-107(A) & (B)
Rule 1.8(g)	EC 5-1, DR 5-106(A)
Rule 1.8(h)	EC 6-6, DR 6-102(A)
Rule 1.8(i)	None
Rule 1.8(j)	EC 5-1, EC 5-7, DR 5-101(A), DR 5-103(A)
Former Client	
Rule 1.9(a)	DR 5-105(C)
Rule 1.9(b)	EC 4-5, EC 4-6
Rule 1.9(c)	None
Imputed Disqualification	
Rule 1.10(a)	EC 4-5, DR 5-105(D)
Rule 1.10(b)	EC 4-5, DR 5-105(D)
Rule 1.10(c)	DR 5-105(A)

TABLE A

(Continued)

ABA MODEL RULES	ABA MODEL CODE
Successive Government and Private Employment	
Rule 1.11(a)	EC 9-3, DR 9-101(B)
Rule 1.11(b)	None
Rule 1.11(c)	EC 8-8
Rule 1.11(d)	None
Rule 1.11(e)	None
Former Judge or Arbitrator	
Rule 1.12(a) & (b)	EC 5-20, EC 9-3, DR 9-101(A) & (B)
Rule 1.12(c)	DR 5-105(D)
Rule 1.12(d)	None
Organization as Client	
Rule 1.13(a)	EC 5-18, EC 5-24
Rule 1.13(b)	EC 5-18, EC 5-24, DR 5-107(B)
Rule 1.13(c)	EC 5-18, EC 5-24, DR 5-105(D), DR 5-107(B)
Rule 1.13(d)	EC 5-16
Rule 1.13(e)	EC 4-4, EC 5-16, DR 5-105(B) & (C)
Disabled Client	
Rule 1.14(a)	EC 7-11, EC 7-12
Rule 1.14(b)	EC 7-12
Safekeeping Property	
Rule 1.15	EC 5-7, EC 9-5, EC 9-7, DR 5-103(A)(1), DR 9-102
Declining or Terminating Representation	
Rule 1.16(a)(1)	EC 2-30, EC 2-31, EC 2-32, DR 2-103(E), DR 2-104(A), DR 2-109(A), DR 2-110(B)(1) & (2)
Rule 1.16(a)(2)	EC 1-6, EC 2-30, EC 2-31, EC 2-32, DR 2-110(B)(3), DR 2-110(C)(4)
Rule 1.16(a)(3)	EC 2-31, EC 2-32, DR 2-110(B)(4)
Rule 1.16(b)(1)	EC 2-31, EC 2-32, DR 2-110(C)(1)(b) & (c), DR 2-110(C)(2)
Rule 1.16(b)(2)	EC 2-31, EC 2-32, DR 2-110(C)(2)
Rule 1.16(b)(3)	EC 2-30, EC 2-31, EC 2-32, DR 2-110(C)(1)(d)

TABLE A

(Continued)

ABA MODEL RULES	ABA MODEL CODE
Rule 1.16(b)(4)	EC 2-31, EC 2-32, DR 2-110(C)(1)(f)(i)(j)
Rule 1.16(b)(5)	EC 2-32, DR 2-110(C)(1)(d) & (e)
Rule 1.16(b)(6)	EC 2-32, DR 2-110(C)(6)
Rule 1.16(c)	EC 2-32, DR 2-110(A)(1)
Rule 1.16(d)	EC 2-32, DR 2-110(A)(2) & (3)
Sale of Law Practice	
Rule 1.17	None
Advisor	
Rule 2.1	EC 5-11, EC 7-3, EC 7-8, DR 5-107(B)
Intermediary	
Rule 2.2(a)(1)	EC 4-2, EC 5-14, EC 5-15, EC 5-16, EC 5-20, DR 5-105(A) & (C)
Rule 2.2(a)(2) & (3)	EC 5-14, EC 5-15, DR 5-105(A) & (C)
Rule 2.2(b)	EC 5-16
Rule 2.2(c)	EC 5-15, EC 5-19, DR 5-105(B) & (C)
Evaluation for Use by Third Persons	
Rule 2.3	None
Meritorious Claims and Contentions	
Rule 3.1	EC 7-1, EC 7-4, EC 7-5, EC 7-14, EC 7-25, DR 5-102(A)(5), DR 2-109(A)(B)(1), DR 7-102(A)(1) & (2)
Expediting Litigation	
Rule 3.2	EC 7-20, DR 1-102(A)(5), DR 7-101(A)(1) & (2)
Candor Toward the Tribunal	
Rule 3.3(a)(1)	EC 7-4, EC 7-32, EC 8-5, DR 1-102(A)(4) & (5), DR 7-102(A)(4) & (5)
Rule 3.3(a)(2)	EC 8-5, DR 1-102(A)(4) & (5), DR 7-102(A)(3), DR 7-102(B)(1), DR 7-109(A)
Rule 3.3(a)(3)	EC 7-23, DR 1-102(A)(5), DR 7-106(B)(1)

TABLE A
(Continued)

ABA MODEL RULES	ABA MODEL CODE
Rule 3.3(a)(4)	EC 7-5, EC 7-26, EC 8-5, DR 1-102(A)(4) & (5), DR 7-102(A)(7), DR 7-102(B)(1)
Rule 3.3(b)	EC 8-5, DR 7-102(B)
Rule 3.3(c)	EC 7-24, EC 7-25
Rule 3.3(d)	EC 7-24, EC 7-27
Fairness to Opposing Party and Counsel	
Rule 3.4(a)	EC 7-6, EC 7-27, DR 1-102(A)(4) & (5), DR 7-106(C)(7), DR 7-109(A) & (B)
Rule 3.4(b)	EC 7-6, EC 7-28, DR 1-102(A)(4), (5) & (6), DR 7-102(A)(6), DR 7-109(C)
Rule 3.4(c)	EC 7-22, EC 7-25, EC 7-38, DR 1-102(A)(5), DR 7-106(A), DR 7-106(C)(5) & (7)
Rule 3.4(d)	DR 1-102(A)(5), DR 7-106(A), DR 7-106(C)(7)
Rule 3.4(e)	EC 7-24, EC 7-25, DR 1-102(A)(5), DR 7-106(C)(1), (2), (3) & (4)
Rule 3.4(f)	EC 7-27, DR 1-102(A)(5), DR 7-104(A)(2), DR 7-109(B)
Impartiality and Decorum	
Rule 3.5(a)	EC 7-20, EC 7-29, EC 7-31, EC 7-32, EC 7-34, DR 7-106, DR 7-108, DR 7-109, DR 7-110, DR 8-101(A)
Rule 3.5(b)	EC 7-35, DR 7-108, DR 7-110(A) & (B)
Rule 3.5(c)	EC 7-20, EC 7-25, EC 7-36, EC 7-37, DR 7-101(A)(1), DR 7-106(C)(6)
Trial Publicity	
Rule 3.6	EC 7-25, EC 7-33, DR 7-107
Lawyer as Witness	
Rule 3.7(a)	EC 5-9, EC 5-10, DR 5-101(B)(1) & (2), DR 5-102
Rule 3.7(b)	EC 5-9, DR 5-101(B), DR 5-102
Special Responsibilities of a Prosecutor	
Rule 3.8(a)	EC 7-11, EC 7-13, EC 7-14, DR 7-103(A)
Rule 3.8(b)	EC 7-11, EC 7-13

TABLE A
(Continued)

ABA MODEL RULES	ABA MODEL CODE
Rule 3.8(c)	EC 7-11, EC 7-13, EC 7-18
Rule 3.8(d)	EC 7-11, EC 7-13, DR 7-103(B)
Rule 3.8(e)	None
Rule 3.8(f)	None
Rule 3.8(g)	EC 7-14
Advocate in Nonadjudicative Proceedings	
Rule 3.9	EC 7-11, EC 7-15, EC 7-16, EC 8-4, EC 8-5, DR 7-106(B)(2), DR 9-101(C)
Truthfulness to Others	
Rule 4.1	EC 7-5, DR 7-102(A)(3), (4), (5) & (7), DR 7-102(B)
Communication with Represented Persons	
Rule 4.2	EC 2-30, EC 7-18, DR 7-104(A)(1)
Dealing with Unrepresented Persons	
Rule 4.3	EC 2-3, EC 7-18, DR 7-104(A)(2)
Respect for Rights of Third Persons	
Rule 4.4	EC 7-10, EC 7-14, EC 7-21, EC 7-25, EC 7-29, EC 7-30, EC 7-37, DR 2-110(B)(1), DR 7-101(A)(1), DR 7-102(A)(1), DR 7-106(C)(2), DR 7-107(D), (E) & (F), DR 7-108(D), (E), & (F)
Responsibilities of a Partner or Supervisory Lawyer	
Rule 5.1(a) & (b)	EC 4-5, DR 4-101(D), DR 7-107(J)
Rule 5.1(c)	DR 1-102(A)(2), DR 1-103(A), DR 7-108(E)
Responsibilities of a Subordinate Lawyer	
Rule 5.2	None
Responsibilities Regarding Nonlawyer Assistants	
Rule 5.3(a)	EC 3-6, EC 4-2, EC 4-5, EC 7-28, DR 4-101(D), DR 7-107(J)

TABLE A
(Continued)

ABA MODEL RULES	ABA MODEL CODE
Rule 5.3(b)	DR 1-102(A)(2), DR 7-107(J), DR 7-108(B), DR 7-108(E)
Rule 5.3(c)	None
Professional Independence of Lawyer	
Rule 5.4(a)	EC 2-33, EC 3-8, EC 5-24, DR 2-103(D)(4)(d), (e) & (f), DR 3-102(A), DR 5-107(C)(3)
Rule 5.4(b)	EC 2-33, EC 3-8, DR 3-103(A)
Rule 5.4(c)	EC 2-33, EC 5-23, DR 2-103(C), DR 5-107(B)
Rule 5.4(d)	EC 2-33, EC 3-8, DR 5-107(C)
Unauthorized Practice of Law	
Rule 5.5	DR 3-101(A) & (B)
Restrictions on Right to Practice	
Rule 5.6	DR 2-108
Responsibilities Regarding Law-Related Services	
Rule 5.7	None
Voluntary Pro Bono Publico Service	
Rule 6.1	EC 1-2, EC 1-4, EC 2-1, EC 2-2, EC 2-16, EC 2-24, EC 2-25, EC 6-2, EC 8-1, EC 8-2, EC 8-3, EC 8-7, EC 8-9
Accepting Appointments	
Rule 6.2 (a)	EC 2-1, EC 2-25, EC 2-27, EC 2-28, EC 2-29, EC 8-3
Rule 6.2(b)	EC 2-16, EC 2-25, EC 2-29, EC 2-30
Rule 6.2(c)	EC 2-25, EC 2-27, EC 2-29, EC 2-30
Membership in Legal Services Organization	
Rule 6.3	EC 2-33, DR 5-101(A)
Law Reform Activities Affecting Client Interests	
Rule 6.4	EC 2-33, DR 5-101(A), DR 8-101

TABLE A
(Continued)

ABA MODEL RULES	ABA MODEL CODE
Communication Concerning Lawyer's Services	
Rule 7.1(a)	EC 2-8, EC 2-9, EC 2-10, DR 2-101(A), (B), (C), (E), (F) & (G), DR 2-102(E)
Rule 7.1(b)	EC 2-5, EC 2-8, EC 2-9, EC 9-4, DR 2-101(A), (B), (C), (E), (F) & (G), DR 9-101(C)
Rule 7.1(c)	EC 2-8, EC 2-9, EC 2-10, DR 2-101(A), (B), (C), (E), (F) & (G)
Advertising	
Rule 7.2(a)	EC 2-1, EC 2-2, EC 2-6, EC 2-7, EC 2-8, EC 2-15, DR 2-101(B) & (H), DR 2-102(A) & (B), DR 2-103(B), DR 2-104(A)(4) & (5)
Rule 7.2(b)	DR 2-101(D)
Rule 7.2(c)	EC 2-8, EC 2-15, DR 2-101(I), DR 2-103(B), (C) & (D)
Rule 7.2(d)	None
Direct Contact with Prospective Clients	
Rule 7.3	EC 2-3, EC 2-4, EC 5-6, DR 2-103(A), DR 2-103(C)(1), DR 2-103(D)(4)(b) & (c), DR 2-104(A)(1), (2), (3) & (5)
Communication of Fields of Practice	
Rule 7.4	EC 2-1, EC 2-7, EC 2-8, EC 2-14, DR 2-101(B)(2), DR 2-102(A)(3), DR 2-102(E), DR 2-105(A)
Rule 7.4(a)	DR 2-105(A)(1)
Rule 7.4(b)	EC 2-14
Rule 7.4(c)	DR 2-105(A)(2) & (3)
Firm Names and Letterheads	
Rule 7.5(a)	EC 2-11, EC 2-13, DR 2-102(A)(4), DR 2-102(B), (D) & (E), DR 2-105
Rule 7.5(b)	EC 2-11, DR 2-102(D)
Rule 7.5(c)	EC 2-11, EC 2-12, DR 2-102(B)
Rule 7.5(d)	EC 2-11, EC 2-13, DR 2-102(C)

TABLE A
(Continued)

ABA MODEL RULES	ABA MODEL CODE
Bar Admission and Disciplinary Matters	
Rule 8.1(a)	EC 1-1, EC 1-2, EC 1-3, DR 1-101(A) & (B)
Rule 8.1(b)	DR 1-102(A)(5), DR 1-103(B)
Judges and Legal Officials	
Rule 8.2(a)	EC 8-6, DR 8-102
Rule 8.2(b)	DR 8-103
Reporting Professional Misconduct	
Rule 8.3	EC 1-3, DR 1-103(A)
Misconduct	
Rule 8.4(a)	EC 1-5, EC 1-6, EC 9-6, DR 1-102(A)(1) & (2), DR 2-103(E), DR 7-102(A) & (B)
Rule 8.4(b)	EC 1-5, DR 1-102(A)(3) & (6), DR 7-102(A)(8), DR 8-101(A)(3)
Rule 8.4(c)	EC 1-5, EC 9-4, DR 1-102(A)(4), DR 8-101(A)(3)
Rule 8.4(d)	EC 3-9, EC 8-3, DR 1-102(A)(5), DR 3-101(B)
Rule 8.4(e)	EC 1-5, EC 9-2, EC 9-4, EC 9-6, DR 9-101(C)
Rule 8.4(f)	EC 1-5, EC 7-34, EC 9-1, DR 1-102(A)(3), (4), (5) & (6), DR 7-110(A), DR 8-101(A)(2)
Jurisdiction	
Rule 8.5	None

TABLE B**

ABA MODEL CODE	ABA MODEL RULES
Canon 1: Integrity of Profession	
EC 1-1	Rules 1.1, 8.1(a)
EC 1-2	Rules 1.1, 6.1, 8.1(a)
EC 1-3	Rules 8.1(a), 8.3
EC 1-4	Rule 6.1
EC 1-5	Rule 8.4(a), (b), (c), (e) & (f)
EC 1-6	Rules 1.16(a)(2), 8.4(a)
DR 1-101	Rule 8.1(a)
DR 1-102(A)(1)	Rule 8.4(a)
DR 1-102(A)(2)	Rules 5.1(c), 5.3(b), 8.4(a)
DR 1-102(A)(3)	Rules 8.4(b) & (f)
DR 1-102(A)(4)	Rules 3.3(a)(1), (2) & (4), 3.4(a) & (b), 8.4(c) & (f)
DR 1-102(A)(5)	Rules 3.1, 3.2, 3.3(a)(1), (2) & (4), 3.4, 8.4(d) & (f)
DR 1-102(A)(6)	Rules 3.4(b), 8.4(b) & (f)
DR 1-103(A)	Rules 5.1(c), 8.3
DR 1-103(B)	Rule 8.1(b)
Canon 2: Making Counsel Available	
EC 2-1	Rules 6.1, 6.2(a), 7.2(a), 7.4
EC 2-2	Rules 6.1, 7.2(a)
EC 2-3	Rules 4.3, 7.3
EC 2-4	Rule 7.3
EC 2-5	Rule 7.1(b)
EC 2-6	Rule 7.2(a)
EC 2-7	Rules 7.2(a), 7.4
EC 2-8	Rules 7.1, 7.2(a) & (c), 7.4
EC 2-9	Rule 7.1
EC 2-10	Rule 7.1(a) & (c)
EC 2-11	Rule 7.5
EC 2-12	Rule 7.5(c)
EC 2-13	Rule 7.5(a) & (d)
EC 2-14	Rule 7.4
EC 2-15	Rule 7.2(a) & (c)
EC 2-16	Rules 1.5(a), 6.1, 6.2(b)

**Table B provides cross-references to related provisions, but only in the sense that the provisions consider substantially similar subject matter or reflect similar concerns. A cross-reference does not indicate that a provision of the ABA Model Code of Professional Responsibility has been incorporated by the provision of a Model Rule. The Canons of the Code are not cross-referenced.

TABLE B
(Continued)

ABA MODEL CODE	ABA MODEL RULES
EC 2-17	Rule 1.5(a)
EC 2-18	Rule 1.5(a)
EC 2-19	Rule 1.5(b)
EC 2-20	Rule 1.5(c) & (d)
EC 2-21	Rules 1.7(b), 1.8(f)
EC 2-22	Rule 1.5(e)
EC 2-23	None
EC 2-24	Rule 6.1
EC 2-25	Rules 6.1, 6.2
EC 2-26	None
EC 2-27	Rule 6.2(a) & (c)
EC 2-28	Rule 6.2(a)
EC 2-29	Rule 6.2
EC 2-30	Rules 1.16(a)(1) & (2), 1.16(b)(3), 4.2, 6.2(b) & (c)
EC 2-31	Rules 1.3, 1.16(a) & (b)
EC 2-32	Rule 1.16(a), (b), (c) & (d)
EC 2-33	Rules 5.4, 6.3, 6.4
DR 2-101(A)	Rule 7.1
DR 2-101(B)	Rules 7.1, 7.2(a)
DR 2-101(C)	Rule 7.1
DR 2-101(D)	Rule 7.2(b)
DR 2-101(E)	Rule 7.1
DR 2-101(F)	Rule 7.1
DR 2-101(G)	Rule 7.1
DR 2-101(H)	Rule 7.2
DR 2-101(I)	Rule 7.2(c)
DR 2-102(A)	Rules 7.2(a), 7.4
DR 2-102(B)	Rules 7.2(a), 7.5(a) & (c)
DR 2-102(C)	Rule 7.5(d)
DR 2-102(D)	Rule 7.5(a) & (b)
DR 2-102(E)	Rules 7.1(a), 7.4, 7.5(a)
DR 2-103(A)	Rule 7.3
DR 2-103(B)	Rule 7.2(a) & (c)
DR 2-103(C)	Rules 5.4(a), 7.2(c), 7.3
DR 2-103(D)	Rules 1.16(a)(1), 5.4(a), 7.2(c), 7.3
DR 2-103(E)	Rules 1.16(a), 7.2(a), 7.3
DR 2-104	Rules 1.16(a), 7.3
DR 2-105	Rule 7.4
DR 2-106(A)	Rule 1.5(a)

TABLE B
(Continued)

ABA MODEL CODE	ABA MODEL RULES
DR 2-106(B)	Rule 1.5(a)
DR 2-106(C)	Rule 1.5(d)
DR 2-107(A)	Rule 1.5(e)
DR 2-107(B)	Rule 5.4(a)(1)
DR 2-108(A)	Rule 5.6
DR 2-108(B)	Rule 5.6
DR 2-109(A)	Rules 1.16(a)(1), 3.1
DR 2-110(A)	Rule 1.16(c) & (d)
DR 2-110(B)	Rules 1.16(a), 3.1, 4.4
DR 2-110(C)	Rules 1.2(e), 1.16(a) & (b)
Canon 3: Unauthorized Practice	
EC 3-1	None
EC 3-2	None
EC 3-3	Rule 8.4(e)
EC 3-4	None
EC 3-5	None
EC 3-6	Rule 5.3(a)
EC 3-7	None
EC 3-8	Rule 5.4(a), (b) & (d)
EC 3-9	Rule 8.4(d)
DR 3-101(A)	Rule 5.5
DR 3-101(B)	Rules 5.5, 8.4(d)
DR 3-102	Rule 5.4(a)
DR 3-103	Rule 5.4(b)
Canon 4: Confidences and Secrets	
EC 4-1	Rule 1.6(a)
EC 4-2	Rules 1.6(a) & (b)(1), 2.2(a)(1), 5.3(a)
EC 4-3	Rule 1.6(a)
EC 4-4	Rules 1.6(a), 1.13(e)
EC 4-5	Rules 1.8(b), 1.9(b), 1.10(a) & (b), 5.1(a) & (c), 5.3(a)
EC 4-6	Rule 1.9(b)
DR 4-101(A)	Rule 1.6(a)
DR 4-101(B)	Rules 1.6(a), 1.8(b), 1.9(b)
DR 4-101(C)	Rules 1.6(a) & (b)
DR 4-101(D)	Rules 5.1(a) & (b), 5.3(a) & (b)

TABLE B
(Continued)

ABA MODEL CODE	ABA MODEL RULES
Canon 5: Independent Judgment	
EC 5-1	Rules 1.7(a) & (b), 1.8(c), (d), (e), (f), (g) & (j)
EC 5-2	Rules 1.7(b), 1.8(c)
EC 5-3	Rules 1.7(b), 1.8(a), (d) & (e)
EC 5-4	Rule 1.8(d)
EC 5-5	Rule 1.8(a) & (c)
EC 5-6	Rules 1.8(c), 7.3
EC 5-7	Rules 1.5(c), 1.8(e) & (j), 1.15
EC 5-8	Rule 1.8(e)
EC 5-9	Rules 1.7(b), 3.7
EC 5-10	Rule 3.7(a)
EC 5-11	Rules 1.7(b), 2.1
EC 5-12	Rule 1.2(a)
EC 5-13	Rule 1.7(b)
EC 5-14	Rules 1.7(a), 2.2(a)
EC 5-15	Rules 1.7, 2.2(a) & (c)
EC 5-16	Rules 1.7(b), 1.10(d), 1.13(d) & (e), 2.2(a)(1) & (b)
EC 5-17	Rule 1.7
EC 5-18	Rule 1.13(a), (b) & (c)
EC 5-19	Rules 1.7(b), 2.2(c)
EC 5-20	Rules 1.12(a) & (b), 2.2(a)(1)
EC 5-21	Rule 1.7
EC 5-22	Rule 1.7
EC 5-23	Rules 1.7(b), 5.4(c)
EC 5-24	Rules 1.13(a),(b) & (c), 5.4(a)
DR 5-101(A)	Rule 1.7, 1.8(j), 6.3, 6.4
DR 5-101(B)	Rules 1.7(b), 3.7
DR 5-102(A)	Rules 1.7(b), 3.7
DR 5-102(B)	Rules.1.7(b), 3.7
DR 5-103(A)	Rules 1.8(j), 1.15
DR 5-103(B)	Rule 1.8(e)
DR 5-104(A)	Rules 1.7(b), 1.8(a)
DR 5-104(B)	Rule 1.8(d)
DR 5-105(A)	Rules 1.7, 1.10(c), 2.2(a)
DR 5-105(B)	Rules 1.7, 1.13(e), 2.2(c)
DR 5-105(C)	Rules 1.7(b), 1.13(e), 1.9(a), 2.2
DR 5-105(D)	Rules 1.10(a), 1.12(c), 1.13(c)
DR 5-106	Rule 1.8(g)

TABLE B
(Continued)

ABA MODEL CODE	ABA MODEL RULES
DR 5-107(A)	Rules 1.7(b), 1.8(f)
DR 5-107(B)	Rules 1.7(a), 1.8(f), 1.13(b) & (c), 2.1, 5.4(c)
DR 5-107(C)	Rule 5.4(a) & (d)
Canon 6: Competence	
EC 6-1	Rule 1.1
EC 6-2	Rules 1.1, 5.1(a) & (b), 6.1
EC 6-3	Rule 1.1
EC 6-4	Rules 1.1, 1.3
EC 6-5	Rule 1.1
EC 6-6	Rule 1.8(h)
DR 6-101	Rules 1.1, 1.3, 1.4(a)
DR 6-102	Rule 1.8(h)
Canon 7: Zeal Within the Law	
EC 7-1	Rules 1.2(d), 1.3, 3.1
EC 7-2	Rule 1.2(d)
EC 7-3	Rule 2.1
EC 7-4	Rules 3.1, 3.3(a)(1)
EC 7-5	Rules 1.2(d), 3.1, 3.3(a)(4), 4.1
EC 7-6	Rule 3.4(a) & (b)
EC 7-7	Rule 1.2(a)
EC 7-8	Rules 1.2(a) & (c), 1.4, 2.1
EC 7-9	Rule 1.2(c)
EC 7-10	Rule 4.4
EC 7-11	Rules 1.14(a), 3.8(a), (b), (c) & (d), 3.9
EC 7-12	Rule 1.14
EC 7-13	Rule 3.8
EC 7-14	Rules 3.1, 3.8(a) & (g), 4.4
EC 7-15	Rule 3.9
EC 7-16	Rule 3.9
EC 7-17	Rule 1.2(b)
EC 7-18	Rule 3.8(c), 4.2, 4.3
EC 7-19	None
EC 7-20	Rules 3.2, 3.5(a) & (c)
EC 7-2	Rule 4.4
EC 7-22	Rules 1.2(d), 3.4(c)
EC 7-23	Rule 3.3(a)(3)

TABLE B
(Continued)

ABA MODEL CODE	ABA MODEL RULES
EC 7-24	Rules 3.3(c) & (d), 3.4(e)
EC 7-25	Rules 3.1, 3.3(c), 3.4(c) & (e), 3.5(c), 3.6, 4.4
EC 7-26	Rule 3.3(a)(4)
EC 7-27	Rules 3.3(d), 3.4(a) & (f)
EC 7-28	Rules 3.4(b), 5.3(a)
EC 7-29	Rules 3.5(a), 4.4
EC 7-30	Rule 4.4
EC 7-31	Rule 3.5(a)
EC 7-32	Rules 3.3(a)(1), 3.5(a)
EC 7-33	Rule 3.6
EC 7-34	Rules 3.5(a), 8.4(f)
EC 7-35	Rule 3.5(b)
EC 7-36	Rule 3.5(c)
EC 7-37	Rules 3.5(c), 4.4
EC 7-38	Rules 1.3, 3.4(c)
EC 7-39	None
DR 7-101(A)	Rules 1.2(a), 1.3, 3.2, 3.5(c), 4.4
DR 7-101(B)	Rules 1.2(b), 1.16(b)
DR 7-102(A)(1)	Rules 3.1, 4.4
DR 7-102(A)(2)	Rule 3.1
DR 7-102(A)(3)	Rules 3.3(a)(2), 4.1
DR 7-102(A)(4)	Rules 3.3(a) & (c), 4.1
DR 7-102(A)(5)	Rules 3.3(a)(1), 4.1
DR 7-102(A)(6)	Rules 1.2(d), 3.4(b)
DR 7-102(A)(7)	Rules 1.2,(d), 3.3(a)(4), 4.1
DR 7-102(A)(8)	Rules 1.2(d), 8.4(a) & (b)
DR 7-102(B)	Rules 1.6(b)(1), 3.3(b), 4.1
DR 7-103(A)	Rule 3.8(a)
DR 7-103(B)	Rule 3.8(d)
DR 7-104	Rules 3.4(f), 4.2, 4.3
DR 7-105	None
DR 7-106(A)	Rules 1.2(d), 3.4(c) & (d), 3.5(a)
DR 7-106(B)	Rules 1.7(b)(2), 3.3(a)(3), 3.9
DR 7-106(C)	Rules 3.4(a), (c), (d) & (e), 3.5(c), 4.4
DR 7-107(A)–(I)	Rule 3.6
DR 7-107(D)–(F)	Rule 4.4
DR 7-107(J)	Rules 5.1(a) & (b), 5.3(a) & (b)
DR 7-108(A)	Rules 3.5(a) & (b)
DR 7-108(B)	Rules 3.5(a), (b), (c), (d) & (f), 5.3(b)

TABLE B
(Continued)

ABA MODEL CODE	ABA MODEL RULES
DR 7-108(C)	Rules 3.5(a) & (b)
DR 7-108(D)	Rule 4.4
DR 7-108(E)	Rules 4.4, 5.1(c), 5.3(b)
DR 7-108(F)	Rule 4.4
DR 7-108(G)	None
DR 7-109(A)	Rules 3.3(a)(2), 3.4(a)
DR 7-109(B)	Rule 3.4(a) & (f)
DR 7-109(C)	Rule 3.4(b)
DR 7-110(A)	Rules 3.5(a), & 8.4(f)
DR 7-110(B)	Rule 3.5(a) & (b)
Canon 8: Improving Legal System	
EC 8-1	Rule 6.1
EC 8-2	Rule 6.1
EC 8-3	Rules 6.1, 6.2(a), 8.4 (d)
EC 8-4	Rule 3.9
EC 8-5	Rules 3.3(a)(1), (2) & (4), 3.3(b), 3.9
EC 8-6	Rule 8.2(a)
EC 8-7	Rule 6.1
EC 8-8	Rule 1.11(c)
EC 8-9	Rule 6.1
DR 8-101	Rules 3.5, 8.4(b), (c) & (f)
DR 8-102	Rule 8.2(a)
DR 8-103	Rule 8.2(b)
Canon 9: Appearance of Impropriety	
EC 9-1	Rule 8.4(f)
EC 9-2	Rules 1.4(a), 8.4(e)
EC 9-3	Rules 1.11(a), 1.12(a) & (b)
EC 9-4	Rules 7.1(b), 8.4(c) & (e)
EC 9-5	Rule 1.15
EC 9-6	Preamble, Rule 8.4(e)
EC 9-7	Rule 1.15
DR 9-101(A)	Rule 1.12(a) & (b)
DR 9-101(B)	Rules 1.11(a), 1.12(a) & (b)
DR 9-101(C)	Rules 1.2(e), 3.9, 7.1(b), 8.4(e)
DR 9-102	Rules 1.4(a), 1.15

APPENDIX C: SUBJECT GUIDE TO THE ABA MODEL RULES OF PROFESSIONAL CONDUCT

A

B

C

D

E

F

G

H

I

M

N

T

U

ABA MODEL CODE OF PROFESSIONAL RESPONSIBILITY

The Model Code of Professional Responsibility was adopted by the House of Delegates of the American Bar Association on August 12, 1969 and was amended by the House of Delegates in February 1970, February 1974, February 1975, August 1976, August 1977, August 1978, February 1979, February 1980, and August 1980.

Contents

Preface

On August 14, 1964, at the request of President Lewis F. Powell, Jr., the House of Delegates of the American Bar Association created a Special Committee on Evaluation of Ethical Standards to examine the then current Canons of Professional Ethics and to make recommendations for changes. That committee produced the Model Code of Professional Responsibility which was adopted by the House of Delegates in 1969 and became effective January 1, 1970. The new Model Code revised the previous Canons in four principal particulars: (1) there were important areas involving the conduct of lawyers that were either only partially covered in or totally omitted from the Canons; (2) many Canons that were sound in substance were in need of editorial revision; (3) most of the Canons did not lend themselves to practical sanctions for violations; and (4) changed and changing conditions in our legal system and urbanized society required new statements of professional principles.

The original 32 Canons of Professional Ethics were adopted by the American Bar Association in 1908. They were based principally on the Code of Ethics adopted by the Alabama State Bar Association in 1887, which in turn has been borrowed largely from the lectures of Judge George Sharswood, published in 1854 under the title of *Professional Ethics*, and from the fifty resolutions included in David Hoffman's *A Course of Legal Study* (2d ed. 1836). Since then a limited number of amendments have been adopted on a piecemeal basis.

As far back as 1934 Mr. Justice (later Chief Justice) Harlan Fiske Stone, in his memorable address entitled *The Public Influence of the Bar*, made this observation:

> Before the Bar can function at all as a guardian of the public interests committed to its care, there must be appraisal and comprehension of the new conditions, and the chained relationship of the lawyer to his clients, to his professional brethren and to the public. That appraisal must pass beyond the petty details of form and manners which have been so largely the subject of our Codes of Ethics, to more fundamental consideration of the way in which our professional activities affect the welfare of society as a whole. Our canons of ethics for the most part are generalizations designed for an earlier era.

Largely in that spirit, the committee appointed by President Powell in 1964 reached unanimous conclusion that further piecemeal amendment of the original Canons would not suffice. It proceeded to compose the Model Code of Professional Responsibility in response to the perceived need for change in the statement of professional principles for lawyers.

While the opinions of the Committee on Professional Ethics of the American Bar Association had been published and given fairly wide distribution with resulting value to the bench and bar, they certainly were not conclusive as to the adequacy of the previous Canons. Because the opinions were necessarily interpretations of the existing Canons, they tended to support the Canons and were critical of them only in the most unusual case. Since a large number of requests for opinions from the Committee on Professional Ethics dealt with the etiquette of law practice, advertising, partnership names, announcements and the like, there had been a tendency for many lawyers to assume that this was the exclusive field of interest of the Committee and that it was not concerned with the more serious questions of professional standards and obligations.

The previous Canons were not an effective teaching instrument and failed to give guidance to young lawyers beyond the language of the Canons themselves. There was no organized interrelationship between the Canons and they often overlapped. They were not cast in language designed for disciplinary enforcement and many abounded with quaint expressions of the past. Those Canons contained, nevertheless, many provisions that were sound in substance, and all of these were retained in the Model Code adopted in 1969. In the studies and meetings conducted by the Committee which developed the present Model Code, the Committee relied heavily upon the monumental *Legal Ethics* (1953) of Henry S. Drinker, who served with great distinction for nine years as Chairman of the Committee on Professional Ethics (known in his day as the Committee on Professional Ethics and Grievances) of the American Bar Association.

The Formal Opinions of the Committee on Ethics and Professional Responsibility were collected and published in a single volume in 1967, and since that time have been published continuously in loose-leaf form. (The name was changed in 1971 to the Standing Committee on Ethics and Professional Responsibility.) The Informal Opinions of the Committee on Ethics and Professional Responsibility were collected and published in a two-volume set in 1975, and since that time new opinions have been published continuously in loose-leaf form.

Since the adoption of the Model Code of Professional Responsibility in 1969 a number of amendments have been required due to decisions of the Supreme Court of the United States and lower courts relating to the provision of group legal services and the provision of additional legal services on a wide scale not only to indigents but also to persons of moderate means. Furthermore, recent decisions of the Supreme Court of the United States on the subject of the constitutionality of restrictive provisions in the Code relating to lawyer advertising have required a substantial revision of Canon 2 and of other portions of the present Model Code. These modifications in the Code are included in the present printing, up to and including the action taken by the House of Delegates in August of 1978. The Committee on Ethics and Professional Responsibility is mandated under the Bylaws of the American Bar Association (Article 30.7) to recommend appropriate amendments to or clarification of the Model Code. Additional changes are under consideration by the Committee with particular cognizance of recent Court decisions.

Preamble[1]

The continued existence of a free and democratic society depends upon recognition of the concept that justice is based upon the rule of law grounded in respect for the dignity of the individual and his capacity through reason for enlightened self-government.[2] Law so grounded makes justice possible, for only through such law does the dignity of the individual attain respect and protection. Without it, individual rights become subject to unrestrained power, respect for law is destroyed, and rational self-government is impossible.

Lawyers, as guardians of the law, play a vital role in the preservation of society. The fulfillment of this role requires an understanding by lawyers of their relationship with and function in our legal system.[3] A consequent obligation of lawyers is to maintain the highest standards of ethical conduct.

In fulfilling his professional responsibilities, a lawyer necessarily assumes various roles that require the performance of many difficult tasks. Not every situation which he may encounter can be foreseen,[4] but fundamental ethical principles are always present to guide him. Within the framework of these principles, a lawyer must with courage and foresight be able and ready to shape the body of the law to the ever-changing relationships of society.[5]

The Model Code of Professional Responsibility points the way to the aspiring and provides standards by which to judge the transgressor. Each lawyer must find within his own conscience the touchstone against which to test the extent to which his actions should rise above minimum standards. But in the last analysis it is the desire for the respect and confidence of the members of his profession and of the society which he serves that should provide to a lawyer the incentive for the highest possible degree of ethical conduct. The possible loss of that respect and confidence is the ultimate sanction. So long as its practitioners are guided by these principles, the law will continue to be a noble profession. This is its greatness and its strength, which permit of no compromise.

Preliminary Statement

In furtherance of the principles stated in the Preamble, the American Bar Association has promulgated this Model Code of Professional Responsibility, consisting of three separate but interrelated parts: Canons, Ethical Considerations, and Disciplinary Rules.[6] The Code is designed to be adopted by appropriate agencies both as an inspirational guide to the members of the profession and as a basis for disciplinary action when the conduct of a lawyer falls below the required minimum standards stated in the Disciplinary Rules.

Obviously the Canons, Ethical Considerations, and Disciplinary Rules cannot apply to non-lawyers; however, they do define the type of ethical conduct that the public has a right to expect not only of lawyers but also of their non-professional employees and associates in all matters pertaining to professional employment. A lawyer should ultimately be responsible for the conduct of his employees and associates in the course of the professional representation of the client.

The Canons are statements of axiomatic norms, expressing in general terms the standards of professional conduct expected of lawyers in their relationships with the public, with the legal system, and with the legal profession. They embody the general concepts from which the Ethical Considerations and the Disciplinary Rules are derived.

The Ethical Considerations are aspirational in character and represent the objectives toward which every member of the profession should strive. They constitute a body of principles upon which the lawyer can rely for guidance in many specific situations.[7]

The Disciplinary Rules, unlike the Ethical Considerations, are mandatory in character. The Disciplinary Rules state the minimum level of conduct below which no lawyer can fall without being subject to disciplinary action. Within the framework of fair trial,[8] the Disciplinary Rules should be uniformly applied to all lawyers,[9] regardless of the nature of their professional activities.[10] The Model Code makes no attempt to prescribe either disciplinary procedures or penalties[11] for violation of a Disciplinary Rule,[12] nor does it undertake to define standards for civil liability of lawyers for professional conduct. The severity of judgment against one found guilty of violating a Disciplinary Rule should be determined by the character of the offense and the attendant circumstances.[13] An enforcing agency, in applying the Disciplinary Rules, may find interpretive guidance in the basic principles embodied in the Canons and in the objectives reflected in the Ethical Considerations.

NOTES

1. The footnotes are intended merely to enable the reader to relate the provisions of this Model Code to the ABA Canons of Professional Ethics adopted in 1908, as amended, the Opinions of the ABA Committee on Professional Ethics, and a limited number of other sources; they are not intended to be an annotation of the views taken by the ABA Special Committee on Evaluation of Ethical Standards. Footnotes citing ABA Canons refer to the ABA Canons of Professional Ethics, adopted in 1908, as amended.

2. *Cf.* ABA CANONS OF PROFESSIONAL ETHICS, Preamble (1908)

3. "[T]he lawyer stands today in special need of a clear understanding of his obligations and of the vital connection between these obligations and the role his profession plays in society." *Professional Responsibility: Report of the Joint Conference*, 44 A.B.A.J. 1159, 1160 (1958).

4. "No general statement of the responsibilities of the legal profession can encompass all the situations in which the lawyer may be placed. Each position held by him makes its own peculiar demands. These demands the lawyer must clarify for himself in the light of the particular role in which he serves." *Professional Responsibility: Report of the Joint Conference*, 44 A.B.A.J. 1159, 1218 (1958).

5. "The law and its institutions change as social conditions change. They must change if they are to preserve, much less advance, the political and social values from which they derive their purpose and their life. This is true of the most important of legal institutions, the profession of law. The profession, too, must change when conditions change in order to preserve and advance the social values that are its reasons for being." Cheatham, *Availability of Legal Services: The Responsibility of the Individual Lawyer and the Organized Bar*. 12 U.C.L.A. L. REV. 438, 440 (1965).

6. The Supreme Court of Wisconsin adopted a Code of Judicial Ethics in 1967. "The code is divided into standards and rules, the standards being statements of what the general desirable level of conduct should be, the rules being particular canons, the violation of which shall subject an individual judge to sanctions." In re Promulgation of a Code of Judicial Ethics, 36 Wis. 2d 252, 255, 153 N.W.2d 873, 874 (1967).

The portion of the Wisconsin Code of Judicial Ethics entitled "Standards" states that "[t]he following standards set forth the significant qualities of the ideal judge . . . ." *Id.*, 36 Wis. 2d at 256, 153 N.W. 2d at 875. The portion entitled "Rules" states that [t]he court promulgates the following rules because the requirements of judicial conduct embodied therein are of sufficient gravity to warrant sanctions if they are not obeyed . . . ." *Id.*, 36 Wis. 2d at 259, 153 N.W.2d at 876.

7. "Under the conditions of modern practice it is peculiarly necessary that the lawyer should understand, not merely the established standards of professional conduct, but the reasons underlying these standards. Today the lawyer plays a changing and increasingly varied role. In many developing fields the precise contribution of the legal profession is as yet undefined." *Professional Responsibility: Report of the Joint Conference*, 44 A.B.A.J. 1159 (1958).

"A true sense of professional responsibility must derive from an understanding of the reasons that lie back of specific restraints, such as those embodied in the Canons. The grounds for the lawyer's peculiar obligations are to be found in the nature of his calling. The lawyer who seeks a clear understanding of his duties will be led to reflect on the special services his profession renders to society and the services it might render if its full capacities were realized. When the lawyer fully understands the nature of his office, he will then discern what restraints are necessary to keep that office wholesome and effective." *Id.*

8. "Disbarment, designed to protect the public, is a punishment or penalty imposed on the lawyer . . . . He is accordingly entitled to procedural due process, which includes fair notice of charge." In re Ruffalo, 390 U.S. 544, 550, 20 L. Ed.2d 117, 122, 88S. Ct. 1222, 1226 (1968), *rehearing denied*, 391 U.S. 961, 20 L. Ed. 2d 874, 88 S. Ct. 1933(1968).

"A State cannot exclude a person from the practice of law or from any other occupation in a manner or for reasons that contravene the Due Process or Equal Protection Clause of the Fourteenth Amendment . . . . A State can require high standards of qualification . . . but any qualification must have a rational connection with the applicant's fitness or capacity to practice law." Schware v. Bd. of Bar Examiners, 353 U.S. 232, 239, 1 L. Ed. 2d 796, 801-02, 77 S. Ct. 752, 756 (1957).

"[A]n accused lawyer may expect that he will not be condemned out of a capricious self-righteousness or denied the essentials of a fair hearing." Kingsland v. Dorsey, 338 U.S. 318, 320, 94 L. Ed. 123, 126, 70 S. Ct. 123, 124-25 (1949).

"The attorney and counsellor being, by the solemn judicial act of the court, clothed with his office, does not hold it as a matter of grace and favor. The right which it confers upon him to appear for suitors, and to argue causes, is something more than a mere indulgence, revocable at the pleasure of the court or at the command of the legislature. It is a right of which he can only be deprived by the judgment of the court for moral or professional delinquency." Ex parte Garland, 71 U.S. (4 Wall.) 333, 378-79,18 L. Ed. 366, 370 (1866).

See generally Comment, *Procedural Due Process and Character Hearings for Bar Applicants*, 15 STAN. L. REV. 500 (1963)

9. "The canons of professional ethics must be enforced by the Courts and must be respected by members of the Bar if we are to maintain public confidence in the integrity and impartiality of the administration of justice." In re Meeker, 76 N. M. 354, 357, 414 P.2d 862, 864 (1966), *appeal dismissed* 385 U.S. 449 (1967).

10. *See* ABA CANONS OF PROFESSIONAL ETHICS, CANON 45 (1908).

11. "Other than serving as a model or derivative source, the American Bar Association Model Code of Professional Responsibility plays no part in the disciplinary proceeding, except as a guide for consideration in adoption of local applicable rules for the regulation of conduct on the part of legal practitioners." ABA COMM. ON PROFESSIONAL ETHICS, INFORMAL OPINION NO. 1420 (1978) [hereinafter each Formal Opinion is cited as "*ABA Opinion*"]. For the purposes and intended effect of the American Bar Association Model Code of Professional Responsibility and of the opinions of the Standing Committee on Ethics and Professional Responsibility, see Informal Opinion No. 1420.

"There is generally no prescribed discipline for any particular type of improper conduct. The disciplinary measures taken are discretionary with the courts, which may disbar, suspend, or merely censure the attorney as the nature of the offense and past indicia of character may warrant." Note, 43 CORNELL L.Q. 489, 495 (1958).

12. The Model Code seeks only to specify conduct for which a lawyer should be disciplined by courts and governmental agencies which have adopted it. Recommendations as to the procedures to be

used in disciplinary actions are within the jurisdiction of the American Bar Association Standing Committee on Professional Discipline.

13. "The severity of the judgment of this court should be in proportion to the gravity of the offenses, the moral turpitude involved, and the extent that the defendant's acts and conduct affect his professional qualifications to practice law." Louisiana State Bar Ass'n v. Steiner, 204 La. 1073, 1092-93, 16 So. 2d 843, 850 (1944) (Higgins, J., concurring in decree).

"Certainly an erring lawyer who has been disciplined and who having paid the penalty has given satisfactory evidence of repentance and has been rehabilitated and restored to his place at the bar by the court which knows him best ought not to have what amounts to an order of permanent disbarment entered against him by a federal court solely on the basis of an earlier criminal record and without regard to his subsequent rehabilitation and present good character . . . . We think, therefore, that the district court should reconsider the appellant's application for admission and grant it unless the court finds it to be a fact that the appellant is not presently of good moral or professional character." In re Dreier, 258 F.2d 68, 69-70 (3d Cir. 1958).

CANON 1
A Lawyer Should Assist in Maintaining the Integrity and Competence of the Legal Profession

ETHICAL CONSIDERATIONS

EC 1-1 A basic tenet of the professional responsibility of lawyers is that every person in our society should have ready access to the independent professional services of a lawyer of integrity and competence. Maintaining the integrity and improving the competence of the bar to meet the highest standards is the ethical responsibility of every lawyer.

EC 1-2 The public should be protected from those who are not qualified to be lawyers by reason of a deficiency in education[1] or moral standards[2] or of other relevant factors[3] but who nevertheless seek to practice law. To assure the maintenance of high moral and educational standards of the legal profession, lawyers should affirmatively assist courts and other appropriate bodies in promulgating, enforcing, and improving requirements for admission to the bar.[4] In like manner, the bar has a positive obligation to aid in the continued improvement of all phases of pre-admission and post-admission legal education.

EC 1-3 Before recommending an applicant for admission, a lawyer should satisfy himself that the applicant is of good moral character. Although a lawyer should not become a self-appointed investigator or judge of applicants for admission, he should report to proper officials all unfavorable information he possesses relating to the character or other qualifications of an applicant.[5]

EC 1-4 The integrity of the profession can be maintained only if conduct of lawyers in violation of the Disciplinary Rules is brought to the attention of the proper officials. A lawyer should reveal voluntarily to those officials all unprivileged knowledge of conduct of lawyers which he believes clearly to be in violation of the Disciplinary Rules.[6] A lawyer should, upon request, serve on and assist committees and boards having responsibility for the administration of the Disciplinary Rules.[7]

EC 1-5 A lawyer should maintain high standards of professional conduct and should encourage fellow lawyers to do likewise. He should be temperate and dignified, and he should refrain from all illegal and morally reprehensible conduct.[8] Because of his position in society, even minor violations of law by a lawyer may tend to lessen public confidence in the legal profession. Obedience to law exemplifies respect for law. To lawyers especially, respect for the law should be more than a platitude.

EC 1-6 An applicant for admission to the bar or a lawyer may be unqualified, temporarily or permanently, for other than moral and educational reasons, such as mental or emotional instability. Lawyers should be diligent in taking steps to see that during a period of disqualification such person is not granted a license or, if licensed, is not permitted to practice.[9] In like manner, when the disqualification has terminated, members of the bar should assist such person in being licensed, or, if licensed, in being restored to his full right to practice.

DISCIPLINARY RULES

DR 1-101 Maintaining Integrity and Competence of the Legal Profession.

(A) A lawyer is subject to discipline if he has made a materially false statement in, or if he has deliberately failed to disclose a material fact requested in connection with, his application for admission to the bar.[10]

(B) A lawyer shall not further the application for admission to the bar of another person known by him to be unqualified in respect to character, education, or other relevant attribute.[11]

DR 1-102 Misconduct.

(A) A lawyer shall not:

(1) Violate a Disciplinary Rule.

(2) Circumvent a Disciplinary Rule through actions of another.[12]

(3) Engage in illegal conduct involving moral turpitude.[13]

(4) Engage in conduct involving dishonesty, fraud, deceit, or misrepresentation.

(5) Engage in conduct that is prejudicial to the administration of justice.

(6) Engage in any other conduct that adversely reflects on his fitness to practice law.

DR 1-103 Disclosure of Information to Authorities.

(A) A lawyer possessing unprivileged knowledge of a violation of DR 1-102 shall report such knowledge to a tribunal or other authority empowered to investigate or act upon such violation.

(B) A lawyer possessing unprivileged knowledge or evidence concerning another lawyer or a judge shall reveal fully such knowledge or evidence upon proper request of a tribunal or other authority empowered to investigate or act upon the conduct of lawyers or judges.

NOTES

1. "[W]e cannot conclude that all educational restrictions [on bar admission] are unlawful. We assume that few would deny that a grammar school education requirement before taking the bar examination was reasonable. Or that an applicant had to be able to read or write. Once we conclude that *some* restriction is proper, then it becomes a matter of degree—the problem of drawing the line.

. . . .

"We conclude the fundamental question here is whether Rule IV, Section 6 of the Rules pertaining to Admission of Applicants to the State Bar of Arizona is 'arbitrary, capricious and unreasonable.' We conclude an educational requirement of graduation from an accredited law school is not." Hackin v. Lockwood, 361 F.2d 499, 503-4(9th Cir. 1966), *cert. denied*, 385 U.S. 960, 17 L. Ed.2d 305, 87 S. Ct. 396 (1966).

2. "Every state in the United States, as a prerequisite for admission to the practice of law, requires that applicants possess 'good moral character.' Although the requirement is of judicial origin, it is now embodied in legislation in most states." Comment, *Procedural Due Process and Character Hearings for Bar Applicants*. 15 STAN. L. REV. 500 (1963).

"Good character in the member of the bar is essential to the preservation of the courts. The duty and power of the court to guard its portals against intrusion by men and women who are mentally and morally dishonest, unfit because of bad character, evidenced by their course of conduct, to participate in the administrative law, would seem to be unquestioned in the matter of preservation of judicial dignity and integrity." In re Monaghan, 126 Vt. 53, 222 A.2d 665, 670 (1966).

"Fundamentally, the question involved in both situations [*i.e.* admission and disciplinary proceedings] is the same—is the applicant for admission or the attorney sought to be disciplined a fit and proper person to be permitted to practice law, and that usually turns upon whether he has committed or is likely to continue to commit acts of moral turpitude. At the time of oral argument the attorney for respondent frankly conceded that the test for admission and for discipline is and should be the same. We agree with this concession." Hallinan v. Comm. of Bar Examiners, 65 Cal.2d 447, 453, 421, P.2d 76, 81, 55 Cal.Rptr. 228, 233 (1966).

3. "Proceedings to gain admission to the bar are for the purpose of protecting the public and the courts from the ministrations of persons unfit to practice the profession. Attorneys are officers of the court appointed to assist the court in the administration of justice. Into their hands are committed the property, the liberty and sometimes the lives of their clients. This commitment demands a high degree of intelligence, knowledge of the law, respect for its function in society, sound and faithful judgment and, above all else, integrity of character in private and professional conduct." In re Monaghan, 126 Vt. 53, 222 A.2d 665, 676 (1966) (Holden, C.J., dissenting).

4. "A bar composed of lawyers of good moral character is objective but it is unnecessary to sacrifice vital freedoms in order to obtain that goal. It is also important both to society and the bar itself that lawyers be unintimidated—free to think, speak, and act as members of an Independent Bar." Konigsberg v. State Bar, 353 U.S. 252, 273, 1 L. Ed. 2d 810, 825, 77 S. Ct. 722, 733 (1957).

5. *See* ABA CANONS OF PROFESSIONAL ETHICS, CANON 29 (1908).

6. ABA CANONS OF PROFESSIONAL ETHICS, CANON 28 (1908) designates certain conduct as unprofessional and then states that: "A duty to the public and to the profession devolves upon every member of the Bar having knowledge of such practices upon the part of any practitioner immediately to inform thereof, to the end that the offender may be disbarred." ABA CANON 29 states a broader admonition: "Lawyers should expose without fear or favor before the proper tribunals corrupt or dishonest conduct in the profession."

7. "It is the obligation of the organized Bar and the individual lawyer to give unstinted cooperation and assistance to the highest court of the state in discharging its function and duty with respect to discipline and in purging the profession of the unworthy." *Report of the Special Committee on Disciplinary Procedures*, 80 A.B.A. REP. 463, 470 (1955).

8. *Cf.* ABA CANONS OF PROFESSIONAL ETHICS, CANON 32 (1908).

9. "We decline, on the present record, to disbar Mr. Sherman or to reprimand him — not because we condone his actions, but because, as heretofore indicated, we are concerned with whether he is mentally responsible for what he has done.

"The logic of the situation would seem to dictate the conclusion that, if he was mentally responsible for the conduct we have outlined, he should be disbarred; and, if he was not mentally responsible, he should not be permitted to practice law.

"However, the flaw in the logic is that he may have been mentally irresponsible [at the time of his offensive conduct] . . . , and, yet, have sufficiently improved in the almost two and one-half years intervening to be able to capably and competently represent his clients.

. . . .

"We would make clear that we are satisfied that a case has been made against Mr. Sherman, warranting a refusal to permit him to further practice law in this state unless he can establish his mental irresponsibility at the time of the offenses charged. The burden of proof is upon him.

"If he establishes such mental irresponsibility, the burden is then upon him to establish his present capability to practice law." In re Sherman, 58 Wash. 2d 1, 6-7, 354 P.2d 888, 890 (1960), *cert. denied*, 371 U.S. 951, 9 L. Ed. 2d 499, 83 S. Ct. 506 (1963).

10. "This Court has the inherent power to revoke a license to practice law in this State, where such license was issued by this Court, and its issuance was procured by the fraudulent concealment, or by the false and fraudulent representation by the applicant of a fact which was manifestly material to the issuance of the license." North Carolina *ex rel.* Attorney General v. Gorson, 209 N.C. 320, 326, 183 S.E. 392, 395 (1936), *cert. denied*, 298 U.S. 662, 80 L.Ed. 1387, 56 S. Ct. 752 (1936).

11. See ABA CANONS OF PROFESSIONAL ETHICS, CANON 29 (1908).

12. In *ABA Opinion* 95 (1933), which held that a municipal attorney could not permit police officers to interview persons with claims against the municipality when the attorney knew the claimants to be represented by counsel, the Committee on Professional Ethics said:

"The law officer is, of course, responsible for the acts of those in his department who are under his supervision and control. *Opinion* 85. *In re Robinson*, 136 N.Y.S. 548 (affirmed 209 N.Y. 354-1912) held that it was a matter of disbarment for an attorney to adopt a general course of approving the unethical conduct of employees of his client, even though he did not actively participate therein.

" '. . . The attorney should not advise or sanction acts by his client which he himself should not do.' *Opinion* 75."

13. "The most obvious non-professional ground for disbarment is conviction for a felony. Most states make conviction for a felony grounds for automatic disbarment. Some of these states, including New York, make disbarment mandatory upon conviction for *any* felony, while others require disbarment only for those felonies which involve moral turpitude. There are strong arguments that some felonies, such as involuntary manslaughter, reflect neither on an attorney's fitness, trustworthiness, nor competence and, therefore, should not be grounds for disbarment but most states tend to disregard these arguments and, following the common law rule, make disbarment mandatory on conviction for any felony." Note, 43 CORNELL L.Q. 489, 490 (1958).

"Some states treat conviction for misdemeanors as grounds for automatic disbarment . . . . However, the vast majority, accepting the common law rule, require that the misdemeanor involve moral turpitude. While the definition of moral turpitude may prove difficult, it seems only proper that those minor offenses which do not affect the attorney's fitness to continue in the profession should not be grounds for disbarment. A good example is an assault and battery conviction which would not involve moral turpitude unless done with malice and deliberation." *Id.* at 491.

"The term 'moral turpitude' has been used in the law for centuries. It has been the subject of many decisions by the courts but has never been clearly defined because of the nature of the term. Perhaps the best general definition of the term 'moral turpitude' is that it imparts an act of baseness, vileness or depravity in the duties which one person owes to another or to society in general, which is contrary to the usual, accepted and customary rule of right and duty which a person should follow. 58 C.J.S. at page 1201. Although offenses against revenue laws have been held to be crimes of moral turpitude, it has also been held that the attempt to evade the payment of taxes due to the government or any subdivision thereof, while wrong and unlawful, does not involve moral turpitude. 58 C.J.S. at page 1205." Comm. on Legal Ethics v. Scheer, 149 W. Va. 721, 726-27, 143 S.E.2d 141, 145 (1965).

"The right and power to discipline an attorney, as one of its officers, is inherent in the court . . . . This power is not limited to those instances of misconduct wherein he has been employed, or has acted, in a professional capacity; but, on the contrary, this power may be exercised where his misconduct outside the scope of his professional relations shows him to be an unfit person to practice law." In re Wilson, 391 S.W.2d 914, 917-18 (Mo. 1965).

14. "It is a fair characterization of the lawyer's responsibility in our society that he stands 'as a shield,' to quote Devlin, J., in defense of right and to ward off wrong. From a profession charged with these responsibilities there must be exacted those qualities of truth-speaking, of a high sense of honor, of granite discretion, of the strictest observance of fiduciary responsibility, that have, throughout the centuries, been compendiously described as 'moral character.'" Schware v. Bd. of Bar Examiners, 353 U.S. 232, 247, 1 L. Ed. 2d 796, 806, 77 S. Ct. 752, 761 (1957) (Frankfurter, J., *concurring*).

"Particularly applicable here is Rule 4.47 providing that 'A lawyer should always maintain his integrity; and shall not willfully commit any act against the interest of the public; nor shall he violate his duty to the courts or his clients; *nor shall he, by any misconduct, commit any offense against the laws of*

Missouri or the United States of America, which amounts to a crime involving acts done by him contrary to justice, honesty, modesty or good morals; nor shall he be guilty of any other misconduct whereby, for the protection of the public and those charged with the administration of justice, he should no longer be entrusted with the duties and responsibilities belonging to the office of an attorney.'" In re Wilson, 391 S.W.2d 914, 917 (Mo. 1965).

15. *See* ABA Canons of Professional Ethics, Canon 29 (1908); *cf.* ABA Canons of Professional Ethics, Canon 28 (1908).

16. Cf. ABA Canons of Professional Ethics, Canons 28 and 29 (1908).

CANON 2
A Lawyer Should Assist the Legal Profession in Fulfilling Its Duty to Make Legal Counsel Available

ETHICAL CONSIDERATIONS

EC 2-1 The need of members of the public for legal services[1] is met only if they recognize their legal problems, appreciate the importance of seeking assistance,[2] and are able to obtain the services of acceptable legal counsel.[3] Hence, important functions of the legal profession are to educate laymen to recognize their problems, to facilitate the process of intelligent selection of lawyers, and to assist in making legal services fully available.[4]

Recognition of Legal Problems

EC 2-2 The legal profession should assist laypersons to recognize legal problems because such problems may not be self-revealing and often are not timely noticed. Therefore, lawyers should encourage and participate in educational and public relations programs concerning our legal system with particular reference to legal problems that frequently arise. Preparation of advertisements and professional articles for lay publications[5] and participation in seminars, lectures, and civic programs should be motivated by a desire to educate the public to an awareness of legal needs and to provide information relevant to the selection of the most appropriate counsel rather than to obtain publicity for particular lawyers. The problems of advertising on television require special consideration, due to the style, cost, and transitory nature of such media. If the interests of laypersons in receiving relevant lawyer advertising are not adequately served by print media and radio advertising, and if adequate safeguards to protect the public can reasonably be formulated, television advertising may serve a public interest.

EC 2-3 Whether a lawyer acts properly in volunteering in-person advice to a layperson to seek legal services depends upon the circumstances.[6] The giving of advice that one should take legal action could well be in fulfillment of the duty of the legal profession to assist laypersons in recognizing legal problems.[7] The advice is proper only if motivated by a desire to protect one who does not recognize that he may have legal problems or who is ignorant of his legal rights or obligations. It is improper if motivated by a desire to obtain personal benefit, secure personal publicity, or cause legal action to be taken merely to harass or injure another. A lawyer should not initiate an in-person contact with a non-client, personally or through a representative, for the purpose of being retained to represent him for compensation.

EC 2-4 Since motivation is subjective and often difficult to judge, the motives of a lawyer who volunteers in-person advice likely to produce legal controversy may well be suspect if he receives professional employment or other benefits as a result.[8] A lawyer who volunteers in-person advice that one should obtain the services of a lawyer generally should not himself accept employment, compensation, or other benefit in connection with that matter. However, it is not improper for a lawyer to volunteer such advice and render resulting legal services to close friends, relatives, former clients (in regard to matters germane to former employment), and regular clients.[9]

EC 2-5 A lawyer who writes or speaks for the purpose of educating members of the public to recognize their legal problems should carefully refrain from giving or appearing to give a general solution applicable to all apparently similar individual problems,[10] since slight changes in fact situations may require a material variance in the applicable advice; otherwise, the public may be misled and misadvised. Talks and writings by lawyers for laymen should caution them not to attempt to solve individual problems upon the basis of the information contained therein.[11]

Selection of a Lawyer

EC 2-6 Formerly a potential client usually knew the reputations of local lawyers for competency and integrity and therefore could select a practitioner in whom he had confidence. This traditional selection process worked well because it was initiated by the client and the choice was an informed one.

EC 2-7 Changed conditions, however, have seriously restricted the effectiveness of the traditional selection process. Often the reputations of lawyers are not sufficiently known to enable laymen to make intelligent choices.[12] The law has become increasingly complex and specialized. Few lawyers are willing and competent to deal with every kind of legal matter, and many laymen have difficulty in determining the competence of lawyers to render different types of legal services. The selection of legal counsel is particularly difficult for transients, persons moving into new areas, persons of limited education or means, and others who have little or no contact with lawyers.[13] Lack of information about the availability of lawyers, the qualifications of particular lawyers, and the expense of legal representation leads laypersons to avoid seeking legal advice.

EC 2-8 Selection of a lawyer by a layperson should be made on an informed basis. Advice and recommendation of third parties—relatives, friends, acquaintances, business associates, or other lawyers—and disclosure of relevant information about the lawyer and his practice may be helpful. A layperson is best served if the recommendation is disinterested and informed. In order that the recommendation be disinterested, a lawyer should not seek to influence another to recommend his employment. A lawyer should not compensate another person for recommending him, for influencing a prospective client to employ him, or to encourage future recommendations.[14] Advertisements and public communications, whether in law lists, telephone directories, newspapers, other forms of print media, television or radio, should be formulated to convey only information that is necessary to make an appropriate selection. Such information includes: (1) office information, such as name, including name of law firm and names of professional associates; addresses; telephone numbers; credit card acceptability; fluency in foreign languages; and office hours; (2) relevant biographical information; (3) description of the practice, but only by using designations and definitions authorized by [the agency having jurisdiction of the subject under state law], for example, one or more fields of law in which the lawyer or law firm practices; a statement that practice is limited to one or more fields of law; and/or a statement that the lawyer or law firm specializes in a particular field of law practice, but only by using designations, definitions and standards authorized by [the agency having jurisdiction of the subject under state law]; and (4) permitted fee information. Self-laudation should be avoided.[15]

Selection of a Lawyer

EC 2-9 The lack of sophistication on the part of many members of the public concerning legal services, the importance of the interests affected by the choice of a lawyer and prior experience with unrestricted lawyer advertising, require that special care be taken by lawyers to avoid misleading the public and to assure that the information set forth in any advertising is relevant to the selection of a lawyer. The lawyer must be mindful that the benefits of lawyer advertising depend upon its reliability and accuracy. Examples of information in lawyer advertising that would be deceptive include misstatements of fact, suggestions that the ingenuity or prior record of a lawyer rather than the justice of the claim are the principal factors likely to determine the result, inclusion of information irrelevant to selecting a lawyer, and representations concerning the quality of service, which cannot be measured or verified. Since lawyer advertising is calculated and not spontaneous, reasonable regulation of lawyer advertising designed to foster compliance with appropriate standards serves the public interest without impeding the flow of useful, meaningful, and relevant information to the public.

EC 2-10 A lawyer should ensure that the information contained in any advertising which the lawyer publishes, broadcasts or causes to be published or broadcast is relevant, is disseminated in an objective and understandable fashion, and would facilitate the prospective client's ability to compare the qualifications of the lawyers available to represent him. A lawyer should strive to communicate such information without undue emphasis upon style and advertising stratagems which serve to hinder rather than to facilitate intelligent selection of counsel. Because technological change is a recurrent feature of communications forms, and because perceptions of what is relevant in lawyer selection may change, lawyer advertising regulations should not be cast in rigid, unchangeable terms. Machinery is therefore available to advertisers and consumers for prompt consideration of proposals to change the rules governing lawyer advertising. The determination of any request for such change should depend upon whether the proposal is necessary in light of existing Code provisions, whether the proposal accords with standards of accuracy, reliability and truthfulness, and whether the proposal would facilitate informed selection of lawyers by potential consumers of legal services. Representatives of lawyers and consumers should be heard in addition to the applicant concerning any proposed change. Any change which is approved should be promulgated in the form of an amendment to the Code so that all lawyers practicing in the jurisdiction may avail themselves of its provisions.

EC 2-11 The name under which a lawyer conducts his practice may be a factor in the selection process.[16] The use of a trade name or an assumed name could mislead laymen concerning the identity, responsibility, and status of those practicing thereunder.[17] Accordingly, a lawyer in private practice should practice only under his own name, the name of a lawyer employing him, a designation containing the name of one or more of the lawyers practicing in a partnership, or, if permitted by law, the name of a professional legal corporation, which should be clearly designated as such. For many years some law firms have used a firm name retaining one or more names of deceased or retired partners and such practice is not improper if the firm is a bona fide successor of a firm in which the deceased or retired person was a member, if the use of the name is authorized by law or by contract, and if the public is not misled thereby.[18] However, the name of a partner who withdraws from a firm but continues to practice law should be omitted from the firm name in order to avoid misleading the public.

EC 2-12 A lawyer occupying a judicial, legislative, or public executive or administrative position who has the right to practice law concurrently may allow his name to remain in the name of the firm if he actively continues to practice law as a member thereof. Otherwise, his name should be removed from the firm name,[19] and he should not be identified as a past or present member of the firm; and he should not hold himself out as being a practicing lawyer.

EC 2-13 In order to avoid the possibility of misleading persons with whom he deals, a lawyer should be scrupulous in the representation of his professional status.[20] He should not hold himself out as being a partner or associate of a law firm if he is not one in fact,[21] and thus should not hold himself out as a partner or associate if he only shares offices with another lawyer.[22]

EC 2-14 In some instances a lawyer confines his practice to a particular field of law.[23] In the absence of state controls to insure the existence of special competence, a lawyer should not be permitted to hold himself out as a specialist or as having official recognition as a specialist, other than in the fields of admiralty, trademark, and patent law where a holding out as a specialist historically has been permitted. A lawyer may, however, indicate in permitted advertising, if it is factual, a limitation of his practice or one or more particular areas or fields of law in which he practices using designations and definitions authorized for that purpose by [the state agency having jurisdiction]. A lawyer practicing in a jurisdiction which certifies specialists must also be careful not to confuse laypersons as to his status. If a lawyer discloses areas of law in which he practices or to which he limits his practice, but is not certified in [the jurisdiction], he, and the designation authorized in [the jurisdiction], should avoid any implication that he is in fact certified.

EC 2-15 The legal profession has developed lawyer referral systems designed to aid individuals who are able to pay fees but need assistance in locating lawyers competent to handle their particular problems. Use of a lawyer referral system enables a layman to avoid an uninformed selection of a lawyer because such a system makes possible the employment of competent lawyers who have indicated an interest in the subject matter involved. Lawyers should support the principle of lawyer referral systems and should encourage the evolution of other ethical plans which aid in the selection of qualified counsel.

Financial Ability to Employ Counsel: Generally

EC 2-16 The legal profession cannot remain a viable force in fulfilling its role in our society unless its members receive adequate compensation for services rendered, and reasonable fees[24] should be charged in appropriate cases to clients able to pay them. Nevertheless, persons unable to pay all or a portion of a reasonable fee should be able to obtain necessary legal services,[25] and lawyers should support and participate in ethical activities designed to achieve that objective.[26]

Financial Ability to Employ Counsel: Persons Able to Pay Reasonable Fees

EC 2-17 The determination of a proper fee requires consideration of the interests of both client and lawyer.[27] A lawyer should not charge more than a reasonable fee,[28] for excessive cost of legal service would deter laymen from utilizing the legal system in protection of their rights. Furthermore, an excessive charge abuses the professional relationship between lawyer and client. On the other hand, adequate compensation is necessary in order to enable the lawyer to serve his client effectively and to preserve the integrity and independence of the profession.[29]

EC 2-18 The determination of the reasonableness of a fee requires consideration of all relevant circumstances,[30] including those stated in the Disciplinary Rules. The fees of a lawyer will vary according to many factors, including the time required, his experience, ability, and reputation, the nature of the employment, the responsibility involved, and the results obtained. It is a commendable and long-standing tradition of the bar that special consideration is given in the fixing of any fee for services rendered a brother lawyer or a member of his immediate family.

EC 2-19 As soon as feasible after a lawyer has been employed, it is desirable that he reach a clear agreement with his client as to the basis of the fee charges to be made. Such a course will not only prevent later misunderstanding but will also work for good relations between the lawyer and the client. It is usually beneficial to reduce to writing the understanding of the parties regarding the fee, particularly when it is contingent. A lawyer should be mindful that many persons who desire to employ him may have had little or no experience with fee charges of lawyers, and for this reason he should explain fully to such persons the reasons for the particular fee arrangement he proposes.

EC 2-20 Contingent fee arrangements[31] in civil cases have long been commonly accepted in the United States in proceedings to enforce claims. The historical bases of their acceptance are that (1) they often, and in a variety of circumstances, provide the only practical means by which one having a claim against another can economically afford, finance, and obtain the services of a competent lawyer to prosecute his claim, and (2) a successful prosecution of the claim produces a *res* out of which the fee can be paid.[32] Although a lawyer generally should decline to accept employment on a contingent fee basis by one who is able to pay a reasonable fixed fee, it is not necessarily improper for a lawyer, where justified by the particular circumstances of a case, to enter into a contingent fee contract in a civil case with any client who, after being fully informed of all relevant factors, desires that arrangement. Because of the human relationships involved and the unique character of the proceedings, contingent fee arrangements in domestic relation cases are rarely justified. In administrative agency proceedings contingent fee contracts should be governed by the same consideration as in other civil cases. Public policy properly condemns contingent fee arrangements in criminal cases, largely on the ground that legal services in criminal cases do not produce a *res* with which to pay the fee.

EC 2-21 A lawyer should not accept compensation or any thing of value incident to his employment or services from one other than his client without the knowledge and consent of his client after full disclosure.[33]

EC 2-22 Without the consent of his client, a lawyer should not associate in a particular matter another lawyer outside his firm. A fee may properly be divided between lawyers[34] properly associated if the division is in proportion to the services performed and the responsibility assumed by each lawyer[35] and if the total fee is reasonable.

EC 2-23 A lawyer should be zealous in his efforts to avoid controversies over fees with clients[36] and should attempt to resolve amicably any differences on the subject.[37] He should not sue a client for a fee unless necessary to prevent fraud or gross imposition by the client.[38]

Financial Ability to Employ Counsel: Persons Unable to Pay Reasonable Fees

EC 2-24 A layman whose financial ability is not sufficient to permit payment of any fee cannot obtain legal services, other than in cases where a contingent fee is appropriate, unless the services are provided for him. Even a person of moderate means may be unable to pay a reasonable fee which is large because of the complexity, novelty, or difficulty of the problem or similar factors.[39]

EC 2-25 Historically, the need for legal services of those unable to pay reasonable fees has been met in part by lawyers who donated their services or accepted court appointments on behalf of such individuals. The basic responsibility for providing legal services for those unable to pay ultimately rests upon the individual lawyer, and personal involvement in the problems of the disadvantaged can be one of the most rewarding experiences in the life of a lawyer. Every lawyer, regardless of professional prominence or professional workload, should find time to participate in serving the disadvantaged. The rendition of free legal services to those unable to pay reasonable fees continues to be an obligation of each lawyer, but the efforts of individual lawyers are often not enough to meet the need.[40] Thus it has been necessary for the profession to institute additional programs to provide legal services.[41] Accordingly, legal aid offices,[42] lawyer referral services, and other related programs have been developed, and others will be developed, by the profession.[43] Every lawyer should support all proper efforts to meet this need for legal services.[44]

Acceptance and Retention of Employment

EC 2-26 A lawyer is under no obligation to act as adviser or advocate for every person who may wish to become his client; but in furtherance of the objective of the bar to make legal services fully available, a lawyer should not lightly decline proffered employment. The fulfillment of this objective requires acceptance by a lawyer of his share of tendered employment which may be unattractive both to him and the bar generally.[45]

EC 2-27 History is replete with instances of distinguished and sacrificial services by lawyers who have represented unpopular clients and causes. Regardless of his personal feelings, a lawyer should not decline representation because a client or a cause is unpopular or community reaction is adverse.[46]

EC 2-28 The personal preference of a lawyer to avoid adversary alignment against judges, other lawyers,[47] public officials, or influential members of the community does not justify his rejection of tendered employment.

EC 2-29 When a lawyer is appointed by a court or requested by a bar association to undertake representation of a person unable to obtain counsel, whether for financial or other reasons, he should not seek to be excused from undertaking the representation except for compelling reasons.[48] Compelling reasons do not include such factors as the repugnance of the subject matter of the proceeding, the identity[49] or position of a person involved in the case, the belief of the lawyer that the defendant in a criminal proceeding is guilty,[50] or the belief of the lawyer regarding the merits of the civil case.[51]

EC 2-30 Employment should not be accepted by a lawyer when he is unable to render competent service[52] or when he knows or it is obvious that the person seeking to employ him desires to institute or maintain an action merely for the purpose of harassing or maliciously injuring another.[53] Likewise, a lawyer should decline employment if the intensity of his personal feeling, as distinguished from a community attitude, may impair his effective representation of a prospective client. If a lawyer knows a client has previously obtained counsel, he should not accept employment in the matter unless the other counsel approves[54] or withdraws, or the client terminates the prior employment.[55]

EC 2-31 Full availability of legal counsel requires both that persons be able to obtain counsel and that lawyers who undertake representation complete the work involved. Trial counsel for a convicted defendant should continue to represent his client by advising whether to take an appeal and, if the appeal is prosecuted, by representing him through the appeal unless new counsel is substituted or withdrawal is permitted by the appropriate court.

EC 2-32 A decision by a lawyer to withdraw should be made only on the basis of compelling circumstances,[56] and in a matter pending before a tribunal he must comply with the rules of the tribunal regarding withdrawal. A lawyer should not withdraw without considering carefully and endeavoring to minimize the possible adverse effect on the rights of his client and the possibility of prejudice to his client[57] as a result of his withdrawal. Even when he justifiably withdraws, a lawyer should protect the welfare of his client by giving due notice of his withdrawal,[58] suggesting employment of other counsel, delivering to the client all papers and property to which the client is entitled, cooperating with counsel subsequently employed, and otherwise endeavoring to minimize the possibility of harm. Further, he should refund to the client any compensation not earned during the employment.[59]

EC 2-33 As a part of the legal profession's commitment to the principle that high quality legal services should be available to all, attorneys are encouraged to cooperate with qualified legal assistance organizations providing prepaid legal services. Such participation should at all times be in accordance with the basic tenets of the profession: independence, integrity, competence and devotion to the interests of individual clients. An attorney so participating should make certain that his relationship with a qualified legal assistance organization in no way interferes with his independent, professional representation of the interests of the individual client. An attorney should avoid situations in which officials of the organization who are not lawyers attempt to direct attorneys concerning the manner in which legal services are performed for individual members, and should also avoid situations in which considerations of economy are given undue weight in determining the attorneys employed by an organization or the legal services to be performed for the member or beneficiary rather than competence and quality of service. An attorney interested in maintaining the historic traditions of the profession and preserving the function of a lawyer as a trusted and independent advisor to individual members of society should carefully assess such factors when accepting employment by, or otherwise participating in, a particular qualified legal assistance organization, and while so participating should adhere to the highest professional standards of effort and competence.[60]

DISCIPLINARY RULES

DR 2-101 Publicity in General.

(A) A lawyer shall not, on behalf of himself, his partner, associate or any other lawyer affiliated with him or his firm, use or participate in the use of any form of public communication containing a false, fraudulent, misleading, deceptive, self-laudatory or unfair statement or claim.

(B) In order to facilitate the process of informed selection of a lawyer by potential consumers of legal services, a lawyer may publish or broadcast, subject to DR 2-103, the following information in print media distributed or over television or radio broadcast in the geographic area or areas in which the lawyer resides or maintains offices of in which a significant part of the lawyer's clientele resides, provided that the information disclosed by the lawyer in such publication or broadcast complies with DR 2-101(A), and is presented in a dignified manner.[61]

(1) Name, including name of law firm and names of professional associates; addresses and telephone numbers;
(2) One or more fields of law in which the lawyer or law firm practices, a statement that practice is limited to one or more fields of law, or a statement that the lawyer or law firm specializes in a particular field of law practice, to the extent authorized under DR 2-105;
(3) Date and place of birth;
(4) Date and place of admission to the bar of state and federal courts;
(5) Schools attended, with dates of graduation, degrees and other scholastic distinctions;
(6) Public or quasi-public offices;
(7) Military service;
(8) Legal authorships;
(9) Legal teaching positions;
(10) Memberships, offices, and committee assignments, in bar associations;
(11) Membership and offices in legal fraternities and legal societies;
(12) Technical and professional licenses;
(13) Memberships in scientific, technical and professional associations and societies;

(14) Foreign language ability;
(15) Names and addresses of bank references;
(16) With their written consent, names of clients regularly represented;
(17) Prepaid or group legal services programs in which the lawyer participates;
(18) Whether credit cards or other credit arrangements are accepted;
(19) Office and telephone answering service hours;
(20) Fee for an initial consultation;
(21) Availability upon request of a written schedule of fees and/or estimate of the fee to be charged for specific services;
(22) Contingent fee rates subject to DR 2-106(C), provided that the statement discloses whether percentages are computed before or after deduction of costs;
(23) Range of fees for services, provided that the statement discloses that the specific fee within the range which will be charged will vary depending upon the particular matter to be handled for each client and the client is entitled without obligation to an estimate of the fee within the range likely to be charged, in print size equivalent to the largest print used in setting forth the fee information;
(24) Hourly rate, provided that the statement discloses that the total fee charged will depend upon the number of hours which must be devoted to the particular matter to be handled for each client and the client is entitled to without obligation an estimate of the fee likely to be charged, in print size at least equivalent to the largest print used in setting forth the fee information;
(25) Fixed fees for specific legal services,* the description of which would not be misunderstood or be deceptive, provided that the statement discloses that the quoted fee will be available only to clients whose matters fall into the services described and that the client is entitled without obligation to a specific estimate of the fee likely to be charged in print size at least equivalent to the largest print used in setting forth the fee information.

(C) Any person desiring to expand the information authorized for disclosure in DR 2-101(B), or to provide for its dissemination through other forums may apply to [the agency having jurisdiction under state law]. Any such application shall be served upon [the agencies having jurisdiction under state law over the regulation of the legal profession and consumer matters] who shall be heard, together with the applicant, on the issue of whether the proposal is necessary in light of the existing provisions of the Code, accords with standards of accuracy, reliability and truthfulness, and would facilitate the process of informed selection of lawyers by potential consumers of legal services. The relief granted in response to any such appli-

* The agency having jurisdiction under state law may desire to issue appropriate guidelihes defining "specific legal services."

cation shall be promulgated as an amendment to DR 2-101(B), universally applicable to all lawyers.**

(D) If the advertisement is communicated to the public over television or radio, it shall be pre-recorded, approved for broadcast by the lawyer, and a recording of the actual transmission shall be retained by the lawyer.[62]

(E) If a lawyer advertises a fee for a service, the lawyer must render that service for no more than the fee advertised.

(F) Unless otherwise specified in the advertisement if a lawyer publishes any fee information authorized under DR 2-101(B) in a publication that is published more frequently than one time per month, the lawyer shall be bound by any representation made therein for a period of not less than 30 days after such publication. If a lawyer publishes any fee information authorized under DR 2-101(B) in a publication that is published once a month or less frequently, he shall be bound by any representation made therein until the publication of the succeeding issue. If a lawyer publishes any fee information authorized under DR 2-101(B) in a publication which has no fixed date for publication of a succeeding issue, the lawyer shall be bound by any representation made therein for a reasonable period of time after publication but in no event less than one year.

(G) Unless otherwise specified, if a lawyer broadcasts any fee information authorized under DR 2-101(B), the lawyer shall be bound by any representation made therein for a period of not less than 30 days after such broadcast.

(H) This rule does not prohibit limited and dignified identification of a lawyer as a lawyer as well as by name:

(1) In political advertisements when his professional status is germane to the political campaign or to a political issue.

(2) In public notices when the name and profession of a lawyer are required or authorized by law or are reasonably pertinent for a purpose other than the attraction of potential clients.

(3) In routine reports and announcements of a bona fide business, civic, professional, or political organization in which he serves as a director or officer.

(4) In and on legal documents prepared by him.

(5) In and on legal textbooks, treatises, and other legal publications, and in dignified advertisements thereof.

(I) A lawyer shall not compensate or give any thing of value to representatives of the press, radio, television, or other communication medium in anticipation of or in return for professional publicity in a news item.

DR 2-102 Professional Notices, Letterheads and Offices

(A) A lawyer or law firm shall not use or participate in the use of[63] profession-

** The agency having jurisidiction under state law should establish orderly and expeditious procedures for ruling on such applications.

al cards, professional announcement cards, office signs, letterheads, telephone directory listings, law lists, legal directory listings, or similar professional notices or devices, except that the following may be used if they are in dignified form:

(1) A professional card of a lawyer identifying him by name and as a lawyer, and giving his addresses, telephone numbers, the name of his law firm, and any information permitted under DR 2-105. A professional card of a law firm may also give the names of members and associates. Such cards may be used for identification.

(2) A brief professional announcement card stating new or changed associations or addresses, change of firm name, or similar matters pertaining to the professional office of a lawyer or law firm, which may be mailed to lawyers, clients, former clients, personal friends, and relatives.[64] It shall not state biographical data except to the extent reasonably necessary to identify the lawyer or to explain the change in his association, but it may state the immediate past position of the lawyer.[65] It may give the names and dates of predecessor firms in a continuing line of succession. It shall not state the nature of the practice except as permitted under DR 2-105.[66]

(3) A sign on or near the door of the office and in the building directory identifying the law office. The sign shall not state the nature of the practice, except as permitted under DR 2-105.

(4) A letterhead of a lawyer identifying him by name and as a lawyer, and giving his addresses, telephone numbers, the name of his law firm, associates and any information permitted under DR 2-105. A letterhead of a law firm may also give the names of members and associates,[67] and names and dates relating to deceased and retired members.[68] A lawyer may be designated "Of Counsel" on a letterhead if he has a continuing relationship with a lawyer or law firm, other than as a partner or associate. A lawyer or law firm may be designated as "General Counsel" or by similar professional reference on stationery of a client if he or the firm devotes a substantial amount of professional time in the representation of that client.[69] The letterhead of a law firm may give the names and dates of predecessor firms in a continuing line of succession.

(B) A lawyer in private practice shall not practice under a trade name, a name that is misleading as to the identity of the lawyer or lawyers practicing under such name, or a firm name containing names other than those of one or more of the lawyers in the firm, except that the name of a professional corporation or professional association may contain "P.C." or "P.A." or similar symbols indicating the nature of the organization, and if otherwise lawful a firm may use as, or continue to include in, its name the name or names of one or more deceased or retired members of the firm or of a predecessor firm in a continuing line of succession.[70] A lawyer who assumes a judicial, legislative, or public executive or administrative post or office shall not permit his name to remain in the name of a law firm or to be used in professional notices of the firm during any significant period in which he is not actively and regularly practicing law as a member of the firm,[71] and during such period other members of the firm shall not use his name in the firm name or in professional notices of the firm.[72]

(C) A lawyer shall not hold himself out as having a partnership with one or more other lawyers or professional corporations[73] unless they are in fact partners.[74]

(D) A partnership shall not be formed or continued between or among lawyers licensed in different jurisdictions unless all enumerations of the members and associates of the firm on its letterhead and in other permissible listings make clear the jurisdictional limitations on those members and associates of the firm not licensed to practice in all listed jurisdictions;[75] however, the same firm name may be used in each jurisdiction.

(E) Nothing contained herein shall prohibit a lawyer from using or permitting the use of, in connection with his name, an earned degree or title derived therefrom indicating his training in the law.[76]

DR 2-103 Recommendation of Professional Employment.[77]

(A) A lawyer shall not, except as authorized in DR 2-101(B), recommend employment, as a private practitioner,[78] of himself, his partner, or associate to a layperson who has not sought his advice regarding employment of a lawyer.[79]

(B) A lawyer shall not compensate or give anything of value to a person or organization to recommend or secure his employment[80] by a client, or as a reward for having made a recommendation resulting in his employment[81] by a client, except that he may pay the usual and reasonable fees or dues charged by any of the organizations listed in DR 2-103(D).[82]

(C) A lawyer shall not request a person or organization to recommend or promote the use of his services or those of his partner or associate, or any other lawyer affiliated with him or his firm, as a private practitioner,[83] except as authorized in DR 2-101, and except that

(1) He may request referrals from a lawyer referral service operated, sponsored, or approved by a bar association and may pay its fees incident thereto.[84]

(2) He may cooperate with the legal service activities of any of the offices or organizations enumerated in DR 2-103(D)(1) through (4) and may perform legal services for those to whom he was recommended by it to do such work if:

(a) The person to whom the recommendation is made is a member or beneficiary of such office or organizations; and

(b) The lawyer remains free to exercise his independent professional judgment on behalf of his client.[85]

(D) A lawyer or his partner or associate or any other lawyer affiliated with him or his firm may be recommended, employed or paid by, or may cooperate with, one of the following offices or organizations that promote the use of his services or those of his partner or associate or any other lawyer affiliated with him or his firm if there is no interference with the exercise of independent professional judgment in behalf of his client:

(1) A legal aid office or public defender office:
  (a) Operated or sponsored by a duly accredited law school.
  (b) Operated or sponsored by a bona fide nonprofit community organization.
  (c) Operated or sponsored by a governmental agency.
  (d) Operated, sponsored, or approved by a bar association.[86]

(2) A military legal assistance office.

(3) A lawyer referral service operated, sponsored, or approved by a bar association.

(4) Any bona fide organization that recommends, furnishes or pays for legal services to its members or beneficiaries[87] provided the following conditions are satisfied:
  (a) Such organization, including any affiliate, is so organized and operated that no profit is derived by it from the rendition of legal services by lawyers, and that, if the organization is organized for profit, the legal services are not rendered by lawyers employed, directed, supervised or selected by it except in connection with matters where such organization bears ultimate liability of its member or beneficiary.
  (b) Neither the lawyer, nor his partner, nor associate, nor any other lawyer affiliated with him or his firm, nor any non-lawyer, shall have initiated or promoted such organization for the primary purpose of providing financial or other benefit to such lawyer, partner, associate or affiliated lawyer.
  (c) Such organization is not operated for the purpose of procuring legal work or financial benefit for any lawyer as a private practitioner outside of the legal services program of the organization.
  (d) The member or beneficiary to whom the legal services are furnished, and not such organization, is recognized as the client of the lawyer in the matter.
  (e) Any member or beneficiary who is entitled to have legal services furnished or paid for by the organization may, if such member or beneficiary so desires, select counsel other than that furnished, selected or approved by the organization for the particular matter involved; and the legal service plan of such organization provides appropriate relief for any member or beneficiary who asserts a claim that representation by counsel furnished, selected or approved would be unethical, improper or inadequate under the circumstances of the matter involved and the plan provides an

appropriate procedure for seeking such relief.

(f) The lawyer does not know or have cause to know that such organization is in violation of applicable laws, rules of court and other legal requirements that govern its legal service operations.

(g) Such organization has filed with the appropriate disciplinary authority at least annually a report with respect to its legal service plan, if any, showing its terms, its schedule of benefits, its subscription charges, agreements with counsel, and financial results of its legal service activities or, if it has failed to do so, the lawyer does not know or have case to know of such failure.[88]

(E) A lawyer shall not accept employment when he knows or it is obvious that the person who seeks his services does so as a result of conduct prohibited under this Disciplinary Rule.

DR 2-104 Suggestion of Need of Legal Services.[89, 90]

(A) A lawyer who has given unsolicited advice to a layman that he should obtain counsel or take legal action shall not accept employment resulting from that advice,[91] except that:

(1) A lawyer may accept employment by a close friend, relative, former client (if the advice is germane to the former employment), or one whom the lawyer reasonably believes to be a client.[92]

(2) A lawyer may accept employment that results from his participation in activities designed to educate laymen to recognize legal problems, to make intelligent selection of counsel, or to utilize available legal services if such activities are conducted or sponsored by a qualified legal assistance organization.[93]

(3) A lawyer who is recommended, furnished or paid by any of the offices or organizations enumerated in DR 2-103(D)(1) through (4)[94] may represent a member or beneficiary thereof, to the extent and under the conditions prescribed therein.

(4) Without affecting his right to accept employment, a lawyer may speak publicly or write for publication on legal topics[95] so long as he does not emphasize his own professional experience or reputation and does not undertake to give individual advice.

(5) If success in asserting rights or defenses of his client in litigation in the nature of a class action is dependent upon the joinder of others, a lawyer may accept, but shall not seek, employment from those contacted for the purpose of obtaining their joinder.[96]

DR 2-105 Limitation of Practice.[97]

(A) A lawyer shall not hold himself out publicly as a specialist, as practicing in certain areas of law or as limiting his practice permitted under DR 2-101(B), except as follows:

(1) A lawyer admitted to practice before the United States Patent and

Trademark Office may use the designation "Patents," "Patent Attorney," or "Patent Lawyer," or "Registered Patent Attorney" or any combination of those terms, on his letterhead and office sign.

(2) A lawyer who publicly discloses fields of law in which the lawyer or the law firm practices or states that his practice is limited to one or more fields of law shall do so by using designations and definitions authorized and approved by [the agency having jurisdiction of the subject under state law].

(3) A lawyer who is certified as a specialist in a particular field of law or law practice by [the authority having jurisdiction under state law over the subject of specialization by lawyers] may hold himself out as such, but only in accordance with the rules prescribed by that authority.[98]

DR 2-106 Fees for Legal Services.[99]

(A) A lawyer shall not enter into an agreement for, charge, or collect an illegal or clearly excessive fee.[100]

(B) A fee is clearly excessive when, after a review of the facts, a lawyer of ordinary prudence would be left with a definite and firm conviction that the fee is in excess of a reasonable fee. Factors to be considered as guides in determining the reasonableness of a fee include the following:

(1) The time and labor required, the novelty and difficulty of the questions involved, and the skill requisite to perform the legal service properly.

(2) The likelihood, if apparent to the client, that the acceptance of the particular employment will preclude other employment by the lawyer.

(3) The fee customarily charged in the locality for similar legal services.

(4) The amount involved and the results obtained.

(5) The time limitations imposed by the client or by the circumstances.

(6) The nature and length of the professional relationship with the client.

(7) The experience, reputation, and ability of the lawyer or lawyers performing the services.

(8) Whether the fee is fixed or contingent.[101]

(C) A lawyer shall not enter into an arrangement for, charge, or collect a contingent fee for representing a defendant in a criminal case.[102]

DR 2-107 Division of Fees Among Lawyers.

(A) A lawyer shall not divide a fee for legal services with another lawyer who is not a partner in or associate of his law firm or law office, unless:

(1) The client consents to employment of the other lawyer after a full disclosure that a division of fees will be made.

(2) The division is made in proportion to the services performed and responsibility assumed by each.[103]

(3) The total fee of the lawyers does not clearly exceed reasonable compensation for all legal services they rendered the client.[104]

(B) This Disciplinary Rule does not prohibit payment to a former partner or associate pursuant to a separation or retirement agreement.

DR 2-108 Agreements Restricting the Practice of a Lawyer.

(A) A lawyer shall not be a party to or participate in a partnership or employment agreement with another lawyer that restricts the right of a lawyer to practice law after the termination of a relationship created by the agreement, except as a condition to payment of retirement benefits.[105]

(B) In connection with the settlement of a controversy or suit, a lawyer shall not enter into an agreement that restricts his right to practice law.

DR 2-109 Acceptance of Employment.

(A) A lawyer shall not accept employment on behalf of a person if he knows or it is obvious that such person wishes to:

(1) Bring a legal action, conduct a defense, or assert a position in litigation, or otherwise have steps taken for him, merely for the purpose of harassing or maliciously injuring any person.[106]

(2) Present a claim or defense in litigation that is not warranted under existing law, unless it can be supported by good faith argument for an extension, modification, or reversal of existing law.

DR 2-110 Withdrawal from Employment.[107]

(A) In general.

(1) If permission for withdrawal from employment is required by the rules of a tribunal, a lawyer shall not withdraw from employment in a proceeding before that tribunal without its permission.

(2) In any event, a lawyer shall not withdraw from employment until he has taken reasonable steps to avoid foreseeable prejudice to the rights of his client, including giving due notice to his client, allowing time for employment of other counsel, delivering to the client all papers and property to which the client is entitled, and complying with applicable laws and rules.

(3) A lawyer who withdraws from employment shall refund promptly any part of a fee paid in advance that has not been earned.

(B) Mandatory withdrawal.

A lawyer representing a client before a tribunal, with its permission if required by its rules, shall withdraw from employment, and a lawyer representing a client in other matters shall withdraw from employment, if:

(1) He knows or it is obvious that his client is bringing the legal action, conducting the defense, or asserting a position in the litigation, or is otherwise having steps taken for him, merely for the purpose of harassing or maliciously injuring any person.

(2) He knows or it is obvious that his continued employment will result in violation of a Disciplinary Rule.[108]

(3) His mental or physical condition renders it unreasonably difficult for

him to carry out the employment effectively.

(4) He is discharged by his client.

(C) Permissive withdrawal.[109]

If DR 2-110(B) is not applicable, a lawyer may not request permission to withdraw in matters pending before a tribunal, and may not withdraw in other matters, unless such request or such withdrawal is because:

(1) His client:

(a) Insists upon presenting a claim or defense that is not warranted under existing law and cannot be supported by good faith argument for an extension, modification, or reversal of existing law.[110]

(b) Personally seeks to pursue an illegal course of conduct.

(c) Insists that the lawyer pursue a course of conduct that is illegal or that is prohibited under the Disciplinary Rules.

(d) By other conduct renders it unreasonably difficult for the lawyer to carry out his employment effectively.

(e) Insists, in a matter not pending before a tribunal, that the lawyer engage in conduct that is contrary to the judgment and advice of the lawyer but not prohibited under the Disciplinary Rules.

(f) Deliberately disregards an agreement or obligation to the lawyer as to expenses or fees.

(2) His continued employment is likely to result in a violation of a Disciplinary Rule.

(3) His inability to work with co-counsel indicates that the best interests of the client likely will be served by withdrawal.

(4) His mental or physical condition renders it difficult for him to carry out the employment effectively.

(5) His client knowingly and freely assents to termination of his employment.

(6) He believes in good faith, in a proceeding pending before a tribunal, that the tribunal will find the existence of other good cause for withdrawal.

NOTES

1. "Men have need for more than a system of law; they have need for a system of law which functions, and that means they have need for lawyers." Cheatham, *The Lawyer's Role and Surroundings*, 25 ROCKY MT. L. REV. 405 (1953).

2. "Law is not self-applying; men must apply and utilize it in concrete cases. But the ordinary man is incapable. He cannot know the principles of law or the rules guiding the machinery of law administration; he does not know how to formulate his desires with precision and to put them into writing, he is ineffective in the presentation of his claims." *Id.*

3. "This need [to provide legal services] was recognized by . . . Mr. [Lewis F.] Powell [Jr., President, American Bar Association, 1963-64], who said: 'Looking at contemporary America realistically, we must admit that despite all our efforts to date (and these have not been insignificant), far too many persons are not able to obtain equal justice under law. This usually results because their poverty or their ignorance has prevented them from obtaining legal counsel.'" Address by E. Clinton Bamberger, Association of

American Law Schools 1965 Annual Meeting, Dec. 28, 1965, in PROCEEDINGS, PART II, 1965, 61, 63-64 (1965).

"A wide gap separates the need for legal services and its satisfaction, as numerous studies reveal. Looked at from the side of the layman, one reason for the gap is poverty and the consequent inability to pay legal fees. Another set of reasons is ignorance of the need for and the value of legal services, and ignorance of where to find a dependable lawyer. There is fear of the mysterious processes and delays of the law, and there is fear of overreaching and overcharging by lawyers, a fear stimulated by the occasional exposure of shysters." Cheatham, *Availability of Legal Services: The Responsibility of the Individual Lawyer and of the Organized Bar*, 12 U.C.L.A. L. REV. 438 (1965).

4. "It is not only the right but the duty of the profession as a whole to utilize such methods as may be developed to bring the services of its members to those who need them, so long as this can be done ethically and with dignity." *ABA Opinion* 320 (1968).

"[T]here is a responsibility on the bar to make legal services available to those who need them. The maxim, 'privilege brings responsibilities,' can be expanded to read, exclusive privilege to render public service brings responsibility to assure that the service is available to those in need of it." Cheatham, *Availability of Legal Services: The Responsibility of the Individual Lawyer and of the Organized Bar*, 12 U.C.L.A. L. REV. 438, 443 (1965).

"The obligation to provide legal services for those actually caught up in litigation carries with it the obligation to make preventive legal advice accessible to all. It is among those unaccustomed to business affairs and fearful of the ways of the law that such advice is often most needed. If it is not received in time, the most valiant and skillful representation in court may come too late." *Professional Responsibility: Report of the Joint Conference*, 44 A.B.A.J. 1159, 1216 (1958).

5. "A lawyer may with propriety write articles for publications in which he gives information upon the law . . . ." ABA CANONS OF PROFESSIONAL ETHICS, CANON 40 (1908).

6. *See* ABA CANONS OF PROFESSIONAL ETHICS, CANON 28 (1908).

7. This question can assume constitutional dimensions: "We meet at the outset the contention that 'solicitation' is wholly outside the area of freedoms protected by the First Amendment. To this contention there are two answers. The first is that a State cannot foreclose the exercise of constitutional rights by mere labels. The second is that abstract discussion is not the only species of communication which the Constitution protects; the First Amendment also protects vigorous advocacy, certainly of lawful ends, against governmental intrusion . . . .

. . . .

"However valid may be Virginia's interest in regulating the traditionally illegal practice of barratry, maintenance and champerty, that interest does not justify the prohibition of the NAACP activities disclosed by this record. Malicious intent was of the essence of the common-law offenses of fomenting or stirring up litigation. And whatever may be or may have been true of suits against governments in other countries, the exercise in our own, as in this case of First Amendment rights to enforce Constitutional rights through litigation, as a matter of law, cannot be deemed malicious." NAACP v. Button, 371 U.S. 415, 429, 439-40, 9 L. Ed. 2d 405, 415-16, 422, 83 S. Ct. 328, 336, 341 (1963).

8. It is disreputable for an attorney to breed litigation by seeking out those who have claims for personal injuries or other grounds of action in order to secure them as clients. or to employ agents or runners, or to reward those who bring or influence the bringing of business to his office . . . . Moreover, it tends quite easily to the institution of baseless litigation and the manufacture of perjured testimony. From early times, this danger has been recognized in the law by the condemnation of the crime of common barratry, or the stirring up of suits or quarrels between individuals at law or otherwise." In re Ades, 6 F.Supp. 467, 474-75 (D. Mary. 1934).

9. "*Rule* 2.

"§a . . . .

"[A] member of the State Bar shall not solicit professional employment by

"(1) Volunteering counsel or advice except where ties of blood relationship or trust make it appropriate." CAL. BUSINESS AND PROFESSIONS CODE §6076 (West 1962).

10. "*Rule 18* . . . A member of the State Bar shall not advise inquirers or render opinions to them through or in connection with a newspaper, radio or other publicity medium of any kind in respect to their specific legal problems, whether or not such attorney shall be compensated for his service." CAL. BUSINESS AND PROFESSIONS CODE §6076 (West 1962).

11. "In any case where a member might well apply the advice given in the opinion to his individual

affairs, the lawyer rendering the opinion [concerning problems common to members of an association and distributed to the members through a periodic bulletin] should specifically state that this opinion should not be relied on by any member as a basis for handling his individual affairs, but that in every case he should consult his counsel. In the publication of the opinion the association should make a similar statement." *ABA Opinion* 273 (1946).

12. "A group of recent interrelated changes bears directly on the availability of legal services . . . . [One] change is the constantly accelerating urbanization of the country and the decline of personal and neighborhood knowledge of whom to retain as a professional man." Cheatham, *Availability of Legal Services: The Responsibility of the Individual Lawyer and of the Organized Bar*, 12 U.C.L.A. L. REV. 438, 440 (1965).

13. *Cf.* Cheatham, *A Lawyer When Needed: Legal Services for the Middle Classes*, 63 COLUM. L. REV. 973, 974 (1963).

14. *See* ABA CANONS OF PROFESSIONAL ETHICS, CANON 28 (1908).

15. Amended, August 1978, House Informational Report No. 118.

16. *Cf. ABA Opinion* 303 (1961).

17. *See* ABA CANONS OF PROFESSIONAL ETHICS, CANON 33 (1908).

18. *Id.*

"The continued use of a firm name by one or more surviving partners after the death of a member of the firm whose name is in the firm title is expressly permitted by the Canons of Ethics. The reason for this is that all of the partners have by their joint and several efforts over a period of years contributed to the good will attached to the firm name. In the case of a firm having widespread connections, this good will is disturbed by a change in firm name every time a name partner dies, and that reflects a loss in some degree of the good will to the building up of which the surviving partners have contributed their time, skill and labor through a period of years. To avoid this loss the firm name is continued, and to meet the requirements of the Canon the individuals constituting the firm from time to time are listed." *ABA Opinion* 267 (1945).

"Accepted local custom in New York recognizes that the name of a law firm does not necessarily identify the individual member of the firm, and hence the continued use of a firm name after the death of one or more partners is not a deception and is permissible . . . . The continued use of a deceased partner's name in the firm title is not affected by the fact that another partner withdraws from the firm and his name is dropped, or the name of the new partner is added to the firm name." *Opinion* No. 45, Committee on Professional Ethics, New York State Bar Ass'n, 39 N.Y.St.B.J. 455 (1967).

Cf. ABA Opinion 258 (1943).

19. *Cf.* ABA CANONS OF PROFESSIONAL ETHICS, CANON 33 (1908) and *ABA Opinion* 315 (1965).

20. *Cf. ABA Opinions* 283 (1950) and 81 (1932).

21. *See ABA Opinion* 316 (1967).

22. "The word 'associates' has a variety of meanings. Principally through custom the word when used on the letterheads of law firms has come to be regarded as describing those who are employees of the firm. Because the word has acquired this special significance in connection with the practice of the law the use of the word to describe lawyer relationships other than employer-employee is likely to be misleading." In re Sussman and Tanner, 241 Ore. 246, 248, 405 P.2d 355, 356 (1965).

According to *ABA Opinion* 310 (1963), use of the term "associates" would be misleading in two situations: (I) where two lawyers are partners and they share both responsibility and liability for the partnership; and (2) where two lawyers practice separately, sharing no responsibility or liability, and only share a suite of offices and some costs.

23. "For a long time, many lawyers have, of necessity, limited their practice to certain branches of law. The increasing complexity of the law and the demand of the public for more expertness on the part of the lawyer has, in the past few years—particularly in the last ten years—brought about specialization on an increasing scale." *Report of the Special Committee on Specialization and Specialized Legal Services*, 79 A.B.A. REP. 582, 584 (1954).

24. *See* ABA CANONS OF PROFESSIONAL ETHICS, CANON 12 (1908).

25. *Cf.* ABA CANONS OF PROFESSIONAL ETHICS, CANON 12 (1908).

26. "If there is any fundamental proposition of government on which all would agree, it is that one of the highest goals of society must be to achieve and maintain equality before the law. Yet this ideal remains an empty form of words unless the legal profession is ready to provide adequate representation for those unable to pay the usual fees." *Professional Representation: Report of the Joint Conference*, 44 A.B.A.J. 1159, 1216 (1958).

27. *See* ABA CANONS OF PROFESSIONAL ETHICS, CANON 12 (1908).

28. *Cf.* ABA CANONS OF PROFESSIONAL ETHICS, CANON 12 (1908).

29. "When members of the Bar are induced to render legal services for inadequate compensation, as a consequence the quality of the service rendered may be lowered, the welfare of the profession injured and the administration of justice made less efficient." *ABA Opinion* 302 (1961).

Cf. ABA Opinion 307 (1962).

30. *See* ABA CANONS OF PROFESSIONAL ETHICS, CANON 12 (1908).

31. *See* ABA CANONS OF PROFESSIONAL ETHICS, CANON 13; *see also* MACKINNON, CONTINGENT FEES FOR LEGAL SERVICES (1964) (A report of the American Bar Foundation).

"A contract for a reasonable contingent fee where sanctioned by law is permitted by *Canon 13*, but the client must remain responsible to the lawyer for expenses advanced by the latter. 'There is to be no barter of the privilege of prosecuting a cause for gain in exchange for the promise of the attorney to prosecute at his own expense.' (Cardozo, C. J. in Matter of Gilman, 251 N.Y. 265, 270-271.)" *ABA Opinion* 246 (1942).

32. *See* Comment, *Providing Legal Services for the Middle Class in Civil Matters: The Problem, the Duty and a Solution.* 26 U. PITT. L. REV. 811, 829 (1965).

33. *See* ABA CANONS OF PROFESSIONAL ETHICS, CANON 38 (1908).

"Of course, as . . . [Informal Opinion 679] points out, there must be full disclosure of the arrangement [that an entity other than the client pays the attorney's fee] by the attorney to the client . . . ." *ABA Opinion* 320 (1968).

34. "Only lawyers may share in . . . a division of fees, but . . . it is not necessary that both lawyers be admitted to practice in the same state, so long as the division was based on the division of services or responsibility." *ABA Opinion* 316 (1967)

35. *See* ABA CANONS OF PROFESSIONAL ETHICS, CANON 34 (1908).

"We adhere to our previous rulings that where a lawyer merely brings about the employment of another lawyer *but renders no service and assumes no responsibility in the matter,* a division of the latter's fee is improper. (*Opinions* 18 and 153).

"It is assumed that the bar, generally, understands what acts or conduct of a lawyer may constitute 'services' to a client within the intendment of *Canon 12*. Such acts or conduct invariably, if not always, involve 'responsibility' on the part of the lawyer, whether the word 'responsibility' be construed to denote the possible resultant legal or moral liability on the part of the lawyer to the client or to others, or the onus of deciding what should or should not be done in behalf of the client. The word 'services' in *Canon 12* must be construed in this broad sense and may apply to the selection and retainer of associate counsel as well as to other acts or conduct in the client's behalf." *ABA Opinion* 204 (1940).

36. *See* ABA CANONS OF PROFESSIONAL ETHICS, CANON 14 (1908).

37. *Cf ABA Opinion* 320 (1968).

38. *See* ABA CANONS OF PROFESSIONAL ETHICS, CANON 14 (1908).

"Ours is a learned profession, not a mere money-getting trade . . . . Suits to collect fees should be avoided. Only where the circumstances imperatively require, should resort be had to a suit to compel payment. And where a lawyer does resort to a suit to enforce payment of fees which involves a disclosure, he should carefully avoid any disclosure not clearly necessary to obtaining or defending his rights." *ABA Opinion* 250 (1943).

But cf. ABA Opinion 320 (1968).

39. "As a society increases in size, sophistication and technology, the body of laws which is required to control that society also increases in size, scope and complexity. With this growth, the law directly affects more and more facets of individual behavior, creating an expanding need for legal services on the part of the individual members of the society. . . . As legal guidance in social and commercial behavior increasingly becomes necessary, there will come a concurrent demand from the layman that such guidance be made available to him. This demand will not come from those who are able to employ the best legal talent, nor from those who can obtain legal assistance at little or no cost. It will come from the large 'forgotten middle income class,' who can neither afford to pay proportionately large fees nor qualify for ultra-low-cost services. The legal profession must recognize this inevitable demand and consider methods whereby it can be satisfied. If the profession fails to provide such methods, the laity will." Comment, *Providing Legal Services for the Middle Class in Civil Matters: The Problem, the Duty and a Solution*, 26 U. PITT. L REV. 811, 811-12 (1965).

"The issue is not whether we shall do something or do nothing. The demand for ordinary everyday legal justice is so great and the moral nature of the demand is so strong that the issue has become whether we devise, maintain, and support suitable agencies able to satisfy the demand or, by our own default, force the government to take over the job, supplant us, and ultimately dominate us." Smith, *Legal Service Offices for Persons of Moderate Means*, 1949 WIS. L REV. 416, 418 (1949).

40. "Lawyers have peculiar responsibilities for the just administration of the law and these responsibilities include providing advice and representation for needy persons. To a degree not always appreciated by the public at large, the bar has performed these obligations with zeal and devotion. The Committee is persuaded, however, that a system of justice that attempts, in mid-twentieth century America, to meet the needs of the financially incapacitated accused through primary or exclusive reliance on the uncompensated services of counsel will prove unsuccessful and inadequate. . . . A system of adequate representation, therefore, should be structured and financed in a manner reflecting its public importance . . . . We believe that fees for private appointed counsel should be set by the court within maximum limits established by the statute." REPORT OF THE ATT'Y GEN'S COMM. ON POVERTY AND THE ADMINISTRATION OF CRIMINAL JUSTICE 41-43 (1963).

41. "At present this representation [of those unable to pay usual fees] is being supplied in some measure through the spontaneous generosity of individual lawyers, through legal aid societies, and—increasingly—through the organized efforts of the Bar. If those who stand in need of this service know of its availability and their need is in fact adequately met, the precise mechanism by which this service is provided becomes of secondary importance. It is of great importance, however, that both the impulse to render this service, and the plan for making that impulse effective, should arise within the legal profession itself." *Professional Responsibility: Report of the Joint Conference*, 44 A.B.A.J. 1159, 1216 (1958).

42. "Free legal clinics carried on by the organized bar are not ethically objectionable. On the contrary, they serve a very worthwhile purpose and should be encouraged." *ABA Opinion* 191 (1939).

43. "Whereas the American Bar Association believes that it is a fundamental duty of the bar to see to it that all persons requiring legal advice be able to attain it, irrespective of their economic status . . . .

"Resolved, that the Association approves and sponsors the setting up by state and local bar associations of lawyer referral plans and low-cost legal service methods for the purpose of dealing with cases of persons who might not otherwise have the benefit of legal advice . . . ." *Proceedings of the House of Delegates of the American Bar Association*, Oct. 30, 1946, 71 A.B.A. REP. 103, 109-10(1946).

44. "The defense of indigent citizens, without compensation, is carried on throughout the country by lawyers representing legal aid societies, not only with the approval, but with the commendation of those acquainted with the work. Not infrequently services are rendered out of sympathy or for other philanthropic reasons, by individual lawyers who do not represent legal aid societies. There is nothing whatever in the Canons to prevent a lawyer from performing such an act, nor should there be." *ABA Opinion* 148 (1935).

45. *But cf.* ABA CANONS OF PROFESSIONAL ETHICS, CANON 31 (1908).

46. "One of the highest services the lawyer can render to society is to appear in court on behalf of clients whose causes are in disfavor with the general public." *Professional Responsibility: Report of the Joint Conference.* 44 A.B.A.J. 1159, 1216 (1958).

One author proposes the following proposition to be included in "A Proper Oath for Advocates": "I recognize that it is sometimes difficult for clients with unpopular causes to obtain proper legal representation. I will do all that I can to assure that the client with the unpopular cause is properly represented, and that the lawyer representing such a client receives credit from and support of the bar for handling such a matter." Thode, *The Ethical Standard for the Advocate*, 39 TEXAS L. REV. 575, 592 (1961).

§6068 . . . . It is the duty of an attorney:

. . . .

"(h) Never to reject, for any consideration personal to himself, the cause of the defenseless or the oppressed." CAL. BUSINESS AND PROFESSIONS CODE §6068 (West 1962). Virtually the same language is found in the Oregon statutes at ORE. REV. STATS. Ch. 9 §9.460(8).

See Rostow, *The Lawyer and His Client.* 48 A.B.A.J. 25 and 146 (1962).

47. *See* ABA CANONS OF PROFESSIONAL ETHICS, CANONS 7 and 29 (1908).

"We are of the opinion that it is not professionally improper for a lawyer to accept employment to compel another lawyer to honor the just claim of a layman. On the contrary, it is highly proper that he do so. Unfortunately, there appears to be a widespread feeling among laymen that it is difficult, if not impossible, to obtain justice when they have claims against members of the Bar because other lawyers will not accept employment to proceed against them. The honor of the profession, whose members proudly style themselves officers of the court, must surely be sullied if its members bind themselves by custom to refrain from enforcing just claims of laymen against lawyers." *ABA Opinion* 144 (1935).

48. ABA CANONS OF PROFESSIONAL ETHICS, CANON 4 (1908) uses a slightly different test, saying, "A lawyer assigned as counsel for an indigent prisoner ought not to ask to be excused for any trivial reason . . . ."

49. *Cf.* ABA CANONS OF PROFESSIONAL ETHICS, CANON 7 (1908).

50. *See* ABA CANONS OF PROFESSIONAL ETHICS, CANON 5 (1908).

51. Dr. Johnson's reply to Boswell upon being asked what he thought of "supporting a cause which you know to be bad" was: "Sir, you do not know it to be good or bad till the Judge determines it. I have said that you are to state facts fairly; so that your thinking, or what you call knowing, a cause to be bad, must be from reasoning, must be from supposing your arguments to be weak and inconclusive. But, Sir, that is not enough. An argument which does not convince yourself, may convince the Judge to whom you urge it: and if it does convince him, why, then, Sir, you are wrong, and he is right." 2 BOSWELL, THE LIFE OF JOHNSON 47-48 (Hill ed. 1887).

52. "The lawyer deciding whether to undertake a case must be able to judge objectively whether he is capable of handling it and whether he can assume its burdens without prejudice to previous commitments . . . ." *Professional Responsibility: Report of the Joint Conference*, 44 A.B.A.J. 1158, 1218 (1958).

53. "The lawyer must decline to conduct a civil cause or to make a defense when convinced that it is intended merely to harass or to injure the opposite party or to work oppression or wrong." ABA CANONS OF PROFESSIONAL ETHICS, CANON 30 (1908).

54. *See* ABA CANONS OF PROFESSIONAL ETHICS, CANON 7 (1908).

55. *Id.*

"From the facts stated we assume that the client has discharged the first attorney and given notice of the discharge. Such being the case, the second attorney may properly accept employment. *Canon 7; Opinions 10, 130, 149."ABA Opinion* 209 (1941).

56. *See* ABA CANONS OF PROFESSIONAL ETHICS, CANON 44 (1908).

"I will carefully consider, before taking a case, whether it appears that I can fully represent the client within the framework of law. If the decision is in the affirmative then it will take extreme circumstances to cause me to decide later that I cannot so represent him." Thode, *The Ethical Standard for the Advocate*, 39 TEXAS L. REV. 575, 592 (1961) (from "A Proper Oath for Advocates").

57. *ABA Opinion* 314 (l965) held that a lawyer should not disassociate himself from a cause when "it is obvious that the very act of disassociation would have the effect of violating *Canon 37*."

58. ABA CANON 44 enumerates instances in which " . . . the lawyer may be warranted in withdrawing on due notice to the client, allowing him time to employ another lawyer."

59. *See* ABA CANONS OF PROFESSIONAL ETHICS, CANON 44 (1908).

60. Amended, February 1975, House Informational Report No. 110.

61. Amended, August 1978, House Informational Report No. 130.

62. *Id.*

63. Amended, February 1976, House Informational Report No. 100.

64. *See ABA Opinion* 301 (1961).

65. "[I]t has become commonplace for many lawyers to participate in government service; to deny them the right, upon their return to private practice, to refer to their prior employment in a brief and dignified manner, would place an undue limitation upon a large element of our profession. It is entirely proper for a member of the profession to explain his absence from private practice, where such is the primary purpose of the announcement, by a brief and dignified reference to the prior employment.

". . . [A]ny such announcement should be limited to the immediate past connection of the lawyer with the government, made upon his leaving that position to enter private practice." *ABA Opinion* 301 (1961).

66. *See ABA Opinion* 251 (1943).

67. "Those lawyers who are working for an individual lawyer or a law firm may be designated on the letterhead and in other appropriate places as 'associates.' " *ABA Opinion* 310 (1963).

68. *See* ABA CANONS OF PROFESSIONAL ETHICS, CANON 33 (1908).

69. *But see ABA Opinion* 285 (1951).

70. *See* ABA CANONS OF PROFESSIONAL ETHICS, CANON 33 (1908); *cf. ABA Opinions* 318 (1967), 267 (1945), 219 (1941), 208 (1940). 192 (1939), 97 (1933), and 6 (1925).

71. *ABA Opinion* 318 (1967) held, "anything to the contrary in Formal Opinion 315 or in the other opinions cited notwithstanding that: 'Where a partner whose name appears in the name of a law firm is elected or appointed to high local, state or federal office, which office he intends to occupy only temporarily, at the end of which time he intends to return to his position with the firm, and provided that

he is not precluded by holding such office from engaging in the practice of law and does not in fact sever his relationship with the firm but only takes a leave of absence, and provided that there is no local law, statute or custom to the contrary, his name may be retained in the firm name during his term or terms of office, but only if proper precautions are taken not to mislead the public as to his degree of participation in the firm's affairs.'"

Cf. ABA Opinion 143 (1935), New York County Opinion 67, and New York City Opinions 36 and 798; *but cf. ABA Opinion* 192 (1939) and Michigan Opinion 164.

72. *Cf.* ABA CANONS OF PROFESSIONAL ETHICS, CANON 33 (1908).

73. Amended, February 1979, House Informational Report No. 123.

74. *See ABA Opinion* 277 (1948); *cf.* ABA CANONS OF PROFESSIONAL ETHICS, CANON 33 (1908) and *ABA Opinions* 318 (1967), 126 (1935), 115 (1934), 106 (1934), and 1383 (1977).

75. *See ABA Opinions* 318 (1967) and 316 (1967); *cf.* ABA CANONS OF PROFESSIONAL ETHICS, CANON 33 (1908).

76. DR 2-102(E) was deleted and DR 2-102(F) was redesignated as DR 2-102(E) in February 1980, House Informational Report No. 107.

77. *Cf.* ABA CANONS OF PROFESSIONAL ETHICS, CANON 28 (1908).

78. "We think it clear that a lawyer's seeking employment in an ordinary law office, or appointment to a civil service position, is not prohibited by . . . [Canon 27]." *ABA Opinion* 197 (1939).

79. "[A] lawyer may not seek from persons not his clients the opportunity to perform . . . a [legal] check-up." *ABA Opinion* 307 (1962).

80. *Cf. ABA Opinion* 78 (1932).

81. "No financial connection of any kind between the Brotherhood and any lawyer is permissible. No lawyer can properly pay any amount whatsoever to the Brotherhood or any of its departments, officers or members as compensation, reimbursement of expenses or gratuity in connection with the procurement of a case.'" In re Brotherhood of R. R. Trainmen, 13 I11. 2d 391, 398, 150 N. E. 2d 163, 167 (1958), *quoted in* In re Ratner, 194 Kan. 362, 372, 399 P.2d 865, 873 (1965).

See ABA Opinion 147 (1935).

82. Amended, February 1975, House Informational Report No. 110.

83. "This Court has condemned the practice of ambulance chasing through the media of runners and touters. In similar fashion we have with equal emphasis condemned the practice of direct solicitation by a lawyer. We have classified both offenses as serious breaches of the Canons of Ethics demanding severe treatment of the offending lawyer." State v. Dawson, 111 So. 2d 427, 431 (Fla. 1959).

84. "Registrants [of a lawyer referral plan] may be required to contribute to the expense of operating it by a reasonable registration charge or by a reasonable percentage of fees collected by them." *ABA Opinion* 291 (1956).

Cf. ABA Opinion 227 (1941).

85. Amended, February 1975, House Informational Report No. 110.

86. *Cf. ABA Opinion* 148 (1935).

87. United Mine Workers v. Ill. State Bar Ass'n, 389 U.S. 217, 19 L. Ed. 2d 426, 88 S. Ct. 353 (1967); Brotherhood of R.R. Trainmen v. Virginia, 371 U.S. 1, 12 L. Ed. 2d 89, 84 S. Ct. 1113 (1964); NAACP v. Button, 371 U.S. 415, 9 L. Ed. 2d 405, 83 S. Ct. 328 (1963). Also *see ABA Opinions* 332 (1973) and 333 (1973).

88. Amended, February 1975, House Informational Report No. 110.

89. "If a bar association has embarked on a program of institutional advertising for an annual legal check-up and provides brochures and reprints, it is not improper to have these available in the lawyer's office for persons to read and take." *ABA Opinion* 307 (1962).

Cf. ABA Opinion 121 (1934).

90. ABA CANONS OF PROFESSIONAL ETHICS, CANON 28 (1908).

91. *Cf. ABA Opinions* 229 (1941) and 173 (1937).

92. "It certainly is not improper for a lawyer to advise his regular clients of new statutes, court decisions, and administrative rulings, which may affect the client's interests, provided the communication is strictly limited to such information . . . .

"When such communications go to concerns or individuals other than regular clients of the lawyer, they are thinly disguised advertisements for professional employment, and are obviously improper." *ABA Opinion* 213 (1941).

"It is our opinion that where the lawyer has no reason to believe that he has been supplanted by another lawyer, it is not only his right, but it might even be his duty to advise his client of any change of fact or law which might defeat the client's testamentary purpose as expressed in the will.

"Periodic notices might be sent to the client for whom a lawyer has drawn a will, suggesting that it might be wise for the client to reexamine his will to determine whether or not there has been any change in his situation requiring a modification of his will." *ABA Opinion* 210 (1941).

Cf. ABA CANONS OF PROFESSIONAL ETHICS, CANON 28 (1908).

93. Amended, March 1974, House Informational Report No. 127.

94. Amended, February 1975, House Informational Report No. 110.

95. *Cf. ABA Opinion* 168 (1937).

96. *But cf. ABA Opinion* 111 (1934).

97. *See* ABA CANONS OF PROFESSIONAL ETHICS, CANON 45 (1908); *cf.* ABA CANONS OF PROFESSIONAL ETHICS, CANONS 43, and 46 (1908).

98. This provision is included to conform to action taken by the ABA House of Delegates at the Mid-Winter Meeting, January, 1969.

99. *See* ABA CANONS OF PROFESSIONAL ETHICS, CANON 12 (1908).

100. The charging of a "clearly excessive fee" is a ground for discipline. State ex rel. Nebraska State Bar Ass'n v. Richards, 165 Neb. 80, 90, 84 N.W.2d 136, 143 (1957).

"An attorney has the right to contract for any fee he chooses so long as it is not excessive (see Opinion 190), and this Committee is not concerned with the amount of such fees unless so excessive as to constitute a misappropriation of the client's funds (see Opinion 27)." *ABA Opinion* 320 (1968).

Cf. ABA Opinions 209 (1940), 190 (1939), and 27 (1930) and State ex rel. Lee v. Buchanan, 191 So. 2d 33 (Fla. 1966).

101. *Cf.* ABA CANONS OF PROFESSIONAL ETHICS, CANON 13 (1908); *see generally* MACKINNON, CONTINGENT FEES FOR LEGAL SERVICES (1964) (A Report of the American Bar Foundation).

102. "Contingent fees, whether in civil or criminal cases, are a special concern of the law . . . .

"In criminal cases, the rule is stricter because of the danger of corrupting justice. The second part of Section 542 of the Restatement [of Contracts] reads: 'A bargain to conduct a criminal case . . . in consideration of a promise of a fee contingent on success is illegal . . . .'" Peyton v. Margiotti, 398 Pa. 86, 156 A.2d 865, 967 (1959).

"The third area of practice in which the use of the contingent fee is generally considered to be prohibited is the prosecution and defense of criminal cases. However, there are so few cases, and these are predominantly old, that it is doubtful that there can be said to be any current law on the subject . . . . In the absence of cases on the validity of contingent fees for defense attorneys, it is necessary to rely on the consensus among commentators that such a fee is void as against public policy. The nature of criminal practice itself makes unlikely the use of contingent fee contracts." MACKINNON, CONTINGENT FEES FOR LEGAL SERVICES 52 (1964) (A Report of the American Bar Foundation).

103. *See* ABA CANONS OF PROFESSIONAL ETHICS, CANON 34 (1908) and *ABA Opinions* 316 (1967) and 294 (1958); *see generally ABA Opinions* 265 (1945), 204 (1940), 190 (1939), 171 (1937), 153 (1936), 97 (1933), 63 (1932), 28 (1930), 27 (1930), and 18 (1930).

104. "*Canon 12* contemplates that a lawyer's fee should not exceed the value of the services rendered . . . .

"*Canon 12* applies, whether joint or separate fees are charged [by associate attorneys] . . . ." *ABA Opinion* 204 (1940).

105. "[A] general covenant restricting an employed lawyer, after leaving the employment, from practicing in the community for a stated period, appears to this Committee to be an unwarranted restriction on the right of a lawyer to choose where he will practice and inconsistent with our professional status. Accordingly, the Committee is of the opinion it would be improper for the employing lawyer to require the covenant and likewise for the employed lawyer to agree to it." *ABA Opinion* 300 (1961).

106. *See* ABA CANONS OF PROFESSIONAL ETHICS, CANON 30 (1908).

"*Rule 13* . . . . A member of the State Bar shall not accept employment to prosecute or defend a case solely out of spite, or solely for the purpose of harassing or delaying another . . . ." CAL. BUSINESS AND PROFESSIONS CODE §6067 (West 1962).

107. *Cf.* ABA CANONS OF PROFESSIONAL ETHICS, CANON 44 (1908).

108. *See also* MODEL CODE OF PROFESSIONAL RESPONSIBILITY, DR 5-102 and DR 5-105.

109. *Cf.* ABA CANONS OF PROFESSIONAL ETHICS, CANON 4 (1908).

110. *Cf.* Anders v. California, 386 U.S. 738, 18 L. Ed. 2d 493, 87 S. Ct. 1396 (1967), *rehearing denied*, 388 U.S. 924, 18 L. Ed. 2d 1377, 87 S. Ct. 2094 (1967).

CANON 3
A Lawyer Should Assist In Preventing the Unauthorized Practice of Law

ETHICAL CONSIDERATIONS

EC 3-1 The prohibition against the practice of law by a layman is grounded in the need of the public for integrity and competence of those who undertake to render legal services. Because of the fiduciary and personal character of the lawyer-client relationship and the inherently complex nature of our legal system, the public can better be assured of the requisite responsibility and competence if the practice of law is confined to those who are subject to the requirements and regulations imposed upon members of the legal profession.

EC 3-2 The sensitive variations in the considerations that bear on legal determinations often make it difficult even for a lawyer to exercise appropriate professional judgment, and it is therefore essential that the personal nature of the relationship of client and lawyer be preserved. Competent professional judgment is the product of a trained familiarity with law and legal processes, a disciplined, analytical approach to legal problems, and a firm ethical commitment.

EC 3-3 A non-lawyer who undertakes to handle legal matters is not governed as to integrity or legal competence by the same rules that govern the conduct of a lawyer. A lawyer is not only subject to that regulation but also is committed to high standards of ethical conduct. The public interest is best served in legal matters by a regulated profession committed to such standards.[1] The Disciplinary Rules protect the public in that they prohibit a lawyer from seeking employment by improper overtures, from acting in cases of divided loyalties, and from submitting to the control of others in the exercise of his judgment. Moreover, a person who entrusts legal matters to a lawyer is protected by the attorney-client privilege and by the duty of the lawyer to hold inviolate the confidences and secrets of his client.

EC 3-4 A layman who seeks legal services often is not in a position to judge whether he will receive proper professional attention. The entrustment of a legal matter may well involve the confidences, the reputation, the property, the freedom, or even the life of the client. Proper protection of members of the public demands that no person be permitted to act in the confidential and demanding capacity of a lawyer unless he is subject to the regulations of the legal profession.

EC 3-5 It is neither necessary nor desirable to attempt the formulation of a single, specific definition of what constitutes the practice of law.[2] Functionally, the practice of law relates to the rendition of services for others that call for the professional judgment of a lawyer. The essence of the professional judgment of the lawyer is his educated ability to relate the general body and philosophy of law to a specific legal problem of a client; and thus, the public interest will be better served if only lawyers are permitted to act in matters involving professional judgment. Where this professional judgment is not involved, non-lawyers, such as court clerks, police officers, abstracters, and many governmental employees, may engage in occupations that require a special knowledge of law in certain areas. But the services of a lawyer are essential in the public interest whenever the exercise of professional legal judgment is required.

EC 3-6 A lawyer often delegates tasks to clerks, secretaries, and other lay persons. Such delegation is proper if the lawyer maintains a direct relationship with his client, supervises the delegated work, and has complete professional responsibility for the work product.[3] This delegation enables a lawyer to render legal service more economically and efficiently.

EC 3-7 The prohibition against a non-lawyer practicing law does not prevent a layman from representing himself, for then he is ordinarily exposing only himself to possible injury. The purpose of the legal profession is to make educated legal representation available to the public; but anyone who does not wish to avail himself of such representation is not required to do so. Even so, the legal profession should help members of the public to recognize legal problems and to understand why it may be unwise for them to act for themselves in matters having legal consequences.

EC 3-8 Since a lawyer should not aid or encourage a layman to practice law, he should not practice law in association with a layman or otherwise share legal fees with a layman.[4] This does not mean, however, that the pecuniary value of the interest of a deceased lawyer in his firm or practice may not be paid to his estate or specified persons such as his widow or heirs.[5] In like manner, profit-sharing retirement plans of a lawyer or law firm which include non-lawyer office employees are not improper.[6] These limited exceptions to the rule against sharing legal fees with laymen are permissible since they do not aid or encourage laymen to practice law.

EC 3-9 Regulation of the practice of law is accomplished principally by the respective states.[7] Authority to engage in the practice of law conferred in any jurisdiction is not per se a grant of the right to practice elsewhere, and it is improper for a lawyer to engage in practice where he is not permitted by law or by court order to do so. However, the demands of business and the mobility of our society pose distinct problems in the regulation of the practice of law by the states.[8] In furtherance of the public interest, the legal profession should discourage regulation that unreasonably imposes territorial limitations upon the right of a lawyer to handle the legal affairs of his client or upon the opportunity of a client to obtain the services of a lawyer of his choice in all matters including the presentation of a contested matter in a tribunal before which the lawyer is not permanently admitted to practice.[9]

DISCIPLINARY RULES

DR 3-101 Aiding Unauthorized Practice of Law.[10]

(A) A lawyer shall not aid a non-lawyer in the unauthorized practice of law.[11]
(B) A lawyer shall not practice law in a jurisdiction where to do so would be in violation of regulations of the profession in that jurisdiction.[12]

DR 3-102 Dividing Legal Fees with a Non-Lawyer.

(A) A lawyer or law firm shall not share legal fees with a non-lawyer,[13] except that:
  (1) An agreement by a lawyer with his firm, partner, or associate may provide for the payment of money, over a reasonable period of time after his death, to his estate or to one or more specified persons.[14]
  (2) A lawyer who undertakes to complete unfinished legal business of a deceased lawyer may pay to the estate of the deceased lawyer that proportion of the total compensation which fairly represents the services rendered by the deceased lawyer.
  (3) A lawyer or law firm may include non-lawyer employees in a retirement plan, even though the plan is based in whole or in part on a profit-sharing arrangement,[15] providing such plan does not circumvent another Disciplinary Rule.[16, 17]

DR 3-103 Forming a Partnership with a Non-Lawyer.

(A) A lawyer shall not form a partnership with a non-lawyer if any of the activities of the partnership consist of the practice of law.[18]

NOTES

1. "The condemnation of the unauthorized practice of law is designed to protect the public from legal services by persons unskilled in the law. The prohibition of lay intermediaries is intended to insure the loyalty of the lawyer to the client unimpaired by intervening and possibly conflicting interests." Cheatham, *Availability of Legal Services: The Responsibility of the Individual Lawyer and of the Organized Bar*, 12 U.C.L.A. L. REV. 438, 439 (1965).

2. "What constitutes unauthorized practice of the law in a particular jurisdiction is a matter for determination by the courts of that jurisdiction." *ABA Opinion* 198 (1939).

"In the light of the historical development of the lawyer's functions, it is impossible to lay down an exhaustive definition of 'the practice of law' by attempting to enumerate every conceivable act performed by lawyers in the normal course of their work." State Bar of Arizona v. Arizona Land Title & Trust Co., 90 Ariz., 76, 87, 366 P.2d 1, 8-9 (1961), *modified*, 91 Ariz. 293, 371 P.2d 1020 (1962).

3. "A lawyer can employ lay secretaries, lay investigators, lay detectives, lay researchers, accountants, lay scriveners, nonlawyer draftsmen or nonlawyer researchers. In fact, he may employ nonlawyers to do any task for him except counsel clients about law matters, engage directly in the practice of law, appear in court or appear in formal proceedings that are a part of the judicial process, so long as it is he who takes the work and vouches for it to the client and becomes responsible to the client." *ABA Opinion* 316 (1967).

ABA Opinion 316 (1967) also stated that if a lawyer practices law as part of a law firm which includes lawyers from several states, he may delegate tasks to firm members in other states so long as he "is the person who, on behalf of the firm, vouched for the work of all of the others and, with the client and in the courts, did the legal acts defined by that state as the practice of law."

"A lawyer cannot delegate his professional responsibility to a law student employed in his office. He may avail himself of the assistance of the student in many of the fields of the lawyer's work, such as examination of case law, finding and interviewing witnesses, making collections of claims, examining court records, delivering papers, conveying important messages, and other similar matters. But the student is not permitted, until he is admitted to the Bar, to perform the professional functions of a lawyer, such as conducting court trials, giving professional advice to clients or drawing legal documents for them. The student in all his work must act as agent for the lawyer employing him, who must supervise his work and be responsible for his good conduct." *ABA Opinion* 85 (1932).

4. "No division of fees for legal services is proper, except with another lawyer . . . ." ABA CANONS OF PROFESSIONAL ETHICS, CANON 34 (1908). Otherwise, according to *ABA Opinion* 316 (1967), "[t]he Canons of Ethics do not examine into the method by which such persons are remunerated by the lawyer . . . . They may be paid a salary, a per diem charge, a flat fee, a contract price, etc."

See ABA CANONS OF PROFESSIONAL ETHICS, CANONS 33 and 47 (1908).

5. "Many partnership agreements provide that the active partners, on the death of any one of them, are to make payments to the estate or to the nominee of a deceased partner on a pre-determined formula. It is only where the effect of such an arrangement is to make the estate or nominee a member of the partnership along with the surviving partners that it is prohibited by *Canon 34*. Where the payments are made in accordance with a pre-existing agreement entered into by the deceased partner during his lifetime and providing for a fixed method for determining their amount based upon the value of services rendered during the partner's lifetime and providing for a fixed period over which the payments are to be made, this is not the case. Under these circumstances, whether the payments are considered to be delayed payment of compensation earned but withheld during the partner's lifetime, or whether they are considered to be an approximation of his interest in matters pending at the time of his death, is immaterial. In either event, as Henry S. Drinker says in his book, LEGAL ETHICS, at page 189: 'It would seem, however, that a reasonable agreement to pay the estate a proportion of the receipts for a reasonable period is a proper practical settlement for the lawyer's services to his retirement or death.'" *ABA Opinion* 308 (1963).

6. *Cf. ABA Opinion* 311 (1964).

7. "That the States have broad power to regulate the practice of law is, of course, beyond question." United Mine Workers v. Ill. State Bar Ass'n, 389 U.S. 217, 222 (1967).

"It is a matter of law, not of ethics, as to where an individual may practice law. Each state has its own rules." *ABA Opinion* 316 (1967).

8. "Much of clients' business crosses state lines. People are mobile, moving from state to state. Many metropolitan areas cross state lines. It is common today to have a single economic and social community involving more than one state. The business of a single client may involve legal problems in several states." *ABA Opinion* 316 (1967).

9. "[W]e reaffirmed the general principle that legal services to New Jersey residents with respect to New Jersey matters may ordinarily be furnished only by New Jersey counsel; but we pointed out that there may be multistate transactions where strict adherence to this thesis would not be in the public interest and that, under the circumstances, it would have been not only more costly to the client but also 'grossly impractical and inefficient' to have had the settlement negotiations conducted by separate lawyers from different states." In re Estate of Waring, 47 N.J. 367, 376, 221 A.2d 193, 197 (1966).

Cf. ABA Opinion 316 (1967).

10. Conduct permitted by Disciplinary Rules of Canons 2 and 5 does not violate DR 3-101.

11. *See* ABA CANONS OF PROFESSIONAL ETHICS, CANON 47 (1908).

12. It should be noted, however, that a lawyer may engage in conduct, otherwise prohibited by this Disciplinary Rule, where such conduct is authorized by preemptive federal legislation. *See* Sperry v. Florida, 373 U.S. 379, 10 L. Ed. 2d 428, 83 S. Ct. 1322 (1963).

13. *See* ABA CANONS OF PROFESSIONAL ETHICS, CANON 34 (1908) and *ABA Opinions* 316 (1967), 180 (1938), and 48 (1931).

"The receiving attorney shall not under any guise or form share his fee for legal services with a lay agency, personal or corporate, without prejudice, however, to the right of the lay forwarder to charge and collect from the creditor proper compensation for non-legal services rendered by the law [*sic*] forwarder which are separate and apart from the services performed by the receiving attorney." *ABA Opinion* 294 (1958).

14. *See ABA Opinion* 266 (1945).
15. *Cf. ABA Opinion* 311 (1964).
16. *See ABA Opinion* 1440
17. Amended, February 1980, House Informational Report No. 107.
18. *See* ABA CANONS OF PROFESSIONAL ETHICS, CANON 33 (1908); *cf. ABA Opinions* 239 (1942) and 201 (1940)

ABA Opinion 316 (1967) states that lawyers licensed in different jurisdictions may, under certain conditions, enter "into an arrangement for the practice of law" and that a lawyer licensed in State A is not, for such purpose, a layman in State B.

CANON 4
A Lawyer Should Preserve the Confidences and Secrets of a Client

ETHICAL CONSIDERATIONS

EC 4-1 Both the fiduciary relationship existing between lawyer and client and the proper functioning of the legal system require the preservation by the lawyer of confidences and secrets of one who has employed or sought to employ him.[1] A client must feel free to discuss whatever he wishes with his lawyer and a lawyer must be equally free to obtain information beyond that volunteered by his client.[2] A lawyer should be fully informed of all the facts of the matter he is handling in order for his client to obtain the full advantage of our legal system. It is for the lawyer in the exercise of his independent professional judgment to separate the relevant and important from the irrelevant and unimportant. The observance of the ethical obligation of a lawyer to hold inviolate the confidences and secrets of his client not only facilitates the full development of facts essential to proper representation of the client but also encourages laymen to seek early legal assistance.

EC 4-2 The obligation to protect confidences and secrets obviously does not preclude a lawyer from revealing information when his client consents after full disclosure,[3] when necessary to perform his professional employment, when permitted by a Disciplinary Rule, or when required by law. Unless the client otherwise directs, a lawyer may disclose the affairs of his client to partners or associates of his firm. It is a matter of common knowledge that the normal operation of a law office exposes confidential professional information to non-lawyer employees of the office, particularly secretaries and those having access to the files; and this obligates a lawyer to exercise care in selecting and training his employees so that the sanctity of all confidences and secrets of his clients may be preserved. If the obligation extends to two or more clients as to the same information, a lawyer should obtain the permission of all before revealing the information. A lawyer must always be sensitive to the rights and wishes of his client and act scrupulously in the making of decisions which may involve the disclosure of information obtained in his professional relationship.[4] Thus, in the absence of consent of his client after full disclosure, a lawyer should not associate another lawyer in the handling of a matter; nor should he, in the absence of consent, seek counsel from another lawyer if there is a reasonable possibility that the identity of the client or his confidences or secrets would be revealed to such lawyer. Both social amenities and professional duty should cause a lawyer to shun indiscreet conversations concerning his clients.

EC 4-3 Unless the client otherwise directs, it is not improper for a lawyer to give limited information from his files to an outside agency necessary for statistical, bookkeeping, accounting, data processing, banking, printing, or other legitimate purposes, provided he exercises due care in the selection of the agency and warns the agency that the information must be kept confidential.

EC 4-4 The attorney-client privilege is more limited than the ethical obligation of a lawyer to guard the confidences and secrets of his client. This ethical precept, unlike the evidentiary privilege, exists without regard to the nature or source of information or the fact that others share the knowledge. A lawyer should endeavor to act in a manner which preserves the evidentiary privilege; for example, he should avoid professional discussions in the presence of persons to whom the privilege does not extend. A lawyer owes an obligation to advise the client of the attorney-client privilege and timely to assert the privilege unless it is waived by the client.

EC 4-5 A lawyer should not use information acquired in the course of the representation of a client to the disadvantage of the client and a lawyer should not use, except with the consent of his client after full disclosure, such information for his own purposes.[5] Likewise, a lawyer should be diligent in his efforts to prevent the misuse of such information by his employees and associates.[6] Care should be exercised by a lawyer to prevent the disclosure of the confidences and secrets of one client to another,[7] and no employment should be accepted that might require such disclosure.

EC 4-6 The obligation of a lawyer to preserve the confidences and secrets of his client continues after the termination of his employment.[8] Thus a lawyer should not attempt to sell a law practice as a going business because, among other reasons, to do so would involve the disclosure of confidences and secrets.[9] A lawyer should also provide for the protection of the confidences and secrets of his client following the termination of the practice of the lawyer, whether termination is due to death, disability, or retirement. For example, a lawyer might provide for the personal papers of the client to be returned to him and for the papers of the lawyer to be delivered to another lawyer or to be destroyed. In determining the method of disposition, the instructions and wishes of the client should be a dominant consideration.

DISCIPLINARY RULES

DR 4-101 Preservation of Confidences and Secrets of a Client.[10]

(A) "Confidence" refers to information protected by the attorney-client privilege under applicable law, and "secret" refers to other information gained in the professional relationship that the client has requested be held inviolate or the disclosure of which would be embarrassing or would be likely to be detrimental to the client.

(B) Except when permitted under DR 4-101(C), a lawyer shall not knowingly:

(1) Reveal a confidence or secret of his client.[11]

(2) Use a confidence or secret of his client to the disadvantage of the client.

(3) Use a confidence or secret of his client for the advantage of himself[12] or of a third person,[13] unless the client consents after full disclosure.

(C) A lawyer may reveal:

(1) Confidences or secrets with the consent of the client or clients affected, but only after a full disclosure to them.[14]

(2) Confidences or secrets when permitted under Disciplinary Rules or required by law or court order.[15]

(3) The intention of his client to commit a crime[16] and the information necessary to prevent the crime.[17]

(4) Confidences or secrets necessary to establish or collect his fee[18] or to defend himself or his employees or associates against an accusation of wrongful conduct.[19]

(D) A lawyer shall exercise reasonable care to prevent his employees, associates, and others whose services are utilized by him from disclosing or using confidences or secrets of a client, except that a lawyer may reveal the information allowed by DR 4-101(C) through an employee.

NOTES

1. *See* ABA CANONS OF PROFESSIONAL ETHICS, CANONS 6 and 37 (1908) and *ABA Opinion* 287 (1953).

"The reason underlying the rule with respect to confidential communications between attorney and client is well stated in MECHEM ON AGENCY, 2d Ed., Vol. 2, §2297, as follows: 'The purposes and necessities of the relation between a client and his attorney require, in many cases, on the part of the client, the fullest and freest disclosures to the attorney of the client's objects, motives and acts. This disclosure is made in the strictest confidence, relying upon the attorney's honor and fidelity. To permit the attorney to reveal to others what is so disclosed, would be not only a gross violation of a sacred trust upon his part, but it would utterly destroy and prevent the usefulness and benefits to be derived from professional assistance. Based upon considerations of public policy, therefore, the law wisely declares that all confidential communications and disclosures, made by a client to his legal adviser for the purpose of obtaining his professional aid or advice shall be strictly privileged;—that the attorney shall not be permitted, without the consent of his client,—and much less will he be compelled—to reveal or disclose communications made to him under such circumstances.' *ABA Opinion* 250(1943).

"While it is true that complete revelation of relevant facts should be encouraged for trial purposes, nevertheless an attorney's dealings with his client, if both are sincere, and if the dealings involve more than mere technical matters, should be immune to discovery proceedings. There must be freedom from fear of revealment of matters disclosed to an attorney because of the peculiarly intimate relationship existing." Ellis-Foster Co. v. Union Carbide & Carbon Corp., 159 F. Supp. 917, 919 (D.N.J. 1958).

Cf. ABA Opinions 314 (1965), 274 (1946) and 268 (1945).

2. "While it is the great purpose of law to ascertain the truth, there is the countervailing necessity of insuring the right of every person to freely and fully confer and confide in one having knowledge of the law, and skilled in its practice, in order that the former may have adequate advice and a proper defense. This assistance can be made safely and readily available only when the client is free from the consequences of apprehension of disclosure by reason of the subsequent statements of the skilled lawyer." Baird v. Koemer, 279 F.2d 623, 629-30 (9th Cir. 1960).

Cf. ABA Opinion 150 (1936).

3. "Where . . . [a client] knowingly and after full disclosure participates in a [legal fee] financing plan which requires the furnishing of certain information to the bank, clearly by his conduct he has waived any privilege as to that information." *ABA Opinion* 320 (1968)

4. "The lawyer must decide when he takes a case whether it is a suitable one for him to undertake and after this decision is made, he is not justified in turning against his client by exposing injurious evidence entrusted to him . . . . [D]oing something intrinsically regrettable, because the only alternative involves worse consequences, is a necessity in every profession." WILLISTON, LIFE AND LAW 271 (1940).

Cf. ABA Opinions 177 (1938) and 83 (1932).

5. *See* ABA CANONS OF PROFESSIONAL ETHICS, CANON 11 (1908).

6. *See* ABA CANONS OF PROFESSIONAL ETHICS, CANON 37 (1908).

7. *See* ABA CANONS OF PROFESSIONAL ETHICS, CANONS 6 and 37 (1908).

"[A]n attorney must not accept professional employment against a client or a former client which will, or even may require him to use confidential information obtained by the attorney in the course of his professional relations with such client regarding the subject matter of the employment . . . ." *ABA Opinion* 165 (1936).

8. *See* ABA CANONS OF PROFESSIONAL ETHICS, CANON 37 (1908).

"Confidential communications between an attorney and his client, made because of the relationship and concerning the subject-matter of the attorney's employment, are generally privileged from disclosure without the consent of the client, and this privilege outlasts the attorney's employment. *Canon 37.*" *ABA Opinion* 154 (1936).

9. *Cf. ABA Opinion* 266 (1945).

10. *See* ABA CANONS OF PROFESSIONAL ETHICS, CANON 37 (1908); *cf.* ABA CANONS OF PROFESSIONAL ETHICS, CANON 6 (1908).

11. "§6068 . . . It is the duty of an attorney:

. . . .

"(e) To maintain inviolate the confidence, and at every peril to himself to preserve the secrets, of his client. CAL. BUSINESS AND PROFESSIONS CODE §6068 (West 1962). Virtually the same provision is found in the Oregon statutes. ORE. REV. STATS. ch. 9 §9.460(5).

"Communication between lawyer and client are privileged (WIGMORE ON EVIDENCE, 3d Ed., Vol. 8,§§2290-2329). The modem theory underlying the privilege is subjective and is to give the client freedom of apprehension in consulting his legal adviser (*ibid.*, §2290, p. 548). The privilege applies to communications made in seeking legal advice for any purpose (*ibid.*, §2294, p.563). The mere circumstance that the advice is given without charge therefor does not nullify the privilege (*ibid.*,§2303)." *ABA Opinion* 216 (1941).

"It is the duty of an attorney to maintain the confidence and preserve inviolate the secrets of his client . . . ." *ABA Opinion* 155 (1936).

12. *See* ABA CANONS OF PROFESSIONAL ETHICS, CANON 11 (1908).

"The provision respecting employment is in accord with the general rule announced in the adjudicated cases that a lawyer may not make use of knowledge or information acquired by him through his professional relations with his client, or in the conduct of his client's business, to his own advantage or profit (7 C.J.S., § 125, p. 958, Healy v. Gray, 184 Iowa 111, 168 N.W 222; Baumgardner v. Hudson, D.C. App., 277 F. 552; Goodrum v. Clement, D.C App., 277 F. 586)" *ABA Opinion* 250 (1943).

13. *See ABA Opinion* 177 (1938).

14. "[A lawyer] may not divulge confidential communications, information, and secrets imparted to

him by the client or acquired during their professional relations unless he is authorized to do so by the client (People v. Gerold, 265 Ill. 448, 107 N.E. 165, 178; Murphy v. Riggs, 238 Mich. 151, 213 N.W. 110, 112; 0pinion of this Committee, No. 91)." *ABA Opinion* 202 (1940).

Cf. ABA Opinion 91 (1933).

15. "A defendant in a criminal case when admitted to bail is not only regarded as in the custody of his bail, but he is also in the custody of the law, and admission to bail does not deprive the court of its inherent power to deal with the person of the prisoner. Being in lawful custody, the defendant is guilty of an escape when he gains his liberty before he is delivered in due process of law, and is guilty of a separate offense for which he may be punished. In failing to disclose his client's whereabouts as a fugitive under these circumstances the attorney would not only be aiding his client to escape trial on the charge for which he was indicted, but would likewise be aiding him in evading prosecution for the additional offense of escape.

"It is the opinion of the committee that under such circumstances the attorney's knowledge of his client's whereabouts is not privileged, and that he may be disciplined for failing to disclose that information to the proper authorities . . . ." *ABA Opinion* 155 (1936).

"We held in Opinion 155 that a communication by a client to his attorney in respect to the future commission of an unlawful act or to a continuing wrong is not privileged from disclosure. Public policy forbids that the relation of attorney and client should be used to conceal wrongdoing on the part of the client.

. . . .

"When an attorney representing a defendant in a criminal case applies on his behalf for probation or suspension of sentence, he represents to the court, by implication at least, that his client will abide by the terms and conditions of the court's order. When that attorney is later advised of a violation of that order, it is his duty to advise his client of the consequences of his act, and endeavor to prevent a continuance of the wrongdoing. If his client thereafter persists in violating the terms and conditions of his probation, it is the duty of the attorney as an officer of the court to advise the proper authorities concerning his client's conduct. Such information, even though coming to the attorney from the client in the course of his professional relations with respect to other matters in which he represents the defendant, is not privileged from disclosure . . . ."

See ABA Opinion 156 (1936).

16. *ABA Opinion* 314 (1965) indicates that a lawyer must disclose even the confidences of his clients if "the facts in the attorney's possession indicate beyond reasonable doubt that a crime will be committed."

See ABA Opinion 155 (1936).

17. *See* ABA CANONS OF PROFESSIONAL ETHICS, CANON 37 (1908) and *ABA Opinion* (1940).

18. *Cf. ABA Opinion* 250 (1943)

19. *See* ABA CANONS OF PROFESSIONAL ETHICS, CANON 37 (1908) and *ABA Opinions* 202 (1940) and 19 (1930).

"[T]he adjudicated cases recognize an exception to the rule [that a lawyer shall not reveal the confidences of his client], where disclosure is necessary to protect the attorney's interests arising out of the relation of attorney and client in which disclosure was made.

"The exception is stated in MECHEM ON AGENCY, 2d Ed., Vol. 2, §2313, as follows: 'But the attorney may disclose information received from the client when it becomes necessary for his own protection, as if the client should bring an action against the attorney for negligence or misconduct, and it became necessary for the attorney to show what his instructions were, or what was the nature of the duty which the client expected him to perform. So if it became necessary for the attorney to bring an action against the client, the client's privilege could not prevent the attorney from disclosing what was essential as a means of obtaining or defending his own rights.'

"Mr Jones, in his COMMENTARIES ON EVIDENCE, 2d Ed., Vol. 5, §2165, states the exception thus: 'It has frequently been held that the rule as to privileged communications does not apply when litigation arises between attorney and client to the extent that their communications are relevant to the issue. In such cases, if the disclosure of privileged communications becomes necessary to protect the attorney's rights, he is released from those obligations of secrecy which the law places upon him. He should not, however, disclose more than is necessary for his own protection. It would be a manifest injustice to allow the client to take advantage of the rule of exclusion as to professional confidence to the prejudice of his attorney, or that it should be carried to the extent of depriving the attorney of the means of obtaining or defending his own rights. In such cases the attorney is exempted from the obligations of secrecy.' " *ABA Opinion* 250 (1943).

CANON 5
A Lawyer Should Exercise Independent Professional Judgment on Behalf of a Client

ETHICAL CONSIDERATIONS

EC 5-1 The professional judgment of a lawyer should be exercised, within the bounds of the law, solely for the benefit of his client and free of compromising influences and loyalties.[1] Neither his personal interests, the interests of other clients, nor the desires of third persons should be permitted to dilute his loyalty to his client.

Interests of a Lawyer That May Affect His Judgment

EC 5-2 A lawyer should not accept proffered employment if his personal interests or desires will, or there is a reasonable probability that they will, affect adversely the advice to be given or services to be rendered the prospective client.[2] After accepting employment, a lawyer carefully should refrain from acquiring a property right or assuming a position that would tend to make his judgment less protective of the interests of his client.

EC 5-3 The self-interest of a lawyer resulting from his ownership of property in which his client also has an interest or which may affect property of his client may interfere with the exercise of free judgment on behalf of his client. If such interference would occur with respect to a prospective client, a lawyer should decline employment proffered by him. After accepting employment, a lawyer should not acquire property rights that would adversely affect his professional judgment in the representation of his client. Even if the property interests of a lawyer do not presently interfere with the exercise of his independent judgment, but the likelihood of interference can reasonably be foreseen by him, a lawyer should explain the situation to his client and should decline employment or withdraw unless the client consents to the continuance of the relationship after full disclosure. A lawyer should not seek to persuade his client to permit him to invest in an undertaking of his client nor make improper use of his professional relationship to influence his client to invest in an enterprise in which the lawyer is interested.

EC 5-4 If, in the course of his representation of a client, a lawyer is permitted to receive from his client a beneficial ownership in publication rights relating to the subject matter of the employment, he may be tempted to subordinate the interests of his client to his own anticipated pecuniary gain. For example, a lawyer in a criminal case who obtains from his client television, radio, motion picture, newspaper, magazine, book, or other publication rights with respect to the case may be influenced, consciously or unconsciously, to a course of conduct that will enhance the value of his publication rights to the prejudice of his client. To prevent these potentially differing interests, such arrangements should be scrupulously avoided prior to the termination of all aspects of the matter giving rise to the employment, even though his employment has previously ended.

EC 5-5 A lawyer should not suggest to his client that a gift be made to himself or for his benefit. If a lawyer accepts a gift from his client, he is peculiarly susceptible to the charge that he unduly influenced or overreached the client. If a client voluntarily offers to make a gift to his lawyer, the lawyer may accept the gift, but before doing so, he should urge that his client secure disinterested advice from an independent, competent person who is cognizant of all the circumstances.[3] Other than in exceptional circumstances, a lawyer should insist that an instrument in which his client desires to name him beneficially be prepared by another lawyer selected by the client.[4]

EC 5-6 A lawyer should not consciously influence a client to name him as executor, trustee, or lawyer in an instrument. In those cases where a client wishes to name his lawyer as such, care should be taken by the lawyer to avoid even the appearance of impropriety.[5]

EC 5-7 The possibility of an adverse effect upon the exercise of free judgment by a lawyer on behalf of his client during litigation generally makes it undesirable for the lawyer to acquire a proprietary interest in the cause of his client or otherwise to become financially interested in the outcome of the litigation.[6] However, it is not improper for a lawyer to protect his right to collect a fee for his services by the assertion of legally permissible liens, even though by doing so he may acquire an interest in the outcome of litigation. Although a contingent fee arrangement[7] gives a lawyer a financial interest in the outcome of litigation, a reasonable contingent fee is permissible in civil cases because it may be the only means by which a layman can obtain the services of a lawyer of his choice. But a lawyer, because he is in a better position to evaluate a cause of action, should enter into a contingent fee arrangement only in those instances where the arrangement will be beneficial to the client.

EC 5-8 A financial interest in the outcome of litigation also results if monetary advances are made by the lawyer to his client.[8] Although this assistance generally is not encouraged, there are instances when it is not improper to make loans to a client. For example, the advancing or guaranteeing of payment of the costs and expenses of litigation by a lawyer may be the only way a client can enforce his cause of action,[9] but the ultimate liability for such costs and expenses must be that of the client.

EC 5-9 Occasionally a lawyer is called upon to decide in a particular case whether he will be a witness or an advocate. If a lawyer is both counsel and witness, he becomes more easily impeachable for interest and thus may be a less effective witness. Conversely, the opposing counsel may be handicapped in challenging the credibility of the lawyer when the lawyer also appears as an advocate in the case. An advocate who becomes a witness is in the unseemly and ineffective position of arguing his own credibility. The roles of an advocate and of a witness are inconsistent; the function of an advocate is to advance or argue the cause of another, while that of a witness is to state facts objectively.

EC 5-10 Problems incident to the lawyer-witness relationship arise at different stages; they relate either to whether a lawyer should accept employment or should withdraw from employment.[10] Regardless of when the problem arises, his decision is to be governed by the same basic considerations. It is not objectionable for a lawyer who is a potential witness to be an advocate if it is unlikely that he will be called as a witness because his testimony would be merely cumulative or if his testimony will relate only to an uncontested issue.[11] In the exceptional situation where it will be manifestly unfair to the client for the lawyer to refuse employment or to withdraw when he will likely be a witness on a contested issue, he may serve as advocate even though he may be a witness.[12] In making such decision, he should determine the personal or financial sacrifice of the client that may result from his refusal of employment or withdrawal therefrom, the materiality of his testimony, and the effectiveness of his representation in view of his personal involvement. In weighing these factors, it should be clear that refusal or withdrawal will impose an unreasonable hardship upon the client before the lawyer accepts or continues the employment.[13] Where the question arises, doubts should be resolved in favor of the lawyer testifying and against his becoming or continuing as an advocate.[14]

EC 5-11 A lawyer should not permit his personal interests to influence his advice relative to a suggestion by his client that additional counsel be employed.[15] In like manner, his personal interests should not deter him from suggesting that additional counsel be employed; on the contrary, he should be alert to the desirability of recommending additional counsel when, in his judgment, the proper representation of his client requires it. However, a lawyer should advise his client not to employ additional counsel suggested by the client if the lawyer believes that such employment would be a disservice to the client, and he should disclose the reasons for his belief.

EC 5-12 Inability of co-counsel to agree on a matter vital to the representation of their client requires that their disagreement be submitted by them jointly to their client for his resolution, and the decision of the client shall control the action to be taken.[16]

EC 5-13 A lawyer should not maintain membership in or be influenced by any organization of employees that undertakes to prescribe, direct, or suggest when or how he should fulfill his professional obligations to a person or organization that employs him as a lawyer. Although it is not necessarily improper for a lawyer employed by a corporation or similar entity to be a member of an organization of employees, he should be vigilant to safeguard his fidelity as a lawyer to his employer, free from outside influences.

Interests of Multiple Clients

EC 5-14 Maintaining the independence of professional judgment required of a lawyer precludes his acceptance or continuation of employment that will adversely affect his judgment on behalf of or dilute his loyalty to a client.[17] This problem arises whenever a lawyer is asked to represent two or more clients who may have differing interests, whether such interests be conflicting, inconsistent, diverse, or otherwise discordant.[18]

EC 5-15 If a lawyer is requested to undertake or to continue representation of multiple clients having potentially differing interests, he must weigh carefully the possibility that his judgment may be impaired or his loyalty divided if he accepts or continues the employment. He should resolve all doubts against the propriety of the representation. A lawyer should never represent in litigation multiple clients with differing interests;[19] and there are few situations in which he would be justified in representing in litigation multiple clients with potentially differing interests. If a lawyer accepted such employment and the interests did become actually differing, he would have to withdraw from employment with likelihood of resulting hardship on the clients; and for this reason it is preferable that he refuse the employment initially. On the other hand, there are many instances in which a lawyer may properly serve multiple clients having potentially differing interests in matters not involving litigation. If the interests vary only slightly, it is generally likely that the lawyer will not be subjected to an adverse influence and that he can retain his independent judgment on behalf of each client; and if the interests become differing, withdrawal is less likely to have a disruptive effect upon the causes of his clients.

EC 5-16 In those instances in which a lawyer is justified in representing two or more clients having differing interests, it is nevertheless essential that each client be given the opportunity to evaluate his need for representation free of any potential conflict and to obtain other counsel if he so desires.[20] Thus before a lawyer may represent multiple clients, he should explain fully to each client the implications of the common representation and should accept or continue employment only if the clients consent.[21] If there are present other circumstances that might cause any of the multiple clients to question the undivided loyalty of the lawyer, he should also advise all of the clients of those circumstances.[22]

EC 5-17 Typically recurring situations involving potentially differing interests are those in which a lawyer is asked to represent co-defendants in a criminal case, co-plaintiffs in a personal injury case, an insured and his insurer,[23] and beneficiaries of the estate of a decedent. Whether a lawyer can fairly and adequately protect the interests of multiple clients in these and similar situations depends upon an analysis of each case. In certain circumstances, there may exist little chance of the judgment of the lawyer being adversely affected by the slight possibility that the interests will become actually differing; in other circumstances, the chance of adverse effect upon his judgment is not unlikely.

EC 5-18 A lawyer employed or retained by a corporation or similar entity owes his allegiance to the entity and not to a stockholder, director, officer, employee, representative, or other person connected with the entity. In advising the entity, a lawyer should keep paramount its interests and his professional judgment should not be influenced by the personal desires of any person or organization. Occasionally a lawyer for an entity is requested by a stockholder, director, officer, employee, representative, or other person connected with the entity to represent him in an individual capacity; in such case the lawyer may serve the individual only if the lawyer is convinced that differing interests are not present.

EC 5–19 A lawyer may represent several clients whose interests are not actually or potentially differing. Nevertheless, he should explain any circumstances that might cause a client to question his undivided loyalty.[24] Regardless of the belief of a lawyer that he may properly represent multiple clients, he must defer to a client who holds the contrary belief and withdraw from representation of that client.

EC 5–20 A lawyer is often asked to serve as an impartial arbitrator or mediator in matters which involve present or former clients. He may serve in either capacity if he first discloses such present or former relationships. After a lawyer has undertaken to act as an impartial arbitrator or mediator, he should not thereafter represent in the dispute any of the parties involved.

Desires of Third Persons

EC 5-21 The obligation of a lawyer to exercise professional judgment solely on behalf of his client requires that he disregard the desires of others that might impair his free judgment.[25] The desires of a third person will seldom adversely affect a lawyer unless that person is in a position to exert strong economic, political, or social pressures upon the lawyer. These influences are often subtle, and a lawyer must be alert to their existence. A lawyer subjected to outside pressures should make full disclosure of them to his client;[26] and if he or his client believes that the effectiveness of his representation has been or will be impaired thereby, the lawyer should take proper steps to withdraw from representation of his client.

EC 5-22 Economic, political, or social pressures by third persons are less likely to impinge upon the independent judgment of a lawyer in a matter in which he is compensated directly by his client and his professional work is exclusively with his client. On the other hand, if a lawyer is compensated from a source other than his client, he may feel a sense of responsibility to someone other than his client.

EC 5-23 A person or organization that pays or furnishes lawyers to represent others possesses a potential power to exert strong pressures against the independent judgment of those lawyers. Some employers may be interested in furthering their own economic, political, or social goals without regard to the professional responsibility of the lawyer to his individual client. Others may be far more concerned with establishment or extension of legal principles than in the immediate protection of the rights of the lawyer's individual client. On some occasions, decisions on priority of work may be made by the employer rather than the lawyer with the result that prosecution of work already undertaken for clients is postponed to their detriment. Similarly, an employer may seek, consciously or unconsciously, to further its own economic interests through the action of the lawyers employed by it. Since a lawyer must always be free to exercise his professional judgment without regard to the interests or motives of a third person, the lawyer who is employed by one to represent another must constantly guard against erosion of his professional freedom.[27]

EC 5-24 To assist a lawyer in preserving his professional independence, a number of courses are available to him. For example, a lawyer should not practice with or in the form of a professional legal corporation, even though the corporate form is permitted by law,[28] if any director, officer, or stockholder of it is a non-lawyer. Although a lawyer may be employed by a business corporation with non-lawyers serving as directors or officers, and they necessarily have the right to make decisions of business policy, a lawyer must decline to accept direction of his professional judgment from any layman. Various types of legal aid offices are administered by boards of directors composed of lawyers and laymen. A lawyer should not accept employment from such an organization unless the board sets only broad policies and there is no interference in the relationship of the lawyer and the individual client he serves. Where a lawyer is employed by an organization, a written agreement that defines the relationship between him and the organization and provides for his independence is desirable since it may serve to prevent misunderstanding as to their respective roles. Although other innovations in the means of supplying legal counsel may develop, the responsibility of the lawyer to maintain his professional independence remains constant, and the legal profession must insure that changing circumstances do not result in loss of the professional independence of the lawyer.

DISCIPLINARY RULES

DR 5-101 Refusing Employment When the Interests of the Lawyer May Impair His Independent Professional Judgment.

(A) Except with the consent of his client after full disclosure, a lawyer shall not accept employment if the exercise of his professional judgment on behalf of his client will be or reasonably may be affected by his own financial, business, property, or personal interests.[29]

(B) A lawyer shall not accept employment in contemplated or pending litigation if he knows or it is obvious that he or a lawyer in his firm ought to be called as a witness, except that he may undertake the employment and he or a lawyer in his firm may testify:

(1) If the testimony will relate solely to an uncontested matter.
(2) If the testimony will relate solely to a matter of formality and there is no reason to believe that substantial evidence will be offered in opposition to the testimony.
(3) If the testimony will relate solely to the nature and value of legal services rendered in the case by the lawyer or his firm to the client.
(4) As to any matter, if refusal would work a substantial hardship on the client because of the distinctive value of the lawyer or his firm as counsel in the particular case.

DR 5-102 Withdrawal as Counsel When the Lawyer Becomes a Witness.[30]

(A) If, after undertaking employment in contemplated or pending litigation, a lawyer learns or it is obvious that he or a lawyer in his firm ought to be called as a witness on behalf of his client, he shall withdraw from the conduct of the trial and his firm, if any, shall not continue the representation in the trial, except that he may continue the representation and he or a lawyer in his firm may testify in the circumstances enumerated in DR 5-101(B)(1) through (4).
(B) If, after undertaking employment in contemplated or pending litigation, a lawyer learns or it is obvious that he or a lawyer in his firm may be called as a witness other than on behalf of his client, he may continue the representation until it is apparent that his testimony is or may be prejudicial to his client.[31]

DR 5-103 Avoiding Acquisition of Interest in Litigation.

(A) A lawyer shall not acquire a proprietary interest in the cause of action or subject matter of litigation he is conducting for a client,[32] except that he may:
(1) Acquire a lien granted by law to secure his fee or expenses.
(2) Contract with a client for a reasonable contingent fee in a civil case.[33]
(B) While representing a client in connection with contemplated or pending litigation, a lawyer shall not advance or guarantee financial assistance to his client,[34] except that a lawyer may advance or guarantee the expenses of litigation, including court costs, expenses of investigation, expenses of medical examination, and costs of obtaining and presenting evidence, provided the client remains ultimately liable for such expenses.

DR 5-104 Limiting Business Relations with a Client.

(A) A lawyer shall not enter into a business transaction with a client if they have differing interests therein and if the client expects the lawyer to exercise his professional judgment therein for the protection of the client, unless the client has consented after full disclosure.
(B) Prior to conclusion of all aspects of the matter giving rise to his employment, a lawyer shall not enter into any arrangement or understanding with a client or a prospective client by which he acquires an interest in publica-

tion rights with respect to the subject matter of his employment or proposed employment.

DR 5-105 Refusing to Accept or Continue Employment if the Interests of Another Client May Impair the Independent Professional Judgment of the Lawyer.

(A) A lawyer shall decline proffered employment if the exercise of his independent professional judgment in behalf of a client will be or is likely to be adversely affected by the acceptance of the proffered employment,[35] or if it would be likely to involve him in representing differing interests,[36] except to the extent permitted under DR 5-105(C).[37]

(B) A lawyer shall not continue multiple employment if the exercise of his independent professional judgment in behalf of a client will be or is likely to be adversely affected by his representation of another client, or if it would be likely to involve him in representing differing interests,[38] except to the extent permitted under DR 5-105(C).[39]

(C) In the situations covered by DR 5-105(A) and (B), a lawyer may represent multiple clients if it is obvious that he can adequately represent the interest of each and if each consents to the representation after full disclosure of the possible effect of such representation on the exercise of his independent professional judgment on behalf of each.

(D) If a lawyer is required to decline employment or to withdraw from employment under a Disciplinary Rule, no partner, or associate, or any other lawyer affiliated with him[40] or his firm, may accept or continue such employment.

DR 5-106 Settling Similar Claims of Clients.[41]

(A) A lawyer who represents two or more clients shall not make or participate in the making of an aggregate settlement of the claims of or against his clients, unless each client has consented to the settlement after being advised of the existence and nature of all the claims involved in the proposed settlement, of the total amount of the settlement, and of the participation of each person in the settlement.

DR 5-107 Avoiding Influence by Others Than the Client.

(A) Except with the consent of his client after full disclosure, a lawyer shall not:
  (1) Accept compensation for his legal services from one other than his client.
  (2) Accept from one other than his client any thing of value related to his representation of or his employment by his client.[42]

(B) A lawyer shall not permit a person who recommends, employs, or pays him to render legal services for another to direct or regulate his professional judgment in rendering such legal services.[43]

(C) A lawyer shall not practice with or in the form of a professional corporation or association authorized to practice law for a profit, if:

(1) A non-lawyer owns any interest therein,[44] except that a fiduciary representative of the estate of a lawyer may hold the stock or interest of the lawyer for a reasonable time during administration;

(2) A non-lawyer is a corporate director or officer thereof;[45] or

(3) A non-lawyer has the right to direct or control the professional judgment of a lawyer.[46]

NOTES

1. *Cf.* ABA Canons of Professional Ethics, Canon 35 (1908).

"[A lawyer's] fiduciary duty is of the highest order and he must not represent interests adverse to those of the client. It is true that because of his professional responsibility and the confidence and trust which his client may legitimately repose in him, he must adhere to a high standard of honesty, integrity and good faith in dealing with his client. He is not permitted to take advantage of his position or superior knowledge to impose upon the client; nor to conceal facts or law, nor in any way deceive him without being held responsible therefor." Smoot v. Lund, 13 Utah 2d 168, 172, 369 P.2d 933, 936 (1962).

"When a client engages the services of a lawyer in a given piece of business he is entitled to feel that, until that business is finally disposed of in some manner, he has the undivided loyalty of the one upon whom he looks as his advocate and champion. If, as in this case, he is sued and his home attached by his own attorney, who is representing him in another matter, all feeling of loyalty is necessarily destroyed, and the profession is exposed to the charge that it is interested only in money." Grievance Comm. v. Rattner, 152 Conn. 59, 65, 203 A.2d 82, 84 (1964).

"One of the cardinal principles confronting every attorney in the representation of a client is the requirement of complete loyalty and service in good faith to the best of his ability. In a criminal case the client is entitled to a fair trail, but not a perfect one. These are fundamental requirements of due process under the Fourteenth Amendment . . . . The same principles are applicable in Sixth Amendment cases (not pertinent herein) and suggest that an attorney should have no conflict of interest and that he must devote his full and faithful efforts toward the defense of his client." Johns v. Smyth, 176 F. Supp. 949, 952 (E.D. Va. 1959), *modified*, United States ex rel. Wilkins v. Banmiller, 205 F. Supp. 123, 128 n.5 (E.D. Pa. 1962), *aff'd,* 325 F.2d 514 (3d Cir. 1963), *cert. denied*, 379 U.S. 847, 13 L. Ed. 2d 51, 85 S.Ct. 87 (1964).

2. "Attorneys must not allow their private interests to conflict with those of their clients . . . . They owe their entire devotion to the interests of their client." United States v. Anonymous, 215 F. Supp. 111, 113 (E.D. Tenn. 1963).

"[T]he court [below] concluded that a firm may not accept any action against a person whom they are presently representing even though there is no relationship between the two cases. In arriving at this conclusion, the court cites an opinion of the Committee on Professional Ethics of the New York County Lawyers' Association which stated in part: 'While under the circumstances . . . there may be no actual conflict of interest . . . "maintenance of public confidence in the Bar requires an attorney who has accepted representation of a client to decline, while representing such client, any employment from an adverse party in any matter even though wholly unrelated to the original retainer." *See* Question and Answer No. 350, N.Y. County L. Ass'n, Question and Answer No. 450 (June 21, 1956).' " Grievance Comm. v. Rattner, 152 Conn. 59, 65, 203 A.2d 82, 84 (1964).

3. "Courts of equity will scrutinize with jealous vigilance transactions between parties occupying fiduciary relations toward each other . . . . A deed will not be held invalid, however, if made by the grantor with full knowledge of its nature and effect, and because of the deliberate voluntary and intelligent desire of the grantor . . . . Where a fiduciary relation exists, the burden of proof is on the grantee of beneficiary of an instrument executed during the existence of such relationship to show the fairness of the transaction, that it was equitable and just and that it did not proceed from undue influence . . . . The same rule has application where an attorney engages in a transaction with a client during the existence of the relation and is benefited thereby . . . . Conversely, an attorney is not prohibited from deal-

ing with his client or buying his property, and such contracts, if open, fair and honest, when deliberately made, are as valid as contracts between other parties . . . . [I]mportant factors in determining whether a transaction is fair include a showing by the fiduciary (1) that he made a full and frank disclosure of all the relevant information that he had; (2) that the consideration was adequate; and (3) that the principal had independent advice before completing the transaction." McFail v. Braden, 19 Ill. 2d 108, 117-18, 166 N.E.2d 46, 52(1960).

4. *See* State ex rel. Nebraska State Bar Ass'n v. Richards, 165 Neb. 80, 94-95, 84 N.W.2d 136, 146 (1957).

5. *See* ABA CANONS OF PROFESSIONAL ETHICS, CANON 9(1908).

6. *See* ABA CANONS OF PROFESSIONAL ETHICS, CANON 10(1908).

7. *See* MODEL CODE OF PROFESSIONAL RESPONSIBILITY, EC 2-20.

8. *See* ABA CANONS OF PROFESSIONAL ETHICS, CANON 42 (1908).

9. "*Rule 3a* . . . . A member of the State Bar shall not directly or indirectly pay or agree to pay, or represent or sanction the representation that he will pay, medical hospital or nursing bills or other personal expenses incurred by or for a client, prospective or existing; provided this rule shall not prohibit a member:

"(1) with the consent of the client, from paying or agreeing to pay to third persons such expenses from funds collected or to be collected for the client; or

(2) after he has been employed, from lending money to his client upon the client's promise in writing to repay such loan; or

(3) from advancing the costs of prosecuting or defending a claim or action. Such costs within the meaning of this subparagraph (3) include all taxable costs or disbursements, costs of investigation and costs of obtaining and presenting evidence." CAL. BUSINESS AND PROFESSIONS CODE §6076 (West Supp. 1967).

10. "When a lawyer knows, prior to trial, that he will be a necessary witness, except as to merely formal matters such as identification or custody of a document or the like, neither he nor his firm or associates should conduct the trial. If, during the trial, he discovers that the ends of justice require his testimony, he should, from that point on, if feasible and not prejudicial to his client's case, leave further conduct of the trial to other counsel. If circumstances do not permit withdrawal from the conduct of the trial, the lawyer should not argue the credibility of his own testimony." *A Code of Trial Conduct: Promulgated by the American College of Trial Lawyers*, 43 A.B.A.J. 223, 224-25 (1957).

11. *Cf.* ABA CANONS OF PROFESSIONAL ETHICS, CANON 19 (1908); "When a lawyer is a witness for his client, except as to merely formal matters, such as the attestation or custody of an instrument and the like, he should leave the trial of the case to other counsel."

12. "It is the general rule that a lawyer may not testify in ligation in which he is an advocate unless circumstances arise which could not be anticipated and it is necessary to prevent a miscarriage of justice. In those rare cases where the testimony of an attorney is needed to protect his client's interests, it is not only proper but mandatory that it be forthcoming." Schwartz v. Wenger, 267 Minn. 40, 43-44, 124 N.W.2d 489, 492 (1963).

13. "The great weight of authority in this country holds that the attorney who acts as counsel and witness, in behalf of his client, in the same cause on a material matter, not of merely formal character, and not in an emergency, but having knowledge that he would be required to be a witness in ample time to have secured other counsel and given up his service in the case, violates a highly important provision of the Code of Ethics and a rule of professional conduct, but does not commit a legal error in so testifying, as a result of which a new trial will be granted." Erwin M. Jennings Co. v. DiGenova, 107 Conn. 491, 499, 141 A. 866, 869 (1928).

14. "[C]ases may arise, and in practice often do arise, in which there would be a failure of justice should the attorney withhold his testimony. In such a case it would be a vicious professional sentiment which would deprive the client of the benefit of his attorney's testimony." Connoly v. Straw, 53 Wis. 645, 649, 11 N.W. 17, 19 (1881).

But see ABA CANONS OF PROFESSIONAL ETHICS, CANON 19 (1908): "Except when essential to the ends of justice, a lawyer should avoid testifying in court in behalf of his client."

15. *Cf.* ABA CANONS OF PROFESSIONAL ETHICS, CANON 7 (1908).

16. *See* ABA CANONS OF PROFESSIONAL ETHICS, CANON 7 (1908).

17. *See* ABA CANONS OF PROFESSIONAL ETHICS, CANON 6 (1908); *cf. ABA Opinions* 261 (1944), 242 (1942), 142 (1935), and 30 (1931).

18. The ABA Canons speak of "conflicting interests" rather than "differing interests" but make no attempt to define such other than the statement in Canon 6: "Within the meaning of this canon, a lawyer represents conflicting interests when, in behalf of one client, it is his duty to contend for that which duty to another client requires him to oppose."

19. "Canon 6 of the Canons of Professional Ethics, adopted by the American Bar Association on September 30, 1937, and by the Pennsylvania Bar Association on January 7, 1938, provides in part that 'It is unprofessional to represent conflicting interests, except by express consent of all concerned given after a full disclosure of the facts. Within the meaning of this Canon, a lawyer represents conflicting interest when, in behalf of one client, it is his duty to contend for that which duty to another client requires him to oppose.' The full disclosure required by this canon contemplates that the possible adverse effect of the conflict be fully explained by the attorney to the client to be affected and by him thoroughly understood . . . .

"The foregoing canon applies to cases where the circumstances are such that possibly conflicting interests may permissibly be represented by the same attorney. But manifestly, there are instances where the conflicts of interest are so critically adverse as not to admit of one attorney's representing both sides. Such is the situation which this record presents. No one could conscionably contend that the same attorney may represent both the plaintiff and defendant in an adversary action. Yet, that is what is being done in this case." Jedwabny v. Philadelphia Transportation Co., 390 Pa. 231, 235, 135 A.2d 252, 254 (1957), *cert. denied*, 355 U.S. 966, 2 L. Ed. 2d 541, 78 S. Ct. 557 (1958).

20. "Glasser wished the benefit of the undivided assistance of counsel of his own choice. We think that such a desire on the part of an accused should be respected. Irrespective of any conflict of interest, the additional burden of representing another party may conceivably impair counsel's effectiveness.

"To determine the precise degree of prejudice sustained by Glasser as a result of the court's appointment of Stewart as counsel for Kretske is at once difficult and unnecessary. The right to have the assistance of counsel is too fundamental and absolute to allow courts to indulge in nice calculations and to the amount of prejudice arising from its denial." Glasser v. United States, 315 U.S. 60, 75-76, 86 L. Ed. 680, 702 S. Ct. 457, 467 (1942).

21. *See* ABA CANONS OF PROFESSIONAL ETHICS, CANON 6 (1908).

22. *Id.*

23. *Cf. ABA Opinion* 282 (1950).

"When counsel, although paid by the casualty company, undertakes to represent the policyholder and files his notice of appearance, he owes to his client, the assured, an undeviating and single allegiance. His fealty embraces the requirement to produce in court all witnesses, fact and expert, who are available and necessary for the proper protection of the rights of his client . . . .

". . . The Canons of Professional Ethics make it pellucid that there are not two standards, one applying to counsel privately retained by a client, and the other to counsel paid by an insurance carrier." American Employers Ins. Co. v. Goble Aircraft Specialties, 205 Misc. 1066, 1075, 131 N.Y.S.2d 393, 401 (1954), *motion to withdraw appeal granted*, 1 App. Div. 2d 1008, 154 N.Y.S.2d 835 (1956).

"[C]ounsel, selected by State Farm to defend Dorothy Walker's suit for $50,000 damages, was apprised by Walker that his earlier version of the accident was untrue and that actually the accident occurred because he lost control of his car in passing a Cadillac just ahead. At that point, Walker's counsel should have refused to participate further in view of the conflict of interest between Walker and State Farm . . . . Instead he participated in the ensuing deposition of the Walkers, even took an *ex parte* sworn statement from Mr. Walker in order to advise State Farm what action it should take, and later used the statement against Walker in the District Court. This action appears to contravene an Indiana attorney's duty 'at every peril to himself, to preserve the secrets of his client'. . . ." State Farm Mut. Auto Ins. Co. v. Walker, 382 F.2d 548, 552 (1967), *cert. denied*, 389 U.S. 1045, 19 L. Ed. 2d 837, 88 S. Ct. 789 (1968).

24. *See* ABA CANONS OF PROFESSIONAL ETHICS, CANON 6 (1908).

25. *See* ABA CANONS OF PROFESSIONAL ETHICS, CANON 35 (1908).

"Objection to the intervention of a lay intermediary, who may control litigation or otherwise interfere with the rendering of legal services in a confidential relationship, . . . derives from the element of pecuniary gain. Fearful of dangers thought to arise from that element, the courts of several States have sustained regulations aimed at these activities. We intimate no view one way or the other as to the merits of those decisions with respect to the particular arrangements against which they are directed. It is enough that the superficial resemblance in form between those arrangements and that at bar cannot obscure the vital fact that here the entire arrangement employs constitutionally privileged means of expression to secure constitutionally guaranteed civil rights." NAACP v. Button, 371 U.S. 415, 441-42, 9 L. Ed. 2d 405, 423-24, 83 S. Ct. 328, 342-43 (1963).

26. *Cf.* ABA CANONS OF PROFESSIONAL ETHICS, CANON 38 (1908).

27. "Certainly it is true that 'the professional relationship between an attorney and his client is highly personal, involving an intimate appreciation of each individual client's particular problem.' And this Committee does not condone practices which interfere with that relationship. However, the mere fact the lawyer is actually paid by some entity other than the client does not affect that relationship, so long as the lawyer is selected by and is directly responsible to the client. See Informal Opinions 469 and 679. Of course, as the latter decision points out, there must be full disclosure of the arrangement by the attorney to the client . . . ." *ABA Opinion* 320 (1968).

"[A] third party may pay the cost of legal services as long as control remains in the client and the responsibility of the lawyer is solely to the client. Informal Opinions 469 ad [*sic*] 679. *See also Opinion* 237." *Id.*

28. *ABA Opinion* 303 (1961) recognized that "[s]tatutory provisions now exist in several states which are designed to make [the practice of law in a form that will be classified as a corporation for federal income tax purpose] legally possible, either as a result of lawyers incorporating or forming associations with various corporate characteristics."

29. Cf. ABA CANONS OF PROFESSIONAL ETHICS, CANON 6 (1908) and *ABA Opinions* 181 (1938), 104 (1934), 103 (1933), 72 (1932), 50 (1931), 49 (1931), and 33 (1931).

"New York County [Opinion] 203 . . . . [A lawyer] should not advise a client to employ an investment company in which he is interested, without informing him of this." DRINKER, LEGAL ETHICS 956 (1953).

"In *Opinions* 72 and 49 this Committee held: The relations of partners in a law firm are such that neither the firm nor any member or associate thereof, may accept any professional employment which any member of the firm cannot properly accept.

"In *Opinion* 16 this Committee held that a member of a law firm could not represent a defendant in a criminal case while was being prosecuted by another member of the firm who was public prosecuting attorney. The Opinion stated that it was clearly unethical for one member of the firm to oppose the interest of the state which another member represented those interests . . . . Since the prosecutor himself could not represent both the public and the defendant, no member of his law firm could either." *ABA Opinion* 296 (1959).

30. *Cf.* ABA CANONS OF PROFESSIONAL ETHICS, CANON 19 (1908) and *ABA Opinions* 220 (1941), 185 (1938), 50 (1931), and 33 (1931); *but cf.* Erwin M. Jennings Co. v. DiGenova, 107 Conn. 491, 498-99, 141 A. 866, 868 (1928).

31. This *Canon* [19] *of Ethics* needs no elaboration to be applied to the facts here. Apparently, the object of this precept is to avoid putting a lawyer in the obviously embarrassing predicament of testifying and then having to argue the credibility and effect of his own testimony. It was not designed to permit a lawyer to call opposing counsel as a witness and thereby disqualify him as counsel." Galarowicz v. Ward, 119 Utah 611, 620, 230 P.2d 576, 580 (1951).

32. ABA CANONS OF PROFESSIONAL ETHICS, CANON 10 (1908) and *ABA Opinions* 279 (1949), 246 (1942), and 176 (1938).

33. *See* MODEL CODE OF PROFESSIONAL RESPONSIBILITY, DR 2-106(C).

34. *See* ABA CANONS OF PROFESSIONAL ETHICS, CANON 42 (1908); *cf. ABA Opinion* 288 (1954).

35. *See* ABA CANONS OF PROFESSIONAL ETHICS, CANON 6 (1908); *cf. ABA Opinions* 167 (1937), 60 (1931), and 40 (1931).

36. Amended, March 1974, House Informational Report No. 127.

37. *ABA Opinion* 247 (1942) held that an attorney could not investigate a night club shooting on behalf of one of the owner's liability insurers, obtaining the cooperation of the owner, and later represent the injured patron in an action against the owner and a different insurance company unless the attorney obtain the "express consent of all concerned given after a full disclosure of the facts," since to do so would be to represent conflicting interests.

See ABA Opinions 247 (1942), 224 (1941), 222 (1941), 218 (1941), 112 (1934), 86 (1932), and 83 (1932).

38. Amended, March 1974, House Information Report No. 127.

39. *Cf. ABA Opinions* 231 (1941) and 160 (1936).

40. Amended, March 1974, House Informational Report No. 127.

41. *Cf. ABA Opinion* 235 (1941).

42. *See* ABA CANONS OF PROFESSIONAL ETHICS, CANON 38 (1908).

"A lawyer who receives a commission (whether delayed or not) from a title insurance company or guaranty fund for recommending or selling the insurance to his client, or for work done for the client or the company, without either fully disclosing to the client his financial interest in the transaction, or crediting the client's bill with the amount thus received, is guilty of unethical conduct." *ABA Opinion* 304 (1962).

43. *See* ABA CANONS OF PROFESSIONAL ETHICS, CANON 35 (1908); *cf. ABA Opinion* 237 (1941).

"When the lay forwarder, as agent for the creditor, forwards a claim to an attorney, the direct relationship of attorney and client shall then exist between the attorney and the creditor, and the forwarder shall not interpose itself as an intermediary to control the activities of the attorney." *ABA Opinion* 294 (1958).

44. "Permanent beneficial and voting rights in the organization set up to practice law, whatever its form, must be restricted to lawyers while the organization is engaged in the practice of law." *ABA Opinion* 303 (1961).

45. "*Canon 33* . . . promulgates underlying principles that must be observed no matter in what form of organization lawyers practice law. Its requirement that no person shall be admitted or held out as a practitioner or member who is not a member of the legal profession duly authorized to practice, and amenable to professional discipline, makes it clear that any centralized management must be in lawyers to avoid a violation of this Canon." *ABA Opinion* 303 (1961).

46. "There is no intervention of any lay agency between lawyer and client when centralized management provided only by lawyers may give guidance or direction to the services being rendered by a lawyer-member of the organization to a client. The language in *Canon 35* that a lawyer should avoid all relations which direct the performance of his duties by or in the interest of an intermediary refers to lay intermediaries and not lawyer intermediaries with whom he is associated in the practice of law." *ABA Opinion* 303 (1961).

CANON 6
A Lawyer Should Represent a Client Competently

ETHICAL CONSIDERATIONS

EC 6-1 Because of his vital role in the legal process, a lawyer should act with competence and proper care in representing clients. He should strive to become and remain proficient in his practice[1] and should accept employment only in matters which he is or intends to become competent to handle.

EC 6-2 A lawyer is aided in attaining and maintaining his competence by keeping abreast of current legal literature and developments, participating in continuing legal education programs,[2] concentrating in particular areas of the law, and by utilizing other available means. He has the additional ethical obligation to assist in improving the legal profession, and he may do so by participating in bar activities intended to advance the quality and standards of members of the profession. Of particular importance is the careful training of his younger associates and the giving of sound guidance to all lawyers who consult him. In short, a lawyer should strive at all levels to aid the legal profession in advancing the highest possible standards of integrity and competence and to meet those standards himself.

EC 6-3 While the licensing of a lawyer is evidence that he has met the standards then prevailing for admission to the bar, a lawyer generally should not accept employment in any area of the law in which he is not qualified.[3] However, he may accept such employment if in good faith he expects to become qualified through study and investigation, as long as such preparation would not result in unreasonable delay or expense to his client. Proper preparation and representation may require the association by the lawyer of professionals in other disciplines. A lawyer offered employment in a matter in which he is not and does not expect to become so qualified should either decline the employment or, with the consent of his client, accept the employment and associate a lawyer who is competent in the matter.

EC 6-4 Having undertaken representation, a lawyer should use proper care to safeguard the interests of his client. If a lawyer has accepted employment in a matter beyond his competence but in which he expected to become competent, he should diligently undertake the work and study necessary to qualify himself. In addition to being qualified to handle a particular matter, his obligation to his client requires him to prepare adequately for and give appropriate attention to his legal work.

EC 6-5 A lawyer should have pride in his professional endeavors. His obligation to act competently calls for higher motivation than that arising from fear of civil liability or disciplinary penalty.

EC 6-6 A lawyer should not seek, by contract or other means, to limit his individual liability to his client for his malpractice. A lawyer who handles the affairs of his client properly has no need to attempt to limit his liability for his professional activities and one who does not handle the affairs of his client properly should not be permitted to do so. A lawyer who is a stockholder in or is associated with a professional legal corporation may, however, limit his liability for malpractice of his associates in the corporation, but only to the extent permitted by law.[4]

DISCIPLINARY RULES

DR 6-101 Failing to Act Competently.

(A) A lawyer shall not:

(1) Handle a legal matter which he knows or should know that he is not competent to handle, without associating with him a lawyer who is competent to handle it.

(2) Handle a legal matter without preparation adequate in the circumstances.

(3) Neglect a legal matter entrusted to him.[5]

DR 6-102 Limiting Liability to Client.

(A) A lawyer shall not attempt to exonerate himself from or limit his liability to his client for his personal malpractice.

NOTES

1. "[W]hen a citizen is faced with the need for a lawyer, he wants, and is entitled to, the best informed counsel he can obtain. Changing times produce changes in our laws and legal procedures. The natural complexities of law require continuing intensive study by a lawyer if he is to render his clients a maximum of efficient service. And, in so doing, he maintains the high standards of the legal profession; and he also increases respect and confidence by the general public." Rochelle & Payne, *The Struggle of Public Understanding*, 25 TEXAS B.J. 109, 160 (1962).

"We have undergone enormous changes in the last fifty years within the lives of most of the adults living today who may be seeking advice. Most of these changes have been accompanied by changes and developments in the law . . . . Every practicing lawyer encounters these problems and is often perplexed with his own inability to keep up, not only with changes in the law, but also with changes in the lives of his clients and their legal problems.

"To be sure, no client has a right to expect that his lawyer will have all of the answers at the end of his tongue or even in the back of his head at all times. But the client does have the right to expect that the lawyer will have devoted his time and energies to maintaining and improving his competence to know where to look for the answers to know how to deal with the problems, and to know how to advise to the best of his legal talents and abilities." Levy & Sprague, *Accounting and Law: Is Dual Practice in the Public Interest?*, 52 A.B.A.J. 1110, 1112 (1966).

2. "The whole purpose of continuing legal education, so enthusiastically supported by the ABA, is to make it possible for lawyers to make themselves better lawyers. But there are no nostrums for proficiency in the law; it must come through the hard work of the lawyer himself. To the extent that work, whether it be in attending institutes or lecture courses, in studying after hours or in the actual day in and day out practice of his profession, can be concentrated within a limited field, the greater the proficiency and expertness that can developed." *Report of the Special Committee on Specialization and Specialized Legal Education*, 79 A.B.A. REP. 582, 588 (1954).

3. "If the attorney is not competent to skillfully and properly perform the work, he should not undertake the service." Design v. Steinbrink, 202 App. Div. 477, 481, 195 N.Y.S. 810, 814 (1922), *aff'd mem.*, 236 N.Y. 669, 142 N.E. 328 (1923).

4. *See ABA Opinion* 303 (1961); *cf.* CODE OF PROFESSIONAL RESPONSIBILITY, EC 2-11.

5. The annual report for 1967-1968 of the Committee on Grievances of the Association of the Bar of the City of New York showed a receipt of 2,232 complaints; of the 828 offenses against clients, 76 involved conversion, 49 involved "overreaching," and 452, or more than half of all such offenses, involved neglect. *Annual Report of the Committee on Grievances of the Association of the Bar of the City of New York*, N.Y.L.J., Sept. 12, 1968, at 4, col. 5.

CANON 7
A Lawyer Should Represent a Client Zealously Within the Bounds of the Law

ETHICAL CONSIDERATIONS

EC 7-1 The duty of a lawyer, both to his client[1] and to the legal system, is to represent his client zealously[2] within the bounds of the law,[3] which includes

Disciplinary Rules and enforceable professional regulations.[4] The professional responsibility of a lawyer derives from his membership in a profession which has the duty of assisting members of the public to secure and protect available legal rights and benefits. In our government of laws and not of men, each member of our society is entitled to have his conduct judged and regulated in accordance with the law;[5] to seek any lawful objective[6] through legally permissible means;[7] and to present for adjudication any lawful claim, issue, or defense.

EC 7-2 The bounds of the law in a given case are often difficult to ascertain.[8] The language of legislative enactments and judicial opinions may be uncertain as applied to varying factual situations. The limits and specific meaning of apparently relevant law may be made doubtful by changing or developing constitutional interpretations, inadequately expressed statutes or judicial opinions, and changing public and judicial attitudes. Certainty of law ranges from well-settled rules through areas of conflicting authority to areas without precedent.

EC 7-3 Where the bounds of law are uncertain, the action of a lawyer may depend on whether he is serving as advocate or adviser. A lawyer may serve simultaneously as both advocate and adviser, but the two roles are essentially different.[9] In asserting a position on behalf of his client, an advocate for the most part deals with past conduct and must take the facts as he finds them. By contrast, a lawyer serving as adviser primarily assists his client in determining the course of future conduct and relationships. While serving as advocate, a lawyer should resolve in favor of his client doubts as to the bounds of the law.[10] In serving a client as adviser, a lawyer in appropriate circumstances should give his professional opinion as to what the ultimate decisions of the courts would likely be as to the applicable law.

Duty of the Lawyer to a Client

EC 7-4 The advocate may urge any permissible construction of the law favorable to his client, without regard to his professional opinion as to the likelihood that the construction will ultimately prevail.[11] His conduct is within the bounds of the law, and therefore permissible, if the position taken is supported by the law or is supportable by a good faith argument for an extension, modification, or reversal of the law. However, a lawyer is not justified in asserting a position in litigation that is frivolous.[12]

EC 7-5 A lawyer as adviser furthers the interest of his client by giving his professional opinion as to what he believes would likely be the ultimate decision of the courts on the matter at hand and by informing his client of the practical effect of such decision.[13] He may continue in the representation of his client even though his client has elected to pursue a course of conduct contrary to the advice of the lawyer so long as he does not thereby knowingly assist the client to engage in illegal conduct or to take a frivolous legal position. A lawyer should never encourage or aid his client to commit criminal acts or counsel his client on how to violate the law and avoid punishment therefor.[14]

EC 7-6 Whether the proposed action of a lawyer is within the bounds of the law may be a perplexing question when his client is contemplating a course of conduct having legal consequences that vary according to the client's intent, motive, or desires at the time of the action. Often a lawyer is asked to assist his client in developing evidence relevant to the state of mind of the client at a particular time. He may properly assist his client in the development and preservation of evidence of existing motive, intent, or desire; obviously, he may not do anything furthering the creation or preservation of false evidence. In many cases a lawyer may not be certain as to the state of mind of his client, and in those situations he should resolve reasonable doubts in favor of his client.

EC 7-7 In certain areas of legal representation not affecting the merits of the cause or substantially prejudicing the rights of a client, a lawyer is entitled to make decisions on his own. But otherwise the authority to make decisions is exclusively that of the client and, if made within the framework of the law, such decisions are binding on his lawyer. As typical examples in civil cases, it is for the client to decide whether he will accept a settlement offer or whether he will waive his right to plead an affirmative defense. A defense lawyer in a criminal case has the duty to advise his client fully on whether a particular plea to a charge appears to be desirable and as to the prospects of success on appeal, but it is for the client to decide what plea should be entered and whether an appeal should be taken.[15]

EC 7-8 A lawyer should exert his best efforts to insure that decisions of his client are made only after the client has been informed of relevant considerations. A lawyer ought to initiate this decision-making process if the client does not do so. Advice of a lawyer to his client need not be confined to purely legal considerations.[16] A lawyer should advise his client of the possible effect of each legal alternative.[17] A lawyer should bring to bear upon this decision-making process the fullness of his experience as well as his objective viewpoint.[18] In assisting his client to reach a proper decision, it is often desirable for a lawyer to point out those factors which may lead to a decision that is morally just as well as legally permissible.[19] He may emphasize the possibility of harsh consequences that might result from assertion of legally permissible positions. In the final analysis, however, the lawyer should always remember that the decision whether to forego legally available objectives or methods because of non-legal factors is ultimately for the client and not for himself. In the event that the client in a non-adjudicatory matter insists upon a course of conduct that is contrary to the judgment and advice of the lawyer but not prohibited by Disciplinary Rules, the lawyer may withdraw from the employment.[20]

EC 7-9 In the exercise of his professional judgment on those decisions which are for his determination in the handling of a legal matter,[21] a lawyer should always act in a manner consistent with the best interests of his client.[22] However, when an action in the best interest of his client seems to him to be unjust, he may ask his client for permission to forego such action.

EC 7-10 The duty of a lawyer to represent his client with zeal does not militate against his concurrent obligation to treat with consideration all persons involved in the legal process and to avoid the infliction of needless harm.

EC 7-11 The responsibilities of a lawyer may vary according to the intelligence, experience, mental condition or age of a client, the obligation of a public officer, or the nature of a particular proceeding. Examples include the representation of an illiterate or an incompetent, service as a public prosecutor or other government lawyer, and appearances before administrative and legislative bodies.

EC 7-12 Any mental or physical condition of a client that renders him incapable of making a considered judgment on his own behalf casts additional responsibilities upon his lawyer. Where an incompetent is acting through a guardian or other legal representative, a lawyer must look to such representative for those decisions which are normally the prerogative of the client to make. If a client under disability has no legal representative, his lawyer may be compelled in court proceedings to make decisions on behalf of the client. If the client is capable of understanding the matter in question or of contributing to the advancement of his interests, regardless of whether he is legally disqualified from performing certain acts, the lawyer should obtain from him all possible aid. If the disability of a client and the lack of a legal representative compel the lawyer to make decisions for his client, the lawyer should consider all circumstances then prevailing and act with care to safeguard and advance the interests of his client. But obviously a lawyer cannot perform any act or make any decision which the law requires his client to perform or make, either acting for himself if competent, or by a duly constituted representative if legally incompetent.

EC 7-13 The responsibility of a public prosecutor differs from that of the usual advocate; his duty is to seek justice, not merely to convict.[23] This special duty exists because: (1) the prosecutor represents the sovereign and therefore should use restraint in the discretionary exercise of governmental powers, such as in the selection of cases to prosecute; (2) during trial the prosecutor is not only an advocate but he also may make decisions normally made by an individual client, and those affecting the public interest should be fair to all; and (3) in our system of criminal justice the accused is to be given the benefit of all reasonable doubts. With respect to evidence and witnesses, the prosecutor has responsibilities different from those of a lawyer in private practice: the prosecutor should make timely disclosure to the defense of available evidence, known to him, that tends to negate the guilt of the accused, mitigate the degree of the offense, or reduce the punishment. Further, a prosecutor should not intentionally avoid pursuit of evidence merely because he believes it will damage the prosecutor's case or aid the accused.

EC 7-14 A government lawyer who has discretionary power relative to litigation should refrain from instituting or continuing litigation that is obviously unfair. A government lawyer not having such discretionary power who believes there is lack of merit in a controversy submitted to him should so advise his superiors and recommend the avoidance of unfair litigation. A government lawyer in a civil action or administrative proceeding has the responsibility to seek justice and to develop a full and fair record, and he should not use his position or the economic power of the government to harass parties or to bring about unjust settlements or results.

EC 7-15 The nature and purpose of proceedings before administrative agencies vary widely. The proceedings may be legislative or quasi-judicial, or a combination of both. They may be *ex parte* in character, in which event they may originate either at the instance of the agency or upon motion of an interested party. The scope of an inquiry may be purely investigative or it may be truly adversary looking toward the adjudication of specific rights of a party or of classes of parties. The foregoing are but examples of some of the types of proceedings conducted by administrative agencies. A lawyer appearing before an administrative agency,[24] regardless of the nature of the proceeding it is conducting, has the continuing duty to advance the cause of his client within the bounds of the law.[25] Where the applicable rules of the agency impose specific obligations upon a lawyer, it is his duty to comply therewith, unless the lawyer has a legitimate basis for challenging the validity thereof. In all appearances before administrative agencies, a lawyer should identify himself, his client if identity of his client is not privileged[26] and the representative nature of his appearance. It is not improper, however, for a lawyer to seek from an agency information available to the public without identifying his client.

EC 7-16 The primary business of a legislative body is to enact laws rather than to adjudicate controversies, although on occasion the activities of a legislative body may take on the characteristics of an adversary proceeding, particularly in investigative and impeachment matters. The role of a lawyer supporting or opposing proposed legislation normally is quite different from his role in representing a person under investigation or on trial by a legislative body. When a lawyer appears in connection with proposed legislation, he seeks to affect the lawmaking process, but when he appears on behalf of a client in investigatory or impeachment proceedings, he is concerned with the protection of the rights of his client. In either event, he should identify himself and his client, if identity of his client is not privileged, and should comply with applicable laws and legislative rules.[27]

EC 7-17 The obligation of loyalty to his client applies only to a lawyer in the discharge of his professional duties and implies no obligation to adopt a personal viewpoint favorable to the interests or desires of his client.[28] While a lawyer must act always with circumspection in order that his conduct will not adversely affect the rights of a client in a matter he is then handling, he may take positions on public issues and espouse legal reforms he favors without regard to the individual views of any client.

EC 7-18 The legal system in its broadest sense functions best when persons in need of legal advice or assistance are represented by their own counsel. For this reason a lawyer should not communicate on the subject matter of the representation of his client with a person he knows to be represented in the matter by a lawyer, unless pursuant to law or rule of court or unless he has the consent of the lawyer for that person.[29] If one is not represented by counsel, a lawyer representing another may have to deal directly with the unrepresented person; in such an instance, a lawyer should not undertake to give advice to the person who is attempting to represent himself,[30] except that he may advise him to obtain a lawyer.

Duty of the Lawyer to the Adversary System of Justice

EC 7-19 Our legal system provides for the adjudication of disputes governed by the rules of substantive, evidentiary, and procedural law. An adversary presentation counters the natural human tendency to judge too swiftly in terms of the familiar that which is not yet fully known;[31] the advocate, by his zealous preparation and presentation of fact and law, enables the tribunal to come to the hearing with an open and neutral mind and to render impartial judgments.[32] The duty of a lawyer to his client and his duty to the legal system are the same; to represent his client zealously within the bounds of the law.[33]

EC 7-20 In order to function properly, our adjudicative process requires an informed, impartial tribunal capable of administering justice promptly and efficiently[34] according to procedures that command public confidence and respect.[35] Not only must there be competent, adverse presentation of evidence and issues, but a tribunal must be aided by rules appropriate to an effective and dignified process. The procedures under which tribunals operate in our adversary system have been prescribed largely by legislative enactments, court rules and decisions, and administrative rules. Through the years certain concepts of proper professional conduct have become rules of law applicable to the adversary adjudicative process. Many of these concepts are the bases for standards of professional conduct set forth in the Disciplinary Rules.

EC 7-21 The civil adjudicative process is primarily designed for the settlement of disputes between parties, while the criminal process is designed for the protection of society as a whole. Threatening to use, or using, the criminal process to coerce adjustment of private civil claims or controversies is a subversion of that process;[36] further, the person against whom the criminal process is so misused may be deterred from asserting his legal rights and thus the usefulness of the civil process in settling private disputes is impaired. As in all cases of abuse of judicial process, the improper use of criminal process tends to diminish public confidence in our legal system.

EC 7-22 Respect for judicial rulings is essential to the proper administration of justice; however, a litigant or his lawyer may, in good faith and within the framework of the law, take steps to test the correctness of a ruling of a tribunal.[37]

EC 7-23 The complexity of law often makes it difficult for a tribunal to be fully informed unless the pertinent law is presented by the lawyers in the cause. A tribunal that is fully informed on the applicable law is better able to make a fair and accurate determination of the matter before it. The adversary system contemplates that each lawyer will present and argue the existing law in the light most favorable to his client.[38] Where a lawyer knows of legal authority in the controlling jurisdiction directly adverse to the position of his client, he should inform the tribunal of its existence unless his adversary has done so; but, having made such disclosure, he may challenge its soundness in whole or in part.[39]

EC 7-24 In order to bring about just and informed decisions, evidentiary and procedural rules have been established by tribunals to permit the inclusion of relevant evidence and argument and the exclusion of all other considerations. The expression by a lawyer of his personal opinion as to the justness of a cause, as to the credibility of a witness, as to the culpability of a civil litigant, or as to the guilt or innocence of an accused is not a proper subject for argument to the trier of fact.[40] It is improper as to factual matters because admissible evidence possessed by a lawyer should be presented only as sworn testimony. It is improper as to all other matters because, were the rule otherwise, the silence of a lawyer on a given occasion could be construed unfavorably to his client. However, a lawyer may argue, on his analysis of the evidence, for any position or conclusion with respect to any of the foregoing matters.

EC 7-25 Rules of evidence and procedure are designed to lead to just decisions and are part of the framework of the law. Thus while a lawyer may take steps in good faith and within the framework of the law to test the validity of rules, he is not justified in consciously violating such rules and he should be diligent in his efforts to guard against his unintentional violation of them.[41] As examples, a lawyer should subscribe to or verify only those pleadings that he believes are in compliance with applicable law and rules; a lawyer should not make any prefatory statement before a tribunal in regard to the purported facts of the case on trial unless he believes that his statement will be supported by admissible evidence; a lawyer should not ask a witness a question solely for the purpose of harassing or embarrassing him; and a lawyer should not by subterfuge put before a jury matters which it cannot properly consider.

EC 7-26 The law and Disciplinary Rules prohibit the use of fraudulent, false, or perjured testimony or evidence.[42] A lawyer who knowingly[43] participates in introduction of such testimony or evidence is subject to discipline. A lawyer should, however, present any admissible evidence his client desires to have presented unless he knows, or from facts within his knowledge should know, that such testimony or evidence is false, fraudulent, or perjured.[46]

EC 7-27 Because it interferes with the proper administration of justice, a lawyer should not suppress evidence that he or his client has a legal obligation to reveal or produce. In like manner, a lawyer should not advise or cause a person to secrete himself or to leave the jurisdiction of a tribunal for the purpose of making him unavailable as a witness therein.[47]

EC 7-28 Witnesses should always testify truthfully[46] and should be free from any financial inducements that might tempt them to do otherwise.[47] A lawyer should not pay or agree to pay a non-expert witness an amount in excess of reimbursement for expenses and financial loss incident to his being a witness; however, a lawyer may pay or agree to pay an expert witness a reasonable fee for his services as an expert. But in no event should a lawyer pay or agree to pay a contingent fee to any witness. A lawyer should exercise reasonable diligence to see that his client and lay associates conform to these standards.[48]

EC 7-29 To safeguard the impartiality that is essential to the judicial process, veniremen and jurors should be protected against extraneous influences.[49] When impartiality is present, public confidence in the judicial system is enhanced. There should be no extrajudicial communication with veniremen prior to trial or with jurors during trial by or on behalf of a lawyer connected with the case. Furthermore, a lawyer who is not connected with the case should not communicate with or cause another to communicate with a venireman or a juror about the case. After the trial, communication by a lawyer with jurors is permitted so long as he refrains from asking questions or making comments that tend to harass or embarrass the juror[50] or to influence actions of the juror in future cases. Were a lawyer to be prohibited from communicating after trial with a juror, he could not ascertain if the verdict might be subject to legal challenge, in which event the invalidity of a verdict might go undetected.[51] When an extrajudicial communication by a lawyer with a juror is permitted by law, it should be made considerately and with deference to the personal feelings of the juror.

EC 7-30 Vexatious or harassing investigations of veniremen or jurors seriously impair the effectiveness of our jury system. For this reason, a lawyer or anyone on his behalf who conducts an investigation of veniremen or jurors should act with circumspection and restraint.

EC 7-31 Communications with or investigations of members of families of veniremen or jurors by a lawyer or by anyone on his behalf are subject to the restrictions imposed upon the lawyer with respect to his communications with or investigations of veniremen and jurors.

EC 7-32 Because of his duty to aid in preserving the integrity of the jury system, a lawyer who learns of improper conduct by or towards a venireman, a juror, or a member of the family of either should make a prompt report to the court regarding such conduct.

EC 7-33 A goal of our legal system is that each party shall have his case, criminal or civil, adjudicated by an impartial tribunal. The attainment of this goal may be defeated by dissemination of news or comments which tend to influence judge or jury.[52] Such news or comments may prevent prospective jurors from being impartial at the outset of the trial[53] and may also interfere with the obligation of jurors to base their verdict solely upon the evidence admitted in the trial.[54] The release by a lawyer of out-of-court statements regarding an anticipated or pending trial may improperly affect the impartiality of the tribunal.[55] For these reasons, standards for permissible and prohibited conduct of a lawyer with respect to trial publicity have been established.

EC 7-34 The impartiality of a public servant in our legal system may be impaired by the receipt of gifts or loans. A lawyer,[56] therefore, is never justified in making a gift or a loan to a judge, a hearing officer, or an official or employee of a tribunal except as permitted by Section C(4) of Canon 5 of the Code of Judicial Conduct, but a lawyer may make a contribution to the campaign fund of a candidate for judicial office in conformity with Section B(2) under Canon 7 of the Code of Judicial Conduct.[57, 58]

EC 7-35 All litigants and lawyers should have access to tribunals on an equal basis. Generally, in adversary proceedings a lawyer should not communicate with a judge relative to a matter pending before, or which is to be brought before, a tribunal over which he presides in circumstances which might have the effect or give the appearance of granting undue advantage to one party.[59] For example, a lawyer should not communicate with a tribunal by a writing unless a copy thereof is promptly delivered to opposing counsel or to the adverse party if he is not represented by a lawyer. Ordinarily an oral communication by a lawyer with a judge or hearing officer should be made only upon adequate notice to opposing counsel, or, if there is none, to the opposing party. A lawyer should not condone or lend himself to private importunities by another with a judge or hearing officer on behalf of himself or his client.

EC 7-36 Judicial hearings ought to be conducted through dignified and orderly procedures designed to protect the rights of all parties. Although a lawyer has the duty to represent his client zealously, he should not engage in any conduct that offends the dignity and decorum of proceedings.[60] While maintaining his independence, a lawyer should be respectful, courteous, and above-board in his relations with a judge or hearing officer before whom he appears.[61] He should avoid undue solicitude for the comfort or convenience of judge or jury and should avoid any other conduct calculated to gain special consideration.

EC 7-37 In adversary proceedings, clients are litigants and though ill feeling may exist between clients, such ill feeling should not influence a lawyer in his conduct, attitude, and demeanor towards opposing lawyers.[62] A lawyer should not make unfair or derogatory personal reference to opposing counsel. Haranguing and offensive tactics by lawyers interfere with the orderly administration of justice and have no proper place in our legal system.

EC 7-38 A lawyer should be courteous to opposing counsel and should accede to reasonable requests regarding court proceedings, settings, continuances, waiver of procedural formalities, and similar matters which do not prejudice the rights of his client.[63] He should follow local customs of courtesy or practice, unless he gives timely notice to opposing counsel of his intention not to do so.[64] A lawyer should be punctual in fulfilling all professional commitments.[65]

EC 7-39 In the final analysis, proper functioning of the adversary system depends upon cooperation between lawyers and tribunals in utilizing procedures which will preserve the impartiality of tribunals and make their decisional processes prompt and just, without impinging upon the obligation of lawyers to represent their clients zealously within the framework of the law.

DISCIPLINARY RULES

DR 7-101 Representing a Client Zealously.

(A) A lawyer shall not intentionally:[66]

(1) Fail to seek the lawful objectives of his client through reasonably available means[67] permitted by law and the Disciplinary Rules, except as provided by DR 7-101(B). A lawyer does not violate this Disciplinary Rule, however, by acceding to reasonable requests of opposing counsel which do not prejudice the rights of his client, by being punctual in fulfilling all professional commitments, by avoiding offensive tactics, or by treating with courtesy and consideration all persons involved in the legal process.

(2) Fail to carry out a contract of employment entered into with a client for professional services, but he may withdraw as permitted under DR 2-110, DR 5-102, and DR 5-105.

(3) Prejudice or damage his client during the course of the professional relationship,[68] except as required under DR 7-102(B).

(B) In his representation of a client, a lawyer may:

(1) Where permissible, exercise his professional judgment to waive or fail to assert a right or position of his client.

(2) Refuse to aid or participate in conduct that he believes to be unlawful, even though there is some support for an argument that the conduct is legal.

DR 7-102 Representing a Client Within the Bounds of the Law.

(A) In his representation of a client, a lawyer shall not:

(1) File a suit, assert a position, conduct a defense, delay a trial, or take other action on behalf of his client when he knows or when it is obvious that such action would serve merely to harass or maliciously injure another.[69]

(2) Knowingly advance a claim or defense that is unwarranted under existing law, except that he may advance such claim or defense if it can be supported by good faith argument for an extension, modification, or reversal of existing law.

(3) Conceal or knowingly fail to disclose that which he is required by law to reveal.

(4) Knowingly use perjured testimony or false evidence.[70]

(5) Knowingly make a false statement of law or fact.

(6) Participate in the creation or preservation of evidence when he knows or it is obvious that the evidence is false.

(7) Counsel or assist his client in conduct that the lawyer knows to be illegal or fraudulent.
(8) Knowingly engage in other illegal conduct or conduct contrary to a Disciplinary Rule.

(B) A lawyer who receives information clearly establishing that:
(1) His client has, in the course of the representation, perpetrated a fraud upon a person or tribunal shall promptly call upon his client to rectify the same, and if his client refuses or is unable to do so, he shall reveal the fraud to the affected person or tribunal, except when the information is protected as a privileged communication.[71,72]
(2) A person other than his client has perpetrated a fraud upon a tribunal shall promptly reveal the fraud to the tribunal.[73]

DR 7-103 Performing the Duty of Public Prosecutor or Other Government Lawyer.[74]

(A) A public prosecutor or other government lawyer shall not institute or cause to be instituted criminal charges when he knows or it is obvious that the charges are not supported by probable cause.

(B) A public prosecutor or other government lawyer in criminal litigation shall make timely disclosure to counsel for the defendant, or to the defendant if he has no counsel, of the existence of evidence, known to the prosecutor or other government lawyer, that tends to negate the guilt of the accused, mitigate the degree of the offense, or reduce the punishment.

DR 7-104 Communicating With One of Adverse Interest.[75]

(A) During the course of his representation of a client a lawyer shall not:
(1) Communicate or cause another to communicate on the subject of the representation with a party he knows to be represented by a lawyer in that matter unless he has the prior consent of the lawyer representing such other party[76] or is authorized by law to do so.
(2) Give advice to a person who is not represented by a lawyer, other than the advice to secure counsel,[77] if the interests of such person are or have a reasonable possibility of being in conflict with the interests of his client.[78]

DR 7-105 Threatening Criminal Prosecution.

(A) A lawyer shall not present, participate in presenting, or threaten to present criminal charges solely to obtain an advantage in a civil matter.

DR 7-106 Trial Conduct.

(A) A lawyer shall not disregard or advise his client to disregard a standing rule of a tribunal or a ruling of a tribunal made in the course of a proceeding, but he may take appropriate steps in good faith to test the validity of such rule or ruling.

(B) In presenting a matter to a tribunal, a lawyer shall disclose:[79]
  (1) Legal authority in the controlling jurisdiction known to him to be directly adverse to the position of his client and which is not disclosed by opposing counsel.[80]
  (2) Unless privileged or irrelevant, the identities of the clients he represents and of the persons who employed him.[81]

(C) In appearing in his professional capacity before a tribunal, a lawyer shall not:
  (1) State or allude to any matter that he has no reasonable basis to believe is relevant to the case or that will not be supported by admissible evidence.[82]
  (2) Ask any question that he has no reasonable basis to believe is relevant to the case and that is intended to degrade a witness or other person.[83]
  (3) Assert his personal knowledge of the facts in issue, except when testifying as a witness.
  (4) Assert his personal opinion as to the justness of a cause, as to the credibility of a witness, as to the culpability of a civil litigant, or as to the guilt or innocence of an accused;[84] but he may argue, on his analysis of the evidence, for any position or conclusion with respect to the matters stated herein.
  (5) Fail to comply with known local customs of courtesy or practice of the bar or a particular tribunal without giving to opposing counsel timely notice of his intent not to comply.[85]
  (6) Engage in undignified or discourteous conduct which is degrading to a tribunal.
  (7) Intentionally or habitually violate any established rule of procedure or of evidence.

DR 7-107 Trial Publicity.[86]

(A) A lawyer participating in or associated with the investigation of a criminal matter shall not make or participate in making an extrajudicial statement that a reasonable person would expect to be disseminated by means of public communication and that does more than state without elaboration:
  (1) Information contained in a public record.
  (2) That the investigation is in progress.
  (3) The general scope of the investigation including a description of the offense and, if permitted by law, the identity of the victim.
  (4) A request for assistance in apprehending a suspect or assistance in other matters and the information necessary thereto.
  (5) A warning to the public of any dangers.

(B) A lawyer or law firm associated with the prosecution or defense of a criminal matter shall not, from the time of the filing of a complaint, information, or indictment, the issuance of an arrest warrant, or arrest until the commencement of the trial or disposition without trial, make or participate in making an extrajudicial statement that a reasonable person would expect to be disseminated by means of public communication and that relates to:

(1) The character, reputation, or prior criminal record (including arrests, indictments, or other charges of crime) of the accused.

(2) The possibility of a plea of guilty to the offense charged or to a lesser offense.

(3) The existence or contents of any confession, admission, or statement given by the accused or his refusal or failure to make a statement.

(4) The performance or results of any examinations or tests or the refusal or failure of the accused to submit to examinations or tests.

(5) The identity, testimony, or credibility of a prospective witness.

(6) Any opinion as to the guilt or innocence of the accused, the evidence, or the merits of the case.

(C) DR 7-107(B) does not preclude a lawyer during such period from announcing:

(1) The name, age, residence, occupation, and family status of the accused.

(2) If the accused has not been apprehended, any information necessary to aid in his apprehension or to warn the public of any dangers he may present.

(3) A request for assistance in obtaining evidence.

(4) The identity of the victim of the crime.

(5) The fact, time, and place of arrest, resistance, pursuit, and use of weapons.

(6) The identity of investigating and arresting officers or agencies and the length of the investigation.

(7) At the time of seizure, a description of the physical evidence seized, other than a confession, admission, or statement.

(8) The nature, substance, or text of the charge.

(9) Quotations from or references to public records of the court in the case.

(10) The scheduling or result of any step in the judicial proceedings.

(11) That the accused denies the charges made against him.

(D) During the selection of a jury or the trial of a criminal matter, a lawyer or law firm associated with the prosecution or defense of a criminal matter shall not make or participate in making an extra-judicial statement that a reasonable person would expect to be disseminated by means of public communication and that relates to the trial, parties, or issues in the trial or other matters that are reasonably likely to interfere with a fair trial, except that he may quote from or refer without comment to public records of the court in the case.

(E) After the completion of a trial or disposition without trial of a criminal matter and prior to the imposition of sentence, a lawyer or law firm associated with the prosecution or defense shall not make or participate in making an extrajudicial statement that a reasonable person would expect to be disseminated by public communication and that is reasonably likely to affect the imposition of sentence.

(F) The foregoing provisions of DR 7-107 also apply to professional disciplinary proceedings and juvenile disciplinary proceedings when pertinent and consistent with other law applicable to such proceedings.

(G) A lawyer or law firm associated with a civil action shall not during its investigation or litigation make or participate in making an extrajudicial statement, other than a quotation from or reference to public records, that a reasonable person would expect to be disseminated by means of public communication and that relates to:

(1) Evidence regarding the occurrence or transaction involved.

(2) The character, credibility, or criminal record of a party, witness, or prospective witness.

(3) The performance or results of any examinations or tests or the refusal or failure of a party to submit to such.

(4) His opinion as to the merits of the claims or defenses of a party, except as required by law or administrative rule.

(5) Any other matter reasonably likely to interfere with a fair trial of the action.

(H) During the pendency of an administrative proceeding, a lawyer or law firm associated therewith shall not make or participate in making a statement, other than a quotation from or reference to public records, that a reasonable person would expect to be disseminated by means of public communication if it is made outside the official course of the proceeding and relates to:

(1) Evidence regarding the occurrence or transaction involved.

(2) The character, credibility, or criminal record of a party, witness, or prospective witness.

(3) Physical evidence or the performance or results of any examinations or tests or the refusal or failure of a party to submit to such.

(4) His opinion as to the merits of the claims, defenses, or positions of an interested person.

(5) Any other matter reasonably likely to interfere with a fair hearing.

(I) The foregoing provisions of DR 7-107 do not preclude a lawyer from replying to charges of misconduct publicly made against him or from participating in the proceedings of legislative, administrative, or other investigative bodies.

(J) A lawyer shall exercise reasonable care to prevent his employees and associates from making an extrajudicial statement that he would be prohibited from making under DR 7-107.

DR 7-108 Communication with or Investigation of Jurors.

(A) Before the trial of a case a lawyer connected therewith shall not communicate with or cause another to communicate with anyone he knows to be a member of the venire from which the jury will be selected for the trial of the case.

(B) During the trial of a case:
  (1) A lawyer connected therewith shall not communicate with or cause another to communicate with any member of the jury.[87]
  (2) A lawyer who is not connected therewith shall not communicate with or cause another to communicate with a juror concerning the case.

(C) DR 7-108(A) and (B) do not prohibit a lawyer from communicating with veniremen or jurors in the course of official proceedings.

(D) After discharge of the jury from further consideration of a case with which the lawyer was connected, the lawyer shall not ask questions of or make comments to a member of that jury that are calculated merely to harass or embarrass the juror or to influence his actions in future jury service.[88]

(E) A lawyer shall not conduct or cause, by financial support or otherwise, another to conduct a vexatious or harassing investigation of either a venireman or a juror.

(F) All restrictions imposed by DR 7-108 upon a lawyer also apply to communications with or investigations of members of a family of a venireman or a juror.

(G) A lawyer shall reveal promptly to the court improper conduct by a venireman or a juror, or by another toward a venireman or a juror or a member of his family, of which the lawyer has knowledge.

DR 7-109 Contact with Witnesses.

(A) A lawyer shall not suppress any evidence that he or his client has a legal obligation to reveal or produce.[89]

(B) A lawyer shall not advise or cause a person to secrete himself or to leave the jurisdiction of a tribunal for the purpose of making him unavailable as a witness therein.[90]

(C) A lawyer shall not pay, offer to pay, or acquiesce in the payment of compensation to a witness contingent upon the content of his testimony or the outcome of the case.[91] But a lawyer may advance, guarantee, or acquiesce in the payment of:
  (1) Expenses reasonably incurred by a witness in attending or testifying.
  (2) Reasonable compensation to a witness for his loss of time in attending or testifying.
  (3) A reasonable fee for the professional services of an expert witness.

DR 7-110 Contact with Officials.[92]

(A) A lawyer shall not give or lend any thing of value to a judge, official, or employee of a tribunal except as permitted by Section C(4) of Canon 5 of the Code of Judicial Conduct, but a lawyer may make a contribution to the campaign fund of a candidate for judicial office in conformity with Section B(2) under Canon 7 of the Code of Judicial Conduct.[93]

(B) In an adversary proceeding, a lawyer shall not communicate, or cause another to communicate, as to the merits of the cause with a judge or an official before whom the proceeding is pending, except:
   (1) In the course of official proceedings in the cause.
   (2) In writing if he promptly delivers a copy of the writing to opposing counsel or to the adverse party if he is not represented by a lawyer.
   (3) Orally upon adequate notice to opposing counsel or to the adverse party if he is not represented by a lawyer.
   (4) As otherwise authorized by law, or by Section A(4) under Canon 3 of the Code of Judicial Conduct.[94, 95]

NOTES

1. "The right to be heard would be, in many cases, of little avail if it did not comprehend the right to be heard by counsel. Even the intelligent and educated layman has small and sometimes no skill in the science of law." Powell v. Alabama, 287 U.S. 45, 68-69, 77 L. Ed. 158, 170, 53 S. Ct. 55, 64 (1932).

2. *Cf.* ABA CANONS OF PROFESSIONAL ETHICS, CANON 4 (1908).

"At times . . . . [the tax lawyer] will be wise to discard some argument and he should exercise discretion to emphasize the arguments which in his judgment are most likely to be persuasive. But this process involves legal judgment rather than moral attitudes. The tax lawyer should put aside private disagreements with Congressional and Treasury policies. His own notions of policy, and his personal view of what the law should be, are irrelevant. The job entrusted to him by his client is to use all his learning and ability to protect his client's rights, not to help in the process of promoting a better tax system. The tax lawyer need not accept his client's economic and social opinions, but the client is paying for the technical attention and undivided concentration upon his affairs. He is equally entitled to performance unfettered by his attorney's economic and social predilections." Paul, *The Lawyer as a Tax Adviser*, 25 ROCKY MT. L. REV. 412, 418 (1953).

3. *See* ABA CANONS OF PROFESSIONAL ETHICS, CANONS 15 and 32 (1908).

ABA Canon 5, although only speaking of one accused of crime, imposes a similar obligation on the lawyer: "[T]he lawyer is bound, by all fair and honorable means, to present every defense that the law of the land permits, to the end that no person may be deprived of life or liberty, but by due process of law.

"Any persuasion of pressure on the advocate which deters him from planning and carrying out the litigation on the basis of 'what, within the framework of the law, is best for my client's interest?' interferes with the obligation to represent the client fully within the law.

"This obligation, in its fullest sense, is the heart of the adversary process. Each attorney, as an advocate, acts for and seeks that which in his judgment is best for his client, within the bounds authoritatively established. The advocate does not *decide* what is in this case—he would be usurping the function of the judge and jury—he acts for and seeks for his client that which he is entitled to under the law. He can do no less and properly represent the client." Thode, *The Ethical Standard for the Advocate*, 39 TEXAS L. REV. 575, 584 (1961).

"The [Texas public opinion] survey indicates that distrust of the lawyer can be traced directly to certain factors. Foremost of these is a basic misunderstanding of the function of the lawyer as an advocate in an adversary system.

"Lawyers are accused of taking advantage of 'loopholes' and 'technicalities' to win. Persons who make this charge are unaware, or do not understand, that the lawyer is hired to win, and if he does not exercise every legitimate effort in his client's behalf, then he is betraying a sacred trust." Rochelle & Payne, *The Struggle of Public Understanding*, 25 TEXAS B.J. 109, 159 (1962).

"The importance of the attorney's undivided allegiance and faithful service to one accused of crime, irrespective of the attorney's personal opinion as to the guilt of his client, lies in Canon 5 of the American Bar Association Canon of Ethics.

"The difficulty lies, of course, in ascertaining whether the attorney has been guilty of an error of judgment, such as an election with respect to trial tactics, or has otherwise been actuated by his conscience or belief that his client should be convicted in any event. All too frequently courts are called upon to review actions of defense counsel which are, at the most, errors of judgment, not properly reviewable on habeas corpus unless the trial is a farce and a mockery of justice which requires the court to intervene . . . . But when defense counsel, in a truly adverse proceeding, admits that his conscience would not permit him to adopt certain customary trial procedures, this extends beyond the realm of judgment and strongly suggests an invasion of constitutional rights." Johns v. Smyth, 176 F. Supp. 949, 952 (E.D. Va. 1959), *modified*, United States ex rel. Wilkins v. Banmiller, 205 F. Supp. 123, 128, n. 5 (E.D. Pa. 1962), *aff'd*, 325 F.2d 514 (3d Cir. 1963), *cert. denied*, 279 U.S. 847, 13 L. Ed. 2d 51, 85 S. Ct. 87 (1964).

"The adversary system in law administration bears a striking resemblance to the competitive economic system. In each we assume that the individual through partisanship or through self-interest will strive mightily for his side, and that kind of striving we must have. But neither system would be tolerable without restraints and modifications, and at times without outright departures from the system itself. Since the legal profession is entrusted with the system of law administration, a part of its task is to develop in its members appropriate restraints without impairing the values of partisan striving. An accompanying task is to aid in the modification of the adversary system or departure from it in areas to which the system is unsuited." Cheatham, *The Lawyer's Role and Surroundings*, 25 ROCKY MT. L. REV. 405, 410 (1953).

4. "Rule 4.15 prohibits, in the pursuit of a client's cause, 'any manner of fraud or chicane'; Rule 4.22 requires 'candor and fairness' in the conduct of the lawyer, and forbids the making of knowing misquotations; Rule 4.47 provides that a lawyer 'should always maintain his integrity,' and generally forbids all misconduct injurious to the interests of the public, the courts, or his clients, and acts contrary to 'justice, honesty, modesty or good morals.' Our Commissioner has accurately paraphrased these rules as follows: 'An attorney does not have the duty to do all and whatever he can that may enable him to win his client's cause or to further his client's interest. His duty and efforts in these respects, although they should be prompted by his "entire devotion" to the interest of his client, must be within and not without the bounds of the law.' " In re Wines, 370 S.W.2d 328, 333 (Mo. 1963).

See Note, 38 TEXAS L. REV. 107,110 (1959).

5. "Under our system of government the process of adjudication is surrounded by safeguards evolved from centuries of experience. These safeguards are not designed merely to lend formality and decorum to the trial of causes. They are predicated on the assumption that to secure for any controversy a truly informed and dispassionate decision is a difficult thing, requiring for its achievement a special summoning and organization of human effort and the adoption of measures to exclude the biases and prejudgments that have free play outside the courtroom. All of this goes for naught if the man with an unpopular cause is unable to find a competent lawyer courageous enough to represent him. His chance to have his day in court loses much of its meaning if his case is handicapped from the outset by the very kind of prejudgment our rules of evidence and procedure are intended to prevent." *Professional Responsibility: Report of the Joint Conference*. 44 A.B.A.J. 1159, 1216 (1958).

6. "[I]t is . . . [the tax lawyer's] positive duty to show the client how to avail himself to the full of what the law permits. He is not the keeper of the Congressional conscience." Paul, *The Lawyer as a Tax Adviser*, 25 ROCKY MT. L. REV. 412, 418 (1953).

7. *See* ABA CANONS OF PROFESSIONAL ETHICS, CANONS 15 and 30 (1908).

8. "The fact that it desired to evade the law, as it is called, is immaterial, because the very meaning of a line in the law is that you intentionally may go as close to it as you can if you do not pass it . . . . It is a matter of proximity and degree as to which minds will differ . . . ." Justice Holmes, in Superior Oil Co. v. Mississippi, 280 U.S. 390, 395-96, 74 L. Ed. 504, 508, 50 S. Ct. 169, 170 (1930).

9. "Today's lawyers perform two distinct types of functions, and our ethical standards should, but in the main do not, recognize these two functions. Judge Philbrick McCoy recently reported to the American Bar Association the need for a reappraisal of the Canons in light of the new and distinct function of counselor, as distinguished from advocate, which today predominates in the legal profession . . . .

". . . In the first place, any revision of the canons must take into account and speak to this new and now predominant function of the lawyer . . . . It is beyond the scope of this paper to discuss the ethical standards to be applied to the counselor except to state that in my opinion such standards should require a greater recognition and protection for the interest of the public generally than is presently expressed in the canons. Also, the counselor's obligation should extend to requiring him to inform and to impress upon the client a just solution of the problem, considering all interests involved." Thode, *The Ethical Standard for the Advocate*, 39 TEXAS L. REV. 575, 578-79 (1961).

"The man who has been called into court to answer for his own actions is entitled to fair hearing. Partisan advocacy plays its essential part in such a hearing, and the lawyer pleading his client's case may properly present it in the most favorable light. A similar resolution of doubts in one direction becomes inappropriate when the lawyer acts as counselor. The reasons that justify and even require partisan advocacy in the trial of a cause do not grant any license to the lawyer to participate as legal advisor in a line of conduct that is immoral, unfair, or of doubtful legality. In saving himself from this unworthy involvement, the lawyer cannot be guided solely by an unreflective inner sense of good faith; he must be at pains to preserve a sufficient detachment from his client's interests so that he remains capable of a sound and objective appraisal of the propriety of what his client proposes to do." *Professional Responsibility: Report of the Joint Conference*, 4 A.B.A.J. 1159, 1161 (1958).

10. "[A] lawyer who is asked to advise his client . . . may freely urge the statement of positions most favorable to the client just as long as there is reasonable basis for those positions." *ABA Opinion* 314 (1965).

11. "The lawyer . . . is not an umpire, but an advocate. He is under no duty to refrain from making every proper argument in support of any legal point because he is not convinced of its inherent soundness . . . . His personal belief in the soundness of his cause or of the authorities supporting it, is irrelevant." *ABA Opinion* 280 (1949).

"Counsel apparently misconceived his role. It was his duty to honorably present his client's contentions in the light most favorable to his client. Instead he presumed to advise the court as to the validity and sufficiency of prisoner's motion, by letter. We therefore conclude that prisoner had no effective assistance of counsel and remand this case to the District Court with instructions to set aside the Judgment, appoint new counsel to represent the prisoner if he makes no objection thereto, and proceed anew." McCartney v. United States, 343 F. 2d 471, 472 (9th Cir. 1965).

12. "Here the court-appointed counsel had the transcript but refused to proceed with the appeal because he found no merit in it . . . . We cannot say that there was a finding of frivolity by either of the California courts or that counsel acted in any greater capacity than merely as *amicus curiae* which was condemned in *Ellis, supra.* Hence California's procedure did not furnish petitioner with counsel acting in the role of an advocate nor did it provide that full consideration and resolution of the matter as is obtained when counsel is acting in the capacity . . . .

"The constitutional requirement of substantial equality and fair process can only be attained where counsel acts in the rule of an active advocate in behalf of his client, as opposed to that of *amicus curiae.* The no-merit letter and the procedure it triggers do not reach that dignity. Counsel should, and can with honor and without conflict, be of more assistance to his client and to the court. His role as advocate requires that he support his client's appeal to the best of his ability. Of course, if counsel finds his case to be wholly frivolous, after a conscientious examination of it, he should so advise the court and request permission to withdraw. That request must, however, be accompanied by a brief referring to anything in the record that might arguably support the appeal. A copy of counsel's brief should be furnished the indigent and time allowed him to raise any points that he chooses; the court—not counsel—then proceeds, after a full examination of all the proceedings, to decide whether the case is wholly frivolous. If it so finds it may grant counsel's request to withdraw and dismiss the appeal insofar as federal requirements are concerned, or proceed to a decision of the merits, if state law so requires. On the other hand, if it finds any of the legal points arguble on their merits (and therefore not frivolous) it must, prior to decision, afford the indigent the assistance of counsel to argue the appeal." Anders v. California, 386 U.S. 738, 744, 18 L. Ed. 2d 493, 498, 87 S. Ct. 1396, 1399-1400 (1967), *rehearing denied*, 388 U.S. 924, 18 L. Ed. 2d 1377, 87 S. Ct. 2094 (1967).

See Paul, *The Lawyer As a Tax Adviser*, 25 ROCKY MT. L. REV. 412, 432 (1953).

13. *See* ABA CANONS OF PROFESSIONAL ETHICS, CANON 32 (1908).

14. "For a lawyer to represent a syndicate notroriously engaged in the violation of the law for the purpose of advising the members how to break the law and at the same time escape it, is manifestly improper. While a lawyer may see to it that anyone accused of crime, no matter how serious and flagrant, has a fair trial, and present all available defenses, he may not co-operate in planning violations of the law. There is a sharp distinction, of course, between advising what can lawfully be done and advising how unlawful acts can be done in a way to avoid conviction. Where a lawyer accepts a retainer from an organization, known to be unlawful, and agrees in advance to defend its members when from time to time they are accused of crime arising out of its unlawful activities, this is equally improper."

"*See also Opinion* 155." *ABA Opinion* 281 (1952).

15. *See* ABA Special Committee on Minimum Standards for the Administration of Criminal Justice, *Standards Relating to Pleas of Guilty,* pp. 69-70 (1968).

16. "First of all, a truly great lawyer is a wise counselor to all manner of men in the varied crises of their lives when they most need disinterested advice. Effective counseling necessarily involves a thoroughgoing knowledge of the principles of the law not merely as they appear in the books but as they actually operate in action." Vanderbilt, *The Five Functions of the Lawyer: Service to Client and the Public,* 40 A.B.A.J. 31 (1954).

17. "A lawyer should endeavor to obtain full knowledge of his client's cause before advising there on . . . ." ABA CANONS OF PROFESSIONAL ETHICS, CANON 8 (1908).

18. "[I]n devising charters of collaborative effort the lawyer often acts where all of the affected parties are present as participants. But the lawyer also performs a similar function in situations where this is not so, as, for example, in planning estates and drafting wills. Here the instrument defining the terms of collaborating may affect persons not present and often not born. Yet here, too, the good lawyer does not serve merely as a legal conduit for his client's desires, but as a wise counselor, experienced in the art of devising arrangements that will put in workable order the entangled affairs and interests of human beings." *Professional Responsibility: Report of the Joint Conference,* 44 A.B.A.J. 1159, 1162 (1958).

19. *See* ABA CANONS OF PROFESSIONAL ETHICS, CANON 8 (1908).

"Vital as is the lawyer's role in adjudication, it should not be thought that it is only as an advocate pleading in open court that he contributes to the administration of the law. The most effective realization of the law's aims often takes place in the attorney's office, where litigation is forestalled by anticipating its outcome, where the lawyer's quiet counsel takes the place of public force. Contrary to popular belief, the compliance with the law thus brought about is not generally lip-serving and narrow, for by reminding him of its long-run costs the lawyer often deters his client from a course of conduct technically permissible under existing law, though inconsistent with its underlying spirit and purpose." *Professional Responsibility: Report of the Joint Conference,* 44 A.B.A.J. 1159, 1161 (1958).

20. "My summation of Judge Sharswood's view of the advocate's duty to the client is that he owes to the client the duty to use all legal means in support of the client's case. However, at the same time Judge Sharswood recognized that many advocates would find this obligation unbearable if applicable without exception. Therefore, the individual lawyer is given the choice of representing his client fully within the bounds set by the law or of telling his client that he cannot do so, so that the client may obtain another attorney if he wishes." Thode, *The Ethical Standard of the Advocate,* 39 TEXAS L. REV. 575, 582 (1961).

Cf. MODEL CODE OF PROFESSIONAL RESPONSIBILITY, DR 2-110(C).

21. *See* ABA CANONS OF PROFESSIONAL ETHICS, CANON 24 (1908).

22. Thode, *The Ethical Standard for the Advocate,* 39 TEXAS L. REV. 575, 592 (1961).

23. *See* ABA CANONS OF PROFESSIONAL ETHICS, CANON 5 (1908) and Berger v. United States, 295 U.S. 78, 79 L. Ed. 1314, 55 S. Ct. 629 (1935).

"The public prosecutor cannot take as a guide for the conduct of his office the standards of an attorney appearing on behalf of an individual client. The freedom elsewhere wisely granted to a partisan advocate must be severely curtailed if the prosector's duties are to be properly discharged. The public prosecutor must recall that he occupies a dual role, being obligated, on the one hand, to furnish that adversary element essential to the informed decision of any controversy, but being possessed, on the other, of important governmental powers that are pledged to the accomplishment of one objective only, that of impartial justice. Where the prosecutor is recreant to the trust implicit in his office, he undermines confidence, not only in his profession, but in government and the very ideal of justice itself." *Professional Responsibility: Report of the Joint Conference,* 44 A.B.A.J. 1159,1218 (1958).

"The prosecuting attorney is the attorney of the state, and it is his primary duty not to convict but to see that justice is done." *ABA Opinion* 150 (1936).

24. As to appearance before a department of government, ABA CANONS OF PROFESSIONAL ETHICS, CANON 26 (1908) provides: "A lawyer openly . . . may render professional services . . . in advocacy of claims before department of government upon the same principles of ethics which justify his appearance before the Courts . . . ."

25. "But as an advocate before a service which itself represents the adversary point of view, where his client's case is fairly arguable, a lawyer is under no duty to disclose its weaknesses, any more than he would be to make such a disclosure to a brother lawyer. The limitations within which he must operate are best expressed in Canon 22 . . . ." *ABA Opinion* 314 (1965).

26. *See* Baird v. Koerner, 279 F.2d 623 (9th Cir.1960).

27. *See* ABA CANONS OF PROFESSIONAL ETHICS, CANON 26 (1908).

28. "Law should be so practiced that the lawyer remains free to make up his own mind how he will vote, what causes he will support, what economic and political philosophy he will espouse. It is one of the glories of the profession that it admits of this freedom. Distinguished examples can be cited of lawyers whose views were at variance from those of their clients, lawyers whose skill and wisdom make them valued advisers to those who had little sympathy with their views as citizens." *Professional Responsibility: Report of the Joint Conference*, 44 A.B.A.J. 1159, 1217 (1958).

"No doubt some tax lawyers feel constrained to abstain from activities on behalf of a better tax system because they think that their clients may object. Clients have no right to object if the tax adviser handles their affairs competently and faithfully and independently of his private views as to tax policy. They buy his expert services, not his private opinions or his silence on issues that gravely affect the public interest." Paul, *The Lawyer as a Tax Adviser*, 25 ROCKY MT. L. REV. 412, 434 (1953).

29. *See* ABA CANONS OF PROFESSIONAL ETHICS, CANON 9 (1908).

30. *Id.*

31. *See Professional Responsibility: Report of the Joint Conference*, 44 A.B.A.J. 1159, 1160 (1958).

32. "Without the participation of someone who can act responsibly for each of the parties, this essential narrowing of the issues [by exchange of written pleading or stipulation of counsel] becomes impossible. But here again the true significance of partisan advocacy lies deeper, touching once more the integrity of the adjudicative process itself. It is only through the advocate's participation that the hearing may remain in fact what it purports to be in theory: a public trial of the facts and issues. Each advocate comes to the hearing prepared to present his proofs and arguments, knowing at the same time that his arguments may fail to persuade and that his proof may be rejected as inadequate . . . . The deciding tribunal, on the other hand, comes to the hearing uncommitted. It has not represented to the public that any fact can be proved, that any argument is sound, or that any particular way of stating a litigant's case is the most effective expression of its merits." *Professional Responsibility: Report of the Joint Conference*, 44 A.B.A.J. 1159, 1160-61 (1958).

33. *Cf.* ABA CANONS OF PROFESSIONAL ETHICS, CANONS 15 and 32 (1908).

34. *Cf.* ABA CANONS OF PROFESSIONAL ETHICS, CANON 21 (1908).

35. *See Professional Responsibility: Report of the Joint Conference*, 44 A.B.A.J. 1159, 1216 (1958).

36. "We are of the opinion that the letter in question was improper, and that in writing and sending it respondent was guilty of unprofessional conduct. This court has heretofore expressed its disapproval of using threats of criminal prosecution as a means of forcing settlement of civil claims . . . .

"Respondent has been guilty of a violation of a principle which condemns any confusion of threats of criminal prosecution with the enforcement of the civil claims. For this misconduct he should be severely censured." Matter of Gelman, 230 App. Div. 524, 527, N.Y.S. 416, 419 (1930).

37. "An attorney has the duty to protect the interests of his client. He has a right to press legitimate argument and to protest an erroneous ruling." Gallagher v. Municpal Court, 31 Cal. 2d 784, 796, 192 P.2d 905, 913 (1948).

"There must be protection, however, in the far more frequent case of the attorney who stands on his rights and combats the order in good faith and without disrespect believing with good cause that it is void, for it is here that the independence of the bar becomes valuable." Note, 39 COLUM. L. REV. 433, 438 (1939).

38. "Too many do not understand that accomplishment of the layman's abstract ideas of justice is the function of the judge and jury, and that it is the lawyer's sworn duty to portray his client's case in its most favorable light." Rochelle & Payne, *The Struggle for Public Understanding*, 25 TEXAS B.J. 109, 159 (1962).

39. "We are of the opinion that this Canon requires the lawyer to disclose such decisions [that are adverse to his client's contentions] to the court. He may, of course, after doing so, challenge the soundness of the decisions or present reasons which he believes would warrant the court in not following them in the pending case." *ABA Opinion* 146 (1935).

Cf. ABA Opinion 280 (1949) and Thode, *The Ethical Standard for the Advocate*, 39 TEXAS L. REV. 575. 585-86 (1961).

40. *See* ABA CANONS OF PROFESSIONAL ETHICS, CANON 15 (1908).

"The traditional duty of an advocate is that he honorably uphold the contentions of his client. He should not voluntarily undermine them." Harders v. State of California, 373 F.2d 839, 842 (9th Cir. 1967).

41. *See* ABA CANONS OF PROFESSIONAL ETHICS, CANON 22 (1908).

42. *Id.*; *cf.* ABA CANONS OF PROFESSIONAL ETHICS, CANON 41 (1908).

43. *See generally ABA Opinion* 287 (1953) as to a lawyer's duty when he unknowingly participates in introducing perjured testimony.

44. "Under any standard of proper ethical conduct an attorney would not sit by silently and permit his client to commit what may have been perjury, and which certainly would mislead the court and opposing party on a matter vital to the issue under consideration . . . .

. . . .

"Respondent next urges that it was his duty to observe the utmost good faith toward his client, and therefore he could not divulge any confidential information. This duty to the client of course does not extend to the point of authorizing collaboration with him in the commission of fraud." In re Carrol, 244 S.W.2d 474,474-75 (Ky. 1951).

45. *See* ABA CANONS OF PROFESSIONAL ETHICS, CANON 5 (1908); *cf. ABA Opinion* 131 (1935).

46. *Cf.* ABA CANONS OF PROFESSIONAL ETHICS, CANON 39 (1908).

47. "The prevalence of perjury is a serious menace to the administration of justice, to prevent which no means have as yet been satisfactorily devised. But there certainly can be no greater incentive to perjury than to allow a party to make payments to its opponent's witnesses under any guise or on any excuse, and at least attorneys who are officers of the court to aid it in the administration of justice, must keep themselves clear of any connection which in the slightest degree tends to induce witnesses to testify in favor of their clients." In re Robinson, 151 App. Div. 589, 600, 136 N.Y.S. 548, 556-57 (1912), *aff'd*, 209 N.Y. 354, 103 N.E. 160 (1913).

48. "It will not do for an attorney who seeks to justify himself against charges of this kind to show that he has escaped criminal responsibility under the Penal Law, nor can he blindly shut his eyes to a system which tends to suborn witnesses, to produce perjured testimony, and to suppress the truth. He has an active affirmative duty to protect the administration of justice from perjury and fraud, and that duty is not performed by allowing his subordinates and assistants to attempt to subvert justice and procure results for his clients based upon false testimony and perjured witnesses." *Id.*, 151 App. Div. at 592, 136 N.Y.S. at 551.

49. *See* ABA CANONS OF PROFESSIONAL ETHICS, CANON 23 (1908).

50. "[I]t is unfair to jurors to permit a disappointed litigant to pick over their private associations in search of something to discredit them and their verdict. And it would be unfair to the public too if jurors should understand that they cannot convict a man of means without risking an inquiry of that kind by paid investigators, with, to boot, the distortions an inquiry of that kind can produce." State v. LaFera, 42 N.J. 97, 107, 199 A.2d 630, 636 (1964).

51. *ABA Opinion* 319 (1968) points out that "[m]any courts today, and the trend is in this direction, allow the testimony of jurors as to all irregularities in and out of the courtroom except those irregularities whose existence can be determined only by exploring the consciousness of a single particular juror, New Jersey v. Kociolek, 20 N.J. 92, 118 A.2d 812 (1955). Model Code of Evidence Rule 301. Certainly as to states in which the testimony and affidavits of jurors may be received in support of or against a motion for new trial, a lawyer, in his obligation to protect his client, must have the tools for ascertaining whether or not grounds for a new trial exist and it is not unethical for him to talk to and question jurors."

52. *Generally see* ABA ADVISORY COMMITTEE ON FAIR TRIAL AND FREE PRESS, STANDARDS RELATING TO FAIR TRIAL AND FREE PRESS (1966).

"[T]he trial court might well have proscribed extrajudicial statements by any lawyer, party, witness, or court official which divulged prejudicial matters . . . . See state v. Van Dwyne. 43 N.J. 369, 389, 204 A.2d 841, 852 (1964), in which the court interpreted Canon 20 of the American Bar Association's Canons of Professional Ethics to prohibit such statements. Being advised of the great public interest in the case, the mass coverage of the press, and the potential prejudicial impact of publicity, the court could also have requested the appropriate city and county officials to promulgate a regulation with respect to dissemination of information about the case by their employees. In addition, reporters who wrote or broadcast prejudicial stories, could have been warned as to the impropriety of publishing material not introduced in the proceedings . . . . In this manner, Sheppard's right to a trial free from outside interference would have been given added protection without corresponding curtailment of the news media. Had the judge, the other officers of the court, and the police placed the interest of justice first, the news media would have soon learned to be content with the task of reporting the case as it unfolded in the courtroom—not pieced together from extrajudicial statements." Sheppard v. Maxwell, 384 U.S. 333,

361-62, 16 L. Ed. 2d 600, 619-20, 86 S. Ct. 1507, 1521-22 (1966).

"Court proceedings are held for the solemn purpose of endeavoring to ascertain the truth which is the *sine qua non* of a fair trial. Over the centuries Anglo-American courts have devised careful safeguards by rule and otherwise to protect and facilitate the performance of this high function. As a result, at this time those safeguards do not permit the televising and photographing of a criminal trial, save in two States and there only under restrictions. The federal courts prohibit it by specific rule. This is weighty evidence that our concepts of a fair trial do not tolerate such an indulgence. We have always held that the atmosphere essential to the preservation of a fair trial—the most fundamental of all freedoms—must be maintained at all costs." Estes v. State of Texas, 381 U.S. 532, 540, 14 L. Ed. 2d 543, 549, 85 S. Ct. 1628, 1631-32 (1965), *rehearing denied*, 382 U.S. 875, 15 L. Ed. 2d 118, 86 S. Ct. 18 (1965).

53. "Pretrial can create a major problem for the defendant in a criminal case. Indeed, it may be more harmful than publicity during the trial for it may well set the community opinion as to guilt or innocence . . . . The trial witnesses present at the hearing, as well as the original jury panel, were undoubtedly made aware of the peculiar public importance of the case by the press and television coverage being provided, and by the fact that they themselves were televised live and their pictures rebroadcast on the evening show." *Id.*, 381 U.S. at 536-37, 14 L. Ed. 2d at 546-47, 85 S. Ct. at 1629-30.

54. "The undeviating rule of this Court was expressed by Mr. Justice Holmes over half a century ago in Patterson v. Colorado, 205 U.S. 454, 462 (1907):

> The theory of our system is that the conclusions to be reached in a case will be induced only by evidence and argument in open court, and not by any outside influence, whether of private talk or public print."

Sheppard v. Maxwell, 384 U.S. 333, 351, 16 L. Ed. 2d 600, 614, 86 S. Ct. 1507, 1516 (1966).

"The trial judge has a large discretion in ruling on the issue of prejudice resulting from the reading by jurors of news articles concerning the trial . . . . Generalizations beyond that statement are not profitable, because each case must turn on its special facts. We have here the exposure of jurors to information of a character which the trial judge ruled was so prejudicial it could not be directly offered as evidence. The prejudice to the defendant is almost certain to be as great when that evidence reaches the jury through news accounts as when it is part of the prosecution's evidence . . . . It may indeed be greater for it is then not tempered by protective procedures." Marshall v. United States, 360 U.S. 310, 312-13, 3 L. Ed. 2d 1252, 79 S. Ct. 1171, 1173 (1959).

"The experienced trial lawyer knows that an adverse public opinion is a tremendous disadvantage to the defense of his client. Although grand jurors conduct their deliberations in secret, they are selected from the body of the public. They are likely to know what the general public knows and to reflect the public attitude. Trials are open to the public, and aroused pubic opinion respecting the merits of a legal controversy creates a court room atmosphere which, without any vocal expression in the presence of the petit jury, makes itself felt and has its effect upon the action of the petit jury. Our fundamental concepts of justice and our American sense of fair play require that the petit jury shall be composed of persons with fair and impartial minds and without preconceived views as to the merits of the controversy, and that it shall determine the issues presented to it solely upon the evidence adduced at the trial and according to the law given in the instructions of the trial judge.

"While we may doubt that the effect of public opinion would sway or bias the judgment of the trial judge in an equity proceeding, the defendant should not be called upon to run that risk and the trial court should not have his work made more difficult by any dissemination of statements to the public that would be calculated to create a public demand for a particular judgment in a prospective or pending case." *ABA Opinion* 199 (1940).

Cf. Estes v. State of Texas, 381 U.S. 532, 544-45, 144 L. Ed. 2d 543, 551, 85 S. Ct. 1628, 1634 (1965), *rehearing denied*, 381 U.S. 875, 15 L. Ed. 2d 118, 86 S. Ct. 18 (1965).

55. *See* ABA CANONS OF PROFESSIONAL ETHICS, CANON 20 (1908).

56. Canon 3 observes that a lawyer "deserves rebuke and denunciation for any device or attempt to gain from a Judge special personal consideration or favor."

See ABA CANONS OF PROFESSIONAL ETHICS, CANON 32 (1908).

57. "*Judicial Canon* 32 provides:

"A judge should not accept any present or favors from litigants, or from lawyers practicing before him or from others whose interests are likely to be submitted to him for judgment.

"The language of this Canon is perhaps broad enough to prohibit campaign contributions by lawyers, practicing before the court upon which the candidate hopes to sit. However, we do not think it was intended to prohibit such contributions when the candidate is obligated, by force of circumstances over which he has no control, to conduct a campaign, the expense of which exceeds that which he should reasonably be expected to personally bear!" *ABA Opinion* 226 (1941).

58. Amended, March 1974, House Informational Report No. 127.

59. *See* ABA CANONS OF PROFESSIONAL ETHICS, CANONS 3 and 32 (1908).

60. *Cf.* ABA CANONS OF PROFESSIONAL ETHICS, CANON 18 (1908).

61. *See* ABA CANONS OF PROFESSIONAL ETHICS, CANONS 1 and 3 (1908).

62. *See* ABA CANONS OF PROFESSIONAL ETHICS, CANON 17 (1908).

63. *See* ABA CANONS OF PROFESSIONAL ETHICS, CANON 24 (1908).

64. *See* ABA CANONS OF PROFESSIONAL ETHICS, CANON 25 (1908).

65. *See* ABA CANONS OF PROFESSIONAL ETHICS, CANON 21 (1908).

66. *See* ABA CANONS OF PROFESSIONAL ETHICS, CANON 15 (1908).

67. *See* ABA CANONS OF PROFESSIONAL ETHICS, CANONS 5 and 15 (1908); *cf.* ABA CANONS 4 and 32 (1908).

68. *Cf.* ABA CANONS OF PROFESSIONAL ETHICS, CANON 24 (1908).

69. *Cf.* ABA CANONS OF PROFESSIONAL ETHICS, CANON 30 (1908).

70. *Cf.* ABA CANONS OF PROFESSIONAL ETHICS, CANONS 22 and 29 (1908).

71. *See* ABA CANONS OF PROFESSIONAL ETHICS, CANON 41 (1908); *cf.* Hinds v. State Bar, 19 Cal.2d 87, 92-93, 119 P.2d 134, 137 (1941); *but see ABA Opinion* 287 (1953) and TEXAS CANON 38. *Also see* MODEL CODE OF PROFESSIONAL RESPONSIBILITY, DR 4-101(C)(2).

72. Amended, March 1974, House Informational Report No. 127.

73. *See* Precision Inst. Mfg. Co. v. Automotive M.M. Co., 324 U.S. 806, 89 L. Ed. 1381, 65 S. Ct. 993 (1945).

74. *Cf.* ABA CANONS OF PROFESSIONAL ETHICS, CANON 5 (1908).

75. "*Rule 12* . . . . A member of the State Bar shall not communicate with a party represented by counsel upon a subject of controversy, in the absence and without the consent of such counsel. This rule shall not apply to communications with a public officer, board committee or body." CAL. BUSINESS AND PROFESSIONAL CODE §6076 (West 1962).

76. *See* ABA CANONS OF PROFESSIONAL ETHICS, CANON 9 (1908); *cf. ABA Opinions* 124 (1934), 108 (1935), 95 (1933), and 75 (1932); *also see* In re Schwabe, 242 Or. 169, 174-75, 408 P.2d 922, 924 (1965).

"It is clear from the earlier opinions of this committee that *Canon* 9 is to be construed literally and does not allow a communication with an opposing party, without the consent of his counsel, though the purpose merely be to investigate the facts. Opinions 117, 55, 66." *ABA Opinion* 187 (1938).

77. *Cf. ABA Opinion* 102 (1933).

78. *Cf.* ABA CANONS OF PROFESSIONAL ETHICS, CANON 9 (1908) and *ABA Opinion* 58 (1931).

79. *Cf.* Note, 38 TEXAS L. REV. 107, 108-09 (1959).

80. "In the brief summary in the 1947 edition of the Committee's decisions (p. 17), *Opinion 146* was thus summarized: *Opinion 146*—A lawyer should disclose to the court a decision directly adverse to his client's case that is unknown to his adversary.

. . . .

"We would not confine the Opinion to 'controlling authorities' — i.e., those decisive of the pending case—but, in accordance with the tests hereafter suggested, would apply it to a decision directly adverse to any proposition of law on which the lawyer expressly relies, which would reasonably be considered important by the judge sitting on the case.

. . . .

". . . The test in every case should be: Is the decision which opposing counsel has overlooked one which the court should clearly consider in deciding the case? Would a reasonable judge properly feel that a lawyer who advanced, as the law, a proposition adverse to the undisclosed decision, was lacking in candor and fairness to him? Might the judge consider himself misled by an implied representation that the lawyer knew of no adverse authority" *ABA Opinion* 280 (1949).

81. "The authorities are substantially uniform against any privilege as applied to the fact of retainer or identity of the client. The privilege is limited to confidential communications, and a retainer is not a confidential communication, although it cannot come into existence without some communication between the attorney and the—at that stage prospective—client" United States v. Pape; 144 F.2d 778, 782 (2d Cir. 1944), *cert. denied,* 323 U.S. 752, 89 L. Ed. 2d 602, 65 S. Ct. 86 (1944).

"To be sure, there may be circumstances under which the identification of a client may amount to the prejudicial disclosure of a confidential communication, as where the substance of a disclosure has already been revealed but not its source." Colton v. United States, 306 F.2d 633, 637 (2d Cir. 1962).

82. *See* ABA CANONS OF PROFESSIONAL ETHICS, CANON 22 (1908); *cf.* ABA CANONS OF PROFESSIONAL ETHICS, CANON 17 (1908).

"The rule allowing counsel when addressing the jury the widest latitude in discussing the evidence and presenting the client's theories falls far short of authorizing the statement by counsel of matter not in evidence, or indulging in argument founded on no proof, or demanding verdicts for purposes other than the just settlement of the matters at issue between the litigants, or appealing to prejudice or passion. The rule confining counsel to legitimate argument is not based on etiquette, but on justice. Its violation is not merely an overstepping of the bounds of propriety, but a violation of a party's rights. The jurors must determine the issues upon the evidence. Counsel's address should help them do this, not tend to lead them astray." Cherry Creek Nat'l Bank v. Fidelity & Cas. Co., 207 App. Div. 787, 790-91, 202 N.Y S. 611, 614 (1924).

83. *Cf.* ABA CANONS OF PROFESSIONAL ETHICS, CANON 18 (1908).

"§6068 . . . . It is the duty of an attorney

. . . .

"(f) To abstain from all offensive personality, and to advance no fact prejudicial to the honor or reputation of a party or witness unless required by the justice of the cause with which he is charged." CAL. BUSINESS AND PROFESSIONS CODE §6068 (West 1962).

84. "The record in the case at bar was silent concerning the qualities and character of the deceased. It is especially improper, in addressing the jury in a murder case, for the prosecuting attorney to make reference to his knowledge of the good qualities of the deceased where there is no evidence in the record bearing upon his character . . . . A prosecutor should never inject into his argument evidence not introduced at the trial." People v. Dukes, 12 Ill. 2d 334, 341, 146 N.E.2d 14, 17-18 (1957).

85. "A lawyer should not ignore known customs or practice of the Bar or of a particular Court, even when the law permits, without giving timely notice to the opposing counsel." ABA CANONS OF PROFESSIONAL ETHICS, CANON 25 (1908).

86. The provisions of Sections (A), (B), (C), and (D) of this Disciplinary Rule incorporate the fair trial-free press standards which apply to lawyers as adopted by the ABA House of Delegates, Feb. 19, 1968, upon the recommendation of the Fair Trial and Free Press Advisory Committee of the ABA Special Committee on Minimum Standards for the Administration of Criminal Justice.

Cf. ABA CANONS OF PROFESSIONAL ETHICS, CANON 20 (1908); *see generally* ABA ADVISORY COMMITTEE ON FAIR TRIAL AND FREE PRESS, STANDARDS RELATING TO FAIR TRIAL AND FREE PRESS (1966).

"From the cases coming here we note that unfair and prejudicial news comment on pending trials has become increasingly prevalent. Due process requires that the accused receive a trial by an impartial jury free from outside influences. Given the pervasiveness of modern communications and the difficulty of effacing prejudicial publicity from the minds of the jurors, the trial courts must take strong measures to ensure that the balance is never weighed against the accused. And appellate tribunals have the duty to make an independent evaluation of the circumstances. Of course, there is nothing that prescribes the press from reporting events that transpire in the courtroom. But where there is a reasonable likelihood that prejudicial news prior to trial will prevent a fair trial the judge should continue the case until the threat abates, or transfer it to another county not so permeated with publicity . . . . The courts must take such steps by rule and regulation that will protect their processes from prejudicial outside interferences. Neither prosecutors, counsel for defense, the accused, witnesses, court staff nor enforcement officers coming under the jurisdiction of the court should be permitted to frustrate its function. Collaboration between counsel and the press as to information affecting the fairness of a criminal trial is not only subject to regulation, but is highly censurable and worthy of disciplinary measures." Sheppard v. Maxwell, 384 U.S. 333, 362-63, 16 L. Ed. 2d 600, 620, 86 S. Ct. 1507, 1522 (1966).

87. *See* ABA CANONS OF PROFESSIONAL ETHICS, CANON 23 (1908).

88. "[I]t would be unethical for a lawyer to harass, entice, induce or exert influence on a juror to obtain his testimony." *ABA Opinion* 319 (1968).

89. *See* ABA CANONS OF PROFESSIONAL ETHICS, CANON 5 (1908).

90. *Cf.* ABA CANONS OF PROFESSIONAL ETHICS, CANON 5 (1908).

"*Rule 15* . . . . A member of the State Bar shall not advise a person, whose testimony could establish or tend to establish a material fact, to avoid service of process, or secrete himself, or otherwise to make his testimony unavailable." CAL. BUSINESS AND PROFESSIONS CODE §6076 (West 1962).

91. *See* In re O'Keefe, 49 Mont. 369, 142 P. 638 (1914).

92. *Cf.* ABA CANONS OF PROFESSIONAL ETHICS, CANON 3 (1908).

93. Amended, March 1974, House Informational Report No. 127.

94. "*Rule 16* . . . . A member of the State Bar shall not, in the absence of opposing counsel, communicate with or argue to a judge or judicial officer except in open court upon the merits of a contested matter pending before such judge or judicial officer; nor shall he, without furnishing opposing counsel with a copy thereof, address a written communication to a judge or judicial officer concerning the merits of a contested matter pending before such judge or judicial officer. This rule shall not apply to ex parte matters." CAL. BUSINESS AND PROFESSIONS CODE §6076 (West 1962).

95. Amended, March 1974, House Informational Report No. 127.

CANON 8
A Lawyer Should Assist in Improving the Legal System

ETHICAL CONSIDERATIONS

EC 8-1 Changes in human affairs and imperfections in human institutions make necessary constant efforts to maintain and improve our legal system.[1] This system should function in a manner that commands public respect and fosters the use of legal remedies to achieve redress of grievances. By reason of education and experience, lawyers are especially qualified to recognize deficiencies in the legal system and to initiate corrective measures therein. Thus they should participate in proposing and supporting legislation and programs to improve the system,[2] without regard to the general interests or desires of clients or former clients.[3]

EC 8-2 Rules of law are deficient if they are not just, understandable, and responsive to the needs of society. If a lawyer believes that the existence or absence of a rule of law, substantive or procedural, causes or contributes to an unjust result, he should endeavor by lawful means to obtain appropriate changes in the law. He should encourage the simplification of laws and the repeal or amendment of laws that are outmoded.[4] Likewise, legal procedures should be improved whenever experience indicates a change is needed.

EC 8-3 The fair administration of justice requires the availability of competent lawyers. Members of the public should be educated to recognize the existence of legal problems and the resultant need for legal services, and should be provided methods for intelligent selection of counsel. Those persons unable to pay for legal services should be provided needed services. Clients and lawyers should not be penalized by undue geographical restraints upon representation in legal matters, and the bar should address itself to improvements in licensing, reciprocity, and admission procedures consistent with the needs of modern commerce.

EC 8-4 Whenever a lawyer seeks legislative or administrative changes, he should identify the capacity in which he appears, whether on behalf of himself, a client, or the public.[5] A lawyer may advocate such changes on behalf of a client even though he does not agree with them. But when a lawyer purports to act on behalf of the public, he should espouse only those changes which he conscientiously believes to be in the public interest.

EC 8-5 Fraudulent, deceptive, or otherwise illegal conduct by a participant in a proceeding before a tribunal or legislative body is inconsistent with fair administration of justice, and it should never be participated in or condoned by lawyers. Unless constrained by his obligation to preserve the confidences and secrets of his client, a lawyer should reveal to appropriate authorities any knowledge he may have of such improper conduct.

EC 8-6 Judges and administrative officials having adjudicatory powers ought to be persons of integrity, competence, and suitable temperament. Generally, lawyers are qualified, by personal observation or investigation, to evaluate the qualifications of persons seeking or being considered for such public offices, and for this reason they have a special responsibility to aid in the selection of only those who are qualified.[6] It is the duty of lawyers to endeavor to prevent political considerations from outweighing judicial fitness in the selection of judges. Lawyers should protest earnestly against the appointment or election of those who are unsuited for the bench and should strive to have elected[7] or appointed thereto only those who are willing to forego pursuits, whether of a business, political, or other nature, that may interfere with the free and fair consideration of questions presented for adjudication. Adjudicatory officials, not being wholly free to defend themselves, are entitled to receive the support of the bar against unjust criticism.[8] While a lawyer as a citizen has a right to criticize such officials publicly,[9] he should be certain of the merit of his complaint, use appropriate language, and avoid petty criticisms, for unrestrained and intemperate statements tend to lessen public confidence in our legal system.[10] Criticisms motivated by reasons other than a desire to improve the legal system are not justified.

EC 8-7 Since lawyers are a vital part of the legal system, they should be persons of integrity, of professional skill, and of dedication to the improvement of the system. Thus a lawyer should aid in establishing, as well as enforcing, standards of conduct adequate to protect the public by insuring that those who practice law are qualified to do so.

EC 8-8 Lawyers often serve as legislators or as holders of other public offices. This is highly desirable, as lawyers are uniquely qualified to make significant contributions to the improvement of the legal system. A lawyer who is a public officer, whether full or part-time, should not engage in activities in which his personal or professional interests are or foreseeably may be in conflict with his official duties.[11]

EC 8-9 The advancement of our legal system is of vital importance in maintaining the rule of law and in facilitating orderly changes; therefore, lawyers should encourage, and should aid in making, needed changes and improvements.

DISCIPLINARY RULES

DR 8-101 Action as a Public Official.

(A) A lawyer who holds public office shall not:

(1) Use his public position to obtain, or attempt to obtain, a special advantage in legislative matters for himself or for a client under circumstances where he knows or it is obvious that such action is not in the public interest.

(2) Use his public position to influence, or attempt to influence, a tribunal to act in favor of himself or of a client.

(3) Accept any thing of value from any person when the lawyer knows or it is obvious that the offer is for the purpose of influencing his action as a public official.

DR 8-102 Statements Concerning Judges and Other Adjudicatory Officers.[12]

(A) A lawyer shall not knowingly make false statements of fact concerning the qualifications of a candidate for election or appointment to a judicial office.

(B) A lawyer shall not knowingly make false accusations against a judge or other adjudicatory officer.

DR 8-103 Lawyer Candidate for Judicial Office.

(A) A lawyer who is a candidate for judicial office shall comply with the applicable provisions of Canon 7 of the Code of Judicial Conduct.[13]

NOTES

1. ". . . . [Another] task of the great lawyer is to do his part individually and as a member of the organized bar to improve his profession, the courts, and the law. As President Theodore Roosevelt aptly put it, 'Every man owes some of his time to the upbuilding of the profession to which he belongs.' Indeed, this obligation is one of the great things which distinguishes a profession from a business. The soundness and the necessity of President Roosevelt's admonition insofar as it relates to the legal profession cannot be doubted. The advances in natural science and technology are so startling and the velocity of change in business and in social life is so great that the law along with the other social sciences, and even human life itself, is in grave danger of being extinguished by new gods of its own invention if it does not awake from its lethargy." Vanderbilt, *The Five Functions of the Lawyer: Service to Client and the Public*, 40 A.B.A.J. 31, 31-32

2. *See* ABA CANONS OF PROFESSIONAL ETHICS, CANON 29 (1908); *cf.* Cheatham, *The Lawyer's Role and Surroundings*, 25 ROCKY MT. L. REV. 405, 406-07 (1953).

"The lawyer tempted by repose should recall the heavy costs paid by his profession when needed legal reform has to be accomplished though the initiative of public-spirited laymen. Where change must be thrust from without upon an unwilling Bar, the public's least flattering picture of the lawyer seems confirmed. The lawyer concerned for the standing of his profession will, therefore, interest himself actively in the improvement of the law. In doing so he will not only help to maintain confidence in the Bar, but will have the satisfaction of meeting a responsibility inhering in the nature of his calling." *Professional Responsibility: Report of the Joint Conference*, 44 A.B.A.J. I 59, 1217 (1958).

3. *See* Stayton, *Cum Honor Officium,* 19 TEX B.J. 76S, 766 (1956); *Professional Responsibility: Report of the Joint Conference,* 44 A.B.A.J. 1159, 1162 (1958); and Paul, *The Lawyer as a Tax Adviser,* 25 ROCKY MT. L. REV. 412, 433-34 (1953).

4. "There are few great figures in the history of the Bar who have not concerned themselves with the reform and improvement of the law. The special obligation of the profession with respect to legal reform rests on considerations too obvious to require enumeration. Certainly it is the lawyer who has both the best chance to know when the law is working badly and the special competence to put it in order." *Professional Responsibility: Report of the Joint Conference,* 44 A.B.A.J. 1159, 1217 (1958).

5. "*Rule 14* . . . . A member of the State Bar shall not communicate with, or appear before, a public officer, board, committee or body, in his professional capacity, without first disclosing that he is an attorney representing interests that may be affected by action of such officer, board, committee or body." CAL. BUSINESS AND PROFESSIONS CODE §6076 (West 1962).

6. *See* ABA CANONS OF PROFESSIONAL ETHICS, CANON 2 (1908).

"Lawyers are better able than laymen to appraise accurately the qualifications of candidates for judicial office. It is proper that they should make that appraisal known to the voters in a proper and dignified manner. A lawyer may with propriety endorse a candidate for judicial office and seek like endorsement from other lawyers. But the lawyer who endorses a judicial candidate or seeks that endorsement from other lawyers should be actuated by a sincere belief in the superior qualifications of the candidate for judicial service and not by personal or selfish motives; and a lawyer should not use or attempt to use the power or prestige of the judicial office to secure such endorsement. On the other hand, the lawyer whose endorsement is sought, if he believes the candidate lacks the essential qualifications for the office or believes the opposing candidate is better qualified, should have the courage and moral stamina to refuse the request for endorsement." *ABA Opinion* 189 (1938).

7. "[W]e are of the opinion that, whenever a candidate for judicial office merits the endorsement and support of lawyers, the lawyers may make financial contributions toward the campaign if its cost, when reasonably conducted, exceeds that which the candidate would be expected to bear personally." *ABA Opinion* 226 (1941).

8. *See* ABA CANONS OF PROFESSIONAL ETHICS, CANON 1 (1908).

9. "Citizens have a right under our constitutional system to criticize governmental officials and agencies. Courts are not, and should not be, immune to such criticism." Konigsberg v. State Bar of California, 353 U.S. 252, 269 (1957).

10. "[E]very lawyer, worthy of respect, realizes that public confidence in our courts is the cornerstone of our governmental structure, and will refrain from unjustified attack on the character of the judges, while recognizing the duty to denounce and expose a corrupt or dishonest judge." Kentucky State Bar Ass'n v. Lewis, 282 S.W. 2d 321, 326 (Ky. 1955).

"We should be the last to deny that Mr. Meeker has the right to uphold the honor of the profession and to expose without fear or favor corrupt or dishonest conduct in the profession, whether the conduct be that of a judge or not . . . . However, this Canon [29] does not permit one to make charges which are false and untrue and unfounded in fact. When one's fancy leads him to make false charges, attacking the character and integrity of others, he does so at his peril. He should not do so without adequate proof of his charges and he is certainly not authorized to make careless, untruthful and vile charges against his professional brethren." In re Meeker, 76 N.M. 354, 364-65, 414 P.2d 862, 869 (1966), *appeal dismissed,* 385 U.S. 449, 17 L. Ed. 2d 510, 87 S. Ct. 613 (1967).

11. "*Opinions 16, 30, 34, 77, 118* and *134* relate to *Canon 6,* and pass on questions concerning the propriety of the conduct of an attorney who is a public officer, in representing private interests adverse to those of the public body which he represents. The principle applied in those opinions is that an attorney holding public office should avoid all conduct which might lead the layman to conclude that the attorney is utilizing his public position to further his professional success or personal interests." *ABA Opinion* 192 (1939).

"The next question is whether a lawyer-member of a legislative body may appear as counsel or co-counsel at hearings before a zoning board of appeals, or similar tribunal, created by the legislative group of which he is a member. We are of the opinion that he may practice before fact-finding officers, hearing bodies and commissioners, since under our views he may appear as counsel in the courts where his municipality is a party. Decisions made at such hearings are usually subject to administrative review by the courts upon the record there made. It would be inconsistent to say that a lawyer-member of a legislative body could not participate in a hearing at which the record is made, but could appear thereafter when the cause is heard by the court on administrative review. This is subject to an important exception. He should not appear as counsel where the matter is subject to review by the legislature body of which he is a member . . . . We are of the opinion that where a lawyer does so appear there would be conflict of interests between his duty as an advocate for his client on the one hand and the obligation to his governmental unit on the other hand." In re Becker, 16 Ill. 2d 488, 494-95, 158 N.E. 2d 753, 756-57 (1959). *Cf. ABA Opinions* 186 (1938), 136 (1935), 118 (1934), and 77 (1932).

12. Cf. ABA CANONS OF PROFESSIONAL ETHICS, CANONS 1 and 2 (1908).

13. Amended, March 1974, House Informational Report No. 127.

CANON 9
A Lawyer Should Avoid Even the Appearance of Professional Impropriety

ETHICAL CONSIDERATIONS

EC 9-1 Continuation of the American concept that we are to be governed by rules of law requires that the people have faith that justice can be obtained through our legal system.[1] A lawyer should promote public confidence in our system and in the legal profession.[2]

EC 9-2 Public confidence in law and lawyers may be eroded by irresponsible or improper conduct of a lawyer. On occasion, ethical conduct of a lawyer may appear to laymen to be unethical. In order to avoid misunderstandings and hence to maintain confidence, a lawyer should fully and promptly inform his client of material developments in the matters being handled for the client. While a lawyer should guard against otherwise proper conduct that has a tendency to diminish public confidence in the legal system or in the legal profession, his duty to clients or to the public should never be subordinate merely because the full discharge of his obligation may be misunderstood or may tend to subject him or the legal profession to criticism. When explicit ethical guidance does not exist, a lawyer should determine his conduct by acting in a manner that promotes public confidence in the integrity and efficiency of the legal system and the legal profession.[3]

EC 9-3 After a lawyer leaves judicial office or other public employment, he should not accept employment in connection with any matter in which he had substantial responsibility prior to his leaving, since to accept employment would give the appearance of impropriety even if none exists.[4]

EC 9-4 Because the very essence of the legal system is to provide procedures by which matters can be presented in an impartial manner so that they may be decided solely upon the merits, any statement or suggestion by a lawyer that he can or would attempt to circumvent those procedures is detrimental to the legal system and tends to undermine public confidence in it.

EC 9-5 Separation of the funds of a client from those of his lawyer not only serves to protect the client but also avoids even the appearance of impropriety, and therefore commingling of such funds should be avoided.

EC 9-6 Every lawyer owes a solemn duty to uphold the integrity and honor of his profession; to encourage respect for the law and for the courts and the judges thereof; to observe the Code of Professional Responsibility; to act as a member of a learned profession, one dedicated to public service; to cooperate with his brother lawyers in supporting the organized bar through the devoting of his time, efforts, and financial support as his professional standing and ability reasonably permit; to conduct himself so as to reflect credit on the legal profession and to inspire the confidence, respect, and trust of his clients and of the public; and to strive to avoid not only professional impropriety but also the appearance of impropriety.[5]

EC 9-7 A lawyer has an obligation to the public to participate in collective efforts of the bar to reimburse persons who have lost money or property as a result of the misappropriation or defalcation of another lawyer, and contribution to a client's security fund is an acceptable method of meeting this obligation.[6]

DISCIPLINARY RULES

DR 9-101 Avoiding Even the Appearance of Impropriety.[7]

(A) A lawyer shall not accept private employment in a matter upon the merits of which he has acted in a judicial capacity.[8]
(B) A lawyer shall not accept private employment in a matter in which he had substantial responsibility while he was a public employee.[9]
(C) A lawyer shall not state or imply that he is able to influence improperly or upon irrelevant grounds any tribunal, legislative body,[10] or public official.

DR 9-102 Preserving Identity of Funds and Property of a Client.[11]

(A) All funds of clients paid to a lawyer or law firm, other than advances for costs and expenses, shall be deposited in one or more identifiable bank accounts maintained in the state in which the law office is situated and no funds belonging to the lawyer or law firm shall be deposited therein except as follows:
   (1) Funds reasonably sufficient to pay bank charges may be deposited therein.
   (2) Funds belonging in part to a client and in part presently or potentially to the lawyer or law firm must be deposited therein, but the portion belonging to the lawyer or law firm may be withdrawn when due

unless the right of the lawyer or law firm to receive it is disputed by the client, in which event the disputed portion shall not be withdrawn until the dispute is finally resolved.

(B) A lawyer shall:

(1)Promptly notify a client of the receipt of his funds, securities, or other properties.

(2) Identify and label securities and properties of a client promptly upon receipt and place them in a safe deposit box or other place of safekeeping as soon as practicable.

(3) Maintain complete records of all funds, securities, and other properties of a client coming into the possession of the lawyer and render appropriate accounts to his client regarding them.

(4) Promptly pay or deliver to the client as requested by a client the funds, securities, or other properties in the possession of the lawyer which the client is entitled to receive.

NOTES

1. "Integrity is the very breath of justice. Confidence in our law, our courts, and in the administration of justice is our supreme interest. No practice must be permitted to prevail which invites towards the administration of justice a doubt or distrust of its integrity." Erwin M. Jennings Co. v. DiGenova, 107 Conn. 491, 499, 141 A. 866, 868 (1928).

2. "A lawyer should never be reluctant or too proud to answer unjustified criticism of his profession, of himself, or of his brother lawyer. He should guard the reputation of his profession and of his brother as zealously as he guards his own." Rochelle & Payne, *The Struggle for Public Understanding*, 25 TEXAS B.J. 109, 162 (1962).

3. *See* ABA CANONS OF PROFESSIONAL ETHICS, CANON 29 (1908).

4. *See* ABA CANONS OF PROFESSIONAL ETHICS, CANON 36 (1908).

5. "As said in Opinion 49, of the Committee on Professional Ethics and Grievances of the American Bar Association, page 134: 'An attorney should not only avoid impropriety but should avoid the appearance of impropriety.' " State ex rel. Nebraska State Bar Ass'n v. Richards, 165 Neb. 80, 93, 84 N.W.2d 136, 145 (1957).

"It would also be preferable that such contribution [to the campaign of a candidate for judicial office] be made to a campaign committee rather than to the candidate personally. In so doing, possible appearances of impropriety would be reduced to a minimum" *ABA Opinion* 226 (1941).

"The lawyer assumes high duties, and has imposed upon him grave responsibilities. He may be the means of much good or much mischief. Interests of vast magnitude are entrusted to him; confidence is reposed in him; life, liberty, character and property should be protected by him. He should guard, with zealous watchfulness, his own reputation, as well as that of his profession." People ex rel. Cutler v. Ford, 54 III. 520, 522 (1870), and also quoted in State Board of Law Examiners v. Sheldon, 43 Wyo. 522, 526, 7 P.2d 226, 227 (1932).

See ABA Opinion 150 (1936).

6. Amended, February 1980, House Informational Report No. 105.

7. *Cf.* MODEL CODE OF PROFESSIONAL RESPONSIBILITY, EC 5-6.

8. *See* ABA CANONS OF PROFESSIONAL ETHICS, CANON 36 (1908).

"It is the duty of the judge to rule on questions of law and evidence in misdemeanor cases and examinations in felony cases. That duty calls for impartial and uninfluenced judgment, regardless of the effect on those immediately involved or others who may, directly or indirectly, be affected. Discharge of that duty might be greatly interfered with if the judge, in another capacity, were permitted to hold himself out to employment by those who are to be, or who may be, brought to trial in felony cases, even though he did not conduct the examination. His private interests as a lawyer in building up his clientele, his duty as such zealously to espouse the cause of his private clients and to defend against charges of crime brought by law enforcement agencies of which he is a part, might prevent, or even destroy, that unbiased judicial judgment which is so essential in the administration of justice.

"In our opinion, acceptance of a judgeship with the duties of conducting misdemeanor trials, and examinations in felony cases to determine whether those accused should be bound over for trial in a higher court, ethically bars the judge from acting as attorney for the defendants upon such trial, whether they were examined by him or by some other judge. Such a practice would not only diminish public confidence in the administration of justice in both courts, but would produce serious conflict between the private interests of the judge as a lawyer, and of his clients, and his duties as a judge in adjudicating important phases of criminal processes in other cases. The public and private duties would be incompatible. The prestige of judicial office would be diverted to private benefit, and the judicial office would be demeaned thereby," *ABA Opinion* 242 (1942).

"A lawyer, who has previously occupied a judicial position or acted in a judicial capacity, should refrain from accepting employment in any matter involving the same facts as were involved in any specific question which he acted upon in a judicial capacity and, for the same reasons, should also refrain from accepting any employment which might reasonably appear to involve the same facts." *ABA Opinion* 49 (1931).

See ABA Opinion 110 (1934).

9. *See ABA Opinions* 135 (1935) and 134 (1935); *cf.* ABA CANONS OF PROFESSIONAL ETHICS, CANON 36 (1980) and *ABA Opinions* 39 (1931) and 26 (1930). *But see ABA Opinion* 37 (1931).

10. "[A statement by a governmental department or agency with regard to a lawyer resigning from its staff that includes a laudation of his legal ability] carries implications, probably not founded in fact, that the lawyer's acquaintance and previous relations with the personnel of the administrative agencies of the government place him in an advantageous position in practicing before such agencies. So to imply would not only represent what probably is untrue, but would be highly reprehensible." *ABA Opinion* 184 (1938).

11. *See* ABA CANONS OF PROFESSIONAL ETHICS, CANON 11 (1908).

"*Rule 9* . . . . A member of the State Bar shall not commingle the money or other property of a client with his own; and he shall promptly report to the client the receipt by him of all money and other property belonging to such client. Unless the client otherwise directs in writing, he shall promptly deposit his client's funds in a bank or trust company . . . in a bank account separate from his own account and clearly designated as 'Clients' Funds Account' or 'Trust Funds Account' or words of similar import. Unless the client otherwise directs in writing, securities of a client in bearer form shall be kept by the attorney in a safe deposit box at a bank or trust company . . . which safe deposit box shall be clearly designated as 'Clients' Account' or 'Trust Account' or words of similar import, and be separate from the attorney's own safe deposit box." CAL. BUSINESS AND PROFESSIONS CODE §6076 (West 1962).

"[C]ommingling is committed when a client's money is intermingled with that of his attorney and its separate identity lost so that it may be used for the attorney's personal expenses or subjected to claims of his creditors . . . . The rule against commingling was adopted to provide against the probability in some cases, the possibility in many cases, and the danger in all cases that such commingling will result in the loss of clients' money. " Black v State Bar, 57 Cal. 2d 219, 225-26, 368 P.2d 118, 122, 18 Cal. Rptr. 518, 522 (1962).

DEFINITIONS*

As used in the Disciplinary Rules of the Model Code of Professional Responsibility:

(1) "Differing interests" include every interest that will adversely affect either the judgment or the loyalty of a lawyer to a client, whether it be a conflicting, inconsistent, diverse, or other interest.

(2) "Law firm" includes a professional legal corporation.

(3) "Person" includes a corporation, an association, a trust, a partnership, and any other organization or legal entity.

(4) "Professional legal corporation" means a corporation, or an association treated as a corporation, authorized by law to practice law for profit.

(5) "State" includes the District of Columbia, Puerto Rico, and other federal territories and possessions.

(6) "Tribunal" includes all courts and all other adjudicatory bodies.

(7) "A Bar association" includes a bar association of specialists as referred to in DR 2-105(A)(1) or (4).[1]

(8) "Qualified legal assistance organization" means an office or organization of one of the four types listed in DR 2-103(D)(1)-(4), inclusive, that meets all the requirements thereof.[2]

NOTES

* "Confidence" and "secret" are defined in DR 4-101(A).

1. Amended, February 1975, House Informational Report No. 110.
2. *Id.*

INDEX

B

C

D

E

F

G

L

M

Q

R

U

V

W

Z

ABA MODEL CODE OF JUDICIAL CONDUCT

The Model Code of Judicial Conduct (1990) was adopted by the House of Delegates of the American Bar Association on August 7, 1990 and amended on August 6, 1997.

PREFACE

The Code of Judicial Conduct was adopted by the House of Delegates of the American Bar Association on August 16, 1972. The Code replaced the Canons of Judicial Ethics, which had been formulated almost 50 years earlier. Although two amendments to the Code have been adopted since 1972, the Code has not been reviewed comprehensively until now.

A survey conducted by the American Bar Association Standing Committee on Ethics and Professional Responsibility in 1986 led to the conclusion that in general the Code had served its purposes well, but that a comprehensive review of the Code was desirable. This review, with an initial grant from the Josephson Institute for the Advancement of Ethics, was funded by the American Bar Association and the State Justice Institute. The Model Code of Judicial Conduct (August 1990) was prepared by the Standing Committee on Ethics and Professional Responsibility and a Subcommittee comprised of several members and former members of the Ethics Committee and several members of the judiciary, with the assistance of a reporter, a research attorney, an advisor and liaisons from other ABA groups and interested organizations.

In the revision process, the Association sought and considered the views of members of the judiciary, the bar and the general public. In the judgment of the Association, this Code, consisting of statements of norms denominated Canons, specific Sections and Commentary, states appropriate ethical obligations of judges.

The general format of the 1972 Code is retained. A Preamble and a Terminology section are added in this revision. An Application Section follows the Canons. An Appendix contains an example of a rule to establish a judicial ethics committee. Its purpose is to assist jurisdictions in establishing judicial ethics advisory committees where none exists, which the Association believes are essential to the proper administration of a code of judicial ethics. The Appendix is not, however, intended to be adopted by jurisdictions as part of the Code.

Contents

PREAMBLE

Our legal system is based on the principle that an independent, fair and competent judiciary will interpret and apply the laws that govern us. The role of the judiciary is central to American concepts of justice and the rule of law. Intrinsic to all sections of this Code are the precepts that judges, individually and collectively, must respect and honor the judicial office as a public trust and strive to enhance and maintain confidence in our legal system. The judge is an arbiter of facts and law for the resolution of disputes and a highly visible symbol of government under the rule of law.

The Code of Judicial Conduct is intended to establish standards for ethical conduct of judges. It consists of broad statements called Canons, specific rules set forth in Sections under each Canon, a Terminology Section, an Application Section and Commentary. The text of the Canons and the Sections, including the Terminology and Application Sections, is authoritative. The Commentary, by explanation and example, provides guidance with respect to the purpose and meaning of the Canons and Sections. The Commentary is not intended as a statement of additional rules. When the text uses "shall" or "shall not," it is intended to impose binding obligations the violation of which can result in disciplinary action. When "should" or "should not" is used, the text is intended as hortatory and as a statement of what is or is not appropriate conduct but not as a binding rule under which a judge may be disciplined. When "may" is used, it denotes permissible discretion or, depending on the context, it refers to action that is not covered by specific proscriptions.

The Canons and Sections are rules of reason. They should be applied consistent with constitutional requirements, statutes, other court rules and decisional law and in the context of all relevant circumstances. The Code is to be construed so as not to impinge on the essential independence of judges in making judicial decisions.

The Code is designed to provide guidance to judges and candidates for judicial office and to provide a structure for regulating conduct through disciplinary agencies. It is not designed or intended as a basis for civil liability or criminal prosecution. Furthermore, the purpose of the Code would be subverted if the Code were invoked by lawyers for mere tactical advantage in a proceeding.

The text of the Canons and Sections is intended to govern conduct of judges and to be binding upon them. It is not intended, however, that every transgression will result in disciplinary action. Whether disciplinary action is appropriate, and the degree of discipline to be imposed, should be determined through a reasonable and reasoned application of the text and should depend on such factors as the seriousness of the transgression, whether there is a pattern of improper activity and the effect of the improper activity on others or on the judicial system. See ABA Standards Relating to Judicial Discipline and Disability Retirement.[+]

[+]Judicial disciplinary procedures adopted in the jurisdictions should comport with the requirements of due process. The ABA Stqandards Relating to ajudicial Discipline and Disability Retirement are cited as an aexample of how these due process requirements may be stasfied.

The Code of Judicial Conduct is not intended as an exhaustive guide for the conduct of judges. They should also be governed in their judicial and personal conduct by general ethical standards. The Code is intended, however, to state basic standards which should govern the conduct of all judges and to provide guidance to assist judges in establishing and maintaining high standards of judicial and personal conduct.

TERMINOLOGY

Terms explained below are noted with an asterisk (*) in the Sections where they appear. In addition, the Sections where terms appear are referred to after the explanation of each term below.

"Appropriate authority" denotes the authority with responsibility for initiation of disciplinary process with respect to the violation to be reported. See Sections 3D(1) and 3D(2).

"Candidate." A candidate is a person seeking selection for or retention in judicial office by election or appointment. A person becomes a candidate for judicial office as soon as he or she makes a public announcement of candidacy, declares or files as a candidate with the election or appointment authority, or authorizes solicitation or acceptance of contributions or support. The term "candidate" has the same meaning when applied to a judge seeking election or appointment to non-judicial office. See Preamble and Sections 5A, 5B, 5C and 5E.

"Continuing part-time judge." A continuing part-time judge is a judge who serves repeatedly on a part-time basis by election or under a continuing appointment, including a retired judge subject to recall who is permitted to practice law. See Application Section C.

"Court personnel" does not include the lawyers in a proceeding before a judge. See Sections 3B(7)(c) and 3B(9).

"De minimis" denotes an insignificant interest that could not raise reasonable question as to a judge's impartiality. See Sections 3E(1)(c) and 3E(1)(d).

"Economic interest" denotes ownership of a more than de minimis legal or equitable interest, or a relationship as officer, director, advisor or other active participant in the affairs of a party, except that:

(i) ownership of an interest in a mutual or common investment fund that holds securities is not an economic interest in such securities unless the judge participates in the management of the fund or a proceeding pending or impending before the judge could substantially affect the value of the interest;

(ii) service by a judge as an officer, director, advisor or other active participant in an educational, religious, charitable, fraternal or civic organization, or service by a judge's spouse, parent or child as an officer, director, advisor or other active participant in any organization does not create an economic interest in securities held by that organization;

(iii) a deposit in a financial institution, the proprietary interest of a policy holder in a mutual insurance company, of a depositor in a mutual savings association or of a member in a credit union, or a similar proprietary interest, is not an economic interest in the organization unless a proceeding pending or impending before the judge could substantially affect the value of the interest;

(iv) ownership of government securities is not an economic interest in the issuer unless a proceeding pending or impending before the judge could substantially affect the value of the securities.

See Sections 3E(1)(c) and 3E(2).

"Fiduciary" includes such relationships as executor, administrator, trustee, and guardian. See Sections 3E(2) and 4E.

"Knowingly," "knowledge," "known" or "knows" denotes actual knowledge of the fact in question. A person's knowledge may be inferred from circumstances. See Sections 3D, 3E(1) and 5A(3).

"Law" denotes court rules as well as statutes, constitutional provisions and decisional law. See Sections 2A, 3A, 3B(2), 3B(6), 4B, 4C, 4D(5), 4F, 4I, 5A(2), 5A(3), 5B(2), 5C(1), 5C(3) and 5D.

"Member of the candidate's family" denotes a spouse, child, grandchild, parent, grandparent or other relative or person with whom the candidate maintains a close familial relationship. See Section 5A(3)(a).

"Member of the judge's family" denotes a spouse, child, grandchild, parent, grandparent, or other relative or person with whom the judge maintains a close familial relationship. See Sections 4D(3), 4E and 4G.

"Member of the judge's family residing in the judge's household" denotes any relative of a judge by blood or marriage, or a person treated by a judge as a member of the judge's family, who resides in the judge's household. See Sections 3E(1) and 4D(5).

"Nonpublic information" denotes information that, by law, is not available to the public. Nonpublic information may include but is not limited to: information that is sealed by statute or court order, impounded or communicated in camera; and information offered in grand jury proceedings, presentencing reports, dependency cases or psychiatric reports. See Section 3B(11).

"Periodic part-time judge." A periodic part-time judge is a judge who serves or expects to serve repeatedly on a part-time basis but under a separate appointment for each limited period of service or for each matter. See Application Section D.

"Political organization" denotes a political party or other group, the principal purpose of which is to further the election or appointment of candidates to political office. See Sections 5A(1), 5B(2) and 5C(1).

"Pro tempore part-time judge." A pro tempore part-time judge is a judge who serves or expects to serve once or only sporadically on a part-time basis under a separate appointment for each period of service or for each case heard. See Application Section E.

"Public election." This term includes primary and general elections; it includes partisan elections, nonpartisan elections and retention elections. See Section 5C.

"Require." The rules prescribing that a judge "require" certain conduct of others are, like all of the rules in this Code, rules of reason. The use of the term "require" in that context means a judge is to exercise reasonable direction and control over the conduct of those persons subject to the judge's direction and control. See Sections 3B(3), 3B(4), 3B(5), 3B(6), 3B(9) and 3C(2).

"Third degree of relationship." The following persons are relatives within the third degree of relationship: great-grandparent, grandparent, parent, uncle, aunt, brother, sister, child, grandchild, great-grandchild, nephew or niece. See Section 3E(1)(d).

CANON 1

A JUDGE SHALL UPHOLD THE INTEGRITY AND INDEPENDENCE OF THE JUDICIARY

A. An independent and honorable judiciary is indispensable to justice in our society. A judge should participate in establishing, maintaining and enforcing high standards of conduct, and shall personally observe those standards so that the integrity and independence of the judiciary will be preserved. The provisions of this Code are to be construed and applied to further that objective.

Commentary:

Deference to the judgments and rulings of courts depends upon public confidence in the integrity and independence of judges. The integrity and independence of judges depends in turn upon their acting without fear or favor. Although judges should be independent, they must comply with the law, including the provisions of this Code. Public confidence in the impartiality of the judiciary is maintained by the adherence of each judge to this responsibility. Conversely, violation of this Code diminishes public confidence in the judiciary and thereby does injury to the system of government under law.

CANON 2

A JUDGE SHALL AVOID IMPROPRIETY AND THE APPEARANCE OF IMPROPRIETY IN ALL OF THE JUDGE'S ACTIVITIES

A. A judge shall respect and comply with the law* and shall act at all times in a manner that promotes public confidence in the integrity and impartiality of the judiciary.

Commentary:

Public confidence in the judiciary is eroded by irresponsible or improper conduct by judges. A judge must avoid all impropriety and appearance of impropriety. A judge must expect to be the subject of constant public scrutiny. A judge must therefore accept restrictions on the judge's conduct that might be viewed as burdensome by the ordinary citizen and should do so freely and willingly.

The prohibition against behaving with impropriety or the appearance of impropriety applies to both the professional and personal conduct of a judge. Because it is not practicable to list all prohibited acts, the proscription is necessarily cast in general terms that extend to conduct by judges that is harmful although not specifically mentioned in the Code. Actual improprieties under this standard include violations of law, court rules or other specific provisions of this Code. The test for appearance of impropriety is whether the conduct would create in reasonable minds a perception that the judge's ability to carry out judicial responsibilities with integrity, impartiality and competence is impaired.

See also Commentary under Section 2C.

B. A judge shall not allow family, social, political or other relationships to influence the judge's judicial conduct or judgment. A judge shall not lend the prestige of judicial office to advance the private interests of the judge or others; nor shall a judge convey or permit others to convey the impression that they are in a special position to influence the judge. A judge shall not testify voluntarily as a character witness.

Commentary:

Maintaining the prestige of judicial office is essential to a system of government in which the judiciary functions independently of the executive and legislative branches. Respect for the judicial office facilitates the orderly conduct of legitimate judicial functions. Judges should distinguish between proper and improper use of the prestige of office in all of their activities. For example, it would be improper for a judge to allude to his or her judgeship to gain a personal advantage such as deferential treatment when stopped by a police officer for a traffic offense. Similarly, judicial letterhead must not be used for conducting a judge's personal business.

A judge must avoid lending the prestige of judicial office for the advancement of the private interests of others. For example, a judge must not use the judge's judicial position to gain advantage in a civil suit involving a member of the judge's family. In contracts for publication of a judge's writings, a judge should retain control over the advertising to avoid exploitation of the judge's office. As to the acceptance of awards, see Section 4D(5)(a) and Commentary.

Although a judge should be sensitive to possible abuse of the prestige of office, a judge may, based on the judge's personal knowledge, serve as a reference or provide a letter of recommendation. However, a judge must not initiate the communication of information to a sentencing judge or a probation or corrections officer but may provide to such persons information for the record in response to a formal request.

Judges may participate in the process of judicial selection by cooperating with appointing authorities and screening committees seeking names for consideration, and by responding to official inquiries concerning a person being considered for a judgeship. See also Canon 5 regarding use of a judge's name in political activities.

A judge must not testify voluntarily as a character witness because to do so may lend the prestige of the judicial office in support of the party for whom the judge testifies. Moreover, when a judge testifies as a witness, a lawyer who regularly appears before the judge may be placed in the awkward position of cross-examining the judge. A judge may, however, testify when properly summoned. Except in unusual circumstances where the demands of justice require, a judge should discourage a party from requiring the judge to testify as a character witness.

C. A judge shall not hold membership in any organization that practices invidious discrimination on the basis of race, sex, religion or national origin.

Commentary:

Membership of a judge in an organization that practices invidious discrimination gives rise to perceptions that the judge's impartiality is impaired. Section 2C refers to the current practices of the organization. Whether an organization practices invidious discrimination is often a complex question to which judges should be sensitive. The answer cannot be determined from a mere examination of an organization's current membership rolls but rather depends on how the organization selects members and other relevant factors, such as that the organization is dedicated to the preservation of religious, ethnic or cultural values of legitimate common interest to its members, or that it is in fact and effect an intimate, purely private organization whose membership limitations could not be constitutionally prohibited. Absent such factors, an organization is generally said to discriminate invidiously if it arbitrarily excludes from membership on the basis of race, religion, sex or national origin persons who would otherwise be admitted to membership. *See New York State Club Ass'n. Inc. v. City of New York*, 108 S. Ct. 2225, 101 L. Ed. 2d 1 (1988); *Board of Directors of Rotary International v. Rotary Club of Duarte*, 481 U.S. 537, 107 S. Ct. 1940, 95 L. Ed. 2d 474(1987); *Roberts v. United States Jaycees*, 468 U.S. 609, 104 S. Ct. 3244, 82 L. Ed. 2d 462 (1984).

Although Section 2C relates only to membership in organizations that invidiously discriminate on the basis of race, sex, religion or national origin, a judge's membership in an organization that engages in any discriminatory membership practices prohibited by the law of the jurisdiction also violates Canon 2 and Section 2A and gives the appearance of impropriety. In addition, it would be a violation of Canon 2 and Section 2A for a judge to arrange a meeting at a club that the judge knows practices invidious discrimination on the basis of race, sex, religion or national origin in its membership or other policies, or for the judge to regularly use such a club. Moreover, public manifestation by a judge of the judge's knowing approval of invidious discrimination on any basis gives the appearance of impropriety under Canon 2 and diminishes public confidence in the integrity and impartiality of the judiciary, in violation of Section 2A.

When a person who is a judge on the date this Code becomes effective [in the jurisdiction in which the person is a judge][1] learns that an organization to which the judge belongs engages in invidious discrimination that would preclude membership under Section 2C or under Canon 2 and Section 2A, the judge is permitted, in lieu of resigning, to make immediate efforts to have the organization discontinue its invidiously discriminatory practices, but is required to suspend participation in any other activities of the organization. If the organization fails to discontinue its invidiously discriminatory practices as promptly as possible (and in all events within a year of the judge's first learning of the practices), the judge is required to resign immediately from the organization.

1. The language within the brackets should be deleted when the jurisdiction adopts this provision.

CANON 3

A JUDGE SHALL PERFORM THE DUTIES OF JUDICIAL OFFICE IMPARTIALLY AND DILIGENTLY

A. Judicial Duties in General. The judicial duties of a judge take precedence over all the judge's other activities. The judge's judicial duties include all the duties of the judge's office prescribed by law.* In the performance of these duties, the following standards apply.

B. Adjudicative Responsibilities.

(1) A judge shall hear and decide matters assigned to the judge except those in which disqualification is required.

(2) A judge shall be faithful to the law* and maintain professional competence in it. A judge shall not be swayed by partisan interests, public clamor or fear of criticism.

(3) A judge shall require* order and decorum in proceedings before the judge.

(4) A judge shall be patient, dignified and courteous to litigants, jurors, witnesses, lawyers and others with whom the judge deals in an official capacity, and shall require* similar conduct of lawyers, and of staff, court officials and others subject to the judge's direction and control.

Commentary:

The duty to hear all proceedings fairly and with patience is not inconsistent with the duty to dispose promptly of the business of the court. Judges can be efficient and businesslike while being patient and deliberate.

(5) A judge shall perform judicial duties without bias or prejudice. A judge shall not, in the performance of judicial duties, by words or conduct manifest bias or prejudice, including but not limited to bias or prejudice based upon race, sex, religion, national origin, disability, age, sexual orientation or socioeconomic status, and shall not permit staff, court officials and others subject to the judge's direction and control to do so.

Commentary:

A judge must refrain from speech, gestures or other conduct that could reasonably be perceived as sexual harassment and must require the same standard of conduct of others subject to the judge's direction and control.

A judge must perform judicial duties impartially and fairly. A judge who manifests bias on any basis in a proceeding impairs the fairness of the proceeding and brings the judiciary into disrepute. Facial expression and body language, in addition to oral communication, can give to parties or lawyers in the proceeding, jurors, the media and others an appearance of judicial bias. A judge must be alert to avoid behavior that may be perceived as prejudicial.

(6) A judge shall require* lawyers in proceedings before the judge to refrain from manifesting, by words or conduct, bias or prejudice based upon race, sex, religion, national origin, disability, age, sexual orientation or socioeconomic status, against parties, witnesses, counsel or others. This Section 3B(6) does not preclude legitimate advocacy when race, sex, religion, national origin, disability, age, sexual orientation or socioeconomic status, or other similar factors, are issues in the proceeding.

(7) A judge shall accord to every person who has a legal interest in a proceeding, or that person's lawyer, the right to be heard according to law*. A judge shall not initiate, permit, or consider ex parte communications, or consider other communications made to the judge outside the presence of the parties concerning a pending or impending proceeding except that:

(a) Where circumstances require, ex parte communications for scheduling, administrative purposes or emergencies that do not deal with substantive matters or issues on the merits are authorized; provided:

(i) the judge reasonably believes that no party will gain a procedural or tactical advantage as a result of the ex parte communication, and

(ii) the judge makes provision promptly to notify all other parties of the substance of the ex parte communication and allows an opportunity to respond.

(b) A judge may obtain the advice of a disinterested expert on the law* applicable to a proceeding before the judge if the judge gives notice to the parties of the person consulted and the substance of the advice, and affords the parties reasonable opportunity to respond.

(c) A judge may consult with court personnel* whose function is to aid the judge in carrying out the judge's adjudicative responsibilities or with other judges.

(d) A judge may, with the consent of the parties, confer separately with the parties and their lawyers in an effort to mediate or settle matters pending before the judge.

(e) A judge may initiate or consider any ex parte communications when expressly authorized by law* to do so.

Commentary:

The proscription against communications concerning a proceeding includes communications from lawyers, law teachers, and other persons who are not participants in the proceeding, except to the limited extent permitted.

To the extent reasonably possible, all parties or their lawyers shall be included in communications with a judge.

Whenever presence of a party or notice to a party is required by Section 3B(7), it is the party's lawyer, or if the party is unrepresented the party, who is to be present or to whom notice is to be given.

An appropriate and often desirable procedure for a court to obtain the advice of a disinterested expert on legal issues is to invite the expert to file a brief amicus curiae.

Certain ex parte communication is approved by Section 3B(7) to facilitate scheduling and other administrative purposes and to accommodate emergencies. In general, however, a judge must discourage ex parte communication and allow it only if all the criteria stated in Section 3B(7) are clearly met. A judge must disclose to all parties all ex parte communications described in Sections 3B(7)(a) and 3B(7)(b) regarding a proceeding pending or impending before the judge.

A judge must not independently investigate facts in a case and must consider only the evidence presented.

A judge may request a party to submit proposed findings of fact and conclusions of law, so long as the other parties are apprised of the request and are given an opportunity to respond to the proposed findings and conclusions.

A judge must make reasonable efforts, including the provision of appropriate supervision, to ensure that Section 3B(7) is not violated through law clerks or other personnel on the judge's staff.

If communication between the trial judge and the appellate court with respect to a proceeding is permitted, a copy of any written communication or the substance of any oral communication should be provided to all parties.

(8) A judge shall dispose of all judicial matters promptly, efficiently and fairly.

Commentary:

In disposing of matters promptly, efficiently and fairly, a judge must demonstrate due regard for the rights of the parties to be heard and to have issues resolved without unnecessary cost or delay. Containing costs while preserving fundamental rights of parties also protects the interests of witnesses and the general public. A judge should monitor and supervise cases so as to reduce or eliminate dilatory practices, avoidable delays and unnecessary costs. A judge should encourage and seek to facilitate settlement, but parties should not feel coerced into surrendering the right to have their controversy resolved by the courts.

Prompt disposition of the court's business requires a judge to devote adequate time to judicial duties, to be punctual in attending court and expeditious in determining matters under submission, and to insist that court officials, litigants and their lawyers cooperate with the judge to that end.

(9) A judge shall not, while a proceeding is pending or impending in any court, make any public comment that might reasonably be expected to affect its outcome or impair its fairness or make any nonpublic comment that might substantially interfere with a fair trial or hearing. The judge shall require* similar abstention on the part of court personnel* subject to the judge's direction and control. This Section does not prohibit judges from making public statements in the course of their official duties or from explaining for public information the procedures of the court. This Section does not apply to proceedings in which the judge is a litigant in a personal capacity.

Commentary:

The requirement that judges abstain from public comment regarding a pending or impending proceeding continues during any appellate process and until final disposition. This Section does not prohibit a judge from commenting on proceedings in which the judge is a litigant in a personal capacity, but in cases such as a writ of mandamus where the judge is a litigant in an official capacity, the judge must not comment publicly. The conduct of lawyers relating to trial publicity is governed by [Rule 3.6 of the ABA Model Rules of Professional Conduct]. (Each jurisdiction should substitute an appropriate reference to its rule.)

(10) A judge shall not commend or criticize jurors for their verdict other than in a court order or opinion in a proceeding, but may express appreciation to jurors for their service to the judicial system and the community.

Commentary:

Commending or criticizing jurors for their verdict may imply a judicial expectation in future cases and may impair a juror's ability to be fair and impartial in a subsequent case.

(11) A judge shall not disclose or use, for any purpose unrelated to judicial duties, nonpublic information* acquired in a judicial capacity.

C. Administrative Responsibilities.

(1) A judge shall diligently discharge the judge's administrative responsibilities without bias or prejudice and maintain professional competence in judicial administration, and should cooperate with other judges and court officials in the administration of court business.

(2) A judge shall require* staff, court officials and others subject to the judge's direction and control to observe the standards of fidelity and diligence that apply to the judge and to refrain from manifesting bias or prejudice in the performance of their official duties.

(3) A judge with supervisory authority for the judicial performance of other judges shall take reasonable measures to assure the prompt disposition of matters before them and the proper performance of their other judicial responsibilities.

(4) A judge shall not make unnecessary appointments. A judge shall exercise the power of appointment impartially and on the basis of merit. A judge shall avoid nepotism and favoritism. A judge shall not approve compensation of appointees beyond the fair value of services rendered.

Commentary:

Appointees of a judge include assigned counsel, officials such as referees, commissioners, special masters, receivers and guardians and personnel such as clerks, secretaries and bailiffs. Consent by the parties to an appointment or an award of compensation does not relieve the judge of the obligation prescribed by Section 3C(4).

D. Disciplinary Responsibilities.

(1) A judge who receives information indicating a substantial likelihood that another judge has committed a violation of this Code should take appropriate action. A judge having knowledge* that another judge has committed a violation of this Code that raises a substantial question as to the other judge's fitness for office shall inform the appropriate authority.*

(2) A judge who receives information indicating a substantial likelihood that a lawyer has committed a violation of the Rules of Professional Conduct [substitute correct title if the applicable rules of lawyer conduct have a different title] should take appropriate action. A judge having knowledge* that a lawyer has committed a violation of the Rules of Professional Conduct [substitute correct title if the applicable rules of lawyer conduct have a different title] that raises a substantial question as to the lawyer's honesty, trustworthiness or fitness as a lawyer in other respects shall inform the appropriate authority.*

(3) Acts of a judge, in the discharge of disciplinary responsibilities, required or permitted by Sections 3D(1) and 3D(2) are part of a judge's judicial duties and shall be absolutely privileged, and no civil action predicated thereon may be instituted against the judge.

Commentary:

Appropriate action may include direct communication with the judge or lawyer who has committed the violation, other direct action if available, and reporting the violation to the appropriate authority or other agency or body.

E. Disqualification.

(1) A judge shall disqualify himself or herself in a proceeding in which the judge's impartiality might reasonably be questioned, including but not limited to instances where:

Commentary:

Under this rule, a judge is disqualified whenever the judge's impartiality might reasonably be questioned, regardless whether any of the specific rules in Section 3E(1) apply. For example, if a judge were in the process of negotiating for employment with a law firm, the judge would be disqualified from any matters in which that law firm appeared, unless the disqualification was waived by the parties after disclosure by the judge.

A judge should disclose on the record information that the judge believes the parties or their lawyers might consider relevant to the question of disqualification, even if the judge believes there is no real basis for disqualification.

By decisional law, the rule of necessity may override the rule of disqualification. For example, a judge might be required to participate in judicial review of a judicial salary statute, or might be the only judge available in a matter requiring immediate judicial action, such as a hearing on probable cause or a temporary restraining order. In the latter case, the judge must disclose on the record the basis for possible disqualification and use reasonable efforts to transfer the matter to another judge as soon as practicable.

(a) the judge has a personal bias or prejudice concerning a party or a party's lawyer, or personal knowledge* of disputed evidentiary facts concerning the proceeding;

(b) the judge served as a lawyer in the matter in controversy, or a lawyer with whom the judge previously practiced law served during such association as a lawyer concerning the matter, or the judge has been a material witness concerning it;

Commentary:

A lawyer in a government agency does not ordinarily have an association with other lawyers employed by that agency within the meaning of Section 3E(1)(b); a judge formerly employed by a government agency, however, should disqualify himself or herself in a proceeding if the judge's impartiality might reasonably be questioned because of such association.

(c) the judge knows* that he or she, individually or as a fiduciary, or the judge's spouse, parent or child wherever residing, or any other member of the judge's family residing in the judge's household,* has an economic interest* in the subject matter in controversy or in a party to the proceeding or has any other more than de minimis* interest that could be substantially affected by the proceeding;

(d) the judge or the judge's spouse, or a person within the third degree of relationship* to either of them, or the spouse of such a person:

(i) is a party to the proceeding, or an officer, director or trustee of a party;

(ii) is acting as a lawyer in the proceeding;

(iii) is known* by the judge to have a more than de minimis* interest that could be substantially affected by the proceeding;

(iv) is to the judge's knowledge* likely to be a material witness in the proceeding.

Commentary:

The fact that a lawyer in a proceeding is affiliated with a law firm with which a relative of the judge is affiliated does not of itself disqualify the judge. Under appropriate circumstances, the fact that "the judge's impartiality might reasonably be questioned" under Section 3E(1), or that the relative is known by the judge to have an interest in the law firm that could be "substantially affected by the outcome of the proceeding" under Section 3E(1)(d)(iii) may require the judge's disqualification.

(2) A judge shall keep informed about the judge's personal and fiduciary* economic interests,* and make a reasonable effort to keep informed about the personal economic interests of the judge's spouse and minor children residing in the judge's household.

F. Remittal of Disqualification. A judge disqualified by the terms of Section 3E may disclose on the record the basis of the judge's disqualification and may ask the parties and their lawyers to consider, out of the presence of the judge, whether to waive disqualification. If following disclosure of any basis for disqualification other than personal bias or prejudice concerning a party, the parties and lawyers, without participation by the judge, all agree that the judge should not be disqualified, and the judge is then willing to participate, the judge may participate in the proceeding. The agreement shall be incorporated in the record of the proceeding.

Commentary:

A remittal procedure provides the parties an opportunity to proceed without delay if they wish to waive the disqualification. To assure that consideration of the question of remittal is made independently of the judge, a judge must not solicit, seek or hear comment on possible remittal or waiver of the disqualification unless the lawyers jointly propose remittal after consultation as provided in the rule. A party may act through counsel if counsel represents on the record that the party has been consulted and consents. As a practical matter, a judge may wish to have all parties and their lawyers sign the remittal agreement.

CANON 4

A JUDGE SHALL SO CONDUCT THE JUDGE'S EXTRA-JUDICIAL ACTIVITIES AS TO MINIMIZE THE RISK OF CONFLICT WITH JUDICIAL OBLIGATIONS

A. Extra-judicial Activities in General. A judge shall conduct all of the judge's extra-judicial activities so that they do not:

(1) cast reasonable doubt on the judge's capacity to act impartially as a judge;

(2) demean the judicial office; or

(3) interfere with the proper performance of judicial duties.

Commentary:

Complete separation of a judge from extra-judicial activities is neither possible nor wise; a judge should not become isolated from the community in which the judge lives.

Expressions of bias or prejudice by a judge, even outside the judge's judicial activities, may cast reasonable doubt on the judge's capacity to act impartially as a judge. Expressions which may do so include jokes or other remarks demeaning individuals on the basis of their race, sex, religion, national origin, disability, age, sexual orientation or socioeconomic status. See Section 2C and accompanying Commentary.

B. Avocational Activities. A judge may speak, write, lecture, teach and participate in other extra-judicial activities concerning the law,* the legal system, the administration of justice and non-legal subjects, subject to the requirements of this Code.

Commentary:

As a judicial officer and person specially learned in the law, a judge is in a unique position to contribute to the improvement of the law, the legal system, and the administration of justice, including revision of substantive and procedural law and improvement of criminal and juvenile justice. To the extent that time permits, a judge is encouraged to do so, either independently or through a bar association, judicial conference or other organization dedicated to the improvement of the law. Judges may participate in efforts to promote the fair administration of justice, the independence of the judiciary and the integrity of the legal profession and may express opposition to the persecution of lawyers and judges in other countries because of their professional activities.

In this and other Sections of Canon 4, the phrase "subject to the requirements of this Code" is used, notably in connection with a judge's governmental, civic or charitable activities. This phrase is included to remind judges that the use of permissive language in various Sections of the Code does not relieve a judge from the other requirements of the Code that apply to the specific conduct.

C. Governmental, Civic or Charitable Activities.

(1) A judge shall not appear at a public hearing before, or otherwise consult with, an executive or legislative body or official except on matters concerning the law,* the legal system or the administration of justice or except when acting pro se in a matter involving the judge or the judge's interests.

Commentary:

See Section 2B regarding the obligation to avoid improper influence.

(2) A judge shall not accept appointment to a governmental committee or commission or other governmental position that is concerned with issues of fact or policy on matters other than the improvement of the law,* the legal system or the administration of justice. A judge may, however, represent a country, state or locality on ceremonial occasions or in connection with historical, educational or cultural activities.

Commentary:

Section 4C(2) prohibits a judge from accepting any governmental position except one relating to the law, legal system or administration of justice as authorized by Section 4C(3). The appropriateness of accepting extra-judicial assignments must be assessed in light of the demands on judicial resources created by crowded dockets and the need to protect the courts from involvement in extra-judicial matters that may prove to be controversial. Judges should not accept governmental appointments that are likely to interfere with the effectiveness and independence of the judiciary.

Section 4C(2) does not govern a judge's service in a nongovernmental position. See Section 4C(3) permitting service by a judge with organizations devoted to the improvement of the law, the legal system or the administration of justice and with educational, religious, charitable, fraternal or civic organizations not conducted for profit. For example, service on the board of a public educational institution, unless it were a law school, would be prohibited under Section 4C(2), but service on the board of a public law school or any private educational institution would generally be permitted under Section 4C(3).

(3) A judge may serve as an officer, director, trustee or non-legal advisor of an organization or governmental agency devoted to the improvement of the law,* the legal system or the administration of justice or of an educational, religious, charitable, fraternal or civic organization not conducted for profit, subject to the following limitations and the other requirements of this Code.

Commentary:

Section 4C(3) does not apply to a judge's service in a governmental position unconnected with the improvement of the law, the legal system or the administration of justice; see Section 4C(2).

See Commentary to Section 4B regarding use of the phrase "subject to the following limitations and the other requirements of this Code." As an example of the meaning of the phrase, a judge permitted by Section 4C(3) to serve on the board of a fraternal institution may be prohibited from such service by Sections 2C or 4A if the institution practices invidious discrimination or if service on the board otherwise casts reasonable doubt on the judge's capacity to act impartially as a judge.

Service by a judge on behalf of a civic or charitable organization may be governed by other provisions of Canon 4 in addition to Section 4C. For example, a judge is prohibited by Section 4G from serving as a legal advisor to a civic or charitable organization.

(a) A judge shall not serve as an officer, director, trustee or non-legal advisor if it is likely that the organization

(i) will be engaged in proceedings that would ordinarily come before the judge, or

(ii) will be engaged frequently in adversary proceedings in the court of

which the judge is a member or in any court subject to the appellate jurisdiction of the court of which the judge is a member.

Commentary:

The changing nature of some organizations and of their relationship to the law makes it necessary for a judge regularly to reexamine the activities of each organization with which the judge is affiliated to determine if it is proper for the judge to continue the affiliation. For example, in many jurisdictions charitable hospitals are now more frequently in court than in the past. Similarly, the boards of some legal aid organizations now make policy decisions that may have political significance or imply commitment to causes that may come before the courts for adjudication.

(b) A judge as an officer, director, trustee or non-legal advisor, or as a member or otherwise:

(i) may assist such an organization in planning fund-raising and may participate in the management and investment of the organization's funds, but shall not personally participate in the solicitation of funds or other fund-raising activities, except that a judge may solicit funds from other judges over whom the judge does not exercise supervisory or appellate authority;

(ii) may make recommendations to public and private fund-granting organizations on projects and programs concerning the law,* the legal system or the administration of justice;

(iii) shall not personally participate in membership solicitation if the solicitation might reasonably be perceived as coercive or, except as permitted in Section 4C(3) (b) (i), if the membership solicitation is essentially a fund-raising mechanism;

(iv) shall not use or permit the use of the prestige of judicial office for fund-raising or membership solicitation.

Commentary:

A judge may solicit membership or endorse or encourage membership efforts for an organization devoted to the improvement of the law, the legal system or the administration of justice or a nonprofit educational, religious, charitable, fraternal or civic organization as long as the solicitation cannot reasonably be perceived as coercive and is not essentially a fund-raising mechanism. Solicitation of funds for an organization and solicitation of memberships similarly involve the danger that the person solicited will feel obligated to respond favorably to the solicitor if the solicitor is in a position of influence or control. A judge must not engage in direct, individual solicitation of funds or memberships in person, in writing or by telephone except in the following cases: 1) a judge may solicit for funds or memberships other judges over whom the judge does not exercise supervisory or appellate authority, 2) a judge may solicit other persons for membership in the organizations described above if neither those persons nor persons with whom they are affiliated are likely ever to appear before the court on which the judge serves and 3) a judge who is an officer of such an organization may send a general membership solicitation mailing over the judge's signature.

Use of an organization letterhead for fund-raising or membership solicitation does not violate Section 4C(3)(b) provided the letterhead lists only the judge's name and office or other position in the organization, and, if comparable designations are listed for other persons, the judge's judicial designation. In addition, a judge must also make reasonable efforts to ensure that the judge's staff, court officials and others subject to the judge's direction and control do not solicit funds on the judge's behalf for any purpose, charitable or otherwise.

A judge must not be a speaker or guest of honor at an organization's fund-raising event, but mere attendance at such an event is permissible if otherwise consistent with this Code.

D. Financial Activities.

(1) A judge shall not engage in financial and business dealings that:

(a) may reasonably be perceived to exploit the judge's judicial position, or

(b) involve the judge in frequent transactions or continuing business relationships with those lawyers or other persons likely to come before the court on which the judge serves.

Commentary:

The Time for Compliance provision of this Code (Application, Section F) postpones the time for compliance with certain provisions of this Section in some cases.

When a judge acquires in a judicial capacity information, such as material contained in filings with the court, that is not yet generally known, the judge must not use the information for private gain. See Section 2B; see also Section 3B(11).

A judge must avoid financial and business dealings that involve the judge in frequent transactions or continuing business relationships with persons likely to come either before the judge personally or before other judges on the judge's court. In addition, a judge should discourage members of the judge's family from engaging in dealings that would reasonably appear to exploit the judge's judicial position. This rule is necessary to avoid creating an appearance of exploitation of office or favoritism and to minimize the potential for disqualification. With respect to affiliation of relatives of judge with law firms appearing before the judge, see Commentary to Section 3E(1) relating to disqualification.

Participation by a judge in financial and business dealings is subject to the general prohibitions in Section 4A against activities that tend to reflect adversely on impartiality, demean the judicial office, or interfere with the proper performance of judicial duties. Such participation is also subject to the general prohibition in Canon 2 against activities involving impropriety or the appearance of impropriety and the prohibition in Section 2B against the misuse of the prestige of judicial office. In addition, a judge must maintain high standards of conduct in all of the judge's activities, as set forth in Canon 1. See Commentary for Section 4B regarding use of the phrase "subject to the requirements of this Code."

(2) A judge may, subject to the requirements of this Code, hold and manage investments of the judge and members of the judge's family,* including real estate, and engage in other remunerative activity.

Commentary:

This Section provides that, subject to the requirements of this Code, a judge may hold and manage investments owned solely by the judge, investments owned solely by a member or members of the judge's family, and investments owned jointly by the judge and members of the judge's family.

(3) A judge shall not serve as an officer, director, manager, general partner, advisor or employee of any business entity except that a judge may, subject to the requirements of this Code, manage and participate in:

(a) a business closely held by the judge or members of the judge's family,* or

(b) a business entity primarily engaged in investment of the financial resources of the judge or members of the judge's family.*

Commentary:

Subject to the requirements of this Code, a judge may participate in a business that is closely held either by the judge alone, by members of the judge's family, or by the judge and members of the judge's family.

Although participation by a judge in a closely-held family business might otherwise be permitted by Section 4D(3), a judge may be prohibited from participation by other provisions of this Code when, for example, the business entity frequently appears before the judge's court or the participation requires significant time away from judicial duties. Similarly, a judge must avoid participating in a closely-held family business if the judge's participation would involve misuse of the prestige of judicial office.

(4) A judge shall manage the judge's investments and other financial interests to minimize the number of cases in which the judge is disqualified. As soon as the judge can do so without serious financial detriment, the judge shall divest himself or herself of investments and other financial interests that might require frequent disqualification.

(5) A judge shall not accept, and shall urge members of the judge's family residing in the judge's household* not to accept, a gift, bequest, favor or loan from anyone except for:

Commentary:

Section 4D(5) does not apply to contributions to a judge's campaign for judicial office, a matter governed by Canon 5.

Because a gift, bequest, favor or loan to a member of the judge's family residing in the judge's household might be viewed as intended to influence the judge, a judge must inform those family members of the relevant ethical constraints upon the judge in this regard and discourage those family members from violating them. A judge cannot, however, reasonably be expected to know or control all of the financial or business activities of all family members residing in the judge's household.

(a) a gift incident to a public testimonial, books, tapes and other resource materials supplied by publishers on a complimentary basis for official use, or an invitation to the judge and the judge's spouse or guest to attend a bar-related function or an activity devoted to the improvement of the law,* the legal system or the administration of justice;

Commentary:

Acceptance of an invitation to a law-related function is governed by Section 4D(5)(a); acceptance of an invitation paid for by an individual lawyer or group of lawyers is governed by Section 4D(5)(h).

A judge may accept a public testimonial or a gift incident thereto only if the donor organization is not an organization whose members comprise or frequently represent the same side in litigation, and the testimonial and gift are otherwise in compliance with other provisions of this Code. See Sections 4A(1) and 2B.

(b) a gift, award or benefit incident to the business, profession or other separate activity of a spouse or other family member of a judge residing in the judge's household, including gifts, awards and benefits for the use of both the spouse or other family member and the judge (as spouse or family member), provided the gift, award or benefit could not reasonably be perceived as intended to influence the judge in the performance of judicial duties;

(c) ordinary social hospitality;

(d) a gift from a relative or friend, for a special occasion, such as a wedding, anniversary or birthday, if the gift is fairly commensurate with the occasion and the relationship;

Commentary:

A gift to a judge, or to a member of the judge's family living in the judge's household, that is excessive in value raises questions about the judge's impartiality and the integrity of the judicial office and might require disqualification of the judge where disqualification would not otherwise be required. See, however, Section 4D(5)(e).

(e) a gift, bequest, favor or loan from a relative or close personal friend whose appearance or interest in a case would in any event require disqualification under Section 3E;

(f) a loan from a lending institution in its regular course of business on the same terms generally available to persons who are not judges;

(g) a scholarship or fellowship awarded on the same terms and based on the same criteria applied to other applicants; or
(h) any other gift, bequest, favor or loan, only if: the donor is not a party or other person who has come or is likely to come or whose interests have come or are likely to come before the judge; and, if its value exceeds $150.00, the judge reports it in the same manner as the judge reports compensation in Section 4H.

Commentary:

Section 4D(5)(h) prohibits judges from accepting gifts, favors, bequests or loans from lawyers or their firms if they have come or are likely to come before the judge; it also prohibits gifts, favors, bequests or loans from clients of lawyers or their firms when the clients' interests have come or are likely to come before the judge.

E. Fiduciary Activities.

(1) A judge shall not serve as executor, administrator or other personal representative, trustee, guardian, attorney in fact or other fiduciary,* except for the estate, trust or person of a member of the judge's family,* and then only if such service will not interfere with the proper performance of judicial duties.
(2) A judge shall not serve as a fiduciary* if it is likely that the judge as a fiduciary will be engaged in proceedings that would ordinarily come before the judge, or if the estate, trust or ward becomes involved in adversary proceedings in the court on which the judge serves or one under its appellate jurisdiction.
(3) The same restrictions on financial activities that apply to a judge personally also apply to the judge while acting in a fiduciary* capacity.

Commentary:

The Time for Compliance provision of this Code (Application, Section F) postpones the time for compliance with certain provisions of this Section in some cases.
The restrictions imposed by this Canon may conflict with the judge's obligation as a fiduciary. For example, a judge should resign as trustee if detriment to the trust would result from divestiture of holdings the retention of which would place the judge in violation of Section 4D(4).

F. Service as Arbitrator or Mediator. A judge shall not act as an arbitrator or mediator or otherwise perform judicial functions in a private capacity unless expressly authorized by law.*

Commentary:

Section 4F does not prohibit a judge from participating in arbitration, mediation or settlement conferences performed as part of judicial duties.

G. Practice of Law. A judge shall not practice law. Notwithstanding this pro-

hibition, a judge may act pro se and may, without compensation, give legal advice to and draft or review documents for a member of the judge's family.*

Commentary:

This prohibition refers to the practice of law in a representative capacity and not in a pro se capacity. A judge may act for himself or herself in all legal matters, including matters involving litigation and matters involving appearances before or other dealings with legislative and other governmental bodies. However, in so doing, a judge must not abuse the prestige of office to advance the interests of the judge or the judge's family. See Section 2(B).

The Code allows a judge to give legal advice to and draft legal documents for members of the judge's family, so long as the judge receives no compensation. A judge must not, however, act as an advocate or negotiator for a member of the judge's family in a legal matter.

*****

Canon 6, new in the 1972 Code, reflected concerns about conflicts of interest and appearances of impropriety arising from compensation for off-the-bench activities. Since 1972, however, reporting requirements that are much more comprehensive with respect to what must be reported and with whom reports must be filed have been adopted by many jurisdictions. The Committee believes that although reports of compensation for extra-judicial activities should be required, reporting requirements preferably should be developed to suit the respective jurisdictions, not simply adopted as set forth in a national model code of judicial conduct. Because of the Committee's concern that deletion of this Canon might lead to the misconception that reporting compensation for extra-judicial activities is no longer important, the substance of Canon 6 is carried forward as Section 4H in this Code for adoption in those jurisdictions that do not have other reporting requirements. In jurisdictions that have separately established reporting requirements, Section 4H(2) (Public Reporting) may be deleted and the caption for Section 4H modified appropriately.

*****

H. Compensation, Reimbursement and Reporting.

(1) Compensation and Reimbursement. A judge may receive compensation and reimbursement of expenses for the extra-judicial activities permitted by this Code, if the source of such payments does not give the appearance of influencing the judge's performance of judicial duties or otherwise give the appearance of impropriety.

(a) Compensation shall not exceed a reasonable amount nor shall it exceed what a person who is not a judge would receive for the same activity.

(b) Expense reimbursement shall be limited to the actual cost of travel, food and lodging reasonably incurred by the judge and, where appropriate to the occasion, by the judge's spouse or guest. Any payment in excess of such an amount is compensation.

(2) Public Reports. A judge shall report the date, place and nature of any activity for which the judge received compensation, and the name of the payor and the amount of compensation so received. Compensation or income of a spouse attributed to the judge by operation of a community property law is not extra-judicial compensation to the judge. The judge's report shall be made at least annually and shall be filed as a public document in the office of the clerk of the court on which the judge serves or other office designated by law.*

Commentary:

See Section 4D(5) regarding reporting of gifts, bequests and loans.

The Code does not prohibit a judge from accepting honoraria or speaking fees provided that the compensation is reasonable and commensurate with the task performed. A judge should ensure, however, that no conflicts are created by the arrangement. A judge must not appear to trade on the judicial position for personal advantage. Nor should a judge spend significant time away from court duties to meet speaking or writing commitments for compensation. In addition, the source of the payment must not raise any question of undue influence or the judge's ability or willingness to be impartial.

I. Disclosure of a judge's income, debts, investments or other assets is required only to the extent provided in this Canon and in Sections 3E and 3F, or as otherwise required by law.*

Commentary:

Section 3E requires a judge to disqualify himself or herself in any proceeding in which the judge has an economic interest. See "economic interest" as explained in the Terminology Section. Section 4D requires a judge to refrain from engaging in business and from financial activities that might interfere with the impartial performance of judicial duties; Section 4H requires a judge to report all compensation the judge received for activities outside judicial office. A judge has the rights of any other citizen, including the right to privacy of the judge's financial affairs, except to the extent that limitations established by law are required to safeguard the proper performance of the judge's duties.

CANON 5[2]

A JUDGE OR JUDICIAL CANDIDATE SHALL REFRAIN FROM INAPPROPRIATE POLITICAL ACTIVITY

A. All Judges and Candidates

(1) Except as authorized in Sections 5B(2), 5C(1) and 5C(3), a judge or a can-

2. Introductory Note to Canon 5: There is wide variation in the methods of judicial selection use, both among jurisdictions and within the jurisdictions themselves. In a given state, judges may be selected by one method initially, retained by a different method, and selected by still another method to fill interim vacancies.

didate* for election or appointment to judicial office shall not:

(a) act as a leader or hold an office in a political organization,*

(b) publicly endorse or publicly oppose another candidate for public office;

(c) make speeches on behalf of a political organization;

(d) attend political gatherings; or

(e) solicit funds for, pay an assessment to or make a contribution to a political organization or candidate, or purchase tickets for political party dinners or other functions.

Commentary:

A judge or candidate for judicial office retains the right to participate in the political process as a voter.

Where false information concerning a judicial candidate is made public, a judge or another judicial candidate having knowledge of the facts is not prohibited by Section 5A(1) from making the facts public.

Section 5A(1)(a) does not prohibit a candidate for elective judicial office from retaining during candidacy a public office such as county prosecutor, which is not "an office in a political organization."

Section 5A(1)(b) does not prohibit a judge or judicial candidate from privately expressing his or her views on judicial candidates or other candidates for public office.

A candidate does not publicly endorse another candidate for public office by having that candidate's name on the same ticket.

(2) A judge shall resign from judicial office upon becoming a candidate* for a non-judicial office either in a primary or in a general election, except that the judge may continue to hold judicial office while being a candidate for election to or serving as a delegate in a state constitutional convention if the judge is otherwise permitted by law* to do so.

(3) A candidate* for a judicial office:

(a) shall maintain the dignity appropriate to judicial office and act in a man-

According to figures compiled in 1987 by the National Center for State Courts, 32 states and the District of Columbia use a merit selection method (in which an executive such as a governor appoints a judge from a group of nominees selected by a judicial nominating commission) to select judges in the state either initially or to fill an interim vacancy. Of those 33 jurisdictions, a merit selection method is used in 18 jurisdictions to choose judges of courts of last resort, in 13 jurisdictions to choose judges of intermediate appellate courts, in 12 jurisdictions to choose judges of general jurisdiction courts and in 5 jurisdictions to choose judges of limited jurisdiction courts.

Methods of judicial selection other than merit selection include nonpartisan election (10 states use it for initial selection at all court levels, another 10 states use it for initial selection for at least one court level) and partisan election (8 states use it for initial selection at all court levels, another 7 states use it for initial selection for at least one level). In a small minority of the states, judicial selection methods include executive or legislative appointment (without nomination of a group of potential appointees by a judicial nominating commission) and court selection. In addition, the federal judicial system utilizes an executive appointment method. See State Court Organization 1987 (National Center for State Courts, 1988).

ner consistent with the integrity and independence of the judiciary, and shall encourage members of the candidate's family* to adhere to the same standards of political conduct in support of the candidate as apply to the candidate;

Commentary:

Although a judicial candidate must encourage members of his or her family to adhere to the same standards of political conduct in support of the candidate that apply to the candidate, family members are free to participate in other political activity.

(b) shall prohibit employees and officials who serve at the pleasure of the candidate,* and shall discourage other employees and officials subject to the candidate's direction and control from doing on the candidate's behalf what the candidate is prohibited from doing under the Sections of this Canon;

(c) except to the extent permitted by Section 5C(2), shall not authorize or knowingly* permit any other person to do for the candidate* what the candidate is prohibited from doing under the Sections of this Canon;

(d) shall not:

(i) make pledges or promises of conduct in office other than the faithful and impartial performance of the duties of the office;

(ii) make statements that commit or appear to commit the candidate with respect to cases, controversies or issues that are likely to come before the court; or

(iii) knowingly* misrepresent the identity, qualifications, present position or other fact concerning the candidate or an opponent;

Commentary:

Section 5A(3)(d) prohibits a candidate for judicial office from making statements that appear to commit the candidate regarding cases, controversies or issues likely to come before the court. As a corollary, a candidate should emphasize in any public statement the candidate's duty to uphold the law regardless of his or her personal views. See also Section 3B(9), the general rule on public comment by judges. Section 5A(3)(d) does not prohibit a candidate from making pledges or promises respecting improvements in court administration. Nor does this Section prohibit an incumbent judge from making private statements to other judges or court personnel in the performance of judicial duties. This Section applies to any statement made in the process of securing judicial office, such as statements to commissions charged with judicial selection and tenure and legislative bodies confirming appointment. See also Rule 8.2 of the ABA Model Rules of Professional Conduct.

(e) may respond to personal attacks or attacks on the candidate's record as long as the response does not violate Section 5A(3)(d).

B. Candidates Seeking Appointment to Judicial or Other Governmental Office.

(1) A candidate* for appointment to judicial office or a judge seeking other governmental office shall not solicit or accept funds, personally or through a committee or otherwise, to support his or her candidacy.

(2) A candidate* for appointment to judicial office or a judge seeking other governmental office shall not engage in any political activity to secure the appointment except that:

(a) such persons may:

(i) communicate with the appointing authority, including any selection or nominating commission or other agency designated to screen candidates;

(ii) seek support or endorsement for the appointment from organizations that regularly make recommendations for reappointment or appointment to the office, and from individuals to the extent requested or required by those specified in Section 5B(2)(a); and

(iii) provide to those specified in Sections 5B(2)(a)(i) and 5B(2)(a)(ii) information as to his or her qualifications for the office;

(b) a non-judge candidate* for appointment to judicial office may, in addition, unless otherwise prohibited by law*:

(i) retain an office in a political organization*,

(ii) attend political gatherings, and

(iii) continue to pay ordinary assessments and ordinary contributions to a political organization or candidate and purchase tickets for political party dinners or other functions.

Commentary:

Section 5B(2) provides a limited exception to the restrictions imposed by Sections 5A(1) and 5D. Under Section 5B(2), candidates seeking reappointment to the same judicial office or appointment to another judicial office or other governmental office may apply for the appointment and seek appropriate support.

Although under Section 5B(2) non-judge candidates seeking appointment to judicial office are permitted during candidacy to retain office in a political organization, attend political gatherings and pay ordinary dues and assessments, they remain subject to other provisions of this Code during candidacy. See Sections 5B(1), 5B(2)(a), 5E and Application Section.

C. Judges and Candidates Subject to Public Election.

(1) A judge or a candidate* subject to public election* may, except as prohibited by law*:

(a) at any time

(i) purchase tickets for and attend political gatherings;

(ii) identify himself or herself as a member of a political party; and

(iii) contribute to a political organization*;

(b) when a candidate for election

(i) speak to gatherings on his or her own behalf;

(ii) appear in newspaper, television and other media advertisements supporting his or her candidacy;

(iii) distribute pamphlets and other promotional campaign literature supporting his or her candidacy; and

(iv) publicly endorse or publicly oppose other candidates for the same judicial office in a public election in which the judge or judicial candidate is running.

Commentary:

Section 5C(1) permits judges subject to election at any time to be involved in limited political activity. Section 5D, applicable solely to incumbent judges, would otherwise bar this activity.

(2) A candidate* shall not personally solicit or accept campaign contributions or personally solicit publicly stated support. A candidate may, however, establish committees of responsible persons to conduct campaigns for the candidate through media advertisements, brochures, mailings, candidate forums and other means not prohibited by law. Such committees may solicit and accept reasonable campaign contributions, manage the expenditure of funds for the candidate's campaign and obtain public statements of support for his or her candidacy. Such committees are not prohibited from soliciting and accepting reasonable campaign contributions and public support from lawyers. A candidate's committees may solicit contributions and public support for the candidate's campaign no earlier than [one year] before an election and no later than [90] days after the last election in which the candidate participates during the election year. A candidate shall not use or permit the use of campaign contributions for the private benefit of the candidate or others.

Commentary:

There is legitimate concern about a judge's impartiality when parties whose interests may come before a judge, or the lawyer who represent such parties, are known to have made contributions to the election campaigns of judicial candidates. This is among the reasons that merit selection of judges is a preferable manner in which to select the judiciary. Notwhithstanding that preference, Section 5C(2) recognizes that in many jurisdictions judicial candidates must raise funds to support their candidacies for election to judicial office. It therefore permits a candidate, other than a candidate for appointment, to establish campaign committees to solicit and accept public support and reasonable financial contributions. In order to guard against the possibility that conflicts of interest will arise, the candidate must instruct his or her campaign committees at the start of the campaign to solicit or accept only contributions that are reasonable and appropriate under the circumstances.

Though not prohibited, campaign contributions of which a judge has knowledge, made by lawyers or others who appear before the judge, may, by virtue of their size or source, raise questions about a judge's impartiality and be cause for disqualification as provided under Section 3E.

Campaign committees established under Section 5C(2) should manage campaign finances responsibly, avoiding deficits that might necessitate post-election fund-raising, to the extent possible. Such committees must at all times comply with applicable statutory provisions governing their conduct.

Section 5C(2) does not prohibit a candidate from initiating an evaluation by a judicial selection commission or bar association, or, subject to the requirements of this Code, from responding to a request for information from any organization.

(3) Except as prohibited by law,* a candidate* for judicial office in a public election* may permit the candidate's name: (a) to be listed on election materials along with the names of other candidates for elective public office, and (b) to appear in promotions of the ticket.

Commentary:

Section 5C(3) provides a limited exception to the restrictions imposed by Section 5A(1).

D. Incumbent Judges. A judge shall not engage in any political activity except (i) as authorized under any other Section of this Code, (ii) on behalf of measures to improve the law,* the legal system or the administration of justice, or (iii) as expressly authorized by law.

Commentary:

Neither Section 5D nor any other section of the Code prohibits a judge in the exercise of administrative functions from engaging in planning and other official activities with members of the executive and legislative branches of government. With respect to a judge's activity on behalf of measures to improve the law, the legal system and the administration of justice, see Commentary to Section 4B and Section 4C(1) and its Commentary.

E. Applicability. Canon 5 generally applies to all incumbent judges and judicial candidates.* A successful candidate, whether or not an incumbent, is subject to judicial discipline for his or her campaign conduct; an unsuccessful candidate who is a lawyer is subject to lawyer discipline for his or her campaign conduct. A lawyer who is a candidate for judicial office is subject to [Rule 8.2(b) of the ABA Model Rules of Professional Conduct]. (An adopting jurisdiction should substitute a reference to its applicable rule.)

APPLICATION OF THE CODE OF JUDICIAL CONDUCT

A. Anyone, whether or not a lawyer, who is an officer of a judicial system[3] and who performs judicial functions, including an officer such as a magistrate, court commissioner, special master or referee, is a judge within the meaning of this Code. All judges shall comply with this Code except as provided below.

Commentary:

The four categories of judicial service in other than a full-time capacity are necessarily defined in general terms because of the widely varying forms of judicial service. For the purposes of this Section, as long as a retired judge is subject to recall the judge is considered to "perform judicial functions." The determination of which category and, accordingly, which specific Code provisions apply to an individual judicial officer, depend upon the facts of the particular judicial service.

B. Retired Judge Subject to Recall. A retired judge subject to recall who by law is not permitted to practice law is not required to comply:

(1) except while serving as a judge, with Section 4F; and
(2) at any time with Section 4E.

C. Continuing Part-time Judge. A continuing part-time judge*:

(1) is not required to comply
(a) except while serving as a judge, with Section 3B(9); and
(b) at any time with Sections 4C(2), 4D(3), 4E(1), 4F, 4G, 4H, 5A(1), 5B(2) and 5D.
(2) shall not practice law in the court on which the judge serves or in any court subject to the appellate jurisdiction of the court on which the judge serves, and shall not act as a lawyer in a proceeding in which the judge has served as a judge or in any other proceeding related thereto.

Commentary:

When a person who has been a continuing part-time judge is no longer a continuing part-time judge, including a retired judge no longer subject to recall, that person may act as a lawyer in a proceeding in which he or she has served as a judge or in any other proceeding related thereto only with the express consent of all parties pursuant to [Rule 1.12(a) of the ABA Model Rules of Professional Conduct]. (An adopting jurisdiction should substitute a reference to its applicable rule).

3. Applicability of this Code to administrative law judges should be determined by each adopting jurisdiction. Administrative law judges generally are affiliated with the executive branch of government rather than the judicial branch and each adopting jurisdiction should consider the unique characteristics of particular administrative law judge positions in adopting and adapting the Code for administrative law judges. See, e.g., Model Code of Judicial Conduct for Federal Administrative Law Judges, endorsed by the National Conference of Administrative Law Judges in February 1989.

D. Periodic Part-time Judge. A periodic part-time judge:*

(1) is not required to comply

(a) except while serving as a judge, with Section 3B(9);

(b) at any time, with Sections 4C(2), 4C(3)(a), 4D(1)(b), 4D(3), 4D(4), 4D(5), 4E, 4F, 4G, 4H, 5A(1), 5B(2) and 5D.

(2) shall not practice law in the court on which the judge serves or in any court subject to the appellate jurisdiction of the court on which the judge serves, and shall not act as a lawyer in a proceeding in which the judge has served as a judge or in any other proceeding related thereto.

Commentary:

When a person who has been a periodic part-time judge is no longer a periodic part-time judge (no longer accepts appointments), that person may act as a lawyer in a proceeding in which he or she has served as a judge or in any other proceeding related thereto only with the express consent of all parties pursuant to [Rule 1.12(a) of the ABA Model Rules of Professional Conduct]. (An adopting jurisdiction should substitute a reference to its applicable rule.)

E. Pro Tempore Part-time Judge. A pro tempore part-time judge*:

(1) is not required to comply

(a) except while serving as a judge, with Sections 2A, 2B, 3B(9) and 4C(1);

(b) at any time with Sections 2C, 4C(2), 4C(3)(a), 4C(3)(b), 4D(1)(b), 4D(3), 4D(4), 4D(5), 4E, 4F, 4G, 4H, 5A(1), 5A(2), 5B(2) and 5D.

(2) A person who has been a pro tempore part-time judge* shall not act as a lawyer in a proceeding in which the judge has served as a judge or in any other proceeding related thereto except as otherwise permitted by [Rule 1.12(a) of the ABA Model Rules of Professional Conduct]. (An adopting jurisdiction should substitute a reference to its applicable rule.)

F. Time for Compliance. A person to whom this Code becomes applicable shall comply immediately with all provisions of this Code except Sections 4D(2), 4D(3) and 4E and shall comply with these Sections as soon as reasonably possible and shall do so in any event within the period of one year.

Commentary:

If serving as a fiduciary when selected as judge, a new judge may, notwithstanding the prohibitions in Section 4E, continue to serve as fiduciary but only for that period of time necessary to avoid serious adverse consequences to the beneficiary of the fiduciary relationship and in no event longer than one year. Similarly, if engaged at the time of judicial selection in a business activity, a new judge may, notwithstanding the prohibitions in Section 4D(3), continue in that activity for a reasonable period but in no event longer than one year.

APPENDIX[4]
Judicial Ethics Committee

A. The [chief judge of the highest court of the jurisdiction] shall appoint a Judicial Ethics Committee consisting of [nine] members. [Five] members shall be judges; [two] members shall be non-judge lawyers; and [two] members shall be public members. Of the judicial members, one member shall be appointed from each of [the highest court, the intermediate levels of courts, and the trial courts]. The remaining judicial members shall be judges appointed from any of the above courts, but not from the [highest court of the jurisdiction]. The [chief judge] shall designate one of the members as chairperson. Members shall serve three-year terms; terms shall be staggered; and no individual shall serve for more than two consecutive terms.

B. The Judicial Ethics Committee so established shall have authority to:

(1) by the concurrence of a majority of its members, express its opinion on proper judicial conduct with respect to the provisions of [the code of judicial conduct adopted by the jurisdiction and any other specified sections of law of the jurisdiction regarding the judiciary, such as financial reporting requirements], either on its own initiative, at the request of a judge or candidate for judicial office, or at the request of a court or an agency charged with the administration of judicial discipline in the jurisdiction, provided that an opinion may not be issued on a matter that is pending before a court or before such an agency except on request of the court or agency;

(2) make recommendations to [the highest court of the jurisdiction] for amendment of the Code of Judicial Conduct [of the jurisdiction]; and

(3) adopt rules relating to the procedures to be used in expressing opinions, including rules to assure a timely response to inquiries.

C. A judge or candidate for judicial office as defined in the Terminology Section of this Code who has requested and relied upon an opinion may not be disciplined for conduct conforming to that opinion.

D. An opinion issued pursuant to this rule shall be filed with [appropriate official of the judicial conference of the jurisdiction]. Such an opinion is confidential and not public information unless [the highest court of the jurisdiction] otherwise directs. However, the [appropriate official of the judicial conference of the jurisdiction] shall cause an edited version of each opinion to be prepared, in which the identity and geographic location of the person who has requested the opinion, the specific court involved, and the identity of other individuals, organizations or groups mentioned in the opinion are not disclosed. Opinions so edited shall be published periodically in the manner [the appropriate official of the judicial conference of the jurisdiction] deems proper.

---

4. Because of the need to encourage the establishment of judicial ethics committees in jurisdictions that do not have such committees either as free-standing entities or in combination with lawyer ethics committees, the following Appendix is provided. It is offered not as a model but simply as an example of provisions that a jurisdiction might adopt. PLEASE NOTE: The Appendix is not a part of the Model Code of Judicial Conduct as adopted on August 7, 1990 by the ABA House of Delegates.

CORRELATION TABLES

The Correlation Tables identify 1990 Code rules that relate to the same subject matter as the corresponding rules of the 1972 Code. The substance of the rules cited is not necessarily identical, and in many instances varies considerably. Although the Commentary is not cross-referenced, the subject matter of certain rules of the 1990 Code may have been addressed by the Commentary in the 1972 Code.

CORRELATION TABLE A

1990 CODE	1972 CODE
Preamble	None
Terminology	Canon 3C(3)(a), (b), (c); 5C(5); 5D
Canon 1	Canon 1
Section 1A	Paragraph to Canon 1
Canon 2	Canon 2
Section 2A	Canon 2A
Section 2B	Canon 2B
Section 2C	None
Canon 3	Canon 3
Section 3A	Paragraph to Canon 3
Section 3B(1)	None
Section 3B(2)	Canon 3A(1)
Section 3B(3)	Canon 3A(2)
Section 3B(4)	Canon 3A(3)
Section 3B(5)	None
Section 3B(6)	None
Section 3B(7)	Canon 3A(4)
Section 3B(7)(a)	None
Section 3B(7)(a)(i)	None
Section 3B(7)(a)(ii)	None
Section 3B(7)(b)	Canon 3A(4)
Section 3B(7)(c)	None
Section 3B(7)(d)	None
Section 3B(7)(e)	None

1990 CODE	1972 CODE
Section 3B(8)	Canon 3A(5)
Section 3B(9)	Canon 3A(6)
Section 3B(10)	None
Section 3B(11)	Canon 5C(7)
Section 3C(1)	Canon 3B(1)
Section 3C(2)	Canon 3B(2)
Section 3C(3)	None
Section 3C(4)	Canon 3B(4)
Section 3D(1)	Canon 3B(3)
Section 3D(2)	Canon 3B(3)
Section 3D(3)	None
Section 3E(1)	Canon 3C(1)
Section 3E(1)(a)	Canon 3C(1)(a)
Section 3E(1)(b)	Canon 3C(1)(b)
Section 3E(1)(c)	Canon 3C(1)(c)
Section 3E(1)(d)	Canon 3C(1)(d)
Section 3E(1)(d)(i)	Canon 3C(1)(d)(i)
Section 3E(1)(d)(ii)	Canon 3C(1)(d)(ii)
Section 3E(1)(d)(iii)	Canon 3C(1)(d)(iii)
Section 3E(1)(d)(iv)	Canon 3C(1)(d)(iv)
Section 3E(2)	Canon 3C(2)
Section 3F	Canon 3D
Canon 4	Canons 4, 5, 6
Section 4A	None
Section 4A(1)	Paragraph to Canon 4; Canon 5B
Section 4A(2)	Canon 5A
Section 4A(3)	Paragraph to Canon 4; Canons 5A, 5B
Section 4B	Canons 4A, 5A
Section 4C(1)	Canon 4B
Section 4C(2)	Canon 5G
Section 4C(3)	Canons 4C, 5B
Section 4C(3)(a)	Canon 5B(1)
Section 4C(3)(a)(i)	Canon 5B(1)
Section 4C(3)(a)(ii)	Canon 5B(1)
Section 4C(3)(b)	Canons 4C, 5B(2)
Section 4C(3)(b)(i)	Canon 4C
Section 4C(3)(b)(ii)	Canon 4C
Section 4C(3)(b)(iii)	None
Section 4C(3)(b)(iv)	Canon 5B(2)

1990 CODE	1972 CODE
Section 4D(1)	Canon 5C(1)
Section 4D(1)(a)	Canon 5C(1)
Section 4D(1)(b)	Canon 5C(1)
Section 4D(2)	Canon 5C(2)
Section 4D(3)	Canon 5C(2)
Section 4D(3)(a)	Canon 5C(2)
Section 4D(3)(b)	Canon 5C(2)
Section 4D(4)	Canon 5C(3)
Section 4D(5)	Canon 5C(4)
Section 4D(5)(a)	Canon 5C(4)(a)
Section 4D(5)(b)	None
Section 4D(5)(c)	Canon 5C(4)(b)
Section 4D(5)(d)	Canon 5C(4)(b)
Section 4D(5)(e)	Canon 5C(4)(b)
Section 4D(5)(f)	Canon 5C(4)(b)
Section 4D(5)(g)	Canon 5C(4)(b)
Section 4D(5)(h)	Canon 5C(4)(c)
Section 4E(1)	Canon 5D
Section 4E(2)	Canon 5D(1)
Section 4E(3)	Canon 5D(2)
Section 4F	Canon 5E
Section 4G	Canon 5F
Section 4H(1)	Paragraph to Canon 6
Section 4H(1)(a)	Canon 6A
Section 4H(1)(b)	Canon 6B
Section 4H(2)	Canon 6C
Section 4I	Canon 5C(6)
Canon 5	Canon 7
Section 5A(1)	Canon 7A(1)
Section 5A(1)(a)	Canon 7A(1)(a)
Section 5A(1)(b)	Canon 7A(1)(b)
Section 5A(1)(c)	Canon 7A(1)(b)
Section 5A(1)(d)	Canon 7A(1)(c)
Section 5A(1)(e)	Canon 7A(1)(c)
Section 5A(2)	Canon 7A(3)
Section 5A(3)	Canon 7B(1)
Section 5A(3)(a)	Canon 7B(1)(a)
Section 5A(3)(b)	Canon 7B(1)(b)
Section 5A(3)(c)	Canon 7B(1)(b)

1990 CODE	1972 CODE
Section 5A(3)(d)	Canon 7B(1)(c)
Section 5A(3)(d)(i)	Canon 7B(1)(c)
Section 5A(3)(d)(ii)	Canon 7B(1)(c)
Section 5A(3)(d)(iii)	Canon 7B(1)(c)
Section 5A(3)(e)	None
Section 5B(1)	None
Section 5B(2)	None
Section 5B(2)(a)	None
Section 5B(2)(a)(i)	None
Section 5B(2)(a)(ii)	None
Section 5B(2)(a)(iii)	None
Section 5B(2)(b)	None
Section 5B(2)(b)(i)	None
Section 5B(2)(b)(ii)	None
Section 5B(2)(b)(iii)	None
Section 5C(1)	Canon 7A(2)
Section 5C(1)(a)	Canon 7A(2)
Section 5C(1)(a)(i)	Canon 7A(2)
Section 5C(1)(a)(ii)	Canon 7A(2)
Section 5C(1)(a)(iii)	Canon 7A(2)
Section 5C(1)(b)	Canon 7A(2)
Section 5C(1)(b)(i)	Canon 7A(2)
Section 5C(1)(b)(ii)	None
Section 5C(1)(b)(iii)	None
Section 5C(1)(b)(iv)	None
Section 5C(2)	Canon 7B(2)
Section 5C(3)	None
Section 5D	Canon 7A(4)
Section 5E	None
Application	Compliance
Section A	Paragraph to Compliance
Section B	Compliance C
Section B(1)	Compliance C
Section B(2)	Compliance C
Section C	Compliance A
Section C(1)	Compliance A(1)
Section C(1)(a)	Compliance A(1)
Section C(1)(b)	Compliance A(1)
Section C(2)	Compliance A(2)

1990 CODE	1972 CODE
Section D	Compliance A
Section D(1)	Compliance A(1)
Section D(1)(a)	Compliance A(1)
Section D(1)(b)	Compliance A(1)
Section D(2)	Compliance A(2)
Section E	Compliance B
Section E(1)	Compliance B(1)
Section E(1)(a)	Compliance B(1)
Section E(1)(b)	Compliance B(1)
Section E(2)	Compliance B(2)
Section F	Effective Date of Compliance

CORRELATION TABLE B

1972 CODE	1990 CODE
Canon 1	Canon 1
Paragraph to Canon 1	Section 1A
Canon 2	Canon 2
Canon 2A	Sections 2A, 2C
Canon 2B	Section 2B
Canon 3	Canon 3
Paragraph to Canon 3	Section 3A
Canon 3A(1)	Section 3B(2)
Canon 3A(2)	Section 3B(3)
Canon 3A(3)	Section 3B(4)
Canon 3A(4)	Sections 3B(7), (b)
Canon 3A(5)	Section 3B(8)
Canon 3A(6)	Section 3B(9)
Canon 3A(7)	None
Canon 3B(1)	Section 3C(1)
Canon 3B(2)	Section 3C(2)
Canon 3B(3)	Sections 3D(1), (2)
Canon 3B(4)	Section 3C(4)
Canon 3C(1)	Section 3E(1)
Canon 3C(1)(a)	Section 3E(1)(a)
Canon 3C(1)(b)	Section 3E(1)(b)
Canon 3C(1)(c)	Section 3E(1)(c)
Canon 3C(1)(d)	Section 3E(1)(d)
Canon 3C(1)(d)(i)	Section 3E(1)(d)(i)
Canon 3C(1)(d)(ii)	Section 3E(1)(d)(ii)
Canon 3C(1)(d)(iii)	Section 3E(1)(d)(iii)
Canon 3C(1)(d)(iv)	Section 3E(1)(d)(iv)
Canon 3C(2)	Section 3E(2)
Canon 3C(3)	Terminology
Canon 3C(3)(a)	Terminology
Canon 3C(3)(b)	Terminology
Canon 3C(3)(c)	Terminology
Canon 3C(3)(c)(i)	Terminology
Canon 3C(3)(c)(ii)	Terminology
Canon 3C(3)(c)(iii)	Terminology
Canon 3C(3)(c)(iv)	Terminology
Canon 3D	Section 3F

1972 CODE	1990 CODE
Canon 4	Canon 4
Paragraph to Canon 4	Section 4A
Canon 4A	Section 4B
Canon 4B	Section 4C(1)
Canon 4C	Sections 4C(3)(b), (i), (ii)
Canon 5	Canon 4
Paragraph to Canon 5	Section 4A
Canon 5A	Section 4B
Canon 5B	Section 4C(3)
Canon 5B(1)	Sections 4C(3)(a), (i), (ii)
Canon 5B(2)	Section 4C(3)(b)
Canon 5B(3)	None
Canon 5C(1)	Section 4D(1)
Canon 5C(2)	Sections 4D(2), (3)
Canon 5C(3)	Section 4D(4)
Canon 5C(4)	Section 4D(5)
Canon 5C(4)(a)	Section 4D(5)(a)
Canon 5C(4)(b)	Sections 4D(5)(c), (d), (e), (f), (g)
Canon 5C(4)(c)	Section 4D(5)(h)
Canon 5C(5)	Terminology
Canon 5C(6)	Section 4I
Canon 5C(7)	Section 3B(11)
Canon 5D	Section 4E(1), Terminology
Canon 5D(1)	Section 4E(2)
Canon 5D(2)	Section 4E(3)
Canon 5E	Section 4F
Canon 5F	Section 4G
Canon 5G	Section 4C(2)
Canon 6	Canon 4
Paragraph to Canon 6	Section 4H(1)
Canon 6A	Section 4H(1)(a)
Canon 6B	Section 4H(1)(b)
Canon 6C	Section 4H(2)
Canon 7	Canon 5
Canon 7A(1)	Section 5A(1)
Canon 7A(1)(a)	Section 5A(1)(a)

1972 CODE	1990 CODE
Canon 7A(1)(b)	Sections 5A(1)(b), (c)
Canon 7A(1)(c)	Sections 5A(1)(d), (e), 5C(1)(a)(i)
Canon 7A(2)	Sections 5C(1)(a), (b)(i)
Canon 7A(3)	Section 5A(2)
Canon 7A(4)	Section 5D
Canon 7B(1)	Section 5A(3)
Canon 7B(1)(a)	Section 5A(3)(a)
Canon 7B(1)(b)	Sections 5A(3)(b), (c)
Canon 7B(1)(c)	Sections 5A(3)(d), (i), (ii), (iii)
Canon 7B(2)	Section 5C(2)
Canon 7B(3)	None
Compliance	Application
Paragraph to Compliance	Section A
Comliance A	Section C
Compliance A(1)	Sections C(1), (b)
Compliance A(2)	Section C(2)
Compliance B	Section E
Comliance B(1)	Sections E(1), (a), (b)
Compliance B(2)	Section E(2)
Compliance C	Sections B, (1), (2)
Effective Date of Compliance	Section F

ABA CANONS OF PROFESSIONAL ETHICS

The Canons of Professional Ethics, to and including Canon 32 were adopted by the American Bar Association at its 31st Annual Meeting on August 27, 1908. Canon 28 was amended and Canons 33 to 45 adopted at the 51st Annual Meeting on July 26, 1928. Canons 11, 13, 34, 35 and 43 were amended and Canon 46 was adopted at the 56th Annual Meeting, on August 31, 1933. Canons 7, 11, 12, 27, 31, 33, 34, 37, 39 and 43 were amended and Canon 47 adopted on September 30, 1937; Canon 27 was amended on September 11, 1940; Canons 27 and 43 were amended on August 27, 1942; Canon 27 on August 25, 1943 and on September 19, 1951; Canon 46 rewritten on February 21, 1956.

Preamble

In America, where the stability of Courts and of all departments of government rests upon the approval of the people, it is peculiarly essential that the system for establishing and dispensing Justice be developed to a high point of efficiency and so maintained that the public shall have absolute confidence in the integrity and impartiality of its administration. The future of the Republic, to a great extent, depends upon our maintenance of Justice pure and unsullied. It cannot be so maintained unless the conduct and the motives of the members of our profession are such as to merit the approval of all just men.

No code or set of rules can be framed, which will particularize all the duties of the lawyer in the varying phases of litigation or in all the relations of professional life. The following canons of ethics are adopted by the American Bar Association as a general guide, yet the enumeration of particular duties should not be construed as a denial of the existence of others equally imperative, though not specifically mentioned.

Canon 1. The Duty of the Lawyer to the Courts.

It is the duty of the lawyer to maintain towards the Courts a respectful attitude, not for the sake of the temporary incumbent of the judicial office, but for the maintenance of its supreme importance. Judges, not being wholly free to defend themselves, are peculiarly entitled to receive the support of the Bar against unjust criticism and clamor. Whenever there is proper ground for serious complaint of a judicial officer, it is the right and duty of the lawyer to submit his grievances to the proper authorities. In such cases, but not otherwise, such charges should be encouraged and the person making them should be protected.

Canon 2. The Selection of Judges.

It is the duty of the Bar to endeavor to prevent political considerations from outweighing judicial fitness in the selections of Judges. It should protect earnestly and actively against the appointment or election of those who are unsuitable for the Bench; and it should strive to have elevated thereto only those willing to forego other employments, whether of a business, political or other character, which may embarrass their free and fair consideration of questions before them for decision. The aspiration of lawyers for judicial positions should be governed by an impartial estimate of their ability to add honor to the office and not by a desire for the distinction the position may bring to themselves.

Canon 3. Attempts to Exert Personal Influence on the Court.

Marked attention and unusual hospitality on the part of a lawyer to a Judge, uncalled for by the personal relations of the parties, subject both the Judge and the lawyer to misconstructions of motive and should be avoided. A lawyer should not communicate or argue privately with the Judge as to the merits of a pending cause, and he deserves rebuke and denunciation for any device or attempt to gain from a Judge special personal consideration or favor. A self-respecting independence in the discharge of professional duty, without denial or diminution of the courtesy and respect due the Judge's station, is the only proper foundation for cordial personal and official relations between Bench and Bar.

Canon 4. When Counsel for an Indigent Prisoner.

A lawyer assigned as counsel for an indigent prisoner ought not to ask to be excused for any trivial reason, and should always exert his best efforts in his behalf.

Canon 5. The Defense of Prosecution of Those Accused of Crime.

It is the right of the lawyer to undertake the defense of a person accused of crime, regardless of his personal opinion as to the guilt of the accused; otherwise, innocent persons, victims only of suspicious circumstances, might be denied proper defense. Having undertaken such defense, the lawyer is bound by all fair and honorable means to present every defense that the law of the land permits, to the end that no person may be deprived of life or liberty, but by due process of law.

The primary duty of a lawyer engaged in public prosecution is not to convict, but to see that justice is done. The suppression of facts or the secreting of witnesses capable of establishing the innocence of the accused is highly reprehensible.

Canon 6. Adverse Influences and Conflicting Interests.

It is the duty of a lawyer at the time of retainer to disclose to the client all the circumstances of his relations to the parties, and any interest in or connection with the controversy, which might influence the client in the selection of counsel.

It is unprofessional to represent conflicting interests, except by express consent of all concerned given after a full disclosure of the facts. Within the meaning of this canon, a lawyer represents conflicting interests when, in behalf of one client, it is his duty to contend for that which duty to another client requires him to oppose.

The obligation to represent the client with undivided fidelity and not to divulge his secrets or confidences forbids also the subsequent acceptance of retainers or employment from others in matters adversely affecting any interest of the client with respect to which confidence has been reposed.

Canon 7. Professional Colleagues and Conflicts of Opinion.

A client's proffer of assistance of additional counsel should not be regarded as evidence of want of confidence, but the matter should be left to the determination of the client. A lawyer should decline association as colleague if it is objectionable to the original counsel, but if the lawyer first retained is relieved, another may come into the case.

When lawyers jointly associated in a cause cannot agree as to any matter vital to the interest of the client, the conflict of opinion should be frankly stated to him for his final determination. His decision should be accepted unless the nature of the difference makes it impracticable for the lawyer whose judgment has been overruled to co-operate effectively. In this event it is his duty to ask the client to relieve him.

Efforts, direct or indirect, in any way to encroach upon the business of another lawyer, are unworthy of those who should be brethren at the Bar; but, nevertheless, it is the right of any lawyer, without fear or favor, to give proper advice to those seeking relief against unfaithful or neglectful counsel, generally after communication with the lawyer of whom the complaint is made.

Canon 8. Advising Upon the Merits of a Client's Cause.

A lawyer should endeavor to obtain full knowledge of his client's cause before advising thereon, and he is bound to give a candid opinion of the merits and probable result of pending or contemplated litigation. The miscarriages to which justice is subject, by reason of surprises and disappointments in evidence and witnesses, and through mistakes of juries and errors of Courts, even though only occasional, admonish lawyers to beware of bold and confident assurances to clients, especially where the employment may depend upon such assurance. Whenever the controversy will admit of fair adjustment, the client should be advised to avoid or to end the litigation.

Canon 9. Negotiations with Opposite Party.

A lawyer should not in any way communicate upon the subject of controversy with a party represented by counsel; much less should he undertake to negotiate or compromise the matter with him, but should deal only with his counsel. It is incumbent upon the lawyer most particularly to avoid everything that may tend to mislead a party not represented by counsel, and he should not undertake to advise him as to the law.

Canon 10. Acquiring Interest in Litigation.

The lawyer should not purchase any interest in the subject matter of the litigation which he is conducting.

Canon 11. Dealing with Trust Property.[1]

The lawyer should refrain from any action whereby for his personal benefit or gain he abuses or takes advantage of the confidence reposed in him by his client.

Money of the client or collected for the client or other just property coming into the possession of the lawyer should be reported and accounted for promptly, and should not under any circumstances be commingled with his own or be used by him.

Canon 12. Fixing the Amount of the Fee.[2]

In fixing fees, lawyers should avoid charges which overestimate their advice and services, as well as those which undervalue them. A client's ability to pay cannot justify a charge in excess of the value of the service, though his poverty may require a less charge, or even none at all. The reasonable requests of brother lawyers, and of their widows and orphans without ample means, should receive special and kindly consideration.

In determining the amount of the fee, it is proper to consider: (1) the time and labor required, the novelty and difficulty of the questions involved and the skill requisite properly to conduct the cause; (2) whether the acceptance of employment in the particular case will preclude the lawyer's appearance for others in cases likely to arise out of the transaction, and in which there is a reasonable expectation that otherwise he would be employed, or will involve the loss of other employment while employed in the particular case or antagonisms with other clients; (3) the customary charges of the Bar for similar services; (4) the amount involved in the controversy and the benefits resulting to the client from the services; (5) the contingency or the certainty of the compensation; and (6) the character of the employment, whether casual or for an established and constant client. No one of these considerations in itself is controlling. They are mere guides in ascertaining the real value of the service.

In determining the customary charges of the Bar for similar services, it is proper

1. Canon 11 was amended at the Fifty-sixth Annual Meeting in 1933.
2. Canon 12 was amended on September 30, 1937.

for a lawyer to consider a schedule of minimum fees adopted by a Bar Association, but no lawyer should permit himself to be controlled thereby or to follow it as his sole guide in determining the amount of his fee.

In fixing fees it should never be forgotten that the profession is a branch of the administration of justice and not a mere money-getting trade.

Canon 13. Contingent Fees.[3]

A contract for a contingent fee where sanctioned by law, should be reasonable under all the circumstances of the case, including the risk and uncertainty of the compensation, but should always be subject to the supervision of a Court, as to its reasonableness.

Canon 14. Suing a Client for a Fee.

Controversies with clients concerning compensation are to be avoided by the lawyer so far as shall be compatible with his self-respect and with his right to receive reasonable recompense for his services; and lawsuits with clients should be resorted to only to prevent injustice, imposition or fraud.

Canon 15. How Far a Lawyer May Go in Supporting a Client's Cause.

Nothing operates more certainly to create or to foster popular prejudice against lawyers as a class, and to deprive the profession of that full measure of public esteem and confidence which belongs to the proper discharge of its duties than does the false claim, often set up by the unscrupulous in defense of questionable transactions, that it is the duty of the lawyer to do whatever may enable him to succeed in winning his client's cause.

It is improper for a lawyer to assert in argument his personal belief in his client's innocence or in the justice of his cause.

The lawyer owes "entire devotion to the interest of the client, warm zeal in the maintenance and defense of his rights and the exertion of his utmost learning and ability," to the end that nothing be taken or be withheld from him, save by the rules of law, legally applied. No fear of judicial disfavor or public unpopularity should restrain him from the full discharge of his duty. In the judicial forum the client is entitled to the benefit of any and every remedy and defense that is authorized by the law of the land, and he may expect his lawyer to assert every such remedy or defense. But it is steadfastly to be borne in the mind that the great trust of the lawyer is to be performed within and not without the bounds of the law. The office of attorney does not permit, much less does it demand of him for any client, violation of law or any manner of fraud or chicane. He must obey his own conscience and not that of his client.

3. Canon 13 was amended at the Fifty-sixth Annual Meeting in 1933.

Canon 16. Restraining Clients From Improprieties.

A lawyer should use his best efforts to restrain and to prevent his clients from doing those things which the lawyer himself ought not to do, particularly with reference to their conduct towards Courts, judicial officers, jurors, witnesses and suitors. If a client persists in such wrongdoing the lawyer should terminate their relation.

Canon 17. Ill Feeling and Personalities Between Advocates.

Clients, not lawyers, are the litigants. Whatever may be the ill-feeling existing between clients, it should not be allowed to influence counsel in their conduct and demeanor toward each other or toward suitors in the cause. All personalities between counsel should be scrupulously avoided. In the trial of a cause it is indecent to allude to the personal history or the personal peculiarities and idiosyncrasies of counsel on the other side. Personal colloquies between counsel which cause delay and promote unseemly wrangling should also be carefully avoided.

Canon 18. Treatment of Witnesses and Litigants.

A lawyer should always treat adverse witnesses and suitors with fairness and due consideration, and he should never minister to the malevolence or prejudices of a client in the trial or conduct of a cause. The client cannot be made the keeper of the lawyer's conscience in professional matters. He has no right to demand that his counsel shall abuse the opposite party or indulge in offensive personalities. Improper speech is not excusable on the ground that it is what the client would say if speaking in his own behalf.

Canon 19. Appearance of Lawyer as Witness for His Client.

When a lawyer is a witness for his client, except as to merely formal matters, such as the attestation or custody of an instrument and the like, he should leave the trial of the case to other counsel. Except when essential to the ends of justice, a lawyer should avoid testifying in court in behalf of his client.

Canon 20. Newspaper Discussion of Pending Litigation.

Newspaper publications by a lawyer as to pending or anticipated litigation may interfere with a fair trial in the Courts and otherwise prejudice the due administration of justice. Generally they are to be condemned. If the extreme circumstances of a particular case justify a statement to the public, it is unprofessional to make it anonymously. An *ex parte* reference to the facts should not go beyond quotation from the records and papers on file in the court; but even in extreme cases it is better to avoid any *ex parte* statement.

Canon 21. Punctuality and Expedition.

It is the duty of the lawyer not only to his client, but also to the Court and to the public to be punctual in attendance, and to be concise and direct in the trial and disposition of causes.

Canon 22. Candor and Fairness.

The conduct of the lawyer before the Court and with other lawyers should be characterized by candor and fairness.

It is not candid or fair for the lawyer knowingly to misquote the contents of a paper, the testimony of a witness, the language or the argument of opposing counsel, or the language of a decision or a textbook; or with knowledge of its invalidity, to cite as authority a decision that has been overruled, or a statute that has been repealed; or in argument to assert as a fact that which has not been proved, or in those jurisdictions where a side has the opening and closing arguments to mislead his opponent by concealing or withholding positions in his opening argument upon which his side then intends to rely.

It is unprofessional and dishonorable to deal other than candidly with the facts in taking the statements of witnesses, in drawing affidavits and other documents, and in the presentation of causes.

A lawyer should not offer evidence which he knows the Court should reject, in order to get the same before the jury by argument for its admissibility, nor should he address to the Judge arguments upon any point not properly calling for determination by him. Neither should he introduce into an argument, addressed to the court, remarks or statements intended to influence the jury or bystanders.

These and all kindred practices are unprofessional and unworthy of an officer of the law charged, as is the lawyer, with the duty of aiding in the administration of justice.

Canon 23. Attitude Toward Jury.

All attempts to curry favor with juries by fawning, flattery or pretended solicitude for their personal comfort are unprofessional. Suggestions of counsel, looking to the comfort or convenience of jurors, and propositions to dispense with argument, should be made to the Court out of the jury's hearing. A lawyer must never converse privately with jurors about the case; and both before and during the trial he should avoid communicating with them, even as to matters foreign to the cause.

Canon 24. Right of Lawyer to Control the Incidents of the Trial.

As to incidental matters pending the trial, not affecting the merits of the cause, or working substantial prejudice to the rights of the client, such as forcing the opposite lawyer to trial when he is under affliction or bereavement; forcing the trial on a particular day to the injury of the opposite lawyer when no harm will result from a trial at a different time; agreeing to an extension of time for signing a bill of exceptions, cross interrogatories and the like, the lawyer must be allowed to judge. In such matters no client has a right to demand that his counsel shall be illiberal, or that he do anything therein repugnant to his own sense of honor and propriety.

Canon 25. Taking Technical Advantage of Opposite Counsel; Agreements with Him.

A lawyer should not ignore known customs or practice of the Bar or of a particular Court, even when the law permits, without giving timely notice to the opposing counsel. As far as possible, important agreements, affecting the rights of clients, should be reduced to writing; but it is dishonorable to avoid performance of an agreement fairly made because it is not reduced to writing, as required by rules of Court.

Canon 26. Professional Advocacy Other Than Before Courts.

A lawyer openly, and in his true character, may render professional services before legislative or other bodies, regarding proposed legislation and in advocacy of claims before departments of government, upon the same principles of ethics which justify his appearance before the Courts; but it is unprofessional for a lawyer so engaged to conceal his attorneyship, or to employ secret personal solicitations, or to use means other than those addressed to the reason and understanding, to influence action.

Canon 27. Advertising, Direct or Indirect[4]

It is unprofessional to solicit professional employment by circulars, advertisements, through touters or by personal communications or interviews not warranted by personal relations. Indirect advertisements for professional employment such as furnishing or inspiring newspaper comments, or procuring his photograph to be published in connection with causes in which the lawyer has been or is engaged or concerning the manner of their conduct, the magnitude of the interest involved, the importance of the lawyer's position, and all other like self-laudation, offend the traditions and lower the tone of our profession and are reprehensible; but the customary use of simple professional cards is not improper.

Publication in reputable law lists in a manner consistent with the standards of conduct imposed by these canons of brief biographical and informative data is permissible. Such data must not be misleading and may include only a statement of the lawyer's name and the names of his professional associates; addresses, telephone numbers, cable addresses; branches of the profession practiced; date and place of birth and admission to the bar; schools attended, with dates of graduation, degrees and other educational distinctions; public or quasi-public offices; posts of honor; legal authorships; legal teaching positions; memberships and offices in bar associations and committees thereof, in legal and scientific societies and legal fraternities; the fact of listings in other reputable law lists; the names and addresses of references; and, with their written consent, the names of clients regularly represented. A certificate of compliance with the Rules and Standards issued by the Special Committee on Law Lists may be treated as evidence that such list is reputable.

It is not improper for a lawyer who is admitted to practice as proctor in admi-

4. Canon 27 was amended to its present form at the annual meeting on August 25, 1943. The last paragraph was added by the amendment of September, 1951.

ralty to use that designation on his letterhead or shingle or for a lawyer who has complied with the statutory requirements of admission to practice before the patent office to so use the designation "patent attorney" or "patent lawyer" or "trademark attorney" or "trademark lawyer" or any combination of those terms.

Canon 28. Stirring Up Litigation, Directly or Through Agents.[5]

It is unprofessional for a lawyer to volunteer advice to bring a lawsuit, except in rare cases where ties of blood, relationship or trust make it his duty to do so. Stirring up strife and litigation is not only unprofessional, but it is indictable at common law. It is disreputable to hunt up defects in titles or other causes of action and inform thereof in order to be employed to bring suit or collect judgment, or to breed litigation by seeking out those with claims for personal injuries or those having any other grounds of action in order to secure them as clients, or to employ agents or runners for like purposes, or to pay or reward, directly or indirectly, those who bring or influence the bringing of such cases to his office, or to remunerate policemen, court or prison officials, physicians, hospital attaches or others who may succeed, under the guise of giving disinterested friendly advice, in influencing the criminal, the sick and the injured, the ignorant or other, to seek his professional services. A duty to the public and to the profession devolves upon every member of the Bar having knowledge of such practices upon the part of any practitioner immediately to inform thereof, to the end that the offender may be disbarred.

Canon 29. Upholding the Honor of the Profession.

Lawyers should expose without fear or favor before the proper tribunals corrupt or dishonest conduct in the profession, and should accept without hesitation employment against a member of the Bar who has wronged his client. The counsel upon the trial of a cause in which perjury has been committed owes it to the profession and to the public to bring the matter to the knowledge of the prosecuting authorities. The lawyer should aid in guarding the Bar against the admission to the profession of candidates unfit or unqualified because deficient in either moral character or education. He should strive at all times to uphold the honor and to maintain the dignity of the profession and to improve not only the law but the administration of justice.

Canon 30. Justifiable and Unjustifiable Litigation.

The lawyer must decline to conduct a civil cause or to make a defense when convinced that it is intended merely to harass or to injure the opposite party or to work oppression or wrong. But otherwise it is his right, and, having accepted retainer, it becomes his duty to insist upon the judgment of the Court as to the legal merits of his client's claim. His appearance in Court should be deemed equivalent to an assertion on his honor that in his opinion his client's cause is one proper for judicial determination.

5. Canon 28 was amended to its present form at this Annual Meeting on July 26, 1928, by inserting the words "or collect judgment" in the 5th line as printed above.

Canon 31. Responsibility for Litigation.[6]

No lawyer is obliged to act either as adviser or advocate for every person who may wish to become his client. He has the right to decline employment. Every lawyer upon his own responsibility must decide what employment he will accept as counsel, what causes he will bring into Court for plaintiffs, what causes he will contest in Court for defendants. The responsibility for advising as to questionable transactions, for bringing questionable suits, for urging questionable defenses, is the lawyer's responsibility. He cannot escape it by urging as an excuse that he is only following his client's instructions.

Canon 32. The Lawyer's Duty in Its Last Analysis.

No client, corporate or individual, however powerful, nor any cause, civil or political, however important, is entitled to receive nor should any lawyer render any service or advice involving disloyalty to the law whose ministers we are, or disrespect of the judicial office, which we are bound to uphold, or corruption of any person or persons exercising a public office or private trust, or deception or betrayal of the public. When rendering any such improper service or advice, the lawyer invites and merits stern and just condemnation. Correspondingly, he advances the honor of his profession and the best interests of his client when he renders service or gives advice tending to impress upon the client and his undertaking exact compliance with the strictest principles of moral law. He must also observe and advise his client to observe the statute law, though until a statute shall have been construed and interpreted by competent adjudication, he is free and is entitled to advise as to its validity and as to what he conscientiously believes to be its just meaning and extent. But above all a lawyer will find his highest honor in a deserved reputation for fidelity to private trust and to public duty, as an honest man and as a patriotic and loyal citizen.

Canon 33. Partnerships—Names.[7]

Partnerships among lawyers for the practice of their profession are very common and are not to be condemned. In the formation of partnerships and the use of partnership names care should be taken not to violate any law, custom, or rule of court locally applicable. Where partnerships are formed between lawyers who are not all admitted to practice in the courts of the state, care should be taken to avoid any misleading name or representation which would create a false impression as to the professional position or privileges of the member not locally admitted. In the formation of partnerships for the practice of law, no person should be admitted or held out as a practitioner or member who is not a member of the legal profession duly authorized to practice, and amenable to professional discipline. In the selection and use of a firm name, no false, misleading, assumed or trade name should be used. The continued use of the name of a deceased or former partner, when permissible

6. Canon 31 was amended on September 30, 1937, by substituting the word "employment" on line 3, for "business."

7. Canon 33 was amended September 30, 1937.

by local custom, is not unethical, but care should be taken that no imposition or deception is practiced through this use. When a member of the firm, on becoming a judge, is precluded from practising law, his name should not be continued in the firm name.

Partnerships between lawyers and members of other professions or non-professional persons should not be formed or permitted where any part of the partnership's employment consists of the practice of law.

Canon 34. Division of Fees.[8]

No division of fees for legal services is proper, except with another lawyer, based upon a division of service or responsibility.

Canon 35. Intermediaries.[9]

The professional services of a lawyer should not be controlled or exploited by any lay agency, personal or corporate, which intervenes between client and lawyer. A lawyer's responsibilities and qualifications are individual. He should avoid all relations which direct the performance of his duties by or in the interest of such intermediary. A lawyer's relation to his client should be personal, and the responsibility should be direct to the client. Charitable societies rendering aid to the indigent are not deemed such intermediaries.

A lawyer may accept employment from any organization, such as an association, club or trade organization, to render legal services in any matter in which the organization, as an entity, is interested, but this employment should not include the rendering of legal services to the members of such an organization in respect to their individual affairs.

"The established custom of receiving commercial collections through a law agency is not condemned hereby."

Canon 36. Retirement from Judicial Position or Public Employment.

A lawyer should not accept employment as an advocate in any matter upon the merits of which he has previously acted in a judicial capacity.

A lawyer, having once held public office or having been in the public employ, should not after his retirement accept employment in connection with any matter which he has investigated or passed upon while in such office or employ.

Canon 37. Confidences of a Client.[10]

It is the duty of a lawyer to preserve his client's confidences. This duty outlasts the lawyer's employment, and extends as well to his employees; and neither of them should accept employment which involves or may involve the disclosure or use of

8. Canon 34 was amended September 30, 1937.
9. Canon 35 was amended August 31, 1933.
10. As amended September 30, 1937.

these confidences, either for the private advantage of the lawyer or his employees or to the disadvantage of the client, without his knowledge and consent, and even though there are other available sources of such information. A lawyer should not continue employment when he discovers that this obligation prevents the performance of his full duty to his former or to his new client.

If a lawyer is accused by his client, he is not precluded from disclosing the truth in respect to the accusation. The announced intention of a client to commit a crime is not included within the confidences which he is bound to respect. He may properly make such disclosures as may be necessary to prevent the act or protect those against whom it is threatened.

Canon 38. Compensation, Commissions and Rebates.

A lawyer should accept no compensation, commission, rebates or other advantages from others without the knowledge and consent of his client after full disclosure.

Canon 39. Witnesses.[11]

A lawyer may properly interview any witness or prospective witness for the opposing side in any civil or criminal action without the consent of opposing counsel or party. In doing so, however, he should scrupulously avoid any suggestion calculated to induce the witness to suppress or deviate from the truth, or in any degree to affect his free and untrammeled conduct when appearing at the trial or on the witness stand.

Canon 40. Newspapers.

A lawyer may with propriety write articles for publications in which he gives information upon the law; but he should not accept employment from such publications to advise inquirers in respect to their individual rights.

Canon 41. Discovery of Imposition and Deception.

When a lawyer discovers that some fraud or deception has been practiced, which has unjustly imposed upon the court or a party, he should endeavor to rectify it; at first by advising his client, and if his client refuses to forego the advantage thus unjustly gained, he should promptly inform the injured person or his counsel, so that they may take appropriate steps.

Canon 42. Expenses of Litigation.

A lawyer may not properly agree with a client that the lawyer shall pay or bear the expenses of litigation; he may in good faith advance expenses as a matter of convenience, but subject to reimbursement.

Canon 43. Approved Law Lists.[12]

It is improper for a lawyer to permit his name to be published in a law list the conduct, management or contents of which are calculated or likely to deceive or injure the

11. Canon 39 was amended on September 30, 1937.
12. Canon 43, with its title, was amended on August 27, 1942.

public or the profession, or to lower the dignity or standing of the profession.

Canon 44. Withdrawal from Employment as Attorney or Counsel.

The right of an attorney or counsel to withdraw from employment, once assumed, arises only from good cause. Even the desire or consent of the client is not always sufficient. The lawyer should not throw up the unfinished task to the detriment of his client except for reasons of honor or self-respect. If the client insists upon an unjust or immoral course in the conduct of his case, or if he persists over the attorney's remonstrance in presenting frivolous defenses, or if he deliberately disregards an agreement or obligation as to fees or expenses, the lawyer may be warranted in withdrawing on due notice to the client, allowing him time to employ another lawyer. So also when a lawyer discovers that his client has no case and the client is determined to continue it; or even if the lawyer finds himself incapable of conducting the case effectively. Sundry other instances may arise in which withdrawal is to be justified. Upon withdrawing from a case after a retainer has been paid, the attorney should refund such part of the retainer as has not been clearly earned.

Canon 45. Specialists.

The canons of the American Bar Association apply to all branches of the legal profession; specialists in particular branches are not to be considered as exempt from the application of these principles.

Canon 46. Notice to Local Lawyers.[13]

A lawyer available to act as an associate of other lawyers in a particular branch of the law or legal service may send to local lawyers only and publish in his local legal journal a brief and dignified announcement of his availability to serve other lawyers in connection therewith. The announcement should be in a form which does not constitute a statement or representation of special experience or expertness.

Canon 47. Aiding the Unauthorized Practice of Law.[14]

No lawyer shall permit his professional services, or his name, to be used in aid of, or to make possible, the unauthorized practice of law by any lay agency, personal or corporate.

13. Canon 46 was amended on February 21, 1956.
14. Adopted September 30, 1937.

ABA STANDARDS FOR IMPOSING LAWYER SANCTIONS

As approved February 10, 1986 and as amended February 4, 1992.

JOINT COMMITTEE ON PROFESSIONAL SANCTIONS

CHAIRMAN
Hon. James Duke Cameron
Phoenix, Arizona

CO-CHAIRMAN
Robert P. Cummins
Chicago, Illinois

MEMBERS
Kurt M. Bulmer
Seattle, Washington

James P. Hargarten
San Francisco, California

Charles W. Kettlewell
Columbus, Ohio

Hon. Richard H. Mills
Springfield, Illinois

Hon. Ben F. Overton
Tallahassee, Florida

Hon. George H. Revercomb
Washington, D.C.

Hon. Florence R. Peskoe
Freehold, New Jersey

John Berry
Tallahassee, Florida
(Liaison from National Organization of Bar Counsel)

Cynthia A. Kelly, *Reporter*
Loyola University School of Law
Chicago, Illinois

CONTENTS

I. PREFACE

A. Background

In 1979, the American Bar Association published the *Standards for Lawyer Discipline and Disability Proceedings.*[1] That book was a result of work by the Joint Committee on Professional Discipline of the American Bar Association. The Joint Committee was composed of members of the Judicial Administration Division and the Standing Committee on Professional Discipline of the American Bar Association. The task of the Joint Committee was to prepare standards for enforcement of discipline in the legal community.

The 1979 standards have been most helpful, and have been used by numerous jurisdictions as a frame of reference against which to compare their own disciplinary systems. Many jurisdictions have modified their procedures to comport with these suggested standards, and the Standing Committee on Professional Discipline of the American Bar Association has assisted state disciplinary systems in evaluating their programs in light of the approved standards.

It became evident that additional analysis was necessary in one important area—that of *appropriate sanctions* for lawyer misconduct. The American Bar Association *Standards for Lawyer Discipline and Disability Proceedings* (hereinafter "Standards for Lawyer Discipline") do not attempt to recommend the type of discipline to be imposed in any particular case. The Standards merely state that the discipline to be imposed "should depend upon the facts and circumstances of the case, should be fashioned in light of the purpose of lawyer discipline, and may take into account aggravating or mitigating circumstances" (Standard 7.1).

For lawyer discipline to be truly effective, sanctions must be based on clearly developed standards. Inappropriate sanctions can undermine the goals of lawyer discipline: sanctions which are too lenient fail to adequately deter misconduct and thus lower public confidence in the profession; sanctions which are too onerous may impair confidence in the system and deter lawyers from reporting ethical violations on the part of other lawyers. Inconsistent sanctions, either within a jurisdiction or among jurisdictions, cast doubt on the efficiency and the basic fairness of all disciplinary systems.

As an example of this problem of inconsistent sanctions, consider the range in levels of sanctions imposed for a conviction for failure to file federal income taxes. In one jurisdiction, in 1979, a lawyer who failed to file income tax returns for one year was suspended for one year,[2] while, in 1980, a lawyer who failed to file income tax returns for two years was merely censured.[3] Within a two-year period, the sanctions imposed on lawyers who converted their clients' funds included disbar-

1. MODEL RULES FOR LAWYER DISCIPLINARY ENFORCEMENT (American Bar Association Standing Committee on Professional Discipline, 1989).

2. *In re* Gold, 77 Ill. 2d 224, 396 N.E.2d 25 (1979).

3. *In re* Oliver, M.R. 2454, 79-CH-6 (1980).

ment,[4] suspension,[5] and censure.[6] The inconsistency of sanctions imposed by different jurisdictions for the same misconduct is even greater.

An examination of these cases illustrates the need for a comprehensive system of sanctions. In many cases, different sanctions are imposed for the same acts of misconduct, and the courts rarely provide any explanation for the selection of sanctions. In other cases, the courts may give reasons for their decisions, but their statements are too general to be useful. In still other cases, the courts may list specific factors to support a certain result, but they do not state whether these factors *must* be considered in every discipline case, nor do they explain whether these factors are entitled to equal weight.

The Joint Committee on Professional Sanctions (hereinafter "Sanctions Committee") was formed to address these problems by formulating standards to be used in imposing sanctions for lawyer misconduct. The Sanctions Committee was composed of members from the Judicial Administration Division and the Standing Committee on Professional Discipline. The mandate given was ambitious: the Committee was to examine the current range of sanctions imposed and to formulate standards for the imposition of appropriate sanctions.

In addressing this task, the Sanctions Committee recognized that any proposed standards should serve as a *model* which sets forth a comprehensive system of sanctions, but which leaves room for flexibility and creativity in assigning sanctions in particular cases of lawyer misconduct. These standards are designed to promote thorough, rational consideration of all factors relevant to imposing a sanction in an individual case. The standards attempt to ensure that such factors are given appropriate weight in light of the stated goals of lawyer discipline, and that only relevant aggravating and mitigating circumstances are considered at the appropriate time. Finally, the standards should help achieve the degree of consistency in the imposition of lawyer discipline necessary for fairness to the public and the bar.

While these standards will improve the operation of lawyer discipline systems, there is an additional factor which, though not the focus of this report, cannot be overlooked. In discussing sanctions for lawyer misconduct, this report assumes that all instances of unethical conduct will be brought to the attention of the disciplinary system. Experience indicates that such is not the case. In 1970, the ABA Special Committee on Evaluation of Disciplinary Enforcement (the Clark Committee) was charged with the responsibility for evaluating the effectiveness of disciplinary enforcement systems. The Clark Committee concluded that one of the most significant problems in lawyer discipline was the reluctance of lawyers and judges to report misconduct.[7] That same problem exists today. It cannot be emphasized strongly enough that lawyers and judges must report unethical conduct to the

4. *In re* Smith, 63 Ill. 2d 250, 347 N.E.2d 133 (1976).

5. *In re* DiBella, 58 Ill. 2d 5, 316 N.E.2d 771 (1974).

6. *In re* Sherman, 60 Ill. 2d 590, 328 N.E.2d 553 (1975).

7. PROBLEMS AND RECOMMENDATIONS IN DISCIPLINARY ENFORCEMENT (Chicago: American Bar Association, Special Committee on Evaluation of Disciplinary Enforcement, 1970), at 167.

appropriate disciplinary agency.[8] Failure to render such reports is a disservice to the public and the legal profession.

Judges in particular should be reminded of their obligation to report unethical conduct to the disciplinary agencies. Under the ABA Model Code of Judicial Conduct, a judge is obligated to "take or initiate appropriate disciplinary measures against a judge or lawyer for unprofessional conduct of which the judge may become aware."[9] Frequently, judges take the position that there is no such need and that errant behavior of lawyers can be remedied solely by use of contempt proceedings and other alternative means. It must be emphasized that the goals of lawyer discipline are not properly and fully served if the judge who observes unethical conduct simply deals with it on an *ad hoc* basis. It may be proper and wise for a judge to use contempt powers in order to assure that the court maintains control of the proceeding and punishes a lawyer for abusive or obstreperous conduct in the court's presence. However, the lawyer discipline system is in addition to and serves purposes different from contempt powers and other mechanisms available to the judge. Only if all lawyer misconduct is in fact reported to the appropriate disciplinary agency can the legal profession have confidence that consistent sanctions are imposed for similar misconduct.

Consistency of sanctions depends on reporting of other types as well. The American Bar Association Center for Professional Responsibility has established a "National Discipline Data Bank" which collects statistics on the nature of ethical violations and sanctions imposed in lawyer discipline cases in all jurisdictions. The information available from the data bank is only as good as the reports which reach it. It is vital that the data bank promptly receive complete, accurate and detailed information with regard to all discipline cases.

Finally, the purposes of lawyer sanctions can best be served, and the consistency of those sanctions enhanced, if courts and disciplinary agencies throughout the country articulate the reasons for sanctions imposed. Courts of record that impose lawyer discipline do a valuable service to the legal profession and the public when they issue opinions in lawyer discipline cases that explain the imposition of a specific sanction. The effort of the Sanctions Committee was made easier by the well-reasoned judicial opinions that were available. At the same time, the Sanctions Committee was frustrated by the fact that many jursidictions do not publish lawyer discipline decisions, and that even published decisions are often summary in nature, failing to articulate the justification for the sanctions imposed.

The *Standards for Imposing Lawyer Sanctions* were amended by the ABA House of Delegates on February 4, 1992. The amendments were proposed by the ABA Standing Committee on Professional Discipline as a result of its ongoing review of

8. Lawyers have a duty to report ethical misconduct of other lawyers under Rule 8.3 of the MODEL RULES OF PROFESSIONAL CONDUCT (American Bar Association, 1983) and under DR 1-103 of the MODEL CODE OF PROFESSIONAL RESPONSIBILITY (American Bar Association, 1981). Judges have a similar duty under the MODEL CODE OF JUDICIAL CONDUCT, Canon 3(D)(2) (American Bar Association, 1990).

9. *Id.,* MODEL CODE OF JUDICIAL CONDUCT.

the courts' use of the Standards in lawyer disciplinary cases to assure their consistency with the developing case law.

B. Methodology

The Standards for Imposing Lawyer Sanctions have been developed after an examination of all reported lawyer discipline cases from 1980 to June 1984, where public discipline was imposed.[10] In addition, eight jurisdictions, which represent a variety of disciplinary systems as well as diversity in geography and population size, were examined in depth. In these jurisdictions—Arizona, California, the District of Columbia, Florida, Illinois, New Jersey, North Dakota, and Utah—all published disciplinary cases from Januar, 1974 through June 1984 were analyzed. In each case, data were collected concerning the type of offense, the sanction imposed, the policy considerations identified, and aggravating or mitigating circumstances noted by the court.[11]

These data were examined to identify the patterns that currently exist among courts imposing sanctions and the policy considerations that guide the courts. In general, the courts were consistent in identifying the following policy considerations: protecting the public, ensuring the administration of justice, and maintaining the integrity of the profession. In the words of the California Supreme Court: "The purpose of a disciplinary proceeding is not punitive but to inquire into the fitness of the lawyer to continue in that capacity for the protection of the public, the courts, and the legal profession."[12] However, the courts failed to articulate any theoretical framework for use in imposing sanctions.

In attempting to develop such a framework, the Sanctions Committee considered a number of options. The Committee considered the obvious possibility of identifying each and every type of misconduct in which a lawyer could engage, then suggesting either a recommended sanction or a range of recommended sanctions to

---

10. See Appendix 3 for a listing of the actual number of reported cases from each jurisdiction. The differences in the number of reported cases among the jurisdictions is a function not only of the differences in lawyer populations, but in the operation of the state discipline systems. States differ dramatically in the sophistication of their disciplinary systems; most importantly for this study, states vary in the extent to which disciplinary orders are published. In those jurisdictions where disciplinary decisions are not published in the regional reporters, summaries in state bar publications or unreported cases (supplied by bar counsel) were examined. (To obtain copies of unreported decisions, contact the ABA Center for Professional Responsibility.) The states in which only reported cases were examined were: Alabama, Alaska, Arkansas, Colorado, Connecticut, Delaware, Georgia, Hawaii, Idaho, Indiana, Iowa, Kansas, Louisiana, Maryland, Minnesota, Mississippi, Missouri, Montana, Nebraska, Nevada, New Jersey, New Mexico, North Carolina, Ohio, Oklahoma, Oregon, Rhode Island, South Carolina, South Dakota, Utah, Vermont, Washington, West Virginia, and Wisconsin. In the following jurisdictions both reported and unreported cases were examined: Arizona, California, District of Columbia, Florida, Illinois, Kentucky, Massachusetts, New York, Pennsylvania, Tennessee, Virginia, and Wyoming. In the following jurisdictions, all data were collected from unreported decisions (supplied by bar counsel or taken from case summaries in bar publications): Maine, Michigan, New Hampshire, and Texas.

11. Because of the difficulty in getting complete factual statements, the report does not include cases which were the result of consent orders, or cases in which reciprocal discipline was imposed.

12. Ballard v. State Bar of California, 35 Cal. 3d 274, 673 P.2d 226, 197 Cal. Rptr. 556 (1983).

deal with that particular misconduct. The Sanctions Committee unanimously rejected that option as being both theoretically simplistic and administratively cumbersome.[13]

The Sanctions Committee next considered an approach that dealt with general categories of lawyer misconduct and applied recommended sanctions to those types of misconduct depending on whether or not—and to what extent—the misconduct resulted from intentional or malicious acts of the lawyer. There is some merit in that approach; certainly, the intentional or unintentional conduct of the lawyer is a relevant factor. Nonetheless, that approach was also abandoned after the Sanctions Committee carefully reviewed the purposes of lawyer sanctions. Solely focusing on the intent of the lawyer is not sufficient, and proposed standards must also consider the damage which the lawyer's misconduct causes to the client, the public, the legal system, and the profession. An approach which looked only at the extent of injury was also rejected as being too narrow.

The Committee adopted a model that looks first at the ethical duty and to whom it is owed, and then at the lawyer's mental state and the amount of injury caused by the lawyer's misconduct. (See Theoretical Framework, p. 5, for a detailed discussion of this approach.) Thus, one will look in vain for a section of this report which recommends a specific sanction for, say, improper contact with opposing parties who are represented by counsel [Rule 4.2/DR 7-104(A)(1)],[14] or for any other specific misconduct. What one will find, however, is an organizational framework that provides recommendations as to the type of sanction that should be imposed based on violations of duties owed to clients, the public, the legal system, and the profession.

To provide support for this approach, the Sanctions Committee has offered as much specific data and guidance as possible from reported cases.[15] Thus, with regard to each category of misconduct, the report provides the following:

13. An example of the problems which would be encountered in such an approach will suffice to demonstrate why that approach was rejected. It is improper for a lawyer to neglect a legal matter entrusted to him (Rule 1.3/DR 6-101 (A)(3)). Sanctions which are imposed for violations of this ethical rule vary dramatically. Such conduct may be an intentional violation of the rule (as where a lawyer takes a client's money never intending to perform the services requested), or it may result from negligence (as where an overworked or inexperienced lawyer does not meet a deadline relating to some aspect of the representation). The Sanctions Committee felt that a listing of sanctions based merely on the type of lawyer misconduct would not adequately differenctiate between conduct which has an extremely deleterious effect on the client, the public, the legal system, and the profession, and conduct which has only a minimal effect. In short, the Sanctions Committee concluded that an approach that reviewed each type of misconduct would result in nothing more than a general statement that the individual circumstances of a case dictate the type of sanction which ought to be imposed.

14. Although the House of Delegates of the American Bar Association adopted the MODEL RULES OF PROFESSSIONAL CONDUCT on August 2, 1983, as the ethical standarads for the legal profession, references to the MODEL CODE OF PROFESSIONAL RESPONSIBILITY are included here because some states' ethical standards still follow the Code in both form and substance.

15. While it is not possible to discuss in detail each of the 2,991 cases which have been examined in preparing this report, statistical summaries are available from the American Bar Association Center for Professional Responsibility.

- discussion of what types of sanctions have been imposed for similar misconduct in reported cases;
- discussion of policy reasons which are articulated in reported cases to support such sanctions; and,
- finally, a recommendation as to the level of sanction imposed for the given misconduct, absent aggravating or mitigating circumstances.

While it is recognized that any individual case may present aggravating or mitigating factors which would lead to the imposition of a sanction different from that recommended, these standards present a model which can be used initially to categorize misconduct and to identify the appropriate sanction. The decision as to the effect of any aggravating or mitigating factors should come only after this initial determination of the sanction.

The Sanctions Committee also recognized that the imposition of a sanction of suspension or disbarment does not conclude the matter. Typically, disciplined lawyers will request reinstatement or readmission. While this report does not include an in-depth study of reinstatement and readmission cases, a general recommendation concerning standards for reinstatement and readmission appears as Standard 2.10.

II. THEORETICAL FRAMEWORK

These standards are based on an analysis of the nature of the professional relationship. Historically, being a member of a profession has meant that an individual is some type of expert, possessing knowledge of high instrumental value such that the members of the community give the professional the power to make decisions for them. In the legal profession, the community has allowed the profession the right of self-regulation. As stated in the Preamble to the ABA Model Rules of Professional Conduct (hereinafter "Model Rules"), "[t]he legal profession's relative autonomy carries with it special responsibilities of self-government. The profession has a responsibility to assure that its regulations are conceived in the public interest and not in furtherance of parochial or self-interested concerns of the bar."[16]

This view of the professional relationship requires lawyers to observe the ethical requirements that are set out in the Model Rules (or applicable standard in the jurisdiction where the lawyer is licensed). While the Model Rules define the ethical guidelines for lawyers, they do not provide any method for assigning sanctions for ethical violations. The Committee developed a model which requires a court imposing sanctions to answer each of the following questions:

(1) What ethical duty did the lawyer violate? (A duty to a client, the public, the legal system, or the profession?)

(2) What was the lawyer's mental state? (Did the lawyer act intentionally, knowingly, or negligently?)

16. Preamble to MODEL RULES, paragraph 11, *supra* note 8.

(3) What was the extent of the actual or potential injury caused by the lawyer's misconduct? (Was there a serious or potentially serious injury?) and

(4) Are there any aggravating or mitigating circumstances?

In determining the nature of the ethical duty violated, the standards assume that the most important ethical duties are those obligations which a lawyer owes to *clients*. These include:

(a) the duty of *loyalty* which (in the terms of the Model Rules and Code of Professional Responsibility) includes the duties to:

  (i) preserve the property of a client [Rule 1.15/DR 9-102],

  (ii) maintain client confidences [Rule 1.6/DR 4-101], and

  (iii) avoid conflicts of interest [Rules 1.7 through 1.13, 2.2, 3.7, 5.4(c) and 6.3/ DR 5-101 through DR 5-105, DR 9-101];

(b) the duty of *diligence* [Rules 1.2, 1.3, 1.4/DR 6-101(A)(3)];

(c) the duty of *competence* [Rule 1.1/DR 6-101(A)(1) & (2)]; and

(d) the duty of *candor* [Rule 8.4(c)/DR 1-102(A)(4) & DR 7-101(A)(3)].

In addition to duties owed to clients, the lawyer also owes duties to the *general public*. Members of the public are entitled to be able to trust lawyers to protect their property, liberty, and their lives. The community expects lawyers to exhibit the highest standards of honesty and integrity, and lawyers have a duty not to engage in conduct involving dishonesty, fraud, or interference with the administration of justice [Rules 8.2, 8.4(b)&(c)/DR 1-102(A)(3)(4)&(5), DR 8-101 through DR 8-103, DR 9-101(c)].

Lawyers also owe duties to the *legal system*. Lawyers are officers of the court, and must abide by the rules of substance and procedure which shape the administration of justice. Lawyers must always operate within the bounds of the law, and cannot create or use false evidence, or engage in any other illegal or improper conduct [Rules 3.1 through 3.6, 3.9, 4.1 through 4.4, 8.2, 8.4(d)(e) & (f)/DR 7-102 through DR 7-110].

Finally, lawyers owe duties to the *legal profession*. Unlike the obligations mentioned above, these duties are not inherent in the relationship between the professional and the community. These duties do not concern the lawyer's basic responsibilities in representing clients, serving as an officer of the court, or maintaining the public trust, but include other duties relating to the profession. These ethical rules concern:

(a) *restrictions on advertising and recommending employment* [Rules 7.1 through 7.5/DR 2-101 through 2-104];

(b) *fees* [Rules 1.5, 5.4 and 5.6/DR 2-106, DR 2-107, and DR 3-102];

(c) *assisting unauthorized practice* [Rule 5.5/DR 3-101 through DR3-103];

(d) *accepting, declining, or terminating representation* [Rules 1.2, 1.14, 1.16/DR 2-110]; and

(e) *maintaining the integrity of the profession* [Rules 8.1&8.3/DR 1-101 and DR 1-103].

The *mental states* used in this model are defined as follows. The most culpable mental state is that of intent, when the lawyer acts with the conscious objective or purpose to accomplish a particular result. The next most culpable mental state is that of knowledge, when the lawyer acts with conscious awareness of the nature or attendant circumstances of his or her conduct both without the conscious objective or purpose to accomplish a particular result. The least culpable mental state is negligence, when a lawyer fails to be aware of a substantial risk that circumstances exist or that a result will follow, which failure is a deviation from the standard of care that a reasonable lawyer would exercise in the situation.

The extent of the *injury* is defined by the type of duty violated and the extent of actual or potential harm. For example, in a conversion case, the injury is determined by examining the extent of the client's actual or potential loss. In a case where a lawyer tampers with a witness, the injury is measured by evaluating the level of interference or potential interference with the legal proceeding. In this model, the standards refer to various levels of injury: "serious injury," "injury," and "little or no injury." A reference to "injury" alone indicates any level of injury greater than "little or no" injury.

As an example of how this model works, consider two cases of conversion of a client's property. After concluding that the lawyers engaged in ethical misconduct, it is necessary to determine what duties were breached. In these cases, each lawyer breached the duty of loyalty owed to clients. To assign a sanction, however, it is necessary to go further, and to examine each lawyer's mental state and the extent of the injuries caused by the lawyers' actions.

In the first case, assume that the client gave the lawyer $100 as an advance against the costs of investigation. The lawyer took the money, deposited it in a personal checking account, and used it for personal expenses. In this case, where the lawyer acted intentionally and the client actually suffered an injury, the most severe sanction—disbarment—would be apropriate.

Contrast this with the case of a second lawyer, whose client delivered $100 to be held in a trust account. The lawyer, in a hurry to get to court, neglected to inform the secretary what to do with these funds and they were erroneously deposited into the lawyer's general office account. When the lawyer needed additional funds he drew against the general account. The lawyer discovered the mistake, and immediately replaced the money. In this case, where there was no actual injury and a potential for only minor injury, and where the lawyer was merely negligent, a less serious sanction should be imposed. The appropriate sanction would be either reprimand or admonition.

In each case, after making the initial determination as to the appropriate sanction, the court would then consider any relevant *aggravating or mitigating factors* (Standard 9). For example, the presence of aggravating factors, such as vulnerability of the victim or refusal to comply with an order to appear before the disciplinary agency, could increase the appropriate sanction. The presence of mitigating factors, such as absence of prior discipline or inexperience in the practice of law, could make a lesser sanction appropriate.

While there may be particular cases of lawyer misconduct that are not easily categorized, the standards are not designed to propose a specific sanction for each of the myriad of fact patterns in cases of lawyer misconduct. Rather, the standards provide a theoretical framework to guide the courts in imposing sanctions. The ultimate sanction imposed will depend on the presence of any aggravating or mitigating factors in that particular situation. The standards thus are not analogous to criminal determinate sentences, but are guidelines which give courts the flexibility to select the appropriate sanction in each particular case of lawyer misconduct.

The standards do not account for multiple charges of misconduct. The ultimate sanction imposed should at least be consistent with the sanction for the most serious instance of misconduct among a number of violations; it might well be and generally should be greater than the sanction for the most serious misconduct. Either a pattern of misconduct or multiple instances of misconduct should be considered as aggravating factors (see Standard 9.22).

III. STANDARDS FOR IMPOSING LAWYER SANCTIONS: BLACK LETTER RULES

DEFINITIONS

"Injury" is harm to a client, the public, the legal system, or the profession which results from a lawyer's misconduct. The level of injury can range from "serious" injury to "little or no" injury; a reference to "injury" alone indicates any level of injury greater than "little or no" injury.

"Intent" is the conscious objective or purpose to accomplish a particular result.

"Knowledge" is the conscious awareness of the nature or attendant circumstances of the conduct but without the conscious objective or purpose to accomplish a particular result.

"Negligence" is the failure of a lawyer to heed a substantial risk that circumstances exist or that a result will follow, which failure is a deviation from the standard of care that a reasonable lawyer would exercise in the situation.

"Potential injury" is the harm to a client, the public, the legal system or the profession that is reasonably foreseeable at the time of the lawyer's misconduct, and which, but for some intervening factor or event, would probably have resulted from the lawyer's misconduct.

A. PURPOSE AND NATURE OF SANCTIONS

1.1 *Purpose of Lawyer Discipline Proceedings.* The purpose of lawyer discipline proceedings is to protect the public and the administration of justice from lawyers who have not discharged, will not discharge, or are unlikely properly to discharge their professional duties to clients, the public, the legal system, and the legal profession.

1.2 *Public Nature of Lawyer Discipline.* Ultimate disposition of lawyer discipline should be public in cases of disbarment, suspension, and reprimand. Only in cases of minor misconduct, when there is little or no injury to a client, the public, the legal system, or the profession, and when there is little likelihood of repetition by the lawyer, should private discipline be imposed.

1.3 *Purpose of These Standards.* These standards are designed for use in imposing a sanction or sanctions following a determination by clear and convincing evidence that a member of the legal profession has violated a provision of the Model Rules of Professional Conduct (or applicable standard under the laws of the jurisdiction where the proceeding is brought). Descriptions in these standards of substantive disciplinary offenses are not intended to create grounds for determining culpability independent of the Model Rules. The Standards constitute a model, setting forth a comprehensive system for determining sanctions, permitting flexibility and creativity in assigning sanctions in particular cases of lawyer misconduct. They are designed to promote: (1) consideration of all factors relevant to imposing the appropriate level of sanction in an individual case; (2) consideration of the appropriate weight of such factors in light of the stated goals of lawyer discipline; (3) consistency in the imposition of disciplinary sanctions for the same or similar offenses within and among jurisdictions.

B. SANCTIONS

2.1 *Scope*

A disciplinary sanction is imposed on a lawyer upon a finding or acknowledgment that the lawyer has engaged in professional misconduct.

2.2 *Disbarment*

Disbarment terminates the individual's status as a lawyer. Where disbarment is not permanent, procedures should be established for a lawyer who has been disbarred to apply for readmission, provided that:

(1) no application should be considered for five years from the effective date of disbarment; and

(2) the petitioner must show by clear and convincing evidence:

  (a) successful completion of the bar examination, and

  (b) rehabilitation and fitness to practice law.

2.3 *Suspension*

Suspension is the removal of a lawyer from the practice of law for a specified minimum period of time. Generally, suspension should be for a period of time equal to or greater than six months, but in no event should the time period prior to application for reinstatement be more than three years. Procedures should be established to allow a suspended lawyer to apply for reinstatement, but a lawyer who has been suspended should not be permitted to return to practice until he has completed a reinstatement process demonstrating rehabilitation and fitness to practice law.

2.4 *Interim Suspension*

Interim suspension is the temporary suspension of a lawyer from the practice of law pending imposition of final discipline. Interim suspension includes:

(a) suspension upon conviction of a "serious crime" or,

(b) suspension when the lawyer's continuing conduct is or is likely to cause immediate and serious injury to a client or the public.

2.5 *Reprimand*

Reprimand, also known as censure or public censure, is a form of public discipline which declares the conduct of the lawyer improper, but does not limit the lawyer's right to practice.

2.6 *Admonition*

Admonition, also known as private reprimand, is a form of non-public discipline which declares the conduct of the lawyer improper, but does not limit the lawyer's right to practice.

2.7 *Probation*

Probation is a sanction that allows a lawyer to practice law under specified conditions. Probation can be imposed alone or in conjunction with a reprimand, an admonition or immediately following a suspension; probation can also be imposed as a condition of readmission or reinstatement.

2.8 *Other Sanctions and Remedies*

Other sanctions and remedies which may be imposed include:

(a) restitution,

(b) assessment of costs,

(c) limitation upon practice,

(d) appointment of a receiver,

(e) requirement that the lawyer take the bar examination or professional responsibility examination,

(f) requirement that the lawyer attend continuing education courses, and

(g) other requirements that the state's highest court or disciplinary board deems consistent with the purposes of lawyer sanctions.

2.9 *Reciprocal Discipline*

Reciprocal discipline is the imposition of a disciplinary sanction on a lawyer who has been disciplined in another jurisdiction.

2.10 *Readmission and Reinstatement*

In jurisdictions where disbarment is not permanent, procedures should be established to allow a disbarred lawyer to apply for readmission. Procedures should be established to allow a suspended lawyer to apply for reinstatement.

C. FACTORS TO BE CONSIDERED IN IMPOSING SANCTIONS

3.0 *Generally*

In imposing a sanction after a finding of lawyer misconduct, a court should consider the following factors:

(a) the duty violated;

(b) the lawyer's mental state;

(c) the potential or actual injury caused by the lawyer's misconduct; and

(d) the existence of aggravating or mitigating factors.

4.0 *Violations of Duties Owed to Clients*

4.1 *Failure to Preserve the Client's Property*

Absent aggravating or mitigating circumstances, upon application of the factors set out in 3.0, the following sanctions are generally appropriate in cases involving the failure to preserve client property:

4.11 Disbarment is generally appropriate when a lawyer knowingly converts client property and causes injury or potential injury to a client.

4.12 Suspension is generally appropriate when a lawyer knows or should know that he is dealing improperly with client property and causes injury or potential injury to a client.

4.13 Reprimand is generally appropriate when a lawyer is negligent in dealing with client property and causes injury or potential injury to a client.

4.14 Admonition is generally appropriate when a lawyer is negligent in dealing with client property and causes little or no actual or potential injury to a client.

4.2 *Failure to Preserve the Client's Confidences*

Absent aggravating or mitigating circumstances, upon application of the factors set out in 3.0, the following sanctions are generally appropriate in cases involving improper revelation of information relating to representation of a client:

4.21 Disbarment is generally appropriate when a lawyer, with the intent to benefit the lawyer or another, knowingly reveals information relating to representation of a client not otherwise lawfully permitted to be disclosed, and this disclosure causes injury or potential injury to a client.

4.22 Suspension is generally appropriate when a lawyer knowingly reveals information relating to the representation of a client not otherwise lawfully permitted to be disclosed, and this disclosure causes injury or potential injury to a client.

4.23 Reprimand is generally appropriate when a lawyer negligently reveals information relating to representation of a client not otherwise lawfully permitted to be disclosed and this disclosure causes injury or potential injury to a client.

4.24 Admonition is generally appropriate when a lawyer negligently reveals information relating to representation of a client not otherwise lawfully permitted to be disclosed and this disclosure causes little or no actual or potential injury to a client.

4.3 *Failure to Avoid Conflicts of Interest*

Absent aggravating or mitigating circumstances, upon application of the factors set out in Standard 3.0, the following sanctions are generally appropriate in cases involving conflicts of interest:

4.31 Disbarment is generally appropriate when a lawyer, without the informed consent of client(s):

(a) engages in representation of a client knowing that the lawyer's interests are adverse to the client's with the intent to benefit the lawyer or another, and causes serious or potentially serious injury to the client; or

(b) simultaneously represents clients that the lawyer knows have adverse interests with the intent to benefit the lawyer or another, and causes serious or potentially serious injury to a client; or

(c) represents a client in a matter substantially related to a matter in which the interests of a present or former client are materially adverse, and knowingly uses information relating to the representation of a client with the intent to benefit the lawyer or another, and causes serious or potentially serious injury to a client.

4.32 Suspension is generally appropriate when a lawyer knows of a conflict of interest and does not fully disclose to a client the possible effect of that conflict, and causes injury or potential injury to a client.

4.33 Reprimand is generally appropriate when a lawyer is negligent in determining whether the representation of a client may be materially affected by the lawyer's own interests, or whether the representation will adversely affect another client, and causes injury or potential injury to a client.

4.34 Admonition is generally appropriate when a lawyer engages in an isolated instance of negligence in determining whether the representation of a client may be materially affected by the lawyer's own interests, or whether the representation will adversely affect another client, and causes little or no actual or potential injury to a client.

4.4 *Lack of Diligence*

Absent aggravating or mitigating circumstances, upon application of the factors set out in Standard 3.0, the following sanctions are generally appropriate in cases involving a failure to act with reasonable diligence and promptness in representing a client:

4.41 Disbarment is generally appropriate when:

(a) a lawyer abandons the practice and causes serious or potentially serious injury to a client; or

(b) a lawyer knowingly fails to perform services for a client and causes serious or potentially serious injury to a client; or

(c) a lawyer engages in a pattern of neglect with respect to client matters and causes serious or potentially serious injury to a client.

4.42 Suspension is generally appropriate when:

(a) a lawyer knowingly fails to perform services for a client and causes injury or potential injury to a client, or

(b) a lawyer engages in a pattern of neglect and causes injury or potential injury to a client.

4.43 Reprimand is generally appropriate when a lawyer is negligent and does not act with reasonable diligence in representing a client, and causes injury or potential injury to a client.

4.44 Admonition is generally appropriate when a lawyer is negligent and does not act with reasonable diligence in representing a client, and causes little or no actual or potential injury to a client.

4.5 *Lack of Competence*

Absent aggravating or mitigating circumstances, upon application of the factors set out in Standard 3.0, the following sanctions are generally appropriate in cases involving failure to provide competent representation to a client:

4.51 Disbarment is generally appropriate when a lawyer's course of conduct demonstrates that the lawyer does not understand the most fundamental legal doctrines or procedures, and the lawyer's conduct causes injury or potential injury to a client.

4.52 Suspension is generally appropriate when a lawyer engages in an area of practice in which the lawyer knows he or she is not competent, and causes injury or potential injury to a client.

4.53 Reprimand is generally appropriate when a lawyer:

(a) demonstrates failure to understand relevant legal doctrines or procedures and causes injury or potential injury to a client; or

(b) is negligent in determining whether he or she is competent to handle a legal matter and causes injury or potential injury to a client.

4.54 Admonition is generally appropriate when a lawyer engages in an isolated instance of negligence in determining whether he or she is competent to handle a legal matter, and causes little or no actual or potential injury to a client.

4.6 *Lack of Candor*

Absent aggravating or mitigating circumstances, upon application of the factors set out in Standard 3.0, the following sanctions are generally appropriate in cases where the lawyer engages in fraud, deceit, or misrepresentation directed toward a client:

4.61 Disbarment is generally appropriate when a lawyer knowingly deceives a client with the intent to benefit the lawyer or another, and causes serious injury or potential serious injury to a client.

4.62 Suspension is generally appropriate when a lawyer knowingly deceives a client, and causes injury or potential injury to the client.

4.63 Reprimand is generally appropriate when a lawyer negligently fails to provide a client with accurate or complete information, and causes injury or potential injury to the client.

4.64 Admonition is generally appropriate when a lawyer engages in an isolated instance of negligence in failing to provide a client with accurate or complete information, and causes little or no actual or potential injury to the client.

5.0 *Violations of Duties Owed to the Public*

5.1 *Failure to Maintain Personal Integrity*

Absent aggravating or mitigating circumstances, upon application of the factors set out in Standard 3.0, the following sanctions are generally appropriate in cases involving commission of a criminal act that reflects adversely on the lawyer's honesty, trustworthiness, or fitness as a lawyer in other respects, or in cases with conduct involving dishonesty, fraud, deceit, or misrepresentation:

5.11 Disbarment is generally appropriate when:

(a) a lawyer engages in serious criminal conduct, a necessary element of which includes intentional interference with the administration of justice, false swearing, misrepresentation, fraud, extortion, misappropriation, or theft; or the sale, distribution or importation of controlled substances; or the intentional killing of another; or an attempt or conspiracy or solicitation of another to commit any of these offenses; or

(b) a lawyer engages in any other intentional conduct involving dishonesty, fraud, deceit, or misrepresentation that seriously adversely reflects on the lawyer's fitness to practice.

5.12 Suspension is generally appropriate when a lawyer knowingly engages in criminal conduct which does not contain the elements listed in Standard 5.11 and that seriously adversely reflects on the lawyer's fitness to practice.

5.13 Reprimand is generally appropriate when a lawyer knowingly engages in any other conduct that involves dishonesty, fraud, deceit, or misrepresentation and that adversely reflects on the lawyer's fitness to practice law.

5.14 Admonition is generally appropriate when a lawyer engages in any other conduct that reflects adversely on the lawyer's fitness to practice law.

5.2 *Failure to Maintain the Public Trust*

Absent aggravating or mitigating circumstances, upon application of the factors set out in Standard 3.0, the following sanctions are generally appropriate in cases involving public officials who engage in conduct that is prejudicial to the administration of justice or who state or imply an ability to influence improperly a government agency or official:

5.21 Disbarment is generally appropriate when a lawyer in an official or governmental position knowingly misuses the position with the intent to obtain a significant benefit or advantage for himself or another, or with the intent to cause serious or potentially serious injury to a party or to the integrity of the legal process.

5.22 Suspension is generally appropriate when a lawyer in an official or governmental position knowingly fails to follow proper procedures or rules, and causes injury or potential injury to a party or to the integrity of the legal process.

5.23 Reprimand is generally appropriate when a lawyer in an official or governmental position negligently fails to follow proper procedures or rules, and causes injury or potential injury to a party or to the integrity of the legal process.

5.24 Admonition is generally appropriate when a lawyer in an official or governmental position engages in an isolated instance of negligence in not following proper procedures or rules, and causes little or no actual or potential injury to a party or to the integrity of the legal process.

6.0 *Violations of Duties Owed to the Legal System*

6.1 *False Statements, Fraud, and Misrepresentation*

Absent aggravating or mitigating circumstances, upon application of the factors set out in Standard 3.0, the following sanctions are generally appropriate in cases involving conduct that is prejudicial to the administration of justice or that involves dishonesty, fraud, deceit, or misrepresentation to a court:

6.11 Disbarment is generally appropriate when a lawyer, with the intent to deceive the court, makes a false statement, submits a false document, or improperly withholds material information, and causes serious or potentially serious injury to a party, or causes a significant or potentially significant adverse effect on the legal proceeding.

6.12 Suspension is generally appropriate when a lawyer knows that false statements or documents are being submitted to the court or that material information is improperly being withheld, and takes no remedial action, and causes injury or potential injury to a party to the legal proceeding, or causes an adverse or potentially adverse effect on the legal proceeding.

6.13 Reprimand is generally appropriate when a lawyer is negligent either in determining whether statements or documents are false or in taking remedial action when material information is being withheld, and causes injury or potential injury to a party to the legal proceeding, or causes an adverse or potentially adverse effect on the legal proceeding.

6.14 Admonition is generally appropriate when a lawyer engages in an isolated instance of neglect in determining whether submitted statements or documents are false or in failing to disclose material information upon learning of its falsity, and causes little or no actual or potential injury to a party, or causes little or no adverse or potentially adverse effect on the legal proceeding.

6.2 *Abuse of the Legal Process*

Absent aggravating or mitigating circumstances, upon application of the factors set out in Standard 3.0, the following sanctions are generally appropriate in cases involving failure to expedite litigation or bring a meritorious claim, or failure to obey any obligation under the rules of a tribunal except for an open refusal based on an assertion that no valid obligation exists:

6.21 Disbarment is generally appropriate when a lawyer knowingly violates a court order or rule with the intent to obtain a benefit for the lawyer or another, and causes serious injury or potentially serious injury to a party or causes serious or potentially serious interference with a legal proceeding.

6.22 Suspension is generally appropriate when a lawyer knows that he or she is violating a court order or rule, and causes injury or potential injury to a client or a party, or causes interference or potential interference with a legal proceeding.

6.23 Reprimand is generally appropriate when a lawyer negligently fails to comply with a court order or rule, and causes injury or potential injury to a client or other party, or causes interference or potential interference with a legal proceeding.

6.24 Admonition is generally appropriate when a lawyer engages in an isolated instance of negligence in complying with a court order or rule, and causes little or no actual or potential injury to a party, or causes little or no actual or potential interference with a legal proceeding.

6.3 *Improper Communications with Individuals in the Legal System*

Absent aggravating or mitigating circumstances, upon application of the factors set out in Standard 3.0, the following sanctions are generally appropriate in cases involving attempts to influence a judge, juror, prospective juror or other official by means prohibited by law:

6.31 Disbarment is generally appropriate when a lawyer:

(a) intentionally tampers with a witness and causes serious or potentially serious injury to a party, or causes significant or potentially significant interference with the outcome of the legal proceeding; or

(b) makes an ex parte communication with a judge or juror with intent to affect the outcome of the proceeding, and causes serious or potentially serious injury to a party, or causes significant or potentially significant interference with the outcome of the legal proceeding; or

(c) improperly communicates with someone in the legal system other than a witness, judge, or juror with the intent to influence or affect the outcome of the proceeding, and causes significant or potentially significant interference with the outcome of the legal proceeding.

6.32 Suspension is generally appropriate when a lawyer engages in communication with an individual in the legal system when the lawyer knows that such communication is improper, and causes injury or potential injury to a party or causes interference or potential interference with the outcome of the legal proceeding.

6.33 Reprimand is generally appropriate when a lawyer is negligent in determining whether it is proper to engage in communication with an individual in the legal system, and causes injury or potential injury to a party or interference or potential interference with the outcome of the legal proceeding.

6.34 Admonition is generally appropriate when a lawyer engages in an isolated instance of negligence in improperly communicating with an individual in the legal system, and causes little or no actual or potential injury to a party, or causes little or no actual or potential interference with the outcome of the legal proceeding.

7.0 *Violations of Duties Owed to the Profession*

Absent aggravating or mitigating circumstances, upon application of the factors set out in Standard 3.0, the following sanctions are generally appropriate in cases involving false or misleading communication about the lawyer or the lawyer's services, improper communication of fields of practice, improper solicitation of professional employment from a prospective client, unreasonable or improper fees, unauthorized practice of law, improper withdrawal from representation, or failure to report professional misconduct.

7.1 Disbarment is generally appropriate when a lawyer knowingly engages in conduct that is a violation of a duty owed as a professional with the intent to obtain a benefit for the lawyer or another, and causes serious or potentially serious injury to a client, the public, or the legal system.

7.2 Suspension is generally appropriate when a lawyer knowingly engages in conduct that is a violation of a duty owed as a professional and causes injury or potential injury to a client, the public, or the legal system.

7.3 Reprimand is generally appropriate when a lawyer negligently engages in conduct that is a violation of a duty owed as a professional and causes injury or potential injury to a client, the public, or the legal system.

7.4 Admonition is generally appropriate when a lawyer engages in an isolated instance of negligence that is a violation of a duty owed as a professional, and causes little or no actual or potential injury to a client, the public, or the legal system.

8.0 *Prior Discipline Orders*

Absent aggravating or mitigating circumstances, upon application of the factors set out in Standard 3.0, the following sanctions are generally appropriate in cases involving prior discipline.

8.1 Disbarment is generally appropriate when a lawyer:

(a) intentionally or knowingly violates the terms of a prior disciplinary order and such violation causes injury or potential injury to a client, the public, the legal system, or the profession; or

(b) has been suspended for the same or similar misconduct, and intentionally or knowingly engages in further similar acts of misconduct that cause injury or potential injury to a client, the public, the legal system, or the profession.

8.2 Suspension is generally appropriate when a lawyer has been reprimanded for the same or similar misconduct and engages in further similar acts of misconduct that cause injury or potential injury to a client, the public, the legal system, or the profession.

8.3 Reprimand is generally appropriate when a lawyer:

(a) negligently violates the terms of a prior disciplinary order and such violation causes injury or potential injury to a client, the public, the legal system, or the profession; or

(b) has received an admonition for the same or similar misconduct and engages in further similar acts of misconduct that cause injury or potential injury to a client, the public, the legal system, or the profession.

8.4 An admonition is generally not an appropriate sanction when a lawyer violates the terms of a prior disciplinary order or when a lawyer has engaged in the same or similar misconduct in the past.

9.0 *Aggravation and Mitigation*

9.1 *Generally*

After misconduct has been established, aggravating and mitigating circumstances may be considered in deciding what sanction to impose.

9.2 *Aggravation*

9.21 *Definition.* Aggravation or aggravating circumstances are any considerations or factors that may justify an increase in the degree of discipline to be imposed.

9.22 *Factors which may be considered in aggravation.* Aggravating factors include:

(a) prior disciplinary offenses;

(b) dishonest or selfish motive;

(c) a pattern of misconduct;

(d) multiple offenses;

(e) bad faith obstruction of the disciplinary proceeding by intentionally failing to comply with rules or orders of the disciplinary agency;

(f) submission of false evidence, false statements, or other deceptive practices during the disciplinary process;

(g) refusal to acknowledge wrongful nature of conduct;

(h) vulnerability of victim;

(i) substantial experience in the practice of law;

(j) indifference to making restitution.

(k) illegal conduct, including that involving the use of controlled substances.

9.3 *Mitigation*

9.31 *Definition.* Mitigation or mitigating circumstances are any considerations or factors that may justify a reduction in the degree of discipline to be imposed.

9.32 *Factors which may be considered in mitigation.* Mitigating factors include:

(a) absence of a prior disciplinary record;

(b) absence of a dishonest or selfish motive;

(c) personal or emotional problems;

(d) timely good faith effort to make restitution or to rectify consequences of misconduct;

(e) full and free disclosure to disciplinary board or cooperative attitude toward proceedings;

(f) inexperience in the practice of law;

(g) character or reputation;

(h) physical disability;

(i) mental disability or chemical dependency including alcoholism or drug abuse when:

(1) there is medical evidence that the respondent is affected by a chemical dependency or mental disability;

(2) the chemical dependency or mental disability caused the misconduct;

(3) the respondent's recovery from the chemical dependency

or mental disability is demonstrated by a meaningful and sustained period of successful rehabilitation; and

(4) the recovery arrested the misconduct and recurrence of that misconduct is unlikely.

(j) delay in disciplinary proceedings;

(k) interim rehabilitation;

(l) imposition of other penalties or sanctions;

(m) remorse;

(n) remoteness of prior offenses.

9.4 *Factors Which Are Neither Aggravating nor Mitigating.*

The following factors should not be considered as either aggravating or mitigating:

(a) forced or compelled restitution;

(b) agreeing to the client's demand for certain improper behavior or result;

(c) withdrawal of complaint against the lawyer;

(d) resignation prior to completion of disciplinary proceedings;

(e) complainant's recommendation as to sanction;

(f) failure of injured client to complain.

APPENDIX 1

Cross-Reference Table: ABA Model Rules of Professional Conduct and Standards for Imposing Sanctions

ABA Model Rules of Professional Conduct	*Standards for Imposing Sanctions*
Competence	
Rule 1.1	Standard 4.5
Scope of Representation	
Rule 1.2(a), (b), (c), (e)	Standard 4.4
Rule 1.2(d)	Standard 6.1
Diligence	
Rule 1.3	Standard 4.4
Communication	
Rule 1.4	Standard 4.4
Fees	
Rule 1.5	Standards 4.6 & 7.0
Confidentiality of Information	
Rule 1.6	Standard 4.2
Conflict of Interest	
Rule 1.7	Standard 4.3
Prohibited Transactions	
Rule 1.8	Standard 4.3
Former Client	
Rule 1.9	Standard 4.3
Imputed Disqualification	
Rule 1.10	Standard 4.3
Successive Government and Private Employment	
Rule 1.11	Standard 4.3
Former Judge or Arbitrator	
Rule 1.12	Standard 4.3
Organization as Client	
Rule 1.13	Standard 4.3
Disabled Client	
Rule 1.14	Standard 7.0
Safekeeping Property	
Rule 1.15	Standard 4.1
Declining or Terminating Representation	
Rule 1.16	Standard 7.0
Advisor	
Rule 2.1	Standard 7.0

ABA Model Rules of Professional Conduct	*Standards for Imposing Sanctions*
Intermediary	
Rule 2.2	Standard 4.3
Evaluation for Use by Third Persons	
Rule 2.3	Standard 7.0
Meritorius Claims and Contentions	
Rule 3.1	Standard 6.2
Expediting Litigation	
Rule 3.2	Standard 6.2
Candor Toward the Tribunal	
Rule 3.3	Standard 6.1
Fairness to Opposing Party and Counsel	
Rule 3.4	Standard 6.2
Impartiality and Decorum	
Rule 3.5	Standard 6.3
Trial Publicity	
Rule 3.6	Standard 6.2
Lawyer as Witness	
Rule 3.7	Standard 4.3
Special Responsibilities of a Prosecutor	
Rule 3.8	Standard 5.2
Advocate in Nonadjudicative Proceedings	
Rule 3.9	Standard 6.2
Truthfulness to Others	
Rule 4.1	Standard 6.1
Communication with Represented Persons	
Rule 4.2	Standard 6.3
Dealing with Unrepresented Persons	
Rule 4.3	Standard 6.3
Respect for Rights of Third Persons	
Rule 4.4	Standard 6.2
Responsibilities of a Partner or Supervisory Lawyer	
Rule 5.1	Standard 7.0
Responsibilities of a Subordinate Lawyer	
Rule 5.2	Standard 7.0
Responsibilities Regarding Nonlawyer Assistants	
Rule 5.3	Standard 7.0
Professional Independence of Lawyer	
Rule 5.4(a), (b)	Standard 7.0
Rule 5.4(c)	Standard 4.3
Rule 5.4(d)	Standard 7.0
Unauthorized Practice of Law	
Rule 5.5	Standard 7.0

ABA Model Rules of Professional Conduct	*Standards for Imposing Sanctions*
Restrictions on Right to Practice	
Rule 5.6	Standard 7.0
Responsibilities Regarding Law-related Services	
Rule 5.7	No Applicable Standard
Pro Bono Publico Service	
Rule 6.1	No Applicable Standard
Accepting Appointments	
Rule 6.2	Standard 7.0
Membership in Legal Services Organization	
Rule 6.3	Standard 4.3
Law Reform Activities Affecting Client Interests	
Rule 6.4	Standard 5.2
Communication Concerning Lawyer's Services	
Rule 7.1	Standard 7.0
Advertising	
Rule 7.2	Standard 7.0
Direct Contact with Prospective Clients	
Rule 7.3	Standard 7.0
Communication of Fields of Practice	
Rule 7.4	Standard 7.0
Firm Names and Letterheads	
Rule 7.5	Standard 7.0
Bar Admission and Disciplinary Matters	
Rule 8.1	Standards 5.1, 7.0
Judges and Legal Officials	
Rule 8.2	Standard 6.1
Reporting Professional Misconduct	
Rule 8.3	Standard 7.0
Misconduct	
Rule 8.4(a)	Standards 4.0, 5.0, 6.0, 7.0
Rule 8.4(b)	Standard 5.1
Rule 8.4(c)	Standards 4.6, 5.1
Rule 8.4(d)	Standard 6.0
Rule 8.4(e), (f)	Standard 6.2
Jurisdiction	
Rule 8.5	None

APPENDIX 2

Cross-Reference Table: ABA Code of Professional Responsibility and Standards for Imposing Sanctions

ABA Model Code of Professional Responsibility	*Standards for Imposing Sanctions*
Canon 1: Integrity of Profession	
DR 1-101	Standard 7.0
DR 1-102	Standards 4.6, 5.1, 6.2
DR 1-103	Standard 7.0
Canon 2: Making Counsel Available	
DR 2-101	Standard 7.0
DR 2-102	Standard 7.0
DR 2-103	Standard 7.0
DR 2-104	Standard 7.0
DR 2-105	Standard 7.0
DR 2-106	Standard 7.0
DR 2-107	Standard 7.0
DR 2-108	Standard 7.0
DR 2-109	Standard 7.0
DR 2-110	Standard 7.0
Canon 3: Unauthorized Practice	
DR 3-101(A)	Standard 7.0
DR 3-101(B)	Standard 8.0
DR 3-102	Standard 7.0
DR 3-103	Standard 7.0
Canon 4: Confidences and Secrets	
DR 4-101	Standard 4.2
Canon 5: Independent Judgment	
DR 5-101	Standard 4.3
DR 5-102	Standard 4.3
DR 5-103	Standard 4.3
DR 5-104	Standard 4.3
DR 5-105	Standard 4.3
DR 5-106	Standard 4.3
DR 5-107	Standard 4.3

ABA Model Code of Professional Responsibility	*Standards for Imposing Sanctions*
Canon 6: Competence	
DR 6-101(A)(1), (2)	Standard 4.5
DR 6-101(A)(3)	Standard 4.4
DR 6-102	Standard 4.3
Canon 7: Zealous Representation	
DR 7-101(A)(1), (2)	Standard 4.4
DR 7-101(A)(3)	Standard 4.6
DR 7-101(B)	Standard 7.0
DR 7-102	Standards 6.1 & 6.2
DR 7-103	Standard 5.2
DR 7-104	Standard 6.3
DR 7-105	Standard 6.2
DR 7-106	Standard 6.2
DR 7-107	Standard 6.2
DR 7-108	Standard 6.3
DR 7-109	Standard 6.3
DR 7-110	Standard 6.3
Canon 8: Improving the Legal System	
DR 8-101	Standard 5.2
DR 8-102	Standard 5.2
DR 8-103	Standard 5.2
Canon 9: Appearance of Impropriety	
DR 9-101(A) & (B)	Standard 4.3
DR 9-101(C)	Standard 5.2
DR 9-102	Standard 4.1

ABA PROFESSIONALISM CODES AND CREEDS

American Bar Association Young Lawyers Division (Annual Meeting 1988)

The Division's second recommendation was amended by the proponents and approved by voice vote. As approved, it reads:

BE IT RESOLVED, That the American Bar Association authorizes the dissemination to the profession of the following "Lawyers' Pledge of Professionalism."

LAWYERS' PLEDGE OF PROFESSIONALISM

1. I will remember that the practice of law is first and foremost a profession, and I will subordinate business concerns to professionalism concerns.
2. I will encourage respect for the law and our legal system through my words and actions.
3. I will remember my responsibilities to serve as an officer of the court and protector of individual rights.
4. I will contribute time and resources to public service, public education, charitable, and pro bono activities in my community.
5. I will work with the other participants in the legal system, including judges, opposing counsel and those whose practices are different from mine, to make our legal system more accessible and responsive.
6. I will resolve matters expeditiously and without unnecessary expense.
7. I will resolve disputes through negotiation whenever possible.
8. I will keep my clients well-informed and involved in making the decisions that affect them.
9. I will continue to expand my knowledge of the law.
10. I will achieve and maintain proficiency in my practice.
11. I will be courteous to those with whom I come into contact during the course of my work.
12. I will honor the spirit and intent, as well as the requirements, of the applicable rules or code of professional conduct for my jurisdiction, and I will encourage others to do the same.

American Bar Association Section of Tort and Insurance Practice (Annual Meeting 1988)

The Section's second recommendation was amended by the proponents and approved by voice vote. As approved, it reads:

BE IT RESOLVED, That the American Bar Association recommend to state and local bar associations that they encourage their members to accept as a guide for the individual conduct, and to comply with, a lawyer's creed of professionalism.

BE IT FURTHER RESOLVED, That nothing contained in such a creed shall be deemed to supersede or in any way amend the Model Rules of Professional Conduct or other disciplinary codes, alter existing standards of conduct against which lawyer negligence might be judged or become a basis for the imposition of civil liability of any kind.

LAWYER'S CREED OF PROFESSIONALISM

Preamble

As a lawyer I must strive to make our system of justice work fairly and efficiently. In order to carry out that responsibility, not only will I comply with the letter and spirit of the disciplinary standards applicable to all lawyers, but I will also conduct myself in accordance with the following Creed of Professionalism when dealing with my client, opposing parties, their counsel, the courts and the general public.

A. With respect to my client:

1. I will be loyal and committed to my client's cause, but I will not permit that loyalty and commitment to interfere with my ability to provide my client with objective and independent advice;

2. I will endeavor to achieve my client's lawful objectives in business transactions and in litigation as expeditiously and economically as possible;

3. In appropriate cases, I will counsel my client with respect to mediation, arbitration and other alternative methods of resolving disputes;

4. I will advise my client against pursuing litigation (or any other course of action) that is without merit and against insisting on tactics which are intended to delay resolution of the matter or to harass or drain the financial resources of the opposing party;

5. I will advise my client that civility and courtesy are not to be equated with weakness;

6. While I must abide by my client's decision concerning the objectives of the

representation, I nevertheless will counsel my client that a willingness to initiate or engage in settlement discussions is consistent with zealous and effective representation.

B. With respect to opposing parties and their counsel:

1. I will endeavor to be courteous and civil, both in oral and in written communications;
2. I will not knowingly make statements of fact or of law that are untrue;
3. In litigation proceedings I will agree to reasonable requests for extensions of time or for waiver of procedural formalities when the legitimate interests of my client will not be adversely affected;
4. I will endeavor to consult with opposing counsel before scheduling depositions and meetings and before re-scheduling hearings, and I will cooperate with opposing counsel when scheduling changes are requested;
5. I will refrain from utilizing litigation or any other course of conduct to harass the opposing party;
6. I will refrain from engaging in excessive and abusive discovery, and I will comply with all reasonable discovery requests;
7. I will refrain from utilizing delaying tactics;
8. In depositions and other proceedings, and in negotiations, I will conduct myself with dignity, avoid making groundless objections and refrain from engaging in acts of rudeness or disrespect;
9. I will not serve motions and pleadings on the other party, or his counsel, at such a time or in such a manner as will unfairly limit the other party's opportunity to respond;
10. In business transactions I will not quarrel over matters of form or style, but will concentrate on matters of substance and content;
11. I will clearly identify, for other counsel or parties, all changes that I have made in documents submitted to me for review.

C. With respect to the courts and other tribunals:

1. I will be a vigorous and zealous advocate on behalf of my client, while recognizing, as an officer of the court, that excessive zeal may be detrimental to my client's interests as well as to the proper function of our system of justice;
2. Where consistent with my client's interests, I will communicate with opposing counsel in an effort to avoid litigation and to resolve litigation that has actually commenced;
3. I will voluntarily withdraw claims or defenses when it becomes apparent that

they do not have merit or are superfluous;

4. I will refrain from filing frivolous motions;
5. I will make every effort to agree with other counsel, as early as possible on a voluntary exchange of information and on a plan for discovery;
6. I will attempt to resolve, by agreement, my objections to matters contained in my opponent's pleadings and discovery requests;
7. When scheduling hearings or depositions have to be canceled, I will notify opposing counsel, and, if appropriate, the court (or other tribunal) as early as possible;
8. Before dates for hearings or trials are set—or if that is not feasible, immediately after such dates have been set—I will attempt to verify the availability of key participants and witnesses so that I can promptly notify the court (or other tribunal) and opposing counsel of any likely problem in that regard;
9. In civil matters, I will stipulate to facts as to which there is no genuine dispute;
10. I will endeavor to be punctual in attending court hearings, conferences and depositions;
11. I will at all times be candid with the court.

D. With respect to the public and to our system of justice:

1. I will remember that, in addition to commitment to my client's cause, my responsibilities as a lawyer include a devotion to the public good;
2. I will endeavor to keep myself current in the areas in which I practice and, when necessary, will associate with, or refer my client to, counsel knowledgeable in anther field of practice;
3. I will be mindful of the fact that, as a member of a self-regulating profession, it is incumbent on me to report violations by fellow lawyers of any disciplinary rule;
4. I will be mindful of the need to protect the image of the legal profession in the eyes of the public and will be so guided when considering methods and content of advertising;
5. I will be mindful that the law is a learned profession and that among its desirable goals are devotion to public service, improvement of administration of justice, and the contribution of uncompensated time and civic influence on behalf of those persons who cannot afford adequate legal assistance.

American Bar Association Standing Committee on Professionalism (Annual Meeting 1995)

RECOMMENDATION

RESOLVED, That the American Bar Association encourages federal, state, territorial and local bar associations and courts to adopt standards of civility, courtesy and conduct as aspirational goals to promote professionalism of lawyers and judges.

REPORT

In 1988 the following recommendation of the American Bar Association Section of Tort and Insurance Practice was approved by the House of Delegates:

BE IT RESOLVED, That the American Bar Association recommend to state and local bar associations that they encourage their members to accept as a guide for their individual conduct, and to comply with, aLawyer's Creed of Professionalism.

BE IT FURTHER RESOLVED, That nothing in such a creed shall be deemed to supersede or in any way amend the Model Rules of Professional Conduct or other disciplinary codes, alter existing standards of conduct against which lawyer negligence might be judged or become a basis for the imposition of civil liability of any kind.

The purpose of this recommendation is to build upon the good work that has been generated by that recommendation (with its accompanying example of a Lawyer's Creed of Professionalism), and the contemporaneous authorization by the House of Delegates of the dissemination of the Lawyers' Pledge of Professionalism proposed by the American Bar Association Young Lawyers Division, by particularly encouraging the courts and those bar associations that have not heretofore provided aspirational standards of civility, courtesy and conduct to their members as a guide, to adopt such standards.

The files of the American Bar Association Center for Professional Responsibility presently show that 88 state and local bar associations and organizations in 38 states, as well as one American Bar Association Section, one American Bar Association division and one Federal Judicial Circuit, have adopted standards of professional conduct in some form.

These standards address and respond to concerns over deteriorating professionalism, a fear that in pursuing the interests of clients or their own self interests, lawyers' regard for the dignity of the justice system and the trust among counsel and the courts engendered to principles of integrity, courtesy and mutual respect may lessen.

The common principles of such standards are:

- A lawyer's duty to represent each client zealously within the bounds of the law is a duty to be honored consistent with the lawyer's responsibility to a justice system;

- In addition to the duties of candor, honesty and diligence that a lawyer owes to the judiciary under rules of professional conduct, a lawyer owes to the judiciary a duty of respect;

- A judge owes to the practicing bar a duty of attentiveness, courtesy, respect and a dedication to the proper administration of the courts;

- A lawyer owes opposing counsel, parties and the courts a duty of courtesy, fairness and cooperation;

- A lawyer owes to the profession adherence to a higher level of conduct than observance of rules of professional conduct.

No documentation of the degree to which regard for the legal profession both among the public and among lawyers and judges has fallen is available, but the observation is virtually uniform. To the extent that lawyers and judges are responsible for the problem, they can take action to correct it.

Adoption of aspirational standards to improve professional conduct of each of us is one measure that the profession can take to address a troublesome issue. The promotion of such standards of conduct demonstrates this Association's concern and its desire to advance the ideals of professionalism.

The recommendation does not attempt to provide a model code of professionalism, of which many splendid examples exist. Rather, the recommendation encourages practicing lawyers and the judiciary to identify standards that go beyond the mere upholding of law and ethics rules and codes that sanction misconduct. The development of codes at the local and state bar levels, judicial circuits and among specialty bars is a healthy and powerful demonstration of a commitment to professionalism.

ABA CLIENT RELATIONS COMMITMENT TO CLIENTS

ABA Client Relations Commitment to Clients+

My Declaration of Commitment to Clients

To treat you with respect and courtesy.

To handle your legal matter competently and diligently, in accordance with the highest standards of the profession.

To exercise independent professional judgment on your behalf.

To charge a reasonable fee and to explain in advance how that fee will be computed and billed.

To return telephone calls promptly.

To keep you informed and provide you with copies of important papers.

To respect your decisions on the objectives to be pursued in your case, as permitted by law and the rules of professional conduct, including whether or not to settle your case.

To work with other participants in the legal system to make our legal system more accessible and responsive.

To preserve the client confiences learned during our lawyer-client relationship.

To exhibit the highest degree of ethical conduct in accordance with the Code of Professional Responsibility/Model Rules of Professional Conduct.

+This Commitment was adopted by the American Bar Association Board of Governors, August 1993, and is subject to the professional rules of conduct in effect in each state.

ABA GUIDELINES FOR LITIGATION CONDUCT

Introduction

The widely-perceived, accelerating decline in professionalism—often denominated "civility"—has been the subject of increasing concern to the profession for many,years. Twice since 1988, the American Bar Association has urged adoption of, and adherence to, civility codes. What has been lacking, however, is an ABA-endorsed model code. The *Guidelines for Litigation Conduct* fill that void.

These *Guidelines* are consensus-driven and state nothing novel or revolutionary. They are purely aspirational and are not to be used as a basis for litigation, liability, discipline, sanctions or penalties of any type. The *Guidelines* are designed not to promote punishment but rather to elevate the tenor of practice—to set a voluntary, higher standard, "in the hope that," in the words of former ABA President John J. Curtin, 46some progress might be made towards greater professional satisfaction."

The *Guidelines for Litigation Conduct* are modeled on the Standards for Professional Conduct adopted by the United States Court of Appeals for the Seventh Circuit, a set of proven aspirational standards. Chief United States District Judge Marvin E. Aspen of Chicago, architect of the Seventh Circuit Standards, has accurately observed that civility in the legal profession is inextricably linked to the manner in which lawyers are perceived by the public—and, therefore, to the deteriorating public confidence that our system of justice enjoys.

Deteriorating civility, in former ABA President Lee Cooper's words, "interrupts the administration ofjustice. It makes the practice of law less rewarding. It robs a lawyer of the sense of dignity and self-worth that should come from a learned profession. Not least of all, it ... brings with it all the problems . . . that accompany low public regard for lawyers and lack of confidence in the justice system."

The problem of incivility is more pervasive, and insidious, than its impact on the legal profession alone. As Justice Anthony M. Kennedy has stressed:

> Civility is the mark of an accomplished and superb professional, but it is more even than this. It is an end in itself. Civility has deep roots in the idea of respect for the individual.

The decline in civility is not limited to the legal profession, but this profession has been in the forefront of those addressing this problem. These *Guidelines* are offered in this spirit.

Gregory P. Joseph
Chair, 1997-1998
Section of Litigation
American Bar Association

American Bar Association
GUIDELINES FOR LITIGATION CONDUCT

August 1998

Preamble

A lawyer's conduct should be characterized at all times by personal courtesy and professional integrity in the fullest sense of those terms. In fulfilling our duty to represent a client vigorously as lawyers, we will be mindful of our obligations to the administration of justice, which is a truth-seeking process designed to resolve human and societal problems in a rational, peaceful, and efficient manner.

A judge's conduct should be characterized at all times by courtesy and patience toward all participants. As judges we owe to all participants in a legal proceeding respect, diligence, punctuality, and protection against unjust and improper criticism or attack.

Conduct that may be characterized as uncivil, abrasive, abusive, hostile, or obstructive impedes the fundamental goal of resolving disputes rationally, peacefully, and efficiently. Such conduct tends to delay and often to deny justice.

The following Guidelines are designed to encourage us, judges and lawyers, to meet our obligations to each other, to litigants and to the system of justice, and thereby achieve the twin goals of civility and professionalism, both of which, are hallmarks of a learned profession dedicated to public service.

We encourage judges, lawyers and clients to make a mutual and firm commitment to these Guidelines.

We support the principles espoused in the following Guidelines, but under no circumstances should these Guidelines be used as a basis for litigation or for sanctions or penalties.

Lawyers' Duties to Other Counsel

1. We will practice our profession with a continuing awareness that our role is to zealously advance the legitimate interests of our clients. In our dealings with others we will not reflect the ill feelings of our clients. We will treat all other counsel, parties, and witnesses in a civil and courteous manner, not only in court, but also in all other written and oral communications. We will refrain from acting upon or manifesting bias or prejudice based upon race, sex, religion, national origin, disability, age, sexual orientation or socioeconomic status toward any participant in the legal process.

2. We will not, even when called upon by a client to do so, abuse or indulge in offensive conduct directed to other counsel, parties, or witnesses. We will abstain

from disparaging personal remarks or acrimony toward other counsel, parties, or witnesses. We will treat adverse witnesses and parties with fair consideration.

3. We will not encourage or knowingly authorize any person under our control to engage in conduct that would be improper if we were to engage in such conduct.

4. We will not, absent good cause, attribute bad motives or improper conduct to other counsel.

5. We will not lightly seek court sanctions.

6. We will in good faith adhere to all express promises and to agreements with other counsel, whether oral or in writing, and to all agreements implied by the circumstances or local customs.

7. When we reach an oral understanding on a proposed agreement or a stipulation and decide to commit it to writing, the drafter will endeavor in good faith to state the oral understanding accurately and completely. The drafter will provide other counsel the opportunity to review the writing. As drafts are exchanged between or among counsel, changes from prior drafts will be identified in the draft or otherwise explicitly brought to other counsel's attention. We will not include in a draft matters to which there has been no agreement without explicitly advising other counsel in writing of the addition.

8. We will endeavor to confer early with other counsel to assess settlement possibilities. We will not falsely hold out the possibility of settlement to obtain unfair advantage.

9. In civil actions, we will stipulate to relevant matters if they are undisputed and if no good faith advocacy basis exists for not stipulating.

10. We will not use any form of discovery or discovery scheduling as a means of harassment.

11. Whenever circumstances allow, we will make good faith efforts to resolve by agreement objections before presenting them to the court.

12. We will not time the filing or service of motions or pleadings in any way that unfairly limits another party's opportunity to respond.

13. We will not request an extension of time solely for the purpose of unjustified delay or to obtain unfair advantage.

14. We will consult other counsel regarding scheduling matters in a good faith effort to avoid scheduling conflicts.

15. We will endeavor to accommodate previously scheduled dates for hearings, depositions, meetings, conferences, vacations, seminars, or other functions that produce good faith calendar conflicts on the part of other counsel.

16. We will promptly notify other counsel and, if appropriate, the court or other persons, when hearings, depositions, meetings, or conferences are to be canceled or postponed.

17. We will agree to reasonable requests for extensions of time and for waiver of procedural formalities, provided our clients' legitimate rights will not be materially or adversely affected.

18. We will not cause any default or dismissal to be entered without first notifying opposing counsel, when we know his or her identity, unless the rules provide otherwise.

19. We will take depositions only when actually needed. We will not take depositions for the purposes of harassment or other improper purpose.

20. We will not engage in any conduct during a deposition that would not be appropriate in the presence of a judge.

21. We will not obstruct questioning during a deposition or object to deposition questions unless permitted under applicable law.

22. During depositions we will ask only those questions we reasonably believe are necessary, and appropriate, for the prosecution or defense of an action.

23. We will carefully craft document production requests so they are limited to those documents we reasonably believe are necessary, and appropriate, for the prosecution or defense of an action. We will not design production requests to place an undue burden or expense on a party, or for any other improper purpose.

24. We will respond to document requests reasonably and not strain to interpret requests in an artificially restrictive manner to avoid disclosure of relevant and non-privileged documents. We will not produce documents in a manner designed to hide or obscure the existence of particular documents, or to accomplish any other improper purpose.

25. We will careftilly craft interrogatories so they are limited to those matters we reasonably believe are necessary, and appropriate, for the prosecution or defense of an action, and we will not design them to place an undue burden or expense on a party, or for any other improper purpose.

26. We will respond to interrogatories reasonably and will not strain to interpret them in an artificially restrictive manner to avoid disclosure of relevant and non-privileged information, or for any other improper purpose.

27. We will base our discovery objections on a good faith belief in their merit and will not object solely for the purpose of withholding or delaying the disclosure of relevant information, or for any other improper purpose.

28. When a draft order is to be prepared by counsel to reflect a court ruling, we will draft an order that accurately and completely reflects the court's ruling. We will promptly prepare and submit aproposed order to other counsel and attempt to reconcile any differences before the draft order is presented to the court.

29. We will not ascribe a position to another counsel that counsel has not taken.

30. Unless permitted or invited by the court, we will not send copies of correspondence between counsel to the court.

31. Nothing contained in these Guidelines is intended or shall be construed to inhibit vigorous advocacy, including vigorous cross-examination.

Lawyers' Duties to the Court

1. We will speak and write civilly and respectftilly in all communications with the court.

2. We will be punctual and prepared for all court appearances so that all hearings, conferences, and trials may commence on time; if delayed, we will notify the court and counsel, if possible.

3 . We will be considerate of the time constraints and pressures on the court and court staff inherent in their efforts to administer justice.

4. We will not engage in any conduct that brings disorder or disruption to the courtroom. We will advise our clients and witnesses appearing in court of the proper conduct expected and required there and, to the best of our ability, prevent our clients and witnesses from creating disorder or disruption.

5. We will not knowingly misrepresent, mischaracterize, misquote, or mis-cite facts or authorities in any oral or written communication to the court.

6. We will not write letters to the court in connection with a pending action, unless invited or permitted by the court.

7. Before dates for hearings or trials are set, or if that is not feasible, immediately after such date has been set, we will attempt to verify the availability of necessary participants and witnesses so we can promptly notify the court of any likely problems.

8. We will act and speak civilly* to court marshals, clerks, court reporters, secretaries, and law clerks with an awareness that they, too, are an integral part of the judicial system.

Courts' Duties to Lawyers

1. We will be courteous, respectful, and civil to lawyers, parties, and witnesses. We will maintain control of the proceedings, recognizing that judges have both the obligation and the authority to insure that all litigation proceedings are conducted in a civil manner.

2. We will not employ hostile, demeaning, or humiliating words in opinions or in written or oral communications with lawyers, parties, or witnesses.

3. We will be punctual in convening all hearings, meetings, and conferences; if delayed, we will notify counsel, if possible.

4. In scheduling all hearings, meetings and conferences we will be considerate of time schedules of lawyers, parties, and witnesses.

5. We will make all reasonable efforts to decide promptly all matters presented to us for decision.

6. We will give the issues in controversy deliberate, impartial, and studied analysis and consideration.

7. While endeavoring to resolve disputes efficiently, we will be considerate of the time constraints and pressures imposed on lawyers by the exigencies of litigation practice.

8. We recognize that a lawyer has a right and a duty to present a cause ftilly and properly, and that a litigant has a right to a fair and impartial hearing. Within the practical limits of time, we will allow lawyers to present proper arguments and to make a complete and accurate record.

9. We will not impugn the integrity or professionalism of any lawyer on the basis of the clients whom or the causes which a lawyer represents.

10. We will do our best to insure that court personnel act civilly toward lawyers, parties, and witnesses.

11. We will not adopt procedures that needlessly increase litigation expense.
12. We will bring to lawyers' attention uncivil conduct which we observe.

Judges' Duties to Each Other

1. We will be courteous, respectful, and civil in opinions, ever mindful that a position articulated by another judge is the result of that judge's earnest effort to interpret the law and the facts correctly.
2. In all written and oral communications, we will abstain from disparaging personal remarks or criticisms, or sarcastic or demeaning comments about another judge.
3. We will endeavor to work with other judges in an effort to foster a spirit of cooperation in our mutual goal of enhancing the administration ofjustice.

SELECTED FEDERAL SANCTIONS AND DISCOVERY PROVISIONS

Selected Federal Rules of Civil Procedure

Rule 11. Signing of Pleadings, Motions, and Other Papers; Representations to Court; Sanctions [effective December 1, 1993]

(a) *Signature.* Every pleading, written motion, and other paper shall be signed by at least one attorney of record in the attorney's individual name, or, if the party is not represented by an attorney, shall be signed by the party. Each paper shall state the signer's address and telephone number, if any. Except when otherwise specifically provided by rule or statute, pleadings need not be verified or accompanied by affidavit. An unsigned paper shall be stricken unless omission of the signature is corrected promptly after being called to the attention of the attorney or party.

(b) *Representations to Court.* By presenting to the court (whether by signing, filing, submitting, or later advocating) a pleading, written motion, or other paper, an attorney or unrepresented party is certifying that to the best of the person's knowledge, information, and belief, formed after an inquiry reasonable under the circumstances,—

(1) it is not being presented for any improper purpose, such as to harass or to cause unnecessary delay or needless increase in the cost of litigation;

(2) the claims, defenses, and other legal contentions therein are warranted by existing law or by a nonfrivolous argument for the extension, modification, or reversal of existing law or the establishment of new law;

(3) the allegations and other factual contentions have evidentiary support or, if specifically so identified, are likely to have evidentiary support after a reasonable opportunity for further investigation or discovery; and

(4) the denials of factual contentions are warranted on the evidence or, if specifically so identified, are reasonably based on a lack of information or belief.

(c) *Sanctions.* If, after notice and a reasonable opportunity to respond, the court determines that subdivision (b) has been violated, the court may, subject to the conditions stated below, impose an appropriate sanction upon the attorneys, law firms, or parties that have violated subdivision (b) or are responsible for the violation.

(1) *How Initiated.*

(A) *By Motion.* A motion for sanctions under this rule shall be made separately from other motions or requests and shall describe the specific conduct alleged to violate subdivision (b). It shall be served as provided in Rule 5, but shall not be filed with or presented to the court unless, within 21 days after service of the motion (or such other period as the court may prescribe), the challenged paper, claim, defense, contention, allegation, or denial is not withdrawn or appropriately corrected. If warranted, the court may award to the party prevailing on the motion the reasonable expenses and attorney's fees incurred in presenting or opposing the motion. Absent exceptional circumstances, a law firm shall be held jointly responsible for violations committed by its partners, associates, and employees.

(B) *On Court's Initiative.* On its own initiative, the court may enter an order describing the specific conduct that appears to violate subdivision (b) and directing an attorney, law firm, or party to show cause why it has not violated subdivision (b) with respect thereto.

(2) *Nature of Sanction; Limitations.* A sanction imposed for violation of this rule shall be limited to what is sufficient to deter repetition of such conduct or comparable conduct by others similarly situated. Subject to the limitations in subparagraphs (A) and (B), the sanction may consist of, or include, directives of a nonmonetary nature, an order to pay a penalty into court, or, if imposed on motion and warranted for effective deterrence, an order directing payment to the movant of some or all of the reasonable attorneys' fees and other expenses incurred as a direct result of the violation.

(A) Monetary sanctions may not be awarded against a represented party for a violation of subdivision (b)(2).

(B) Monetary sanctions may not be awarded on the court's initiative unless the court issues its order to show cause before a voluntary dismissal or settlement of the claims made by or against the party which is, or whose attorneys are, to be sanctioned.

(3) *Order.* When imposing sanctions, the court shall describe the conduct determined to constitute a violation of this rule and explain the basis for the sanction imposed.

(d) *Inapplicability to Discovery.* Subdivisions (a) through (c) of this rule do not apply to disclosures and discovery requests, responses, objections, and motions that are subject to the provisions of Rules 26 through 37.

Rule 26. General Provisions Governing Discovery; Duty of Disclosure [effective December 1, 1993]

(a) *Required Disclosures; Methods to Discover Additional Matter.*

(1) *Initial Disclosures.* Except to the extent otherwise stipulated or directed by order or local rule, a party shall, without awaiting a discovery request, provide to other parties:

(A) the name and, if known, the address and telephone number of each individual likely to have discoverable information relevant to disputed facts alleged with particularity in the pleadings, identifying the subjects of the information;

(B) a copy of, or a description by category and location of, all documents, data compilations, and tangible things in the possession, custody, or control of the party that are relevant to disputed facts alleged with particularity in the pleadings;

(C) a computation of any category of damages claimed by the disclosing party, making available for inspection and copying as under Rule 34 the documents or other evidentiary material, not privileged or protected from disclosure, on which such computation is based, including materials bearing on the nature and extent of injuries suffered; and

(D) for inspection and copying as under Rule 34 any insurance agreement under which any person carrying on an insurance business may be liable to satisfy part or all of a judgment which may be entered in the action or to indemnify or reimburse for payments made to satisfy the judgment. Unless otherwise stipulated or directed by the court, these disclosures shall be made at or within 10 days after the meeting of the parties under subdivision (f). A party shall make its initial disclosures based on the information then reasonably available to it and is not excused from making its disclosures because it has not fully completed its investigation of the case or because it challenges the sufficiency of another party's disclosures or because another party has not made its disclosures.

(2) *Disclosure of Expert Testimony.*

(A) In addition to the disclosures required by paragraph (1), a party shall disclose to other parties the identity of any person who may be used at trial to present evidence under Rules 702, 703, or 705 of the Federal Rules of Evidence.

(B) Except as otherwise stipulated or directed by the court, this disclosure shall, with respect to a witness who is retained or specially employed to provide expert testimony in the case or whose duties as an employee of the party regularly involve giving expert testimony, be accompanied by a written report prepared and signed by the witness. The report shall contain a complete statement of all opinions to be expressed and the basis and reasons therefor; the data or other information considered by the witness in forming the opinions; any exhibits to be used as a summary of or support for the opinions; the qualifications of the witness, including a list of all publications authored by the witness within the preceding ten years; the compensation to be paid for the study and testimony; and a listing of any other cases in which the witness has testified as an expert at trial or by deposition within the preceding four years.

(C) These disclosures shall be made at the times and in the sequence directed by the court. In the absence of other directions from the court or stipulation by the parties, the disclosures shall be made at least 90 days before the trial date or the date the case is to be ready for trial or, if the evidence is intended solely to contradict or rebut evidence on the same subject matter identified by another party under paragraph (2)(B), within 30 days after the disclosure made by the other party. The parties shall supplement these disclosures when required under subdivision (e)(1).

(3) *Pretrial Disclosures.* In addition to the disclosures required in the preceding paragraphs, a party shall provide to other parties the following information regarding the evidence that it may present at trial other than solely for impeachment purposes:

(A) the name and, if not previously provided, the address and telephone number of each witness, separately identifying those whom the party expects to present and those whom the party may call if the need arises;

(B) the designation of those witnesses whose testimony is expected to be presented by means of a deposition and, if not taken stenographically, a transcript of the pertinent portions of the deposition testimony; and

(C) an appropriate identification of each document or other exhibit, including summaries of other evidence, separately identifying those which the party expects to offer and those which the party may offer if the need arises. Unless otherwise directed by the court, these disclosures shall be made at least 30 days before trial. Within 14 days thereafter, unless a different time is specified by the court, a party may serve and file a list disclosing (i) any objections to the use under Rule 32(a) of a deposition designated by another party under subparagraph (B) and (ii) any objection, together with the grounds therefor, that may be made to the admissibility of materials identified under subparagraph (C). Objections not so disclosed, other than objections under Rules 402 and 403 of the Federal Rules of Evidence, shall be deemed waived unless excused by the court for good cause shown.

(4) *Form of Disclosures; Filing.* Unless otherwise directed by order or local rule, all disclosures under paragraphs (1) through (3) shall be made in writing, signed, served, and promptly filed with the court.

(5) *Methods to Discover Additional Matter.* Parties may obtain discovery by one or more of the following methods: depositions upon oral examination or written questions; written interrogatories; production of documents or things or permission to enter upon land or other property under Rule 34 or 45(a)(1)(C), for inspection and other purposes; physical and mental examinations; and requests for admission.

(b) *Discovery Scope and Limits.* Unless otherwise limited by order of the court in accordance with these rules, the scope of discovery is as follows:

(1) *In General.* Parties may obtain discovery regarding any matter, not privileged, which is relevant to the subject matter involved in the pending action, whether it relates to the claim or defense of the party seeking discovery or to the claim or defense of any other party, including the existence, description, nature, custody, condition, and location of any books, documents, or other tangible things and the identity and location of persons having knowledge of any discoverable matter. The information sought need not be admissible at the trial if the information sought appears reasonably calculated to lead to the discovery of admissible evidence.

(2) *Limitations.* By order or by local rule, the court may alter the limits in these rules on the number of depositions and interrogatories and may also limit the length of depositions under Rule 30 and the number of requests under Rule 36. The frequency or extent of use of the discovery methods otherwise permitted under these rules and by any local rule shall be limited by the court if it determines that: (i) the discovery sought is unreasonably cumulative or duplicative, or is obtainable from some other source that is more convenient, less burdensome, or less expensive; (ii) the party seeking discovery has had ample opportunity by

discovery in the action to obtain the information sought; or (iii) the burden or expense of the proposed discovery outweighs its likely benefit, taking into account the needs of the case, the amount in controversy, the parties' resources, the importance of the issues at stake in the litigation, and the importance of the proposed discovery in resolving the issues. The court may act upon its own initiative after reasonable notice or pursuant to a motion under subdivision (c).

(3) *Trial Preparation: Materials.* Subject to the provisions of subdivision (b)(4) of this rule, a party may obtain discovery of documents and tangible things otherwise discoverable under subdivision (b)(1) of this rule and prepared in anticipation of litigation or for trial by or for another party or by or for that other party's representative (including the other party's attorney, consultant, surety, indemnitor, insurer, or agent) only upon a showing that the party seeking discovery has substantial need of the materials in the preparation of the party's case and that the party is unable without undue hardship to obtain the substantial equivalent of the materials by other means. In ordering discovery of such materials when the required showing has been made, the court shall protect against disclosure of the mental impressions, conclusions, opinions, or legal theories of an attorney or other representative of a party concerning the litigation. A party may obtain without the required showing a statement concerning the action or its subject matter previously made by that party. Upon request, a person not a party may obtain without the required showing a statement concerning the action or its subject matter previously made by that person. If the request is refused, the person may move for a court order. The provisions of Rule 37(a)(4) apply to the award of expenses incurred in relation to the motion. For purposes of this paragraph, a statement previously made is (A) a written statement signed or otherwise adopted or approved by the person making it, or (B) a stenographic, mechanical, electrical, or other recording, or a transcription thereof, which is a substantially verbatim recital of an oral statement by the person making it and contemporaneously recorded.

(4) *Trial Preparation: Experts.*

(A) A party may depose any person who has been identified as an expert whose opinions may be presented at trial. If a report from the expert is required under subdivision (a)(2)(B), the deposition shall not be conducted until after the report is provided.

(B) A party may, through interrogatories or by deposition, discover facts known or opinions held by an expert who has been retained or specially employed by another party in anticipation of litigation or preparation for trial and who is not expected to be called as a witness at trial, only as provided in Rule 35(b) or upon a showing of exceptional circumstances under which it is impracticable for the party seeking discovery to obtain facts or opinions on the same subject by other means.

(C) Unless manifest injustice would result, (i) the court shall require that the party seeking discovery pay the expert a reasonable fee for time spent in responding to discovery under this subdivision; and (ii) with respect to discovery obtained under subdivision (b)(4)(B) of this rule the court shall require the party seeking discovery to pay the other party a fair portion of the fees and expenses reasonably incurred by the latter party in obtaining facts and opinions from the expert.

(5) *Claims of Privilege or Protection of Trial Preparation Materials.* When a party withholds information otherwise discoverable under these rules by claiming that it is privileged or subject to protection as trial preparation material, the party shall make the claim expressly and shall describe the nature of the documents, communications, or things not produced or disclosed in a manner that, without revealing information itself privileged or protected, will enable other parties to assess the applicability of the privilege or protection.

(c) *Protective Orders.* Upon motion by a party or by the person from whom discovery is sought, accompanied by a certification that the movant has in good faith conferred or attempted to confer with other affected parties in an effort to resolve the dispute without court action, and for good cause shown, the court in which the action is pending or alternatively, on matters relating to a deposition, the court in the district where the deposition is to be taken may make any order which justice requires to protect a party or person from annoyance, embarrassment, oppression, or undue burden or expense, including one or more of the following:

(1) that the disclosure or discovery not be had;

(2) that the disclosure or discovery may be had only on specified terms and conditions, including a designation of the time or place;

(3) that the discovery may be had only by a method of discovery other than that selected by the party seeking discovery;

(4) that certain matters not be inquired into, or that the scope of the disclosure or discovery be limited to certain matters;

(5) that discovery be conducted with no one present except persons designated by the court;

(6) that a deposition, after being sealed, be opened only by order of the court;

(7) that a trade secret or other confidential research, development, or commercial information not be revealed or be revealed only in a designated way; and

(8) that the parties simultaneously file specified documents or information enclosed in sealed envelopes to be opened as directed by the court.

If the motion for a protective order is denied in whole or in part, the court may, on such terms and conditions as are just, order that any party or other person provide or permit discovery. The provisions of Rule 37(a)(4) apply to the award of expenses incurred in relation to the motion.

(d) *Timing and Sequence of Discovery.* Except when authorized under these rules or by local rule, order, or agreement of the parties, a party may not seek discovery from any source before the parties have met and conferred as required by subdivision (f). Unless the court upon motion, for the convenience of parties and witnesses and in the interests of justice, orders otherwise, methods of discovery may be used in any sequence, and the fact that a party is conducting discovery, whether by deposition or otherwise, shall not operate to delay any other party's discovery.

(e) *Supplementation of Disclosures and Responses.* A party who has made a disclosure under subdivision (a) or responded to a request for discovery with a disclosure or response is under a duty to supplement or correct the disclosure or response to include information thereafter acquired if ordered by the court or in the following circumstances:

(1) A party is under a duty to supplement at appropriate intervals its disclosures under subdivision (a) if the party learns that in some material respect the information disclosed is incomplete or incorrect and if the additional or corrective information has not otherwise been made known to the other parties during the discovery process or in writing. With respect to testimony of an expert from whom a report is required under subdivision (a)(2)(B) the duty extends both to information contained in the report and to information provided through a deposition of the expert, and any additions or other changes to this information shall be disclosed by the time the party's disclosures under Rule 26(a)(3) are due.

(2) A party is under a duty seasonably to amend a prior response to an interrogatory, request for production, or request for admission if the party learns that the response is in some material respect incomplete or incorrect and if the additional or corrective information has not otherwise been made known to the other parties during the discovery process or in writing.

(f) *Meeting of Parties; Planning for Discovery.* Except in actions exempted by local rule or when otherwise ordered, the parties shall, as soon as practicable and in any event at least 14 days before a scheduling conference is held or a scheduling order is due under Rule 16(b), meet to discuss the nature and basis of their claims and defenses and the possibilities for a prompt settlement or resolution of the case, to make or arrange for the disclosures required by subdivision (a)(1), and to develop a proposed discovery plan. The plan shall indicate the parties' views and proposals concerning:

(1) what changes should be made in the timing, form, or requirement for disclosures under subdivision (a) or local rule, including a statement as to when disclosures under subdivision (a)(1) were made or will be made;

(2) the subjects on which discovery may be needed, when discovery should be completed, and whether discovery should be conducted in phases or be limited to or focused upon particular issues;

(3) what changes should be made in the limitations on discovery imposed under these rules or by local rule, and what other limitations should be imposed; and

(4) any other orders that should be entered by the court under subdivision (c) or under Rule 16(b) and (c).

The attorneys of record and all unrepresented parties that have appeared in the case are jointly responsible for arranging and being present or represented at the meeting, for attempting in good faith to agree on the proposed discovery plan, and for submitting to the court within 10 days after the meeting a written report outlining the plan.

(g) *Signing of Disclosures, Discovery Requests, Responses, and Objections.*

(1) Every disclosure made pursuant to subdivision (a)(1) or subdivision (a)(3) shall be signed by at least one attorney of record in the attorney's individual name, whose address shall be stated. An unrepresented party shall sign the disclosure and state the party's address. The signature of the attorney or party constitutes a certification that to the best of the signer's knowledge, information, and belief, formed after a reasonable inquiry, the disclosure is complete and correct as of the time it is made.

(2) Every discovery request, response, or objection made by a party represented by an attorney shall be signed by at least one attorney of record in the attorney's individual name, whose address shall be stated. An unrepresented party shall sign the request, response, or objection and state the party's address. The signature of the attorney or party constitutes a certification that to the best of the signer's knowledge, information, and belief, formed after a reasonable inquiry, the request, response, or objection is:

(A) consistent with these rules and warranted by existing law or a good faith argument for the extension, modification, or reversal of existing law;

(B) not interposed for any improper purpose, such as to harass or to cause unnecessary delay or needless increase in the cost of litigation; and

(C) not unreasonable or unduly burdensome or expensive, given the needs of the case, the discovery already had in the case, the amount in controversy, and the importance of the issues at stake in the litigation.

If a request, response, or objection is not signed, it shall be stricken unless it is signed promptly after the omission is called to the attention of the party making the request, response, or objection, and a party shall not be obligated to take any action with respect to it until it is signed.

(3) If without substantial justification a certification is made in violation of the rule, the court, upon motion or upon its own initiative, shall impose upon the person who made the certification, the party on whose behalf the disclosure, request, response, or objection is made, or both, an appropriate sanction, which may include an order to pay the amount of the reasonable expenses incurred because of the violation, including a reasonable attorney's fee.

Rule 37. Failure to Make Disclosure or Cooperate in Discovery: Sanctions [effective December 1, 1993]

(a) *Motion For Order Compelling Disclosure or Discovery.* A party, upon reasonable notice to other parties and all persons affected thereby, may apply for an order compelling disclosure or discovery as follows:

(1) *Appropriate Court.* An application for an order to a party shall be made to the court in which the action is pending. An application for an order to a person who is not a party shall be made to the court in the district where the discovery is being, or is to be, taken.

(2) *Motion.*

(A) If a party fails to make a disclosure required by Rule 26(a), any other party may move to compel disclosure and for appropriate sanctions. The motion must include a certification that the movant has in good faith conferred or attempted to confer with the party not making the disclosure in an effort to secure the disclosure without court action.

(B) If a deponent fails to answer a question propounded or submitted under Rule 30 or 31, or a corporation or other entity fails to make a designation under Rule 30(b)(6) or 31(a), or a party fails to answer an interrogatory submitted under Rule 33, or if a party, in response to a request for inspection submitted under Rule 34, fails to respond that inspection will be permitted as requested or fails to permit inspection as requested, the discovering party may move for an order compelling an answer, or a designation, or an order compelling inspection in accordance with the request. The motion must include a certification that the movant has in good faith conferred or attempted to confer with the person or party failing to make the discovery in an effort to secure the information or material without court action. When taking a deposition on oral examination, the proponent of the question may complete or adjourn the examination before applying for an order.

(3) *Evasive or Incomplete Disclosure, Answer, or Response.* For purposes of this subdivision an evasive or incomplete disclosure, answer, or response is to be treated as a failure to disclose, answer, or respond.

(4) *Expenses and Sanctions.*

(A) If the motion is granted or if the disclosure or requested discovery is provided after the motion was filed, the court shall, after affording an opportunity to be heard, require the party or deponent whose conduct necessitated the motion or the party or attorney advising such conduct or both of them to pay to the moving party the reasonable expenses incurred in making the motion, including attorney's fees, unless the court finds that the motion was filed without the movant's first making a good faith effort to obtain the disclosure or discovery without court action, or that the opposing party's nondisclosure, response, or objection was substantially justified, or that other circumstances make an award of expenses unjust.

(B) If the motion is denied, the court may enter any protective order authorized under Rule 26(c) and shall, after affording an opportunity to be heard, require the moving party or the attorney filing the motion or both of them to pay to the party or deponent who opposed the motion the reasonable expenses incurred in opposing the motion, including attorney's fees, unless the court finds that the making of the motion was substantially justified or that other circumstances make an award of expenses unjust.

(C) If the motion is granted in part and denied in part, the court may enter any protective order authorized under Rule 26(c) and may, after affording an opportunity to be heard, apportion the reasonable expenses incurred in relation to the motion among the parties and persons in a just manner.

(b) *Failure to Comply With Order.*

(1) *Sanctions by Court in District Where Deposition Is Taken.* If a deponent fails to be sworn or to answer a question after being directed to do so by the court in the district in which the deposition is being taken, the failure may be considered a contempt of that court.

(2) *Sanctions by Court in Which Action Is Pending.* If a party or an officer, director, or managing agent of a party or a person designated under Rule 30(b)(6) or 31(a) to testify on behalf of a party fails to obey an order to provide or permit discovery, including an order made under subdivision (a) of this rule or Rule 35, or if a party fails to obey an order entered under Rule 26(f), the court in which the action is pending may make such orders in regard to the failure as are just, and among others the following:

(A) An order that the matters regarding which the order was made or any other designated facts shall be taken to be established for the purposes of the action in accordance with the claim of the party obtaining the order;

(B) An order refusing to allow the disobedient party to support or oppose designated claims or defenses, or prohibiting that party from introducing designated matters in evidence;

(C) An order striking out pleadings or parts thereof, or staying further proceedings until the order is obeyed, or dismissing the action or proceeding or any part thereof, or rendering a judgment by default against the disobedient party;

(D) In lieu of any of the foregoing orders or in addition thereto, an order treating as a contempt of court the failure to obey any orders except an order to submit to a physical or mental examination;

(E) Where a party has failed to comply with an order under Rule 35(a) requiring that party to produce another for examination, such orders as are listed in paragraphs (A), (B), and (C) of this subdivision, unless the party failing to comply shows that that party is unable to produce such person for examination.

In lieu of any of the foregoing orders or in addition thereto, the court shall require the party failing to obey the order or the attorney advising that party or both to pay the reasonable expenses, including attorney's fees, caused by the failure, unless the court finds that the failure was substantially justified or that other circumstances make an award of expenses unjust.

(c) *Failure to Disclose; False or Misleading Disclosure; Refusal to Admit.*

(1) A party that without substantial justification fails to disclose information required by Rule 26(a) or 26(e)(1) shall not, unless such failure is harmless, be permitted to use as evidence at a trial, at a hearing, or on a motion any witness or information not so disclosed. In addition to or in lieu of this sanction, the court, on motion and after affording an opportunity to be heard, may impose other appropriate sanctions. In addition to requiring payment of reasonable expenses, including attorney's fees, caused by the failure, these sanctions may include any of the actions authorized under subparagraphs (A), (B), and (C) of subdivision (b)(2) of this rule and may include informing the jury of the failure

to make the disclosure.

(2) If a party fails to admit the genuineness of any document or the truth of any matter as requested under Rule 36, and if the party requesting the admissions thereafter proves the genuineness of the document or the truth of the matter, the requesting party may apply to the court for an order requiring the other party to pay the reasonable expenses incurred in making that proof, including reasonable attorney's fees. The court shall make the order unless it finds that (A) the request was held objectionable pursuant to Rule 36(a), or (B) the admission sought was of no substantial importance, or (C) the party failing to admit had reasonable ground to believe that the party might prevail on the matter, or (D) there was other good reason for the failure to admit.

(d) *Failure of Party to Attend at Own Deposition or Serve Answers to Interrogatories or Respond to Request for Inspection.* If a party or an officer, director, or managing agent of a party or a person designated under Rule 30(b)(6) or 31(a) to testify on behalf of a party fails (1) to appear before the officer who is to take the deposition, after being served with a proper notice, or (2) to serve answers or objections to interrogatories submitted under Rule 33, after proper service of the interrogatories, or (3) to serve a written response to a request for inspection submitted under Rule 34, after proper service of the request, the court in which the action is pending on motion may make such orders in regard to the failure as are just, and among others it may take any action authorized under subparagraphs (A), (B), and (C) of subdivision (b)(2) of this rule. Any motion specifying a failure under clause (2) or (3) of this subdivision shall include a certification that the movant has in good faith conferred or attempted to confer with the party failing to answer or respond in an effort to obtain such answer or response without court action. In lieu of any order or in addition thereto, the court shall require the party failing to act or the attorney advising that party or both to pay the reasonable expenses, including attorney's fees, caused by the failure unless the court finds that the failure was substantially justified or that other circumstances make an award of expenses unjust.

The failure to act described in this subdivision may not be excused on the ground that the discovery sought is objectionable unless the party failing to act has a pending motion for a protective order as provided by Rule 26(c).

(e) [Abrogated]

(f) [Repealed. Pub. L. No. 96-481, Title II, § 205(a), Oct. 21, 1980, 94 Stat. 2330].

(g) *Failure to Participate in the Framing of a Discovery Plan.* If a party or a party's attorney fails to participate in good faith in the development and submission of a proposed discovery plan as required by Rule 26(f), the court may, after opportunity for hearing, require such party or attorney to pay to any other party the reasonable expenses, including attorney's fees, caused by the failure.

(As amended Dec. 29, 1948, eff. Oct. 20, 1949; Mar. 30, 1970, eff. July 1, 1970; Apr. 29, 1980, eff. Aug. 1, 1980; Pub. L. No. 96-481, Title II, § 205(a), Oct. 21, 1980, 94 Stat. 2330; Mar. 2, 1987, eff. Aug. 1, 1987.)

Federal Rules of Appellate Procedure

Rule 38. Damages and Costs for Frivolous Appeals

If a court of appeals determines that an appeal is frivolous, it may, after a separately filed motion or notice from the court and reasonable opportunity to respond, award just damages and single or double costs to the appellee.

Rule 46. Attorneys

(a) *Admission to the Bar of a Court of Appeals; Eligibility; Procedure for Admission.* An attorney who has been admitted to practice before the Supreme Court of the United States, or the highest court of a state, or another United States court of appeals, or a United States district court (including the district courts for the Canal Zone, Guam and the Virgin Islands), and who is of good moral and professional character, is eligible for admission to the bar of a court of appeals.

An applicant shall file with the clerk of the court of appeals, on a form approved by the court and furnished by the clerk, an application for admission containing the applicant's personal statement showing eligibility for membership. At the foot of the application the applicant shall take and subscribe to the following oath or affirmation:

I, ____________________, do solemnly swear (or affirm) that I will demean myself as an attorney and counselor of this court, uprightly and according to law; and that I will support the Constitution of the United States.

Thereafter, upon written or oral motion of a member of the bar of the court, the court will act upon the application. An applicant may be admitted by oral motion in open court, but it is not necessary that the applicant appear before the court for the purpose of being admitted, unless the court shall otherwise order. An applicant shall upon admission pay to the clerk the fee prescribed by rule or order of the court.

(b) *Suspension or Disbarment.* When it is shown to the court that any member of its bar has been suspended or disbarred from practice in any other court of record, or has been guilty of conduct unbecoming a member of the bar of the court, the member will be subject to suspension or disbarment by the court. The member shall be afforded an opportunity to show good cause, within such time as the court shall prescribe, why the member should not be suspended or disbarred. Upon the member's response to the rule to show cause, and after hearing, if requested, or upon expiration of the time prescribed for a response if no response is made, the court shall enter an appropriate order.

(c) *Disciplinary Power of the Court Over Attorneys.* A court of appeals may, after reasonable notice and an opportunity to show cause to the contrary, and after hearing, if requested, take any appropriate disciplinary action against any attorney who practices before it for conduct unbecoming a member of the bar or for failure to comply with these rules or any rule of the court.

NEW YORK DOMESTIC RELATIONS PROCEDURES

New York Codes, Rules and Regulations: Procedure for Attorneys in Domestic Relations Matters

§1400.1 Application.

This Part shall apply to all attorneys who, on or after November 30, 1993, undertake to represent a client in a claim, action or proceeding, or preliminary to the filing of a claim, action or proceeding, in either Supreme Court or Family Court, or in any court of appellate jurisdiction, for divorce, separation, annulment, custody, visitation, maintenance, child support, or alimony, or to enforce or modify a judgment or order in connection with any such claims, actions or proceedings. This Part shall not apply to attorneys representing clients without compensation paid by the client, except that where a client is other than a minor, the provisions of section 1400.2 of this Part shall apply to the extent they are not applicable to compensation.

§1400.2 Statement of client's rights and responsibilities.

An attorney shall provide a prospective client with a statement of client's rights and responsibilities, in a form prescribed by the Appellate Divisions, at the initial conference and prior to the signing of a written retainer agreement. If the attorney is not being paid a fee from the client for the work to be performed on the particular case, the attorney may delete from the statement those provisions dealing with fees. The attorney shall obtain a signed acknowledgement of receipt from the client. The statement shall contain the following:

Statement of Client's Rights and Responsibilities

Your attorney is providing you with this document to inform you of what you, as a client, are entitled to by law or by custom. To help prevent any misunderstanding between you and your attorney please read this document carefully.

If you ever have any questions about these rights, or about the way your case is being handled, do not hesitate to ask your attorney. He or she should be readily available to represent your best interests and keep you informed about your case.

An attorney may not refuse to represent you on the basis of race, creed, color, sex, sexual orientation, age, national origin or disability.

You are entitled to an attorney who will be capable of handling your case; show you courtesy and consideration at all times; represent you zealously; and preserve your confidences and secrets that are revealed in the course of the relationship.

You are entitled to a written retainer agreement which must set forth, in plain language, the nature of the relationship and the details of the fee arrangement. At your request, and before you sign the agreement, you are entitled to have your attorney clarify in writing any of its terms, or include additional provisions.

You are entitled to fully understand the proposed rates and retainer fee before you sign a retainer agreement, as in any other contract.

You may refuse to enter into any fee arrangement that you find unsatisfactory.

Your attorney may not request a fee that is contingent on the securing of a divorce or on the amount of money or property that may be obtained.

Your attorney may not request a retainer fee that is nonrefundable. That is, should you discharge your attorney, or should your attorney withdraw from the case, before the retainer is used up, he or she is entitled to be paid commensurate with the work performed on your case and any expenses, but must return the balance of the retainer to you. However, your attorney may enter into a minimum fee arrangement with you that provides for the payment of a specific amount below which the fee will not fall based upon the handling of the case to its conclusion.

You are entitled to know the approximate number of attorneys and other legal staff members who will be working on your case at any given time and what you will be charged for the services of each.

You are entitled to know in advance how you will be asked to pay legal fees and expenses, and how the retainer, if any, will be spent.

At your request, and after your attorney has had a reasonable opportunity to investigate your case, you are entitled to be given an estimate of approximate future costs of your case, which estimate shall be made in good faith but may be subject to change due to facts and circumstances affecting the case.

You are entitled to receive a written, itemized bill on a regular basis, at least every 60 days.

You are expected to review the itemized bills sent by counsel, and to raise any objections or errors in a timely manner. Time spent in discussion or explanation of bills will not be charged to you.

You are expected to be truthful in all discussions with your attorney, and to provide all relevant information and documentation to enable him or her to competently prepare your case.

You are entitled to be kept informed of the status of your case, and to be provided with copies of correspondence and documents prepared on your behalf or received from the court or your adversary.

You have the right to be present in court at the time that conferences are held.

You are entitled to make the ultimate decision on the objectives to be pursued in your case, and to make the final decision regarding the settlement of your case.

Your attorney's written retainer agreement must specify under what circumstances he or she might seek to withdraw as your attorney for nonpayment of legal fees. If an action or proceeding is pending, the court may give your attorney a "charging lien," which entitles your attorney to payment for services already rendered at the end of the case out of the proceeds of the final order or judgment.

You are under no legal obligation to sign a confession of judgment or promissory note, or to agree to a lien or mortgage on your home to cover legal fees. Your attorney's written retainer agreement must specify whether, and under what circumstances, such security may be requested. In no event may such security interest be obtained by your attorney without prior court approval and notice to your adversary. An attorney's security interest in the marital residence cannot be foreclosed against you.

You are entitled to have your attorney's best efforts exerted on your behalf, but no particular results can be guaranteed.

If you entrust money with an attorney for an escrow deposit in your case, the attorney must safeguard the escrow in a special bank account. You are entitled to a written escrow agreement, a written receipt, and a complete record concerning the escrow. When the terms of the escrow agreement have been performed, the attorney must promptly make payment of the escrow to all persons who are entitled to it.

In the event of a fee dispute. you may have the right to seek arbitration. Your attorney will provide you with the necessary information regarding arbitration in the event of a fee dispute, or upon your request.

Receipt Acknowledged:

____

Attorney's signature

____

Client's signature

____

Date

§1400.3 Written retainer agreement.

An attorney who undertakes to represent a party and enters into an arrangement for, charges or collects any fee from a client shall execute a written agreement with the client setting forth in plain language the terms of compensation and the nature of services to be rendered. The agreement, and any amendment thereto, shall be signed by both client and attorney, and, in actions in Supreme Court, a copy of the signed agreement shall be filed with the court with the statement of net worth. Where substitution of counsel occurs after the filing of the net worth statement, a signed copy of the attorney's retainer agreement shall be filed with the court within 10 days of its execution. A copy of a signed amendment shall be filed within 15 days of signing. A duplicate copy of the filed agreement and any amendment shall be provided to the client. The agreement shall be subject to the provisions governing confidentiality contained in Domestic Relations Law, section 235(1). The agreement shall contain the following information:

Retainer Agreement

1. Names and addresses of the parties entering into the agreement;
2. Nature of the services to be rendered;
3. Amount of the advance retainer, if any, and what it is intended to cover;
4. Circumstances under which any portion of the advance retainer may be refunded. Should the attorney withdraw from the case or be discharged prior to the depletion of the advance retainer, the written retainer agreement shall provide how the attorney's fees and expenses are to be determined, and the remainder of the advance retainer shall be refunded to the client;
5. Client's right to cancel the agreement at any time; how the attorney's fee will be determined and paid should the client discharge the attorney at any time during the course of the representation;
6. How the attorney will be paid through the conclusion of the case after the retainer is depleted; whether the client may be asked to pay another lump sum;
7. Hourly rate of each person whose time may be charged to the client; any out-of-pocket disbursements for which the client will be required to reimburse the attorney. Any changes in such rates or fees shall be incorporated into a written agreement constituting an amendment to the original agreement, which must be signed by the client before it may take effect;
8. Any clause providing for a fee in addition to the agreed-upon rate, such as a reasonable minimum fee clause, must be defined in plain language and set forth the circumstances under which such fee may be incurred and how it will be calculated;
9. Frequency of itemized billing, which shall be at least every 60 days; the client may not be charged for time spent in discussion of the bills received;
10. Client's right to be provided with copies of correspondence and documents relating to the case, and to be kept apprised of the status of the case;
11. Whether and under what circumstances the attorney might seek a security interest from the client, which can be obtained only upon court approval and on notice to the adversary;
12. Under what circumstances the attorney might seek to withdraw from the case for nonpayment of fees, and the attorney's right to seek a charging lien from the court.
13. Should a dispute arise concerning the attorney's fee, the client may seek arbitration, which is binding upon both attorney and client; the attorney shall provide information concerning fee arbitration in the event of such dispute or upon the client's request.

§1400.4 Nonrefundable retainer fee

An attorney shall not enter into an arrangement for, charge or collect a nonrefundable retainer fee from a client. An attorney may enter into a "minimum fee" arrangement with a client that provides for the payment of a specific amount below which the fee will not fall based upon the handling of the case to its conclusion.

§1400.5 Security interests.

(a) An attorney may obtain a confession of judgment or promissory note, take a lien on real property, or otherwise obtain a security interest to secure his or her fee only where:

(1) the retainer agreement provides that a security interest may be sought;

(2) notice of an application for a security interest has been given to the other spouse; and

(3) the court grants approval for the security interest after submission of an application for counsel fees.

(b) Notwithstanding the provisions of subdivision (a) of this section, an attorney shall not foreclose on a mortgage placed on the marital residence while the spouse who consents to the mortgage remains the titleholder and the residence remains the spouse's primary residence.

§1400.6 Closing statement.

[Section deleted effective March 1, 1997.]

§1400.7 Fee arbitration.

In the event of a fee dispute between attorney and client, the client may seek to resolve the dispute by arbitration, which shall be binding upon both attorney and client and subject to review under CPLR article 75, pursuant to a fee arbitration program established and operated by the Chief Administrator of the Courts and subject to the approval of the justices of the Appellate Divisions.

ABA FORMAL ETHICS OPINIONS

Formal Opinion 92-364 July 6, 1992
Sexual Relations with Clients

A sexual relationship between lawyer and client may involve unfair exploitation of the lawyer's fiduciary position, and/or significantly impair a lawyer's ability to represent the client competently, and therefore may violate both the Model Rules of Professional Conduct and the Model Code of Professional Responsibility.

The Committee has been asked whether a lawyer violates the ABA Model Rules of Professional Conduct (1983, amended 1991) or the ABA Model Code of Professional Responsibility (1969, amended 1980) by entering into a sexual relationship with a client during the course of representation.[1] In the opinion of the Committee, such a relationship may involve unfair exploitation of the lawyer's fiduciary position and presents a significant danger that the lawyer's ability to represent the client adequately may be impaired, and that as a consequence the lawyer may violate both the Model Rules and the Model Code. The roles of lover and lawyer are potentially conflicting ones as the emotional involvement that is fostered by a sexual relationship has the potential to undercut the objective detachment that is often demanded for adequate representation.

Although no detailed statistics are presently available to document the incidence of sexual relations between clients and their lawyers, there is information enough to substantiate both the existence and the seriousness of problems in this area.[2] Recent efforts in several states to draft rules addressing these problems have highlighted the need to clarify the ethical precepts that govern attorney conduct in this area.[3]

---

1. A sexual relationship predating the professional relationship could, in some circumstances, raise the same ethical problems as are here considered. Because the likelihood of this happening should be considerably less when the sexual relationship predates the professional one, this opinion focuses primarily on sexual relationships that develop after the formation of the professional relationship.

2. The Illinois Attorney Registration and Disciplinary Commission received approximately 50 complaints about lawyer sexual misconduct in 1989 alone as reported in the 1990 Report of the Illinois Task Force on Gender Bias in the Courts at 54. The Commission called the problem a "systemic, unchanging and consistent trend" in the domestic relations field. In addition, anecdotal evidence illustrates the acute nature of the problem. *See* Jorgenson & Sutherland, *Fiduciary Theory Applied to Personal Dealings: Attorney-Client Sexual Contact*, 45 ARK. L. REV. 459 (1992); Dubin, *Sex and the Divorce Lawyer: Is the Client Off Limits?*, 3 GEO. J. LEG. ETHICS 585 (1988); Lyon, *Sexual Exploitation of Divorce Clients: The Lawyer's Prerogative*, 10 HARV. WOMEN'S L.J. 159 (1987); A. Stone, *Law, Psychiatry and Morality* 199 (1984).

3. California, Illinois and Oregon all have recently attempted to draft rules covering attorney-client sexual relations. *See, e.g.,* California Proposed Rule 3-120; Illinois Proposed Rule 1.17; Oregon Proposed Rule 107-139. *See also* McDaniel v. Gile, 281 Cal. Rptr. 242, 230 Cal. App. 3d 363 (1991); Suppressed v. Suppressed, 206 Ill. App. 3d 918, 565 N.E.2d 101 (1990).

The Committee recognizes that no provision in either the Rules or the Code specifically addresses, let alone prohibits, sexual relationships between lawyer and client. However, there are several provisions of the Model Rules that may be implicated by a sexual relationship, particularly one that arises after the formation of the attorney-client relationship. First, because of the dependence that so often characterizes the attorney-client relationship, there is a significant possibility that the sexual relationship will have resulted from exploitation of the lawyer's dominant position and influence and, thus, breached the lawyer's fiduciary obligations to the client. Second, a sexual relationship with a client may affect the independence of the lawyer's judgment. Third, the lawyer's engaging in a sexual relationship with a client may create a prohibited conflict between the interests of the lawyer and those of the client. Fourth, a non-professional, yet emotionally charged, relationship between attorney and client may result in confidences being imparted in circumstances where the attorney-client privilege is not available, yet would have been, absent the personal relationship.

The Lawyer Has Fiduciary Obligations to the Client that Require, *Inter Alia*, that the Lawyer not Take Advantage of His or Her Dominant Position or Exploit the Dependent and Vulnerable Position of the Client

It is axiomatic that the attorney-client relationship is a fiduciary one in which the client places his or her trust and confidence in the lawyer in return for the lawyer's undertaking to place the interest of the client ahead of any self-interest of the lawyer.[4] This fiduciary relationship imposes the highest standards of ethical conduct on the lawyer.

> A lawyer is bound to conduct himself as a fiduciary or trustee occupying the highest position of trust and confidence, so that, in all his relations with his client, it is his duty to exercise and maintain the utmost good faith, honesty, integrity, fairness and fidelity . . . . This fiduciary or trust relationship precludes the attorney from personal interests antagonistic to those of the client or from obtaining personal advantage or profit out of the relationship.

Hafter v. Farkas, 498 F.2d 587, 589 (2d Cir. 1974); *see also Singleton v. Foreman*, 435 F.2d 962, 970 (5th Cir. 1970). The lawyer's position of trust places the burden

4. This fiduciary relationship arises from principles of common law. As stated by the Supreme Court in 1850: "There are few business relations of life involving a higher trust and confidence than those of attorney and client, or generally speaking one more honorably and faithfully discharged, few more anxiously guarded by the law or governed by sterner principles of morality and justice; and it is the duty of the court to administer them in a corresponding spirit, and to be watchful and industrious, to see that confidence thus reposed shall not be used to the detriment of prejudice of the rights of the party bestowing it." Stockton v. Ford, 52 U.S. (11 How.) 232, 247 (1850); *see also* Maritrans GP Inc. v. Pepper, Hamilton & Scheetz, 602 A.2d 1277, 1283 (Pa. 1992) (citing *Stockton* with approval); *In re* Education Law Center, Inc., 86 N.J. 124, 429 A.2d 1051 (1981) (same); 98 A.L.R. 2d 1235 (1964) (collecting cases).

on the lawyer to ensure that all attorney-client dealings are fair and reasonable[5] and do not interfere with competent representation.[6]

The attorney-client relationship is not merely one that necessarily imposes fiduciary obligations but also one that is often inherently unequal. The client comes to a lawyer because he or she needs help to resolve a problem. The client puts his or her faith in the lawyer's ability to think reasonably and objectively for the client's benefit. The client relies on the lawyer's special knowledge, skills and access to the courts to solve the client's problem. The lawyer encourages this special relationship, offering to lead the client through a complex legal system.

The factors leading to the client's trust and reliance on the lawyer also have the potential for placing the lawyer in a position of dominance and the client in a position of vulnerability. All of the positive characteristics that the lawyer is encouraged to develop so that the client will be confident that he or she is being well served can reinforce a feeling of dependence. While there are situations, especially in the commercial business setting, in which the sophisticated corporate client representative has little or no sense of dependence, there is also a broad range of situations in which the client, by virtue of his or her emotional state, educational level, age or social status, feels particularly dependent and disarmed vis-à-vis the attorney.

The nature of the matter can also affect the degree of dependence. An individual client, in particular, is likely to have retained a lawyer at a time of crisis. The divorce client's marriage is disintegrating. The criminal client may have just been arrested and could be facing the possibility of jail. The probate client is dealing with the loss of a loved one. The immigration client may be in fear of deportation. Other clients may be trying to save a business or salvage a reputation. The corporate employee may see his or her employment on the line depending on the outcome of the transactions or litigation, viewing the lawyer as a potential savior of the employee's job.

The fiduciary obligation inherent in the lawyer's role is heightened if the client is emotionally vulnerable in a way that affects the client's ability to make reasoned judgements about the future. Model Rule 1.14(a) provides that

> [w]hen a client's ability to make adequately considered decisions in connection with the representation is impaired, whether because of minority, mental disability or for some other reason, the lawyer shall, as far as reasonably possible, maintain a normal client-lawyer relationship with the client.[7]

---

5. *See* Comment to Model Rule 1.8: "As a general principle, all transactions between client and lawyer should be fair and reasonable to the client."

6. Model Rule 1.1 states that a lawyer shall provide competent representation to a client.

7. There is no direct counterpart to this rule in the disciplinary rules of the Model Code. EC 7-12, however, states that any mental or physical condition of a client that renders him incapable of making a considered judgment on his own behalf casts additional responsibility upon the lawyer.

Similarly, the ABA standards relating to disciplinary sanctions assert that any special vulnerability of the victim should be considered an aggravating circumstance when imposing attorney discipline. *See* ABA Standards for Imposing Lawyer Sanctions §9.22(h) (1986, amended 1992).

Thus, the more vulnerable the client, the heavier the obligation of the lawyer to avoid engaging in any relationship other than that of attorney-client.[8] If the lawyer permits the otherwise benign and even recommended client reliance and trust to become the catalyst for a sexual relationship with a client, the lawyer may violate one of the most basic ethical obligations, i.e., not to use the trust of the client to the client's disadvantage.[9] This obligation has deep historical roots:

> [A] most scrupulous fidelity must be forever observed on the part of the lawyer toward his client so that he shall never betray or take advantage [of the client] neither in word or deed . . . good policy would seem to require, as well as every principle of honour and fair dealing, that the counsel or attorney should not be permitted to do anything that would tend to prejudice the interest of his client or occasion a loss to him.[10]

The principle rests on public policy, and is "intended as a protection to the client against the strong influence to which the confidential relation naturally gives rise."[11] It was formalized in Canon 11 of the Canons of Professional Ethics, which provided that "the lawyer should refrain from any action whereby for his personal benefit or gain he abuses or takes advantage of the confidence reposed in him by his client." *See also* ABA Comm. on Professional Ethics, Informal Op. C-804 (1964) (lawyers are obligated to refrain from actions that would abuse the confidence and trust reposed in the lawyer by the client).

This fundamental principle of fiduciary obligation is recognized in both the Model Rules and the Model Code. Rule 1.8(b) and DR 4-101(B)(2) both provide that a lawyer may not use client confidences to the disadvantage of the client. Both Model Rule 1.7(b) and DR 5-101 prohibit a lawyer from representing a client when the representation may be limited by the lawyer's own interests.

These rules reflect the fundamental obligation of a lawyer not to exploit a client's trust for the lawyer's benefit. The same principle underlies the rules that

8. Similar concerns about a lawyer's taking advantage of those who are emotionally vulnerable have led to a prohibition on the immediate solicitation of relatives of victims of mass accidents. Solicitation of clients is restricted until the relatives are less wracked with emotion and more capable of reasoned judgment. *See, e.g., In re* Anis, 599 A.2d 1265 (N.J. 1992) (imposing a two-week waiting period on attorneys before solicitation is allowed). Model Rule 7.3 (b).

9. *See, e.g.,* DR 7-101(a)(3) stating that a lawyer shall not intentionally prejudice or damage his client during the course of the professional relationship.

10. Galbraith v. Elder, 8 Watts (Pa.) 81, 94 (1830).

11. Thomas v. Turner's Adm'r, 87 Va. 1, 12 (1980) (dealings between attorney and client that benefit attorney are presumptively invalid; the presumption can be overcome only by clear evidence).

seek to ensure that lawyers not take financial advantage of their clients. Business transactions concurrent with the attorney-client relationship are inherently suspect. Generally, a lawyer who benefits from a financial transaction with a client must show that the transaction was fair, equitable and just, and that it did not proceed from undue influence. Thus, Rule 1.8(a) prohibits business transactions unless full disclosure is made, the client is advised to seek the advice of independent counsel, and the client's written consent is obtained. Disciplinary Rule 5-104(a) and EC 5-3 of the Code impose similar requirements. These provisions safeguard clients from lawyers who abuse their ability to influence their client for their own financial gain. This protection is called for because the unequal nature of the lawyer-client relationship makes it particularly susceptible to abuse.

The same fundamental principle of fiduciary obligation that underlies the specific rules governing attorney-client financial dealings implies as well that a lawyer should not abuse the client's trust by taking sexual or emotional advantage of a client. Protecting a client's emotional and physical well-being is surely as important as protecting the client's financial well-being.[12] The inherently unequal attorney-client relationship allows the unethical lawyer just as easily to exploit the client sexually as financially. The trust and confidence reposed in a lawyer can provide an opportunity for the lawyer to manipulate a client emotionally for the lawyer's sexual benefit. Moreover, the client may not feel free to rebuff unwanted sexual advances because of fear that such a rejection will either reduce the lawyer's ardor for the client's cause or, worse yet, require finding a new lawyer, causing the client to lose the time and money that has already been invested in the present representation and possibly damaging the client's legal position.[13]

Such an abuse of client trust, even though not explicitly prohibited by any ethical rule, would nonetheless be inconsistent with the fiduciary obligation reflected in both the Model Rules and the Model Code. Moreover, such a sexual relationship, whether or not resulting from an abuse of trust, poses a variety of risks to the attorney-client relationship.

Risks to the Attorney-Client Relationship that May Result from Sexual Relations

The existence of a sexual relationship between lawyer and client may make it impossible for the attorney to provide the competent representation of the client that is ethically required.[14] This may be so for several different reasons.

12. *See, e.g.*, Hafter v. Farkas, 498 F.2d 587 (2d Cir. 1974); Singleton v. Foreman, 435 F.2d 962, 970 (5th Cir. 1970) ("custom requires that the attorney treat his clients with civility, common decency and loyalty, both as to legal problems and as to their personal relationship").

13. The client might also fear that the lawyer, in retaliation for any rejection of sexual advances, will disclose information given in confidence. *See* Kentucky State Bar Association v. Meredith, 752 S.W.2d 786 (Ky. 1988) (attorney who had had sexual relationship with client disciplined for revealing privileged information about client after his discharge).

14. *See* Rule 1.1 and DR 6-101 stating that a lawyer should provide competent representa-

1. A Sexual Relationship May Deprive the Lawyer of Independent Judgment.

Emotional detachment is essential to the lawyer's ability to render competent legal services. One of the most important aspects of the attorney-client relationship is the attorney's duty to exercise independent professional judgment.[15] Thus, Model Rule 2.1 states that when representing a client "a lawyer shall exercise independent professional judgment and render candid advice." *Id.* The lawyer must evaluate the client's situation, objectively and reasonably, fairly considering all possible courses of action.

It can be difficult, however, to separate sound judgment from the emotion or bias that may result from a sexual relationship. A lawyer involved in a sexual and emotional relationship with a client may encounter particular difficulty in providing the "straightforward advice" which "often involves unpleasant facts and alternatives that a client may be disinclined to confront." Rule 2.1 comment. Because of a desire to preserve the relationship, the lawyer may "be deterred from giving candid advice by the prospect that the advice will be unpalatable to the client." *Id.* Thus, a lawyer who engages in a sexual relationship with a client during the course of representation risks losing the objectivity and reasonableness that form the basis of the lawyer's independent professional judgment.

2. A Sexual Relationship Creates Risks that the Lawyer Will Be Subject to a Conflict of Interest.

One of the hallmarks of the legal profession is the obligation of a lawyer to exercise professional judgment solely on behalf of the client. ABA Comm. on Ethics and Professional Responsibility, Informal Op. 1482 (1982). A sexual relationship between the parties may hinder the attorney's ability to meet this obligation. "It cannot be proper for a lawyer to represent a client when the lawyer's own interest may tempt him to temper his efforts to promote to the utmost his client's interest." ABA Comm. on Professional Ethics and Grievances, Formal Op. 132 (1935). Certainly the lawyer's interest in preserving the sexual relationship can rise to this level.

Rule 1.7(b) states that a lawyer shall not represent a client if the representation of the client may be materially limited by the lawyer's own interests. DR 5-101(A) similarly obligates the lawyer not to accept employment if the exercise of the lawyer's professional judgment on behalf of the client will be, or reasonably may be, affected by the lawyer's own personal interest. If the lawyer's interests in the relationship interfere with decisions that must be made for the client,

tion to the client; *see also* EC 1.1 ("maintaining the integrity and improving the competency of the bar is the ethical responsibility of every lawyer"); EC 6.1 ("a lawyer should act with competence and proper care in representing clients").

15. *See also* DR 5-107 (prohibiting situations that could adversely affect the exercise of the lawyer's independent judgment on behalf of the client).

the representation will have been impaired.

While it may be argued that such a conflict only arises in the special situations presented, for example, by divorce proceedings, the fact is that these conflicting interests can arise even in seemingly benign settings. For instance, although it is generally thought that the ethical concerns raised by a sexual relationship are not present in the commercial corporate setting, a sexual relationship with a corporate client's representative can be just as problematic as in other contexts.

In the corporate setting the lawyer's client is the corporation, not any individual employee. Model Rule 1.13(a). And even in less extreme situations than those contemplated by Rule 1.13, as a result of instructions from the client the lawyer may be obliged to follow the established corporate chain of command in fulfilling counsel's obligation to report to the entity client. A potential conflict of interest arises if the lawyer, engaging in a sexual relationship with a corporate client's representative, learns information which may redound to the detriment of the sexual partner, but which should be reported to a higher authority.

Lawyers recognize how difficult it is to deal with such a situation in a representation free from a sexual relationship. When the corporate employee shares information with the company's lawyer and asks the lawyer either not to pass it on or pass it on anonymously, the corporate lawyer is conflicted enough in reconciling the lawyer's duty to the corporate client with the trust the corporate employee has reposed. Such a conflict can only be compounded when a sexual relationship is also involved.

A related danger resulting from the blurring of relationships and one where the lover becomes a participant adverse to the client is presented in divorce cases where the attorney engaging in a sexual relationship with a client may risk becoming an adverse witness to the client on issues of adultery and child custody.[16]

3. A Sexual Relationship May Risk Unwarranted Expectations Regarding the Preservation of Confidences and Related Dangers.

A sexual relationship between the parties may also have the potential to blur the contours of the attorney-client relationship. Client confidences are protected by privilege only when they are imparted in the context of the attorney-client relationship. The courts will not protect confidences given as part of a personal relationship; except for that of husband and wife, there is no privilege for lovers.[17] A blurred line between any professional and personal relationship may make it difficult to predict to what extent client confidences will be protected. Expectations of confidences will be forced to rest on ever shifting sands.

---

16. *See* Model Rule 3.7, which requires that a lawyer terminate representation if the attorney is likely to be called as a witness against his client. *See also* DR 5-102(B) (adding the requirement that the testimony be prejudicial).

17. *See, e.g., In re* Marriage of Kantar, 581 N.E.2d 6, 14 (Ill. App. 1991); *In re* Pump, 120 Wis. 2d 422, 355 N.W.2d 248 (1984), *see also* C. WOLFRAM, MODERN LEGAL ETHICS, 252

Conclusion

It is apparent that a sexual relationship during the course of representation can seriously harm the client's interests. Therefore, the Committee concludes that because of the danger of impairment to the lawyer's representation associated with a sexual relationship between lawyer and client, the lawyer would be well advised to refrain from such a relationship. If such a sexual relationship occurs and the impairment is not avoided, the lawyer will have violated ethical obligations to the client.[18]

The client's consent to sexual relations alone will rarely be sufficient to eliminate this danger. In many cases, the client's ability to give meaningful consent is vitiated by the lawyer's potential undue influence and/or the emotional vulnerability of the client. The lawyer may, therefore, be called upon in a disciplinary or other proceeding to show that the client consented, that the consent was freely given based on full and reasonable disclosure of the risks involved, and that any ensuing sexual relationship did not in any way disadvantage the client in the representation; that is, the attorney's judgment remained independent, the representation proceeded free of conflicts, the privilege was not compromised and the other ethical obligations to the client were fulfilled.

(1986) ("Even if the confidential relationship of lawyer and client is indisputably formed, it does not follow that every communication between them will be privileged. Some communication may have nothing to do with the lawyer's legal services").

18. Some other professions, most notably the medical profession, that have considered this issue have found that in their fields the potential ethical problems associated with a client-professional sexual relationship warrant an absolute ban on such relationships. *See Report of the Council on Ethical and Judicial Affairs* as adopted by the American Medical Association House of Delegates on December 4, 1990 (finding all sexual relationships between doctor and patient to be potentially exploitative and detrimental to the physician's medical judgement and to the patient's trust); *see also* R. GORLIN, CODES OF PROFESSIONAL RESPONSIBILITY, 217, 226-228, 281 (2d ed. 1990) (prohibiting professional-client sexual relationship for social workers and mental health workers).

Formal Opinion 92-368 Inadvertent Disclosure of Confidential Materials

November 10, 1992

A lawyer who receives materials that on their face appear to be subject to the attorney-client privilege or otherwise confidential, under circumstances where it is clear they were not intended for the receiving lawyer, should refrain from examining the materials, notify the sending lawyer and abide the instructions of the lawyer who sent them.

The Committee has been asked to opine on the obligations under the Model Rules of Professional Conduct of a lawyer who comes into possession of materials that appear on their face to be subject to the attorney-client privilege or otherwise confidential, under circumstances where it is clear that the materials were not intended for the receiving lawyer. The question posed includes situations in which the sending lawyer has notified the receiving lawyer of the erroneous transmission and has requested return of the materials sent as well as those situations in which the inadvertent sending lawyer and his client remain ignorant that the materials were missent. It also extends to situations in which the receiving lawyer has already reviewed the materials as well as those in which the sending lawyer intercedes before the receiving lawyer has had such an opportunity. This opinion is intended to answer a question which has become increasingly important as the burgeoning of multi-party cases, the availability of xerography and the proliferation of facsimile machines and electronic mail make it technologically ever more likely that through inadvertence, privileged or confidential materials will be produced to opposing counsel by no more than the pushing of the wrong speed dial number on a facsimile machine.

A satisfactory answer to the question posed cannot be drawn from a narrow, literalistic reading of the black letter of the Model Rules. But it is useful, and necessary, to bear in mind the thoughts in the Preamble to the Model Rules that "many difficult issues of professional discretion . . . must be resolved through the exercise of sensitive professional and moral judgment guided by the basic principles underlying the Rules," and that "the Rules do not exhaust the moral and ethical considerations that should inform a lawyer, for no worthwhile human activity can be completely defined by legal rules." In that larger, and more fundamental, framework, the Committee's views, expressed in this opinion, have been informed by (i) the importance the Model Rules give to maintaining client confidentiality, (ii) the law governing waiver of the attorney-client privilege, (iii) the law governing missent property, (iv) the similarity between the circumstances here addressed and other conduct the profession universally condemns, and (v) the receiving lawyer's obligations to his client.

Giving due weight to each of the foregoing considerations, it is the view of the Committee that the receiving lawyer, as a matter of ethical conduct contemplated by the precepts underlying the Model Rules, (a) should not examine the materials once the inadvertence is discovered, (b) should notify the sending lawyer of their receipt and (c) should abide by the sending lawyer's instructions as to their disposition.

I. Confidentiality

The concept of confidentiality is a fundamental aspect of the right to the effective assistance of counsel. As reflected in each iteration of the rules of professional responsibility, the obligation of the lawyer to maintain and to refuse to divulge client confidences is virtually absolute.

The confidentiality principle rests on the vital importance society places upon the "full, free and frank" exchange between lawyer and client, shielded from the intrusive eyes and ears of adverse parties, the government, the media and the public. The principle's primary basis is that, absent the guarantee of confidentiality, critical discussions will be either proscribed, circumscribed or intruded upon in a way that will impact directly on the ability of the lawyer to serve his or her client. If the lawyer cannot gather all the necessary information and is not free to explore with the client the client's options, free from the threat that these confidential communications will be shared with those whose interests may be adverse to the client, the chilling effect on the lawyer-client relationship becomes plain. The benefits of confidentiality were recognized over 150 years ago when Justice Shaw observed in *Hatton v. Robinson*, 31 Mass. (14 Pick.) 416, 422 (1833):

> This principle we take to be this; that so numerous and complex are the laws by which the rights and duties of citizens are governed, so important is it that they should be permitted to avail themselves of the superior skill and learning of [attorneys] both in ascertaining their rights in the country, and maintaining them most safely in court . . . that the law has considered it the wisest policy to encourage and sanction this confidence, by requiring that on such facts the mouth of the attorney should be forever sealed.

Model Rule 1.6 codifies a lawyer's obligation to keep the confidences of his client.[1] The rule of keeping client's confidences confidential is mandatory; while

---

1. The full text of Rule 1.6 is as follows:

(a) A lawyer shall not reveal information relating to representation of a client unless the client consents after consultation, except for disclosures that are impliedly authorized in order to carry out the representation, and except as stated in paragraph (b).

(b) A lawyer may reveal such information to the extent the lawyer reasonably believes necessary:

(1) to prevent the client from committing a criminal act that the lawyer believes is likely to result in imminent death or substantial bodily harm; or

(2) to establish a claim or defense on behalf of the lawyer in a controversy between the lawyer and the client, to establish a defense to a criminal charge or civil claim against the lawyer based upon conduct in which the client was involved, or to respond to allegations in any proceeding concerning the lawyer's representation of the client.

section (b) lists limited scenarios in which a lawyer *may* choose to breach client confidences, such disclosure is not mandatory but optional. The Comment to Rule 1.6 states that the Rule "applies not merely to matters communicated in confidence by the client but also to all information relating to the representation, whatever its source." Rule 1.6 broadens the obligations imposed by DR 4-101 of the Model Code of Professional Responsibility, which prohibited only a lawyer's disclosure of a client's "confidence" (defined as "information protected by the attorney-client privilege") or "secret" (defined as "other information gained in the professional relationship that the client has requested be held inviolate or the disclosure of which would be embarrassing or would be likely to be detrimental to the client").

A. Competing Principles

If the Committee were to countenance, or indeed encourage, conduct on the part of the receiving lawyer which was in derogation of this strong policy in favor of confidentiality, the Committee would have to identify a more important principle which supports an alternative result. As the Committee examines the potentially competing principles, we conclude that their importance pales in comparison to the importance of maintaining confidentiality.

First, it might be argued that keeping the confidential materials and not letting the sending lawyer know they were received will punish carelessness on the part of the sending lawyer and those with whom that lawyer works. However, loss of confidentiality is a very high penalty to pay for a mere slip, particularly when the person or entity paying the "price" is not the individual lawyer responsible for the inadvertent conduct, but rather the client who presumably had nothing to do with the mis-sending of the materials.

Second, it could be asserted that letting the receiving lawyer keep the confidential materials in this situation will encourage more careful conduct on the part of other counsel in the future. Once the catastrophic consequences of a misstep are recognized, lawyers and their clients will conform their future conduct to avoid such an unfortunate result. However, this rationale undervalues the lawyer's existing strong motivation.

Lawyers already have significant incentives to protect confidential materials, not the least of which is the mandate of Model Rule 1.6 itself. Having an inadvertent disclosure act as a total waiver of confidentiality can add little to this equation. The argument also ignores the persistence of human frailty. The possibility of "punishment," no matter how severe, will never prevent, in this modern age of electronic transmission, unlimited photocopies and cases with hundreds of parties, accidents from occurring. The wrong number on the facsimile machine will still be "mis-speed-dialed"; the contents of two envelopes will get switched; "send copies to all defense counsel" will be misunderstood as "send copies to all counsel."

Third, it may be asserted that once confidential materials are missent there is nothing really to protect. Of course, this argument does not apply if the receiving lawyer becomes aware of the inadvertence before the materials are examined. If the facsimile cover sheet says "to All Defense Counsel" and the receiving lawyer represents the plaintiff, the confidentiality can be completely protected so long as the lawyer refrains from giving in to temptation. But even where the receiving lawyer examines the materials before discovering that they were missent, there is still value in maintaining what confidentiality remains.

First, disclosure to counsel does not have to result in disclosure to counsel's client. Second, there is a significant difference between a lawyer's knowing the contents of documents and that lawyer's being able to use them, for example, at trial either as a basis for questions or by presentation of them to a fact finder. Third, inadvertent disclosure to one counsel or party does not necessarily lead to disclosure to other parties or their counsel if precautions, such as those in confidentiality orders, are taken.

Finally, it might be urged that a receiving lawyer has an obligation to maximize the advantage his client will gain from careful scrutiny of the missent materials. While the "zealous" representation of Canon 7 of the Model Code of Professional Responsibility does not appear *in haec verba* in the Model Rules, it could be argued that a lawyer's "commitment and dedication to the interests of the client," referred to in the Comment to Model Rule 1.3 (calling on a lawyer to act with "reasonable promptness and diligence"), includes an obligation to capitalize on an error of this sort on the part of opposing counsel.

However, there are many limitations on the extent to which a lawyer may go "all out" for the client. The examples cited in Part IV of this opinion are all "opportunities" the lawyer may not seize. Similarly, the Model Rules carefully circumscribe factual and legal representations a lawyer may make, people counsel may contact and clients counsel can represent. The limitation contemplated by this opinion is entirely consistent with these ethical restraints on uncontrolled advocacy.

B. The Analogy to Inadvertent Waiver of the Attorney-Client Privilege

In concluding that inadvertent disclosure of confidential materials should not result in the loss of their confidential character we find persuasive the manner in which courts have treated the inadvertent disclosure of materials subject to the attorney-client privilege. While the privilege is a rule of evidence which addresses when an attorney can be compelled to disclose otherwise protected material, whereas confidentiality is a principle designed to govern the lawyer's voluntary conduct, both concepts are designed to further the attorney-client relationship in a similar manner and for the same reasons.

A review of the relevant cases demonstrates, with few exceptions, an unwillingness to permit mere inadvertence to constitute a waiver.[2] Something more, like a failure of counsel to spend any time reviewing the documents to be produced in discovery, is required before a waiver is found. An example of this approach is the decision by the New Mexico Supreme Court in *Hartman v. El Paso Natural Gas Co.*, 107 N.M. 679, 763 P.2d 1144, 1152 (1988) in which the court explained how it would examine counsel's conduct in determining if there is a waiver:

> [There are] five factors which should assist a court in determining whether a document has lost its privilege: (1) The reasonableness of the precautions taken to prevent inadvertent disclosure in view of the extent of the document production; (2) the number of inadvertent disclosures; (3) the extent of the disclosure; (4) any delay and measures taken to rectify the disclosures; (5) whether the overriding interests of justice would be served by relieving a party of its error.

The Committee recognizes that the view that inadvertence should not necessarily give rise to a waiver of the attorney-client is not universally accepted.[3] Some cases and commentators endorse Wigmore's view that "the privilege stands in derogation of the public's right to everyman's evidence," that the privilege results in the suppression of evidence, that the cost of the privilege is clear: evidence which would have been used in the search for truth is excluded. This contrary view finds its philosophical expression in the writings of Judge Marvin E. Frankel who observed:

> The effect of every evidentiary privilege, every grant in the law of a right to withhold information, is an added barrier to the search for truth. The lawyer is authorized and required by the privilege to cover up what may be evil and needed facts. The interests injured by the cover-up may be precious ones.

M. Frankel, *Partisan Justice* 64 (1980).

---

2. *See* R. Franco & M. Pringle, *The Inadvertent Waiver of Privilege*, 26 TORT & INS. L.J. 637 (1991); W. Ayers, *Attorney Client Privilege: The Necessity of Intent to Waive the Privilege in Inadvertent Disclosure Cases*, 18 PAC. L.J. 59 (1986); J. Grippando, *Attorney-Client Privilege: Implied Waiver Through Inadvertent Disclosure of Documents*, 39 U. MIAMI L. REV. 511 (1985); Note, *Inadvertent Disclosure of Documents Subject to the Attorney-Client Privilege*, 82 MICH. L. REV. 598 (1983).

3. There are also a minority of cases which would never find waiver unless such a result was intended by counsel.

> We are taught from first year law school that waiver imports the "intentional relinquishment or abandonment of a known right." Inadvertent production is the antithesis of that concept . . . . Mendenhall's lawyer (not trial counsel) might well have been negligent in failing to cull the files of the letters before turning over the files. But if we are serious about the attorney-client privilege and its relation to the client's welfare, we should require more than such negligence by counsel before the client can be deemed to have given up the privilege.

Mendenhall v. Barber-Greene Co., 531 F. Supp. 951, 959 (N.D. Ill. 1982).

The cases reflecting what appears to be the minority view conclude that any unforced disclosure of attorney-client privileged communications destroys confidentiality and terminates the privilege, not only for the communications disclosed but also for all related communications.

> [I]f a client wishes to preserve the privilege, it must treat the confidentiality of attorney-client communications like jewels—if not crown jewels. Short of court compelled disclosure, [citation omitted] or equally extraordinary circumstances, we will not distinguish between various degrees of "voluntariness" in waivers of the attorney-client privilege. *In re Sealed Case*, 877 F.2d 976, 980 (D.C. Cir. 1989).

The fact that this result is reached is not surprising if one starts with hostility to the privilege. However, the Model Rules certainly reflect a far more positive view toward the importance of maintaining the confidentiality of attorney-client communications, one that this Committee must reflect as it interprets and explicates the Model Rules.

II. Law Governing Missent Property

While the Committee does not answer questions of law, this principle does not preclude consideration, for present purposes, of the black letter of the law of bailment as it applies to missent property. Indeed, examination of the law of bailment proves instructive in suggesting how, as a matter of ethics, the receiving lawyer should conduct himself when he receives materials clearly not intended for him. That law defines the relationship between sending and receiving lawyer, the rights of the receiving lawyer with respect to the missent property and the obligations receiving lawyer has with respect to its use.

In the question presented to the Standing Committee, the receiving lawyer lawfully possesses the missent materials, but the sending lawyer clearly did not intend to relinquish title to them, either the physical objects or the ideas reflected on each page, such that they would become the "property" of the receiving attorney. The common law of bailments characterizes such mistaken possession as a bailment implied by law, or a constructive bailment.

> When possession of personal property of another is acquired and held under circumstances where the recipient, on principles of justice, ought to keep it safely and restore or deliver it to the owner, as, for example, where possession has been acquired accidentally, gratuitously, *through mistake*, or by agreement since terminated for some other purpose than bailment, the law, irrespective of any actual meeting of the minds, any voluntary undertaking, or any reasonable basis for implying mutual benefit, imposes on the recipient the duties and obligations of a bailee. Such bailments are known as constructive and involuntary bailments, and ordinarily the party in possession of the property is regarded as a gratuitous bailee . . . .

8 Am. Jur. 2d *Bailments* § 64 (1980) (emphasis added).

An essential element of the bailment relationship is the absolute obligation of the bailee to return the subject matter of the bailment upon termination of the bailment. *Id.* § 178 (1980). This obligation to return the property is necessarily implied from the mere fact of lawful possession of personal property of another. *Id.* § 178. Where the bailment is not for any particular time, the bailor may terminate it at will. *Id.* § 292. Indeed, the bailment terminates when an unauthorized use is made of the property. *Id.* § 295. If the bailee refuses to return the property, makes an unauthorized disposition of it, or uses it for purposes other than those agreed on, he may be liable for its conversion. *Id.* § 178.

The right of a bailee to use the bailed property and the extent to which it may be used is governed by the intention of the parties to the bailment. *Id.* § 207. In the absence of any express agreement between the parties, as is the case in the question presented the Committee, no rule of universal application can be laid down:

> Each case must be governed by its own circumstances, such as the character and purpose of the bailment and the nature of the property, in connection with other attending incidents. One test or principle applicable to the subject is whether, from the circumstances, *the consent of the owner to the use may be fairly presumed.*

Id. § 207 (emphasis added).

The sending lawyer here, of course, cannot begin to be presumed to have consented to any use of the missent materials by the receiving lawyer. Indeed, the only "use" to which the sending lawyer could be presumed to have consented is the immediate return of the missent property. Any attempt by the receiving lawyer to use the missent letter for his own purposes would thus constitute an "unauthorized use."

III. Analogous Cases

The present issue is not unlike that presented to the Standing Committee in Informal Opinion 86-1518, Notice to Opposing Counsel of Inadvertent Omission of Contract Provision (February 9, 1986). In that case a contract was negotiated including one hotly disputed provision insisted upon by B. When B's lawyer forwarded a draft of the agreement to A's lawyer, the key provision, though agreed to, was missing. The Committee was asked what duty, if any, A's lawyer had in the circumstances.

The opinion concluded that A's lawyer had no duty to notify A of the error under Model Rule 1.4 because the client has no decision to make. Nor was the lawyer barred by the confidentiality provisions of Model Rule 1.6 from informing the other side because this disclosure was "impliedly authorized" by the representation. Because under Model Rule 1.2 the lawyer has the authority to decide the technical means to carry out the representation and because the client's right under the same Model Rule to committed and dedicated representation is not unlimited, the opinion concluded that the "error is appropriate for correction between the lawyers without client consultation." In reaching this result the opinion was concerned that to do otherwise and "capitalize on the clerical error," might violate the proscription of Model Rule 1.2(d) not to counsel the client to engage in conduct the lawyer knows is fraudulent as well as the admonishment of Model Rule 4.1(b) not knowingly to fail to disclose a material fact when disclosure is necessary to avoid a client fraud.

While Informal Opinion 86-1516 is not on all fours with the instant situation, its charitable view toward inadvertence, its unwillingness to permit parties to capitalize on errors, its recognition of a limitation on client decision-making authority and its respect for the role of counsel all support the position advanced in this opinion as to counsel's proper conduct upon the inadvertent receipt of confidential information.

The Committee has also considered other hypothetical situations in which an opposing lawyer may have opportunity to "take advantage" of a chance to review and use confidential information. It is the view of the Committee that its dim view of a lawyer's doing so in each of these examples supports the conclusion reached by this opinion. For example, if during a lunch break in a deposition, lawyer B left notes or other materials in a conference room, either in an unlocked briefcase or on the conference room table, there is no respectable argument that competent and diligent representation requires or even permits lawyer A, arriving back from lunch early, to review the materials to which he now has easy access. Nor if, after a closing at lawyer A's office, lawyer B accidentally leaves a file or a briefcase behind would it be proper to assert that lawyer A could take advantage of this inadvertence and rifle the file or inspect the briefcase before returning it. Indeed, in the view of the Committee that lawyer would have an obligation to notify the lawyer who left her briefcase that it had been found. Finally, if in positioning an overhead projector on a shared counsel table in a courtroom during a recess, court personnel inadvertently move the prosecutor's notes into a position in front of the defense counsel's place at the table, it seems clear to the Committee that defense counsel would have an absolute obligation to return the materials without any examination or copying.

IV. Good Sense and Reciprocity

The analysis of this issue as an ethical matter should not obscure some more practical considerations that suggest the correct course for the receiving lawyer is to inform sending lawyer and return the documents. The immediate reaction of receiving counsel might be that the use of the missent materials can only serve to advantage his client. Nonetheless, it is clear there are advantages to doing just the opposite. First, instances of inadvertent production of documents tend not to occur only on one side. While a lawyer today may be the beneficiary of the opposing lawyer's misstep, tomorrow the shoe could be on the other foot. Second, when it is discovered that the confidential materials were retained and used the result could be similar to that which occurred recently in Baltimore when the court learned after jury selection that defendants' jury selection strategy was misdirected to plaintiffs' counsel by fax. "I find that the plaintiffs' attorneys have an advantage over the defense attorneys. Specifically, the plaintiffs know pretty well which prospective jurors the defense is going to strike . . . . They knew the inner-most thinking of the defense counsel." Baltimore City Personal Injury and Wrongful Death Asbestos Cases, Pretrial Hearing, June 5, 1991, Transcript at 4521, Circuit Court for Baltimore City, File No. 89236704. The judge struck the jury and ordered the entire process to begin again, at no small cost to plaintiffs, a cost that would have been expanded exponentially if the judge had not learned of this fact until the trial was over or when it was on appeal. Of similar effect is the recent example involving the Washington, D.C. office of a Texas law firm. Though in that case the confidential materials were intentionally delivered and, because they were from the government, special statutory provisions were involved, the fact that the firm felt compelled to withdraw because the firm was exposed to these materials, suggests the hazardous pathway which one must traverse after receipt of confidential materials.[4] "Taking a bet" on what reaction a court may have when an inadvertent disclosure becomes known can be a risky proposition indeed. Third, the credibility and professionalism inherent in doing the right thing can, in some significant ways, enhance the strength of one's case, one's standing with the other party and opposing counsel, and one's stature before the court.

Conclusion

The preamble to the Model Rules correctly notes that "virtually all difficult ethical problems arise from the conflict between a lawyer's responsibility to clients, to the legal system and to the lawyer's interest in remaining an upright person while earning a satisfactory living." Similarly, the same introduction observes that "a lawyer is also guided by personal conscience and the approbation of professional peers." In this instance, those principles, as well as the Model Rules, the law of bailment and good sense all come together to support our conclusion that receiving counsel's obligations under those circumstances are to avoid reviewing the materials, notify sending counsel if sending counsel remains ignorant of the problem and abide sending counsel's direction as to how to treat the disposition of the confidential materials. This result not only fosters the important principle of confidentiality, avoids punishing the innocent client and conforms to the law of bailment, but also achieves a level of professionalism which can only redound to the lawyer's benefit.

---

4. Jonathan Groner, *Akin, Gump Returns "Hot" Documents to Sender*, LEGAL TIMES (Washington, D.C.), October 5, 1992, at 8.

Formal Opinion 93-379 December 6, 1993
Billing for Professional Fees, Disbursements and Other Expenses

Consistent with the Model Rules of Professional Conduct, a lawyer must disclose to a client the basis on which the client is to be billed for both professional time and any other charges. Absent a contrary understanding, any invoice for professional services should fairly reflect the basis on which the client's charges have been determined. In matters where the client has agreed to have the fee determined with reference to the time expended by the lawyer, a lawyer may not bill more time than she actually spends on a matter, except to the extent that she rounds up to minimum time periods (such as one-quarter or one-tenth of an hour). A lawyer may not charge a client for overhead expenses generally associated with properly maintaining, staffing and equipping an office; however, the lawyer may recoup expenses reasonably incurred in connection with the client's matter for services performed in-house, such as photocopying, long distance telephone calls, computer research, special deliveries, secretarial overtime, and other similar services, so long as the charge reasonably reflects the lawyer's actual cost for the services rendered. A lawyer may not charge a client more than her disbursements for services provided by third parties like court reporters, travel agents or expert witnesses, except to the extent that the lawyer incurs costs additional to the direct cost of the third-party services.

The legal profession has dedicated a substantial amount of time and energy to developing elaborate sets of ethical guidelines for the benefit of its clients. Similarly, the profession has spent extraordinary resources on interpreting, teaching and enforcing these ethics rules. Yet, ironically, lawyers are not generally regarded by the public as particularly ethical. One major contributing factor to the discouraging public opinion of the legal profession appears to be the billing practices of some of its members.

It is a common perception that pressure on lawyers to bill a minimum of hours and on law firms to maintain or improve profits may have led some lawyers to engage in problematic billing practices. These include charges to more than one client for the same work or the same hours, surcharges on services contracted with outside vendors, and charges beyond reasonable costs for in-house services like photocopying and computer searches. Moreover, the bases on which these charges are to be assessed often are not disclosed in advance or are disguised in cryptic invoices so that the client does not fully understand exactly what costs are being charged to him.

The Model Rules of Professional Conduct provide important principles applicable to the billing of clients, principles which, if followed, would ameliorate many of the problems noted above. The Committee has decided to address several practices that are the subject of frequent inquiry, with the goal of helping the profession adhere to its ethical obligations to its clients despite economic pressures.

The first set of practices involves billing more than one client for the same hours spent. In one illustrative situation, a lawyer finds it possible to schedule court appearances for three clients on the same day. He spends a total of four hours at the courthouse, the amount of time he would have spent on behalf of each client had it not been for the fortuitious circumstance that all three cases were scheduled on the same day. May he bill each of the three clients, who otherwise understand that they will be billed on the basis of time spent, for the four hours be spent on them collectively? In another scenario, a lawyer is flying cross-country to attend a deposition on behalf of one client, expending travel time she would ordinarily bill to that client. If she decides not to watch the movie or read her novel, but to work instead on drafting a motion for another client, may she charge both clients, each of whom agreed to hourly billing, for the time during which she was traveling on behalf of one and drafting a document on behalf of the other? A third situation involves research on a particular topic for one client that later turns out to be relevant to an inquiry from a second client. May the firm bill the second client, who agreed to be charged on the basis of time spent on his case, the same amount for the recycled work product that it charged the first client?

The second set of practices involves billing for expenses and disbursements, and is exemplified by the situation in which a firm contracts for the expert witness services of an economist at an hourly rate of $200. May the firm bill the client for the expert's time at the rate of $250 per hour? Similarly, may the firm add a surcharge to the cost of computer-assisted research if the per-minute total charged by the computer company does not include the cost of purchasing the computers or staffing their operation?

The questions presented to the Committee require us to determine what constitute reasonable billing procedures; that is, what are the services and costs for which a lawyer may legitimately charge, both generally and with regard to the specific scenarios? This inquiry requires an elucidation of the Rule of Professional Conduct 1.5,[1] and the Model Code of Professional

1. Rule 1.5 states in relevant part:

(a) A lawyer's fee shall be reasonable. The factors to be considered in determining the reasonableness of a fee include the following:

(1) the time and labor required, the novelty and difficulty of the questions involved, and the skill requisite to perform the legal service properly;

(2) the likelihood, if apparent to the client, that the acceptance of the particular employment will preclude other employment by the lawyer;

(3) the fee customarily charged in the locality for similar legal services;

(4) the amount involved and the results obtained;

Responsibility DR 2-106.[2]

Disclosure of the Bases of the Amounts to Be Charged

At the outset of the representation the lawyer should make disclosure of the basis for the fee and any other charges to the client. This is a two-fold duty, including not only an explanation at the beginning of engagement of the basis on which fees and other charges will be billed, but also a sufficient explanation in the statement so that the client may reasonably be expected to understand what fees and other charges the client is actually being billed.

Authority for the obligation to make disclosure at the beginning of a representation is found in the interplay among a number of rules. Rule 1.5(b) provides that

> When the lawyer has not regularly represented the client, the basis or rate of the fee shall be communicated to the client, preferably in writing, before or within a reasonable time after commencing the representation.

The Comment to Rule 1.5 gives guidance on how to execute the duty to communicate the basis of the fee:

> In a new client-lawyer relationship . . . an understanding as to the fee should be promptly established. It is not necessary to recite all the factors that underlie the basis of the fee, but only those that are directly involved in its computation. It is sufficient, for example, to state that the basic rate is an hourly charge or a fixed amount or an estimated amount, or to identify the factors that may be taken into account in finally fixing the fee. When developments occur during the representation that render an earlier estimate substantially inaccurate, a revised estimate should be provided to the client. A written statement concerning the fee reduces the possibility of misunderstanding. Furnishing the client with a simple memorandum or a copy of the lawyer's customary fee schedule is sufficient if the basis or rate of the fee is set forth.

This obligation is reinforced by reference to Model Rule 1.4(b) which provides that

> A lawyer shall explain a matter to the extent reasonably necessary to permit

---

(5) the time limitations imposed by the client or by the circumstances;

(6) the nature and length of the professional relationship with the client;

(7) the experience, reputation, and ability of the lawyer or lawyers performing the services; and

(8) whether the fee is fixed or contingent.

(b) When the lawyer has not regularly represented the client, the basis or rate of the fee shall be communicated to the client, preferably in writing, before or within a reasonable time after commencing the representation.

2. DR 2-106 contains substantially the same factors listed in Rule 1.5 to determine reasonableness, but does not require that the basis of the fee be communicated to the client "preferably in writing" as Rule 1.5 does.

the client to make informed decisions regarding the representation.

While the Comment to this Rule suggests its obvious applicability to negotiations or litigation with adverse parties, its important principle should be equally applicable to the lawyer's obligation to explain the basis on which the lawyer expects to be compensated, so the client can make one of the more important decisions "regarding the representation."

An obligation of disclosure is also supported by Model Rule 7.1, which addresses communications concerning a lawyer's services, including the basis on which fees would be charged. The rule provides:

> A lawyer shall not make a false or misleading communication about the lawyer or the lawyer's services. A communication is false or misleading if it:
>
> (a) contains a material misrepresentation of fact or law, or omits a fact necessary to make the statement considered as a whole not materially misleading.

It is clear under Model Rule 7.1 that in offering to perform services for prospective clients it is critical that lawyers avoid making any statements about fees that are not complete. If it is true that a lawyer when advertising for new clients must disclose, for example, that costs are the responsibility of the client, *Zauderer v. Office of Disciplinary Counsel*, 471 U.S. 626 (1985), it necessarily follows that in entering into an actual client relationship a lawyer must make fair disclosure of the basis on which fees will be assessed.

A corollary of the obligation to disclose the basis for future billing is a duty to render statements to the client that adequately apprise the client as to how that basis for billing has been applied. In an engagement in which the client has agreed to compensate the lawyer on the basis of time expended at regular hourly rates, a bill setting out no more than a total dollar figure for unidentified professional services will often be insufficient to tell the client what he or she needs to know in order to understand how the amount was determined. By the same token, billing other charges without breaking the charges down by type would not provide the client with the information the client needs to understand the basis for the charges.

Initial disclosure of the basis for the fee arrangement fosters communication that will promote the attorney-client relationship. The relationship will be similarly benefitted if the statement for services explicitly reflects the basis for the charges so that the client understands how the fee bill was determined.

Professional Obligations Regarding the Reasonableness of Fees

Implicit in the Model Rules and their antecedents is the notion that the attorney-client relationship is not necessarily one of equals, that it is built on trust, and that the client is encouraged to be dependent on the lawyer, who is dealing with matters of great moment to the client. The client should only be charged a reasonable fee for the legal services performed. Rule 1.5 explicitly addresses the reasonableness of legal fees. The rule deals not only with the determination of a reasonable hourly rate, but also with total cost to the client. The Comment to the rule states, for example, that "[a] lawyer should not exploit a fee arrangement based primarily on hourly charges by using wasteful procedures." The goal should be solely to compensate the lawyer fully for time reasonably expended, an approach that if followed will not take advantage of the client.

Ethical Consideration 2-17 of the Model Code of Professional Responsibility provides a framework for balancing the interests between the lawyer and client in determining the reasonableness of a fee arrangement:

> The determination of a proper fee requires consideration of the interests of both client and lawyer. A lawyer should not charge more than a reasonable fee, for excessive cost of legal service would deter laymen from utilizing the legal system in protection of their rights. Furthermore, an excessive charge abuses the professional relationship between lawyer and client. On the other hand, adequate compensation is necessary in order to enable the lawyer to serve his client effectively and to preserve the integrity and independence of the profession.

The lawyer's conduct should be such as to promote the client's trust of the lawyer and of the legal profession. This means acting as the advocate for the client to the extent necessary to complete a project thoroughly. Only through careful attention to detail is the lawyer able to manage a client's case properly. An unreasonable limitation on the hours a lawyer may spend on a client should be avoided as a threat to the lawyer's ability to fulfill her obligation under Model Rule 1.1 to "provide competent representation to a client." "Competent representation requires the legal knowledge, skill, thoroughness and preparation necessary for the representation." Model Rule 1.1. Certainly either a willingness on the part of the lawyer, or a demand by the client, to circumscribe the lawyer's efforts, to compromise the lawyer's ability to be as thorough and as prepared as necessary, is not in the best interests of the client and may lead to a violation of Model Rule 1.1 if it means the lawyer is unable to provide competent representation. The Comment to Model Rule 1.2, while observing that "the scope of services provided by a lawyer may be limited by agreement," also notes that an agreement "concerning the scope of representation must accord with the Rules . . . . Thus, the client may not be asked to agree to representation so limited in scope as to violate Rule 1.1 . . . ."[3]

On the other hand, the lawyer who has agreed to bill on the basis of hours expended does not fulfill her ethical duty if she bills the client for more time than

3. Beyond the scope of this opinion is the question whether a lawyer, with full disclosure to a sophisticated client of the risks involved, can agree to undertake at the request of the client only ten hours of research, when the lawyer knows that the resulting work product does not fulfill the competent representation requirement of Model Rule 1.1.

she actually spent on the client's behalf.[4] In addressing the hypotheticals regarding (a) simultaneous appearance on behalf of three clients, (b) the airplane flight on behalf of one client while working on another client's matters and (c) recycled work product, it is helpful to consider these questions, not from the perspective of what a client could be forced to pay, but rather from the perspective of what the lawyer actually earned. A lawyer who spends four hours of time on behalf of three clients has not earned twelve billable hours. A lawyer who files for six hours for one client, while working for five hours on behalf of another, has not earned eleven billable hours. A lawyer who is able to reuse old work product has not re-earned the hours previously billed and compensated when the work product was first generated. Rather than looking to profit from the fortuity of coincidental scheduling, the desire to get work done rather than watch a movie, or the luck of being asked the identical question twice, the lawyer who has agreed to bill solely on the basis of time spent is obliged to pass the benefits of these economies on to the client. The practice of billing several clients for the same time or work product, since it results in the earning of an unreasonable fee, therefore is contrary to the mandate of the Model Rules. Model Rule 1.5.

Moreover, continuous toil on or overstaffing a project for the purpose of churning out hours is also not properly considered "earning" one's fees. One job of a lawyer is to expedite the legal process. Model Rule 3.2. Just as a lawyer is expected to discharge a matter on summary judgment if possible rather than proceed to trial, so too is the lawyer expected to complete other projects for a client efficiently. A lawyer should take as much time as is reasonably required to complete a project, and should certainly never be motivated by anything other than the best interests of the client when determining how to staff or how much time to spend on any particular project.

It goes without saying that a lawyer who has undertaken to bill on an hourly basis is never justified in charging a client for hours not actually expended. If a lawyer has agreed to charge the client on this basis and it turns out that the lawyer is particularly efficient in accomplishing a given result, it nonetheless will not be permissible to charge the client for more hours than were actually expended on the matter. When that basis for billing the client has been agreed to, the economies associated with the result must inure to the benefit of the client, not give rise to an opportunity to bill a client phantom hours. This is not to say that the lawyer who agreed to hourly compensation is not free, with full disclosure, to suggest additional compensation because of a particularly efficient or outstanding result, or because the lawyer was able to reuse prior work product on the client's behalf. The point here is that fee enhancement cannot be accomplished simply by presenting the client with a statement reflecting more billable hours than were actually expended. On the other hand,

4. Rule 1.5 clearly contemplates that there are bases for billing clients other than the time expended. This opinion, however, only addresses issues raised when it is understood that the client will be charged on the basis of time expended.

if a matter turns out to be more difficult to accomplish than first anticipated and more hours are required than were originally estimated, the lawyer is fully entitled (though not required) to bill those hours unless the client agreement turned the original estimate into a cap on the fees to be charged.

Charges Other Than Professional Fees

In addition to charging clients fees for professional services, lawyers typically charge their clients for certain additional items which are often referred to variously as disbursements, out-of-pocket expenses or additional charges. Inquiries to the Committee demonstrate that the profession has encountered difficulties in conforming to the ethical standards in this area as well. The Rules provide no specific guidance on the issue of how much a lawyer may charge a client for costs incurred over and above her own fee. However, we believe that the reasonableness standard explicitly applicable to fees under Rule 1.5(a) should be applicable to these charges as well.

The Committee, in trying to sort out the issues related to these charges, has identified three different questions which must be addressed. First, which items are properly subject to additional charges? Second, to what extent, if at all, may clients be charged for more than actual out-of-pocket disbursements? Third, on what basis may clients be charged for the provision of in-house services? We shall address these one at a time.

A. General Overhead

When a client has engaged a lawyer to provide professional services for a fee (whether calculated on the basis of the number of hours expended, a flat fee, a contingent percentage of the amount recovered or otherwise) the client would be justifiably disturbed if the lawyer submitted a bill to the client which included, beyond the professional fee, additional charges for general office overhead. In the absence of disclosure to the client in advance of the engagement to the contrary, the client should reasonably expect that the lawyer's cost in maintaining a library, securing malpractice insurance, renting of office space, purchasing utilities and the like would be subsumed within the charges the lawyer is making for professional services.

B. Disbursements

At the beginning of the engagement lawyers typically tell their clients that they will be charged for disbursements. When that term is used clients justifiably should expect that the lawyer will be passing on to the client those actual payments of funds made by the lawyer on the client's behalf. Thus, if the lawyer hires a court stenographer to transcribe a deposition, the client can reasonably expect to be billed as a disbursement the amount the lawyer pays to the court reporting service. Similarly, if the lawyer flies to Los Angeles for the client, the client can reasonably expect to be billed as a disbursement the amount of the airfare, taxicabs, meals and hotel room.

It is the view of the Committee that, in the absence of disclosure to the contrary, it would be improper if the lawyer assessed a surcharge on these disbursements over and above the amount actually incurred unless the lawyer herself incurred additional expenses beyond the actual cost of the disbursement item. In the same regard, if a lawyer receives a discounted rate from a third-party provider, it would be improper if she did not pass along the benefit of the discount to her client rather than charge the client the full rate and reserve the profit to herself. Clients quite properly could view these practices as an attempt to create additional undisclosed profit centers when the client had been told he would be billed for disbursements.

C. In-House Provision of Services

Perhaps the most difficult issue is the handling of charges to clients for the provision of in-house services. In this connection the Committee has in view charges for photocopying, computer research, on-site meals, deliveries and other similar items. Like professional fees, it seems clear that lawyers may pass on reasonable charges for these services. Thus, in view of the Committee, the lawyer and the client may agree in advance that, for example, photocopying will be charged at $.15 per page, or messenger services will be provided at $5.00 per mile. However, the question arises what may be charged to the client, in the absence of a specific agreement to the contrary, when the client has simply been told that costs for these items will be charged to the client. We conclude that under those circumstances the lawyer is obliged to charge the client no more than the direct cost associated with the service (i.e., the actual cost of making a copy on the photocopy machine) plus a reasonable allocation of overhead expenses directly associated with the provision of the service (e.g., the salary of a photocopy machine operator).

It is not appropriate for the Committee, in addressing ethical standards, to opine on the various accounting issues as to how one calculates direct cost and what may or may not be included in allocated overhead. These are questions which properly should be reserved for our colleagues in the accounting profession. Rather, it is the responsibility of the Committee to explain the principles it draws from the mandate of Model Rule 1.5's injunction that fees be reasonable. Any reasonable calculation of direct costs as well as any reasonable allocation of related overhead should pass ethical muster. On the other hand, in the absence of an agreement to the contrary, it is impermissible for a lawyer to create an additional source of profit for the law firm beyond that which is contained in the provision of professional services themselves. The lawyer's stock in trade is the sale of legal services, not photocopy paper, tuna fish sandwiches, computer time or messenger services.

Conclusion

As the foregoing demonstrates, the subject of fees for professional services and other charges is one that is fraught with tension between the lawyer and the client. Nonetheless, if the principles outlined in this opinion are followed, the ethical resolution of these issues can be achieved.

Formal Opinion 94-389 December 5, 1994
Contingent Fees

It is ethical to charge contingent fees as long as the fee is appropriate and reasonable and the client has been fully informed of the availability of alternative billing arrangements. The fact that a client can afford to compensate the lawyer on another basis does not render a contingent fee arrangement for such a client unethical. Nor is it unethical to charge a contingent fee when liability is clear and some recovery is anticipated. If the lawyer and client so contract, a lawyer is entitled to a full contingent fee on the total recovery by the client, including that portion of the recovery that was the subject of an early settlement offer that was rejected by the client. Finally, if the lawyer and client agree, it is ethical for the lawyer to charge a different contingent fee at different stages of a matter, and to increase the percentage taken as a fee as the amount of the recovery or savings to the client increases.

A. Introduction

The term contingent fees evokes an almost instantaneous visceral response among lawyers. Some view the contingent fee as the salvation of the impecunious,[1] a means to redress great wrongs, vindicate rights and reform the law.[2] Others view it as an inducement to frivolous lawsuits which abuse tort laws,[3] and a means of exacting outrageously high fees for already overpaid lawyers.[4] This

1. As stated by the Pennsylvania Supreme Court:

> If it were not for contingent fees, indigent victims of tortious accidents would be subject to the unbridled, self-willed partisanship of their tortfeasors. The person who has, without fault on his part, been injured and who, because of his injury, is unable to work, and has a large family to support, and has no money to engage a lawyer, would be at the mercy of the person who disabled him because, being in a superior economic position, the injuring person could force on his victim, desperately in need of money to keep the candle of life burning in himself and his dependent ones, a wholly unconscionable meager sum in settlement or even refuse to pay him anything at all. Any society, and especially a democratic one, worthy of respect in the spectrum of civilization, should never tolerate such a victimization of the weak by the mighty.

Richette v. Solomon, 187 A.2d 910, 919 (Pa. 1963).

2. *See* Comment, *Judicial Regulation of Contingent Fee Contracts*, 48 J.AIR L. & COMM. 151, 158 (1982); Pollack, *Book Review*, 90 HARV. L. REV. 482, 484 (1976); Corboy, *Contingency Fees: The Individual's Key to the Courthouse,* 2 LITIGATION 27 (1976); R. KEETON, VENTURING TO DO JUSTICE: REFORMING PRIVATE LAW (1969).

3. *See* Statements of Barry Keene, leader of the Association for California Tort Reform, that restrictions on contingent fees are necessary to "reduce financial incentives that encourage lawyers to file unnecessary, unwarranted and unmeritorious suits." 9 ABA/BNA LAWYERS' MANUAL ON PROFESSIONAL CONDUCT No. 20 at 320 (1993).

4. *See* Brickman, *Contingent Fees Without Contingencies: Hamlet Without the Prince of Denmark*, 37 U.C.L.A. L. REV. 29, 32-33 (1989); Grady, *Some Ethical Questions About Percentage Fees*, 2 LITIGATION 20 (1976). A study by the Rand Corporation, however, suggests

Committee does not propose in this opinion to take a role in this often intense public policy debate, which has been and will continue to be played out in Congress, state legislatures and other places in the political arena and within the profession.

Rather, the Committee confines its discussion here, in accordance with the specific question addressed to it, to the circumstances under which the charging of contingent fees could violate either the ABA Model Rules of Professional Conduct (1983, as amended) or the ABA Model Code of Professional Responsibility (1980). In particular, the Committee has been asked if it is an ethical violation for a lawyer to charge a contingent fee a) to a client who can otherwise afford to pay on a non-contingent basis or b) in a matter where liability is clear and some recovery is likely. The Committee has also been asked c) whether a personal injury lawyer operating under a contingent fee agreement is obligated to solicit an early settlement offer and d) whether the same lawyer can charge a contingent fee on the amount of recovery that was the subject of a rejected early settlement offer. Finally, the Committee has been asked if it is ethical to charge a contingent fee whose percentage increases e) as the litigation proceeds and f) as the recovery increases.

These are all appropriate questions of professional ethics, properly addressed to this Committee. Without taking sides on the inflammatory and divisive policy issues these questions may evoke, the Committee can answer the questions in the hope of reminding the profession of important client safeguards that come into play in the contingent fee area. These safeguards, if followed, may go a long way toward reducing the larger controversy generated by contingent fees.

In the opinion of the Committee, the charging of a contingent fee, in personal injury and in all other permissible types of litigation, as well as in numerous non-litigation matters, does not violate ethical standards as long as the fee is appropriate in the circumstances and reasonable in amount, and as long as the client has been fully advised of the availability of alternative fee arrangements. The mere fact that liability may be clear does not, by itself, render a contingent fee inappropriate or unethical. Nor does the possibility that, as some have suggested, the profession's obligation to assure appropriateness and reasonableness is sometimes honored in its breach mean that contingent fees are inherently ethically questionable. Rather, any lapse from the applicable requirements by some members of the profession simply suggests that the profession should redouble its efforts to assure that the ethical obligations associated with entering into a con-

---

that compensation received by attorneys on a contingent fee basis, if averaged over all cases, is similar to that received by attorneys compensated on an hourly basis. *See* P. Danzon, Rand Corporation Institute for Civil Justice, *Contingent Fees for Personal Injury Litigation*, Govt. Publication No. R-2458-HCFA at viii (June 1980). The study also suggests that prohibitions on contingency fees are likely to produce suboptimal compensation for plaintiffs and, hence, suboptimal deterrence of negligent actions because a substantial number of low and middle income plaintiffs would be deterred from filing suit. *Id. See also* Report of the Secretary's Commission on Medical Malpractice, U.S. Dep't. of Health Education and Welfare, *The Medical Malpractice Legal System* at 87, 154 (Jan. 16, 1973).

tingent fee arrangement are fully understood and observed.

B. Contingent Fees Are Employed in Multiple Situations

It should be recognized at the outset that when we address contingent fees we are talking about a wide variety of situations. Contingent fees are no longer, if ever they were, limited to personal injury cases. Nor are contingent fees limited to suits involving tortious conduct. Contingent fees are now commonly offered to plaintiff-clients in collections, civil rights, securities and anti-trust class actions, real estate tax appeals and even patent litigation.

Nor is this compensation arrangement limited to plaintiffs. In this Committee's recent Formal Opinion 93-373, the Committee considered the ethical issues raised by the increasingly employed so-called "reverse contingent fees," in which defendants hire lawyers who will be compensated by an agreed upon percentage of the amount the client saves. The Committee concluded that as long as the fee arrangement reached between the lawyer and client realistically estimates the exposure of the defendant client, such a fee is consistent with the Model Rules.

Moreover, contingent fees are not limited to litigation practice. Fees in the mergers and acquisitions arena are often either partially or totally dependent on the consummation of a takeover or successful resistance of such a takeover. Additionally, fees on public offerings are often tied to whether the stocks or bonds come to market and to the amount generated in the offering. Banks are also hiring lawyers to handle loan transactions in which the fee for the bank's lawyers is dependent in whole or part on the consummation of the loan.

The use of contingent fees in these areas, for plaintiffs and defendants, impecunious and affluent alike, reflects the desire of clients to tie a lawyer's compensation to her performance and to give the lawyer incentives to improve returns to the client. The trend also may reflect a growing dissatisfaction with hourly rate billing.[5] Because of the growing importance and widespread use of contingent

5. For example, Zoe Baird, General Counsel of Aetna Casualty & Surety Co., at the 1992 ABA Annual Meeting asserted that billing based on hourly fees is a "deeply flawed economic system" which instead of focusing lawyers on resolving client problems, encourages "too much time spent on discovery, complicated and unproductive meetings, and long uncommunicative briefs." *See* ABA/BNA LAWYERS' MANUAL ON PROFESSIONAL CONDUCT, 8 CUR. REPS. 286-87 (9/9/92).

Shelby Rogers, General Counsel of Texas Commerce Bancshares, and Francis H. Musselman, Managing Partner of Milbank, Tweed, Hadley & McCoy, have similarly criticized the present system of hourly billing and advocated the use of contingent fees and "success bonuses" as a means of ensuring a correlation between attorney work and value received by the client. *See* ABA/BNA LAWYERS' MANUAL ON PROFESSIONAL CONDUCT, 9 CUR. REPS. 254-55 (9/8/93); *see also* SALOP & LITAN, MORE VALUE FOR THE LEGAL DOLLAR: A NEW LOOK AT ATTORNEY CLIENT FEES AND RELATIONSHIPS (Brookings Institute 1992). This Committee has recently identified some ethical abuses that can accompany hourly billing in ABA Standing Committee on Ethics and Professional Responsibility Formal Opinion No. 93-379 ("Billing for Professional Fees, Disbursements and Other Expenses").

fees, the Committee will first address in detail the factors that should be considered before a lawyer and client enter into such a fee arrangement, and then address the specific questions occasioning this opinion.

C. The Decision by the Client to Enter Into a Contingent Fee Agreement Must Be an Informed One

Nothing in the Model Rules expressly prohibits a lawyer from entering into a contingent fee agreement with any client. Nevertheless, the lawyer must recognize that not all matters are appropriate for a contingent fee. For example, Model Rule 1.5(d) makes it clear that a contingent fee may never be agreed to, charged or collected in a criminal matter or divorce proceeding.[6] More to the point, in Informal Opinion 86-1521 this Committee concluded that, "when there is any doubt whether a contingent fee is consistent with the client's best interest," and the client is able to pay a reasonable fixed fee, the lawyer "must offer the client the *opportunity* to engage counsel on a reasonable fixed fee basis before entering into a contingent fee arrangement" (emphasis added). The Opinion pointed out that a client with a meritorious claim:

> is entitled to representation and should not be required to relinquish a share of the claim to get representation if the client has the money to pay a reasonable fixed fee and is willing to assume the contingency risk. It may also be in some cases that a contingent fee arrangement is the only practical basis upon which a matter can be handled, but that decision should be made after consideration of the relevant facts and circumstances in consultation with the client . . . .

In other words, regardless of whether the lawyer, the prospective client, or both, are initially inclined towards a contingent fee, the nature (and details) of the compensation arrangement should be fully discussed by the lawyer and client before any final agreement is reached.

The extent of the discussion, of course, will depend on whether it is the lawyer or the client who initiated the idea of proceeding with the contingent fee arrangement, the lawyer's prior dealings with the client (including whether there has been any prior contingent fee arrangement), and the experience and sophistication of the client with respect to litigation and other legal matters.[7] Among the factors that should be considered and discussed are the following:

---

6. The Model Code contains similar provisions in DR 2-106(C) and EC 2-20.

7. This procedure meets the lawyer's fiduciary obligations to the client without unnecessarily interfering with the lawyer's right to charge reasonable fees, Model Rule 1.5; ABA Standing Committee on Ethics and Professional Responsibility Formal Opinion 329; or the freedom of contract enjoyed by both lawyer and client. *See* Venegas v. Mitchell, 495 U.S. 82, 88 (1990) (parties are free to assign part of their recovery to an attorney if they believe that the contingency agreement will increase their likelihood of recovery); Wells v. Sullivan, 907 F.2d 367, 369-370 (2d Cir. 1990) ("absent fraud or overreaching, courts must enforce such private contingency fee

a. The likelihood of success;
b. The likely amount of recovery or savings, if the case is successful;
c. The possibility of an award of exemplary or multiple damages and how that will affect the fee;
d. The attitude and prior practices of the other side with respect to settlement;
e. The likelihood of, or any anticipated difficulties in, collecting any judgement;
f. The availability of alternative dispute resolution as a means of achieving an earlier conclusion to the matter;
g. The amount of time that is likely to be invested by the lawyer;
h. The likely amount of the fee if the matter is handled on a non-contingent basis;
i. The client's ability and willingness to pay a non-contingent fee;
j. The percentage of any recovery that the lawyer would receive as a contingent fee and whether that percentage will be fixed or on a sliding scale;
k. Whether the lawyer's fees would be recoverable by the client by reason of statute or common law rule;
l. Whether the jurisdiction in which the claim will be pursued has any rules or guidelines for contingent fees; and
m. How expenses of the litigation are to be handled.

Notwithstanding the foregoing, however, the inquiries prompting this opinion take the position that there are two particular circumstances where contingent fee arrangements are inappropriate. To these we now turn.

D. Contingent Fees May Be Appropriate When the Client Can Afford to Pay on Another Basis

Is a contingent fee appropriate when a client can afford to pay the lawyer on a non-contingent basis? Some commentators have suggested that because one of the fundamental reasons for allowing contingent fees is that they provide the poor equal access to the court system, such a fee may be inappropriate and unethical when the client is relatively well off or otherwise able to afford a lawyer.[8] However, as discussed above, there is nothing in the Model Rules to prevent a lawyer from entering into a contingent fee agreement with any client, regardless of the client's means, so

---

agreements, which are, after all, embodiments of the intentions and wishes of the parties . . . . [T]o deny [plaintiffs] the option of entering contingent fee arrangements would tend to defeat the general remedial purpose of the statute by unnecessarily restricting claimants' options in securing adequate counsel or counsel of their choice").

8. *See* G. HAZARD & W.W. HODES, 2 LAW OF LAWYERING §1.5 at 118, 122-23 (1993 Supp.) (suggesting that lawyers should use a different fee system for clients who can afford to bear costs); J. O'CONNELL, THE INJURY INDUSTRY 48 (1971) ("[L]awyers will not normally take a per-

long as the client's decision to enter into the arrangement is an informed one.

Moreover, to state that contingent fees are only appropriate for the indigent would ignore the reality of how expensive present day litigation can be. It is not uncommon for expenses and legal fees to total hundreds of thousands of dollars through trial.[9] Also, it is often difficult at the outset of a matter for the lawyer to estimate accurately how much time will be expended. Therefore, it may very well be in the client's best interests, whatever the client's apparent ability to pay the fee, to agree to pay a fixed percentage of any possible recovery, rather than assume liability for a possibly prohibitively expensive legal bill that will be owed even if the client recovers nothing.

The contingent fee system essentially shifts the risk of litigation or other legal endeavor from a risk averse client to the lawyer who may be more risk neutral because of his ability to recoup his losses through his handling of other legal matters on a contingent basis.

Even for those who can well afford to pay legal fees on a pay as you go basis, such as large corporations, the client's best interests may still be served by a contingent fee arrangement. In this way the corporation can use its financial resources, which would otherwise be spent in paying for legal services, for other business purposes until such time as the merger may be consummated or an identifiable fund is available from the proceeds of a public offering.

Furthermore, both the wealthy and the impecunious client may share the desire to give their lawyers the incentive to increase the actual proceeds to the client. At least some clients think contingent fee agreements are the best, if not the only way, to give such incentives. In their view the interests of the lawyer and the interests of the client are only in true alignment when the lawyer's fee is totally contingent on a successful outcome for the client.

Thus, as discussed above, while the client's inability to pay legal fees on a non-contingent basis may be the determining factor in a conclusion that a contingent fee is appropriate, the fact that the client is able to pay such fees does not necessarily make a contingent fee inappropriate. Barring contingent fees for other than the impecunious would deny important benefits to which the well-to-do as well as the poor client are clearly entitled.

E. In a Case in Which Liability Is Clear and Some Recovery Is Certain, a Fee Based on a Percentage of the Recovery Can Be Ethically Proper

The Committee has also been asked to consider whether it is ethical for a lawyer

---

sonal injury case on other than a contingency fee no matter how wealthy the client . . . [this] suggests . . . that its use is so widespread today because it is profitable for lawyers"); Comment, *Are Contingent Fees Ethical Where Client Is Able to Pay a Retainer?* 20 OHIO ST. L.J. 329 (1959).

9. Fees and expenses can be especially high in certain hard fought and groundbreaking litigation. A prime example is the cigarette liability litigation which has cost law firms working on a contingent fee basis millions of dollars that has not been offset by any judgment or settlement. *See The Heat Is On*, A.B.A. J., Sept. 1994, at 59.

to accept a matter on a contingent fee basis when liability is clear and some recovery is certain. The argument put forward is that since the lawyer is sure that the matter will result in some recovery, there is no real contingency; thus, there is no justification for a contingent fee arrangement. A variation of this argument discussed more fully under caption G below, is found in a recent inquiry to this Committee which asks whether a lawyer to be compensated under a contingent fee arrangement is ethically obligated to solicit early settlement offers and whether a lawyer should be prohibited from charging a contingent fee on the amount of such offer, even if it is not accepted and the same amount is recovered after the case must go to trial.[10]

First, neither the Model Rules nor the Model Code mention any requirements regarding solicitation of early settlement offers and there is no valid basis for inferring such a requirement. *See* ABA Formal Opinion 329 (1972) (no reasonable method of fixing fees which takes into account the relevant factors set forth in the ethical rules is proscribed).

Second, the Committee is of the view that the argument may rest on a faulty notion as to the number of cases regarding which at the onset of the engagement the lawyer can say with certainty that the client will recover.[11] Defendants often vigorously defend and even win cases where liability seems certain.[12] Additionally, a previously undiscovered fact or an unexpected change in the law can suddenly transform a case that seemed a sure winner at the outset of representation into a certain loser. *See, e.g., Central Bank of Denver v. First Interstate Bank of Denver*, 114 S. Ct. 1439 (1994) (where the Supreme Court held that a private plaintiff may not maintain an aiding and abetting suit under §10(b) of the Securities Act of 1934, overruling every circuit court which for decades had allowed such suits).

Moreover, even in cases where there is no risk of non-recovery, and the lawyer and client are certain that liability is clear and will be conceded, a fee arrangement contingent on the amount recovered may nonetheless be reasonable.[13] As the increasing popularity of reverse contingent fees demonstrates, for almost all cases there is a range of possible recoveries. Since the amount of the recovery

10. *See* BRICKMAN, HOROWITZ & O'CONNELL, RETHINKING CONTINGENCY FEES, at 28 (The Manhattan Institute 1994) (proposing that "[w]hen plaintiffs reject defendants' early offers, contingency fees may only be charged against net recoveries in excess of such offers").

11. A recent study indicates that the probability of recovery is presently decreasing, rather than increasing, in many types of lawsuits that are traditionally handled on a contingent fee basis. *See Stingier Jurors Doling Out Fewer Awards*, A.B.A. JOURNAL, Sept. 1994 at 20. This study shows that in medical malpractice cases the probability of recovery at trial has decreased from 37% to 31%, and, in products liability cases from 51% to 43%. *Id.*

12. In a study of 8,231 closed medical malpractice cases in the State of New Jersey from 1977 to 1992, almost 10% of patients received no recovery at all in cases where the defendant doctors' conduct was rated indefensible. *See* M.I. Taragin, L.R. Willet, A. Pwilczek, R. Trout and J.L. Carson, *The Influence of Standard of Care and Severity of Injury on the Resolution of Medical Malpractice Claims*, 1992 ANNALS OF AMER. MED. 780-784.

13. Evidence that, in such cases, free market forces may result in a substantially reduced contingent fee can be found in airline liability cases. In cases where airline insurers voluntari

will be largely determined by the lawyer's knowledge, skill, experience and time expended, both the defendant and the plaintiff may best be served by a contingency fee arrangement that ties the lawyer's fee to the amount recovered.[14]

Also, an early settlement offer is often prompted by the defendant's recognition of the ability of the plaintiff's lawyer fairly and accurately to value the case and to proceed effectively through trial and appeals if necessary. There is no ethical reason why the lawyer is not entitled to an appropriate consideration for this value that his engagement has brought to the case, even though it results in an early resolution.

Given the foregoing, the Committee concludes that as a general proposition contingent fees are appropriate and ethical in situations where liability is certain and some recovery is likely.

That having been said, there may nonetheless be special situations in which a contingent fee may not be appropriate. For example, if in a particular instance a lawyer was reasonably confident that as soon as the case was filed the defendant would offer an amount that the client would accept, it might be that the only appropriate fee would be one based on the lawyer's time spent on the case since, from the information known to the lawyer, there was little risk of non-recovery and the lawyer's efforts would have brought little value to the client's recovery.[15] And even if, in such circumstances, after a full discussion, it were agreed between lawyer and client that a contingent fee was appropriate, the fee arrangement should recognize the likelihood of an early favorable result by providing for a significantly smaller percentage recovery if the anticipated offer is received and accepted than if the case must go forward through discovery, trial and appeal.[16]

---

ly sent out the "Alpert letter" which makes an early settlement offer and concedes all legal liability, average contingent fee rates dropped to 17% and were often only charged on a portion of the recovery. *See* L. Kriendler, *The Letter: It Shouldn't Be Sent*, 12 THE BRIEF 4, 38 (November 1982).

14. Similarly, in the case of reverse contingent fee arrangements, some savings from the amount the plaintiff demands is almost always a certainty, yet as this Committee opined in Formal Opinion 93-373, there is nothing ethically improper about entering into a fee agreement that compensates the lawyer based on a percentage of the total saved.

15. Similar reasoning has led many courts to find that it is inappropriate to charge a contingent fee in cases involving first party insurance benefits where there is no risk of non-recovery and the lawyer merely submits the claim on behalf of the client. But courts have also found that contingent fees may be appropriate in these types of cases, if the lawyer performs additional services relating to the recovery by the client. *See In re* Doyle, 581 N.E.2d 669 (Ill. 1991).

16. A recognition of the amount of additional work required to take a case through trial and appeals is reflected by several states which cap percentage fees in certain types of cases but allow the percentage charged to rise after certain milestones, i.e., 25% if settled before trial, 33 1/2% if tried. *See* New Jersey Ct. R. 1.27(C)(f) (limiting fees in tort cases involving minors). States have also mandated differing percentages depending on the amount recovered. *See* N.Y. Jud. L. § 474-A (McKinneys 1994 Supp.); Conn. Gen. St. Ann. §52-251(c) (1991).

F. Following an Early Settlement Offer Which the Client Rejects, It Is Ethical for a Lawyer to Collect a Contingent Fee Based on the Entire Recovery, Including That Portion Which Was the Subject of an Early Settlement Offer

The analysis in the preceding section regarding early settlement offers, however, does not mean, as an inquirer[17] has suggested, that in order to pass ethical muster a contingent fee agreement must limit the percentage recovery on the amount originally offered to the same small percentage suggested in Part E, if the client rejects the early offer, takes the case to trial and recovers no more than what was originally offered. In that example it would be ethical for the lawyer to provide for a significantly higher percentage contingent fee on the amount originally offered if the client chooses to go the full trial route. This higher fee would recognize the substantial time and effort that is required to take the matter to trial as well as the lawyer's assumption of the real risk that the plaintiffs will lose on the merits or that any judgment at trial may be less than the early offer.

The problem created by the inquirer's proposed limitation of the lawyer's contingent fee is that such a limitation penalizes both plaintiff and lawyer in cases where, even though liability is clear, there is an honest disagreement between the parties as to the amount owed in damages. Under those circumstances the plaintiff is entitled to reject the early offer and take his claim to a judge or jury represented by a fully compensated lawyer of his choosing. The circumstance that the fact finder eventually agrees with the defendant's evaluation of the case provides no ethical reason to interfere with a mutually agreed-upon contingent fee arrangement that was reasonable and appropriate at the onset of representation.[18] Such interference is particularly inappropriate given the fact that Model Rule 1.2 makes it clear that all decisions regarding the objectives of representation, including the acceptance and rejection of settlement offers, are solely those of the client. It is the lawyer who is bound by the client's decision, not the other way around. The inquirer's proposal, however, results in the lawyer being penalized because she is required to pass on the client's rejection of the early offer and press forward with the litigation to a stage of the proceedings that the client chooses.

The argument for limiting contingent fees on the amount of an early offer finds no support in the ethical rules and seems to be based on the assumption that by making an early offer the defendant is conceding all liability up to that amount, thereby eradicating the possibility of non-recovery by the plaintiff. But early settlement offers are made for numerous reasons besides a concession of liability. And as any experienced trial lawyer knows, once an early settlement offer is

---

17. *See* note 10, *supra*.

18. It should be noted that under one suggested proposal the plaintiff's lawyer is penalized even if the fact finder agrees with the plaintiff's valuation of the case, because the proposal would limit any fee on the portion of the judgment which equals the early settlement offer even if much more is awarded after trial. *See* Brickman et al. *supra* note 10.

rejected, the defendant and its lawyer will, in most cases, do their best to defend both against the fact of liability and the amount of damages owed. There is generally a real risk to the client and to the lawyer being paid on a contingent fee basis that such a defense will be successful. It is ethical for the lawyer to be compensated for both the time she expends to defeat any such defenses and the risk she assumes that the plaintiff will not prevail at trial or that a judgment awarded may never be collected.

The lawyer is also being compensated for the risk she assumes that the client will fire the lawyer, a right the client might exercise at any time. *See Hiscott & Robinson v. King*, 626 A.2d 1235 (Pa. Super. 1993); *Covington v. Rhodes*, 247 S.E.2d 305 (N.C. App. 1978); Comment on Model Rule 1.16(a)(3) ("a client has a right to discharge a lawyer at any time, with or without cause"); DR 2-110(B)(4), or that the client will insist on proceeding with the litigation through appeals or otherwise longer than the lawyer would proceed, if it were the lawyer's, rather than the client's decision.[19] *See* Model Rule 1.2. Additionally, the lawyer is being compensated for the often lengthy delay between the time work is performed and the time a fee is received.

G. There Is No Ethical Requirement for a Plaintiff's Lawyer Whose Compensation Agreement Is Contingent on the Recovery to Solicit an Early Settlement Offer from the Defendant

An inquirer has asked whether, as an ethical matter, the plaintiff's lawyer must solicit an early offer of settlement. The Committee concludes that there is no such ethical requirement. First, neither the Model Rules nor the Model Code requires any such solicitation. Second, the suggestion seems inequitable as no reciprocal requirement for the defendant to make an early settlement offer is imposed. Any requirement to seek an early settlement offer would raise fundamental problems. Plaintiff's counsel, whether proceeding on a contingent fee basis or not, must be free (with appropriate consultation with the client) to select her own strategy. It may be that at the outset of the litigation, she doesn't have enough information about the defendant's conduct to make an intelligent evaluation of a settlement offer. For example, she may not know whether liability is clear or uncertain or whether exemplary damages may be available. Additionally, the plaintiff's damages at that juncture may still be a matter of significant uncertainty, with respect to either extent, permanence, or both. Finally, the plaintiff may have decided that he does not, under any circumstances, wish to settle or enter into settlement negotiations.

---

19. "The ordinary rule of construction of contingent fee contracts is that, absent an express provision otherwise, services rendered by the attorney in upholding a judgment on appeal are within the underlying contract." Attorney Grievance Commission v. Korotki, 569 A.2d 1224 (Md. 1990). *See also* New York City Ethics Opinion 1986-6; Michigan State Bar Committee on Professional & Judicial Ethics Formal Opinion R-11 (1991). Conversely, if the client decides to voluntarily dismiss a case that the lawyer considers meritorious and likely to succeed, the lawyer cannot recover on a contingent fee contract.

As an ethical matter, these are all matters to be decided between lawyer and client; there is no ground in the Model Rules for suggesting that the lawyer who is retained on a contingent basis and the plaintiff who retained her should be any less free than a lawyer who is compensated on some other basis to decide with her client whether and when to solicit or make a settlement offer. While the ethical rules require that any strategy pursued by the lawyer be directed to the client's best interests, it is not the role of the ethical rules to force lawyers to follow any specific litigation strategy or approach. Additionally, any proposed rule that seeks to dictate a particular strategy in all cases would be in conflict with Model Rule 2.1 which requires a lawyer to exercise her independent professional judgment on behalf of her client.

H. The Contingent Fee Arrangement Must Be Reasonable

In addition to the requirement that a fee be appropriate, Model Rule 1.5 requires that the fee, whether based on an hourly rate, a contingent percentage or some other basis, "shall be reasonable." Similarly, DR 2-106 prohibits a "clearly excessive fee," which is in turn defined as a "fee . . . in excess of a reasonable fee."[20]

In deciding whether a contingent fee arrangement is reasonable the lawyer must consider the following factors set forth in Model Rule 1.5(a):

(1) the time and labor required, the novelty and difficulty of the questions involved, and the skill requisite to perform the legal service properly;
(2) the likelihood, if apparent to the client, that the acceptance of the particular employment will preclude other employment by the lawyer;
(3) the fee customarily charged in the locality for similar legal services;
(4) the amount involved and the results obtained;
(5) the time limitations imposed by the client or by the circumstances;
(6) the nature and length of the professional relationship with the client;
(7) the experience, reputation, and ability of the lawyer or lawyers performing the services.

Additionally, the lawyer must look again at, and discuss with the client, the factors that were considered in reviewing the appropriateness of the fee, discussed in Section C above.

We stress that the lawyer should take all these factors into account in evaluating every case. *See* ABA Formal Opinion 329 (1972). For this reason, a lawyer who always charges the same percentage of recovery regardless of the particulars of a case should consider whether he is charging a fee that is, in an ethical context, a reasonable one. One standard fee for all cases may have the effect, given the difference among cases, of both over- and under-compensating the lawyer. *Cf. In re Recorder's Court Bar Association v. Wayne Circuit Court*, 503 N.W.2d 885

20. DR 2-106 provides that "[a] lawyer shall not enter into an agreement for, charge, or collect an illegal or clearly excessive fee." A fee is "clearly excessive" under DR 2-106 "when, after a review of the facts, a lawyer of ordinary prudence would be left with a definite and firm conviction that the fee is in excess of a reasonable fee."

(Mich. 1993) (finding that a fixed fee system for compensating attorneys who represented indigent defendants that did not take into account the particulars of the case was unreasonable).

As with the question of appropriateness, the mere fact that liability may be clear and that some recovery is likely does not *per se* make any given contingent fee unreasonable. It is important to keep in mind that the reasonableness as well as the appropriateness of a fee arrangement necessarily must be judged at the time it is entered into. All contingent fee agreements carry certain risks: the risk that the case will require substantially more work than the lawyer anticipated; the risk that there will be no judgment, or only an unenforceable one; the risk of changes in the law; the risk that the client will dismiss the lawyer, and the risk that the client will require the lawyer to reject what the lawyer considers a good settlement or otherwise to continue the proceedings much further than in the lawyer's judgment they should be pursued. If a lawyer accepts a given risk—for example, the risk posed by the fact that the opposing party has a reputation for being intransigent in its approach to settlement—and offers a fee contract reflecting that risk, which is accepted by a fully informed client, the lawyer should not be required as a matter of ethics to give up the benefit of the agreement because the opposing party, to everyone's surprise, offers an early settlement that is acceptable to the client.[21] By the same token, a later development that increases the risk to the lawyer—for example, a statutorily imposed cap on liability, the loss of a summary judgment motion everyone expected to win, or the need to take three times the number of depositions originally anticipated—should not permit the lawyer to demand a new, more generous fee arrangement.[22]

I. The Percentage of a Contingent Fee May as an Ethical Matter Be Increased On the Basis of How Far the Lawyer Must Proceed in Prosecuting the Case

The Committee has also been asked whether it is ethical for a lawyer and client to enter into a fee agreement that provides for higher contingent fees after spe-

21. Brickman, *supra* note 4, at 87 ("It is not the actual effort expended by the attorney that is determinative of the legitimacy of the fee, but what a good faith, professionally informed estimate of anticipated effort and risk of non-recovery would have been prior to the *commencement of representation*"). (Emphasis added.)

22. *See, e.g.*, Chase v. Gilbert, 499 A.2d 1203 (D.C. 1985) (A lawyer cannot modify a fee agreement even if he ends up performing significantly more services than were contemplated when agreement was entered into). Because reasonableness is judged at the time the contract is entered into, there is nothing necessarily unethical about charging a contingent fee on the portion of any recovery that is equal to an early settlement offer. *See* ABA Formal Opinion 329 ("[n]o reasonable method of fixing fees which takes into account the factors of DR 2-106(B) is proscribed by the Code of Professional Responsibility"). It should be noted, however, that extreme changes in circumstances occurring after negotiation of the fee agreement may lead a reviewing court to decide, ex post facto, that payment of the fee is unreasonable. *See, e.g.*, Mckenzie Construction Inc. v. Maynard, 758 F.2d 97 (3d Cir.1985).

cific benchmarks, for example, 25% if the case settles within six months and 33% after trial. The higher contingent fee at advanced stages of the matter is meant to compensate the lawyer for the additional time and labor necessary in the case. As demonstrated in the factors set forth in Model Rule 1.5(a) set out above, the time and labor involved in a matter are among the reasonable bases for setting a fee. Therefore, it is the Committee's opinion that such a fee agreement is ethical as long as the overall fee is appropriate and reasonable. *See, e.g.,* Philadelphia Bar Association Ethics Opinion 93-11 (approving such a fee arrangement).

J. The Percentage of a Contingent Fee May Increase with the Amount of the Recovery

Finally, the Committee has been asked whether it is ethical for a lawyer to enter into a fee agreement that provides for a higher percentage fee as the amount of the recovery goes up or the amount of the savings increases: for example, 15% on the first $100,000 recovered or saved, 20% on the next hundred thousand, and 25% on everything thereafter. Such an arrangement on its face runs contrary to what several states have mandated in terms of reducing the percentage recovery as the amount recovered rises.[23] Nonetheless, as a matter of ethics, the Committee is of the view that a percentage that increases with the amount of the recovery can be permissible. Model Rule 1.5(a) refers, in connection with the reasonableness of a fee, to "results obtained," and the "ability of the lawyer or lawyers performing the services" as factors that may be considered. Since a higher recovery would, by definition, reflect the first of these factors and, in all likelihood, reflect the other as well, the Committee is of the view that such a fee agreement is ethical, so long as the matter for which the fee is charged is appropriate and the amount of the fee is reasonable. Indeed, many would say that this form of contingent fee agreement more closely rewards the effort and ability the lawyer brings to the engagement than does a straight percentage fee arrangement, since everyone would agree that it is the last dollars, not the first dollars, of recovery that require the greatest effort and/or ability on the part of the lawyer. It may be that any lawyer would have been able to achieve a $100,000 verdict for a given plaintiff's injuries, but that only the most skilled would have been able to secure a $500,000 award plus an additional sum for exemplary damages.

K. Conclusion

A lawyer entering into a contingent fee arrangement complies with the ethical standards set forth in both the Model Rules of Professional Conduct and the Model Code of Professional Responsibility if the fee is both appropriate and reasonable and if the client has been fully informed of all appropriate alternative billing arrangements and their implications. Contingent fee arrangements are appropriate for both the affluent and those who cannot otherwise afford the lawyer's services.

23. *See* Calif. Bus. & Prof. Code §6146 (West 1990); *see also* note 16, *supra.*

It is not necessarily unethical to charge a contingent fee when liability is clear and some recovery is anticipated. A lawyer compensated on a contingent basis has no obligation to solicit on behalf of the client an early settlement offer; further, she may collect a contingent fee on the total recovery, including any amount that was the subject of an early settlement offer. Finally, a lawyer may charge a different contingent fee at different stages of a matter, and may increase the percentage taken as a fee as the amount of the recovery or savings to the client increases.

Formal Opinion 95-390 January 25, 1995
Conflicts of Interest in the Corporate Family Context

A lawyer who represents a corporate client is not by that fact alone necessarily barred from a representation that is adverse to a corporate affiliate of that client in an unrelated matter. However, a lawyer may not accept such a representation without consent of the corporate client if the circumstances are such that the affiliate should also be considered a client of the lawyer; or if there is an understanding between the lawyer and the corporate client that the lawyer will avoid representations adverse to the client's corporate affiliates; or if the lawyer's obligations to either the corporate client or the new, adverse client, will materially limit the lawyer's representation of the other client. Even if the circumstances are such that client consent is not ethically required, as a matter of prudence and good practice a lawyer who contemplates undertaking a representation adverse to a corporate affiliate of a client will be well advised to discuss the matter with the client before undertaking the representation.

The Committee has been asked whether a lawyer who represents a corporate client may undertake a representation that is adverse to a corporate affiliate of the client in an unrelated matter, without obtaining the client's consent.

The issue is one that has arisen with increasing frequency because of "[t]he proliferation of national or multi-national public corporations owning or partially owning subsidiaries which may also be national or multi-national [and] the spawning of varied types of corporate affiliates . . . ." *Pennwalt Corp. v. Plough, Inc.*, 85 F.R.D. 264, 267 (D. Del. 1980). Although, in the sense described in *Pennwalt*, the problem has been "created" by modern corporations, the onus is squarely on the lawyer to anticipate and resolve conflicts of interest involving corporate affiliates. *Id.* at 273. As stated in the Comment to Rule 1.7 of the Model Rules of Professional Conduct (1983, amended 1994):

> The lawyer should adopt reasonable procedures, appropriate for the size and type of firm and practice, to determine in both litigation and non-litigation matters the parties and issues involved and to determine whether there are actual or potential conflicts of interest.

In addition to the ethical questions that a lawyer may face in undertaking a representation adverse to an affiliate of an existing corporate client, the lawyer also faces a potential motion to disqualify. Indeed, these circumstances have been considered most often in the context of such a motion.[1]

1. *E.g.*, Vanderveer Group, Inc. v. Petruny, No. Civ. A. 93-3677, 1993 WL 308720 (E.D. Pa. Aug. 13, 1993); Stratagem Dev. Corp. v. Heron Int'l N.V., 756 F. Supp. 789 (S.D.N.Y. 1991); Teradyne, Inc. v. Hewlett-Packard Co., 20 U.S.P.Q.2d (BNA) 1143 (N.D. Cal. 1991); Gould, Inc. v. Mitsui Mining & Smelting Co., 738 F. Supp. 1121 (N.D. Ohio 1990); Hartford Accident

Clearly, the best solution to the problems that may arise by reason of clients' corporate affiliations is to have a clear understanding between lawyer and client, at the very start of the representation, as to which entity or entities in the corporate family are to be the lawyer's clients, or are to be so treated for conflicts purposes. This Opinion is principally addressed to those circumstances where there are not such clear governing terms to the engagement. Such circumstances will frequently obtain simply because the relationship with the client is of long standing, antedating the time when letters of engagement came into common use; or because there is a change in the identity or the corporate affiliations of the client, through acquisitions, mergers and the like.

Even in circumstances where there is no established understanding about the lawyer's obligations toward affiliates of the client, considerations of client relations will ordinarily dictate the lawyer's course of action, without the occasion even arising to consider whether the Model Rules forbid the contemplated new representation. Nonetheless, there will sometimes be circumstances where the requirements of the Model Rules rather than considerations of client relations will govern: for example, where by virtue of merger or acquisition the corporate affiliation of the client changes.

It is the Committee's opinion that the Model Rules of Professional Conduct do not prohibit a lawyer from representing a party adverse to a particular corporation merely because the lawyer (or another lawyer in the same firm) represents, in an unrelated matter, another corporation that owns the potentially adverse corporation, or is owned by it, or is, together with the adverse corporation, owned by a third entity.[2] The fact of corporate affiliation, without more, does not make all of a corporate client's affiliates into clients as well. Nonetheless, the circumstances of a particular representation may be such that the corporate client has a reasonable expectation that the affiliates will be treated as clients, either generally or for purposes of avoidance of conflicts, and the lawyer is aware of the expectation.

In any event, although the ethical propriety of a given representation will

& Indem. Co. v. RJR Nabisco, Inc., 721 F. Supp. 534 (S.D.N.Y. 1989); Pennwalt Corp. v. Plough, Inc., 85 F.R.D. 264 (D. Del. 1980).

2. We here principally address, for simplicity of analysis, situations where the subsidiaries in the corporate family are wholly owned by the corporate parent. Corporate affiliations involving lesser degrees of ownership may of course present the same issues, and involve in some degree the same analysis, as those involving whole ownership. The circumstance of only partial ownership, however, is a variable that may affect the result in a particular case. *E.g.*, Whiting Corp. v. White Mach. Corp., 567 F.2d 713, 714-15 (7th Cir. 1977) (court refused to disqualify counsel where counsel represented both plaintiff and a corporation that owned 20% of the defendant corporation's stock and had the right to elect 40% of its board of directors); *see also* Vanderveer Group, Inc. v. Petruny, No. Civ.A 93-3677, 1993 WL 308720 (E.D. Pa. Aug. 13, 1993) (a law firm's representation of defendant company's 51%-owned subsidiary does not require the firm's disqualification from representing the plaintiff; the decision does not, however, rely on the degree of ownership).

depend on the particular circumstances, the Committee believes that as a general matter, in the absence of a clear understanding otherwise, the better course is for a lawyer to obtain the corporate client's consent before the lawyer undertakes a representation adverse to its affiliate.

The Requirements of Rule 1.7

The key provision of the Model Rules is Rule 1.7, which provides in pertinent part as follows:

(a) A lawyer shall not represent a client if the representation of that client will be directly adverse to another client, unless:
  (1) the lawyer reasonably believes the representation will not adversely affect the relationship with the other client; and
  (2) each client consents after consultation.

(b) A lawyer shall not represent a client if the representation of that client may be materially limited by the lawyer's responsibilities to another client or to a third person . . . unless:
  (1) the lawyer reasonably believes the representation will not be adversely affected; and
  (2) the client consents after consultation.

Rule 1.7 is a rule of general applicability, governing lawyers' conduct whether they represent individuals or entities. The touchstone of the Rule, as the Comment to it makes clear, is loyalty to the client.

When requested to undertake a new representation that may adversely affect the interests of an existing client, a lawyer must first consider Rule 1.7(a). Under that provision, representation of a party "directly adverse to another client" is prohibited unless a lawyer concludes that his relationship with the existing client will not be "adversely affected" by the new representation, and both clients consent. The use of the term "directly adverse" in Rule 1.7(a) clearly differentiates the more general or indirect adverseness which is addressed in paragraph (b) of the Rule, discussed below. The Comment to Rule 1.7 confirms this interpretation of the term "directly," noting that "a lawyer ordinarily may not act as advocate against a person the lawyer represents in some other matter, even if it is wholly unrelated," but "simultaneous representation in unrelated matters of clients whose interests are only generally adverse, such as competing economic enterprises, does not require consent of the respective clients."

Where there is direct adverseness, so that Rule 1.7(a) applies, the lawyer may not take on the new representation unless two tests are met. First, the lawyer must reasonably believe that his new assignment will not adversely affect his relationship with his existing client. The lawyer's subjective judgment is not necessarily dispositive: his belief must be a reasonable one. *See Clay v. Doherty*, 608 F. Supp. 295, 302 (N.D. Ill. 1985); Charles W. Wolfram, *Modern Legal Ethics* § 7.2.3 (Student ed. 1986).

Second, both clients must consent after "consultation," which means that there has been "communication of information reasonably sufficient to permit the client to appreciate the significance of the matter in question." Model Rules, Terminology.

If the provisions of Rule 1.7(a) do not apply because the affiliate is not a client, the lawyer must nonetheless consider, under Rule 1.7(b), whether either the subsisting representation or the prospective one may be "materially limited by the lawyer's responsibilities to another client or to a third person." Loyalty to a client is impaired not only when a lawyer undertakes a representation directly adverse to the client, but also "when a lawyer cannot consider, recommend or carry out an appropriate course of action for the client because of the lawyer's other responsibilities or interests." Comment to Model Rule 1.7. Where the new representation will be materially limited by the lawyer's responsibilities to an existing client, the new representation is prohibited by Rule 1.7(b) unless the lawyer reasonably believes that the new representation will not be "adversely affected" by the limitations flowing from his duties to another client or third person, and the new client consents. Conversely, the lawyer must also consider under Rule 1.7(b) whether the lawyer's representation of his existing client would be materially limited by his duties to the new client.[3] By its terms, Rule 1.7(b) requires the consent only of the client whose representation may be materially limited by the lawyer's other duties, but the lawyer must consider the effect of the simultaneous representation of two clients on each of them, and obtain consent where required by the Rule.

* * *

The application of these provisions in the circumstances before us can best be addressed in relation to three questions: (1) Is the corporate client's affiliate also a client, or entitled to be so treated for purposes of Rule 1.7? (2) If the affiliate is not a client, is the representation adverse to the affiliate also "directly adverse" to the corporate client, so as to bring it under Rule 1.7(a)? (3) If Rule 1.7(a) is not applicable, will the lawyer's responsibilities to one or the other client nonetheless materially limit the lawyer's representation so as to bring Rule 1.7(b) into play?

(1) Is the Corporate Client's Affiliate Also a Client?

Since a lawyer owes a duty of loyalty only to the lawyer's client, it is necessary to determine at the outset of analysis whether the affiliate of the lawyer's corporate client is also a client. As explained below, we conclude that the fact of corporate affiliation, without more, does not necessarily make the affiliate of a corporate client also a client. Nonetheless, the particular circumstances may be such that the affiliate also should be considered a client. It may also be the case that the corporate client has an expectation, binding on the lawyer in the circumstances, that its affiliates will be treated as clients for purposes of addressing con-

3. As the Comment makes clear, Rule 1.7 applies not merely to new representations but also to conflicts arising after a representation has commenced.

flicts under Rule 1.7, even though there is not a full-fledged client-lawyer relationship with the affiliates.

As to whether the fact of corporate affiliation *ipso facto* creates a client-lawyer relationship with every member of a corporate family when one of its members is formally represented by the lawyer, the Model Rules are silent. It is possible to read the following passage in the Comment to Rule 1.7 as assuming that such a relationship necessarily exists:

> Ordinarily, a lawyer may not act as advocate against a client the lawyer represents in some other matter, even if the other matter is wholly unrelated. However, there are circumstances in which a lawyer may act as advocate against a client. For example, *a lawyer representing an enterprise with diverse operations may accept employment as an advocate against the enterprise in an unrelated matter if doing so will not adversely affect the lawyer's relationship with the enterprise . . . and if both clients consent upon consultation.* (Emphasis added.)

The statement that a representation adverse to "an enterprise with diverse operations" requires the consent of both clients may be taken to imply that a lawyer who represents a corporation represents all of its affiliates, since in this context the term "enterprise" can be understood as referring not merely to a corporation with various divisions or product lines but also to a family of corporations. However, the use of "enterprise" in this connection does not refer to a corporate conglomerate; the term is used in the Model Rules, in distinction from "corporation" and "organization," to denote profit-making entities, which may include not only corporations but also partnerships, joint ventures and the like.[4]

Moreover, Rule 1.13 squarely states that when a lawyer represents an "organization"—a term that clearly includes corporations—it is the organization that is the lawyer's client. Its constituents, including its stockholders, are not also the lawyer's clients solely because of their relationship to the client. Rule 1.13(e) contemplates that a client-lawyer relationship between a constituent, including a stockholder, and corporate counsel, must be specifically formed, rather than arising automatically by virtue of the client-lawyer relationship with the organization.[5]

To be sure, Rule 1.13 does not directly address the question of when an affiliate of a corporate client is also a client, for the thrust of the Rule is to require the lawyer to distinguish between the corporation or other organization, which is his

4. *See* Comments to Rule 1.5, Rule 2.2, and Rule 5.1. Where a generic term including not only corporations and other profit-making enterprises but non-profit entities as well is called for, the term "organization" is used in the Model Rules: *see, e.g.,* Rule 1.13.

5. Rule 1.13(e) provides:

> A lawyer representing an organization may also represent any of its directors, officers, employees, members, shareholders or other constituents, subject to the provisions of Rule 1.7. If the organization's consent to the dual representation is required by Rule 1.7, the consent shall be given by an appropriate official of the organization other than the individual who is to be represented, or by the shareholders.

client, and the human representatives of the corporation, with whom the lawyer works and often forms personal relationships.[6]

Nonetheless, in light of the general proposition embodied in Model Rule 1.13, that an organization is separate from its constituents, construing the Comment to Rule 1.7 as establishing that all of a corporate client's affiliates should be considered clients of a lawyer is unwarranted. No court or ethics committee that has considered the general question of representation of corporate affiliates has given this construction to the Comment to Rule 1.7.

We conclude, therefore, that whether a lawyer represents a corporate affiliate of his client, for purposes of Rule 1.7, depends not upon any clearcut per se rule but rather upon the particular circumstances.

The Model Rules do not directly address the question of when or how a client-lawyer relationship has been established: that is a matter governed by substantive law outside the Model Rules. *See* Model Rules, Scope Section:

> [F]or purposes of determining the lawyer's authority and responsibility, principles of substantive law external to these Rules determine whether a client-lawyer relationship exists. . . . Whether a client-lawyer relationship exists for any specific purpose can depend on the circumstances and may be a question of fact.

The client-lawyer relationship is principally a matter of contract, and the contract may be either express or implied. Thus, the entities within a corporate family that are to be considered clients may have been expressly identified as clients, or they may have become entitled to be so treated by reason of the way the representation of one of the members of the corporate family has been handled. In addition, it may be one of the terms of the engagement that the corporate client expects some or all of its affiliates to be treated as clients *for purposes of Rule 1.7*—i.e., that the lawyer will not accept engagements that would be prohibited by that Rule if the affiliates were clients.[7]

Clearly, a corporate affiliate must be treated as a client, whether generally or only for purposes of Rule 1.7, if the lawyer has agreed so to treat it, regardless of whether any actual work has been or is to be performed for the affiliate. Clearly also, it is important that lawyer and client share an understanding as to whether

6. *See* ABA/BNA LAW. MAN. ON PROF. CONDUCT 91:2002 (1994):

> Because a lawyer who represents a corporation necessarily must deal with individuals—be they directors, officers and other employees, or shareholders—it is tempting to view some of them, or all of them collectively, as clients. Absent special circumstances, however, the rule of law applied by the courts, and the rule of professional responsibility that guides disciplinary authorities, is that the lawyer must view the corporation itself as the client, and in his or her representation must work for the best interest of the corporation.

7. Such an understanding between the lawyer and the corporate client that the lawyer will refrain from representations adverse to the corporate affiliates of the client does not in itself establish a full-fledged client-lawyer relationship with the affiliates.

the client expects the lawyer to observe obligations to persons or entities other than the client itself, for that information is necessary for the lawyer to make the appropriate inquiries under Model Rule 1.7 to determine whether he can undertake the representation. Moreover, a client that has such an expectation has an obligation to keep the lawyer apprised of changes in the composition of the corporate family. While competent general counsel can be expected to be familiar with the corporate family and the expectations of one member as to the treatment of other members, outside lawyers who are performing only a limited role for a single aspect of the business, no matter how well-intentioned, should not be expected to be current on all of the names, relationships and ownership interests among a client's varied and sometimes far-flung business interests. A lawyer who has no reason to know that his potential adversary is an affiliate of his client will not necessarily violate Rule 1.7 by accepting the new representation without his client's consent. *See, e.g., Pennwalt Corp. v. Plough, Inc.*, 85 F.R.D. 264, 266 (D. Del. 1980).

A client-lawyer relationship does not, however, require an explicit agreement, let alone a written letter of engagement: it may come into being as a result of reasonable expectations and a failure of the lawyer to dispel those expectations. *See* Restatement (Third) of The Law Governing Lawyers § 26 (Tent. Draft No. 5, 1992):

§26. Formation of a Client-Lawyer Relationship

A relationship of client and lawyer arises when:

(1) *A person manifests to a lawyer the person's intent that the lawyer provide legal services for the person; and*

(2) (a) *The lawyer* manifests to the person consent to do so, or (b) *fails to manifest lack of consent to do so, when the lawyer knows or reasonably should know that the person reasonably relies on the lawyer to provide the services*, or (c) a tribunal with power to do so appoints the lawyer to provide the services. (Emphasis added.)

See also Westinghouse Elec. Corp. v. Kerr-McGee Corp., 580 F.2d 1311 (7th Cir.), *cert. denied*, 439 U.S. 955 (1978):

> [A]n attorney-client relationship does not arise only in the agency manner such as when the parties expressly or impliedly consent to its formation . . . . [It] is not dependent upon the payment of fees [or] . . . upon the execution of a formal contract.

Thus, when a lawyer is considering whether he can assume the representation adverse to a corporate affiliate of a client, he must consider not merely the terms of his engagement to that client but in addition whether the circumstances are such that the affiliate has reason to believe, on the basis of the nature of the lawyer's dealings with it, that it has a client-lawyer relationship with the lawyer.

Our Formal Opinions 91-361 (Representation of a Partnership) (1991) and 92-365 (Trade Associations as Clients) (1992) identify some of the circumstances that will bear on whether an affiliate of a lawyer's corporate client must also be considered a client of the lawyer.

In Formal Opinion 91-361, we considered whether a lawyer who represents a partnership also represents the individual partners. We concluded that the lawyer does not represent the partners merely because he represents the partnership, but that in particular circumstances the lawyer might be found to represent individual partners as well. We stated:

> Whether such a relationship has been created almost always will depend on an analysis of the specific facts involved. The analysis may include such factors as whether the lawyer affirmatively assumed a duty of representation to the individual partner, whether the partner was separately represented by other counsel when the partnership was created or in connection with its affairs, whether the lawyer had represented an individual partner before undertaking to represent the partnership, and whether there was evidence of reliance by the individual partner on the lawyer as his or her separate counsel, or evidence of the partner's expectation of personal representation.

Similarly, in Formal Opinion 92-365, we opined that a lawyer who represents a trade association does not merely by reason of that fact have a client-lawyer relationship with individual members of the association. We stated:

> [D]etermining whether and to what extent the individual member has become a client requires careful examination of all of the circumstances of the lawyer's relationship to and representation of the trade association. Particularly important is an inquiry into what the member may have disclosed to the lawyer, under what circumstances and with what expectations.
>
> * * *
>
> A fiduciary relationship may result because of the nature of the work performed and the circumstances under which confidential information is divulged.

The analysis in those Opinions is equally applicable here. Thus, the nature of the lawyer's dealings with affiliates of the corporate client may be such that they have become clients as well. This may be the case, for example, where the lawyer's work for the corporate parent—say, on a stock issue or bank financing—is intended to benefit all subsidiaries, and involves collecting confidential information from all of them.

Even if the subject matter of the lawyer's representation of the corporate client does not involve the affiliate at all, however, the lawyer's relationship with the corporate affiliate may lead the affiliate reasonably to believe that it is a client of the lawyer. For example, the fact that a lawyer for a subsidiary was engaged by and reports to an officer or general counsel for its parent may support the inference that the corporate parent reasonably expects to be treated as a client. *See, e.g., Teradyne, Inc. v. Hewlett-Packard Co.*, 20 U.S.P.Q. 2d (BNA) 1143, 1144-45 (N.D. Cal. 1991); *Hartford Accident & Indem. Co. v. RJR Nabisco, Inc.*, 721 F. Supp. 534, 540 (S.D.N.Y. 1989).

A client-lawyer relationship with the affiliate may also arise because the affiliate imparted confidential information to the lawyer with the expectation that the lawyer would use it in representing the affiliate. *See, e.g., Westinghouse Elec. Corp. v. Kerr-McGee Corp.*, 580 F.2d 1311 (7th Cir.), *cert. denied*, 439 U.S. 955 (1978). Additionally, even if the affiliate confiding information does not expect that the lawyer will be *representing* the affiliate, there may well be a reasonable view on the part of the client that the information was imparted in furtherance of the representation, creating an ethically binding obligation that the lawyer will not use the information against the interests of any member of the corporate family.

Finally, the relationship of the corporate client to its affiliate may be such that the lawyer is required to regard the affiliate as his client. This would clearly be true where one corporation is the alter ego of the other. It is not necessary, however, for one corporation to be the alter ego of the other as a matter of law in order for both to be considered clients. A disregard of corporate formalities and/or a complete identity of managements and boards of directors could call for treating the two corporations as one. As stated by the court in *Teradyne*, supra (quoting Formal Opinion No. 1989-113 of the State Bar of California Standing Committee on Professional Responsibility and Conduct):

> In determining whether there is a sufficient unity of interests to require an attorney to disregard separate corporate entities for conflict purposes, the attorney should evaluate whether corporate formalities are observed, the extent to which each entity has distinct and independent managements and boards of directors and whether, for legal purposes, one entity could be considered the alter ego of the other.

20 U.S.P.Q. 2d at 1146.

The fact that the corporate client wholly owns, or is wholly owned by, its affiliate does not in itself make them alter egos. However, whole ownership may well entail not merely a shared legal department but a management so intertwined that all members of the corporate family effectively operate as a single entity; and in those circumstances representing one member of the family may effectively mean representing all the others as well. Conversely, where two corporations are related only through stock ownership, the ownership is less than a controlling interest and the lawyer has had no dealing whatever with the affiliate, there will rarely be any reason to conclude that the affiliate is the lawyer's client.[8]

8. *Cf.* Whiting Corp. v. White Mach. Corp., 567 F.2d 713, 714-15 (7th Cir. 1977) (court refused to disqualify counsel where counsel represented both plaintiff and a corporation which owned 20% of the defendant corporation and had the power to appoint 40 percent of its Board).

(2) Is the Representation Affecting the Affiliate "Directly Adverse" to the Client?

Even though the corporation against which the lawyer is considering an adverse representation clearly is not the lawyer's client (or entitled for purposes of Rule 1.7 to be treated as such), the corporation that is a client may argue that the representation is nonetheless "directly adverse" to it, because any potential economic impact on the affiliate entails an impact on the corporation itself.

The paradigm situation here is presented by a lawyer's bringing a lawsuit, unrelated in substance to the lawyer's representation of a corporate client, seeking substantial money damages against a wholly owned subsidiary of the client: if the suit is successful, this will affect adversely not only the subsidiary but the parent as well, in the sense that one of its assets is the equity in the subsidiary, and its consolidated financial statements may (unless the subsidiary has applicable insurance coverage) reflect the impact of material adverse judgments against the subsidiary. *See Stratagem Dev. Corp. v. Heron Int'l N.V.*, 756 F. Supp 789, 792 (S.D.N.Y. 1991) ("the liabilities of a subsidiary corporation directly affect the bottom line of the corporate parent").[9] It may also be the case, although less often, that a suit against a *parent* corporation will have a similarly direct economic impact on a wholly-owned subsidiary (absent an "alter ego" situation),[10] or that a corporation will be directly affected by a suit against a sibling corporation.[11]

The critical question is whether, in any of the situations referred to above, the representation is, as to the corporate client, *directly* adverse, so as to fall under Rule 1.7(a); or only *indirectly* adverse, so that Rule 1.7(b) is the only potentially applicable provision. Although there is room for dispute on the point, we believe the better view is that the adverseness in such circumstances is indirect, and not direct.

This Committee has not previously addressed this question, although it has considered the general issue of direct and indirect adverseness in two recent opinions. In Formal Opinion 92-367 (Lawyer Examining a Client as an Adverse Witness (1992), or Conducting Third Party Discovery of the Client), we addressed the question whether a lawyer representing a client in litigation in which another client is a nonparty witness may cross-examine, or seek nonparty discovery from, that other client. We opined that the general circumstances (two clients involved in the same litigation, but one as a party and the other as a nonparty witness) might involve either direct or indirect adverseness, so as to fall under either Rule 1.7(a) or 1.7(b). If the representation involved attacking the conduct or credibility of the

9. *See also* Telesat Cable Television, Inc. v. Opryland, USA, Inc., No. 90-137-CIV-ORL-19, 1990 WL 303150 (M.D. Fla. July 25, 1990) (holding impermissible a representation adverse to the interests of a third-tier subsidiary of a client).

10. *Cf.* Vanderveer Group, Inc. v. Petruny, No. Civ.A. 93-3677, 1993 WL 308720 at *3 (E.D. Pa. Aug. 13, 1993) (rejecting claim that suit against corporate parent of a client was "directly adverse" to the client).

11. *Cf.* Pennwalt Corp. v. Plough, Inc., 85 F.R.D. 264 (D. Del 1980) (declining to disqualify a firm from a representation adverse to a sibling of the firm's corporate client).

second client, or seeking to compel resisted discovery from the client, we concluded that the representation would be "directly adverse" to the witness client, because "any advantage gained by the lawyer in representation of the litigation client necessarily entails some concrete disadvantage to the [witness] client." In Formal Opinion 93-377 (Positional Conflicts) (1993), on the other hand, we held that representation of two clients in different suits, where one suit may create a legal precedent that materially undercuts the position being advanced for the client in the other suit, presents a conflict under Rule 1.7(b), not a "directly adverse" representation under Rule 1.7(a). We there explained (in footnote 4):

> Where there is such a conflict between separate representations, in the Committee's view the provision of Rule 1.7 that is potentially applicable is not paragraph (a), but paragraph (b). The former, in referring to a representation that is "directly adverse" to another client, contemplates litigating, or maintaining a position, in a given matter, on behalf of one client against a person or entity which is a client of the lawyer (or her firm) in another matter. The test under paragraph (b), on the other hand, is whether the representation of a client in one matter may be "materially limited" by the lawyer's responsibilities to another client in another matter, and the Committee views the impairment of a representation as a material limitation within the meaning of that paragraph.

Thus, we have interpreted "directly adverse" to refer not merely to the practical impact (on the adversely affected client) but also to the circumstances in which the conflict arises, and specifically the closeness of the connection between the lawyer's actions and the adverse effect on the client. As a prominent treatise observes in this connection,

> The direct-remote distinction . . . calls attention not simply to the clients' general economic interests, but specifically to the transactions in which the clients employ the lawyer's services.

1 Geoffrey C. Hazard & William W. Hodes, *The Law of Lawyering* § 1.7.203 (2d ed. 1990).[12]

We conclude, then, that although in situations involving an unrelated suit against an affiliate of a corporate client, the client may be adversely affected, that adverseness is, for purposes of Rule 1.7, indirect rather than direct, since its immediate impact is on the affiliate, and only derivatively upon the client. The phrasing of Rule 1.7(a) is not ambiguous: the reference to a representation that is "directly adverse" clearly draws a distinction between direct and indirect adverse-

12. *See also* ANNOTATED MODEL RULES OF PROFESSIONAL CONDUCT RULE 1.7 at 112-13 (2d ed. 1992):

> Simultaneous representation of clients in different lawsuits but which involve a related matter can also give rise to the direct, impermissible conflict proscribed by Rule 1.7(a).

ness, and thereby draws a bright line striking a balance between the interests of lawyer and client. If the proposed representation is directly adverse to a client, the client may veto its opponent's choice of counsel. A lawyer may not undertake litigation against a client without that client's consent, and the client may decline consent for any reason or no reason at all. Rule 1.7(a) thus establishes a per se rule, but its reach is appropriately limited to cases in which a lawyer is asked to undertake a matter that is "directly adverse" to an existing client. In all other cases, the client's only recourse is to fire the lawyer who undertakes a matter that displeases the client. Moreover, we see no principled way otherwise to draw a line short of the point where *any* discernible economic impact on a client arising from another representation (however slight or remote) must be treated as direct adverseness, requiring application of Rule 1.7(a) rather than Rule 1.7(b).

We recognize that there is some authority for a broader reading of "directly adverse."[13] However, we think the foregoing analysis represents a sounder approach to Rule 1.7.

(3) If Rule 1.7(a) Is Not Applicable, Is the Representation Nonetheless Barred by Rule 1.7(b)?

As has been discussed above, even if it is determined that Rule 1.7(a) does not bar a particular representation adverse to an affiliate of a corporate client, because the affiliate is not also a client and the representation is not directly adverse to the corporate client, the lawyer must also be sure that the representation does not fall afoul of Rule 1.7(b). The lawyer must consider whether the representation that is adverse to the affiliate may be materially limited by the lawyer's responsibilities to the corporate client, or, correlatively, the representation of the corporate client may be materially limited by the representation of the client adverse to the affiliate; and if so in either case, the lawyer may not take on the adverse representation unless the lawyer reasonably concludes that the representation will not be adversely affected, and the potentially affected client consents.

What triggers Rule 1.7(b) is a lawyer's recognition of the possibility that a particular representation *may be materially limited* by the lawyer's responsibilities to another client. As the Comment to the Rule makes clear, the reference is to situations "when a lawyer cannot consider, recommend or carry out an appropriate course of action for the client because of the lawyer's other responsibilities or interests." Such a material limitation on the lawyer's ability properly to represent a client could arise, for example, if the lawyer's concern for remaining in the good graces of client A was likely to impair the independence of judgment or the zeal

13. *See, e.g.,* North Star Hotels Corp. v. Mid-City Hotel Associates, 118 F.R.D. 109 (D. Minn. 1987) (law firm disqualified from suing a limited partnership when a general partner of that partnership, who would have personal liability, was also a general partner in two other partnerships that were represented by the law firm); Cincinnati Bell, Inc. v. Anizter Bros., Inc., No. C-1-93-0871 (S.D. Ohio, June 27, 1994) (law firm disqualified for representation of opponent's sister corporation in an unrelated matter); *Telesat Cable Television*, cited in note 9, *supra*.

that the lawyer could bring to bear on behalf of client B. Thus, Rule 1.7(b) might come into play if the lawyer had reason to believe that, even though there was no understanding as to how the corporate client's affiliates were to be treated, nonetheless the corporate client would resent the lawyer's undertaking any representation that threatened, even indirectly, any adverse effect on either the financial well-being or the programmatic purposes of the corporate client; and if, because of this belief, there was a significant risk that the lawyer's diligence or judgment on behalf of his new client would be adversely affected by his awareness of the corporate client's displeasure.

The foregoing discussion recognizes that Rule 1.7(b) must be considered by the lawyer whenever a representation adverse to a corporate client is considered; it should not, of course, be taken to imply that Rule 1.7(b) requires the lawyer to seek consent from either the new client or the existing corporate client whenever a proposed representation is adverse to an affiliate of a corporate client. It is only when there is a threat of material limitation on the lawyer's ability properly to represent a client because of his responsibilities to another client that the Rule requires the lawyer to seek consent.

Conclusion

The provisions of both paragraphs of Rule 1.7 emphasize the paramount importance of preserving a lawyer's relationship with his client. In that light, doubts about whether one or another requirement of the Rule applies should be resolved by a presumption that favors the client who will be adversely affected by the prospective representation.

A lawyer should not strain to conclude that a proposed representation will not adversely affect his relationship with that client.[14] Where it is difficult to ascertain whether a matter will be directly adverse to an existing client, or to judge whether taking on the matter will affect the lawyer's relationship with the client, a lawyer ordinarily would be well advised as a matter of prudence and good practice to discuss the matter with his existing client before undertaking a representation adverse to an affiliate of the client, even though consent may not be ethically required. We hasten to add that the fact that the lawyer has as a matter of prudence and good practice sought consent where consent was not ethically required does not make the lawyer's undertaking the new representation in the absence of consent a disciplinable ethical violation. However, in any instance where the lawyer concludes that no client consent is required, under either paragraph of Rule 1.7, the lawyer should be prepared to show how he was able to make the various determinations required without contacting the client for information or consent—par-

14. Lawyers who have taken an overly narrow view of what is "directly adverse" have found themselves disqualified in reported cases—*e.g.*, Fund of Funds, Ltd. v. Arthur Andersen & Co., 567 F.2d (2d Cir. 1977); Stratagem Dev. Corp. v. Heron Int'l N.V., 756 F. Supp. 789 (S.D.N.Y. 1991); North Star Hotels Corp. v. Mid-City Hotel Assoc., 118 F.R.D. 109, 111 (D. Minn. 1987). Where disqualification is not available, of course, a client can simply choose to discharge counsel.

ticularly determinations (a) that the client does not have an expectation that the corporate affiliate will be treated as a client, and (b) that the proposed representation adverse to the affiliate will not have a material adverse effect on the representation of the client.

Assuming that obtaining client consent is the preferable course would have several practical benefits. Loyalty is an essential element in a lawyer's representation of any client. Disloyalty is easily perceived by a client, whether or not that perception is wellfounded. As this Committee noted in Formal Opinion 91-361 (Representation of a Partnership) (1991), if a lawyer explains the implications of a dual representation and obtains the informed consent of both parties, "the likelihood of perceived ethical impropriety on the part of the lawyer should be significantly reduced."

Concurring in Part and Dissenting in Part

I dissent from that portion of the Committee's opinion which concludes that consultation with a client is solely a matter of prudence—not ethics—when a lawyer has difficulty making any of the judgments which are required by Rule 1.7. There are many such judgments, including whether the adverse party in the new matter is, or should be, treated as an existing client, and whether a lawyer's accepting the new matter will adversely affect the lawyer's relationship with his corporate client. Indeed, the issue of whether or not an action against a corporate affiliate would be "directly adverse" to a corporate client is a very difficult one, and the Committee's opinion, while announcing a decision on this point, hardly settles the matter, as my Colleagues' dissents well illustrate.

There is no doubt that accepting a new engagement adverse to an affiliate of a corporate client, without consultation with and the consent of that client, is business folly. This fact alone should impel most practitioners to call their clients before accepting such work. However, I submit that a lawyer has an ethical duty to consult with his client, and obtain consent, whenever the extent of the lawyer's representation of one or more members of a corporate family has not been clearly limited by prior agreement between the lawyer and client or circumstances known to and reasonably understood by both lawyer and client.

A lawyer's unilateral decision to take on a matter adverse to an affiliate of an existing client, made on the basis of imperfect information about how his client will regard that decision, can easily have significant ethical repercussions. Rule 1.4 states that "A lawyer shall explain a matter to the extent reasonably necessary to permit the client to make informed decisions regarding the representation." A lawyer's failure to consult his client about a new representation adverse to its affiliate deprives the client of the ability freely to make an "informed decision regarding the representation." Instead, the client is forced to decide between discharging the lawyer, even if such discharge will have a material adverse effect on its interests (a circumstance in which the lawyer would not have been permitted to withdraw), or acquiescing in the lawyer's continuing to represent it, with whatever impairment of communication, cooperation and diligence, and whatever threat to confidentiality, results. It cannot be consistent with a lawyer's ethical duties for a lawyer to force his client to such a decision.

Deborah A. Coleman

DISSENTS

This Committee has struggled for more than two years to formulate an answer to the submission which a majority of the Committee can agree upon. What the majority of this Committee has finally agreed upon is a departure from its tradition of interpreting the Model Rules in an aspirational manner.

The majority view, when reduced to its most simplistic terms, is as follows: XYZ Corporation is represented by the law firm of Roe & Doe. XYZ has a number of subsidiaries which the majority characterizes as "corporate affiliates." One of them is about to be sued by another client of Roe & Doe in an "unrelated matter." In such a case, the majority opines that even if the suit threatens to adversely impact XYZ's economic interest, the conflict is governed not by Model Rule 1.7(a) which would require the consent of XYZ, but by Model Rule 1.7(b) which does not require the consent of XYZ, thus depriving it of a veto power which would prevent Roe & Doe from suing its subsidiary.

It may very well be that in the rarified Fortune 500 world, a suit against a subsidiary might be considered as having only a derivative impact upon the parent, but outside those elevated precincts most parent companies would view such a suit as outrageous and a clear conflict of interest. The majority suggests that the parent corporation might avoid this unhappy situation by arriving at an "understanding" with their lawyers that they "will avoid representations adverse to the client's corporate affiliates." In the most elementary terms, what the majority is doing is shifting the lawyer's burden of protecting the client to the client, who must now protect itself against its own lawyer. If there is one clear message to be drawn from the majority opinion, it is that all corporate in-house counsel and all corporate officers having responsibility for their company's relationship with their attorneys, should promptly review their retainer agreements and amend them in order to protect their "corporate affiliates" from their own lawyers.

The majority's repeated use of the term "corporate affiliate" must be viewed as an elevation of form over substance. Even the majority doesn't go so far as to suggest that if the XYZ Corporation had a number of divisions under its corporate umbrella, a suit brought by its lawyers, Roe & Doe, against one of those divisions would be indirectly adverse. [Rule 1.7(b)]. What they do say is that because XYZ chose to or was by law required to operate via corporate subsidiaries, if a profitable case against XYZ's subsidiary comes to Roe & Doe, it is free to make a business decision to take that case without XYZ's consent and the only recourse

XYZ has is to discharge Roe & Doe or move to disqualify it. This "solution" ignores the fact that XYZ may be represented by Roe & Doe in other matters where the involvement in time and money makes it economically unrealistic to terminate the relationship. Thus, XYZ may be economically bound to a law firm which is suing its subsidiary—with both the law firm and the client unhappy with the relationship.

The majority is of the view that while the claim against the subsidiary is direct, the adverseness against the parent is "for the purpose of Rule 1.7, indirect rather than direct, since its immediate impact is upon the affiliate and only derivatively upon the client." I am hard put to understand what that means in the real world. I assume that if XYZ is maintaining a subsidiary, it does so with the expectancy that the subsidiary's profits will add to the bottom line of XYZ's annual report and that the subsidiary's reputation will add to the luster of XYZ's reputation. From XYZ's point of view, the suit against the subsidiary will always have a direct impact on it and no matter what the majority opines, will be a conflict of interest.

In the conclusion of the opinion, an effort is made to palliate the impact in the interest of "preserving a lawyer's relationship with his client." Doubts as to whether Rule 1.7(a) or 1.7(b) applies "should be resolved by a presumption that favors the client who will be adversely affected by the prospective representation."

Then, the majority suggests, if it is difficult to ascertain "whether a matter will be directly adverse to an existing client or to judge whether taking on the matter will affect the lawyer's relationship with the client," Roe & Doe "ordinarily would be well advised as a matter of prudence and good practice" to discuss the matter with XYZ "before assuming a representation adverse to an affiliate" of XYZ "even though such consent may not be ethically required." The majority "hastens to add" that the fact that Roe & Doe sought XYZ's consent "where such consent was not ethically required" (relying upon the majority opinion) does not subject Roe & Doe to a "disciplinable ethical violation" if it proceeds with the new representation without XYZ's consent.

The foregoing invites a visit to the following scenario. Roe calls XYZ's President and says "Remember that little company you purchased a few years ago? We have just been retained by a major client to sue it for unfair competition. I hope you don't mind." XYZ's President explodes saying there is no way his Board of Directors is going to stand still for its lawyers suing its subsidiary and suggests that Roe & Doe are in a conflict of interest situation. Roe responds that their ethics partners have carefully reviewed the situation and in reliance upon an opinion of the American Bar Association's Standing Committee on Ethics and Professional Responsibility (handing XYZ's President a copy of the majority opinion appropriately underlined), Roe & Doe need not obtain XYZ's consent and the fact that they asked for it but didn't get it and proceeded with the action is not ethically disciplinable. So much for client relations—so much for enhancing the reputation of the profession.

Conclusion

The majority opinion fails to furnish bright line guidance in the complex and confused area of conflicts of interest. Stripped of its elegant verbiage, the opinion opens a Pandora's Box of unintended consequences which most assuredly will return to vex us in the future. Admittedly, Model Rule 1.7 problems do not always fit into precise categories, but to paraphrase an oft-quoted sentence from a Supreme Court opinion, I may have difficulty defining a conflict but I know one when I see one. The majority opinion sends our profession the wrong message at the wrong time. For the foregoing reasons, I respectfully dissent therefrom.

Richard L. Amster

* * *

This Standing Committee on Ethics and Professional Responsibility has wrestled with the issues of conflict of interest in the corporate family context for years. Now it issues an opinion which, I am sad to report, prompts this member's first dissent. What makes this doubly sad is the fact that the opinion contains so much laudable practical advice regarding the lawyer's better course of action, what should be done when lawyers confront representations adverse to corporate affiliates of corporate clients, and how considerations of client relations will ordinarily dictate proper conduct. All of this "advice" would be ethically mandated as well, if the majority had not strained the meaning of Model Rule 1.7 to permit what everyone on this Committee agrees is ill-advised: suits against corporate affiliates of corporate clients.

Yet when the Committee's opinion is distilled and the hortatory language is removed, we learn that it is the opinion of the majority that when a lawyer represents less than all members of a corporate family that lawyer is free to take a position adverse to those non-client members of the corporate family *without contacting the client member* on the ground that the adverse effect of such representation on the client member is "indirect rather than direct, since its immediate impact is on the affiliate, and only derivatively upon the client." Op. at 21. Thus, in one unfortunate opinion the majority has turned a Rule of Professional Conduct designed to protect clients into one that can be used to permit lawyers freely, and without consultation, to take positions which destroy traditional notions of client loyalty and client concern.

The majority's opinion starts from a premise that is so flawed it can only be explained by the fact that its proponents imagine its conclusion only to apply to the largest of America's corporate conglomerates; then the majority compounds this error by assuming that companies that are part of these very large conglomerates do not very much care what happens to other members of the corporate family who are in different lines of business or in different geographical areas or led by different management, but just happen to be part of the same corporate enterprise.

The first problem with this approach is that the opinion as written applies to all corporate families regardless of their size or the nature of their businesses. Thus, even if one could imagine a special rule for "nasty" big companies, a possibility this writer rejects out of hand, that is not what the majority has crafted. The second problem is that the majority opinion fails to recognize the fact that corporate families are financially totally inter-dependent and that the sole purpose for the existence of these corporate families is economic success. Thus, when the majority opinion argues that an event economically adverse to subsidiary "A" only indirectly affects subsidiary "B,"[15] it clearly ignores the fact that for members of a corporate family the location of a corporate family's losses are totally irrelevant to the impact on the bottom line. Parents are directly dependent on the health of their subsidiaries; subsidiaries are directly dependent on the health of the parent; and subsidiaries are directly dependent on the health of other subsidiaries. For the last proposition one need look no further than the drastic effects on General Electric Credit Corporation of the widely publicized events at Kidder, Peabody.

All members of this Committee agree that a lawyer may never take a position directly adverse to a client corporation no matter how minor the matter and no matter how distant geographically, by industry or by personnel, the new proposed representation is from the original one the lawyer is handling. Not only is that the rule, but that is what the rule should be. If the client wishes to consent to the representation because of those factors or because it otherwise wishes to accommodate the lawyer's desire to take on the new representation, that is something for the client to decide, giving the client the full protection of the rules governing conflicts of interest.

But today the majority announces a rule that would result in no call to the client, no request for a waiver of a conflict, no opportunity to determine what the client thinks about the proposed representation adverse to an affiliate of the client, no opportunity to condition the representation on reasonable safeguards like voluntary screening or an agreement not to sue for punitive damages. Rather, the majority empowers the lawyer at precisely the time when the lawyer's objectivity can be seen to be the most compromised, simply to take a position adverse to the client's corporate affiliate on the ground that as a matter of ethics and, therefore, as a matter not requiring any further inquiry, the effect on the client is merely indirect.

The invalidity of this result can be seen in a hypothetical: A lawyer regularly defends dealer termination litigation for the Lincoln Mercury Division of the Ford Motor Company. She receives a call from a friend whose mother-in-law was just injured in an automobile accident. She was driving a Jaguar, the friend relates, and the brakes failed. The mother-in-law wants to sue the manufacturer claiming

15. The "directly adverse/indirectly adverse" distinction is at the heart of this dispute since, if the proposed representation is directly adverse to the client, Model Rule 1.7(a), with its requirement that the client consent, is triggered. Under Model Rule 1.7(b) only the new client that is taking a position adverse to a corporate affiliate of the old client need consent.

faulty brake design. Lawyer consults a recent annual report of Ford and this Committee's majority opinion and replies that, since Jaguar is a subsidiary of Ford, he can take the case because any impact on his present client, Ford, will be at best indirect.

Two days later the same friend calls to tell lawyer that his mother-in-law has just been released from the hospital, her delusions of grandeur have disappeared and she now remembers that she was, in fact, driving a Ford Escort at the time of the accident. The friend wants confirmation that lawyer will still take the case. Lawyer again consults the majority opinion and replies that now, since Ford is a division of Ford Motors, she cannot take the case because the adverse effect of the representation will now be direct. Friend, a non-lawyer, asks for an explanation of the different results and when he is told the distinction the ABA Ethics Committee drew between subsidiaries of clients and divisions of clients in drafting its corporate family opinion, the friend remarks that the result exalts form over substance.

The friend is quite correct. Taking the profession where no prior opinion has ever tread, the majority today condones lawyers taking positions adverse to the parents, subsidiaries and siblings of their corporate clients on the ground that doing so is only indirectly adverse because it involves economic harm to a subsidiary, parent or sibling. The sole reason for corporate existence is the maximization of economic success. Thus, when a corporation is harmed economically it is being hurt in the only way that counts. Yet somehow because the corporation has decided to, been forced to or, indeed, been counseled by its own lawyer to conduct its affairs through subsidiaries, it has lost the protection the majority concedes it would enjoy if its various businesses were organized as divisions. Why a corporation with subsidiaries may be so "punished" is nowhere explained by the majority. Nor is it explained why the suit against the Ford Division of Ford, even if it is for $100, results in direct adverseness while the suit against Jaguar, even if it is for $100,000,000, is indirect.

It is the conclusion of the majority opinion that the way a client chooses, is advised or is forced to organize its business is determinative of how the company should be treated for conflict of interest purposes. Yet every lawyer knows that there will be almost no cases where, *from the client's perspective*, that should be so. And it is clients, not lawyers, that the conflict of interest rules are supposed to protect.

The existence of subsidiaries often reflects regulatory requirements, historical accidents or considerations of limiting liability. They will almost never reflect a client judgment that what happens to the subsidiary, parent or sibling is not a matter that it cares about very much indeed. Just as Ford undoubtedly cares as much about what happens at its Jaguar subsidiary as it does about what happens at its Lincoln Mercury Division, so, too, is this the case in virtually every wholly owned corporate family. In the final analysis the enterprise is simply one economic conglomerate whose sole reason for being is earning profits for its shareholders.

The majority's reliance on Formal Opinions 91-361 (Representation of a Partnership) (1991) and 92-365 (Trade Association as Clients) (1992) is clearly misplaced. In each of those cases the Committee considered whether an individual partner of a multi-partner partnership or an individual member of a multi-member trade association would become a client of the lawyer who represented, respectively, the partnership or the trade association. The author of this dissent agrees that in those two situations a careful analysis of other facts is required to determine whether the partner or the member become clients. But here we are talking about a wholly owned corporate family. The only analogies that would be apt here are a single partner partnership or a single member trade association. In each of those cases, there is no doubt that the lone partner or the lone member must either be considered a client of the lawyer or, at a minimum, a person who would suffer a direct adverse effect if any action were taken adverse to the partnership or trade association.

It is also surprising that the majority relies on Formal Opinion 92-367 (Lawyer Examining a Client as an Adverse Witness, or Conducting Third Party Discovery of the Client) (1992) in support of its position. In that opinion this Committee concluded that the cross examination of one's client, a non-party witness, in a case on behalf of another client, would be "directly adverse" to the client non-party witness because "any advantage gathered by the lawyer in representation of the litigation client necessarily entails some concrete disadvantage to the [witness] client." If attacking the credibility of a witness, who is not a party, is said to entail a concrete disadvantage then suing the subsidiary of a client for damages surely entails an even greater and more concrete disadvantage. In the former case, by definition, the witness has no stake in the litigation and so at worst some feelings get bruised or one's reputation tarnished; but in the latter the lawyer who is suing the subsidiary of a parent client is literally putting her hand in her client's pocketbook. Short of physical injury, it does not get more concrete than that.

One of the biggest problems with the majority approach is that those clients that are the most sophisticated and the least in need of protection, the very independent Fortune 500 companies that the majority thinks are indifferent to lawsuits against corporate family affiliates, will be able to protect themselves from this opinion by sending each lawyer the company engages a letter telling the lawyer to treat all of the corporate affiliates listed on an annexed chart as clients for purposes of Rule 1.7. It is only the unsophisticated, those corporate families which do not have legions of in-house lawyers, who will be caught in the trap this opinion creates. It is they who will naively hire a lawyer, assume total loyalty and find out much to their surprise that the lawyer feels completely free to sue another member of the corporate family simply because the economic impact on the "client" was indirect.

The majority, of course, thinks this conflict result can be ameliorated because the client who learns its lawyer is suing a member of the corporate family can simply fire the lawyer for this unfortunate conduct. Op. at 22. However, as all lawyers recognize, firing one's counsel is rarely a satisfactory solution and often an impossibility, given the pressures of time and the extraordinary costs associated with hiring new counsel. Moreover, the last thing this Committee should ever condone is a device which would permit lawyers, who wish to take on a new, more lucrative engagement from which they are precluded because of some conflict, to place their clients in a position where they have a Hobson's choice of waiving the conflict or firing their lawyers.

The final ironic infirmity in the majority opinion is its recognition that the lawyer might run afoul of Model Rule 1.7(b)'s material limitation language because the client might "resent the lawyer's undertaking any representation that threatened, even indirectly, any adverse effect on . . . the financial well-being . . . of the corporate client," while at the same time the opinion fails to recognize how much the client might resent far more the fact that the lawyer, according to the majority, is not even required to call the client before undertaking the "indirectly adverse" representation. The truth is both slights will be resented and justifiably so. Yet the majority deliberately eschews the only way that client resentment can be avoided: for the lawyer to be required to notify the client and then use all her advocacy power to persuade the client she should be allowed to undertake the adverse representation. If she succeeds, fine; if she fails, client loyalty will be preserved. Nothing less should be required.

Conclusion

It is the view of this writer that the majority opinion misinterprets Model Rule 1.7(a) when it concludes that the rule's interdiction of conduct directly adverse to a client does not include taking a position directly adverse to a corporate affiliate of the client. Perhaps another Standing Committee on Ethics and Professional Responsibility on another day will see the error of the majority's ways and correct it. Until then, this dissent is offered as a call to the profession to follow the dissent's bright line rule whenever the profession approaches conflicts of interest in the corporate family context. The last thing our profession needs is another black eye caused by jettisoned client loyalty in the name of economic expediency.

Lawrence J. Fox

* * *

I concur in the dissents of Messrs. Amster and Fox.

Kim Taylor-Thompson

Formal Opinion 95-396 July 28, 1995
Communications With Represented Persons

Rule 4.2 prohibits a lawyer from knowingly communicating with a represented person about the subject matter of the representation without the consent of that person's lawyer. This prohibition applies to the conduct of lawyers in both civil and criminal matters, and covers any person known to be represented by a lawyer with respect to the matter to be discussed.

In the context of criminal investigations, nonetheless, it must be recognized that the Rule has been interpreted by some courts not to prohibit contacts by investigative agents acting under the general direction of a lawyer, with a person known to be represented in the matter being investigated, prior to arrest or the institution of formal charges.

The communicating lawyer is not barred from communicating with the represented person absent actual knowledge of the representation. Such knowledge may, however, be inferred from the circumstances; thus, a lawyer may not avoid the need to secure consent of counsel by closing her eyes to circumstances that make it obvious that the person to be communicated with is represented with respect to the matter in question.

The communicating lawyer is not barred from communicating with a represented person about topics that are not the subject of the representation.

When a corporation or other organization is known to be represented with respect to a particular matter, the bar applies only to communications with those employees who have managerial responsibility, those whose act or omission may be imputed to the organization, and those whose statements may constitute admissions by the organization with respect to the matter in question. Thus, a lawyer representing the organization cannot insulate all employees from contacts with opposing lawyers by asserting a blanket representation of the organization.

The fact that the represented person is the one who initiates a communication does not render inapplicable the prohibition on communicating about the subject matter of the representation.

When a person known to have been represented initiates contact with a lawyer and declares that she has terminated or intends to terminate the representation, the lawyer should obtain reasonable assurance that the representation has in fact been terminated before engaging in substantive discussion of the subject of the representation.

A lawyer may not direct an investigative agent to communicate with a represented person in circumstances where the lawyer herself would be prohibited from doing so. Whether in a civil or a criminal matter, if the investigator acts as the lawyer's "alter ego," the lawyer is ethically responsible for the investigator's conduct.

The bar against contacts with represented persons applies to all communications relating to the subject matter of the representation except those that fall within the narrow category of being "authorized by law." Communications "authorized by law" include communications that are constitutionally protected, and in addition, communications that are specifically authorized by statute, court rule, court order, statutorily authorized regulation or judicial decisional precedent.

Recent controversy concerning Rule 4.2 of the Model Rules of Professional Conduct (1983, as amended) has prompted this Committee to undertake a comprehensive consideration of the proper scope of the Rule.[1] The Rule as it now stands provides:

Communication with Person Represented by Counsel

In representing a client, a lawyer shall not communicate about the subject matter of the representation with a party the lawyer knows to be represented by another lawyer in the matter, unless the lawyer has the consent of the other lawyer or is authorized by law to do so.[2]

The questions framing this examination of the Rule are these: (1) Does Rule 4.2 apply to the conduct of lawyers in criminal as well as civil matters? (2) Does a represented "party," under the Rule, mean only a person who is a formally designated party to an adjudicative proceeding, contract or negotiation, or does it apply more broadly to any person who is represented by counsel with respect to the matter that is the subject of the communication? (3) In the context of criminal investigations, does the prohibition apply differently before arrest or the fil-

1. This opinion was prompted in part by the dialogue between the American Bar Association and the United States Department of Justice in connection with the promulgation of the Department's regulations on Communications with Represented Persons, 28 C.F.R. Part 77.

2. This Committee has proposed an amendment to the Rule, to substitute "person" for "party" in the text of the Rule. That proposal will be submitted to the House of Delegates for consideration in August 1995. The change would resolve the ambiguity in the present Rule that is discussed in Part II of this Opinion. The Committee's proposal would also amend the Comment to the Rule to clarify certain matters regarding its proper scope as discussed in this Opinion in the text accompanying notes 36 and 38.

ing of formal charges than it does after those events? (4) Does the prohibition apply if the communicating lawyer does not have definite knowledge that the person with whom she wishes to communicate is represented in the matter to be discussed? (5) What is the scope of the subject matter about which communication is prohibited? (6) May a lawyer representing a corporation or other organization bar communication with all employees of the organization by declaring a blanket representation of the organization and its employees? (7) May a lawyer communicate with a represented person absent consent of that person's lawyer if that person initiates the contact? (8) May a lawyer communicate with a person known to have been represented in the matter to be discussed who states that she has terminated or intends to terminate the representation? (9) To what extent does the prohibition on a lawyer's communicating with a represented person apply also to investigative agents acting under the direction of a lawyer? (10) What communications with represented persons fall within the "authorized by law" exception in Rule 4.2?

The Background and Purposes of the Anti-Contact Rule

While the debate about the scope and application of Rule 4.2's prohibition on contacts with represented parties has been heated, the controversy appears to be of relatively recent vintage. The ethical prohibition against such contacts has enjoyed a long history and broad acceptance. Its origin appears to be found in Hoffman's treatise, in 1836:

> I will never enter into any conversation with my opponent's client, relative to his claim or defence, except with the consent, and in the presence of his counsel.[3]

Every ethical code promulgated by the American Bar Association has contained an anti-contact provision. Thus, the Canons of Professional Ethics, promulgated in 1908, included the following provision in Canon 9:

> A lawyer should not in any way communicate upon the subject of controversy with a party represented by counsel; much less should he undertake to negotiate or compromise the matter with him, but should deal only with his counsel.

Since that time, rules embodying this fundamental ethical precept, usually following one or another of the models offered by the ABA, have been adopted in every state.[4]

In DR 7-104(A)(1) of the ABA Model Code of Professional Responsibility,

3. 2 DAVID HOFFMAN, A COURSE OF LEGAL STUDY ADDRESSED TO STUDENTS AND THE PROFESSION GENERALLY 771 (2d ed. Baltimore 1836), quoted in John Leubsdorf, *Communicating with Another Lawyer's Client: the Lawyer's Veto and the Client's Interests*, 127 U. PA. L. REV. 683, 684 n. 6 (1979).

4. *See* Roger C. Cramton & Lisa K. Udell, *State Ethics Rules and Federal Prosecutors: The Controversies Over the Anti-Contact and Subpoena Rules*, 53 U. PITT. L. REV. 291, 292 n. 3 (1992).

which superseded the 1908 Canons and in turn anteceded the Model Rules, the language closely resembles what is now found in Rule 4.2:

> Communicating With One of Adverse Interest.
>
> (A)During the course of his representation of a client a lawyer shall not:
>
> (1) Communicate or cause another to communicate on the subject of the representation with a party he knows to be represented by a lawyer in the matter unless he has the prior consent of the lawyer representing such other party or is authorized by law to do so.

In addition, EC 7-18 of the Model Code set out the central proposition on which all of the anti-contact rules have rested:

> The legal system in its broadest sense functions best when persons in need of legal advice or assistance are represented by their own counsel.

Implementing this fundamental premise, the anti-contact rules provide protection of the represented person against overreaching by adverse counsel, safeguard the client-lawyer relationship from interference by adverse counsel, and reduce the likelihood that clients will disclose privileged or other information that might harm their interests.[5]

I. The Bar Against Communication With Represented Parties Applies to Criminal As Well As Civil Matters

Model Rule 4.2, like its predecessors, seeks to maintain a real barrier between the opposing lawyer and the represented person. In the context of a civil matter, the rule has been described as perhaps the sole barrier between the client and an overreaching opponent.[6] Similarly, the prohibition against communications with represented persons operates in a criminal matter to protect a represented person against harmful admissions and waivers of privilege that may result from interference with the client-lawyer relationship. Recognizing that communications in a criminal case may entail significant consequences for the represented person, the Department of Justice has noted that the reasons for an anti-contact rule apply to criminal proceedings, "perhaps with more force than in the civil context."[7]

Although there have been holdings to the contrary,[8] the Committee believes it

5. Cramton & Udell, *supra* note 4 at 325.

6. *Id. See also* Polycast Technology Corp. v. Uniroyal, Inc., 129 F.R.D. 621, 625 (S.D.N.Y. 1990) (stating that the anti-contact rule prevents lawyers from using superior skills and training to obtain "unwise statements" from an opposing party, protects privileged information, and aids in settlements by allowing lawyers skilled in negotiating to conduct discussions about the matter).

7. 4 Op. Off. Legal Counsel 576, 584 (1980) (concluding, however, that DR 7-104 did not prohibit federal criminal investigative activities because such activities are "authorized by law").

8. *See, e.g.,* State v. Richmond, 560 P.2d 41, 46 (Ariz. 1976), *cert. denied,* 433 U.S. 915 (1977); State v. Nicholson, 463 P.2d 633, 636 (Wash. 1969).

is clear that Rule 4.2 applies to the conduct of lawyers in criminal as well as civil matters, including both federal and state prosecutors. It has been argued that, because the Rule applies to a lawyer only "[i]n representing a client," the Rule does not reach the conduct of a prosecutor since she does not represent a "client" in the ordinary sense.[9] However, the history of the Rule and its predecessors offers no support for any assertion that it was intended to exempt prosecutors. Moreover, a majority of court decisions have concluded that Rule 4.2 and its predecessor anti-contact rules apply to both federal and state prosecutors;[10] even though, as discussed in part III below, some decisions have also limited the Rule's application in the context of criminal investigations prior to arrest or indictment.

Defense counsel in criminal cases of course are also subject to the provisions of Rule 4.2. For example, suppose that co-Defendants Able and Baker are charged with a crime, and Lawyer representing Defendant Able wishes to communicate with Defendant Baker because she has reason to believe that he may be able to exculpate her client. If Lawyer knows that Defendant Baker is represented in that matter, she may not engage in any communications with Baker without the consent of Baker's lawyer.[11]

II. The Bar Applies to Communications Not Only with Formal "Parties" but Also with Any Person Known to Be Represented with Respect to the Matter to Be Discussed

Although most frequently encountered in the context of litigation, Rule 4.2 applies (as have its predecessor anti-contact rules) in transactional circumstances as well. For example, suppose Buyer and Seller in a real estate transaction are each represented by counsel. The lawyer who represents Seller contacts Buyer, without leave of Buyer's lawyer, to suggest postponement of the closing. That communication would be prohibited under Rule 4.2 absent the consent of Buyer's lawyer. The same would of course apply to separately represented parties to nego-

9. *See* F. Dennis Saylor, IV & J. Douglas Wilson, *Putting a Square Peg in a Round Hole: The Application of Model Rule 4.2 to Federal Prosecutors*, 53 U. Pitt. L. Rev. 459 (1992).

10. *See generally*, United States v. Hammad, 858 F.2d 834 (2d Cir. 1988), *cert. denied*, 498 U.S. 871 (1990); United States v. Thomas, 474 F.2d 110 (10th Cir.), *cert. denied*, 412 U.S. 932 (1973); *In re* Doe, 801 F. Supp. 478 (D.N.M. 1992); United States v. Lopez, 765 F. Supp. 1433 (N.D. Cal. 1991), *rev'd on other grounds*, 4 F.3d 1455 (9th Cir. 1993); Suarez v. State, 481 So. 2d 1201 (Fla. 1985), *cert. denied*, 476 U.S. 1178 (1986); People v. Green, 274 N.W.2d 448 (Mich. 1979).

11. *See* United States v. Santiago-Lugo, Crim. No. 95-029 (D.P.R. June 6, 1995), 11 ABA/BNA Law. Man. Prof. Conduct 192 (criminal defense counsel who conducted ex parte interviews with co-defendants of their client censured for violating Rule 4.2); *but cf.* Grievance Comm. for the Southern District of New York v. Simels, 48 F.3d 640 (2d Cir. 1995) (holding that the lawyer for a criminal defendant was not barred from interviewing, without consent of his lawyer, a potential witness against his client in one matter, who was also a potential co-defendant of his client in another matter, since in neither case was this individual a "party" in the same "matter" as the lawyer's client within the meaning of DR 7-104(A)).

tiations leading to a closing, or to any other transaction or potential transaction.

Moreover, even in a litigation context, the application of the Rule does not depend on a proceeding having actually commenced, so that those involved in a dispute have become formal "parties." The Comment to Rule 4.2 makes plain that "the rule covers any person, whether or not a party to a formal proceeding, who is represented by counsel concerning the matter in question."[12]

Much of the controversy regarding the scope of Rule 4.2 has turned on its use of the term "party." There is case law holding that in order for a person to be deemed a "party" under the Rule or its predecessors, at least in the criminal context, formal proceedings must have been initiated in which that person is named as a party.[13] A majority of the Committee believe, however, that the term "party," as used in Rule 4.2, should not be given so narrow a meaning. As pointed out above, the Comment to the Rule states that it applies to "any person, whether or not a party to a formal proceeding." And the word "party" has a broad as well as a narrow sense.[14]

The Committee recognizes that, as just indicated, the word "party" as used in the Rule is ambiguous—an ambiguity compounded by the fact that the caption of the Rule refers to a "person" represented by counsel.[15] The key to resolving this ambiguity, the Committee believes, is consideration of the purposes intended to

---

12. Rule 4.2 cmt [3].

13. *See* United States v. Ryans, 903 F.2d 731, 739 (10th Cir.), *cert. denied*, 498 U.S. 855 (1990) ("We are not convinced that the language of [DR 7-104(A)(1)] calls for its application to the investigative phase of law enforcement" because "the rule appears to contemplate an adversarial relationship between litigants, whether in a criminal or a civil setting"). *But see* United States v. Hammad, 858 F.2d 834 (2d Cir. 1988), *cert. denied*, 498 U.S. 871 (1990) (DR 7-104(A)(1) applies prior to filing of formal charges).

14. Thus, the term "party" is commonly used to refer to persons beyond the technical parties involved in a matter. For example, "third party discovery" is frequently used with the same meaning as "non-party discovery." Moreover, the definition of "party" appears in *Black's Law Dictionary* (6th ed. 1990) as "[a] person concerned or having or taking part in any affair, matter, transaction, or proceeding, considered individually."

See also CHARLES W. WOLFRAM, MODERN LEGAL ETHICS 611 (1986) (observing that "party" is a lawyerism that is intended to refer broadly to any "person" represented by a lawyer in a matter, and suggesting that while DR 7-104(A)(1) of the Model Code of Professional Responsibility "probably" prohibited contact with *any* represented person, Model Rule 4.2 clearly does); N.Y. State Bar Ass'n Comm. on Prof. Ethics, Op. 656 (1993) (interpreting N.Y. Disciplinary Rule 7-104(A)(1) as applying to communications between lawyer representing parent in child custody proceeding and child for whom a law guardian had been appointed even though the child is not a "party" to the proceeding); N.Y. State Bar Ass'n Comm. on Prof. Ethics, Op. 463 (1977) (describing DR 7-104(A)(1) as an absolute proscription against communications with a represented person, not merely a technical party).

15. The comprehensive record of the deliberations of the Kutak Commission casts no light on the reason why the word "person" was used in the caption of the Rule while "party" was used in its text.

be served by the Rule. In this light, the broader sense of the word "party," taking it as equivalent to "person," is clearly the appropriate one.[16] The reasons for protecting uncounselled persons against overreaching by adverse counsel, protecting the client-lawyer relationship from interference by such counsel, and protecting clients from disclosing privileged information that might harm their interests, are not limited to circumstances where the represented person is a party to an adjudicative or other formal proceeding. The interests that the Rule seeks to protect are engaged when litigation is simply under consideration, even though it has not actually been instituted, and the persons who are potentially parties to the litigation have retained counsel with respect to the matter in dispute.[17]

The harms that may flow from the disparity in sophistication and skill between a lay person and a lawyer are as likely to occur prior to the initiation of formal proceedings as they are following the filing of papers. Indeed, the critical phase in the representation of a client may be precisely the period when a lawyer, using her professional skills and training, attempts to avoid the filing of a suit entirely or to shape prospective litigation. In such circumstances, a lawyer may, intentionally or otherwise, take advantage of unsophisticated persons who are represented by counsel and thereby circumvent the client-lawyer relationship. Rule 4.2 should, therefore, operate to prevent a lawyer from adversely affecting the relationship between a client and her lawyer even in the absence of a formal proceeding.[18]

If the Rule is to serve its intended purpose, it should have broad coverage, protecting not only parties to a negotiation and parties to formal adjudicative proceedings, but any person who has retained counsel in a matter and whose interests are potentially distinct from those of the client on whose behalf the communicating lawyer is acting. Such persons would include targets of criminal investi-

---

16. In order to eliminate the ambiguity arising from use of the term "party," described in the accompanying text, the Committee has proposed that the Rule be amended to substitute the word "person" for "party" in the body of the Rule. *See* note 2, *supra*.

17. *See, e.g.*, United States v. Jamil, 546 F. Supp. 646, 654 (E.D.N.Y. 1982), *rev'd on other grounds*, 707 F.2d 638 (2d Cir. 1983) (stating that DR 7-104(A)(1) protects a person who is a potential litigant); Florida State Bar Assoc. Comm. on Prof. Ethics, Op. 78-4 (1978) (stating that DR 7 104(A)(1) applies "whenever an attorney-client relationship has been established . . . regardless of whether or not litigation has commenced."); Mississippi State Bar, Op. 141 (1988) ("The actual filing of a lawsuit or intent to file a lawsuit is irrelevant to the question of whether the lawyer may communicate with the adverse party."); Texas State Bar Prof. Ethics Comm., Op. 492 (1994) (prohibitions of the Texas anti-contact rule, which is similar to Rule 4.2, apply "despite the fact that litigation is neither in progress nor contemplated.").

18. *See* Geoffrey C. Hazard, Jr. & W. William Hodes, The Law of Lawyering: A Handbook on the Model Rules of Professional Conduct 730 (1993 Supp.). *See, e.g.*, Comm. on Prof. Ethics and Conduct of the Iowa State Bar Assoc. v. Shepler, 519 N.W.2d 92 (Iowa 1994) (attorney's violation of DR 7-104(A)(1) resulted in disbarment when he obtained personal gain in a direct transaction with an elderly woman after being instructed to contact either her family or attorney regarding business matters).

gations,[19] potential parties to civil litigation,[20] and witnesses who have hired counsel in the matter.[21] In sum, the Rule's coverage should extend to any represented person who has an interest in the matter to be discussed, who is represented with respect to that interest, and who is sought to be communicated with by a lawyer representing another party.[22]

III. The Bar May Have a More Limited Application to Criminal Investigations Prior to Arrest or the Filing of Criminal Charges

As has been noted, the reasons for the prohibition on contacts with represented persons apply at least as forcefully in the criminal as in the civil context; and in both contexts they apply *before* formal proceedings have been initiated as well as afterward. Nonetheless, a number of court decisions, mainly involving the conduct of undercover investigators or informants acting in concert with prosecutors, have limited the applicability of the Rule or its predecessor anti-contact rules in the criminal context, either holding the prohibition wholly inapplicable to all pre-indictment non-custodial contacts,[23] or holding it inapplicable to some such contacts by informants or undercover agents.[24] Some cases note that the Rule would apply if the communication had been made by the prosecutor himself, or at his specific direction.[25] Some courts have specifically relied upon the Rule's use of

---

19. *See, e.g.*, United States v. Jacobs, 547 F.2d 772 (2d Cir. 1976), *cert. dismissed as improvidently granted*, 436 U.S. 31 (1978). *But see* the discussion in Part III *infra*, regarding decisional authority limiting the Rule's application in criminal investigations prior to arrest or the filing of formal charges.

20. *See, e.g.*, Triple A Machine Shop, Inc. v. State, 261 Cal. Rptr. 493, 498 (Ct. App. 1989) (California anti-contact rule's prohibitions "attached once an attorney knew that an opposing party was represented by counsel even where no formal action had been filed."). *See also* decisions cited in note 17, *supra*.

21. *See, e.g.*, United States v. Pinto, 850 F.2d 927 (2d Cir.), *cert. denied*, 488 U.S. 867 (1988) (holding that DR 7-104 applied where the prosecutor interviewed a represented witness who was a potential defendant); ABA Formal Op. 187 (1938) (holding that the prohibition in Canon 9 covers a party in a civil case who also is a prospective witness in the matter).

22. In the Committee's view, the decision in the *Simels* case, *supra* note 11, took an unduly narrow view of the anti-contact rule there involved, DR 7-104, in declining to hold the rule applicable to contact with a represented adverse witness and potential co-defendant.

23. *See* United States v. Ryans, 903 F.2d 731, 740 (10th Cir.), *cert. denied*, 498 U.S. 855 (1990) (DR 7-104(A)(1) does not apply "during the investigation process before the initiation of criminal proceedings"); United States v. Heinz, 983 F.2d 609, 613 (5th Cir. 1993) (following *Ryans*).

24. *See* United States v. Jamil, 707 F.2d 638, 645-46 (2d Cir. 1983) (communication by undercover informant in pre-indictment non-custodial setting did not violate DR 7-104(A)(1) where informant was not acting as "alter ego" of prosecutor); United States v. Lemonakis, 485 F.2d 941, 954-56 (D.C. Cir. 1973), *cert. denied*, 415 U.S. 989 (1974) (DR 7-104 did not prohibit use of undercover informant in a pre-indictment, noncustodial circumstance because the informant's instructions from the prosecutor were not such as to make him the prosecutor's alter ego).

25. *See* United States v. Hammad, 858 F.2d 834, 838-40 (2d Cir. 1988), *cert. denied*, 498

the word "party" (as opposed to "person") to reach the conclusion that the Rule was not intended to apply to non-custodial pre-indictment communications with represented persons in the criminal context.[26] But at least one court has held that an anti-contact rule using the term "person" rather than "party" has no application to pre-indictment non-custodial investigations.[27] Some courts have appeared to take the view that since non-custodial pre-indictment communications with persons known to be represented would not violate the Sixth Amendment, such contacts should not be considered violative of anti-contact rules.[28] And some courts have expressed the view that applying a no-contact rule before indictment would unduly limit the government's ability to investigate suspected criminal activity.[29]

The Committee believes that to the extent those decisions suggest that the Rule has no application at all in the criminal context, or that it does not come into play until Sixth Amendment rights attach, they are not sound.[30] As one court has noted, since prosecutors have substantial control over the timing of an indictment, limiting the Rule to post-indictment communications could allow the government to "manipulate grand jury proceedings to avoid its encumbrances."[31] Moreover,

---

U.S. 871 (1990) (DR 7-104(A)(1) applies prior to filing of formal charges, and undercover informant's use of sham subpoena, under specific direction of prosecutor, to trick suspect contributed to the informant's becoming the prosecutor's alter ego); United States v. Jamil, 546 F. Supp. 646, 654 (E.D.N.Y. 1982), *rev'd on other grounds*, 707 F.2d 638 (2d Cir. 1983) ("Any direct communication between the Assistant United States Attorney, or a representative of his office, and the defendant occurring after the government became aware that he was represented by counsel would constitute a violation of DR 7-104(A)(1)."); People v. White, 567 N.E.2d 1368, 1386-87 (Ill. App.), *appeal denied*, 575 N.E.2d 922 (Ill. 1991) (holding, following *Hammad*, that DR 7-104 applies prior to filing of formal charges, but is only violated by use of an informer in such circumstances when the attorney/prosecutor is "intimately involved in the investigation," so as to make the informer his alter ego). *See also* United States v. Heinz, 983 F.2d at 615 (Parker, J., concurring in part and dissenting in part) (prosecutor's use of lawyer as undercover informant violated DR 7-104 because he was able to act as a "prosecutorial alter ego" for the government).

26. *See, e.g.,* United States v. Ryans, 903 F.2d at 739 ("We are not convinced that the language of [DR 7-104(A)(1)] calls for its application to the investigative phase of law enforcement" because the rule's use of the word "party" "appears to contemplate an adversarial relationship between litigants, whether in a criminal or a civil setting.").

27. *See In re* Disciplinary Proceedings regarding John Doe, 876 F. Supp. 265 (M.D. Fla. 1993) (Florida version of Model Rule 4.2 should be interpreted consistently with that Rule in other circuits, notwithstanding the fact that it uses the word "person" rather than "party").

28. *See, e.g.,* United States v. Dobbs, 711 F.2d 84 (8th Cir. 1983); United States v. Kenny, 645 F.2d 1323 (9th Cir.), *cert. denied*, 452 U.S. 920 (1981); United States v. Heinz, 983 F.2d 609 (5th Cir. 1993).

29. *See, e.g.,* United States v. Ryans, 903 F.2d at 739-40; United States v. Jamil, 707 F.2d at 745.

30. *Accord* ABA Informal Op. 1373 (1976) (finding that Canon 9 bars a prosecutor from sending a letter containing a plea offer to a represented person, even though the communication was pre-indictment).

31. United States v. Hammad, 858 F.2d at 839.

applying the Rule to prohibit only post-indictment communications would render the rule of little use in the criminal context.[32]

The Committee also believes that, in criminal cases, Rule 4.2 is not simply coextensive with the Fifth and Sixth Amendments. While the Fifth and Sixth Amendments provide protections to individuals in the context of a criminal case, the Constitution establishes only the "minimal historic safeguards" that defendants must receive rather than the outer limits of those they may be afforded.[33] Ethics rules, on the other hand, seek to regulate the conduct of lawyers according to the standards of the profession quite apart from other laws or rules that may also govern a lawyer's actions. Consequently, by delineating a lawyer's duties to maintain standards of ethical conduct, ethical rules like Rule 4.2 may offer protections beyond those provided by the Constitution.[34]

The Committee recognizes that prohibitions against communications with a represented person can be an obstacle to investigation, but the search for truth is not the only value to which lawyers, including government lawyers, must respond. Indeed, the Sixth Amendment right to counsel puts limits on the government's investigatory efforts. The filing of an indictment, which triggers that constitutional right, may mean that the government can establish a prima facie case against the person charged, but more investigation is generally required ultimately to prove the person's guilt beyond a reasonable doubt. Thus, it could be argued that but for the attachment of the right to counsel, lawyers could arrange for undercover investigations involving contacts with the charged person. However, despite the resulting investigatory problems, the Sixth Amendment bars lawyers from "deliberately eliciting" information from a person who is represented unless her counsel is

---

32. *See* Alafair S.R. Burke, *Reconciling Professional Ethics and Prosecutorial Power: The Non-Contact Rule Debate*, 46 STAN. L. REV. 1635, 1642-45 (1994).

It should be noted that the Department of Justice's regulations on Communications with Represented Persons recognize that in limited circumstances, an anti-contact prohibition applies pre-indictment. Specifically, although the regulations take a categorical position that no one is a "party" until there is a formal proceeding in which he is named as such, 28 C.F.R. § 77.3(a), they prohibit negotiation of a plea agreement, settlement, immunity agreement and other disposition of potential criminal charges with a represented *person* unless the communication was initiated by that person and the procedure referred to in the text, *infra* at note 51, has been followed, 28 C.F.R. § 77.8. In addition, the accompanying amendments to the United States Attorneys' Manual forbid *ex parte* contacts with represented "targets" of investigations in all but exceptional circumstances. U.S.A.M. 9-13.240 Overt Communications with Represented Targets. The manual defines a target as a person against whom the lawyer for the government "(a) has substantial evidence linking that person to the commission of a crime or to other wrongful conduct; and (b) anticipates seeking an indictment or naming as a defendant in a civil law enforcement proceeding."

33. United States v. Hammad, 858 F.2d at 839 (quoting McNabb v. United States, 318 U.S. 332, 340 (1943)).

34. *Id. See also* 4 Op. Off. Legal Counsel 576, 581 (1980) (stating that "DR 7-104, as generally interpreted, provides suspects and defendants with protections that the Constitution does not.").

present or she expressly waives her right to counsel.[35] There are also statutory limitations on investigative techniques, which go beyond constitutional requirements.[36] And other ethical prohibitions indubitably restrict prosecutors' activities.[37] Similarly, Rule 4.2 imposes an additional burden on the opposing counsel to use investigatory means other than direct contact with a represented person.

All this said, the Committee recognizes that there is a body of decisional law that in effect concludes that the public interest in investigating crime may outweigh the interests served by the Rule in the criminal context, at least where the contacts are made with represented persons who have been neither arrested nor formally charged, and the contacts are made by undercover agents or informants and not by the government lawyers themselves (or by agents acting so closely under the lawyers' direction as to be their "alter egos"). Accordingly, the Committee believes that so long as this body of precedent remains good law, it is appropriate to treat contacts that are recognized as proper by such decisional authority as being "authorized by law" within the meaning of that exception stated in the Rule.[38]

IV. The Bar Applies Only if the Communicating Lawyer Knows That the Person Sought To Be Communicated With Is Represented By Counsel in the Matter To Be Discussed; But Such Knowledge May Be Inferred from the Circumstances

The Rule's requirement of securing permission of counsel is limited to those circumstances where the inquiring lawyer "knows" that the person to whom he wants to speak is represented by counsel with respect to the subject of the communication.[39]

---

35. *See* Maine v. Moulton, 474 U.S. 159 (1985); Brewer v. Williams, 430 U.S. 387 (1977); Massiah v. United States, 377 U.S. 201 (1964).

36. *E.g.,* 18 U.S.C. § 2511 (prohibiting wiretapping without a warrant); 12 U.S.C. § 3402 (limiting governmental access to financial records of customers of financial institutions).

37. *E.g.,* Model Rule 3.8 (Special Responsibilities of a Prosecutor); Model Rule 4.1(a) (Truthfulness in Statements to Others); Model Rule 4.3 (Dealing with Unrepresented Persons); Model Rule 4.4 (Respect for Rights of Third Persons).

38. The Committee's proposal for amendment of Rule 4.2, discussed in note 2, *supra*, includes a proposed amendment to Comment [2] to the Rule, to recognize as "authorized by law" governmental investigative activities prior to the commencement of criminal proceedings and in addition civil enforcement proceedings when they have been held permissible by such judicial authority.

39. The purposes of the Rule, which is to say the reasons for requiring consent of counsel representing the person with whom communication is sought, clearly apply whether or not the inquiring lawyer is aware of the representation. Thus, the requirement that that lawyer *know* of the representation serves not to implement the purposes of the Rule but only to frame a rule of conduct that can as a practical matter reasonably be imposed. It would not, from such a practical point of view, be reasonable to require a lawyer in all circumstances where the lawyer wishes to speak to a third person in the course of his representation of a client first to inquire whether the person is represented by counsel: among other things, such a routine inquiry would unnecessarily complicate perfectly routine fact-finding, and might well unnecessarily obstruct

The term "knows" is defined in the Terminology section of the Model Rules as follows:

> "Knowingly," "known," or "knows" denotes actual knowledge of the fact in question. A person's knowledge may be inferred from the circumstances.

"Know" does not mean "reasonably should know," which is also a defined term in the rules that does not appear in the text of Rule 4.2 although it does appear in Rule 4.3, "Dealing with Unrepresented Person" (which applies to the communication if the lawyer does *not* know that the person contacted is represented by counsel).[40] The Terminology provides that

> "Should have known," when used in reference to a lawyer denotes that a lawyer of reasonable prudence and competence would ascertain the matter in question.

Thus, in the Committee's view, Rule 4.2 does not, like Rule 4.3, imply a duty to inquire. Nonetheless, it bears emphasis that, as stated in the definition of "knows" (set out above), actual knowledge may be inferred from the circumstances. It follows, therefore, that a lawyer may not avoid Rule 4.2's bar against communication with a represented person simply by closing her eyes to the obvious.[41]

V. The Bar Is Limited to Communications Related to the Subject Matter of Both Representations

Rule 4.2 makes reference to the subject matter of two representations, and requires a link between them. Thus, it provides that "in representing a client," a lawyer shall not communicate "about the subject of the representation"—referring to the lawyer's representation of her client. It goes on to refer to communications with one whom the lawyer knows to be "represented in the matter"—requiring that the second representation be within the compass of the inquiring lawyer's representation. This required connection between the two representations, imparted by the phrase "in the matter," significantly limits the scope of the prohibition.

---

such fact-finding by conveying a suggestion that there was a need for counsel in circumstances where there was none, thus discouraging witnesses from talking.

40. Rule 4.3 provides:

> Dealing with Unrepresented Person
>
> In dealing on behalf of a client with a person who is not represented by counsel, a lawyer shall not state or imply that the lawyer is disinterested. When the lawyer knows or reasonably should know that the unrepresented person misunderstands the lawyer's role in the matter, the lawyer shall make reasonable efforts to correct the misunderstanding.

41. The Committee's proposed amendment to Rule 4.2 to substitute "person" for "party," discussed in note 2, *supra*, would also amend the Comment to deal more clearly with the requirement that the communicating lawyer *know* of the representation.

If a person is represented by counsel on a particular matter, that representation does not bar communications on other, unrelated matters. For example, suppose a lawyer represents Defendant on a charge involving crime A. Under Rule 4.2, another lawyer may not, pursuant to a representation, either as prosecutor or as counsel for a co-defendant involving crime A, communicate with Defendant about that crime without leave of Defendant's lawyer. However, if the communicating lawyer represents a client with respect to a separate and distinct crime B and wishes to contact Defendant regarding that crime, the representation by counsel in crime A does not bar communications about crime B. Similarly, the fact that Defendant had been indicted on crime A would not prevent the prosecutor from communicating with Defendant, directly or through investigative agents, regarding crime B.[42]

Questions regarding the scope of representation "in the matter" have arisen in the context of investigations of ongoing criminal enterprises. Can a lawyer representing persons believed to be involved in organized crime bar communications with her clients by advising the prosecutor that she represents these clients in all matters, without specification of what the matters are? Or may an individual insulate herself from undercover investigation in a criminal matter by retaining "house counsel"? The Committee believes that in both situations, and quite apart from the latitude that, as explained in part III above, the courts have allowed for undercover investigative contacts before arrest or indictment, the prosecutor is not barred from communicating under the Rule.

By prohibiting communication about the subject matter of the representation, the Rule contemplates that the matter is defined and specific, such that the communicating lawyer can be placed on notice of the subject of representation. Thus, if the representation is focused on a given matter, such as one involving past conduct, and the communicating lawyer is aware of this representation, she may not communicate with the represented person absent consent of the representing lawyer. However, where the representation is general—such as where the client indicates that the lawyer will represent her in all matters—the subject matter lacks sufficient specificity to trigger the operation of Rule 4.2.

Similarly, retaining counsel for "all" matters that might arise would not be sufficiently specific to bring the rule into play. In order for the prohibition to apply, the subject matter of the representation needs to have crystallized between the client and the lawyer. Therefore, a client or her lawyer cannot simply claim blanket, inchoate representation for all future conduct whatever it may prove to be, and expect the prohibition on communications to apply. Indeed, in those circumstances, the communicating lawyer could engage in communications with the

42. As a practical matter, in the course of contact with a person represented by counsel in another matter, the communicating lawyer would be well advised to take care not to elicit comments or attempt to communicate about crime A. However, Rule 4.2 does not preclude discussions of crime B.

represented person without violating the rule.

In the civil context also, the "matter" with which the representation is concerned must have been concretely identified. For example, suppose that Corporation A wishes to purchase a subsidiary of Corporation B. Corporation B has an on-going relationship with outside counsel, law firm XYZ, such that the firm represents the corporation on all of its legal matters. In addition, Corporation A knows that XYZ law firm always represents Corporation B in its legal matters. However, Corporation A has not broached with Corporation B the possible purchase of Corporation B's subsidiary, and thus the general counsel for Corporation A has no reason to believe, let alone to know, that Corporation B has consulted its counsel regarding such an acquisition. In such circumstances, because the representation by outside counsel is not specifically focused on the matter, the general counsel for Corporation A is not barred by Rule 4.2 from contacting the president of Corporation B to initiate discussions without asking law firm XYZ for its consent. Correspondingly, the XYZ firm cannot preclude such a communication by announcing that it represents Corporation B for all purposes. A similar analysis applies as respects in-house general counsel, who represent the corporation for all purposes.[43]

VI. Representation of an Organization Does Not Bar Communications with All Employees of the Organization

Questions arise as to the manner in which the Rule applies when the represented party is a collective entity, such as a corporation, rather than an individual. Specifically, the Committee has considered whether a lawyer's representation of an organization extends the Rule's prohibition, either automatically or upon the declaration of the organization's lawyer, to cover communications with all employees or members of that organization.

Some courts addressing this issue have found that the represented party is limited to corporate employees who fall within the "control group": those employees who manage and speak for the corporation.[44] The Comment to Rule 4.2, however, makes plain that the term represented party refers not only to those with managerial responsibilities but to anyone who may legally bind the organization with respect to the matter in question.[45] Consequently, when the party is an organization, the bar against communication covers not only the control group but in addition

---

43. As a practical matter, to be sure, a lawyer wishing to open a dialogue with a person or entity known to be generally represented by a particular firm or by in-house counsel may find it more expeditious and less likely to generate dispute to communicate through counsel.

44. *See, e.g.*, Wright *ex rel.* Wright v. Group Health Hosp., 691 P.2d 564 (Wash. 1984) (applying Model Code of Professional Responsibility DR 7-104(A)).

45. Comment [2] provides:

> In the case of an organization, this Rule prohibits communications by a lawyer for one party concerning the matter in representation with persons having a managerial responsibility on behalf of the organization, and with any other person whose act or omission in connection with that matter may be imputed to the organization for purposes of civil or

anyone "whose act or omission in connection with that matter may be imputed to the organization for purposes of civil or criminal liability or whose statement may constitute an admission on the part of the organization."[46]

Expansive though the Rule's coverage is with respect to officers and employees of a represented organization, the Rule does not contemplate that a lawyer representing the entity can invoke the rule's prohibition to cover all employees of the entity, by asserting a blanket representation of all of them. So, for example, if in-house counsel for the XYZ corporation announces that no one may talk to any XYZ employee without obtaining in-house counsel's permission, the communicating lawyer is not barred from communicating with all employees. If an employee cannot by statement, act or omission bind the organization with respect to the particular matter, then that employee may ethically be contacted by opposing counsel without the consent of in-house counsel. Of course, if individual employees have their own counsel in the matter, then the bar against communication would apply absent consent of that separate counsel. But the fact that an entity is represented by counsel does not prevent communication with all current employees of the represented corporation.[47]

VII. Initiation of the Contact by the Represented Person Does Not Remove the Bar

Another issue arising under the Rule is whether the prohibition against communications with represented persons applies if the represented person initiates contact with the communicating lawyer. Rule 4.2 exempts communications if the *lawyer* representing the contacted person consents; but the Rule says nothing about permitting the represented person to forego the protection accorded him by the ethical responsibilities of the communicating lawyer. This Committee concluded in Formal Opinion 108 (1934) that the anti-contact rule does not contemplate such a waiver.

Since then, a number of courts have similarly found that because the ethical

---

criminal liability or whose statement may constitute an admission on the part of the organization. If an agent or employee of the organization is represented in the matter by his or her own counsel, the consent by that counsel to a communication will be sufficient for purposes of this Rule. Compare Rule 3.4(f).

46. *Accord*, Upjohn Co. v. United States, 449 U.S. 383 (1981); Chancellor v. Boeing Co., 678 F. Supp. 250, 253 (D. Kan. 1988); Shearson Lehman Bros., Inc. v. Wasatch Bank, 139 F.R.D. 412 (D. Utah 1991); Morrison v. Brandeis University, 125 F.R.D. 14, 16-17 (D. Mass. 1989); Niesig v. Team I, 76 N.Y.2d 363 (1990). *See* ABA Informal Op. 1410 (1978) (stating that DR 7-104(A)(1) bars communication with an officer or employee of a corporation in a particular situation unless the communicating lawyer has the prior consent of the lawyer representing the corporation).

47. It should be noted that Rule 4.2 does not prohibit contacts with former officers or employees of a represented corporation, even if they were in one of the categories with which communication was prohibited while they were employed. This Committee so concluded in ABA Formal Op. 91-359 (1991).

prohibition is designed, in part, to protect the effectiveness of the lawyer's representation, the represented person may not waive it.[48]

While the Committee recognizes that not allowing the represented person to waive the Rule's protection may be seen as paternalistic, it believes that Rule 4.2 requires that result. Reflecting the concern that the represented person may not be in a position to make an informed waiver of the presence of counsel, the Rule operates to reduce the likelihood of the represented person engaging in communications that might ultimately prove harmful to her cause by imposing a strict ethical obligation on the communicating lawyer.[49]

VIII. When Contact Is Initiated by a Person Who Is Known to Have Been Represented by Counsel in the Matter But Who Declares that the Representation Has Been or Will Be Terminated, the Communicating Lawyer Should Not Proceed Without Reasonable Assurance that the Representation Has in Fact Been Terminated

Of course, any represented person retains the right to terminate the representation. In the event that such a termination has occurred, the communicating lawyer is free to communicate with, and to respond to communications from, the former represented person. The communicating lawyer's conduct would then be governed by Rule 4.3, Communications with Unrepresented Persons.[50]

As a practical matter, a sensible course for the communicating lawyer would generally be to confirm whether in fact the representing lawyer has been effectively discharged. For example, the lawyer might ask the person to provide evidence that the lawyer has been dismissed. The communicating lawyer can also contact the representing lawyer directly to determine whether she has been informed of the discharge. The communicating lawyer may also choose to inform the person that she does not wish to communicate further until he gets another lawyer.

There are some circumstances where the communicating lawyer may need to go beyond determining that the person has discharged her lawyer. One is that in

48. *See, e.g.*, United States v. Lopez, 4 F.3d 1455, 1459 (9th Cir. 1993) ("the trust necessary for a successful attorney-client relationship is eviscerated when the client is lured into clandestine meetings with the lawyer for the opposition. As a result, uncurbed communications with represented parties could have deleterious effects well beyond the context of the individual case . . . ."); People v. Green, 274 N.W.2d 448, 453 (Mich. 1991) (defendant's willingness to speak does "not excuse compliance with the standard of professional conduct prescribed by DR 7-104(A)(1)"); United States v. Thomas, 474 F.2d 110, 111 (10th Cir.), *cert. denied*, 412 U.S. 932 (1973); United States v. Batchelor, 484 F. Supp. 812 (E.D. Pa. 1980); State v. Morgan, 646 P.2d 1064, 1068-70 (Kan. 1982); State v. Ford, 793 P.2d 397, 401 n.4 (Utah App. 1990).

49. *See Lopez*, 4 F.3d at 1462 (finding that "[t]he rule against communicating with represented parties is fundamentally concerned with the duties of attorneys, not with the rights of parties").

50. *See* note 40, *supra*.

a criminal case where the court has appointed a lawyer to represent the client, the lawyer is not relieved as counsel of record until the court grants her leave to withdraw. Consequently, even if the contacted person tells the communicating lawyer that she has fired her lawyer, the communicating lawyer may not proceed without reasonable assurance that the court has granted the lawyer leave to withdraw. Similarly, if retained counsel has entered an appearance in a matter, whether civil or criminal, and remains counsel of record, with corresponding responsibilities, the communicating lawyer may not communicate with the person until the lawyer has withdrawn her appearance. In addition, if a communicating lawyer knows that the represented person is incompetent, that person's statement regarding the status of her representation may not be sufficiently reliable to allow the communicating lawyer to assume that she is free to engage in communications with the person.

On the other hand, there may be situations, particularly in the criminal context, in which the represented person is reluctant to terminate her relationship with counsel, or wishes to negotiate with the prosecutor without the knowledge of her counsel, because of doubt as to whether the lawyer representing her is in fact concerned with protecting her interests as distinct from protecting the interests of others who may have arranged for her representation. Even in such circumstances, the prohibition of Rule 4.2 against communications with the represented party applies, at least until the lawyer seeking to communicate with that person has assurance that the representation that the person is seeking to disclaim has been either terminated or superseded by a new representation. A useful course of action in such circumstances may be to request a court (if there is one with jurisdiction) to hold an *ex parte* hearing to appoint new counsel or give approval to the communication without counsel.[51] While arranging for such a hearing, the communicating lawyer should refrain from offering advice or engaging in other substantive discussions with the person in question until the court has acted.[52]

IX. A Lawyer Is Ethically Responsible for Contacts by Investigators Acting Under Her Instructions That Would Violate the Bar If Made by a Lawyer

The next issue the Committee has undertaken to address concerns the applicability of Rule 4.2 to the activities of investigators working with lawyers; and in particular, the circumstances where a lawyer may be held vicariously responsible if an investigator collaborating with her communicates with a represented person without the consent of the representing lawyer.

There is no doubt that the use of investigators in civil and criminal matters is normal and proper. Particularly in the criminal context, there are legitimate rea-

51. The Department of Justice regulations on Communications with Represented Persons contemplate such a procedure. 28 C.F.R. § 77.6(c).

52. *Accord*, Mich. State Bar Comm. on Prof. and Jud'l. Ethics, Op. 202 (April 5, 1965).

sons not only for the use of undercover agents to conduct investigations, but for lawyers to supervise the acts of those agents.[53] And the investigators themselves are not directly subject to Rule 4.2, even if they happen to be admitted to the Bar (as many FBI agents are), because they are not, in their investigative activities, acting as lawyers: they are not "representing a client."[54] However, when the investigators are directed by lawyers, the lawyers may have ethical responsibility for the investigators' conduct.

Such responsibility will ordinarily arise under Rule 5.3, which provides in part:

> Responsibilities Regarding Nonlawyer Assistants
>
> With respect to a nonlawyer employed or retained by or associated with a lawyer:
>
> * * *
>
> (b) a lawyer having direct supervisory authority over the nonlawyer shall make reasonable efforts to ensure that the person's conduct is compatible with the professional obligations of the lawyer; and
>
> (c) a lawyer shall be responsible for conduct of such a person that would be a violation of the rules of professional conduct if engaged in by a lawyer if:
>
> (1) the lawyer orders or, with the knowledge of the specific conduct, ratifies the conduct involved; or
>
> (2) the lawyer is a partner in the law firm in which the person is employed, or has direct supervisory authority over the person, and

---

53. Lawyer supervision of the activities of investigators is likely to make their work product more useful, and to provide assurance against the commission of improprieties by the investigators.

54. Although there appears to be no decisional authority on the point, it seems clear, and widely understood, that the fact that an investigator is also a member of the bar does not render him, in his activities as an investigator, subject to those ethical rules—the overwhelming majority of the provisions of the Model Rules—that apply only to a lawyer "representing a client." Such an investigator would nonetheless be subject to those few provisions of the Model Rules, such as portions of Rule 8.4 (Misconduct) that apply to lawyers even when they are not acting as such. *See, e.g.*, Rule 8.4(b): "It is professional misconduct for a lawyer to . . . commit a criminal act that reflects adversely on the lawyer's honesty, trustworthiness or fitness as a lawyer in other respects."

Thus, the Department of Justice regulations on Communications with Represented Persons exclude from the defined term "attorney for the government" (with whose activities the regulations are principally concerned), "any attorney employed by the Department of Justice as an investigator or other law enforcement agent who is not authorized to represent the United States in criminal or civil law enforcement litigation or to supervise such proceedings." 28 C.F.R. § 77.2(a).

knows of the conduct at a time when its consequences can be avoided or mitigated but fails to take reasonable remedial action.

Under these provisions, if the lawyer has direct supervisory authority over the investigator, then in the context of contacts with represented persons, the lawyer would be ethically responsible for such contacts made by the investigator if she had not made reasonable efforts to prevent them (Rule 5.3(b)); if she instructed the investigator to make them (Rule 5.3(c)(1)); or if, specifically knowing that the investigator planned to make such contacts she failed to instruct the investigator not to do so (Rule 5.3(c)(2)).

The Committee believes, however, that if, despite instruction to the contrary, an investigator under her direct supervisory authority (or one not under such authority) made such contacts, she would not be prohibited by Rule 5.3 from making use of the result of the contact.[55] Rule 8.4(a) imposes similar, albeit narrower, ethical limits on what a lawyer can direct an investigator to do. Rule 8.4(a) provides:

Misconduct

It is professional misconduct for a lawyer to:

(a) violate or attempt to violate the Rules of Professional Conduct, knowingly assist or induce another to do so, or do so through the acts of another.

Since a lawyer is barred under Rule 4.2 from communicating with a represented party about the subject matter of the representation, she may not circumvent the Rule by sending an investigator to do on her behalf that which she is herself forbidden to do.[56] Whether in a civil or a criminal matter, if the investigator acts as the lawyer's "alter-ego," the lawyer is ethically responsible for the investigator's conduct.

---

55. Although the question is a close one, the Committee does not believe that a lawyer's making use of evidence offered by an investigative agent by means that would have been forbidden to the lawyer herself but in which she was not complicitous would constitute "ratification" under Rule 5.3(c)(1).

"Ratify" is defined by BLACK'S LAW DICTIONARY (6th ed. 1990) as:

> To approve and sanction; to make valid; to confirm; to give sanction to. To authorize or otherwise approve, retroactively, an agreement or conduct either expressly or by implication.

56. *See* ABA Informal Op. 663 (finding that Canon 9 prohibits employment of investigator in defense of malpractice suit to communicate with plaintiff who was represented by counsel); ABA Formal Op. 95 (1933) (finding that it is improper under Canon 9 for a municipal lawyer to permit police officers to obtain written statements from persons having personal injury claims against the municipality when the lawyer knows that the claimants are represented by counsel). *See, e.g.,* Shantz v. Eyman, 418 F.2d 11, 13 (9th Cir. 1969), *cert. denied*, 397 U.S. 1021 (1970) (finding that a prosecutor acted unethically by sending a psychiatrist to speak with a represented defendant without counsel's knowledge).

X. There Are Several Categories of Communications That Are "Authorized by Law"

The final issue the Committee has undertaken to address is the scope of the exception in Rule 4.2 permitting otherwise prohibited communications if they are "authorized by law." That exception first appeared in the black letter text of DR 7-104(A)(1), but had been found to be implied in Canon 9[57] and is now to be found in the anti-contact rule of every jurisdiction but one.[58]

The Comment to Rule 4.2 identifies, as an example of a communication authorized by law, "the right of a party to a controversy with a government agency to speak with government officials about the matter"—the right in question being First Amendment right of petition.[59] The "authorized by law" exception to the Rule is also satisfied by a constitutional provision, statute or court rule, having the force and effect of law, that expressly allows a particular communication to occur in the absence of counsel—such as court rules providing for service of process on a party,[60] or a statute authorizing a government agency to inspect certain regulated premises.[61] Further, in appropriate circumstances, a court order could provide the necessary authorization.[62]

As has been explained in part III above, an additional category of circumstances that appear to be fairly treated as "authorized by law" are those where courts have held that certain criminal investigative activities prior to arrest or the filing of formal charges, such as the use of undercover agents or informers not acting as the prosecutor's "alter ego," are not prohibited by the Rule.

A more difficult issue is raised by the Department of Justice regulations on Communications with Represented Persons,[63] which are evidently intended to rest squarely on the "authorized by law" exception in Rule 4.2. That issue is what, if any, directives by a governmental department or agency purporting to permit contacts with represented parties fall within the "authorized by law" exception? The Committee believes that such directives will qualify as "law" for purposes of the Rule only when embodied in formal regulations that have been properly pro-

---

57. *See* ABA Informal Op. 985 (1967) (opining that a formal offer of judgment could, consistently with Canon 9, be served directly upon a represented opposing party, but only if this was *specifically* authorized by statute, and if a copy was simultaneously served on counsel).

58. The single exception is Florida. *See* Florida Rules of Prof. Conduct, Rule 4-4.2. *See also In re* Disciplinary Proceedings regarding John Doe, 876 F. Supp. 265 (M.D. Fla. 1993), discussed in note 27, *supra.*

59. Rule 4.2 cmt. [2]. *See also* WOLFRAM, *supra* note 14, at 614-15.

60. *See* HAZARD & HODES, *supra* note 18, at § 4.2.109 (1994 Supp.)

61. *See* ABA Informal Op. 1496 (1983) (an agency lawyer may conduct an inspection of regulated business premises without first contacting the lawyer for the business).

62. *See* United States v. Lopez, 989 F.2d 1032, 1099 amended, 4 F.2d 1455 (9th Cir. 1993) (noting that a court order, if it is to authorize an exception to the Rule's prohibition, must be based upon accurate, and not misleading, information).

63. 28 C.F.R. Part 77.

mulgated pursuant to statutory authority that contemplates regulation of the character in question. Were any other regulation or fiat by an agency head to be considered an authorization by law, any government agency could "authorize" its lawyers to engage in conduct expressly prohibited by ethical codes simply by promulgating a regulation or policy.[64]

The Committee's view finds support in *Chrysler v. Brown*, 441 U.S. 281, 198 (1979), where the Supreme Court rejected the view that any agency conduct that has been directed or approved by an agency head is "authorized by law," within the meaning of a statute prohibiting such conduct except where "authorized by law." Rather, the Court held that for a government agency's regulation to have the force and effect of law, it must be a substantive regulation, which has been adopted in accordance with the procedural requirements imposed by Congress, and also rooted in a Congressional grant of authority. *Chrysler v. Brown* teaches that when an agency promulgates regulations purporting to authorize conduct in derogation of other law, those regulations must be grounded in a statute which contemplates regulations of the kind issued. A general grant of regulatory authority to an agency is not sufficient to support the issuance of regulations that permit what other law forbids. Although in *Chrysler v. Brown* the federal agency regulations in issue would have overridden requirements of a federal statute, the Committee believes the same result should be reached if the other law involved were rules of professional conduct adopted by state courts—or, for that matter, federal courts.[65]

CONCURRENCE

This is an important opinion addressing critical issues arising under Model Rule 4.2 and putting to rest a series of misguided notions that have been asserted by those who seek to undermine the sanctity of the lawyer-client relationship embodied in the provisions of Model Rule 4.2. There is nothing more central to what it means to be a client in the American system of justice than to know that, having hired a lawyer, the client need not worry about being taken advantage of by lawyers, with special skills and training, who represent others. Once the client's representation is disclosed, all lawyers are on notice that they must deal with the client's lawyer on all matters, unless the represented person's lawyer provides oth-

64. As has been noted above, ethical rules prohibiting communications with represented persons have been adopted in every state as a part of comprehensive ethics regulations. Lawyers representing the federal government are governed by these rules as a result of the specific requirement by Congress that federal attorneys be "duly licensed and authorized to practice as an attorney under the laws of a State, territory, or the District of Columbia." Department of Justice Appropriation Authorization Act, Fiscal Year 1980, Pub. L. No. 96-132, §3(a), 93 Stat. 1044, as carried forward in Pub. L. No. 103-317, § 102, 108 Stat. 1734 (1994).

65. Although the Committee believes, as stated, that the *Chrysler v. Brown* test is an appropriate one for interpreting the term "authorized by law" in Rule 4.2, we express no view as to whether the Department of Justice regulations have sufficient statutory authorization to meet that test.

erwise. Whether the matter is civil, criminal or transactional, whether a complaint has been filed, an indictment brought, a tax audit commenced or an agreement of sale signed, whether an adverse party, a co-defendant or plaintiff, a witness or a participant in a transaction, all clients who have hired lawyers should benefit from the protection of Rule 4.2. Nor may a lawyer avoid the rule by using non-lawyer agents to undertake what the lawyer is prohibited from doing, by maintaining studied ignorance of the representation, or by claiming the represented person initiated the contact.

This concurrence is filed to address several points on which the author believes the majority opinion and the dissents do not have it quite right. First, the Committee observes in the headnote that "the Rule has been interpreted by some courts not to prohibit contacts by investigative agents acting under the general direction of a lawyer with a person known to be represented . . . ." While this statement is correct, it doesn't explain to the unsuspecting, who might only read the syllabus, that almost all of those cases rely on reasoning which this opinion rejects, reasoning which this Committee, in issuing this Opinion describing what it believes to be the correct interpretation of the Rule, hopes courts in the future will also reject.

For too long, the mere repetition of the words "legitimate needs of prosecutors" has been used by the opponents of the principles of Model Rule 4.2 to undermine the protections the Rule is intended to provide. In responding to this litany, some of these courts, quite incorrectly, have eviscerated the Rule in the very situations where it is most needed: to protect from improper contacts those represented persons who face the awesome power of the government. Once a person has retained a lawyer in a matter, as this Opinion so carefully reasons, then all contacts are to be through that lawyer, and any contacts that are made on any basis other than through the lawyer, are in violation of the Rule.

Second, the majority opinion addresses by indirection the Department of Justice regulations on Communications with Represented Persons, regulations which by their terms are premised on so-called principles that are rejected out-of-hand in this opinion. More important, those regulations are clearly not authorized by law. There is no Congressional grant of authority to the Justice Department to issue regulations undermining the fundamental rights of clients to be represented by counsel. Moreover, regulation of lawyers, including Justice Department lawyers, has been traditionally and quite properly left to the states. Indeed, in the author's view, there could never be a delegation to the Justice Department or other law enforcement agency to set its own ethics rules unilaterally. When the drafters of Model Rule 4.2 inserted the words "authorized by law" they must have had in mind law established by either the courts or the legislature.

The Department of Justice regulations demonstrate the evil of having one party to disputed matters have that power. The regulations provide for loopholes so large that in some contexts they render the protections of Model Rule 4.2 meaningless. To ever permit a litigant (particularly one as powerful and capable of threatening represented parties as the Justice Department) to decide what rules will govern its own lawyers unbalances the judicial process in a fundamental, unfortunate and inequitable way.

Third, addressing Mr. Elliot's dissent, its flawed interpretation of Model Rule 4.2 as limited to "parties," not "persons," becomes apparent if one analyzes one of his opinion's examples. In trying to explain how, on the basis of principle, he is able to decide who is a party (and therefore entitled to the protection of the rule) and who is a person (and therefore not), Mr. Elliot explains that "[i]n a real estate transaction, the buyer and seller would be 'parties,' and, if represented, could not be contacted by the other's attorney absent consent of their own attorney. The buyer's mortgagee bank and the seller's bank whose mortgage the buyer would have to pay off would not be 'parties,' even if represented." This result will come as a great surprise to those in our profession who represent lenders, underwriters and other key "players" in transactions; in those situations, when it is made known that the bank or investment company will be represented by counsel, there should be every expectation, based on Model Rule 4.2, that lawyers for the buyer and seller would not be contacting the bank or investment company directly. If Mr. Elliot thinks otherwise, then that is but one more reason to conclude that Model Rule 4.2 was intended to reach these "persons" as well as the buyer and seller "parties." The buyer, the seller, the bank, the title company, the investment banker, the auditor and any other represented persons to a transaction, by the sole fact they choose to be represented by counsel, are entitled to the full protection of Model Rule 4.2, whether they meet Mr. Elliot's strained interpretation of party or not.

Finally, addressing Mr. Amster's dissent, while I share his view that the protections of Model Rule 4.2 are even more important in the criminal context, this does not mean that those protections should not be available to all clients, including organizations. The Rule recognizes, quite properly it seems, that the lawyer who represents an organization should not be able to prevent unsupervised contacts with all organization employees. By the same token, it recognizes that in order for an organization's lawyer to provide effective representation, contacts with employees having managerial responsibility, and any person whose act or omission in connection with the matter may be imputed to the organization or whose statement may constitute an omission must be prohibited. Any other rule would make it impossible for organization clients to receive the same level and quality of representation accorded to individuals. This may, as Mr. Amster notes, interfere with informal fact gathering but the need to resort to formal fact gathering is a very small price to pay for the important protections Model Rule 4.2 provides.

Lawrence J. Fox
Kim Taylor-Thompson

DISSENTS

I cannot go along with this opinion. It is overbroad and obstructs the legitimate search for the facts and the truth in civil litigation. In concentrating upon the applicability of Rule 4.2 in the criminal context where the constraint upon communication with represented persons is based upon the Constitution and concern for the rights of criminal defendants which might be overwhelmed by the resources of law enforcement agencies, this Committee has overlooked its impact upon the pursuit of the truth and facts in civil litigation. The opinion provides counsel for organizations with even broader power to isolate potential adverse witnesses than presently exists under Rule 4.2.[66] By erecting this wall blocking the fact-seeker from persons who may have knowledge of the matter in both criminal and civil litigation, the Committee has thrown out the baby with the bath water. This opinion in the civil context protects lawyers and their clients rather than individuals who might shed light on the factual basis of civil litigation.

Some members of the majority have asserted that the above-cited comment to Rule 4.2 fixed the direction of this opinion and that this dissent should have been directed at the rule rather than the opinion. If that is so, somewhere in this opinion the Committee should have suggested modifications to the rule which would have made it less onerous to a fact-seeker in civil litigation, especially one with limited resources. Not only did they not do so, but they compounded the problem by opining that even if the contact is initiated by a low-level employee of a represented organization, the rule bars any contact. This means that in the run-of-the-mill civil case, where a lawyer announces that he represents the organization in all personal injury matters, it will be more time-consuming and expensive to marshall facts from persons who in many cases will be best situated to witness the event which resulted in the litigation, i.e., low-level employees of a represented organization who may be willing to tell what they know about the incident.

During the Committee's lengthy discussions, a paragraph was suggested which would exempt communication initiated by a whistle-blower for the purpose of disclosing wrongdoing on the part of a corporation. Such a provision to this writer made common sense, but a majority of the Committee voted to delete the paragraph. The opinion also fails to take into account the endless variety of factual situations where a noncontrol employee far down on the food chain might provide relevant information in civil litigation and makes it almost impossible to develop the facts without the oversight of lawyers thus making the search for the truth an obstacle course.

66. Comment to Rule 4.2 provides that in the case of a represented organization, communications are prohibited with "persons having managerial responsibility on behalf of the organization and with any other person whose act or omission in connection with this matter may be imputed to the organization for purposes of civil or criminal liability or whose statement may constitute an admission on the part of the organization."

In addition to my substantive concern about this opinion, its length and complexity requires some comment. Several members of this committee tried their hand at writing an opinion upon which a majority of the committee might agree, and it is fair to say that the opinion ultimately took on a life of its own. The end result is a protracted and global interpretation of Rule 4.2 which is so convoluted and complex that it provides little comfort for the lawyer seeking facts to support his client's case as to precisely what conduct is permissible.

I envisage that the role of this committee is to furnish *all* members of the legal profession with guidelines which if followed would aid the ordinary practicing lawyer to comply with those ethical standards embodied in the Model Rules. This opinion is more appropriate for a learned legal periodical and does not take into account the real world where individual lawyers are confronted with time constraints in making hard decisions in the field of ethics. It just does not show them the way; to the contrary, it will add to their confusion.

The committee might have been better off had it abandoned its efforts and not written this opinion once the problems which gave rise to our interminable discussions and revisions surfaced. Unfortunately, it did not do so, and we are now issuing this massive work product which, in this writer's opinion, creates more problems for the average practicing attorney than it solves.

In light of the foregoing, I dissent.

Richard L. Amster

* * *

The fundamental premise of much, if not most, of the Committee's opinion is the proposition that when Rule 4.2 uses the word "party," it really means "any person." The distinguished American writer, thinker and philosopher, Johnny Carson, was wont to observe: "You buy the premise, you buy the joke." I do not buy the premise. Accordingly, I dissent.

My dissent, however, is limited to the premise. I have no quarrel with the reasoning of the Committee on those points that do not require its latitudinarian interpretation of the word "party." Indeed, if I were to accede to that definitional view, I would have no quarrel with the elaboration of those points that do depend upon that premise. My dissent is simply based upon the fact that despite best efforts at textual archeology, the Committee can find no basis whatsoever in legislative history for its conclusion; the conclusion it reaches violates basic and universally-applied canons of statutory construction that govern the interpretation of these Rules; other jurisdictions have, by their actions on the Rules of Professional Conduct, recognized that "party" does not mean "any person"; and the conclusion itself is reduced in the end to a desperate exercise in wish fulfillment. The Model Rules, for better or worse, are not and never have been a wishing well.

Legislative History

The Committee concedes, as it must, that it hasn't a clue as to why Rule 4.2 uses the word "party" instead of "person" when describing the protected communicatee. It recognizes that Canon 9 of the 1908 Canons of Professional Ethics used the word "party," and did so in a context clearly disclosing that the "party" was one with whom a dispute or transaction was involved. That same word "party" was repeated in DR 7-104(A)(1) under the title "Communicating With One of Adverse Interest." The word "party" again was employed in Model Rule 4.2, this time under the title "Communicating With Person Represented by Counsel." The Committee can find no discussion in the legislative history as to the meaning of "party" in any of these iterations of the rule.

Canons of Construction

In light of the fact that throughout the Model Rules the word "person" is frequently used, but the word "party" is used in Rule 4.2, canons of statutory construction, universally applied as well in construing court rules like the Model Rules of Professional Conduct, compel the conclusion that "party" means something different from "person."

There is a presumption of purpose behind every sentence, clause or phrase of a rule, and no word in a rule is to be treated as superfluous. *DeSisto College, Inc. v. Town of Howey-in-the-Hills*, 706 F. Supp. 1479, 1495 (M.D. Fla. 1989), *affirmed,* 888 F.2d 766; *Fox-Knapp, Inc. v. Employees Mutual Casualty Co.*, 725 F. Supp. 706, 709 (S.D.N.Y. 1989), *affirmed,* 893 F.2d 14; *Peck v. Jacquemin*, 196 Conn. 53, 64, 491 A.2d 1043 (1985). The use of different words in the same Rules must indicate a difference in legislative intent. *BFP Resolution Trust Corp.*, 114 S. Ct. 1757, 1761 (1994); *Lankford v. Law Enforcement Assistance Administration*, 620 F.2d 35, 36 (4th Cir. 1980); *Tafoya v. U.S. Dep't of Justice, LEAA*, 748 F.2d 1389, 1392 (10th Cir. 1984); *Fritz v. Madow*, 179 Conn. 269, 272, 426 A.2d 268 (1979); *Hinchcliffe v. American Motors Corporation*, 184 Conn. 607, 613, 440 A.2d 810 (1981); *Farricielli v. Personnel Appeal Board*, 186 Conn. 198, 203, 440 A.2d 286 (1982).

We are not permitted to "torture words to import ambiguity where the ordinary meaning leaves no room for it." *Mingachos v. CBS, Inc.*, 196 Conn. 91, 98, 481 A.2d 368 (1985). A rule does not become ambiguous solely because people disagree as to its meaning. As much as we may think a rule *should* have meant something else, its intent is to be found not in what its enactors *meant* to say, but in the meaning of what they *did* say. We are not permitted to read into the terms of a rule something which manifestly is not there in order to reach what we think would be a just result. *In re Pederson*, 875 F.2d 781, 784 (9th Cir. 1989). *Commissioner v. Freedom of Information Commission*, 204 Conn. 609, 620, 529 A.2d 692 (1987). Neither does a rule become ambiguous simply because different courts might have interpreted it differently. *Jones v. Brown*, 41 F.3d 634, 639 (Fed. Cir. 1994).

Fidelity to the canons of construction which govern courts in interpreting the Model Rules, and therefore ought to govern this Committee, compels the conclusion that this Committee cannot impose upon the word "party" the meaning of "any person."

As a simple matter of logic, the Committee cannot, by the *ipse dixit* of an opinion, ignore the fact that for almost 90 years a different word—"party"—has been used in Rule 4.2 and its antecedents at the same time that the Committee's favored word—"person"—has been used elsewhere in the same Canons, Code and Rules by the same authors. To import synonymy where the drafters used *different* words is resolutely to close one's eyes to the obvious, and to flout the canons of construction that govern our deliberations.

What Other Jurisdictions Have Done

That "party" does not mean "any person" is demonstrated as well by the understanding of the jurisdictions—now, some 40—which have adopted the Model Rules or variants of them. Simply put, when these jurisdictions wanted Rule 4.2 to protect more than just parties, they amended Rule 4.2 to say so. Thus, Alaska Rule 4.2 ("party or person"); Texas Rule 4.2 ("person, organization or entity of government"); Florida Rule 4-4.2 ("person"); and see Oregon DR 7-104(A)(1) ("person"). This Committee itself has—in what one presumes is not an act of supererogation—proposed to the House of Delegates in August 1995 changing the word "party" to "person" in Model Rule 4.2.

Presumably, the 40 or so jurisdictions that have adopted the Model Rules—indeed those still operating under the Code of Professional Responsibility—have long understood that "party" is a subset, and not a synonym, of "person." Those who wanted a more expansive protection have amended the rule. Amendment, not wish-fulfilling interpretation, is the way to pour the new wine of "person" into the old bottle of "party."

Unambiguous Meaning

The Committee for some reason (probably because it wants an excuse to construe it so that it can then apply it as it does in the Opinion) and contrary to universally-applied canons of construction, *supra*, purports to find the word "party" ambiguous, and finds the ambiguity "compounded" by use of the word "person" in the title to the Rule. But that latter fact should not affect the meaning of "party" in the Rule. All parties are persons, but not all persons are parties. The overall title to the section comprising Model Rules 4.1 - 4.4 is "Transactions With Persons Other Than Clients."

The Committee chooses to treat "party" as meaning "person" despite the fact that the drafters knew full well how to employ the broader "person" when they meant "person"—they used that word in Rules. 4.1, 4.3 and 4.4—but avoided using it in Rule 4.2. The Committee, seeking to buttress the logic of interpreting "party" to mean "person," notes that the word "party" is used as a synonym for "person" in the phrase "third party discovery." In the Model Rules, however, when "third person" is meant, "third person" is the phrase the drafters use. *See, e.g.*, Model Rules 4.1(a) and (b) and 4.4.

Seeking support for its expansive interpretation, the Committee cites part, but not all, of the *Black's Law Dictionary* definition of "party." A more instructive citation would have included the entire definition:

> Party, n. A person concerned or having or taking part in any affair, matter, transaction, or proceeding, considered individually. A "party" to an action is a person whose name is designated on record as plaintiff or defendant. M & A Elec. Power Co-op v. True, Mo. App., 480 S.W.2d, 310, 314. Term, in general, means one having right to control proceedings, to make defense, to adduce and cross-examine witnesses, and to appeal from judgment. City of Chattanooga v. Swift, 223 Tenn. 46, 442 S.W.2d 257, 258.
>
> "Party" is a technical word having a precise meaning in legal parlance; it refers to those by or against whom a legal suit is brought, whether in law or in equity, the party plaintiff or defendant, whether composed of one or more individuals and whether natural or legal persons; all others who may be affected by the suit, indirectly or consequently, are persons interested but not parties. Golatte v. Mathews, D.C. Ala. 394 F. Supp. 1203, 1207.

See also Nominal defendant; Parties; Prevailing party.

Black's Law Dictionary (5th ed.)

When we accept the lexicographers' invitation to see related words and turn to "parties" we find a definition which, quite rightly, takes the word beyond the confines of litigation:

> Parties. The persons who take part in the performance of any act, or who are directly interested in any affair, contract, or conveyance, or who are actively concerned in the prosecution and defense of any legal proceeding. Green v. Bogue, 158 U.S. 478, 15 S. Ct. 975, 39 L. Ed. 1061. See also Party.

Id.

Indeed, in light of the clearly limited meaning of "party" as a common law term, the Committee's *diktat* that "party" means "any person" contravenes yet another canon of statutory construction: that unless those promulgating a rule make minifest an intent to the contrary, a presumption obtains that when they use a common law term, they intend to use it in its common law sense. *United States v. Shabani*, 115 S.Ct. 382, 385 (1994); *Resolution Trust Corp. v. Diamond*, 45 F.3d 665, 672 (2 Cir. 1995); *Citizens Action League v. Kizer*, 887 F.2d 1003, 1006 (9 Cir. 1989), *cert. denied; Department of Health Services of California v. Citizens Action League*, 110 S. Ct. 1524; *U.S. v. Patterson*, 882 F.2d 595, 603 (1 Cir. 1989), *cert. denied,* 110 S. Ct. 737; and see *Gilbert v. United States*, 370 U.S. 650, 655 (1962).

The Committee's discussion is also unpersuasive because the Committee appears constantly to be shifting ground in identifying the concept against which it is fighting. Too often the Committee seeks to justify its "person" choice by arguing that for policy reasons the communicatee need not be a "party to an adjudicative or other formal proceeding." But the Comment already says *that*. The issue, with which the Committee never comes to grips, is whether by using the word "party" the drafters intended to mean a person who had an interest in the matter—be it a lawsuit, a contract negotiation, a real estate closing, or whatever—which it was the purpose and foreseeable outcome of the matter significantly and directly to affect. *Such* persons would have an interest *qualitatively* different from others in the matter, a qualitative difference signified by the word "party." The Committee neither acknowledges nor addresses this natural—and in my view, correct—rationale for the use consistently since 1908 of the word "party" instead of the word "person." Such an interpretation, however, is exactly what "parties," *supra*, is defined as meaning.

In this scenario, for instance, a plaintiff and defendant in a lawsuit would be "parties," because the purpose and foreseeable outcome would directly affect their interests. The fact or expert witness would not be a "party," even if for whatever reason he had retained a lawyer to advise him in his capacity as a witness. In a matrimonial case, where custody, visitation rights or support are issues, the represented children of the marriage would be parties because of the centrality of their interests to the matter, even though they are not formal parties to the litigation.

In a real estate transaction, the buyer and seller would be "parties," and, if represented, could not be contacted by the other's attorney absent consent of their own attorney. The buyer's mortgagee bank and the seller's bank whose mortgage the buyer would have to pay off would not be "parties," even if represented, so that the buyer's lawyer could contact directly the seller's mortgage officer to find out the precise amount of the pay-off figure without the intermediation of the bank's lawyer. While both banks have an interest in the transaction, the interest is qualitatively ancillary to the central interest of the buyer and the seller.

As a *policy* matter, of course, it might conceivably be better if the word "person" were used in Rule 4.2 instead of "party." It certainly would be easier to apply the Rule (though the consequences of such a broad applicability have only begun to be discerned in the Committee's opinion). Indeed, the Committee has proposed changing the Rule to *substitute* "person" for "party," and if that change is adopted, this discussion will be moot for the *Model* Rule, though still relevant in the vast majority of jurisdictions which have adopted Rule 4.2 using "party."

But ease of application and logical consistency cannot effect a change in the meaning of a word used consistently since 1908 in this particular rule, especially where, as here, there is a perfectly normal, natural meaning to be accorded to the word "party" that acknowledges its more limited ambit as a subset, instead of a synonym, of "person."

Conclusion

If the Committee's expansive reading of "party" to mean "person" is correct, there is no need for the House of Delegates in August of 1995 to change the text of Model Rule 4.2, as proposed by the Committee. If the Committee's reading is correct, the Judges of Oregon, Alaska and Texas did not know what they were doing when they amended their rules, thinking they were expanding "party." If the Committee's reading is correct, the ABA House of Delegates stands accused of bizarre and irrational behavior for using the word "party" in Rule 4.2 to mean the same thing as that for which everywhere else it had used "person" (and so do the Houses that adopted the Model Code and the Canons).

Of course, this is not so. This Committee, in proposing the rule change, understood that it was proposing just that: a change in the rule. The Judges of Alaska, Oregon and Texas did not engage in futile gestures of rule-making. The House of Delegates in adopting Model Rule 4.2 and deliberately using the word "party" where everywhere else it had used the word "person" clearly intended a difference in meaning.

If my colleagues want Model Rule 4.2 to protect "any person," their remedy is not to imagine ambiguity in the current term "party" and then through construction transform it into the broader term "person." Their remedy is to proselytize the members of the House to change the words as the Committee has proposed. Theirs must be the route of legislation, not interpretation.

Ralph G. Elliot

ABA STANDING COMMITTEE ON ETHICS AND PROFESSIONAL RESPONSIBILITY

COMPOSITION AND JURISDICTION

The Standing Committee on Ethics and Professional Responsibility, which consists of ten members, may:

(1) by the concurrence of a majority of its members, express its opinion on proper professional or judicial conduct, either on its own initiative or when requested to do so by a member of the bar or the judiciary;

(2) periodically publish its issued opinions to the profession in summary or complete form and, on request, provide copies of opinions to members of the bar, the judiciary and the public;

(3) provide under its supervision informal responses to ethics inquiries the answers to which are substantially governed by applicable ethical codes and existing written opinions;

(4) on request, advise or otherwise assist professional organizations and courts in their activities relating to the development, modification and interpretation of statements of the ethical standards of the profession such as the Model Rules of Professional Conduct, the predecessor Model Code of Professional Responsibility and the Code of Judicial Conduct;

(5) recommend amendments to or clarifications of the Model Rules of Professional Conduct or the Code of Judicial Conduct; and

(6) adopt rules relating to the procedures to be used in issuing opinions, effective when approved by the Board of Governors.

[The above Composition and Jurisdiction statement is found at §31.7 of the Bylaws of the Association. The Rules of Procedure are not incorporated into the Bylaws.]

RULES OF PROCEDURE

1. The Committee may express its opinion on questions of proper professional and judicial conduct. The Model Rules of Professional Conduct and the Code of Judicial Conduct, as they may be amended or superseded, contain the standards to be applied. For as long as a significant number of jurisdictions continue to base their professional standards on the predecessor Model Code of Professional Responsibility, the Committee will continue to refer also to the Model Code in its opinions.

2. The Committee may issue an opinion on its own initiative or upon a request from a member of the bar or the judiciary or from a professional organization or a court.

3. The Committee may issue opinions of two kinds: Formal Opinions and Informal Opinions. Formal Opinions are those upon subjects the Committee determines to be of widespread interest or unusual importance. Other opinions are Informal Opinions. The Committee will assign to each opinion a non-duplicative identifying number, with distinction between Formal Opinions and Informal Opinions.

4. The Committee will not usually issue an opinion on a question that is known to be pending before a court in a proceeding in which the requestor is involved. The Committee's published opinions will not identify the person who was the requestor or whose conduct is the subject of the opinion. The Committee will not issue an opinion on a question of law.

5. The Committee may invite or accept written information relevant to a particular opinion from a person or persons interested in such an opinion before the Committee begins its work on an opinion. Ordinarily, the Committee will not invite anyone to make an oral presentation or argument in support of that position.

6. When a Committee or staff member receives an inquiry about the status of a draft opinion from anyone outside the Committee, the member may inform the inquirer that the Committee is considering the question. Draft opinions may, in appropriate circumstances, be shown to other interested ABA Committees and entities. Committee and staff members shall not, absent unusual circumstances, discuss the substance of pending opinions with the public, but may mention topics related to pending opinions in a general fashion.

7. Before issuing an opinion with respect to judicial conduct the Committee will submit the proposed opinion to the Judges' Advisory Committee and consider any objection or comment from the Judges' Advisory Committee and any member of it. The Committee may assume that the Judges' Advisory Committee and its members have no objection or comment if none is received by the Committee within 30 days after the submission.

8. If the Committee decides not to issue a requested opinion the requestor will be promptly notified.

9. The Committee will issue an opinion only with the concurrence of six members in a vote taken at a meeting or in a telephone conference call. When a Committee member votes against a position declaring a Committee policy, that vote may be recorded in the minutes, which may include the name of the dissenting Committee member. The minutes shall not reflect the names of Committee members voting for or against any non-Committee policy question except that a member's vote shall be recorded and identified at the member's request.

When drafting an opinion, policy statement or other document to be publicly disseminated, the Committee shall make every effort to reach a consensus. When, after a full examination of the issue and an exchange of views, the Committee cannot reach a consensus, a dissenting opinion may be appropriate to express the views of a Committee member or members. A member may place a statement of dissent in the Committee file or request that the dissent be published with the opinion.

10. The Chair may assign to one or more members the responsibility of preparing a proposed opinion for consideration by the Committee. The Committee will issue a requested opinion as promptly as feasible.

11. A Formal Opinion overrules an earlier Formal Opinion or Informal Opinion to the extent of conflict. An Informal Opinion overrules an earlier Informal Opinion to the extent of conflict but does not overrule an earlier Formal Opinion.

12. Opinions of the Committee issued before the effective dates of the Model

Rules of Professional Conduct, the predecessor Model Code of Professional Responsibility and the Code of Judicial Conduct continue in effect to the extent not inconsistent with those standards and not overruled or limited by later opinions.

13. The Committee will make opinions and/or summaries of opinions available for publication in the *American Bar Association Journal.* The Committee will cause Formal Opinions and Informal Opinions to be published in loose-leaf form.

14. The Committee may through its staff arrange to provide informal responses to ethics inquiries the answers to which are substantially governed by applicable ethical codes and opinions of this Committee or other ethics committees. The staff will maintain a log of such inquiries that will periodically be reviewed by the Committee.

15. Information contained in Committee files relating to requests for opinions that would disclose the identity of the inquirer or the person whose conduct is the subject of the opinion will not voluntarily be disclosed by the Association without the consent of the affected persons.

REVIEW QUESTIONS WITH ANALYSIS

REVIEW QUESTIONS ON PROFESSIONAL RESPONSIBILITY

*by Professor Nathan M. Crystal**

Editor's Note

The multiple choice questions that follow can be used to review doctrinal issues taught in most professional responsibility or legal ethics courses and to prepare for the Multistate Professional Responsibility examination prepared by the National Conference of Bar Examiners. Answers with analysis follow the questions.

Terminology

The questions use terminology that is similar to the terminology used on the Multistate Examination. In answering the questions, choose the answer that seems best even if you do not completely agree with all of the alternatives. Comments to the Model Rules should be consulted for guidance in interpreting the Rules. In answering the questions, the following terms apply:

- "**Subject to Discipline**" asks whether the conduct referred to or described in the question subjects the attorney to discipline under the American Bar Association Model Rules of Professional Conduct or the judge to discipline under the American Bar Association Model Code of Judicial Conduct.

- "**Proper**" asks whether the conduct referred to or described in the question is professionally appropriate in that it:
  (a) would not subject an attorney to discipline;
  (b) would not subject a judge to discipline.

- "**Subject to liability**" asks whether the conduct referred to or described in the question subjects the attorney to civil liability for damages, whether for negligence, breach of fiduciary duty, violation of Rule 11 of the Federal Rules of Civil Procedure, or other theory of recovery.

*Nathan M. Crystal is the Roy Webster Professor of Law at the University of South Carolina School of Law.

Questions

Confidentiality

(1) L is defending D in a prosecution for murder. D informs L that D has committed several other murders that have not yet been solved by the police.

I. L is subject to discipline if L informs the authorities that D committed these crimes.

II. L is subject to discipline if L conducts an investigation to determine whether D is telling the truth about the murders.

III. L can be compelled to testify about D's admissions because the attorney-client privilege does not apply.

(A) I only.
(B) II only.
(C) III only.
(D) II and III, but not I.

Conflicts of Interests

(2) Lawson, an attorney with Law Firm A is defending A Corporation in a products liability action. B Corporation wishes to retain Anderson, another attorney employed by Law Firm, to handle a breach of contract action against A Corporation.

I. It would be proper for Anderson to represent B Corporation in the breach of contract action against A Corporation so long as the breach of contract action and the products liability action that Law Firm is handling for A Corporation are not related in any way.

II. It would be proper for Anderson to represent B Corporation in the breach of contract action against A Corporation so long as the firm screens Anderson from any access to A Corporation's files.

III. It would be proper for Anderson to represent B Corporation provided B Corporation consents after consultation about Law Firm's representation of A Corporation.

(A) I only.
(B) II only.
(C) III only.
(D) Neither I, II, or III.

(3) The Lawson Law Firm is deciding whether to hire a new associate A, who

currently works for the Anderson Law Firm. The Lawson Law Firm is handling a products liability action against one of the clients of the Anderson Law Firm. A has had no involvement and no knowledge whatsoever about the products liability case.

(A) The Lawson firm will be disqualified from handling the products liability case if A works on the matter when she joins the Lawson firm.
(B) The Lawson firm will be disqualified from handling the products liability case unless it promptly establishes appropriate procedures to screen A from any participation in the matter.
(C) The Lawson firm will be disqualified from handling the products liability case if A joins the firm, regardless of the steps the firm takes.
(D) The Lawson firm will not be disqualified from handling the products liability case if A joins the firm.

(4) C retains L to prepare an insurance trust to hold a large life insurance policy for which C has applied. During the course of representation L learns that C has failed to disclose serious health problems on C's insurance application.

I. L is subject to discipline if L prepares the insurance trust and assists C in transferring ownership of the policy to the trust.
II. L is subject to discipline if L fails to inform the insurance company of C's failure to disclose C's health problems.
III. It would be proper for L to continue to represent C in completing the insurance trust so long as L does not make any misrepresentations to the insurance company.
(1) I only.
(2) II only.
(3) III only.
(4) I and II, but not III.

(5) L represents Corporation (C) in a number of small debt collection actions. X has asked L to represent her against C in a breach of contract action. Is L subject to discipline if he represents X against C in the contract action while also representing C in the debt collection matters?

(1) No, if the breach of contract action and the debt collection matters are not substantially related.
(2) No, if L reasonably believes that he can adequately represent X and X consents after full disclosure of the conflict.
(3) Yes, because simultaneous representation of adverse parties even in unrelated matters is a conflict of interest.
(4) Yes, because of the appearance of impropriety.

Fees, Expenses, and Client Property

(6) In which of the following situations is a state court judge required subject to discipline for failure to recuse herself from hearing the case?

I. The judge's first cousin is a party to the case.

II. The judge's former law partner represents one of the parties in the case.

III. The judge's knows that her husband owns 10 shares of stock in a corporation that is a party to the case. The stock is worth less than $250.

(1) I only.

(2) II only.

(3) III only.

(4) Neither I, II, or III.

Limitations on Zealous Representation

(7) L represents the plaintiff in a products liability action against C Corporation. C Corporation is represented by A. E is the chief engineer in charge of product design for C Corporation. Without informing A, L contacts E and asks to interview E about the company's product design procedures. E refuses because A has previously asked E not to voluntarily give any information to L.

(A) L is subject to discipline for contacting E, and A is also subject to discipline for asking E not to voluntarily give information to L.

(B) L is subject to discipline for contacting E, but A acted properly in asking E not to voluntarily give information to L.

(C) L acted properly in contacting E, but A is subject to discipline for asking E not to voluntarily give information to L.

(D) Both L and A acted properly.

Advertising, Solicitation, Firm Names and Unauthorized Practice

(8) L runs a television advertisement in which L states that L's firm is "one of the most outstanding products liability firms in the country" and that the firm has obtained "numerous multimillion-dollar settlements and judgments."

I. L is subject to discipline for advertising that the firm is "one of the most outstanding products liability firms in the country."

II. L is subject to discipline for advertising that the firm has obtained "numerous multimillion-dollar settlements and judgments."

III. L's advertisement is constitutionally protected under the *Bates* decision.

(A) I only.

(B) II only.

(C) III only.

(D) I and II, but not III.

(9) A local bank has a staff of attorneys that it employs on salaried basis. Management of the bank has decided to offer its customers a "will preparation service." For a fee paid to the bank, lawyers on the bank's staff will prepare wills for the bank's customers. Is it proper for these lawyers to participate in this service?

(A) Yes, so long as it is clear that the lawyers are representing the customers, not the bank.
(B) Yes, because the lawyers are salaried employees of the bank.
(C) No, because the bank is involved in the unauthorized practice of law.
(D) No, because the plan involves improper solicitation.

Law Firm Matters

(10) L, a sole practitioner, has decided to retire. L enters into an agreement to sell L's practice to C. As part of the agreement, L promises not to practice law in the city in which L formerly practiced.

I. L and C are subject to discipline for entering into an agreement to sell L's practice.
II. L and C are subject to discipline for entering into an agreement that restricts L's right to practice law.
III. L and C are subject to discipline unless all of C's clients consent in writing to the sale.

(A) I only.
(B) II only.
(C) III only.
(D) Neither I, II, or III

Answers with Analysis

Confidentiality

(1) A

I is correct. MR 1.6 does not have an exception for past criminal conduct; thus, the general duty of confidentiality applies. L would violate the duty of confidentiality by revealing the information to the authorities.

II is incorrect. It would be improper for L to engage in criminal conduct or to attempt to cover up the crime, but investigation of the client's story does not involve either of these forms of misconduct. Whether L should conduct an investigation seems to be a strategic choice for L to make, depending on whether L could make some use of the information that could be acquired through the investigation.

III is incorrect. D's communications seem to fall squarely within the attorney-client privilege. D made communications to L in confidence for the purpose of seeking legal advice. The crime/fraud exception to the privilege only applies when the advice is sought to carry out a criminal or fraudulent scheme, not when advice is sought about past conduct.

Conflicts of Interest

(2) D

I is incorrect. The "substantial relationship" test applies to representation against a former client. Representation directly adverse to a current client without that client's consent is improper, regardless of whether the matters are related or not; such representation violates the lawyer's duty of loyalty. MR 1.7(a) and Comment 3.

II is incorrect. The Model Rules reject "screening" of a disqualified lawyer as a solution to conflict of interest problems except in the case of the former government lawyer. *See* 1 HAZARD & HODES, THE LAW OF LAWYERING §1.10:207, at 334; *see also* Model Rule 1.11(a). Despite the Model Rules, however, a few courts have allowed firms to avoid disqualification of a firm by screening a disqualified lawyer. *See Cromley v. Board of Education of Lockport Township High School District* 205, 17 F.3d 1059 (7th Cir. 1994). These cases, however, typically involve former rather than current clients.

III is incorrect. Consent by B Corporation is necessary but not sufficient. A corporation also has an interest in Law Firm's undivided loyalty. Thus, both A Corporation and B Corporation must consent to the representation after consultation with Law Firm. *See* Model Rule 1.7(a)(2).

(3) D

(1) is incorrect. This answer flows from Model Rules 1.9(a) and (b) and Model Rule 1.10(a). Under Model Rule 1.10(a), to determine whether a firm is disqualified, it is necessary to determine if any member of the firm is disqualified. Thus, the issue is whether A would be disqualified if A joined the firm. Model Rule 1.9(a) provides that a lawyer is disqualified if the lawyer formerly represented the client in a substantially related matter. That Rule does not apply to A because A did not represent the client while a member of the Anderson firm. Model Rule 1.9(b) provides that when a lawyer leaves a firm the lawyer may not undertake representation against a client of the lawyer's former firm if the lawyer acquired confidential information. This Rule also does not apply because A does not have any knowledge about the case. Since A would not be disqualified under either Model Rules 1.9(a) or 1.9(b), then the Lawson firm would not be disqualified if A joined the firm.

(2) is incorrect. For the reasons set forth in (1) above, A is not personally disqualified, so screening procedures are unnecessary. Further, the Model Rules do not authorize screening as a solution to conflict of interest problems except in the case of the former government lawyer. *See* 1 HAZARD & HODES, THE LAW OF LAWYERING §1.10:207, at 334; *see also* Model Rule 1.11(a).

(3) is incorrect. For the reasons set forth in (1) above, A is not personally disqualified, so the firm is not disqualified.

(4) is correct.

(4) 1

I is correct. Lawyers may not "counsel or assist" clients in conduct that they know is criminal or fraudulent. MR 1.2(d). By preparing the trust that will receive the policy and by participating in the transfer, the lawyer is assisting in conduct that the lawyer knows is fraudulent.

II is incorrect. The information relates to L's representation, so it is subject to the duty of confidentiality. MR 1.6(a). Neither of the exceptions in MR 1.6(b) applies. Note that even if C's conduct is considered to be a continuing crime, L could still not disclose the information under MR 1.6(b)(1) because C is committing a financial fraud rather than an act involving death or substantial bodily harm. Under the Code of Professional Responsibility and under the rules of ethics adopted in some states, the exception for future wrongful acts is broader than that found in MR 1.6(b)(1). DR 4-101(C)(3), for example, provided that a lawyer may reveal confidential information to prevent the client from committing a crime. Under these broader rules L would have discretion to reveal C's conduct.

III is incorrect. It would be improper for L to make misrepresentations to the insurance company. *See* MR 4.1(a) and MR 8.4(c). However, even if L does not engage in active misrepresentation, L is still required not to counsel or assist a client in fraudulent or criminal conduct. See the discussion above. In other words, the duty not to counsel or assist in fraud is independent of and in addition to the duty not to engage in misrepresentation.

(5) 3
(1) is incorrect. The "substantial relationship" test applies to representation against a former client. Representation directly adverse to a current client without that client's consent is improper, regardless of whether the matters are related or not; such representation violates the lawyer's duty of loyalty. MR 1.7(a) and comment 3.
(2) is incorrect. While disclosure and consent of X is necessary, L has a duty of loyalty to C which requires disclosure and consent by C.
(3) is correct. *See* MR 1.7(a) and comment 3.
(4) is incorrect. The appearance of impropriety is found in Canon 9 of the Code of Professional Responsibility, but the concept is not found in the Model Rules. In fact, the drafters of the Model Rules deleted the concept because of its vagueness. *See* Comment 5 to Model Rule 1.9.

Fees, Expenses, and Client Property

(6) 4
I is incorrect. Canon 3(E)(1) deals with judicial disqualification. Section (d) states that a judge shall disqualify herself when a "person within the third degree of relationship" to the judge is a party to the proceeding. The Terminology section defines third degree of relationship and does not include first cousins. The judge must still determine whether the relationship with the cousin is sufficiently close that the judge's "impartiality might reasonably be questioned." Canon 3(E)(1).
II is incorrect. Canon 3(E)(1)(b) deals with situations in which relationships with former partners require disqualification. That section only requires disqualification if the matter before the judge was one being handled by the former partner while the judge was associated with the lawyer. The mere fact that a former partner appears before the judge does not require disqualification. The judge must still determine whether the relationship with the former partner is sufficiently close that the judge's "impartiality might reasonably be questioned." Canon 3(E)(1). In Informal Opinion 87-1524 the ABA Committee on Ethics and Professional Responsibility ruled that a judge was not required to disqualify himself simply because the judge had been associated with counsel for one of the parties two years earlier. The Committee indicated that a period of one or two years after termination of professional association was appropriate, depending on factors such as the closeness of the relationship and the amount of continued contact.
III is incorrect. Canon 3(E)(1)(c) deals with financial disqualification. The Canon requires disqualification if the judge or the judge's spouse has an "economic interest" in a party. The Terminology section defines "economic interest" to mean more than a "*de minimis* legal or equitable interest." Here the interest of the judge's spouse seems *de minimis*. Note that this represents a change made by the 1990 Model Code of Judicial Code over the 1972 Code. Under the 1972 Code, a financial interest "however small" required disqualification. Note also that the "however small" standard still applies to federal judges. *See* 28 U.S.C. §455(b)(4).

Limitations on Zealous Representation

(7) B

L is subject to discipline. Model Rule 4.2 states that a lawyer "shall not communicate about the subject of the representation with a person the lawyer knows to be represented by another lawyer in the matter, unless the lawyer has the consent of the other lawyer or is authorized by law to do so." Comment 4 states that "[i]n the case of an organization, this Rule prohibits communications by a lawyer for another person or entity concerning the matter in representation with persons having a managerial responsibility on behalf of the organization, and with any other person whose act or omission in connection with that matter may be imputed to the organization for purposes of civil or criminal liability or whose statement may constitute an admission on the part of the organization." Since E is the chief engineer for product design, E almost certainly qualifies as a person with managerial responsibility. In addition, E's acts with regard to product design could be imputed to the organization.

A is not subject to discipline. Model Rule 3.4(f)(1) states that a lawyer shall not request a person to refrain from voluntarily giving relevant information unless "the person is a relative or an employee or other agent of a client." Since E is an employee of A's client, A's request is proper under Rule 3.4(f)(1). Some critics of the Model Rules have pointed to the disparity between these rules as evidence of a pro-defense slant in the Model Rules.

Advertising, Solicitation, Firm Names and Unauthorized Practice

(8) D

I is correct. Model Rule 7.1 states that a lawyer shall not make a false or misleading advertisement. Rule 7.1(c) states that an advertisement is false or misleading if it "compares the lawyer's services with other lawyers' services, unless the comparison can be factually substantiated." How can the firm substantiate factually that it is one of the most outstanding firms in the country?

II is correct. Model Rule 7.1(b) states that a lawyer shall not make an advertisement that is "likely to create an unjustified expectation about results the lawyer can achieve." *See also* Comment to Rule 7.1.

III is incorrect. The Court in *Bates* specifically refused to pass on the constitutional protection of media advertising because such advertising posed special problems: "The special problems of advertising on the electronic broadcast media will warrant special consideration." *Bates v. State Bar of Arizona*, 433 U.S. at 383-84 (1977). Indeed, the Supreme Court to date has not ruled on the scope of constitutional protection for media advertising. Further, under *Bates* false or misleading advertisements are not constitutionally protected.

(9) C

(1) is incorrect or at least not the best answer. While the lawyers would have an obligation to make sure that it was clear that they represented the bank's customers, and not the bank, *see* Model Rule 1.8(f), that action does not solve the unauthorized practice problem discussed below.

(2) is incorrect. Just because the lawyers are salaried employees of the bank does not eliminate the requirement that they comply with the rules of professional conduct, including the prohibition against assisting a nonlawyer in the unauthorized practice of law. Model Rule 5.5.

(3) is correct. The bank would be performing legal services for others through its lawyer-employees for a fee. The lawyer-employees would be assisting in this conduct, in violation of Model Rule 5.5(b). Note that Model Rule 5.4(b) states that it is improper for a lawyer to form a partnership with a nonlawyer if the activities of the partnership involve the practice of law. Since it is unethical to form a partnership with a nonlawyer, it is even more clearly unethical for the lawyer to be in the position of an employee of an entity performing legal services for a third party. Note also that the rules do not prohibit commercial entities from hiring lawyers to perform legal services for the entity itself. The prohibition only applies when the entity attempts to perform legal services for others. Also relevant is Model Rule 5.4(a), which prohibits fee spitting with nonlawyers.

(4) is incorrect. No evidence of improper solicitation exists. The plan could be offered through advertisement rather than personal contact. Further, if it were offered through personal contact with bank customers, arguably the "prior professional relationship" exception to the prohibition on solicitation would apply. Model Rule 7.3(a).

Law Firm Matters

(10) D

I is incorrect. Model Rule 1.17 allows lawyers to enter into agreements to sell their practices, including goodwill. The Rule, which was adopted in 1990 by the ABA based on California Rule 2-300, changes the long-standing professional prohibition against sale of professional goodwill. The rationale given for the Rule was to eliminate disparity between law firms, which had built-in mechanisms for dealing with lawyer retirement, and sole practitioners, who did not have this advantage. Only a few states have adopted the Rule; in other states the prohibition on sale of a practice remains in effect. In such states, lawyers can accomplish the same result as a direct sale through proper retirement planning. The successor lawyer can form a partnership before the retiring lawyer leaves practice. See Model Rule 5.4, which allows payments to nonlawyers through retirement plans.

II is incorrect. While agreements that restrict the right of lawyers to practice law are generally unethical, such agreements are not improper when part of the sale of a law practice under Model Rule 1.17. *See* Model Rule 5.6, Comment 3.

III is incorrect. Under Model Rule 1.17(c)(4), clients are entitled to receive notice of the sale, but they do not have to consent in writing. Their consent is presumed unless they object within 90 days after receiving notice.

SAMPLE MPRE QUESTIONS AND ANSWERS

MPRE Sample Questions*

Question 1

Attorney Alpha represents Plaintiff in a personal injury action against Defendant, the defendant, who is represented by Attorney Beta. Alpha had heard that Defendant was anxious to settle the case and believed that Beta had not informed Defendant of a reasonable settlement offer made by Alpha. Alpha instructed Alpha's nonlawyer investigator, Inv, to tell Defendant about the settlement offer so Alpha could be sure that Beta does not force the case to trial merely to increase Beta's fee. Inv talked to Defendant as instructed.

Is Alpha subject to discipline?

A. Yes, because Defendant was represented by counsel.
B. Yes, because Alpha was assisting Inv in the unauthorized practice of law.
C. No, because Inv is not a lawyer.
D. No, if Alpha reasonably believed Beta was not keeping Defendant informed.

Question 2

Attorney placed Associate, recently admitted to the bar, in complete charge of the work of the paralegals in Attorney's office. That work consisted of searching titles to real property, an area in which Associate had no familiarity. Attorney instructed Associate to review the searches prepared by the paralegals, and thereafter to sign Attorney's name to the required certifications of title if Associate was satisfied that the search accurately reflected the condition of the title. This arrangement enabled Attorney to lower office operating expenses. Attorney told Associate that Associates should resolve any legal questions that might arise because Attorney was too busy handling major litigation.

Is it proper for Attorney to assign Associate this responsibility?

A. Yes, if the paralegals are experienced in searching titles.
B. Yes, because Attorney is ultimately liable for the accuracy for the title searches.
C. No, unless it enables Attorney to charge lower fees for title certification.
D. No, because Attorney is not adequately supervising the work of Associate.

MPRE SAMPLE QUESTIONS contains over 150 previously published MPRE questions from actual exams (including the 10 questions published in this volume). To order, contact the National Conference of Bar Examiners at 333 North Michigan Avenue, Suite 1025, Chicago, Illinois 60601-4090.

Question 3

During the closing argument to the jury in a civil tax fraud case, Attorney, representing the government, quoted a portion of Defendant's testimony and then said:

I. "That testimony of Defendant directly contradicts the testimony of two witnesses for the government."

II. "I ask you, who has the reason to lie, the two witnesses for the government or Defendant"?

III. "I can truthfully say I have never seen a witness less worthy of belief."

Which of the above statements by Attorney would be proper?

A. I only
B. I and II, but not III
C. II and III, but not I
D. I, II, and III

Question 4

Attorney represents Defendant, a prominent businessman, in a civil paternity suit brought by Plaintiff, who was formerly Defendant's employee. Blood tests did not exclude Defendant's paternity, and the case is being tried before a jury. The result turns on questions of fact. Defendant has steadfastly denied that he had sexual relations with Plaintiff, while Plaintiff has testified that they had sexual relations while on business trips and in her home. The trial has generated great public interest and is closely followed by the news media.

When Plaintiff completed her testimony, Attorney was interviewed by a newspaper reporter.

Which of the following statements, if believed by Attorney to be true, would be proper for attorney to make?

I. "As stated in our pleadings, we expect to prove that other men could be the father of Plaintiff's child."

II. "We have a scientific medical test proving that Defendant is sterile."

III. "We have been unable to locate several people whose testimony will be helpful to us, and I implore them to contact me immediately."

A. II only
B. III only
C. I and III, but not II
D. I, II, and III

Question 5

Attorney Alpha is a lawyer running for election as a state judge. Attorney Beta, who practices law in the same community as Alpha, has frequently observed Alpha's courtroom demeanor in litigation cases. Based on those experiences, Beta believes that Alpha does not have a proper judicial temperament. A local news reporter asked Beta how Beta would rate the candidates, and Beta responded in good faith, "I think Alpha is unsuited for the bench. Alpha lacks the proper judicial temperament and would make a very poor judge." A local newspaper with a wide circulation quoted Beta's remarks?

Were Beta's remarks proper?

A. Yes, because Beta was not seeking judicial office.
B. Yes, because Beta believed Alpha was unsuited for the bench.
C. No, because the remarks serve to bring the judiciary into disrepute.
D. No, because a lawyer should not publicly comment on candidates for judicial office.

Question 6

Two years ago, Attorney was employed by State's Department of Transportation (DOT) to search title to several tracts of land. Attorney has not been employed by DOT during the last year. Recently, DOT instituted proceedings to condemn a tract, owned by Owner, for a new highway route. Owner asked Attorney to represent her in obtaining the highest amount of compensation for the condemnation. Owner's tract is one of the tracts on which Attorney searched title two years ago. Attorney remembers that Engineer, a DOT engineer, once drafted a confidential memorandum advising against running a new highway across Owner's land because of potential adverse environmental impact. Because of this information, Attorney believes it is possible to prevent the condemnation of Owner's land or to increase the settlement amount.

It is proper for Attorney to:

A. represent Owner on the issue of damages only and not disclose the information that might prevent the condemnation.
B. represent Owner and attempt to prevent the condemnation by using the information about the adverse environmental impact.
C. refuse to represent Owner but disclose to Owner the information about the adverse environmental impact.
D. refuse to represent Owner and not disclose the information about the adverse environmental impact.

Question 7

Attorney, who had represented Testator for many years, prepared Testator's will and acted as one of two subscribing witnesses to its execution. Testator's sister and brother were his sole heirs. The will left Testator's entire estate to his sister and nothing to his brother. Upon Testator's death two years later, Executor, the executor named in the will, asked Attorney to act as his lawyer in the probate of the will and the administration of the estate. At that time, Executor informed Attorney that Testator's brother would concede that the will was properly executed but intended to contest the will on the ground that he has been excluded because of fraud previously practiced on Testator by Testator's sister. The other subscribing witness to the will predeceased Testator," and Attorney will be called as a witness solely for the purpose of establishing the due execution of the will.

Is it proper for Attorney to accept the representation?

A. Yes, if there is no contested issue of fact with respect to the formal execution of the will.

B. Yes, because Executor has no beneficial interest under the will.

C. No, unless Attorney's services are necessary to avoid substantial hardship to Executor.

D. No, because Attorney will be called as a witness in the case.

Question 8

Attorney represented Plaintiff in an action against several defendants. The retainer agreement provided the Plaintiff would pay all costs and expenses of litigation and would, on demand, reimburse Attorney for any costs or expenses advanced by Attorney. After serving process on two defendants, Attorney had difficulty locating and serving the remaining defendants. Plaintiff approved the hiring of an investigator to locate and serve the defendants, and Attorney advanced the costs for the investigator. When Attorney asked Plaintiff for reimbursement, Plaintiff refused to pay. Attorney then told Plaintiff that Attorney would do no more work on the case until Attorney was reimbursed for the amount advanced.

Thereafter, one of the defendants filed a counterclaim that required a responsive pleading within thirty days. Because Attorney had not been paid, Attorney permitted the time to respond to the counterclaim to expire without filing a responsive pleading, and a default was entered on the counterclaim. Later, Plaintiff reimbursed Attorney for the costs Attorney had advanced, and Attorney was successful in having the default on the counterclaim set aside. The case was tried, and Plaintiff prevailed on Plaintiff's complaint, and the counterclaimant recovered nothing.

Is Attorney subject to discipline for not initially filing a responsive pleading to the counterclaim?

A. Yes, because Attorney neglected Plaintiff's case.

B. Yes, unless Attorney had asked leave of court to withdraw.

C. No, because Plaintiff breached the agreement to reimburse Attorney.

D. No, because Plaintiff did not sustain any prejudice as a result of Attorney's action.

Question 9

Judge, prior to her recent appointment to the federal court, had been an outspoken and effective opponent of the racial segregation policies of Gov, a foreign country's government. As part of its worldwide tour, Gov's national soccer team scheduled a soccer team match with a team in this country. Several civil rights groups have applied to judge for an order enjoining the playing of the proposed match. The matter is now pending. Only legal issues are presented. Judge, after painstaking consideration, has privately concluded that she cannot decide the legal questions without bias against the representatives of Gov's government. However, no one has made a motion to disqualify judge.

Should Judge recuse herself in the pending matter?

A. Yes, unless Judge believes she has greater expertise than other judges on the court in legal issues involving racial segregation.

B. Yes, because Judge believes that she cannot be impartial.

C. No, because the only issues presented for decision are legal questions.

D. No, because none of the interested parties has moved to disqualify judge.

Question 10

Candidate, a member of the bar, is a candidate for judicial office in an election. Candidate personally asked several of his friends to contribute $1,000 each to kick off his campaign. After Candidate's friends made the contributions, Candidate, who was elated by the support, formed a committee to collect more contributions. Candidate then turned over the contributions to the committee and began campaigning in earnest.

Is Candidate subject to discipline?

A. No, because Candidate turned over the funds to his committee.

B. No, unless the committee includes lawyers likely to practice before Candidate.

C. Yes, unless none of the original contributors was a lawyer.

D. Yes, because Candidate personally solicited funds.

Answers

1. A
2. D
3. B
4. C
5. B
6. D
7. A
8. A
9. B
10. D

STATUS OF THE ADOPTION OF THE ABA MODEL RULES OF PROFESSIONAL CONDUCT

DATES OF ADOPTION OF THE MODEL RULES OF PROFESSIONAL CONDUCT

(Alphabetical)

Alabama	5/2/90
Alaska	4/14/93
Arizona	9/7/84
Arkansas	12/16/85
Colorado	5/7/92
Connecticut	6/23/86
Delaware	9/12/85
District of Columbia	3/1/90
Florida	7/17/86
Hawaii	12/6/93
Idaho	9/3/86
Illinois	2/8/90
Indiana	11/25/86
Kansas	1/29/88
Kentucky	6/12/89
Louisiana	12/18/86
Maryland	4/15/86
Massachusetts	6/9/97
Michigan	3/11/88
Minnesota	6/13/85
Mississippi	2/18/87
Missouri	8/7/85
Montana	6/6/85
Nevada	1/26/86
New Hampshire	1/16/86
New Jersey	7/12/84
New Mexico	6/26/86
North Carolina	10/7/85
North Dakota	5/6/87
Oklahoma	3/10/88
Pennsylvania	10/16/87
Rhode Island	11/1/88
South Carolina	1/9/90
South Dakota	12/15/87
Texas	6/20/89
Utah	3/20/87
Vermont (effective 9/1/99)	3/9/99
Virgin Islands	1/28/91
Virginia	1/25/99
Washington	7/25/85
West Virginia	6/30/88
Wisconsin	6/10/87
Wyoming	11/7/86

DATES OF ADOPTION OF THE MODEL RULES OF PROFESSIONAL CONDUCT

(Chronological)

New Jersey	7/12/84
Arizona	9/7/84
Montana	6/6/85
Minnesota	6/13/85
Washington	7/25/85
Missouri	8/7/85
Delaware	9/12/85
North Carolina	10/7/85
Arkansas	12/16/85
New Hampshire	1/16/86
Nevada	1/26/86
Maryland	4/15/86
Connecticut	6/23/86
New Mexico	6/26/86
Florida	7/17/86
Idaho	9/3/86
Wyoming	11/7/86
Indiana	11/25/86
Louisiana	12/18/86
Mississippi	2/18/87
Utah	3/20/87
North Dakota	5/6/87
Wisconsin	6/10/87
Pennsylvania	10/16/87
South Dakota	12/15/87
Kansas	1/29/88
Oklahoma	3/10/88
Michigan	3/11/88
West Virginia	6/30/88
Rhode Island	11/1/88
Kentucky	6/12/89
Texas	6/20/89
South Carolina	1/9/90
Illinois	2/8/90
District of Columbia	3/1/90
Alabama	5/2/90
Virgin Islands	1/28/91
Colorado	5/7/92
Alaska	4/14/93
Hawaii	12/6/93
Massachusetts	6/9/97
Virginia	1/25/99
Vermont (effective 9/1/99)	3/9/99